Studies in Byzantine Intellectual History

Professor Milton V. Anastos

Milton V. Anastos

Studies in Byzantine Intellectual History

VARIORUM REPRINTS
London 1979

British Library CIP data   Anastos, Milton V
                                    Studies in Byzantine intellectual history.
                                    — (Collected studies series; CS88)
                                    1. Byzantine Empire — Intellectual life
                                    I. Title
                                    180   DF531

                                    ISBN 0-86078-031-7

161312.

Preface and Complementary notes copyright © 1979 Variorum Reprints

Published in Great Britain by   Variorum Reprints
                                    21a Pembridge Mews London W11 3EQ

Printed in Great Britain by   Kingprint Ltd
                                    Richmond Surrey TW9 4PD

VARIORUM REPRINT CS88

CONTENTS

This volume contains a total of 432 pages

PREFACE

For many years I have been collecting material for an intellectual history of the Byzantine Empire, which I have entitled the *Mind of Byzantium* (MOB). The papers in this volume represent ventures into this field, which has special appeal because the most distinctive features of Byzantine civilization, it seems to me, concern the realm of ideas.

The three most notable of these in my opinion are art (including architecture), law, and theology, in all of which Byzantium made contributions of permanent value and direct contemporaneous relevance. Byzantine art is perhaps the best known of the three, and popular interest in the visual remains of Byzantine civilization, small and large, is mounting steadily. Of even greater importance, however, is the *Corpus Iuris Civilis*, the customary designation for the great collection of laws assembled, revised, and arranged by Justinian and his jurisconsults between 528 and 534 for the purpose of governing the Empire. By this great work of codification, Justinian not only eliminated uncertainty and disorder from the practice of law in his own day, but also provided the basic text, now literally translated into various languages and somewhat revised, of the codes of law current in most of modern Europe, the whole of Latin America, and the sovereign state of Louisiana. This *Corpus* is one of the mightiest achievements of the mind of man and worthy of comparison with the Anglo-American common law, although it lacks concern for what we today call civil rights and liberties, which rank high among the chief glories of modern civilization.

In theology, the Byzantine definitions of the dogmas of the Trinity and the Incarnation (i.e., the doctrine of the person of Jesus Christ), as formulated at the Seven Oecumenical Councils (325-787), remain authoritative to this day and command the adherence of approximately a billion people throughout the world belonging to the major churches of Christendom, including the Greek Orthodox (with its numerous national branches), the Roman, the Episcopal, and many others. It should be remembered that these councils were convoked by the Byzantine emperor and attended almost exclusively by Byzantine, i.e., Greek-speaking bishops. The Roman pope was represented at all of the Councils except the Second (in 381) and the Fifth (in 553), but only a very few Latin bishops were present at any one of these. Hence, the basic doctrine of the Christian Church at large was drafted by Byzantine theologians. It was approved by the Roman Church, and some Roman theological ideas were incorporated into the Oecumenical Creeds, which, however, were written originally in Greek and are Byzantine in both language and style.

In my own work, despite my great interest in the subject, I have not done much with the arts, which I leave to the archaeologists and historians of art, except that I have made an effort to deal with the problem created by the iconoclasts, who threatened to do away with religious art altogether. On the other hand, I have examined some aspects of the influence exerted by the three forces which constitute the major sources of Byzantine culture: the tradition of ancient Greece, the legal and political institutions of pagan Rome, and Christianity.

Accordingly, in I, I analyze Porphyry's attack on the Bible, which is a diabolically incisive, if often captious, criticism of Christianity based upon a profound knowledge of the New Testament. Number II in the collection concerns the Edict of 313, which is one of the most important documents in the history of the Early Church. As I try to show against the "paradoxographers," it was promulgated by both Constantine and Licinius in 313, in all probability as an *edictum*, although in the fourth century the technical differences between *edictum* and other imperial *constitutiones* had been blurred and were no longer of much moment. Special interest attaches also the numismatic evidence I assemble in my addendum to II, which, I believe, in itself, even apart from other powerful arguments that have recently been made, conclusively demonstrates the authenticity of Eusebius's account of Constantine's vision and dream (*Vita*, 1, 28-31).

In the next section, I discuss the Byzantine concept of the process by which the emperor was said to have been chosen by God (III), review a few illustrations of the way the emperor ruled over the Church (IV), and comment upon some of the Biblical texts which lay behind the Byzantine theory of autocracy (V).

My principal objective in the articles on theology has been to uphold the validity of a number of disputed or controversial theses. In VI, I contend that Nestorius would have accepted the Creed of 451 without qualms and should be granted the same indulgence for his inconsistency in the use of theological terms that the Church has always been willing to accord to Cyril. It must be admitted, however, that Nestorius's method of argumentation and his tortuous style are hazards which are not easily surmounted. Despite all that has been written about him, much remains to be done. A serious inquiry, for example, should be undertaken to demonstrate whether or not Nestorius, when properly understood, could be proved to have been in substantial agreement with Cyril's *Third Letter* (including its *Twelve Anathemas*), which did not gain oecumenical sanction until 553. In addition, it would be interesting to determine, on the basis of historical and textual analysis, rather than confessional bias, whether the hypostasis of Jesus Christ can be regarded as belonging to the Logos, as some hold, or whether this idea is not more consistent with mono-physite than with orthodox Christology.

In VII, I maintain that the anathemas of the Creed of 325 justify Justinian in condemning Theodore of Mopsuestia, and in VIII I draw attention to a passage in the *Liber Pontificalis*, which in my judgment proves that the Emperor Leo issued a decree against the images in 726-27. It is strange that none of the proponents of the view that there was no iconoclastic edict before 730 ever cite the decisive words in the *Liber Pontificalis* (decreverat imperator ut nulla imago cuiuslibet sancti aut martyris aut angeli haberetur), on which I rely to show that there was such an edict, or ever attempt to explain them away – if, indeed, it be possible to do so. No one has attempted to refute VIII, except that one reviewer, in a notice of nine printed lines (*BZ*, 65 [1972], 173), suggests without any proof whatever that the compilers of the *Liber Pontificalis* deliberately distorted the record and mentioned iv

a decree against the icons in 726-27 in order to exculpate the popes for refusing to pay taxes to Byzantium thereafter. I should perhaps add that several years ago, when I showed an early version of VIII to Professor Georg Ostrogorsky, the chief recent exponent of the theory that there was no iconoclastic legislation in 726-27, whom, needless to say, I greatly admire and respect, he graciously conceded that I had proved my point.

In IX I argue that Illyricum, Calabria, and Sicily were transferred to the ecclesiastical jurisdiction of Constantinople in 732-33. I then (X) turn to the later phase of iconoclasm and the Christological arguments advanced by the iconoclasts in the reign of the Emperor Constantine V (741-75), which were subsequently taken over with virtually no change by the Emperor Leo V in 815 (XI).

In a study of Byzantine influence on the Latin West during the twelfth century (XII), I summarize what is known about Latin translations from the Greek, and quote a few texts in which Latins expressed hostility to both the Greeks and their language. I devote several pages to the debate on the addition of *Filioque* to the Creed and to the use Latin theologians made of basic theological principles set forth by John of Damascus.

In the next section (XIII-XVII), I identify some of the ancient geographical and astronomical texts used by Cosmas Indicopleustes, Pletho, and a few other Byzantine scholars, and conclude with proof that Pletho at the Council of Ferrara-Florence in 1438-39 set in motion forces which led to the discovery of America by Christopher Columbus in 1492.

In short, I hope that the material presented in these papers, along with other evidence of the same sort, will demonstrate that Byzantium was by no means intellectually sterile and that the Byzantines made cultural contributions of far-reaching significance.

MILTON V. ANASTOS

Los Angeles
October, 1978

PAGANISM AND CHRISTIANITY

I

Porphyry's Attack
on the Bible

LONG before the Emperor Constantine I in 313 put an end to the persecution of the Christians and granted the Church the right to exist alongside of the then dominant, but faltering, heathen cults of the Roman Empire, thoughtful pagans were aware of the appeal of the new religion; and some, like Porphyry (d. c. 304), the celebrated Neoplatonist and author of the *Eisagoge* to Aristotle's *Categories,* devoted much subtlety and zeal to a hostile critique of the Old and New Testaments, which they studied carefully in search of suitable targets for criticism and ridicule.[1]

* I am grateful for the opportunity of paying homage to my good friend, Professor Caplan, whose erudition, wit, and kind heart have enriched all who are acquainted with him or his work. He is a man of such urbanity, that he, I know, and others, I hope, will find Porphyry's jibes of some interest, if not amusing, even when they are most offensive. I have tried to reproduce Porphyry's argument and that of the opposition fairly and disinterestedly without obtruding my value judgments at every point. As a humanist, I give Porphyry full παρρησία; personally, I repudiate him. But I am a historian, not an apologist, and therefore make no effort, except by the omission of wearisome details, to strengthen Macarius' hand, even when he is most desperately in need of assistance.

The present paper is from the first chapter of Part IV of my book, *The Mind of Byzantium*, which is in preparation.

[1] There is no satisfactory study available of the conflict between paganism and Christianity, or of the influence of the former on the latter during the Middle Ages. On the survival in the Byzantine Empire, however, of pagan forms, customs, and religious practices, we have the monumental work of Phaidon Kukules, *Life and Culture of the*

422

About a century earlier (c. 175), the scholar Celsus wrote a treatise (now lost) against Christianity, which the great theologian Origen of Alexandria deemed so important that he subjected it to minute analysis, and about the year 248 replied in a lengthy volume, which has survived the ages intact.[2] But neither Origen, despite his learning and dialectical skill, nor any of his successors, was ever able to still the voice of paganism altogether, and, throughout the mediaeval period, there was abundant evidence of the perseverance of heathenism in one form or another.[3] Pagan opposition to Christian beliefs and practices never ceased.

Byzantines 1–6 (in Greek) (Athens, 1948–57), which is based upon an exhaustive study of Byzantine sources. Cf. also Kukules, *Folklore in the Works of Eustathius of Thessalonike* 1–2 (in Greek) (Society of Macedonian Studies, *Epistemonikai pragmateiai,* Philological and Theological Ser. 5–6; Athens, 1950). On the early period, especially on the first three or four centuries, there is an abundant literature. Note especially: Karl Prümm, *Religionsgeschichtliches Handbuch für den Raum der altchristlichen Umwelt* (2nd ed.; Rome, 1954); Karl Schneider, *Geistesgeschichte des antiken Christentums* I–II (Munich, 1954); Wilhelm Krause, *Die Stellung der frühchristlichen Autoren zur heidnischen Literatur* (Vienna, 1958); Pierre de Labriolle, *La réaction païenne: étude sur la polémique antichrétienne du i[er] au vi[e] siècle* (Paris, 1934).

[2] On this polemical literature in general, besides the works noted above, and as supplements to the fundamental book of Labriolle, see Heinrich O. Schroeder, "Celsus und Porphyrius als Christengegner," *Die Welt als Geschichte* 17 (1957), 190–202; Gustave Bardy, "Chrétiens et païens à la fin du ive siècle," *L'année théologique* 4 (1943), 457–503; Wilhelm Nestle, "Die Haupteinwände des antiken Denkens gegen das Christentum," *Archiv für Religionswissenschaft* 37 (1941–2), 51–100; Friedrich Anwander, "Die literarische Bekämpfung des Christentums in der Antike," *Benediktinische Monatschrift* 6 (1924), 297–320. For an anthology of texts see Antonio Quacquarelli, *La polemica pagano-cristiana: da Plotino ad Agostino* (Milan, 1952). On Origen's *apologia* see P. Koetschau in *GCS* 2–3 (Leipzig, 1899), and Jean Scherer, *Extraits des livres I et II d. Contre Ceise d'Origène d'après le papyrus no. 88747 du Musée du Caire* (Institut français d'Archéologie orientale, Bibliothèque d'étude 28; Cairo, 1956). The best translation is by Henry Chadwick, *Origen: Contra Celsum* (Cambridge, Eng., 1953); see the classified bibliography by Henri Crouzel, *Origène et la "connaissance mystique"* (Museum Lessianum, sec. théol. 56; Paris and Bruges, 1960). On Celsus see Robert Bader, *Der ΑΛΗΘΗΣ ΛΟΓΟΣ des Kelsos* (Tübinger Beiträge zur Altertumswissenschaft 33; Stuttgart and Berlin, 1940), and Carl Andresen, *Logos und Nomos: Die Polemik des Kelsos wider das Christentum* (Arbeiten zur Kirchengeschichte 30; Berlin, 1955). For Porphyry's use of Celsus see Georg Loesche, "Haben die späteren neuplatonischen Polemiker gegen das Christentum das Werk des Celsus benutzt?," *Zeitschrift für wissenschaftliche Theologie* 27 (1883), 257–302. See also p. 450 below.

[3] In my forthcoming book, I devote much space to a consideration of these survivals, and I hope to treat them in detail in a series of projected volumes on the history of the pagan Greek tradition during the Middle Ages.

One of the most formidable of the pagan opponents of Christianity on the threshold of the Middle Ages, was the mentioned Porphyry, the disciple of Plotinus. Authorities differ whether Plotinus did or did not direct some of his shafts against the Christians.[4] Of Porphyry's attitude, however, there is no doubt, since we know that he wrote an erudite and caustic polemic against Christianity in fifteen books. Unfortunately, this work, entitled *Against the Christians* (Κατὰ Χριστιανῶν), which is of inestimable value in appraising the nature of the pagan criticism of Christian doctrine, was systematically destroyed in accordance with an edict of the Emperor Constantine I in 325,[5] after the Council of Nicaea, and again in 448 by order of the Emperors Valentinian III and Theodosius II.[6]

The enforcement of these two edicts was so effective that only a scant 105 fragments now remain,[7] most of which have been preserved by Jerome in several of his works and by Macarius Magnes (i.e., of Magnesia, in Asia Minor) in his Ἀποκριτικὸς ἢ Μονογενὴς πρὸς Ἕλληνας περὶ τῶν ἐν τῷ Εὐαγγελίῳ ζητημάτων καὶ λύσεων (*Refutation or Only-begotten against the Pagans, on Problems relating to the Gospel and their Solution*), probably dating from the beginning of the fifth century, rather than from the early years of the fourth, as it once had been

[4] Labriolle, *La réaction païenne* (Paris, 1934), 228–31.

[5] The text of Constantine's Edict is extant only in Socrates, *Historia ecclesiastica* 1, 9, 31, ed. Robert Hussey (Oxford, 1853), 69 (*PG* 67.88C), and in that of Gelasius 2, 36, ed. Theodor Mommsen (*GCS* 9; Leipzig, 1903). The authenticity of this pronouncement has been doubted without reason, since it is cited by Athanasius, a contemporary, in the *Historia Arianorum ad monachos* 51, which dates from 358 (*PG* 25.753D), and was referred to by the Emperor Theodosius in 435 (*Codex Theodosianus* 16.5.66). See Labriolle, *op. cit.*, 242f.

[6] *Codex Iustinianus* 1.1.3.

[7] The fragments have been collected and edited by Adolf von Harnack, *Porphyrius "Gegen die Christen," 15 Bücher* (*Abhandlungen der königlich-preussischen Akademie der Wissenschaften*, Philosophisch-historische Klasse, Nr. 1; Berlin, 1916); Harnack, "Neue Fragmente des Werks des Porphyrius gegen die Christen: die Pseudo-Polycarpiana und die Schrift des Rhetors Pacatus gegen Porphyrius," *Sitzungsberichte der preuss. Ak. der Wiss.* (Berlin, 1921), 266–84, with *Supplement*, 834f. (I have not discussed these five fragments in the present paper.) Harnack translated the extant remains into German in his *Kritik des Neuen Testaments von einem griechischen Philosophen des 3. Jahrh.* (*TU* 37, 4; Leipzig, 1911); criticized, with emendations, by Felix Scheidweiler, "Zu Porphyrios κατὰ χριστιανῶν," *Philologus* 99 (1954–5), 304–12. Note also Franz Altheim and Ruth Stiehl, "Neue Bruchstücke aus Porphyrios' κατὰ χριστιανούς" [*sic*], ΑΠΑΡΧΑΙ: *Untersuchungen zur klassischen Philologie und Geschichte des Altertums* 4 (Tübingen, 1961), 23–38. See also P. Nautin, "Trois autres fragments du livre de Porphyre *Contre les chrétiens*," *Revue Biblique* 57 (1950), 409–16.

thought.[8] Nearly half of the *Apokritikos* has perished, and neither Macarius, who wrote in Greek, nor Jerome, who wrote in Latin, had access to the complete text of Porphyry's treatise. But Macarius apparently used an anonymous abridgment of Porphyry; and Jerome found quotations from Porphyry imbedded in the refutations by Methodius of Olympus, Eusebius of Caesarea, and Apollinaris of Laodicea, which, though originally considerable in extent (10,000 lines, 25 books, and 30 books respectively), have disappeared almost without a trace.[9] Nevertheless, what has survived of Porphyry's *Against the Christians* is sufficient to indicate the general tenor of his attack.

There is no mystery about the disappearance of the original text of Porphyry's diatribe, which had twice been struck down by imperial proscription. The loss of the lengthy works that Methodius, Eusebius, and Apollinaris directed against it is more curious, but is probably to be explained by the fact that Porphyry's jibes were so sharp and penetrating that they were painful to contemplate even in the context of the Christian counterattack. It must be admitted also that much of what is extant of the latter is feeble, and would not have satisfied the subtler intellects within the Christian fold. It may well be that Chris-

[8] *Macarii Magnetis quae supersunt,* ed. C. Blondel (Paris, 1876), is valuable, since the Greek MS on which it is based has been lost. See the abridged English translation by T. W. Crafer, *The Apocriticus of Macarius Magnes* (London and New York, 1919), who is usually dependable, although he often gives a paraphrase or a summary instead of a translation. On Macarius see Francesco Corsaro, "La dottrina eucaristica di Macario di Magnesia," *Convivium Dominicum: Studi sull' eucarestia nei padri della chiesa antica e miscellanea patristica* (Catania, 1959), 67–86; Corsaro, "L'Apocritico di Macario di Magnesia e le sacre Scritture," *Nuovo Didaskaleion* 7 (1957), 1–24; Paolo Frassinetti, "Sull' autore delle questioni pagane conservate nell' Apocritico di Macario di Magnesia, *ibid.* 3 (1949), 41–56: on the basis of fragment 35 (Macarius 4, 2: "330 years after Paul"), Frassinetti dates Macarius c. 380; he also makes an ingenious but unsuccessful attempt to show that Julian, not Porphyry, was the author of the pagan criticism. Cf. also Giovanni Mercati, "Per L'Apocritico di Macario Magnete, una tavola dei capi dei libri i, ii e iii," *Nuove note di letteratura biblica e cristiana antica* (Studi e Testi 95 [1941]), 49–84; Gustave Bardy, "Les objections d'un philosophe païen d'après l'Apocriticus de Macaire de Magnésie," *Bulletin d' ancienne littérature et d' archéologie chrétiennes* 3 (1913), 95–111. S. Pezzella, "Il problema del *Kata Christianon* di Porfirio," *Eos* 52 (1962), 87–104, assumes that while certain fragments in Macarius' work are indeed derived from Porphyry, others are culled from Hierocles' *Philalethes* and other apologists no longer extant. On textual problems, see Jonas Palm, *Textkritisches zum Apokritikos des Makarios Magnes* (Scripta minora Regiae Societatis Humaniorum Litterarum Ludensis 1959–60:4).

[9] On these, see Harnack, *Porphyrius,* 3–21, 35 n. xv.

tian scholars and scribes were so dissatisfied with the writings of their co-religionists on this subject that they deliberately chose not to transscribe them. This lack of enthusiasm on their part probably accounts for the fact that the modern editor of Macarius' *Apokritikos* could find only one manuscript on which to base his edition, and that even this has now vanished.

In what follows I analyze some of the more interesting fragments. Occasionally, for the sake of clarity, I abridge the original considerably, and give only a few representative examples of Macarius' rather peculiar allegorical interpretations of perplexing Biblical passages. The reader should remember that Macarius was addressing himself to a Christian audience, rather than to hostile pagans. His style was loose, verbose, and homiletical; and he made little effort to construct a tightly reasoned defense of his position. In general, Macarius fails to turn to the commonest, and perhaps most relevant, weapons in the armory of Christian apologetics, i.e., that the New Testament records the fulfillment by Christ of what the prophets had written about him, that God's ways are inscrutable, that mortal man cannot hope to penetrate the divine mysteries, and that Christians accept the Bible and its contents on faith, which cannot be analyzed.

Porphyry was far from being a friendly critic,[10] even if he had ever been a Christian who relapsed into paganism (he was born a pagan) in anger, after a thrashing at the hands of some Christians in Palestine, as the historian Socrates relates.[11] In view of the acerbity of some of his remarks about Christ, there are no grounds for assuming, as some have done, that Porphyry was well disposed toward Christ but hostile to his

[10] For the latest literature on Porphyry in general, see A. R. Sodano, ed., *Porphyrii in Platonis Timaeum Commentariorum fragmenta* (Naples, 1964); *idem*, ed. and trans., *Porfirio, lettera ad Anebo* (Naples, 1958); and Heinrich Dörrie, *Porphyrios' "Symmikta Zetemata" (Zetemata* 20 [Munich, 1959]). Of the vast bibliography I refer to: Pierre Courcelle, "Critiques exégétiques et arguments anti-chrétiens rapportés par Ambrosiaster," *Vigiliae Christianae* 13 (1959), 133–69; Courcelle, "Propos anti-chrétiens rapportés par Saint Augustin," *Recherches Augustiniennes* (Suppl. à la *Revue des études augustiniennes* 1, 1958), 149–86: most of these are derived from Porphyry. See furthermore John J. O'Meara, *Porphyry's Philosophy from Oracles in Augustine* (Paris, 1959), and Paolo Frassinetti, "Porfirio esegeta del profeta Daniele," *Istituto Lombardo: Rendiconti, classe di lettere e scienze morali e storiche* 86 (1953), 194–210. For Emperor Julian's anti-Christian polemic and its relationship to Porphyry see Loesche (above n. 2) and Rudolf Asmus, *Julians Galiläerschrift im Zusammenhang mit seinen übrigen Werken* in *Beilage zum Jahresbericht des Grossherzoglichen Gymnasiums zu Freiburg* (Freiburg im Br., 1904).

[11] Socrates, *Historia ecclesiastica* 3, 23; *PG* 67.444.

disciples and the Evangelists,[12] who, he objects, were not the historians, but rather the inventors of the episodes they set forth from the life of Jesus.[13]

In view of the fragmentary state of Porphyry's diatribe, it is difficult to deal systematically with it. I consider the topics he covers in the following order:

I. The errors and inconsistencies in the Christian view of life, as seen (a) in the Bible, (b) in the contradictory behavior of Peter and Paul, (c) in the Christian use of the Old Testament, (d) in the insistence of the Christians that they worshipped only one God, although they were really polytheists, and (e) in the delay of the promulgation of the Gospel.

II. His attack on Christian practice with regard to (a) prayer and ethics, (b) baptism, and (c) the eucharist.

III. On the Christian doctrine of immortality, especially as demonstrated through the life, crucifixion, and resurrection of Jesus Christ (a–g).

I (a). *Errors and inconsistencies in the Bible.* Porphyry makes much of errors and contradictions he discovers in the Bible, and condemns the disciples of Jesus as ignorant men, unworthy of respect, who performed miracles by magical arts and thereby persuaded wealthy women to give them their property.[14] He criticizes Matthew (13:35) for ascribing to Isaiah a passage which occurs in the Psalms,[15] and Mark (1:2f.)[16] for quoting as from Isaiah alone a text derived partly from Malachi (3:1—"Behold, I send my messenger before thy face, who shall prepare thy way before thee") and partly from Isaiah (40:3— "The voice of one crying in the wilderness; prepare ye the way of the Lord: make his paths straight"). In both instances Porphyry had reference to a Greek text (with variants) which is not reproduced by the English versions.

[12] L. Vaganay, "Porphyre," *Dictionnaire de théologie catholique* 12, 2 (Paris, 1935), 2570–72.

[13] Unless otherwise stated, the references are to Harnack's ed. of 1916: frag. 1.14ff.; frag. 15.1ff. (Macarius Magnes 2, 12).

[14] Cf. Harnack, p. 28.10ff., 25ff.; frag. 4, Jerome on Psalm 81, ed. G. Morin, *Corpus Christianorum, Series Latina* 87 (Turnholt, 1958), 89, lines 225ff.; *PL* 26.1130CD; cf. frag. 97.

[15] Frag. 10, Jerome on Psalm 77, ed. G. Morin, *CCL* 87, 66, 73ff.; *PL* 26.1108BC.

[16] Frag. 9 (Jerome, *Tract. in Marci Evangelium* I, 1–12, ed. G. Morin, *CCL* 88, 452, 30ff.; Jerome, *In Matheum* 1, 3, 3, *CCL* 77 (1969), 16,229 – 17,241; *PL* 26.29f.).

The Christian apologists enter a general denial to these charges, and refute them point by point. In meeting the specific accusation of garbling Biblical quotations Jerome, for example, contends that the mistakes were not made by the Evangelists but by copyists, who incorrectly wrote Isaiah in Matthew for Asaph (an ancient musician to whom several of the Psalms were traditionally ascribed), and wrongly introduced the name of Isaiah into Mark.[17] Porphyry commented adversely also on the discrepancy between Acts (1:18), according to which Judas was said to have burst asunder, and Matthew (27:5), who described him as having hanged himself.[18]

Macarius' rebuttal with regard to Judas has been lost, but we have more documentation on other points at issue, as for example in his summary and criticism of Porphyry's animadversions on the account of the healing of the demoniac named Legion. Porphyry, Macarius reports, draws attention to the inconsistency between Matthew, who speaks of two demoniacs, and Mark who refers to only one.[19]

Porphyry is skeptical also about Mark's statement (5:8ff.) that there were two thousand pigs which the demoniac spirits, expelled by Jesus, drove off the cliff into the Sea of Tiberias, both because Matthew (8:28ff.; cf. Luke 8:32) merely mentions "many pigs," and because he doubted that so large a number of pigs could have been assembled in a land inhabited by Jews, who regarded swine as unclean and unfit for food. He censures Jesus for harkening to the evil demons and allowing them to enter the swine, as they requested, instead of casting them into the abyss (Luke 8:31), of which they stood in dread. Furthermore he chides Jesus for bringing destruction upon dumb animals in this way and creating confusion among the swineherds and townspeople, as the Gospels say he did. He sees no virtue in curing some men and inflicting evil simultaneously upon others, as in this miracle.

He finds fault also with Mark for describing the body of water in Galilee near Tiberias as a sea (Mark 6:47ff.; cf. Matt. 14:24ff.; John 6:19), although it is only a small lake, which can be crossed easily by small boats in a couple of hours at the most.[20] He therefore brands

---

[17] Jerome, on Psalm 77, *Tract. in Marci Evang.,* and *On Matthew.*
[18] See texts cited in notes 15f. above.
[19] Frag. 49 (Macarius 3, 4).
[20] Frag. 55 (Macarius 3, 6).

Mark's account of the storm which would have threatened the lives of the disciples, had it not been stilled by Jesus, as a ridiculous fable typical of what he takes to be the general undependability of the Gospels as a whole. It is somewhat curious that he does not take special notice of Christ's walking on the water, which forms the kernel and most striking feature of the episode under discussion. He may have done so in a portion of the text that has been lost; or perhaps his silence here may indicate that this particular miracle was so similar to the numerous epiphanies recounted in pagan mythology as to seem relatively commonplace.

Macarius takes up Porphyry's questions seriatim.[21] In the first place, it is immaterial, he asserts, whether the Gospels record two demoniacs (as in Matt. 8:28) or only one (as in Mark 5) in view of the frequent use of singular nouns for the plural. Thus, for example, it is possible to speak of "the barbarian's reply to the emperor," when the reference is not to *one* barbarian, but to the barbarians as a group; and "man" may refer to mankind as a whole (hence, to many men), rather than to a single individual. Secondly, the pigs belonged to Roman troops stationed in that area, not to the Jews. Thirdly, Jesus refrained from commanding the demons to fall off a nearby cliff (or into a ravine or canyon, ἄβυσσος) and cast them, at their request, into the swine for several reasons: to make clear that they were unable, of themselves, without his command, to enter even such a wretched creature as a pig; and to discourage the prudent from wishing to lead a pig's life ($\text{χοιρώδη πολιτείαν καὶ ῥυπαρὰν μιμήσασθαι}$). Finally, when the demons left their human abode to lodge within the pigs, and sank into the sea with the latter, there was no room for doubt that they had truly been expelled from their dwelling place among men permanently and irretrievably. Had they been plunged into the ravine, it might have been thought that they had merely moved on to another locality to torture other men.

Even if the "Sea" of Tiberias were only a lake, Macarius retorts, it was also a sea, since it was tossed by the winds and bore fishing-ships like a sea.[22] But he soon loses sight of this point, and launches into an exposition of the miracle on the sea as an elaborate allegory of Christ's mission: The sea symbolizes the bitterness of human existence; the night is life; the ship is the universe; those who sail in it all night long

[21] Macarius 3, 11.
[22] Macarius 3, 13; n.b. Blondel, 84.9ff., 88.24ff.

denote man in the span of his life; the contrary wind is the opposition of the devil; and the fourth watch is the coming of the Saviour. In fact, the lake is an ellipse 21 kilometres long by 9.5 in breadth, has a depth averaging from 50 to 70 metres, reaching as much as 250 metres at some points, and is subject to furious storms, which can be dangerous.[23]

I (*b*). *Contradictions in the behavior of Peter and Paul.* Porphyry had no respect for either Peter or Paul, and ascribes the conflict between them (cf. Gal. 2) to Paul's jealousy of Peter.[24] A totally different theory about these disagreements is presented by Jerome, who was of the opinion that Peter and Paul only pretended to disagree on the observance of the Jewish law (Peter *pro,* Paul *contra*), in order to facilitate the conversion and rehabilitation of the Jews. Jerome clung to this hypothesis despite the fact that his friend Augustine was convinced that the two apostles actually did differ in their attitude toward the validity and applicability of the Mosaic Code.[25]

Porphyry contrasts Peter's high position among the apostles with his weakness in denying Christ three times and his pitiless execution of Ananias and Sapphira (Acts 5:1-10) merely because they had withheld for their daily needs a small portion of the money received from the sale of their property.[26] He judges Ananias and Sapphira guiltless in this matter but remarks that, even if what they did had constituted a sin, they should have been forgiven this one lapse, since, he notes (carrying out the multiplication in Christ's injunction to forgive "until seventy times seven": Matt. 18:22), Christ had commanded Peter to forgive as many as 490 offences. Porphyry is critical of Peter's conduct in general and deplores what he takes to have been Peter's act of cruelty in cutting off the ear of the high priest's servant, who was only carrying out orders (John 18:10; cf. Matt. 26:51; Mark 14:47;

---

[23] See F. Vigouroux, *Dictionnaire de la Bible* 5 (Paris, 1912), 2209-11.

[24] Frag. 21, n.b. B: Jerome, *Epistola* 112, 4-11, ed. Isidor Hilberg (*CSEL* 55; Vienna and Leipzig, 1912), 370-80; Jerome, *Comm. in Epist. ad Gal.,* PL 26.334f. (prologus), 363ff. (on 2, 11ff.).

[25] Augustine, *Epistulae* 28, 3f.; 40, 3-7; and 82, 4ff., ed. Al. Goldbacher, *CSEL* 34, 1 (p. 107-10); *CSEL* 34, 2 (pp. 71-8, 355ff.). Augustine's *Epp.* 28, 40, 82 appear as *Epp.* 56, 67, 116 in the Hieronyman collection *CSEL* 54 (498-502; 668-72); and *CSEL* 55 (399ff.). Jerome's *Ep.* 112-75 in the Augustinian collection *CSEL* 34, 2 (280ff.). Cf. J. Forget, "Jérôme (Saint)," *Dictionnaire de théologie catholique* 8, 1 (Paris, 1923), 902f.; Ferd. Cavallera, *Saint Jérôme, sa vie et son oeuvre* I (*Spicilegium sacrum Lovaniense: Études et documents* 1, 1922), 297.

[26] Frags. 23 and 25 (Macarius 3, 19 and 21).

I

430

Luke 22:50).[27] He wonders how Jesus could have entrusted such a man with the keys of heaven (Matt. 16:19), and mocks Christ for upbraiding Peter as "Satan" and a scandal (Matt. 16:23), immediately after having called him "blessed," and the foundation of his church (Matt. 16:17f.). Porphyry concludes that Jesus either was under the influence of wine when he rebuked Peter as Satan or was dreaming when he bestowed the keys of the kingdom of heaven upon such a person.[28]

In defence of Peter, whose guilt would, he admits, if substantiated, contaminate the whole company of apostles and all but tear out the roots of the Christian faith, Macarius distinguishes between Christ's praise of Peter for acknowledging him to be "the Christ, the Son of the living God" at Caesarea Philippi (Matt. 16:16), and the rebuke with which he repelled the suggestion that he should not undergo the passion (Matt. 16:22: "Be it far from thee, Lord: this shall not be unto thee").[29] In the former instance, Peter was rewarded when Christ said, "Blessed art thou, Simon Barjona: for flesh and blood hath not revealed [this mystery] unto thee" (Matt. 16:17), nor any of the angels or the supracosmic powers, but the Father in heaven.

At the same time, in perhaps the most celebrated pun in the literature of the world, Christ said to him, "Thou art Peter (in Greek, *Petros*) and upon this rock (in Greek, *petra*) I will build my Church; and the gates of hell shall not prevail against it. And I will give thee the keys of the kingdom of heaven: and whatsoever thou shalt bind on earth shall be bound in heaven: and whatsoever thou shalt loose on earth shall be loosed in heaven" (Matt. 16:18f.). Macarius explains that Peter was so named because "he had a mind and power of reasoning that could not be moved, and in giving witness to the immutability of the divine nature, revealed an impregnable and unshakable rock to all the world." A couple of pages later, Macarius adds that this apostle was called Peter because he "proclaimed the eternal character of the unshakable rock." Thus, Macarius's exegesis supports both those (i.e., many Protestants) who say that Christ or his divinity was the rock, and those (the Roman Catholics) who say that Peter himself was the rock.

[27] Frag. 24 (Macarius 3, 20). In frag. 24, read ὠμόν with Harnack instead of μῶμον; on other episodes in Peter's life see frags. 23 and 26 (Macarius 3, 19, and 22).

[28] Frags. 23 and 26.

[29] Macarius 3, 27. Cf. Johannes Betz, "Christus-petra-Petrus," *Kirche und Überlieferung,* ed. Johannes Betz and Heinrich Fries (Freiburg im Br., Basel, and Vienna, 1960), 1–21.

In the second of the texts cited by Porphyry, however, Macarius holds, Christ reprimanded Peter because the crucifixion was part of the divine scheme and was destined to break the power of Satan. Realizing that Christ's passion would overthrow the empire of wickedness, Satan prompted Peter to speak out against the crucifixion. But Christ recognized the devil's hand here, and was addressing the devil when he said, "Get thee behind me, Satan" (Matt. 16:23). Then, Macarius goes on, Christ directed the rest of the verse to Peter: "thou art an offence unto me: for thou savourest not the things that be of God, but those that be of men." This was the way he chided Peter for having been deceived by the devil. For the words of sympathy in which Peter attempted to dissuade Christ from submitting to death would have damaged mankind by depriving it of Christ's resurrection and ascension, along with the salvation which was to be gained thereby. Christ reproved Peter similarly in healing the high priest's servant, whose ear Peter had cut off. But on this occasion he did not utter a reproach in words, since he knew what Peter really intended.

In attempting to justify Peter's behavior with regard to Ananias and Sapphira, Macarius argues that they had joined a society in which the possession of wealth was abhorrent, and had voluntarily decided to present the total value of the land they owned to Christ.[30] Once they had taken this step, their offering became irrevocable, and they were guilty of sacrilege in making a gift to God of which the whole community had been informed, while at the same time secretly retaining a portion of it for themselves.

Peter was obliged to make a public exposé in order to eliminate this kind of corruption, which was like a disease or a weed that might, if unchecked, poison the whole of Christian society. Moreover, since the crime was not committed against Peter, but against God and the faith, Peter had no opportunity to exercise forgiveness. If Ananias and Sapphira had not been punished, it would have seemed that Christ had no knowledge of deeds done secretly, and Ananias would not only have proceeded to further acts of wickedness but would have influenced other men to imitate his nefarious example. In the last paragraph of this section, Macarius acquits Peter of responsibility as executioner. Peter did not execute the guilty pair with a sword, as Porphyry claims. All he did was to remind them that they had sinned against the Holy Spirit (Acts 5:9; cf. 5:3); and it was their conscience, not Peter, which killed them.

[30] Macarius 3, 28.

Porphyry is no less critical of Paul, whom he ridicules for indecision with regard to circumcision,[31] meat offered to idols,[32] marriage, and virginity.[33] In his anxiety to be all things to all men, Porphyry complains, and in asserting himself to be now a Jew, then a Roman, Paul ends up being a liar, and undermines his proud boast, "I speak the truth in Christ; I lie not" (Rom. 9:1).[34] He is equally caustic about Paul's contradictory judgments on the Jewish law, which he condemns as involving a curse (Gal. 3:10; cf. 3:1; 5:3) and then pronounces to be holy (Rom. 7:12) and spiritual (7:14).[35]

With regard to Paul's apparently conflicting statements about circumcision, Macarius urges that Paul is to be compared to a teacher, physician, or general, who makes concessions to his pupils, patients, or foes, in order to advance his cause.[36] Often a harmful drug, when combined with another, will cure stubborn illnesses. In like manner, Paul yields to the Gentiles whenever he can, so as to convert them, and is even willing to combine circumcision with the Gospel, to which it is admittedly alien, in the hope of conciliating the Jews.

Neither Porphyry nor Macarius understood Paul's teaching on meat offered to idols, which was somewhat at variance with the decision of the Council of Antioch (Acts 15:29; cf. 15:20). The Council forbade the eating of such meat, but Paul had no objection, if its connection with pagan sacrifices was not blatantly proclaimed. For this reason he advised his followers to buy meat freely even from pagan butchers, and to accept meat at the table of their pagan friends without asking embarrassing questions about its origin, even when the probability was great that it had been used in pagan sacrifice.[37] To Paul it made little difference how such meat had been slaughtered, whether as a sacrificial offering or not. The important thing in his judgment was not to offend Christians who might feel that such meat was unsuitable. Only in association with people of strict observance would Paul counsel abstention from meat that might have been contaminated by heathen religious associations.

But instead of interpreting Paul's apparently contradictory re-

[31] Macarius 3, 30.

[32] Macarius 3, 35.

[33] Macarius 3, 36.

[34] Macarius 3, 31. Cf. G. Kehnscherper, "Der Apostel Paulus als römischer Bürger," *Studia evangelica* 2, ed. Frank Cross (*TU* 87; Berlin, 1964), 411–40.

[35] Macarius 3, 33, 34.

[36] Macarius 3, 37.

[37] Cf. Rom. 14:14–21; I Cor. 8:1–13; Acts 15:24.

marks along these lines, Macarius distinguishes between meat offered to idols (εἰδωλόθυτα), which he says Paul forbade, and meat presented for sale by butchers, which was not forbidden to Christians.[38] Then he descants at length upon the various kinds of pagan sacrifice, and concludes, after further discussion of the Pauline distinction, with the observation that butchers slaughter animals for profit, not in order to serve demons.

In absolving Paul from blame for favoring virginity but also recommending marriage, Macarius pleads that celibacy is difficult and unnatural and was for this reason not required by Christ.[39] Notwithstanding this admission, virginity remained in his eyes a higher mode of existence and one which, being optional, merited high praise. He disputes Porphyry's verdict that Paul was a liar but strangely fails to stress the fact that a Jew could be a Roman citizen, although he comes close to saying this, and this may be what he meant.[40]

With regard to Porphyry's taunts on Paul's contradictory pronouncements about the Jewish law, Macarius concedes that the law itself was indeed holy, as Paul had declared it to be, because the Holy One (Christ) had fulfilled it.[41] But it was so detailed, so complex, so inconsistent, so impossible to read through and remember, that no one could hope to carry out all its provisions. Moreover, since Christ freed mankind from all obligation to Jewish law, any attempt to follow it was tantamount to rebellion against Christ and would imply that he had not truly accomplished his mission.

I (c). *Christian misuse of the Old Testament.* Despite his own extensive use of allegory in expounding ancient lore,[42] Porphyry upbraids Origen, whom he had known personally, for reading a hidden meaning into the Old Testament, that is, presumably, for interpreting much of it as prophetic of Christ. Eusebius, our source for this excerpt from Porphyry,[43] brushes aside Porphyry's judgment on Origen without further comment on the validity of the allegorical method, which he himself found especially congenial. Porphyry impugns the traditional date for the composition of the Book of Daniel, which he puts, quite

---

[38] Macarius 3, 42.

[39] Macarius 3, 43.

[40] Macarius 3, 38.

[41] Macarius 3, 40; cf. 3, 39 and 41.

[42] As, for example, in *De antro nympharum*, ed. A. Nauck, *Porphyrii philosophi Platonici opuscula selecta* (Leipzig, 1886), 53–81.

[43] Frag. 39 (Eusebius, *Historia ecclesiastica* 6, 19, 2ff.).

434

correctly, in the time of Antiochus Epiphanes,[44] and thus was the first scholar to divine its true place in history. His long *Commentary on Daniel* has disappeared except for the excerpts quoted by Jerome, who, however, dissents vigorously from Porphyry on numerous details, and cleaves to the conservative view that the Book of Daniel was written in the sixth century B.C., and was an elaborate historical prophecy, not a chronicle of events that had already taken place, as Porphyry believed it to be.

Then, aiming at the heart and core of the Old Testament, Porphyry declares that none of the writings of Moses survived the destruction of the temple, and that the works which bear his name were written 1,180 years after his death by Ezra and the latter's associates.[45] But even, he says, if we were to accept the Mosaic authorship of these books, they contain no reference to Christ as God, God the Word, or Creator, or to his crucifixion.

Porphyry's barbs here were directed against John 5:46f. ("If ye believed Moses, ye would have believed me, for he wrote concerning me"), which Macarius finds unobjectionable. He grants that what Moses wrote was destroyed in the Babylonian Captivity, but he claims that the same spirit which inspired Moses guided Ezra, and dictated the identical text to both.[46] Moreover, he summarizes several passages in the Pentateuch which he regarded as prefiguring Christ's incarnation and crucifixion, and quotes others in which Christ, according to his exegesis, is called God (Psalm 19:7 LXX; Isaiah 2:3: references to the "Lord's Christ" and the "Lord's Word"), none of which, it must be admitted, strengthens his argument. His citation of Psalm 44:8 LXX refers to a royal anointment and is completely irrelevant.

I (d). *Christian polytheism.* In Porphyry's view the Christian faith was irrational, and the Christians themselves, despite their professed monotheism, were in reality polytheists.[47] He imputes polytheism to them for several reasons. In the first place, he contends, the monarchy of God, on which the Christians insisted, necessarily involved rule over other gods.[48] A monarch is not one who *is* alone, but one who, like

---

[44] Frag. 43; cf. James A. Montgomery, *A Critical and Exegetical Commentary on the Book of Daniel* (New York, 1927), 107; for Porphyry's commentary on Daniel, ed. F. Glorie, *CCL* 75A (Turnholt, 1964), see Paolo Frassinetti, *loc. cit.*, n. 10 above, and Jean Lataix, "Le commentaire de Saint Jérôme sur Daniel," *Revue d'histoire et de littérature religieuses* 2 (1897), 164–73, 268–77.

[45] Frag. 68 (Macarius 3, 3).

[46] Macarius 3, 10.

[47] Frags. 1.17f., 52 (Macarius 4, 9), 73.

[48] Frag. 75 (Macarius 4, 20).

the Roman Emperor Hadrian, rules alone over other human beings. Hence, God would not have been called a monarch unless he ruled over other gods.

Secondly, both the Old Testament and the New refer to other gods, as, for example, in Joshua 24:14: "Fear him and worship him alone, and put away the gods whom your fathers worshipped" (slightly abridged but not distorted by Porphyry).[49] He also quotes Exodus 22:28 and Jeremiah 7:6 to the same effect, along with I Corinthians 8:5f. ("For though there are many who are called gods and many who are called lords, whether on earth or in heaven, but we have one God and Father, of whom are all things" [also somewhat amended]). Thirdly, rulers and masters do not shrink from having the same names as their subjects and slaves, and we can hardly suppose God to be less gracious in such matters than men.

Finally, the angels are nothing less than gods.[50] In such matters, the designation is of no consequence. The Greeks, for example, speak of Athena; the Romans call the same goddess Minerva. The Egyptians, the Syrians, and the Thracians use other names, but she is designated as a divinity nevertheless. Similarly, it makes no difference whether the angels are *called* gods or not since they are said to have a divine nature, and are impassible, immortal, and incorruptible.

He then proceeds, on this basis, to an apologia in defense of statues (βρέτας, ἄγαλμα, ξόανα) of divine beings. The logical link here is somewhat obscure, but the relevance of this discussion will become clear if we supply as a connection the unexpressed assumption on Porphyry's part that, where there is a plurality of gods, there must be images. He vigorously denies that anyone would believe that the gods reside in these representations, any more than anyone would suppose that the person portrayed in a painting (εἰκόνα) dwells therein. In both instances, the image is intended to honor the person represented, or to serve as a reminder of the divinity portrayed. On the other hand, in his view, sacrifices are offered to gods, not so much to honor them as to symbolize the good wishes and gratitude of their worshippers.

Statues of gods are rightly cast in human form, since man is deemed to be the fairest of all animals and the image of god. Furthermore, he says, the Christian God has fingers, as is proved by the verse,

[49] Frag. 78 (Macarius 4, 23).
[50] Frag. 76 (Macarius 4, 21). On the anthropomorphic nature of images cf. also Porphyry, *De imaginibus,* frag. 2.8, etc., ed. J. Bidez, *Vie de Porphyre* (Université de Gand: *Recueil de travaux publiés par la Faculté de philosophie et lettres* 43; Gand and Leipzig, 1913), 2*.

I

436

"He gave Moses . . . two tablets written with the finger of God" (Exodus 31:18); and the Christians imitate the pagan temples by building huge houses of worship, although it was possible for them to say their prayers at home, since their God hears them wherever they may be. But, he adds, even if any pagan were so idiotic as to imagine that the gods dwelt in their statues, this conception is far purer than that of the Christians, who believe that the divine descended into the womb of the Virgin Mary, became an embryo, was born, and was soiled by blood, the afterbirth, bile, and worse.[51]

Against Porphyry's first point (n. 48 above), that the "monarchy" of God necessarily involves polytheism, Macarius tries to show that identity of name or designation does not imply identity of nature.[52] A fire, for example, is warm, as is a man who stands close to it; but only the former is warm by nature (φύσει). The latter is warm by position (θέσει). Similarly, God is the only true God, and he alone is uncreated. Though he does not begrudge the name of God or Lord to those who draw close to him, they are all beings whom he has created, and he rules over them, not merely as one of them. Macarius here apparently was referring to I Corinthians 8:5, but he probably had in mind also John 10:34 and Psalms 82:6: "Ye are gods." He then rejects Porphyry's analogy of earthly rulers like Hadrian, because they govern tyrannically and by force over ordinary men like themselves. God, on the other hand, rules with love over beings he has created, who are unlike him. Just as the sun imparts brightness to the objects it illumines, without receiving illumination from them or sharing its own being with them, God gives the angels a kind of reflected divinity, but does not receive any part of his nature from them or yield any of it to them since they are gods "by position, not by nature," and he alone is truly God.

In rebutting Porphyry's second point (n. 49 above), Macarius ignores all but one (Exod. 22:28) of the Biblical witnesses to polytheism cited, and says that the "gods" here ("Thou shalt not revile the gods") are those to whom the word of God has come, just as those are warm who have been heated by the fire.[53]

In taking up Porphyry's fourth point (about the angels, n. 50 above), Macarius rejects Porphyry's theory of pagan images (as he had done also in refuting the second point), and repudiates the notion

[51] Frag. 77 (Macarius 4, 22); cf. Porphyry, *Ad Marcellam*, 17f., ed. Nauck, *op. cit.*, 285f.
[52] Macarius 4, 26.   [53] Macarius 4, 29.

that God actually has physical fingers.[54] The Biblical allusions to them, like the references to God's hands, feet, voice, and hearing, must be taken figuratively. God is incorporeal and invisible; he is spoken of in physical terms only to help man lift his mind to the realm of the divine. As for the angels, he holds, it is futile to try to represent in tactile form incorporeal beings who cannot be touched. It was for this reason that, after his meeting with the three angels (Gen. 18), Abraham quite properly refrained from attempting to reproduce their corporeal likeness in a painting or statue but fixed recollection of them "in the secret treasury of his soul."

In combating Porphyry's view that the incarnation involved great impurity, Macarius argues that Christ did not contaminate himself in becoming flesh.[55] On the contrary, what he did was to free human flesh from its defects and confer immortality upon it. Besides, Macarius adds, there is an exact pagan parallel in the myth of the miraculous birth of the goddess Athena from the head of Zeus, which caused no scandal or difficulties about physical impurities.

I (*e*). *Postponement of the Gospel.* Another type of inconsistency which vexed Porphyry, as we learn from Jerome and Augustine, was that involved in the long delay before the promulgation of the Gospel. If no one could be saved except by Christ, he asked, why was salvation postponed so long, and what became of the innumerable souls which existed before Christ came to the earth, and could not be blamed for having been born too soon, to say nothing of remote regions like Britain and Scotland, to which the work of Moses and the prophets had never penetrated.[56]

Jerome dismisses this query by an appeal to the wisdom of God. But Augustine gives it serious attention, and demonstrates that both the pagans and the Christians had to face this difficulty, and both dealt with it in much the same way. The pagans claimed that their divinities had always existed and that variety of nomenclature, cult, and practice did not affect essentials. Similarly, the Christians maintain that Christ spoke by his prophets from the beginning of the human race and had followers among men as early as the time of Adam, who won salvation by believing in him. Despite differences of one sort or other, and although it was more obscurely revealed and less widely disseminated before his incarnation, the religion of Christ has

---

[54] Macarius 4, 27.
[55] Macarius 4, 28.
[56] Frags. 81f.

always been the same. Augustine admits, however, that in some regions and some periods of time, the gospel of Christ was not preached, because it was foreknown that they would not be receptive to it.[57]

II (a). *Christian practices attacked: prayer and ethics.* In attacking the practices of the Christian churches, Porphyry expresses scorn for Christian standards of faith, and ridicules Christ's teaching on the power of prayer.[58] If it really be true, he says, that a man of faith can move mountains (Matt. 17:20; Mark 11:23), the Christian who has not moved his mountain is unworthy of a place in the company of the faithful. Hence, no Christian, not even a single priest or bishop, would have the right to be called a believer. Porphyry was in error, Macarius rejoins, in taking the reference to mountains literally. Jesus was obviously speaking allegorically here, since he never made any topographical changes of this kind himself.

Porphyry takes particular delight in scoffing at Christian ethics and the famous verse, "It is easier for a camel to go through [Porphyry omits "the eye of"] a needle than for a rich man to enter into the kingdom of heaven" (Matt. 19:24; Mark 10:25; Luke 18:25), which he interprets as signifying that the wealthy, however virtuous, are barred from heaven by reason of their wealth alone, and that the poor, however wicked, gain entry to heaven solely because of their poverty.[59] This means, he says, that it is not virtue, but lack of possessions, which opens the door to salvation, and that the way to be saved is to ignore virtue, behave immorally, and cleave to poverty. Accordingly, he refuses to believe that Jesus ever uttered these words, and prefers to attribute them to poor men, eager to lay their hands on the property of the wealthy. He renders the same judgment on the injunction, "Go sell what thou hast, and give to the poor, and thou shalt have treasure in heaven" (Matt. 19:21; Mark 10:21; Luke 18:22; cf. Luke 12:33), which he cannot accept as genuine and ascribes to some indigent woman, not to Jesus.

This interpretation is unsound, Macarius protests.[60] It is the behavior of both rich and poor which determines whether they are to be admitted to heaven, not their wealth or poverty. What matters is not

[57] Jerome, *Epistola* 133, 9, ed. Hilberg (*CSEL* 56; 1918), 255f.; Augustine, *Epistola* 102, 8–15 (Quaestio 2), to Deogratias, ed. Al. Goldbacher (*CSEL* 34, 2; Prague, Vienna, Leipzig, 1898), 551–58.

[58] Frag. 95 (Macarius 3, 17); and Macarius, 3, 25.

[59] Frag. 58 (Macarius 3, 5).

[60] Macarius 3, 12; quotation, Blondel, *op. cit.,* 83.18f.

a man's wealth or poverty but the way he conducts himself. If a rich man is selfish and ignores the need and entreaties of the poor, he will be excluded from heaven. There are rich men who have been admitted to the kingdom of heaven, and poor men who have been excluded, Macarius says, but the "poor are the advocates of the rich without whom wealth is profitless in the sight of God." He also admits at the end of his argument that wealth is burdensome in many ways, and creates the presumption of greed, so that it is actually better for a rich man to divest himself of his wealth if he really aspires to heaven.

One of Porphyry's most insidious sneers was based on Matthew 9:12f. and Luke 5:31f. ("They that be whole need not a physician, but they that are sick. I am not come to call the righteous, but sinners to repentance").[61] If this be so, he says, the necessary inference is that Christ came only for the sake of sinners and the sick. Since it is the sinners who are called and the sick who are healed, and since the righteous are not called, it follows that he who is neither called nor in need of therapy is righteous and in good health. Thus, he who does not require healing turns away from the Gospel; and the more completely he rejects it, the more righteous and healthy he will be.

Macarius makes no attempt to cope with Porphyry's pungently stated paradox.[62] Instead, he contents himself with a tedious affirmation of the proposition that all men are sinners. John Chrysostom (d. 407) solves the problem in the same terms but much more succinctly.[63] It is unfortunate that in addressing himself to this question, Macarius failed to offer some exegesis of the word "righteous" (δίκαιος), which in this context had reference to those who sought justification by observance of the Jewish law, that is the Pharisees and the scribes, who opposed Jesus at every step. This is in effect what Cyril of Alexandria does in his remarks on the passage.[64] Cyril also draws attention to the fact that Jesus deliberately sought out men like the publicans "who had not been purified" and whom the Jewish law abominated, in order to give them grace and compassion, which were not otherwise available to them.

---

[61] Frag. 87 (Macarius 4, 10).

[62] Macarius 4, 18.

[63] Chrysostom, *Commentarius in Sanctum Matthaeum Evangelistam, homilia* 30 (31), *PG* 57.365D. Cf. Édouard Massaux, *L'Influence de l'Évangile de saint Matthieu sur la littérature chrétienne avant saint Irénée* (*Universitas Catholica Lovaniensis* 2, 42; Louvain, 1950), 140f.

[64] Joseph Reuss, *Matthäus-Kommentare aus der griechischen Kirche* (*TU* 61; 5. Reihe, 6; Berlin, 1957), 186f.; *Explanatio in Lucae Evangelium* 5, 30, *PG* 72.569C–72A.

II (b). *Baptism.* Addressing himself to I Corinthians 6:11 ("But such [wicked] were some of you: but ye are washed, but ye are sanctified, but ye are justified in the name of the Lord Jesus, and by the Spirit of our God"), Porphyry condemns Christian baptismal theory as immoral because it provides too easy an escape from the burden of previous offences, which, he observes, the newly baptized sloughed off like a serpent shedding its skin.[65] He objects also that it encouraged depravity and undermined the legal foundations of society by assuring men that, however wantonly they behaved, they could obtain full remission for all their misdeeds simply by believing, calling upon the name of Jesus, and being baptized. Porphyry's jeers were probably prompted in part by his disapproval of the practice, common among Christians in his day, of postponing baptism until the end of their lives, in order to avoid the risk of committing mortal sin after the cleansing waters of baptism had washed away all the sins of the past.

Responding to Porphyry in behalf of the sacrament of baptism, Macarius compares its expiatory effect to the pardon granted by the Roman emperor to persons sentenced to death under the law.[66] In baptism the name of Christ invests ordinary water with power to wipe away the stains of wickedness, just as the signature of the emperor transforms a mere piece of paper into an official certificate of pardon. He even likens the name of Christ invoked upon the baptismal water to soda (the chemical compound, i.e., not the beverage), which, when added to water, removes dirt. Similarly, he says the name of Christ in the water of baptism removes sin, purifies the baptized person, and gives him the power to overcome evil in the future.

II (c). *The eucharist.* Most of all, Porphyry was repelled by the Johannine account of the eucharist: "Except ye eat my flesh and drink my blood, ye have no life in you" (John 6:53, in Porphyry's paraphrase).[67] It is hardly credible that he was sincere in making this

---

[65] Frag. 88 (Macarius 4, 19). On postponement of baptism see Eusebius, *Vita Constantini* 4, 61ff., ed. Ivar A. Heikel, (*GCS* 7; Leipzig, 1902); *PG* 20.1212ff. Christian criticism of such postponement: Pseudo-Basil, *Homilia* 13, 1ff., *PG* 31.425Bff.; Gregory of Nazianzus, *Oratio* 40, 11–46, *PG* 36.372–425; Gregory of Nyssa, *Adversus eos qui different baptismum*, *PG* 46.416–32. The subject is discussed by Franz J. Dölger, "Die Taufe Konstantins und ihre Probleme," *Konstantin der Grosse und seine Zeit* (*Römische Quartalschrift*, Suppl. 19; Freiburg im Br., 1913), 377–447.

[66] Macarius 4, 25.

[67] Frag. 69 (Macarius 3, 15). I have given Porphyry's version of John 6:53, which in all of the best MSS has "the flesh of the Son of man" and "his blood." On cannibalism, see Porphyry, *De abstinentia* 2, 8; 4, 21, ed. Nauck, *op. cit.,* 138f., 266f.

charge. Perhaps he could not resist the temptation to put the old pagan anti-Christian libel into a somewhat more respectable form. Anyway, he at least pretends that the eucharist was cannibalistic, unprecedentedly barbarous, and worse than the Thyestean banquet of human flesh of which Tereus partook unwillingly, or the grim meal consisting of his son's body which Harpagus, tricked by Astyages, consumed. These pagan instances of cannibalism Porphyry extenuates as involuntary, and contrasts with the Christian eucharist, which he terms abominable, even if interpreted allegorically. Not even animals are autophagous in the direst famine, he says; and Matthew, Mark, and Luke deliberately omitted the Johannine eucharistic imagery because they were outraged by it.

It is true that none of the "Synoptic" Gospels includes the words from John reprehended by Porphyry. But Macarius unaccountably neglects to remind his readers that Matthew and Mark (supported in essentials by Luke and Paul) contain an account of the Last Supper in which Christ describes the eucharist as "my body" and "my blood," which he commanded his disciples to eat and drink in his memory (Matt. 26:26ff.; Mark 14:22ff.; Luke 22:19ff.; I Cor. 11:23ff.).[68] Instead, he makes the retort that infants feed on the flesh and blood of their mother. He weakens the effect of his argument by spinning it out too far, and tries to show that milk is really the same as blood because the latter is physiologically transformed into the former in the mother's breast. He then loses himself in a fog of allegory, whereby he identifies the body and the blood of Christ (whom he here designates as *sophia* [wisdom]) with the words of the Old and New Testament, which he likens to the breasts of *sophia* (which in Greek is feminine). He also offers the suggestion that the bread and wine of the eucharist may properly be described as Christ's body and blood because he created them and made use of them for his own body. He could have presented the Christian position more effectively had he openly admitted that the transformation of the bread and wine into the "body and blood of Christ" is a mystery inaccessible except by an act of faith.

III. *Immortality, crucifixion, and resurrection.* Porphyry's most telling blows were struck at the doctrine of the immortality of the body and

[68] Macarius 3, 23. Cf. Hippocrates, περὶ ἀδένων (on the glands), 16, ed. É. Littré, *Oeuvres complètes d'Hippocrate* 8 (Paris, 1853), 572f.: καὶ τὴν τροφήν, ἥν τινα ἕλκουσιν [sc. οἱ μαζοὶ] ἐπὶ σφᾶς, ἀλλοιοῦσιν ἐς τὸ γάλα ("The breasts transform into milk all the nourishment they take in").

the Gospel account of Christ's crucifixion and resurrection.[69] These basic articles of Christian belief were repugnant to Porphyry because they were in conflict with the Platonic theory that the body perishes after death and that immortality is limited to the soul. He also questions the value of the incarnation and the crucifixion, and asks how Christ, who was the Son of God and impassible ("incapable of suffering"), could have been contained by a body for a brief period of time and subjected to pain. And why, he inquires, was Christ crucified and not punished in some other way?

III (a). *Incarnation and crucifixion in general.* In the few extant pages of Pseudo-Methodius' treatise *Against Porphyry* we have a sample of early Christian reasoning on these matters.[70] Christ became man, Methodius says, in order to free human nature from domination by demons, conquer death, and offer mankind a way to heavenly life. He died on the cross because the cross was a symbol of victory. Indeed, so successful was it in scattering all kinds of evil that it was adopted by terrestrial rulers as the model for battle standards. In accordance with traditional exegesis, Methodius denies that the Logos himself suffered on the cross. It was the flesh which suffered, while the Logos remained impassible. He then supplements the tradition with a theory of his own, which is perhaps not entirely fatuous. His idea was that it is impossible to damage fire or air, for example, by stone, iron, wood, or the like, since air and fire offer no resistance and yield before the blow. It is all the more unlikely that the Divine Wisdom could be injured in any way, even when associated with a body that was crucified.

III (b). *Cosmic cataclysm.* Porphyry then turns his attention to the question of the destruction of the universe, which served in Christian eschatology as the prelude to the last judgment and the general resurrection.[71] He was repelled by this hypothesis because it seemed to

---

[69] Frag. 84; *Methodius,* ed. N. Bonwetsch (*GCS,* 27; Leipzig, 1917), 503 n., 505 n. Bonwetsch, *Die Theologie des Methodius von Olympus* (Abhandlungen der königlichen Gesellschaft der Wissenschaften zu Göttingen, philolog.-hist. Kl., N.F. 7, 1; Berlin, 1903), 52f., briefly summarizes the fragments traditionally ascribed to Methodius. But Vinzenz Buchheit, *Studien zu Methodios von Olympos* (*TU* 69, 5.R., 14; Berlin, 1958), 120–29, argues on sytlistic grounds that this attribution is incorrect.

[70] Methodius, ed. Bonwetsch, *op. cit.,* 503–7. On early Christian ideas of the cross, see Carlo Cecchelli, *Il trionfo della croce* (Rome, 1954).

[71] Frag. 93, *Quaestiones gentiles ad Christianos* 14, *Corpus apologetarum Christianorum saeculi secundi,* ed. I. C. T. de Otto 5 (3rd ed.; Jena, 1881), 328–30. For the identity of Pseudo-Justin, see Johannes Quasten, *Patrology* 3 (1960), 549; Gustave Bardy, "La littérature patristique des 'Quaestiones et responsiones' sur l'Écriture Sainte," *Revue*

presuppose a defect in the creator, which was for him metaphysically inadmissible. If such a cosmic catastrophe were to take place, he reasoned, whatever its immediate cause, the responsibility would ultimately lie with the creator, either for having been evil himself, or for having left a fatal imperfection in his creation, or for having been too weak to overcome whatever external force it was which opposed him and destroyed what he had created. Porphyry's unknown Christian opponent, now usually styled Pseudo-Justin, to whom we owe the fragment under review, repudiates his adversary's analysis of the logical errors in the Christian expectation of a cataclysmic destruction of the universe.[72] For, according to him, the eventual dissolution of the cosmos is attributable, not to a flaw either in its creator or in creation itself, but to the ordinance of God.

III (*c*). *Resurrection of the flesh.* These Christian beliefs ran counter to Porphyry's conviction that the cosmos was ordained of God, and hence could neither be condemned nor annihilated, as if it were the work of a mortal man. Moreover, he objects, the Christians failed to explain how it was possible that all men would be restored to life in the flesh simultaneously, so that Priam and Nestor, for example, who had died thousands of years previously, would resume their living bodies along with someone who had died only three days before the resurrection.

In Porphyry's judgment, the Christian dogma of the resurrection of the flesh leads to absurdity if examined critically.[73] Suppose, for instance, he suggests, that a shipwrecked man is devoured by fish and that the latter are eaten by fishermen, who die and are consumed by dogs, which, in turn, fall prey to crows and vultures. How could a body that has suffered such vicissitudes, or one that was burned or eaten by worms, ever be put together again? Such questions cannot be parried, Porphyry warns, by saying that God is omnipotent and can do anything, for this is not true. God cannot now bring it about that Homer was not a poet, that Troy was not captured, or that two times two make five. Nor can he sin or be evil if he wishes, since he is

---

Biblique 42 (1933), 211–19. On the cosmological questions at issue see A. Luneau, "Les âges du monde: état de la question à l'aurore de l'ère patristique," *Studia Patristica* 5 (*TU* 80; Berlin, 1962), 509–18; Wolfgang Marcus, "Typen altchristlicher Kosmologie in den Genesis-Kommentaren," *Philosophisches Jahrbuch der Görresgesellschaft* 65 (1956), 106–19.

[72] *Quaestiones* 10 (14), *op. cit.,* 348.
[73] Frag. 94 (Macarius 4, 24).

I

444

good. But even if it were possible for God to destroy heaven, earth, and the stars, and thereafter to bring the bodies of all men back to life, how could the earth hold all the population of the world born since its creation?

Realizing the gravity of Porphyry's onslaught on the doctrine of the resurrection, Macarius devotes the longest chapter in his book to a consideration of this dogma, which he admits is exceedingly difficult.[74] He fails to discuss what Porphyry took to be the logical objections to the Christian theory that God at the end of time would destroy the world he had created. Instead, he begins by assuming that God, as the creator of mankind and the universe *ex nihilo*, would naturally wish to improve what he had created by purging it of its flaws. Moreover, the immortality of human beings, together with the resurrection and rebirth of the universe along new lines, was essential to wash away corruption, reward the virtuous, punish the wicked, and bring about cosmic renewal, harmony, and beauty. When man is made immortal, it is only fitting that the universe, which was created for him, be made over and beautified to accommodate itself to his new condition.

Since a thousand years are as one day with the Lord and vice versa (II Pet. 3:8), it makes no difference whether a man died three days before the resurrection or a thousand years ago, like Priam and Nestor, especially since everyone will be rewarded according to his deserts. Nor does Macarius see any merit in Porphyry's question about the shipwrecked man and the itinerary of his body through the digestive systems of fish, men, dogs, and birds of prey. God has the power to reassemble the dispersed members of such a man, both because he is omnipotent and because man is his most treasured creation. On this particular point Pseudo-Justin adds that it is no more of a task for God to reconstitute the elements of which the bodies of men and fish are formed than to put them together in the first place, at the time of creation.[75] Unlike Porphyry, Macarius believed God to be omnipo-

[74] Macarius 4, 30.

[75] *Quaestiones* II (15), *op. cit.* 5, 348–50. Porphyry's diabolical question concerning the reconstitution of the human body after the *resurrectio carnis* was not original with him, and may have been based upon Celsus, ed. Bader, 128f., cf. 205f. (from Origen, *Contra Celsum* 5, 14; cf. 8, 49). See Henry Chadwick, "Origen, Celsus, and the Resurrection of the Body," *Harvard Theological Review* 41 (1948), 83–102. The argument exactly in the form in which it was presented by Porphyry is mentioned by Athenagoras of Athens, *De resurrectione mortuorum*, 4f., ed. Otto, *op. cit.* 7 (Jena, 1857), 200ff., cf. cc. 3ff., *ibid.*, 198ff. See Quasten, *Patrology* 1 (Westminster, Utrecht, Brussels, 1950),

tent.[76] But his reasoning on this head is obscure, and he fails to grapple with Porphyry's formulation of the logical and metaphysical implications inherent in the concept of omnipotence.

III (*d*). *The crucifixion narrative in the Gospels.* Porphyry caustically reviews the numerous differences among the four Gospels in the account of the crucifixion, and concludes therefrom that the four Evangelists were completely unreliable in this as well as in other matters.[77] The narrative is so inconsistent, he concludes, that it is not clear whether only one man had been crucified or several.

Macarius vindicates the Gospel description of the crucifixion on two grounds.[78] First, he rules out the disparity noted by Porphyry with regard to what Christ was offered to drink on the cross, whether vinegar (Mark 15:36; John 19:29) or wine mixed with gall (Matt. 27:33), since, in his view, they all amounted in the end to the same thing. Secondly, and more sweepingly, he holds that the incidents and words recorded in the Gospels correspond exactly with what the Evangelists saw and heard. They merely related their experiences without attempting to reconcile apparent inconsistencies or excise anything that seemed strange, although he concedes that their equilibrium was disturbed by the earthquake, the eclipse of the sun, and other frightening phenomena attendant upon the crucifixion. Still, their account of the events they witnessed, however devoid of literary merit (a strange and unnecessary admission), had the advantage of presenting the facts without distortion. They were not educated men, but even if they had been, it was their task to give a simple, unvarnished report of what had happened. This is exactly what they did, for they realized that such a narrative, which did not attempt to gloss over difficulties, would be more convincing than an elaborately contrived literary composition.

235f.; Pseudo-Athanasius, *Quaestiones ad Antiochum ducem* 114, *PG* 28.668Dff.; Gregory of Nyssa, *De anima et resurrectione, PG* 46.72C–76B, 80A, 108A, 108C–109A, 156C–157B, 160ABC: on the general proposition; on the specific point raised by Porphyry: Gregory of Nyssa, *De hominis opificio,* 26, cf. 25 and 27, *PG* 44.224f., 213–29; Anastasius Sinaita, *Interrogationes et responsiones, Quaestio* 92, *PG* 89.725Bff. A study of the sources and mutual relationship of these passages would be of great interest. See Robert M. Grant, *Miracle and Natural Law in Graeco-Roman and early Christian Thought* (Amsterdam, 1952).

[76] Macarius 4, 30.
[77] Frag. 15 (Macarius 2, 12).
[78] Macarius 2, 17.

III (e). *Christ's attitude toward death.* In dealing with Christ's conduct in the face of death, Porphyry finds his behavior inexplicable and
completely out of character for a divine being or even for one of the
heroes of ancient times.[79] He cannot understand why Christ failed to
take advantage of the temptation by Satan (Matt. 4:6). If Christ had
really been a miracle worker, he says, and able to bring back the dead
to life by a mere word, he ought to have plunged from the top of the
temple and demonstrated by landing safely that he was truly the son
of God, and had been carried by the angels in their hands. In this way
he could have proved that he had the power to save himself and others
from harm. By failing to do so, Porphyry concludes, Christ convicted
himself of cowardice.

It would have been improper for Christ to cast himself down, as
the devil urged him to do, Macarius retorts, because he would then
have been yielding to his adversary.[80] Still worse, had he hearkened
to Satan in this temptation, and also in the preceding one (v. 3: "Make
these stones into bread"), he would have been compelled to yield also
with regard to the third, which was Satan's true goal (i.e.: ". . . fall
down and worship me"). It is true that by jumping from the pinnacle
of the temple he would have fulfilled the prophecy (Psalms 91:11f.) as
quoted in Matthew 4:6 ("He shall give his angels charge concerning
thee . . . and in their hands they shall bear thee up, lest at any time
thou dash thy foot against a stone"). But the devil had chosen this text
precisely in order to trick Christ by means of the Scriptures into offering him worship. Christ saw through the deception and avoided
the trap.

Porphyry finds fault with several aspects of Christ's demeanor in
the Garden of Gethsemane (Matt. 26:36ff.; Luke 22:44).[81] But his
chief target is Christ's agony in the face of death, which led him to
ignore his own precept ("Fear not them which kill the body"—Matt.
10:28), and to pray (Matt. 26:39) that he might not have to undergo
the passion. Christ's words on this occasion were unworthy of the Son
of God, he says, or even of a wise man who scorned death.

A theologian like Athanasius would have disposed of Porphyry's
accusation of cowardice by assigning the expressions of fear and
anguish in this context to Christ's human nature, and denying that

[79] Frag. 48 (Macarius 3, 18).

[80] Macarius 3, 26; M. Steiner, *La tentation de Jésus dans l'interprétation patristique de
saint Justin à Origène* (Paris, 1962); V. Kesich, "Empire-Church relations and the Third
Temptation," *Studia patristica* 4 (*TU* 79; Berlin, 1961), 465–71.

[81] Frag. 62 (Macarius 3, 2).

they affected his divinity in any way. But Macarius, probably under the influence of Gregory of Nyssa, chose to follow another tack, and relied instead on the so-called "fishhook" (ἄγκιστρον) theory of atonement, which, though less illuminating, perhaps, for the modern reader, has considerable significance in the history of theology.[82] According to this doctrine, the devil was frightened by Christ's miracles and became reluctant to press on to the foreordained passion, lest he discover, when it was too late, that his intended victim was not a man, as he had thought, but truly God and the Son of God. Under these circumstances, there was danger that the crucifixion might never take place, and that man would, as a result, fail to attain salvation.

In order to avoid these dire consequences, Christ *pretended* to be afraid of death. Like an angler, he wrapped a worm as bait (his body) around the fishhook of his divinity, in order to entice the devil to swallow the hook. The scheme worked, the devil lunged after the worm, and was hooked (Macarius cites Job 41:1, slightly altered: "Thou shalt catch a dragon with a hook"). This stratagem was foreshadowed by Psalms 22:6 ("But I am a worm, and no man"), Macarius adds, "and the worm [*sc.* on the hook of Christ's manhood] devoured the tree of death" (the tree, he means, whose fruit corrupted Adam and all of mankind, through Adam). That is, Macarius says, repeating the traditional formula, Christ by one tree (that which witnessed his crucifixion and resurrection) destroyed the tree of sin and death, by which Satan had got his hold on the human race.

III (*f*). *Crucifixion and resurrection*. Porphyry deemed it unbecoming for a sage or a divine person to have suffered himself to be condemned, beaten by a reed, spat upon, and crowned with thorns (Matt. 27:26ff.; Mark 15:15ff.) without uttering some inspiring statement to his judges and tormentors.[83] He contrasts what he regards as ignominious conduct on the part of Jesus with the courageous bearing

---

[82] Macarius 3, 9. Cf. Jean Daniélou, "Das Leben, das am Holze hängt, Dt 28, 66 in der altchristlichen Katechese," *Kirche und Überlieferung*, ed. Johannes Betz and Heinrich Fries (Freiburg im Br., Basel, Vienna, 1960), 22–34. On this theory of redemption see Athanasius, *Vita S. Antonii* 24, *PG* 26, 880A; Gregory of Nyssa, *Oratio catechetica* 15–27, n.b. 21–24, ed. James H. Srawley, *The Catechetical Oration of Gregory of Nyssa* (Cambridge, Eng., 1903), 63ff., n.b. 81ff., 93.3ff.; *PG* 45.48ff., 57ff., 65A; J. Rivière, *Le dogme de la rédemption chez saint Augustin* (3rd ed.; Paris, 1933), 252, 373–91; Johannes B. Aufhauser, *Die Heilslehre des hl. Gregor von Nyssa* (Munich, 1910), 111. Note also G. W. H. Lampe, *A Patristic Greek Lexicon* I (Oxford, 1961), 20, s.v. ἄγκιστρον.

[83] Frag. 63 (Macarius 3, 1); cf. Philostratus, *Life of Apollonius* 8, 10ff., tr. by F. C. Conybeare, (Loeb Classical Library) II, 356–64.

I

of Apollonius of Tyana, who spoke out boldly before the court of the Emperor Domitian in Rome, then suddenly vanished, and appeared some hours later at Dicearchia (Puteoli). Even if he were bound by the will of God to undergo suffering, Porphyry insists, Christ should have addressed Pilate with wisdom and courage rather than submit cravenly to humiliation.

On the contrary, Macarius demurs, Christ had to submit to abasement in order to fulfill the prophecies of the Old Testament, according to which he was "without form or comeliness," and was "led as a sheep to the slaughter" (Isa. 53:2; Jer. 11:19).[84] Besides, had he loosed his full power against his enemies, no one would have dared to crucify him, and salvation would never have been won. He refrained from behaving like Apollonius in order to avoid appearing to be a mere magician or trickster. Nevertheless, Jesus was untouched by opprobrium and contumely, because God dwelled within him, and God is impervious to human insults. Hence Jesus was no more affected by the attempts to humiliate him than is a rock traversed by reptiles, which bears no mark or trace of their passage over it because of its hardness.

Above all, Porphyry remonstrates, after his resurrection Christ should have revealed himself to Pilate, Herod, the High Priest, or better to the Roman Senate and to the people, rather than to the humble Mary Magdalene, who had been possessed by seven demons, to the other Mary, and to a few other ordinary folk.[85] Had he displayed himself after the resurrection to men of high rank, he would have converted the world, and his disciples would not have been persecuted by Roman judges as inventors of monstrous fables. For surely, Porphyry adds satirically, neither God nor a wise man is pleased if many undergo heavy penalties for his sake.

Macarius offers a two-fold explanation of Christ's failure to appear to Pilate and other notables after his resurrection.[86] He did not exhibit himself to prominent Palestinians in order to avoid the suspicion that, either by error, trickery, or collusion, someone else had been substituted for him and crucified in his place. This is hardly very convincing. But the second argument has more cogency. According to this, Christ disclosed himself to humble folk, not to men of distinction, so as to emphasize the divine nature of his mission, which did not need testi-

[84] Macarius 3, 8.
[85] Frag. 64 (Macarius 2, 14); cf. 65 (*PG* 89.233).
[86] Macarius 2, 19.

monials from famous personages. If he had made a demonstration
before the Roman Senate, and had won official sponsorship, it would
have seemed that the Gospel owed its success to powerful human supporters rather than to its divine origin.

III (*g*). *Second Coming*. Porphyry was contemptuous also of the
description of Christ's Second Coming (*Parusia*) as portrayed by Paul
in I Thessalonians 4:16f., which predicts that Christ "shall descend
from heaven with a shout . . . and the dead in Christ shall rise first:
Then we who are alive and remain shall be caught up together with
them in the clouds, to meet the Lord in the air and so shall we ever be
with the Lord." [87] Porphyry ridicules this conception of Christ and
mortal men riding on a cloud through the sky as if they were sailing
over the ocean. Such a prodigy would upset the natural balance of the
universe, since nature had from the beginning assigned all creatures
to the regions best suited to them: the sea for those which live in the
water, the earth for those on dry land, the air for winged animals, and
the aether for heavenly bodies. Nor would the divine Logos (Christ)
ever so far violate the rule of order as to transfer the denizens of one
sphere from their natural habitat to another. Anyhow, Porphyry observes sardonically, Paul is a liar, since it is three hundred years since
he made this prediction and neither he nor anyone else has been
lifted up into heaven.

In a lengthy statement, not all of which is relevant, Macarius attempts to confute Porphyry by means of the allegorical method.[88]
According to him, the word "clouds" in I Thessalonians 4:17 is not to
be taken literally. It signifies angels in this context, he claims, and the
passage as a whole means that, at Christ's Second Coming, mankind
will be liberated from death by angels. Paul did not intend to suggest
that men actually were to ride on the clouds, nor did he lie when he
wrote, "We shall be caught up," since these words referred to mankind as a whole, not specifically to himself or his contemporaries.

Porphyry had an encyclopaedic knowledge of the Bible and the
Christian cultus, and in his own circle the κατὰ Χριστιανῶν must have
seemed irrefutable. But he was overliteral in his approach; and in the
end, despite all his erudition, subtlety, and dialectical virtuosity, he
proved to be no more successful than Celsus in the previous century
or the Emperor Julian, a hundred years later, in providing paganism

[87] Frag. 35 (Macarius 4, 2).
[88] Macarius 4, 12.

with a formula that would enable it to survive on equal terms with the new religion. On the other hand, though Macarius moved on a humbler plane, he stubbornly contested every point, and even managed to make a few penetrating thrusts of his own. Nevertheless, as he would have been the first to concede, the eventual victory was won, not because of any merit on his part, but because of the superiority of the cause he championed.

University of California at Los Angeles

COMPLEMENTARY NOTE

In the editorial process, reference to the following works unaccountably disapeared from my article:

Joseph R. Laurin, Orientations maîtresses des apologistes chrétiens de 270 à 361 (Analecta Gregoriana, 61) (Rome,1954),discusses Porphyry at many points most eruditely but in a manner totally different from mine; and Pierre Courcelle,"Anti-Christian arguments and Christian Platonism: from Arnobius to St. Ambrose," in Arnaldo Momigliano,ed., The Conflict between Paganism and Christianity in the Fourth Century (Oxford,1963), 156, refers to Porphyry only once, but the whole volume is of interest in a general way.

II

THE EDICT OF MILAN (313)

A DEFENCE OF ITS TRADITIONAL AUTHORSHIP AND DESIGNATION ([1])

This paper is intended as a refutation of the modern paradoxographers (2) who have been seduced by the temptation of trying to

(1) I am deeply indebted to the John Simon Guggenheim Foundation for indispensable support (in 1954-55 and 1966-67) of my study of Byzantine intellectual history, the *Mind of Byzantium*, of which this paper forms a part.

I acknowledge gratefully assistance from my colleague, Professor Lynn White, Jr., Director of the Center for Medieval and Renaissance Studies, UCLA, who has made a number of valuable suggestions.

The most convenient text of the Edict is to be found in Lactance, *De la mort des persécuteurs*, 48, ed. with French translation and notes by Jacques Moreau, *Sources Chrétiennes*, 39, vols. 1-2 (Paris, 1954); and in Greek in Eusebius, HE, 10, 5, 2-14, ed. Eduard Schwartz, *Die griechischen christlichen Schriftsteller der ersten drei Jahrhunderte*, 9, 2 (Berlin 1908); with English translation by J. E. L. Oulton and H. J. Lawlor, *Eusebius, the Ecclesiastical History*, 2 (Loeb Classical Library, 1932); with French translation by Gustave, Bardy, *Sources chrétiennes*, 55 (Paris, 1958). P. R. Coleman-Norton, *Roman State & Christian Church*, 1 (London, 1966), 30-35, gives an English translation of Lactantius's version of the Edict and Eusebius's variants therefrom.

Of the vast bibliography on the Edict, I cite the following works, both for their importance in the history of the subject and for their references to the older literature, which it is profitless to repeat: Mario Agnes, "Alcune considerazioni sul cosiddetto 'Editto' di Milano", *Studi romani*, 13 (1965), 424-32: does not discuss the "problem" of the Edict; Salvatore Calderone, *Costantino e il cattolicesimo*, 1 (*Pubblicazioni dell' Istituto di storia dell' Università di Messina*, 3 [Florence, 1962]); Mario Amelotti, "Da Diocleziano a Costantino, note in tema di costituzioni imperiali", *Studia et documenta historiae et iuris*, 27 (1961), 241-323; Maurilio Adriani, "La storicità dell' Editto di Milano", *Studi Romani*, 2 (1954), 18-32; Herbert Nesselhauf, "Das Toleranzgesetz des Licinius", *Historisches Jahrbuch*, 74 (1954), 44-61; Andreas Alföldi, *The conversion of Constantine* (Oxford, 1948), 37 f., 129 n. 13; J. R. Palanque, "A propos du prétendu Édit de Milan", *Byzantion*, 10 (1935), 607-16; Norman H. Baynes, *Constantine the Great and the Christian Church* (*Proceedings of the British Academy*, 15 [London, 1929]), 11, 69-74 (the lecture was delivered in 1930); Richard Laqueur, "Die beiden Fassungen des sog. Toleranzedikts von Mailand", ΕΠΙΤΥΜΒΙΟΝ *Heinrich Swoboda dargebracht* (Reichenberg, 1927), 132-41: I see no way to reconcile with texts or logic L's tortuous theory (n. b. p. 140) that Eusebius's version of the Edict included interpolations from Maximinus's rescript to Sabinus (HE, 9, 9a, 1-9), which L deems to have been issued *before* the Edict but dishonestly represented by the Constantinian party (and Eusebius) as Maximinus's reply to the Edict (HE, 9, 9, 12f.; 9, 9a, 10-12); John R. Knipfing, "Das angebliche 'Mailänder Edikt' v. J. 313 im Lichte der neueren Forschung", *Zeitschrift für Kirchengeschichte*, 40 (1922), 206-18; Émile Chénon, "Les conséquences juridiques de l'Édit de Milan (313), *Nouvelle Revue historique de droit français et étranger*, 38 (1914-15), 255-63; Pierre Batiffol, *La paix constantinienne et le catholicisme*, 2d ed. (Paris, 1914), 203-67, n. b. 229 ff.; G. L. Perugi, "La fonte giuridica dell' Editto di Milano", *Roma e l'Oriente*, 6, fasc. 35-36 (1913), 13-40: chiefly of interest for detailed references to the earlier bibliography; Carlo Santucci, "L'Editto di Milano nei riguardi del diritto", *Nuovo Bullettino di Archeologia cristiana*, 19 (1913), 71-75; Joseph Wittig, "Das Toleranzreskript von Mailand 313", *Konstantin der Grosse und seine Zeit*, ed. Franz J. Dölger (Freiburg im Br., 1913), 40-65; Valerian Şesan, *Die Religionspolitik der christlich-röm. Kaiser von Konstantin d. Gr. bis Theodosius d. Gr. (313-380) (Kirche und Staat im römisch-byzantinischen Reiche*

prove that, despite his friendly disposition towards the Christian Church, Constantine did not issue the * Edict of Milan (313) but that Licinius, whom Eusebius condemns as a persecutor ** (HE, 10, 8, 8-9, 9; see n. 11 below), did. This is a titillating conceit, heightened by the additional paradox, that Constantine did not even participate in the Edict (Seeck, *loc. cit.* in n. 2: "diese [Urkunde] ist erstens kein Edikt, zweitens nicht in Mailand erlassen, drittens nicht von Konstantin"). But, except possibly for the second proposition in this quotation from Seeck, these elements of the modern paradoxographic tradition concerning Constantine can be justified by neither the sources nor *a priori* considerations.

On the contrary, I hope to show (I) that Constantine was one of the authors of the Edict, (II) that he must be regarded as having published it in his part of the Empire, (III) that his version of it was in essentials identical with, or very similar, to that reproduced by Eusebius in HE, 10, 5, 2-14 and by Lactantius in MP, 48, (IV) that these two texts not only constitute the Edict of Milan, but also are properly so designated, and (V) that the celebrated phrase, *instinctu*

---

seit Konstantin dem Grossen und bis zum Falle Konstantinopels, 1 [Czernowitz, 1911]), 128-237; Guglielmo Schnyder, "L'Editto di Milano, ed i recenti studi critici che lo riguardano", *Dissertazioni della Pontificia Accademia Romana di Archeologia*, S. 2, 8 (1903), 149-79; A. Crivellucci, "L'Editto di Milano", *Studi Storici*, I (1892), 239-50; *idem*, "Intorno all' Editto di Milano", *ibid.*, 4 (1895), 267-73. A. H. M. Jones, *The Later Roman Empire (284-602)*, I (Oxford, 1964), 80 f., simply describes it as an edict without discussion. Heinz Kähler, "Konstantin 313", *Jahrbuch des deutschen archäologischen Instituts*, 67, (1952), 1-30, does not deal with the Edict, but with proof that the colossal statue of Constantine, fragments of which are preserved in the Palazzo dei Conservatori, was produced ca. 313 and set up in the (western) apse of the Basilica of (Maxentius) Constantine.

(2) The *Fons et origo* of this school was Otto Seeck, "Das sogenannte Edikt von Mailand", *Zeitschrift für Kirchengeschichte*, 12 (1891), 381-86, whose thesis was taken up enthusiastically by Henri Grégoire in *Byzantion*, 7 (1932), 645-61; 10 (1935), 616-19 (see also bibliography in Moreau, SC, 39, 1, 159 f.); and then in three papers by Jacques Moreau, "Zur Religionspolitik Konstantins des Grossen", *Annales Universitatis Saraviensis, Philosophie et Lettres*, 1 (1952), 160-68 (*idem, Scripta minora*, ed. Walter Schmitthenner, *Annales U. Saraviensis, Reihe: Philosophische Fakultät*, 1 [Heidelberg, 1964], 106-13); "Les 'Litterae Licinii' ", AUS, 2 (1935), 100-105 (*Scripta minora*, 99-105, n. b. 102: "Licinius, et Licinius seul, est l'auteur de l'acte de tolérance de 313"); "Vérité historique et propagande politique chez Lactance et dans la Vita Constantini ", AUS, 4 (1955), 89-97 (*Scripta minora*, 135-43); and in his notes on the MP in SC, 39, 2, 456-64, n. b. 458. The most recent exponent of these views about the Edict is Joseph Vogt, *Constantin der Grosse* (see next note), 168 f., 284. Cf. n. 13 below.

Seeck and Vogt, however, were content to attack the view that Constantine was the author of the Edict or issued it in his own realm. They accept the other elements of the historical tradition about Constantine (the conversion, etc.), which Grégoire and Moreau reject.

* To which I will refer below as the Edict or, occasionally, to avoid ambiguity, as the Edict of 313.

** HE = Eusebius's *Ecclesiastical History* (ἐκκλησιαστικὴ ἱστορία).

MP = Lactantius's *De mortibus persecutorum*.

divinitatis, in the inscription on the Arch of Constantine was in all probability derived from the Edict, which the Roman senators took delight in imitating because by so doing they were enabled to pay a particularly delicate compliment to the Emperor Constantine, whom they *knew* to be its author.

In venturing to reopen these time-worn questions once again, I lay little claim to originality, and rely on only one small point, which, however, I believe to be decisive. My cardinal principle here, and in my whole approach to historical research in general, is that the ancient and mediaeval historians who were contemporaries of the events they report, especially when uncontradicted by other authorities of equal weight, deserve considerably more respect than certain scholars have in recent years been willing to accord them.

I have reference above all to Eusebius, who, after a generation of abuse at the hands of scholars of high repute, is at last being vindicated (3) against his detractors. From the first, I have agreed with Norman H. Baynes, who was the most important of the earlier champions of Eusebius, that the latter's account of the life of Constantine is not to be rejected except for the most compelling reasons, and I

(3) Of the many excellent scholars who have devoted themselves to this task, the latest is Friedhelm Winkelmann, beginning with his dissertation, *Die Vita Constantini des Eusebius, ihre Authentizität, ihre Textbezeugung* (Halle, 1959); then in *Die Textbezeugung der Vita Constantini des Eusebius von Caesarea (Texte und Untersuchungen*, 84 [Berlin, 1962]), and also in a number of articles: "Die Beurteilung des Eusebius von Cäsarea und seiner Vita Constantini im griechischen Osten, ein Beitrag zur Untersuchung der griechischen hagiographischen Vitae Constantini", *Byzantinistische Beiträge* (Berlin, 1964), 91-119; "Zur Geschichte des Authentizitätsproblems der Vita Constantini", *Klio*, 40 (1962), 187-243: an admirable and fair-minded survey of the literature; "Konstantins Religionspolitik und ihre Motive im Urteil der literarischen Quellen des iv. und v. Jahrhunderts", *Acta Antiqua Academiae Scientiarum Hungaricae*, 9 (1961), 239-56. Among his most notable predecessors *nota bene*: Joseph Vogt, "Pagans and Christians in the family of Constantine the Great", *The conflict between paganism and Christianity in the fourth century*, ed. Arnaldo Momigliano (Oxford, 1963), 38-54; *idem, Constantin der Grosse*, 2d ed. (Munich, 1960); *idem*, "Constantinus der Grosse", *Reallexikon für Antike und Christentum*, 3 (Stuttgart, 1957), 306-79; *idem*, "Die constantinische Frage", Comitato Internazionale di Scienze Storiche, *X Congresso Internazionale di Scienze Storiche* (Rome), *Relazioni*, 6 (Florence, 1955), 731-79; Kurt Aland, *Kirchengeschichtliche Entwürfe* (Gütersloh, 1960), 165-239, including a reprint of his paper, "Die religiöse Haltung Kaiser Konstantins", from *Studia Patristica (Texte und Untersuchungen*, 63 [Berlin, 1957]); Heinz Kraft, *Kaiser Konstantins religiöse Entwicklung (Beiträge zur historischen Theologie*, 20 [Tübingen, 1955]); Johannes Straub, "Konstantins Verzicht auf den Gang zum Kapitol", *Historia*, 4 (1955), 297-313; *idem, Vom Herrscherideal in der Spätantike (Forschungen zur Kirchen- und Geistesgeschichte*, 18 [Stuttgart, 1939, reprinted 1964]); Hermann Dörries, *Das Selbstzeugnis Kaiser Konstantins (Abhandlungen der Akademie der Wissenschaften in Göttingen, Philologisch-historische Klasse*, 3. F., 34 [Göttingen, 1954]); A.H.M. Jones, "Notes on the genuineness of the Constantinian documents in Eusebius's Life of Constantine", *Journal of ecclesiastical history*, 5 (1954), 196-200 (With an appendix by T.C. Skeat); A.H.M. Jones, *Constantine and the conversion of Europe* (reprinted, N.Y., 1962); Friedrich Vittinghoff, "Eusebius als Verfasser der Vita Constantini", *Rheinisches Museum*, N.F., 96 (1953), 330-73; Andrew Alföldi, *The conversion of Constantine and pagan Rome* (Oxford, 1948); Norman H. Baynes, *Constantine the Great* (n. 1 above).

16

rejoice that a new generation of critics has been piling up impressive evidence in support of this position.

Specifically, with regard to the Edict, I maintain that the critical passage on which the entire decision rests, is to be found in Eusebius's preface to a collection of legal texts (HE, 10, 5, 1):

Φέρε δή, λοιπὸν καὶ τῶν βασιλικῶν διατάξεων Κωνσταντίνου καὶ Λικιννίου τὰς ἐκ τῆς Ῥωμαίων φωνῆς μεταληφθείσας ἑρμηνείας παραθώμεθα.

ΑΝΤΙΓΡΑΦΟΝ ΒΑΣΙΛΙΚΩΝ ΔΙΑΤΑΞΕΩΝ ΕΚ ΡΩΜΑΙΚΗΣ ΓΑΩΤΤΗΣ ΜΕΤΑΑΗΦΘΕΙΣΩΝ.

(i. e., "Now, then, let us quote the translations that have been made from the Latin of the imperial laws of Constantine and Licinius. *Copy of the imperial laws translated from the Latin language*").

The first of these laws is the Edict, which begins (HE, 10, 5, 4), after a brief introductory paragraph as follows:

Ὁπότε εὐτυχῶς ἐγὼ Κωνσταντῖνος ὁ Αὔγουστος κἀγὼ Λικίννιος ὁ Αὔγουστος ἐν τῇ Μεδιολάνῳ ἐληλύθειμεν καὶ πάντα ὅσα πρὸς τὸ λυσιτελὲς καὶ τὸ χρήσιμον τῷ κοινῷ διέφερεν, ἐν ζητήσει ἔσχομεν, ταῦτα μεταξὺ τῶν λοιπῶν ἅτινα ἐδόκει ἐν πολλοῖς ἅπασιν ἐπωφελῆ εἶναι, μᾶλλον δὲ ἐν πρώτοις διατάξαι ἐδογματίσαμεν, οἷς ἡ πρὸς τὸ θεῖον αἰδώς τε καὶ τὸ σέβας ἐνείχετο, τοῦτ' ἔστιν, ὅπως δῶμεν καὶ τοῖς Χριστιανοῖς καὶ πᾶσιν ἐλευθέραν αἵρεσιν τοῦ ἀκολουθεῖν τῇ θρησκείᾳ ᾗ δ' ἂν βουληθῶσιν, ὅπως ὅ τί ποτέ ἐστιν θειότητος καὶ οὐρανίου πράγματος, ἡμῖν καὶ πᾶσι τοῖς ὑπὸ τὴν ἡμετέραν ἐξουσίαν διάγουσιν εὐμενὲς εἶναι δυνηθῇ.

Eusebius differs from the Latin (see below) principally in mis-'reading *omnibus* for *hominibus* and substituting a binomial expression ὅπως ὅ τί ποτέ ἐστιν θειότητος καὶ οὐρανίου πράγματος, for the simpler *quicquid < est > diuinitatis*. Then, in a reversal of technique, he reduces the Latin *placatum ac propitium* to a single adjective in Greek. In my translation, I have followed the Latin:

" When I Constantine Augustus and I Licinius Augustus (4) had met under happy auspices at Milan and discussed all questions pertaining to the general welfare and the security of the state, we decided that,

---

(4) It makes no difference to my argument whether Emperor Maximinus's name was included in the pro-oimion of the Edict, as some contend. But I doubt that it was, since none of the texts above quoted refer to it. Knipfing, ZKG, 40 (1922), 213-15, lists authorities on both sides of this question. Moreau, SC, 39, 2, 457, agrees that Maximinus was not mentioned. For the latter's defeat by Licinius on April 30, 313, near Adrianople, in the Campus Ergenus (MP, 47), erroneously called Campus Serenus by Lactantius (MP, 46, 9), see Moreau, SC, 39, 1, 130, 28 f.; Grégoire, *Byzantion*, 13 (1938), 585.

among the other things we knew would benefit the majority of men,
first consideration should be given to the regulation of the affairs
which affect the worship of divinity. [Hence, we resolved] to grant the
Christians and all [others] the right to follow freely whatever religion
they wished, so that whatever divinity there be in heaven might be
favorable and propitious to us and to all of our subjects. "

In all material respects, then, Eusebius's Greek translation is a
faithful and accurate rendering of the Latin text of the Edict as
represented by Lactantius in his MP 48, 2-12. The fidelity of the
Greek to the Latin can be illustrated by the corresponding portion
of the Edict as it appears in Lactantius:

Cum feliciter tam ego [quam] Constantinus Augustus quam etiam
ego Licinius Augustus apud Mediolanum conuenissemus atque uniuersa
quæ ad commoda et securitatem publicam pertinerent, in tractatu
haberemus, hæc inter cetera quæ uidebamus pluribus hominibus
profutura, uel in primis ordinanda esse credidimus, quibus diuinitatis
reuerentia continebatur, ut daremus et christianis et omnibus liberam
potestatem sequendi religionem quam quisque uoluisset, quo quicquid
< est > diuinitatis in sede cælesti, nobis atque omnibus qui sub
potestate nostra sunt constituti, placatum ac propitium possit existere.

Despite close agreement on all essential matters, there remain
enough minor discrepancies (5) (like those noted above) between
Eusebius's Greek and Lactantius's Latin to demonstrate that Eusebius's source could not have been the Edict as found in MP, 48.
Hence, we have at least two separate and independent witnesses to the
wording of this important document, which corroborate each other
most impressively on all the principal questions at issue although
neither was copied or transcribed from the other. The exact relationship, however, between HE, 10, 5, 2-4, and MP, 48 cannot be
precisely determined.

(5) For a list of these with discussion, see I.A. Heikel, *De Constantini imperatoris scriptis
edendis* (Helsinki, 1916), 17-28; Wittig, *loc.cit.* (n. 1 above), 58-61; Şesan, *Kirche und Staat*,
1, 169-73, 226 f. Cf. also Moreau, *Scripta minora*, 103 f., nn. 27 f.; and *idem*, SC, 39, 2, 456 ff.
Şesan, *op. cit.*, 175 ff., 189-216, concludes from the differences between the two texts, especially from the omission in MP, 48 of the preface to the Edict as given in HE, 10, 5, 2, that
Eusebius had translated directly from the original Edict of Milan, not from Licinius's
version thereof (as in MP, 48) or any other such copy. Somewhat similarly, J. Maurice,
"Note sur le préambule placé par Eusèbe en tête de l'Édit de Milan", *Bulletin d'ancienne
littérature et d'archéologie chrétiennes*, 4 (1914), 45-47, looks upon the presence of this preface
in HE, 10, 5, 2 f., and its omission in MP, 48, as proof that Eusebius' text represents the
Litterae Constantini, which Constantine had addressed to the governors of the Western
provinces, as contrasted with the *Litterae Licinii*, which Licinius promulgated in his part
of the Empire.

18

In view of the plain meaning and obvious implications of the texts quoted, it is a great disservice to historical scholarship to belittle, minimize, or ignore them; and my principal service in what follows is merely to insist not only that the passages I have cited from the HE and MP mean what they say but also that they cannot be, and have not been, refuted.

I.-II. *Constantine co-author of the Edict and his promulgation of it in his own realm.*

These excerpts from Eusebius and Lactantius prove beyond all doubt (1) that the Edict was issued by both Constantine and Licinius and (2) that their versions of it (on this point see p. 26 below), as posted individually and separately by Constantine and Licinius in their respective jurisdictions, must have been identical or nearly so. Otherwise, Eusebius would not have included this text among what he calls the laws of both Constantine and Licinius, nor would both emperors have stated in so many words, as they do (« I Constantine Augustus and I Licinius Augustus »), that they had actively collaborated in this project. In other words, these passages from the HE and MP make it altogether impossible to deny that Constantine was one of the authors of this ordinance, or that he published it as a law for the portion of the Empire over which he ruled. (See also notes 7 a and 10 below.)

These conclusions follow inevitably from the opening sentence of the Edict (as quoted above), in which the two emperors declare that their chief objective was to grant religious freedom to all of their subjects, in order that by so doing they might win divine favor for the Empire and all of its inhabitants. It is difficult to imagine how Constantine could have discussed these matters with Licinius in Milan and then drafted, or assented to, a law couched in these terms, as both Eusebius and Lactantius agree that he did, without enacting it in his own name for his own part of the Empire.

It is much more likely that Constantine arranged the conference in Milan, as well as the matrimonial alliance between his half-sister and Licinius, at least in part so as to win over his imperial colleague to the policy of religious toleration which he had already adopted. Whether this really was his aim or not, it is inconceivable that Constantine, the first and greatest imperial benefactor (6) of the Christian

(6) For the gifts, privileges, and immunities Constantine bestowed upon the Christian Church, see Ludwig Voelkl, *Die Kirchenstiftungen des Kaisers Konstantin im Lichte des*

Church, and in all probability its most influential patron in the early centuries, apart from its Founder, could have failed in his own realm to promulgate this great charter of Christian liberty and privilege (7),

römischen Sakralrechts (Arbeitsgemeinschaft für Forschung des Landes Nordrhein-Westfalen, Geisteswissenschaften, 117 [Cologne-Opladen, 1964]); Clémence Dupont, "Les donations dans les constitutions de Constantin", *Revue internationale des droits de l'antiquité*, S. 3, 9 (1962), 291-324, n. b. 319 ff.; Biondo Biondi, *Il diritto romano cristiano*, 1 (Milan, 1952), 21-30, 358, 361 f.; Jean Gaudemet, "La législation religieuse de Constantin", *Revue d'histoire de l'Église de France*, 33 (1947), 25-61.

On Constantine as a lawgiver in general, see Gudrun Stühff, *Vulgarrecht im Kaiserrecht unter besonderer Berücksichtigung der Gesetzgebung Konstantins des Grossen (Forschungen zum römischen Recht*, 21 [Weimar, 1966]); Clémence Dupont, "Les successions dans les constitutions de Constantin", *Ivra*, 15 (1964), 57-116; four volumes by *eadem*, published in Lille: *La réglementation économique dans les constitutions de Constantin* (1963); *Le droit criminel dans les constitutions de Constantin, Les infractions* (1953); *Les peines* (1955); *Les constitutions de Constantin et le droit privé au début du IVe siècle* (1937); Arnold Ehrhardt, "Constantin d. Gr. Religions-politik und Gesetzgebung", *Zeitschrift der Savigny-Stiftung für Rechtsgeschichte, Romanistische Abteilung*, 72 (1955), 154-90; Joseph Vogt, "Zur Frage des christlichen Einflusses auf die Gesetzgebung Konstantins des Grossen", *Münchener Beiträge zur Papyrusforschung und antiken Rechtsgeschichte*, 35, *Festschrift für Leopold Wenger*, 2 (Munich, 1945), 118-48. Cf. E. Volterra, "Quelques remarques sur le style des Constitutions de Constantin", *Droits de l'antiquité et de sociologie juridique, Mélanges Henri Lévy-Bruhl (Publications de l'Institut de droit romain de l'Université de Paris*, 17 [Paris, 1959]), 325-34; Manlio Sargenti, *Il diritto privato nella legislazione di Costantino; persone e famiglia (Pubblicazioni dell' Istituto di diritto romano dei diritti dell' Oriente mediterraneo e di storia del diritto*, 3 [Milan, 1938]).

The vast literature on the *episcopalis audientia* is summarized by Max Kaser, *Das römische Zivilprozessrecht* (Iwan von Müller, Walter Otto, Hermann Bengtson, edd., *Handbuch der Altertumswissenschaft*, 10, 3, 4 [Munich, 1966]), 527-29; see also J. N. Bakhuizen van den Brink, "Episcopalis audientia," *Mededelingen der koninklijke Nederlandse Akademie van Wetenschappen, Afdeling Letterkunde, Nieuwe Reeks*, 19, 8 (Amsterdam, 1956), 245-301.

(7) Émile Chénon, « Les conséquences juridiques de l'édit de Milan, » *Nouvelle Revue historique de droit français et étranger*, 38 (1914-15), 255-63, suggests that the Edict has great significance because it constitutes the first formal recognition of the Christian Church as a legal corporation authorized to receive, hold, and administer property. It is possible that it should be so regarded since Constantine's order to Anulinus (HE, 10, 5, 15-17) is limited in scope (see section 4 below) and does not connect the grant of these rights with freedom of worship. But this is not altogether certain, nor have scholars been able to explain satisfactorily the legal basis or origin of the system by which the Christian communities acquired and held real estate and other property during the first three centuries of their existence.

In view of these uncertainties, I refrain from pressing this argument, despite its appeal. On the legal status implied by Constantine's Edict to Anulinus, see Ehrhardt, *loc. cit.* (in previous n.), 172 f., who takes (τὸ δίκαιον) here as the equivalent of *corpus* or σῶμα (corporation), though it is nevertheless interesting, and surely significant, that Eusebius uses this term in preference to σῶμα, which occurs in his translation of the Edict (HE, 10, 5, 10-12). See note 48 below.

On this topic see the following (with references to the older literature): Giannetto Longo, "Sul diritto sepolcrale romano", *Ivra*, 15 (1964), 137-58; *idem*, "Communità cristiane primitive e 'res religiosae'," *Bullettino dell' Istituto di diritto romano*, N.S., 18-19 = 59-60 (1956), 237-57; W. W. Buckland, *A text-book of Roman Law from Augustus to Justinian*, 3rd ed. by Peter Stein (Cambridge, England, 1963), 177-79; Charles Saumagne, "Corpus Christianorum," *Revue internationale des droits de l'antiquité*, S. 3, 7 (1960), 437-78; S. 3, 8 (1961), 257-79; Max Kaser, *Das römische Privatrecht* (Iwan von Müller, etc., edd., *Handbuch der Altertumswissenschaft*, 10, 3, 3, 2 [Munich, 1959]), 105, nn. 17-22, 106, 348, n. 21; Arnold Ehrhardt, "Das Corpus Christi und die Korporationen im spät-römischen Recht," *Zeitschrift der Savigny-Stiftung für Rechtsgeschichte, Romanistische Abteilung*, 70 (1953), 299-

20

which explicitly and systematically enacted into law the principles of which he was the most notable exponent.

If this reasoning be sound, as I believe it is, we are compelled to assume that Constantine would have taken action by means of a separate Edict of his own, specifically addressed to the people or to an official of his own portion of the Empire. This he would have had to do because, as it has been proved conclusively, in the years during which Constantine and Licinius were co-emperors (and also from 338 to 468), a law like Licinius's edition of the Edict (MP, 48), published as it was Nicomedia (MP, 48, 1), was valid only for the jurisdiction of the emperor who issued it, i.e., for Licinius and in his own *pars imperii*. It had no validity outside of his domain, and would not have taken effect in the regions ruled by Constantine. For in legal documents of this kind, the names of other emperors often listed in the preface or at other points in the text did not signify that the law applied to the entire Empire (7a).

In each case, the place of emission recorded in a constitution indicates the sphere in which it was intended to operate. Hence, if it was posted in the Eastern half of the Empire (like MP, 48), it had binding effect only there and not in the West as well. Only very rarely, and under the most unusual circumstances, which do not affect the general

347; 71 (1954), 25-40; Alexander Philipsborn, "Der Begriff der juristischen Person im römischen Recht", *ibid.*, 71 (1954), 41-70; Hans-Rudolf Hagemann, *Die Stellung der Piae Causae nach justinianischem Rechte (Basler Studien zur Rechtswissenschaft*, 37 [Basel, 1953]); Maurizio Borda, "Collegia funeraticia", *Enciclopedia Cattolica*, 3 (1949), 1950-52; Giuseppe Bovini, *La proprietà ecclesiastica e la condizione giuridica della chiesa in età precostantiniana* (Milan, 1949); *idem*, s.v. Chiesa, A, VI, "Posizione giuridica della Chiesa fino a Giustiniano," *Enciclopedia Cattolica*, 3 (1949), 1504-6, who gives the bibliography of the subject and a summary of the leading theories up to his time; Gerda Krüger, *Die Rechtsstellung der vorkonstantinischen Kirchen (Kirchenrechtliche Abhandlungen*, 115-16 [Stuttgart, 1935]), 234-42; J. P. Waltzing, "Collegia," DACL, 3, 2 (1914), 2107-40; Carlo Carassai, "La politica religiosa di Costantino il Grande e la proprietà della Chiesa," *Archivio della R. Società Romana di Storia Patria*, 24 (1901), 95-157. Cf. also Fernand de Visscher, *Le droit des tombeaux romains* (Milan, 1963), 261-76.

(7a) Against the older view that the constitutions of every emperor applied automatically to the entire Empire, without specific enactment in each part thereof, it has now been proved that imperial legislation (from 338 on) was valid only for the jurisdiction of the emperor who issued it, i. e., in his own *pars imperii*. This principle was established by M. Antonio de Dominicis, « Il problema dei rapporti burocratico-legislativi tra 'occidente ed oriente' nel basso impero romano alla luce delle inscriptiones e subscriptiones delle costituzioni imperiali », *Istituto Lombardo di scienze e lettere, Rendiconti, Classe di lettere e Scienze Morali e Storiche*, S. 3, 18=87 (1954), 329-487. Similar conclusions were reached independently by Jean Gaudemet, « Le partage législatif au Bas-Empire d'après un ouvrage récent », SDHI, 21(1955), 319-31; *idem*, « Le partage législatif dans la seconde moitié du IVe siècle », *Studi in onore di Pietro de Francisci*, 2 (Milan, 1956), 317-54 (with particular attention to the years 364-95); *idem, La formation du droit séculier et du droit de l'Église au IVe et Ve siècles, (Institut de droit romain de l'Université de Paris*, 15 [Paris, 1957]), 17-26; *idem*, « Orthodoxie èt interpolations (à propos de CTh. xvi, 1, 4 et xvi, 4, 1) », *Mélanges en l'honneur de*

rule under consideration, did an emperor of one *pars imperii* address a law to an official in another. Similarly, if two emperors wished to enact the same regulation, they would and did promulgate separate laws for this purpose, each in his own territory, as Licinius did in his Edict (MP, 48) and Constantine inevitably would have done in his.

Less important than this basic matter of Constantine's direct personal connection with the Edict are two subsidiary questions which unfortunately cannot be answered categorically.

(1) The first of these concerns the date and place of promulgation of Constantine's own copy of the Edict, as distinguished from that which Licinius, as we learn from MP, 48, 1, posted in Nicomedia on June 13, 313 (8) in Constantine's name and his own. None of the extant sources gives any precise information on these matters. But it seems logical to assume that Constantine must have issued his version of the Edict in Rome some time after his victory over Maxentius on October 28, 312, either (*a*) late in 312 (9) and prior to his

---

S. E. *le Cardinal André Jullien, Revue de droit canonique,* 10, 3-4; 11, 1 (1960-61), 163 f.; *idem, Institutions de l'antiquité* (Paris, 1967), 673; Giovanni Gualandi, « Privilegi imperiali e dualità legislativa nel Basso Impero alla luce di alcuni testi di Libanio », *Archivio giuridico « Filippo Serafini »,* s. 6, 25=156 (1959), 5-34; Ernst Levy, « West-östliches Vulgarrecht und Justinian », ZSS, RA, 76 (1959), 2-5.

(8) Moreau in his translation, SC, 39, 1, 131 f., translates *die Iduum 'Iuniarum* by *le quinze juin,* momentarily forgetting the school-boy rule that the Ides fall on the thirteenth, except in March, May, July, and October, although he subsequently gives the date correctly, SC, 39, 2, 464.

The *terminus a quo* is October 28, 312, the day of Constantine's victory over Maxentius. This traditional date, called into question by Patrick Bruun, "The Battle of the Milvian Bridge," *Hermes,* 88 (1960), 361-65; *idem, Studies in Constantinian chronology (Numismatic Notes and Monographs,* 146 [New York, 1961]), 7, who pushes it back one year to October 28, 311, has, however, been vindicated by Roberto Andreotti, "Recenti contributi alla cronologia costantiniana," *Latomus,* 23 [(1964), 537-42; Maria R. Alföldi, *Die constantinische Goldprägung* (Mainz, 1963), 32; *eadem* and Dietmar Kienast, "Zu P. Bruuns Datierung der Schlacht an der Milvischen Brücke," *Jahrbuch für Numismatik und Geldgeschichte,* 11 (1961), 33-41.

(9) Calderone, *Costantino* (n. 1 above), 157-64; Şesan, *Kirche und Staat,* 1, 216-21, 358 f. (published by Constantine and Licinius). See also Nesselhauf, n. 13 below. Karl Bihlmeyer, "Das angebliche Toleranzedikt Konstantins von 312. Mit Beiträgen zur Mailänder Konstitution (313)," *Theologische Quartalschrift,* 96 (1914), 65-100, 198-224, denies that Constantine issued any such a law in 312 either before the Battle of the Milvian Bridge or thereafter. Knipfing, ZKG, 40 (1922), 209 f., agrees with Bihlmeyer and lists the modern authorities on both sides of this question.

Theoretically conceivable but hardly worthy of consideration is a third possibility, that Constantine might have held back his own Edict until after June 13. Such a delay on his part is extremely improbable because, unlike Licinius (see note 16 below), he exercised full dominion in his territories as early as October 28-29, 312. The uprising in Gaul with which he had to contend in the spring and summer of 313 affected only a small area and did not loosen his grip on Italy and North Africa, in which he legislated freely and without hindrince. For his legislation in the early months of 313, see T. Mommsen, *op. cit.* in note 10 below, vol. 1, 1, p. ccix; Seeck, *op. cit.* in note 15 below, 160 f. The insurrection in Gaul is mentioned by Ernest Stein, *Histoire du Bas-Empire,* 1, 1 (1959), 92; 1, 2, 459, n. 145; *Panegyrici latini,* XII (IX), 21, 5-23, 4, ed. Mynors (see n. 51 below), 286-88; IX (12), ed. Galletier,

meeting with Licinius in Milan, or (*b*) shortly thereafter, but presumably before June 13, 313, the day on which the Licinian draft of the Edict was made public. On the former supposition, Constantine would have drawn up the Edict himself very much in its present form and then persuaded Licinius to join him in sponsoring it.

In view of Constantine's attitude towards the Christians as demonstrated throughout his career from October 28, 312 on (see n. 7 above), alternative (*a*) seems more likely than (*b*), though neither is capable of proof, and both are legally (10) defensible since the emperor of one part of the Empire could, as we have seen (note 7*a* above), publish a law independently of his imperial colleague, who would not be bound thereby unless he wished to adopt it by a separate enactment of his own.

Both hypotheses (*a*) and (*b*), it should be emphasized, are consistent with the unambiguous statements of Eusebius (HE, 9, 9, 12; 10, 5, 1 et 4) and Lactantius (MP, 48, 2), quoted on pp. 16-17, that Constantine and Licinius were jointly responsible for the Edict. The language used in these passages goes far beyond the normal heading of an ordinary law (as, e.g., *Codex Theodosianus*, 10.19.10 of August 29, 382 : *Imperatores Gratianus, Valentinianus et Theodosius Augusti Floro Praefecto Praetorio... Dat. iiii Kal. Sept. Constantinopoli...*, which concerned Theodosius's part of the Empire alone, as can be seen from reference to Constantinople as the place of emission: see note 7*a*), and proves that both emperors actively took part in the issuance of the Edict.

Nevertheless, whichever of these two alternatives may appear

---

v. 2, p. 106, 140 ff.; Zosimus, *Historia nova*, 17, 2 f., ed. L. Mendelssohn (Leipzig, 1887), 74.15 ff. Cf. *Excerpta Valesiana*, 13, ed. Jacques Moreau (Leipzig, 1961), 4.17 f.; Camille Jullian, *Histoire de la Gaule*, 7 (reprinted Brussels, 1964 without date of original edition), 111. Of course, there was nothing to prevent an emperor from legislating even in unsettled times.

(10) H. F. Jolowicz, *Historical introduction to the study of Roman law*, 2d ed. (Cambridge, England, 1952), 438, 481. See also *Codex Theodosianus*, 1. 1. 5; *Leges Novellae Theodosii II*, 1, 5; 2 pr.; *Leges Novellae Valentiniani III*, 26 (Haenel 25), ed. T. Mommsen & P. M. Meyer, *Theodosiani libri xvi... et Leges Novellae ad Theodosianum pertinentes*, 1, 2 (reprinted, Berlin, 1954), 29, 4-10; 2 (*ibid.*), 4f., 6, 121 f., Cf. for Zeno Biondo Biondi, "La L. 12 cod. de aed. priv. 8, 10 e la questione delle relazioni legislative tra le due parti dell' impero," *Bullettino dell' Istituto di diritto romano*, 44 (1936-37), 363-84; M. A. von Bethmann-Hollweg, *Der Civilprozess des gemeinen Rechts*, 3, *Der römische Civilprozess* (Bonn, 1866), 215 f. Fritz von Schwind, *Zur Frage der Publikation im römischen Recht (Münchener Beiträge zur Papyrusforschung und antiken Rechtsgeschichte*, 31 [1940]), 157 ff. (on the *Publikation der kaiserlichen Edikte*), provides no information on publication during the Dominate. The view held by Jolowicz and von Bethmann-Hollweg, *loc. cit.*, that the system of promulgation discussed in the text was a later development and did not obtain ca. 313 is erroneous. See note 7*a* above.

the more plausible, (a) is greatly to be preferred to the hypothesis
recklessly advanced (11) without proof that the initiative for the
Edict somehow lay with Licinius, who ended his days, Eusebius
charges, as a persecutor of the Church. Whether this accusation be
altogether just or not, there is not the slightest evidence which indicates that Licinius ever of his own accord took any action of any
kind that was favorable to the Christians.

(2) Secondly, commentators do not agree on the identification of
the "most perfect and fully detailed law on behalf of the Christians",
which, Eusebius says (HE, 9, 9, 12; cf. 9, 9a, 12) "Constantine himself
and Licinius with him... with one will and purpose together drew
up" (Καὶ δὴ ἐπὶ τούτοις αὐτός τε Κωνσταντῖνος καὶ σὺν αὐτῷ βασιλεὺς
Λικίννιος, ...ἄμφω μιᾷ βουλῇ καὶ γνώμῃ νόμον ὑπὲρ Χριστιανῶν τελεώτατον
πληρέστατα διατυποῦνται...).

Although Eusebius does not further identify this "most perfect
law", he does say (HE, 9, 9, 9-12) that Constantine and Licinius
issued it soon after (ἐπὶ τούτοις) Constantine's victory over Maxentius on October 28, 312. This description of the circumstances makes
it probable that he was referring thereby to the Edict, which is the

(11) Moreau, *Scripta minora*, 102 f.; Seeck, ZKG, 12 (1891), n.b. 381, 386. *Contra*, see
inter alios Joseph Vogt, *Constantin der Grosse*, 168 f., 284; Calderone, *Costantino*, 164 f.;
Dörries, *Selbstzeugnis* (n. 1 above), 229 ff.; J. R. Palanque, « A propos du prétendu Édit
de Milan. » *Byzantion*, 10 (1935), 612 ff.; André Piganiol. *L'empereur Constantin* (Paris,
1932), 92-97; Pierre Batiffol, *La paix constantinienne et le catholicisme*, 2d ed. (Paris, 1914),
231.

See also Marcello Fortina, "La politica religiosa dell' imperatore Licinio," *Rivista di
studi classici*, 7 (1959), 245-65; 8 (1960), 3-23. On the almost hopeless task of attempting
to determine whether some of the legal texts now attributed to Constantine had originally
been issued by Licinius, see Roberto Andreotti, "L'imperatore Licinio ed alcuni problemi
della legislazione costantiniana," *Studi in onore di Emilio Betti*, 3 (Milan, 1962), 41-63;
Mario Amelotti, *SDHI*, 27 (1961), 300-23; Jean Gaudemet, "Constantin, restaurateur de
l'ordre," *Studi in onore di Siro Solazzi nel cinquantesimo anniversario del suo insegnamento
universitario (1899-1948)* (Naples, 1948), 652-74, who analyzes the Constantinian legislation which he believes annulled and replaced the laws enacted by Maxentius and Licinius.

On Licinius as persecutor, see Eusebius, HE, 10, 8, 8-9, 9, etc., with discussion by Calderone, *Costantino*, 205-30, who, however, is too eager to explain away all the data Eusebius
presents on Licinius's harshness towards the Church. From what Eusebius says, it appears
that, though Licinius did not persecute the Christians in the manner of the earlier pagan
emperors, he was unsympathetic towards them and enacted a number of measures which
were designed to harass them. The best recent study of the whole career of Licinius is that
by Roberto Andreotti, s.v., in the *Dizionario epigrafico di antichità romane*, 4, fasc. 31-33
(Rome, 1958-59), 979-1041, n.b. 994-97 on the Edict.

It cannot be proved that Constantine was the first to terminate active persecution of
the Christians. He seems to have done so ca. 306-7, but apparently no sooner and no more
completely than did his rival, Maxentius, who may once have outstripped him in the positive encouragement of Christianity. See HE, 8, 14, 1 and Hans von Schoenebeck, *Beiträge
zur Religionspolitik des Maxentius und Constantin*, *Klio*, Beiheft 43 (1939, reprinted Aalen,
1962), 4-27; Alberto Pincherle, "La politica ecclesiastica di Massenzio," in *idem*, *Cristianesimo
antico e moderno* (Rome, 1956), 38-50.

only joint declaration of these two emperors on religious liberty that he quotes. Likewise, this same text (HE, 9, 9, 9-12) makes it obvious that Eusebius could not possibly have been thinking here(a), as some have rashly supposed (12), of Galerius's Edict of 311, which preceded by over a year the above-mentioned defeat of Maxentius. This fatal objection to the proposed identification of the "most perfect law" with Galerius's Edict is fully borne out by internal evidence (to be discussed below, 5 (a)-(e)).

Likewise to be rejected (b) is the possibility that Eusebius had in mind the non-existing law which many believe (see (1) (a) above) Constantine issued on his own initiative, without reference to Licinius, late in 312 or early in 313, since Eusebius would never have confused such an enactment with one promulgated, as he says, by *both* of the emperors. Calderone argues (see n. 9) that Constantine acted in this instance by himself, on his own authority as senior Augustus, without consulting Licinius, but that, in accordance with the normal procedure (see n. 10), he then inserted Licinius's name *pro forma* in the text which he made public.

According to a somewhat similar theory (13), Eusebius deliberately added Licinius's name to HE, 9, 9, 12 as co-author with Constantine of the "most perfect law" in order to ingratiate himself with Licinius under whose jurisdiction he was residing at the time he was writing this portion of his HE. It is not clear why Licinius should have been pleased by a back-handed compliment of this kind. However that may be, both of these guesses fall wide of the mark because of Eusebius's express statement, as above quoted, that Licinius acted jointly in this matter with Constantine (Κωνσταντῖνος καὶ σὺν αὐτῷ βασιλεὺς Λικίννιος) and that they both had agreed to publish the legislation in question (ἄμφω μιᾷ βουλῇ καὶ γνώμῃ νόμον... διατυποῦνται). Eusebius would never have used such specific language if Licinius had not

(12) E.g., Moreau, *Scripta minora*, 102 f., without proof and relying on Grégoire, *Byzantion*, 7 (1932), 649, who guesses that Eusebius did not reproduce the text of this "most perfect law" since it was nothing but Galerius's Edict of 311. So universal is the respect and admiration for the erudition of the effervescent Henri Grégoire and his faithful disciple that their error about the Edict of Galerius has not previously been refuted.

(13) Nesselhauf, HJ, 74 (1954), 51 f., 54. Many authorities, e.g., Calderone, *Costantino*, 163-204, Nesselhauf, *loc. cit.*, Ehrhardt, ZSS, RA, 71 (1954), 38, & 72 (1955), 171 f., and Jochen Martin, "Toleranzedikt v. Mailand," *Lexikon für Theologie und Kirche*, 2d ed., 10 (Freiburg im Br., 1965), 246, believe that Constantine issued a law in 312 which served as the model for the Edict (attributed to Licinius by all four).

A curiosity worthy of mention is Eusebius's remark (HE, 9, 10, 6) that Maximinus, whom he denounces elsewhere as a stubborn enemy of the Church, legislated for the Christians "in the fullest and most perfect manner" (τελεώτατα καὶ πληρέστατα διαταξάμενος).

actively participated in the formulation of this law, at least to the extent postulated in I (a) above.

Nor (c) could there have been an earlier and now no longer surviving "most perfect law". For there is no known reason why the two emperors, after turning out one "most perfect law" (at the earliest late in 312, subsequent to Constantine's victory over Maxentius; see HE, 9, 9, 12), should only a few months later have deemed it necessary to frame a revised version thereof, i. e., our extant Edict of 313. Surely, if such a putative previous "most perfect law" had ever existed or had been "more perfect" than other such legislation, Eusebius would have wished to quote it, alongside of, or in preference to, the Edict of 313. Obviously, he would have preferred to transcribe the truly "most perfect law" and actually, I conclude, did so--in the text of the extant Edict of 313.

Such uncertainty as there is on this point arises from the fact that, by some accident in the transmission of the original manuscripts, the Edict (and a number of other legal documents), which should logically have followed closely upon Eusebius's reference to the "most perfect law", have been shifted to their present position (HE, 10, 5-7). Attempts (14) have been made to determine how and why this displacement came about, but none of the theories that

---

(14) Henri Grégoire, Byzantion, 7 (1932), 649, and Jacques Moreau, Scripta minora, 102 f., make much of the fact that some MSS omit HE, 10, 5, 1-7, 2 (which contains the Edict and a number of laws issued by Constantine alone). But these omissions by no means prove that the Edict is not fully attested since, of course, it still remains in MP, 48 and five out of nine MSS and versions of the HE.

Hugh J. Lawlor, Eusebiana, essays on the Ecclesiastical History of Eusebius, Bishop of Caesarea (Oxford, 1912), 243-54, holds that there was only one edition of HE, 10, but that some MSS are defective. His argument is directed against Eduard Schwartz, RE, 6, 1 (Stuttgart, 1907), 1405 f., and idem, Die griechischen christlichen Schriftsteller, 9, 3 (Leipzig, 1909), xlviii-l, who maintains that the passages in question were eliminated by Eusebius in the fourth and last edition of the HE, so as to remove all references favorable to Licinius, whose name would have been obnoxious to Constantine after the war of 324. ¶ But Schwartz's argument is unconvincing since, apart from the Edict itself HE (10, 5, 2-14), the portion of the HE that is missing in some of the MSS consists entirely of decrees of various kinds (HE, 10, 5, 15-7, 2) by which Constantine conferred on the Church special benefits of which he would have been proud (restoration of confiscated property, convocation of ecclesiastical synods, grants of money, immunity of the clergy from public offices). Hence, it seems better to suppose, with Lawlor, that the omissions in the defective MSS are to be attributed to accident rather than design. Even if Schwartz's theory were tenable, however, the text of the Edict (in HE, 10, 5, 1-14) cannot be impugned, as he himself concedes (GCS, 9, 3, xlviii-l). ¶ Cf. Richard Laqueur, Eusebius als Historiker seiner Zeit (Arbeiten zur Kirchengeschichte, 11 [Berlin-Leipzig, 1929]), 201 ff., 207 f., who argues, quite implausibly, that the Edict was omitted in the last edition of the HE, not because of the damnatio memoriae of Licinius, but because ca. 324 (his date for the last edition of the HE) these laws on Christian freedom of worship were taken for granted and no longer seemed vital or relevant. For a brief summary see Gustave Bardy, Sources Chrétiennes, 55 (Paris, 1958), 104-13; 73 (1960), 129-32.

have been propounded has won unanimous acceptance. Nor does any of them affect the reliability or authenticity of the crucial texts from Eusebius cited above.

Hence, the principal thesis of this paper, that Constantine was directly connected with the Edict and published a version of it in his own territories, stands, whatever the time and place of its promulgation and whatever the identity of the "most perfect and fully detailed law".

III.-IV. *The Edict of Milan: Constantinian and Licinian texts identical.*

As we learn from both Eusebius (HE, 10, 5, 4) and Lactantius (MP, 48, 2), the Edict was based upon conversations between Constantine and his co-emperor Licinius that took place in Milan (15), sometime early in 313, if not in the latter part of 312, as some believe. The exact date cannot be ascertained, although it has been thought that Constantine would presumably have been present in Rome on January 1, 313, the day on which he assumed his third consulship. But this is by no means certain; and he might well have left the capital long before this, just as his predecessor, Diocletian, had absented himself therefrom (MP, 17, 2) at the beginning of the year (304) in which he became consul for the ninth time. Similarly, there is no necessity for assuming that Constantine must have been in Rome as late as January 18, 313 simply because one of his constitutions *ad populum*, of which two fragments have been preserved, was published *(proposita)* in Rome on that day (CT, 10. 10. 1; CJ, 11. 58. 1 = CT, 13. 10. 1). For it was not essential that the emperor be at hand when his laws were publicly posted.

Actually, the sources do not provide sufficient information for an accurate chronology of Constantine's travels at this period. There is no doubt, however, that Constantine and Licinius did meet in Milan, either late in the year 312 or more probably early in 313 (16), in order to celebrate the marriage of the latter to the former's half-

---

(15) The date is fully discussed by Calderone, *Costantino*, 158-63. Otto Seeck, *Regesten der Kaiser und Päpste für die Jahre 311 bis 476 n. Chr.* (Stuttgart, 1919), 50, 35 ff., contends that the texts cited indicate that Constantine was in Rome on January 18, 313. On posting, etc., see *idem*, 8 ff.

(16) The long delay between the sessions in Milan (which were held in January, 313, or possibly even as late as February or March) and June 13, on which Licinius's Edict appeared, is best to be explained as the interval Licinius needed to bring Maximinus's part of the Empire under his effective control. See Calderone, *Costantino*, 182 ff.

sister, Constantia (17). At the same time, they took advantage of the opportunity thus afforded them to discuss the general situation and, above all, the status of religion in the Empire. (See the texts quoted above, pp. 16-17).

It has been argued (18) that Eusebius's version of the Edict should be regarded as the Greek translation of the original Edict which was promulgated by Constantine at Milan early in 313. But this conclusion is far from inevitable, and there is in fact no surviving document which can be *proved* without question to have been the original Edict of Milan.

Nevertheless, this traditional title for our Edict is not inappropriate if by it is understood the joint imperial Edict of toleration which, as a consequence of the understandings reached in Milan by Constantine and Licinius, became effective throughout the Empire upon promulgation by each of the emperors separately in his own realm. So much at the very least is undeniable.

But the traditional designation can, and probably should, be vindicated even more completely. This possibility of vindication arises because, as it should be obvious after reflection upon the normal procedures followed by lawyers and lawmakers, the results of the Milanese conversations between Constantine and Licinius must have been put into writing (19) before the parties separated. For two Roman emperors intent upon establishing a new imperial policy to be sanctioned by a law could never have been satisfied with anything less than a written and carefully worded record of the points on which they had agreed. This would hardly have been less than a formal text of the law that was soon to be proclaimed.

Hence, we are entitled to conjecture, each of the two emperors, or their respective legal secretaries, carried away from Milan a copy

---

(17) *Excerpta Valesiana*, 4, 13, ed. Jacques Moreau (Leipzig, 1961), 4, 12-18; Zosimus, *Historia nova*, 2, 17, 2, ed. L. Mendelssohn (Leipzig, 1887), 74, 15 ff.; *Epitome de Caesaribus*, 41, 1, edd. F. Pichlmayr and R. Gruendel, with Sextus Aurelius Victor (Leipzig, 1961), 166, 12 ff. Constantia is not mentioned by name in MP, 43, 2 or 45, 1 f. Constantia, the daughter of Constantius Chlorus and Theodora, is not to be confused with Constantine's daughter of the same name: Adolf Lippold, s.v. Constantia, *Der Kleine Pauly*, edd. K. Ziegler & W. Sontheimer, 1 (Stuttgart, 1964), 1283 f.

(18) By Şesan, *Kirche und Staat*, 1, 181-207, 207 ff., n. b. 190-92. See n. 5 above. Wittig, *loc. cit.* (n. 1 above), agrees with Sesan except that he prefers to describe this law as a rescript rather than an edict, and ascribes it to Licinius rather than to Constantine.

(19) So *inter alios* J. Maurice "Note sur le préambule placé par Eusèbe en tête de l'Édit de Milan¹", *Bulletin d'ancienne littérature et d'archéologie chrétiennes*, 4 (1914), 45. So also Hermann Dörries, *Wort und Stunde*, 1 (Göttingen, 1966), 20 n. 35, who goes almost as far as I do when he says (*ibid.*, 23) "Der herkömmliche Name 'Mailänder Edikt' ist zwar formal unrichtig, sachlich aber völlig zutreffend."

II

28

of an officially prepared text, which was then in all probability reproduced practically verbatim not only by Licinius in the Edict as we know it from MP, 48 but also by Constantine in his own no longer extant version thereof. These two promulgations, having been transcribed from the articles of agreement drawn up at Milan, would as a matter of course have been all but identical. Consequently, since our Edict (HE, 10, 5, 2-14; MP, 48) must have been a transcript of the meticulously articulated and officially approved memorandum worked out by the emperors in Milan, it deserves to be recognized as the "Edict of Milan", although it was not promulgated in this city.

Of course, there is no formal proof that the Edict actually took shape in this way. But the logic of the situation and the clear implication of the Edict, both as quoted above (HE, 10, 5, 4; MP, 48, 2) and as analyzed below with respect to *placuisse nobis* and its specific provisions, which are too detailed and too circumstantial to have been transmitted orally (pp. 31-32 below), lead inevitably to this conclusion.

On the other hand, it is not surprising that there are minor but not substantial discrepancies (see n. 5 above) between the Eusebian and Lactantian texts of the Edict, just as there undoubtedly must have been between the Licinian and Constantinian forms thereof. Absolute identity in such texts is all but unattainable, as anyone knows who has ever revised even an ordinary typescript, and then tried to incorporate all the final changes and *retouches* into all the carbon copies.

Some have argued **(1)** that this law of 313 was not an edict *(edictum)* but a rescript (20) *(rescriptum)* or a *mandatum* (21). Others hold **(2)** that it was nothing more than a statement of principle without legal consequences (22), or **(3)** that it was intended solely for Licinius's part of the Empire (23), or that Constantine would not have taken the trouble to promulgate the Edict himself (24), which would

(20) Vogt, *Constantin*, 170.
(21) Ernest Stein and J. R. Palanque, *Histoire du Bas-Empire*, 1, 2 (n. p., 1959), 458, n. 143; Moreau, *Scripta minora*, 103.
(22) So Vogt, *Constantin*, 169, who concludes of Constantine and Licinius at Milan: "dass sie auf die Abfassung eines Edikts verzichteten und sich damit begnügten, die Grundlinien einer künftigen Politik zu umreissen."
(23) Moreau, *Scripta minora*, 101-103; SC, 39, 2, 458.
* It is usually so described, though Eusebius (HE, 10, 5, 15) calls it a διάταξις (= constitutio), and it probably merits the designation edict as much as the Edict of 313. See notes 28-33 below and Ehrhardt, *loc. cit.* (n. 6 above), 171.(Reference to p. 29 below.)
(24) Baynes, *Constantine the Great*, 11, 74 f.; Moreau, *Scripta minora*, 102.

have been pointless and repetitious for him, since he had anticipated
it **(4)** in the rescript* addressed to Anulinus (HE, 10, 5, 15-17),
and above all **(5)** in the Edict of Sardica (25) of 311, to which his
name had been attached, along with those of Galerius (the senior
Emperor, its principal sponsor) and Licinius (26). Moreover, some
critics maintain **(6)** (27), this Galerian law of 311 was still in force
in Africa in 314 (or rather, 315; see n. 43) and could not, therefore,
have been superseded by the Edict, which, according to them, was
for this reason devoid of legal significance.

Of course, as its advocates seem not to realize, point **(5)** above
could equally well be used to support the impossible proposition,
favored by no one, that Licinius himself, having already legislated
sufficiently on this subject by joining Galerius and Constantine in
promulgating the Edict of 311, would merely have extended this
Edict to apply to his newly-conquered lands, as they argue Constantine had done, and would not subsequently have published the Edict
of 313, from which no one has ever thought of dissociating him.
Nor do they explain why Constantine could not have issued more
than one law on religious toleration especially if the successive enact-
ments were drafted in different terms or were designed to meet
special requirements, as even the most radical critics concede he
did, since no one denies that he was responsible for both the Edict
to Anulinus (312-313) and that of 311 (on which his name appears
along with those of Galerius and Licinius; see n. 26 above).

This logical flaw is characteristic of all six of these objections,
not one of which can withstand critical examination. **(1)** In the
first place, according to the usage of the Later Empire, such an

(25) Moreau, *Scripta minora*, 101-3; Seeck, ZKG, 12 (1891), 381-86.
(26) Eusebius, HE, 8, 17, 3-5. Some of the MSS (see GCS and LCL editions) omit Licinius's
name.
(27) Erich Caspar, *Geschichte des Papsttums*, 1 (Tübingen, 1930), 581, followed by Jacques Moreau, *Scripta minora*, 101, who does not attempt to deal with J. R. Palanque's
ingenious refutation of Caspar's theory in *Byzantion*, 10 (1935), 607-16; but see n. 44 below.
Vogt, *Constantin der Grosse*, 2d ed. (Munich, 1960), 169, 284, accepts Caspar's conclusion
without discussion, although he *cites* Palanque.
   In BZ, 32 (1932), 117 f., Ernest Stein accepts Caspar's argument that the Edict of Galerius was being cited in Africa in 314 (as we now know 315: see n. 43 below). But he interprets
this circumstance as proof that the Edict of 313 was then actually in effect. According to
him, since the *actorum rescissio* operated to expunge all the legislation of a tyrant (in this
case, Maxentius), Galerius's Edict could not have been re-instated after the death of Maxentius except by a law of Constantine, i.e., by the Edict of 313. This is a complex notion,
and it is difficult to follow Stein's argument that Constantine's Edict of 313 re-instated
Galerius's Edict, which it simultaneously replaced. On the *rescissio*, see Calderone, *Costantino*, 152-55; Theodor Mommsen, *Römisches Staatsrecht*, 2, 2, 3rd ed. (reprinted, Graz,
1952, with no reference to the original date), 1129-32.

enactment would have been regarded as an edict. The opposition
to this term in the present context rests mainly upon the theory (28)
that it should be restricted to documents which begin *Imperator
Caesar... dicit* (i.e., "the Emperor... says"). On this account, some
have thought, *mandatum* (29) would be a more accurate term than
edict. But this suggestion overlooks the fact that by this time (30)
mandata had become quite rare, and did not re-enter popular usage
until the reign of Justinian. Furthermore, since the *mandatum* was
the medium for transmitting administrative instructions to provincial magistrates, it would have been unsuitable for a formal pronouncement like the Edict of 313, which applied to the Empire as a
whole. It may also be relevant that, by a terminological accident,
the *mandatum* was never described as a *constitutio* (imperial enactment)
by a Roman writer, whereas the Edict is defined by Eusebius (HE,
10, 5, 1) as a διάταξις, i.e., as a *constitutio* (see n. 35 below).

Likewise, it is not likely that the legal provisions arising out of
the conference of Constantine and Licinius in Milan would have
been set forth in a rescript (31), which was the form customarily
used by the emperors to reply to queries from officials or petitions
from private persons.

These proposals of alternative and putatively preferable designations for the Edict look back primarily to the practice of the earlier
Empire (32), in which several types of laws (*edicta, decreta, rescripta,*
etc.) had been distinguished. In later times, however, the difference
between one form and another became less significant, and after
the reign of Diocletian (284-305) the principal distinction was between
laws of general application (the *leges generales*) (33), which were
promulgated for the Empire as a whole, and those which were granted

(28) On this definition of the imperial edict, see Leopold Wenger, *Die Quellen des römischen Rechts* (*Oesterreichische Akademie der Wissenschaften, Denkschriften der Gesamtakademie*, 2 [Vienna, 1953]), 425, n. 2.

(29) So, e.g., Seeck, ZKG, 12 (1891), 381-86. For the *mandatum*, see Wenger, *op. cit.*, 425 f.

(30) Jolowicz, *op. cit.* (n. 10 above), 376, 380 f., 480; Jean Gaudemet, *La formation du droit séculier et du droit de l'église aux IVᵉ et Vᵉ siècles* (*Institut de droit romain de l'Université de Paris*, 15 [1957]), 26 f.; *idem, Institutions de l'antiquité* (Paris, 1967), 481, 585, 733.

(31) On rescripts, see Wenger, *op. cit.*, 427-32; Jolowicz, *op. cit.*, 378-80, 479; Adolf Berger, *Encyclopedic dictionary of Roman law* (*Transactions of the American Philosophical Society*, N.S. 43, 2 [Philadelphia, 1953]), 574, 680.

(32) Jolowicz, *op. cit.*, 479, cf. 376 ff.; Kipp, s.v. Edictum, RE, 5, 2 (Stuttgart, 1905), 1947. 64 ff.

(33) Jolowicz, *op. cit.*, 478 f.; Wenger, *op. cit.*, 433 f. F. Martroye, "A propos de 'l'édit de Milan,' " *Bulletin d'ancienne littérature et d'archéologie chrétiennes*, 4 (1914), 48 f., inexplicably denies that the Edict "s'agit... d'une déclaration de droits s'adressant à la population tout entière."

ad hoc to bestow a favor or to deal with some extraordinary situation, but were not intended to serve as legal precedents that would be regularly applicable in the future.

A *lex generalis* could be issued in various ways, and if it was specifically so designated or promulgated as a law of general application, it had the force of an edict. This definition was laid down in a constitution of 426 (CJ, 1.14.3), which provided: *Sed et si generalis lex vocata est vel ad omnes iussa est pertinere, vim obtineat edicti.* These conditions were clearly fulfilled by the Edict of 313 since it prescribed rules that were directed to all the inhabitants of the Empire, to whom it specifically referred (as *omnibus* ["all"] twice in MP, 48, 2, and as *quisque* ["each"] thrice: MP, 48, 2, 4, 6), etc., and was therefore indubitably *ad omnes iussa est pertinere.*

(2) Actually, whether or not this definition is relevant for the fourth century, as it probably is, there is no need to quibble about terminology, since, under the Dominate (i.e., from the time of Diocletian) and even before, the legal channel by which the emperor chose to proceed was of little consequence and could not affect the final result. For no one could challenge his authority; and whatever method he preferred or the moment seemed to demand — whether he chose to take action through an edict or some other legal device — his decision as thus expressed became without question (34) the law of the Empire. This principle, which is traceable to Gaius and Ulpian, is set forth twice in the *Corpus Iuris Civilis*, in the *Institutes* (1.2.6) and in the *Digest* (1.4.1), and is almost too well-known to quote: *Quod principi placuit legis habet vigorem* ("What the emperor ordains (35) has the force of law").

It is significant, therefore, that the emperors used this technical term (in this instance, *placuisse nobis:* MP, 48, 4) to introduce the

---

(34) On this text, see Fritz Schulz, "Bracton on kingship", *L'Europa e il diritto romano, Studi in memoria di Paolo Koschaker*, 1 (Milan, 1954), 44 ff.; Pietro de Francisci, *Arcana imperii*, 3, 2 (Milan, 1948), 203-23.

(35) It is hardly necessary to warn the reader that *Quod principi placuit* is not to be translated crudely and unidiomatically, "What has *pleased* the king," as many of even the most erudite scholars persist in rendering it. The impersonal *placet* here is used in the technical meaning of *rule, determine, decide, ordain,* etc.; and the clause as a whole means: "What the emperor rules," i.e., what he has determined in his judicial capacity as lawgiver, presumably after consultation with his legal advisers (CJ, 1. 14. 2) or at least after due reflection on juridical matters. The full text is of great importance: *Institutiones*, 1. 2. 6: Sed et quod principi placuit legis habet vigorem, cum lege regia, quae de imperio eius lata est, populus ei et in eum omne suum imperium et potestatem concessit. Quodcumque igitur imperator per epistulam constituit vel cognoscens decrevit vel edicto praecepit, legem esse constat: haec sunt quae constitutiones appellantur. The parallel text, *Digest*, 1. 4. 1, differs in only a few minor particulars.

principal subject of their Edict (vid., that the restrictions on the Christians were to be removed). For, as any bureaucrat or educated man of the fourth century would have recognized at once, these two words (whose legal significance has been ignored by nearly (36) all of the modern commentators on the Edict) invest the text under consideration with full legal authority as a law. This would have been obvious to any Romanist, not only from the use of the wholly unambiguous *terminus technicus* just cited, but also from the form of the preface, the stress on its universal application, and a number of other legal tags (37). ¶ There is, of course, it should be added to conclude this phase of the argument, no reason to object that what we have been describing as the Edict cannot be accepted as such because it is otherwise unattested. For, as every student of Roman history knows, there is a huge corpus (38) of materials which by one accident or another were never taken up into any of the existing codes of law, and are known only from inscriptions, papyri, or the works of historians, whose authority, as in this instance, cannot be questioned.

(3) Thirdly, although the Edict was, according to Lactantius (MP, 48, 1), addressed to the governor of Bithynia, it is not reasonable to infer that it was on this account restricted to Licinius's portion of the Empire. If any such limitation had been envisaged, Eusebius would hardly have failed to draw attention to it. But he does not even mention the addressee designated by Lactantius. Besides, even in the Lactantian text (MP, 48, 2), both Constantine and Licinius are named as the authors of the Edict (tam ego Constantinus Augustus quam etiam ego Licinius Augustus... ordinanda esse credidimus), in a manner which proves that this was not a purely formal listing of the reigning monarchs but an official statement of actual collaboration and joint sponsorship. (See also HE, 10, 5, 1, quoted on p.16 above.)

(36) An exception is Amelotti, SDHI, 27 (1961), 288-95, n. b. 292, n. 142, 308 (who ascribes it to Licinius alone, but admits it to have been an edict); Adriani, SR, 2 (1954), 24 ff., accepts it as an edict, as does Ehrhardt, ZSS, RA, 72 (1955), 171. Even Moreau, who argues that this document cannot be described as an edict, himself (SC, 39, 2, 459, on 1, 15), refers to it as *l'édit*, and fails to comment on either CJ, 1. 14. 2 f. or *placuisse nobis*, which provide the key to its legal character.
A detailed study of the phraseology of the Edict and its use of legal terminology would be rewarding.
(37) Nesselhauf, HJ, 74 (1954), 46 f.
(38) See Gustav Haenel, *Corpus legum ab imperatoribus romanis ante Iustinianum latarum quae extra constitutionum codices supersunt*, 2 vols. (Leipzig, 1857, repr. Aalen, 1965); 1, 187 ff.

(4) Fourthly, the letter (HE, 10, 5, 15-17) to Anulinus (39), pro-consul of Africa, which some (see n. 24 f. above) deem to have been sufficient expression of Constantine's official attitude on toleration to have precluded his active collaboration in the Edict of 313, cannot be dated with certainty. Though Eusebius, our sole source for this document, quotes it *after* the Edict (HE, 10, 5, 15-17), logically, it would appear to be prior thereto, since it deals *ad hoc* with only one of the problems with which the Edict was concerned (i.e., with nothing but the restoration of Christian properties that had been seized by the State during the persecutions) and would in all likelihood have been unnecessary thereafter. ¶ Moreover, it lacks two of the most characteristic and indispensable elements of the Edict, (a) the promise of indemnification for pagans whose interests were damaged by the execution of this measure, and (b) the unequivocal declaration of the principle of absolute equality in the law to all religions. It was this last provision, which went far beyond the mere toleration already accorded by Galerius and Maxentius, that makes the Edict one of the most memorable monuments in the history of human freedom. No one in the fourth century, therefore, for which egalitarian ideas were, it need hardly be said, incomparably more revolutionary than they are in the twentieth, could ever have supposed that Constantine's simple instructions on a single point of law constituted an adequate substitute for the Edict.

In addition, the proponents of **(4)** overlook the fact that, as the emperors explain (HE, 10, 5, 2 f.; MP, 48, 4), the Edict was needed in order to remove certain *condiciones* in a previous enactment of theirs which had denied freedom of worship to many Christians. Thus, the emperors would have felt obliged to issue the Edict, even if the letter to Anulinus had been far more satisfactory a pronouncement on the religious question than it really was.

There is some dispute as to what these vexatious *condiciones* (40)

---

(39) On this document, see, Calderone, *Costantino*, 144 f.; Ehrhardt, ZSS, RA, 72 (1955), 171-73; Baynes, *Constantine the Great and the Christian Church*, 10, 68 f.; Kraft, *Kaiser Konstantins religiöse Entwicklung*, 160 f.; Dörries, *Selbstzeugnis*, 16.

(40) According to Knipfing, ZKG, 40 (1922), 211, the letter stated by Eusebius to have required correction is the one Sabinus sent at Maximinus's behest to replace the Edict of Galerius (HE, 9, 1-6). But I fail to see why Constantine and Licinius would have assumed responsibility for this document, with which they had had no connection.

Salvatore Calderone, "ΑΙΡΕΣΙΣ — 'condicio' nelle *Litterae Licinii*," *Helikon*, 1 (1961), 283-94, suggests that the word *condiciones* (in MP, 48, 4), which Eusebius translates by αἱρέσεις (HE, 10, 5, 6), in this context means, not *condition, stipulation, proviso*, etc., as it usually does, but something like *social condition* and, hence, *heretical sect*. This exegesis requires us to suppose that the law to which the emperors refer (said by C. to have been

34

were. But the most reasonable explanation seems to be that the clauses to which the emperors objected were contained in the special instructions (§e in the section immediately following) Galerius (41) sent his governors to supplement the Edict of 311.

(5) The same objections that have been urged against (4) in the preceding paragraphs apply *a fortiori* against the contention that Constantine was content merely to reinstate Galerius's Edict of 311 (42) and felt no necessity to issue the Edict of 313. This hypothesis, though confidently asserted, is purely an assumption, rests on no ancient or mediaeval evidence, and completely ignores the fact, which is obvious on even a casual examination, that the Edict of 313 is fuller, more decisive, and more advanced (in terms of the relations between Christianity and the State) than any of the previous constitutions which had dealt with this problem. None of the critics explains why Constantine should have preferred the inadequate measure grudgingly yielded to the Christians by one of the most ruthless persecutors of the Church to the much more humane document (the Edict of 313) which bears his own name (HE, 10, 5, 2-14; MP, 48).

Indisputably, Constantine would have found Galerius's Edict

that promulgated by Constantine alone in 312) put limitations on freedom of worship because it listed certain Christian sects which were to be tolerated but did not, and could not, include them all. The notion then arose, C. theorizes, that only the groups named were to be free. Accordingly, the clause, *amotis omnibus omnino condicionibus* (ἀφαιρεθεισῶν παντελῶς τῶν αἱρέσεων), means that the Edict eliminated this catalogue and thereby extended the scope of the religious privileges which it granted.

This is an ingenious hypothesis. But it is unnecessarily complicated, and assumes that Eusebius, or his translator, on coming upon *condicio* in the Latin original, took it to be the equivalent of *secta*. No one, it may be said categorically, would ever arrive at such a translation automatically, or without protest, even after the lexicographical analysis that has been mustered in its behalf.

Somewhat similarly, Ch. Saumagne, "Du mot αἱρεσις dans l'édit licinien de l'année 313," *Theologische Zeitschrift*, 10 (1954), 376-87, maintains that Lactantius saw *amotis omnibus omnino sectis* in the text of the Edict which he was transcribing but could not understand it and therefore corrected *sectis* to *condicionibus*.

My view is that the latter word stood in the original Edict and that αἱρέσεων in Eusebius's translation is to be understood as *restriction, condition*, etc., a sense which the word can, and does occasionally, bear (see Saumagne, *loc. cit.*, 382). But it must be admitted that αἱρεσις does not normally have this connotation. Perhaps, Eusebius, or his Latinist, simply made a mistake.

(41) Against this assumption, Knipfing, ZKG, 40 (1922), 210 f., argues, *inter alia*, that Galerius died too soon after issuing his Edict ·to have had an opportunity to circulate the letters in question. It seems more probable, however, that Galerius had these special instructions in mind from the very beginning and sent them out simultaneously with the Edict.

(42) For the text see HE, 8, 17, 3-11; MP, 34, with textual notes in Moreau, SC, 39, 1, 117; Haenel, *Corpus legum*, 1, 185. The latest study is Hans U. Instinsky, *Die alte Kirche und das Heil des Staates* (Munich, 1963). Karl Bihlmeyer, "Das Toleranzedikt des Galerius von 311," *Theologische Quartalschrift*, 94 (1912), 411-27, 527-89, still merits attention.

intolerable and in need of emendation for several reasons. (*a*) It granted the Christians nothing for their own sake and was, as Galerius frankly admitted, nothing but a last desperate attempt on his part to win over the Christians in the hope that they might then pray for his recovery from a foul disease. (*b*) It contained harsh language on the stubbornness and folly of the Christians in abandoning the [heathen] religion of their ancestors (HE, 8, 17, 6 f., 9; MP, 34, 1f., 4). (*c*) In a manner that could only have been offensive, it authorized them to "resume being Christians and build their meeting-places, on condition that they refrain from disorderly conduct" (HE, 8, 17, 9; MP, 34, 4: *ut denuo sint christiani et conuenticula sua componant, ita ut ne quid contra disciplinam agant*). (*d*) It ignored the problem of the restoration of the property which the Christians had forfeited to the government in previous years. (*e*) It tied the new privileges now vouchsafed to other, but unspecified and no longer extant, requirements, which Galerius said he would communicate to his governors (HE, 8, 17, 9; MP, 34, 5: *Per aliam autem epistulam iudicibus significaturi sumus quid debeant obseruare*).

These imperfections are so numerous and so glaring that Eusebius could not possibly have pronounced the document embracing them to be "the most perfect and fully articulated law" promulgated by Constantine and Licinius in behalf of the Christians (HE, 9, 9, 12; cf. 9a, 9, 12). The scholars who have propounded this unfortunate theory did not compare the two texts and, still worse, detached Eusebius's sentence on the most perfect law from the paragraph in which Eusebius makes it clear (see p. 23 above) that the "most perfect law" appeared some one and a half years later than Galerius's Edict.

Indeed, the very existence of the Edict of 311, bearing his name as one of its imperial sponsors, would have been enough to persuade Constantine of the necessity for superseding it with one that would be more expressive of his own sentiments. He had joined Galerius in the pronouncement of 311 *bon gré mal gré*, when, as a junior Augustus, he had no alternative but to accede to the senior Emperor's demands. But after he had won his way to the rank of senior Augustus as a result of his victory over Maxentius (MP, 44, 11), he would surely have wished to assert himself in the spirit of his overwhelming spiritual experience on the eve of October 28, 312.

Notwithstanding all the compelling reasons Constantine would have had for preparing new legislation of his own on religious freedom, it has been argued that he never did so, that Galerius's edict of 311 was still in force as late as 315 (n. 27 above), and that it had not been superseded by Constantine's Edict of 313, which, accordingly, it is said, never had the force of law. Proof of these propositions is found in the proceedings of a trial held in 315 before a certain Aelian, who was proconsul in Carthage and is quoted as having said (43): *Constantinus Maximus semper Augustus et Licinius Caesares ita pietatem christianis exhibere dignantur, ut disciplinam corrumpi nolint, sed potius obseruari relegionem (sic) istam et coli uelint.*

These words have been taken to be a citation of the Edict of Galerius *(ita ut ne quid contra disciplinam agant)*. Even if this interpretation be correct, however, and even if Aelian was not merely giving his own exegesis of the Edict of 313 (which, like any other new law, overthrew certain regulations without abolishing the legal system as a whole), it has been shown (44), he was not citing the Edict of Galerius as his authority on religious toleration (since this was not at issue) but only as his justification for requiring the Christians, like all others, to obey the ordinary civil law.

In this case, a certain Ingentius, a Donatist who had forged a letter libelling Bishop Felix of Aptungi as a *traditor* (i.e., one who had "handed over" the Scriptures to imperial officials in order to escape persecution), pleaded that he was a Christian in order to avoid confessing the crime of which he had been guilty. To this defence Aelian replied (45): *Noli itaque tibi blandiri, quod cum mihi dicas dei cultorem te esse, [ac delendum] propterea non possis torqueri. Torqueris, ne mentiaris, quod alienum christianis esse uidetur. Et ideo dic simpliciter, ne torquearis.* ("Don't deceive yourself that, since you tell me you are a worshipper of God, you are for this reason exempt from torture. The rack is to prevent lies, which, I hear, the

---

(43) *Acta purgationis Felicis*, ed. C. Ziwsa, *S. Optati Milevitani libri vii (Corpus Scriptorum Ecclesiasticorum Latinorum*, 26 [1893]), 203, 5 ff. On the identity of Ingentius, Bishop Felix of Aptungi, etc., see Ernst L. Grasmück, *Coercitio, Staat und Kirche im Donatistenstreit (Bonner historische Forschungen*, 22 [Bonn, 1964]), 65 ff., 68 ff., and passim, who puts this episode in 315 rather than 314 (p. 68, n. 300); W. H. Frend, *The Donatist Church* (Oxford, 1952), 150 ff.

(44) By J. R. Palanque, in a masterly article, "A propos du prétendu Édit de Milan," *Byzantion*, 10 (1935), 607-16. In *Histoire de l'Église*, 3, edd. A. Fliche & V. Martin, *De la paix Constantinienne à la mort de Théodose* (Paris, 1935), 23 f., however, he abandons his former position, which was sound, and attributes the Edict to Licinius. But Ernest Stein, *Histoire du Bas-Empire*, 1, *De l'État romain à l'État byzantin (284-476)* ([Bruges], 1959), 92, 458, edited by Palanque, still clings "à la réalité de la décision de tolérance de Milan," which he ascribes to both Constantine and Licinius, although he prefers to call it a *mandatum* rather than an edict.

(45) CSEL, 26, 203, 8 ff.

Christians abhor. So, tell the truth, and you will not be tortured.")
Ergo, this allusion to the Edict of Galerius (if that is what it really
be), does not by any means prove that Aelian was unaware of the
Edict of 313, but only that, as a competent magistrate, he knew
what precedents to cite on the precise question that was being adju-
dicated.

Since we have disposed of all possible objections, there can be
no doubt that in 313 Constantine and Licinius issued an Edict which
clarified and restated in new terms the principle of religious freedom
as set forth by Galerius in 311. What the two emperors now did was
to put the Christians on a plane of complete equality with the pagans
in all matters of religion and worship (HE, 10, 5, 4-8; MP, 48, 2-6).
At the same time, the restrictions previously imposed upon the
Christians were lifted, and immediate restitution was ordered of
all the property which had been confiscated from the churches (HE,
10, 5, 9-11; MP, 48, 7-11). Pagans who suffered financial loss as a
result of complying with this regulation were to be indemnified by
the State (HE, 10, 5, 10f., MP, 48, 8f.).

Nothing was said about making similar amends to individual
Christians (46). But the Christian communities as a whole gained
immeasurably more than this in now being accorded by both emperors
the status of legal corporations (47) (*corpus*, σῶμα in Greek: HE, 10
5, 10-12; MP, 48, 8-10). It has been argued (48) that Constantine had
granted this right to the Christians of Africa somewhat earlier, in his
Edict to Anulinus (HE, 10, 5, 15-17). But there are objections to this
view, and the Edict is the first document that indubitably recognizes
both the corporate legal capacity of the Church and the principle of
freedom of worship.

At the same time, the new privilege of religious liberty granted
the Christians was specifically extended to all others (HE, 10, 5, 4 f.,
8; MP, 48), so that no one might feel any restraint in the free exercise
of his predilections with regard to belief or cultus. On the contrary,

(46) It was not until a few years later, ca. 319, that Constantine ordered that indemnification be made to private individuals: *Vita Constantini*, 1, 41, 3; 2, 20, 2, ed. Ivar A. Heikel,
Eusebius Werke, 1 (*Die griechischen christlichen Schriftsteller der ersten drei Jahrhunderte*,
7 [Leipzig, 1902]), 27, 10 ff., 49, 13 ff., discussed by Arnold Ehrhardt, ZSS, RA, 72 (1955),
171-75.

(47) See literature cited in n. 7 above.

(48) So Ehrhardt, ZSS, RA, 72 (1955), 172 f. Ludwig Schnorr von Carolsfeld, *Geschichte
der juristischen Person*, 1 (Munich, 1933), 206 f., denies that τὸ δίκαιον in HE, 10, 5, 15-17
can be equated with *corpus* and σῶμα in the sense of a legal corporation, as does Artur Steinwenter, "Die Rechtsstellung der Kirchen und Klöster nach den Papyri", ZSS, KA, 19
(1930), 31-35.

the emperors expressed the hope (HE, 10, 5, 4f., 13; MP, 48, 2f., 11, quoted above) that in this way they might placate for themselves and their subjects every form of divinity that there might be, and thus hold the favor of the highest divinity, to which, they averred without naming it, they paid homage without reserve *(summa diuinitas, cuius religioni liberis mentibus obsequimur)*. Eusebius omits the last relative clause and the adjective *summa*, but he shares with Lactantius the abstract noun *diuinitas*, which he translates simply by τὸ θεῖον.

Although the Edict guaranteed freedom to all religions, the emphasis throughout is on the Christians, who had never before been granted this privilege so unreservedly. The studied ambiguity in the references to the Godhead, on the other hand (HE, 10, 5, 4 & 5; Greek quoted above; MP, 48, 2: *quicquid est diuinitatis in sede caelesti; ibid.*, 3: *summa diuinitas)*, as many have remarked, was both acceptable to the Christians, whom it was the primary purpose of the Edict to conciliate, and also at the same time inoffensive to the pagans, who were too numerous (49) to alienate. Since the latter constituted the majority throughout the Empire, especially in his portion of it, Constantine, despite the sincerity of his conversion to Christianity, would have made a special effort (as in the choice of an innocuous substitute for the divine name in this Edict) to avoid alarming them or goading them into rebellion under the banner of the ancient gods. Similar considerations would have weighed heavily also with Licinius, in whose part of the Empire the Christians, though more numerous than in the West, were nevertheless outnumbered by the pagans.

V. *Imitation of the Edict on the Arch of Constantine.*

Under these circumstances, it was inevitable that Constantine's panegyrists and others who wished to honor him (like the designers of the Arch of Constantine [dedicated in 315]) (50) would have imitated

(49) The best and most detailed treatment of the size of the Christian population remains Adolf von Harnack, *Mission und Ausbreitung des Christentums in den ersten drei Jahrhunderten*, 4th ed. (Leipzig, 1924), 2, 946-58. For later surveys, see B. Kötting, "Christentum I (Ausbreitung)," *Reallexikon für Antike und Christentum*, 2 (Stuttgart, 1954), 1138-59; Kenneth S. Latourette, *A history of the expansion of Christianity*, 1 (New York, 1937), 158-60 and passim.

(50) Hans P L'Orange and Armin von Gerkan, *Der spätantike Bildschmuck des Konstantinsbogens (Studien zur spätantiken Kunstgeschichte*, 10 [Berlin, 1939]), 4-28; Antonio Giuliano, *Arco di Costantino* (Milan, 1955). Alföldi, *The conversion of Constantine*, 69 ff., comes close to enunciating my theory of the connection between Constantine's Edict and the Arch.

the terminology which the Edict had by its example established as
proper for reference to the imperial tutelary deity. In other words,
there can be little doubt that the Edict was the obvious, but so far
as I can see hitherto unrecognized, source for the new caution in the
use of religious language which now came into style.

Thus, in an oration delivered soon after the Edict, in the summer
or fall of 313, an unknown panegyrist (51), addressing Constantine
directly, asks what god or favoring divinity it was which inspired
him to make his daring assault upon Rome [in October, 312], against
the advice of his advisers and soothsayers:

> Quisnam te deus, quae tam praesens hortata
> [est?] maiestas ut... contra consilia hominum,
> contra haruspicum monita ipse per temet
> liberandae urbis tempus uenisse sentires (2,4).

Later, the orator touches upon the *diuina praecepta* (4, 4) to which
Constantine hearkened, and the divine guidance which directed
him *(*11, 4: *diuino monitus instinctu)*. Likewise in the spirit of
the Edict, at the end of this discourse, there is an apostrophe (26)
to the lord of the universe, who is described as either some divine
force or intellect or a power exalted above the heavens, in whom
the highest goodness dwells. Several years later, in 321, the panegyrist
Nazarius (52) took over the same terminology: *illa diuinitas* (13, 5),
diuinitus (14,1), *uis diuinitatis* (27, 5).

The influence of the Edict upon these vague and circumlocutory
expressions can be illustrated by comparison with two other panegyrics, both anonymous, which were pronounced in 310 and 312, respectively. In the former of these (53), the unknown author, while cele-

---

(51) *XII panegyrici latini*, ed. R.A.B. Mynors (Oxford, 1964), no. XII (IX), p. 271 ff.;
Panégyriques latins, ed. with French translation, by Édouard Galletier, 2 (Paris, 1952),
no. IX (12), p. 103 ff. (with essay on the date, etc., 105 ff.). The passage summarized in
the text (26, 1) runs: Quamobrem te, summe rerum sator, cuius tot nomina sunt quot gentium
linguas esse uoluisti (quem enim te ipse dici uelis, scire non possumus), siue tute quaedam
uis mensque diuina es, ... siue aliqua supra omne caelum potestas es quae hoc opus tuum
ex altiore Naturae arce despicias... Et certe summa in te bonitas est et potestas (26, 3).

On the emperor as deus, etc., see François Burdeau, "L'empereur d'après les panégyriques latins," *Aspects de l'empire romain (Travaux et recherches de la faculté de droit et des
sciences économiques de Paris, Sciences historiques*, 1 [Paris, 1964]), 1-60, n. b. 10 ff.; and
on the panegyrists in general, besides the introductions in Galletier's edition, cf. René Pichon,
Les derniers écrivains profanes (Paris, 1906), 97 f., 101 f., 103-8. On the passages cited in
notes 50-55, see also Johannes Straub, *Vom Herrscherideal in der Spätantike* (n. 3 above),
99 ff.

(52) Mynors, IV (x), p. 145 ff.; Galletier, X (4), v. 2, 147 ff.

(53) Mynors, VI (vii), p. 186 ff.; Galletier, VII (6), v. 2, p. 31 ff.

brating Constantine's virtues, catalogues his divine sponsors without reticence and lists, among others, Jupiter (7, 3; 8, 5; cf. 15, 6), the *di boni* (8, 2; 9, 4), Iris (8, 5), Ceres (9, 2), Liber, i.e., Bacchus (9, 2 & 4), Mercury (9, 4), Apollo (21, 4 & 7; 22, 1), the *di immortales* (22, 1), and so on. In the second of these, the anonymous *Gratiarum Actio Constantino Augusto* (54), mention is made of the *di immortales* (7, 6; 13, 1), the "statues of all our gods" (8, 4: *omnium deorum nostrorum simulacra*), and Jupiter (13, 6).

The new restraint and meticulous avoidance of the names of the pagan divinities which characterizes the oration of 313 are inexplicable except as an acknowledgement of Constantine's momentous experience on the eve of October 28, 312, and, more particularly, as a sign of deference to his terminological approach to divinity in the Edict.

Even more striking is the celebrated inscription on the Arch of Constantine (55), which copied the ambiguous and neutral language of the Edict of 313 in declaring that Constantine had won his victory over Maxentius at the Milvian Bridge (on October 28, 312) *instinctu divinitatis* ("under the guidance [or inspiration] of divinity "). Obviously, these ambivalent words were chosen deliberately in order to express gratitude for supernatural intervention without indicating a preference for either the Christian God or any of the pagan divinities. This is exactly the kind of appeal to unnamed divine powers which Constantine and Licinius had made in the Edict.

The reappearance of *divinitas* in this inscription is doubly significant, since the Roman Senate was predominantly pagan (56). Hence, their adoption of this equivocal term proves that the senators, like the anonymous panegyrist of 313, had been informed about Constantine's religious experience on the eve of October 28, 312. In addition, and more specifically, they showed thereby that they were consciously following the Constantinian religious policy and deferring to his method of referring to God as set forth in the Edict. For this reason, in order not to offend the Emperor or violate the terms and spirit of the Edict, they scrupulously refrained from naming his former divine champion (*Sol Invictus* (the unconquered, i.e., unconquerable Sun), whom they would presumably have found congenial. At the

(54) Mynors, V (VIII), p. 174 ff.; Galletier, VIII (5), v. 2, p. 76 ff.
(55) For the text of the inscription, see Hermann[us] Dessau, *Inscriptiones latinae selectae*, 3rd ed. (repr. Berlin, 1962, original date unfortunately not given), no. 694.
(56) On the paganism of the Senate, see Alföldi, *The conversion of Constantine*, 61-73.

same time, they also abstained from mentioning the Emperor's new God, and no doubt were pleased to be able to cloak their own religious feelings under the ambiguity of the colorless *divinitas*, which Constantine had invested with imperial sanction in the Edict.

It is therefore improper to interpret the inscription on the Arch as if it were connected with the solar iconography (57) of the fourth century. The attempt to read elements of a Neoplatonized solar mysticism into *instinctu divinitatis* has been popular in recent years. But this interpretation ignores both the political consequences of Constantine's conversion on the night of October 27-28, 312, and the true significance of the Edict. The solar and lunar sculptural elements in the decoration of the Arch were from Constantine's point of view purely adventitious, like most of the sculptures on this famous monument, which, as L'Orange and von Gerkan have demonstrated, were taken from other imperial structures of various kinds.

Therefore, the panegyric of 313 and the inscription of 315 prove not only that Constantine's subjects in the West were aware of the revolutionary change that had taken place in his religious beliefs in 312, but also that they realized that he was the author of the Edict.

University of California.
Los Angeles.

(57) E. g., L'Orange and von Gerkan, *op. cit.* (n. 50 above), 5 f., 174 ff.; Franz Altheim *Aus Spätantike und Christentum* (Tübingen, 1951), 49 ff. Bernard Berenson, *The Arch of Constantine, or the decline of form* (London, 1954), who concerns himself with style rather than iconography, is unsympathetic to the art of the fourth century.

IIa

COMPLEMENTARY NOTE

In a brief critique of the above article (BZ, 61(1968),408),H.G.Beck flippantly suggests that the whole question of Constantine's attitude towards Christianity (i.e., more specifically, I suppose, of the trust-worthiness of Eusebius's VC 1,28-31 -Constantine's vision and dream on the eve of the Battle of Milvian Bridge- and related texts) is a matter of fluctuating styles, which are subject to change with the passage of time.

But this judgment ignores the logical weakness of the "paradoxogra - phic" method and the vast literature of recent years (p.15 n.3 above) which has completely vindicated the authenticity of the passages in Eusebius's VC attacked by the paradoxographers as interpolations of the latter part of the fourth century or the beginning of the fifth.

Consider two of the paradoxes. Grégoire claims without any docu-mentary proof that Licinius was responsible for the Edict of 311,although Lactantius ascribes it to Galerius (MP,33f.;cf. Eusebius,HE,8,17,1-11). Then he insists, as does Moreau, that Licinius alone was the author of the Edict of 313, despite its ascription to both Constantine and Licinius by Eusebius and Lactantius (pp.16f. above). The argument they make for their theory of Licinian authorship is that there was no need for Const-antine to issue a new edict of toleration in 313, in his realm, i.e.,in the West, since the Edict of 311 was still in force there. At the same time, they contend that it was necessary for Licinius to do so because he had to remedy the defects of the Edict of 311 (Grégoire,"La 'conversion' de Constantin," German version in Heinrich Kraft,op. cit.,208,213, Moreau, Scripta minora, 162f.).

Their only explanation for this paradox is that Constantine had alrea-dy taken some steps in this direction. But Eusebius was well aware of what Constantine had done and gives the text of the measures to which the paradoxographers refer. Nevertheless,he names Constantine as the co-author of the Edict of 313,which deals comprehensively with the pro-blem of religious toleration as a whole and would for this reason have been far more satisfactory legally and administratively than a number of disparate laws amending and revising the obsolete Edict of 311.

For the latest refutation of the paradoxographers,see,inter alios, Friedhelm Winkelmann's new edition of the Vita , Die griechischen christlichen Schriftsteller der ersten Jahrhunderte,Eusebius Werke,1, 1 (Berlin,1975),LVIf., and the papers by Joseph Vogt,Hermann Dörries (Konrad Kraft,"Das Silbermedaillon Constantins des Grossen mit dem Christusmonogram auf dem Helm" from Jahrbuch für Numismatik und Geldgeschichte,5-6 (1954-55),151-78), and Arnold Ehrhardt (above,p. 19 n.6),reprinted by Heinrich Kraft,Konstantin der Grosse (Wege der Forschung,131 (Darmstadt,1974).

Special mention should be made also of Pio Franchi de' Cavalieri, Constantiniana, Studi e Testi,171 (Vatican City,1953), who meticulously refutes the arguments of the paradoxographers on the autenticity of VC 1, 28-31 point by point,and shows that their entire case rests upon careless or incomplete reading of the relevant texts.

As a result of the detailed argumentation and analysis by these scholars and the authorities they cite, too numerous to list here, it has become clear that the VC as we now have it is essentially what Eusebius wrote. Such interpolations as there may be are inconsequential.

This verdict is not affected,e.g., by the argument of Andreas Alföldi in his valuable paper, "Hoc signo victor eris," Pisciculi (Antike und Christentum, Supplement 1 (Münster in Westfalen,1939),1-18 (reprinted by H. Kraft, op.cit.), in which he maintains that Eusebius was mistaken in inferring from Constantine's report of his dream (VC,1,28-31) that the device to be reproduced on the shields of his soldiers was a cross rather than a Christogram (as described by Lactantius,MP,44,5f.). Alföldi is of the opinion that this was either an honest error on Eusebius's part or a pious exaggeration, which, of course, does not invalidate the VC in general.

Against Alföldi,Vogt, Mélanges Grégoire,1,cited below,606,stoutly maintains that the heavenly sign of Constantine's vision and dream was a cross, as Eusebius says it was, and not a Christogram. It is interesting to note that Alföldi does not use HOC SIGNO VICTOR ERIS on the coins (see below) as testifying to the reliability of VC,1,28-31, probably because he regards it as indisputable and in no need of external corroboration.

It is difficult to determine whether a cross or a Christogram was intended. It should be emphasized, however, that the paradoxographers devoted most of their energy to attaking Eusebius. But they have been unable to undermine the authority of Lactantius,MP,44,5f. (on the Christogram Constantine was advised in a dream to inscribe on the shields of his troops before marching out against Maxentius), which by itself impressively confirms the major points of VC,1,28-31 (i.e., Constantine's dream and divine revelation).

One very important proof that VC,1,28-31 was not a later addition has never been sufficiently stressed,although many have referred to it. This is found on the coins. Vogt (Kraft,op.cit.,366) says that Vetranio's coins of the year 350 with the legend,HOC SIGNO VICTOR ERIS,prove that Eusebius's version of Constantine's vision and dream was well known. (This legend is a latin translation ("by this sign you shall be the victor") of τούτῳ νίκα ("by this sign conquer"),the words which Eusebius said (VC,1,28,1f.) Constantine had sworn to him were inscribed upon the figure of the cross he and his troops had seen in the sky around noon on October 27,312.)

It is upon this latin inscription that Vogt and Franchi de' Cavalieri, op.cit.,28,93,100,130, rely for evidence that the Latin West was familiar

with the principal features of Eusebius's account of Constantine's vision
and dream in 350,i.e., only about a decade after Eusebius's death,even
if, de'Cavalieri adds, these coins do not necessarily signify that the VC
itself had already been published and had reached the West by this time.
But they do indicate that VC,1,28-31 could not have been an interpolation
which, as the paradoxographers claim, was made a few generations after
the event.

Actually, these numismatic data go much further than this. Coins with
this reverse legend were struck not only by Vetranio and Constantius II in
Siscia in 1350 but also in Sirmium,between 351 and 354, by the Caesar,
Constantius Gallus, who in 351 married his cousin, Constantia,the daughter of Constantine I and sister of Constantius II. On the obverse these
coins represent the head of Vetranio, Constantius II, and Constantius
Gallus,respectively. (Vetranio was probably responsible for both his own
coins and those issued with the portrait of Constantius, which he in all
likelihood intended as a mark of deference to the latter, who was the sole
legitimate emperor.)

On the reverse, all of these coins are iconographically very similar
and present one of the three above-mentioned royal personages in military garb facing forward, with head left , carrying a vertical labarum with
the Christogram in his right hand and a staff or scepter held transversely
in his left. Behind him, facing left, is a female figure of the winged Victory with her right hand raised in the act of placing a wreath upon his
head and holding a palm frond in her left. All three types have the reverse
legend, HOC SIGNO VICTOR ERIS.

The obvious source for this iconography and also for the Latin translation of Eusebius's τούτῳ νίκα,since Latin was Constantine's native language and presumably that of his daughter,was Constantia, who, in order
to help her brother Constantius II in his struggle against the usurper Magnentius (350-353), had made Vetranio Caesar in 350 (Philostorgius,HE,3,
22) and thus influenced Constantius to send him the imperial diadem.
Somewhat later,she apparently persuaded her husband, Constantius Gallus,
to strike coins of the same type. Under these circumstances, there can be
little doubt that it was Constantia who related to Vetranio and to her husband, Constantine I's nephew (if the latter had not heard it himself in the
circle of the family) the substance of her father's vision and dream much
as they are reported by Eusebius in VC,1,28-31.

It is this circumstance that is of the highest significance in the present
context. For it provides unimpeachable archaeological corroboration of
Eusebius's dependability that goes back to Constantine's immediate entou-
rage and thence to Constantine himself. This would seem to be self-evident.
But it is a crucial point which has not been previously made, not even by
Alföldi in his many important works on Constantine. Neither the Christ-
ograms on Constantine's coins in general nor that on his helmet in these
extant silver medallions, though impressive witness to his commitment to
Christianity,give support to VC,1,28-31 so completely and so directly as

do the coins of 350 with their Latin translation of τούτῳ νίϰα.

The logical inference is that Constantine had told his children of his anxieties on October 27 and the early hours of the 28th and of the vision and dream he had had or claimed that he had had on that occasion. In view of the numismatic evidence, it is extremely unlikely that he would have invented such a tale and much more probable that he actually underwent this experience, for which he had been conditioned by his fears and aspirations as he was preparing to engage in a battle with Maxentius on the following day, that was to have enormous consequences for him personally, for the Empire and indeed, as we now know, for the entire history of Western civilization.

Accordingly, whether Constantine imagined the vision and dream or not, the inscription, HOC SIGNO VICTOR ERIS, on the coins must have originated with one or more of his sons or daughters, who had heard his version of this affair and had discussed it with Vetranio and others in the West

In urging Vetranio to use this Constantinian symbolism on his coins, Constantia in all likelihood thought that it would serve to demonstrate his loyalty to Constantius and the Constantinian line. For a brief time Vetranio wavered slightly in his fidelity but soon reverted to what seems to have been his original position, which he had adopted at Constantia's behest, of serving primarily as Constantius's ally, whose chief function it was to hold the West for Constantius until the latter was in a position to take personal command of the war against Magnentius.

As soon as he was able to do so, Constantius proceeded to Serdica and then to Naïssus, where he met with Vetranio, who then complaisant- ly gave up the throne and retired to a peaceful and affluent life in Bithynia after having been emperor for almost ten months (from March 1 until December 25,350). Constantius Gallus's coins with this reverse are probably to be explained similarly as an attempt to wave the Constantin- ian banner and so to placate the Emperor Constantius, who had been ali- enated by the former's wanton behavior and was fearful of his intentions.

Grégoire (Byzantion,7 (1932),647) argues that these coins refer, not to VC,1,28-31, but to the statue of Constantine set up in Rome,presuma- bly in the Forum,in the right hand of which, according to Eusebius (HE, 9,9,10f.),the Emperor had ordered that the sōtērion sēmeion ("the sign of salvation")be placed, together with the inscription "by this sign of salvation (tutō tō sōteriōdei sēmeiō) have I liberated your city..." But nota bene :it is not this text which is translated on the coins but tutō nika ("by this sign conquer"). The inscription on the statue lacks the key word, conquer. Moreover, as Vogt has pointed out (Kraft, op.cit., 366f.),Eusebius refers to the "sign of salvation ... the standard of victory" Christ gave to Constantine,by which the enemy and the demons were conquered in his Oration on the thirtieth anniversary of Constant- ine's succession,6,21, ed. I.A. Heikel,GCS,7,212.4-9. (See n.1 below). This passage (if not HE,9,9,10f.,quoted above, as well) is an indubitable

5

reminiscence of VC,1,28-31 in a genuine work of Eusebius and thus in
itself demolishes the paradoxographic argument that Eusebius himself
knew nothing of VC,1,28-31.

We advance one step further with the coins, which demonstrate that
Eusebius was relying, as he said, upon Constantine's oath (VC,1,28,1)
and that VC,1,28-31 as a whole was neither fabricated by Eusebius nor
a pious fraud of later date. On these coins,see J.P.C. Kent, Max and
Albert Hirmer,Roman Coins (London,1978, revised from the German
edition, Munich,1973), #681,pl.173,p.335 (Constantius,reverse);Wen-
delin Kellner,Libertas und Christogramm (Karlsruhe,1968),102,105,107,
162f.; Guido Bruck,Die spätrömische Kupferprägung (Graz,1961),xxiii,
44; P.V. Hill,J.P.C. Kent and R.A. Carson Late Roman Bronze Coinage,
(London,1960),70,76,109,pl.III,1178; G. Mazzini, Monete imperiali
romane,5 (Milan,1958),189,205,pl. LI,4;LV,34 (Vetranio and C.
Gallus); Henry Cohen,Description historique des monnaies frappées
sous l'Empire Romain,7 (Paris,1888,reprinted Graz,1955),461,8;2nd.
ed. (Paris,1892,reprinted Graz,1955),4,4;36,33; Ioseph(us) Eckhel,
Doctrina numorum veterum ,2nd. ed. (Vienna,1828),116f.,120,126.
For Vetranio see Wilhelm Ensslin,s.v.,RE,S.2,16 (=8A2) (Stuttgart,
1958),1838-40; for Constantius Gallus, Otto Seeck, "Constantius 5",
RE,7 (=4,1),(Stuttgart,1900),1094-99.

The vision of the cross seen by the inhabitants of Palestine mentioned
by Cyril of Jerusalem in a letter to Constantius II (PG,33,1165-76) does
not impugn the testimony of the coins of 350 since it was written in 351
or, more probably, as late as 353; see Franchi de' Cavalieri, op.cit.,
86f., and J. Vogt,"Berichte über Kreuzeserscheinungen aus dem 4.
Jahrhundert n. Chr.," Mélanges Henri Grégoire,1 (Annuaire de l'Institut de philologie et d'histoire orientales et slaves, 9 (Brussels,1949),
293-606,n.b. 596-604. The latter argues, against Grégoire, that Cyril's
vision of the cross was dependent upon Eusebius's account of the heavenly sign (VC,1,28-31), which he regards as authentically Eusebian.

It should be noted also (pp.28-32) that Galerius's law of 311 does
not conform to the ordinary definition of an edict,although it is described as such by Lactantius (MP,34). Would it not have been reasonable,therefore, for Constantine and Licinius to have replaced it with a
law of the same type,i.e., by another edict ?

On another point (p.20 above),the question of the actual publication
of the Edict by Constantine and Licinius in their respective realms, the
general view now is that, in the early Dominate, at least,beginning with
Diocletian (284-305),the Maximus Augustus had the exclusive right to
promulgate leges (i.e.,laws for the Empire as a whole). Neither the
junior Augustus (e.g.,Maximianus Herculius,286-305) nor the Caesars
shared this prerogative:Ernst Kornemann, Doppelprinzipat und Reich-
steilung im Imperium Romanum (Leipzig-Berlin,1930),111;Otto Seeck,
Geschichte des Untergangs der antiken Welt,1,4th ed.(Stuttgart,1921,
reprinted 1966),27,33,except that they could issue rescripts;idem,

"Die Zeitfolge der Gesetze Constantins,"Zeitschrift der SSRG ,Romanis-
tische Abt.,10 (1889),178f. So also William Seston, Dioclétien et la
tétrarchie (Bibliothèque des Ecoles françaises d'Athènes et de Rome,
162)(Paris,1946),233f.; and Mario Amelotti, Per l'interpretazione
della legislazione privatistica di Diocleziano (Fondazione Guglielmo
Castelli,26) (Milan,1960),13. Francesco de Martino, Storia della
costituzione romana, 5 (Naples,1975)86f., with a slight change of emphasis,distinguishes between edicts dealing with matters of imperial policy as a whole ("che hanno fini politici"), which he assigns to the Maximus Augustus, and administrative regulations which he says were put
out by both Augusti.

Since the Roman Senate voted Constantine the rank "of the first name,"
i.e.,that of Maximus Augustus (Lactantius,MP,44,11;Kornemann,op.cit.,
125), it must be assumed that, whether or not he was the only one em-
powered to make the laws until 314, as Kornemann maintains (p.126),he
would at the very least have legislated for his own realm, if not for the
whole Empire.

On pp.23f. above:n.b. Richard Klein, "Der νόμος τελεώτατος
Konstantins für die Christen im Jahre 312," Römische Quartalschrift,67
(1972),1-28, who maintains that this "most perfect law" is no longer extant and can no longer be completely reconstructed, although he acknow-
ledges that much of it has been preserved in other documents and especially in the Edict of 313 ("besonders in das sogenannte Mailänder Edikt
mit eingeflossen"). He does not cite, or attempt to deal with, my article.

The inevitable conclusion is that the case of the paradoxographers has
failed utterly, and that the reliability of the text of Eusebius in the matters
at issue remains unshaken. As far as my article is concerned, I hold to
what I have written. But even if what I have been describing as the Edict
of 313 is not, as I contend, an actual edict within the strict definition of
this term, it cannot be denied that it does truly constitute a law or legal
enactment of some kind providing for the toleration of Christianity alongside the pagan religions, and that it was issued jointly by Constantine and
Licinius in Milan, as both Eusebius and Lactantius clearly state (pp.16f.
above). I prefer to trust the testimony of the two ancient historians who
worked independently and support each other without any substantial deviation, rather than the fragile hypotheses concocted by modern writers
who have not made full or careful use of the sources.

I now find that my argument (pp.38-41) about the close relation between the inscription on the Arch of Constantine and the language of the
panegyrists, on the one hand, and the Edict of 313, on the other, had
been anticipated by Franchi de' Cavalieri,op.cit.,121-23.

One last word needs to be said about the "most perfect and fully detailed law on behalf of the Christians,"which Eusebius says (pp.23f.
above)"Constantine himself and Licinius with him...with one will and
purpose together drew up" subsequent to October 28,312. Grégoire, I
note, admits that this was actually later than the Battle of the Milvian

Bridge. But he insists that it was identical with Galerius's Edict of 311. For the reasons set forth above (pp.34-37), the one indefectibly certain fact is that this "most perfect and fully detailed law" could not have satisfied Constantine after his victory on October 28. It is much more probable, as I have argued, that it was the Edict of 313.

(1)   Vogt cites also <u>ibid</u>.,11,1,223.23-29, in which Eusebius addresses Constantine, to whom, he says, God, through Christ, disclosed the holy secrets by divine revelation. But since this divine revelation is described as having frequently(πολλαχῶς)enlightened Constantine, it is by no means certain that Eusebius had VC,1,28-31 in mind here.

POLITICAL THEORY

III

VOX POPULI VOLUNTAS DEI
AND THE ELECTION OF THE BYZANTINE EMPEROR

Vox populi (vel tyranni vel imperatoris vel Augustae) voluntas Dei:
observations on the election and coronation of the Byzantine Emperor

It is a great satisfaction for me to be able to contribute to this series
of volumes in honor of my good friend, Professor Morton Smith, whose
versatility, decisive manner, and vast erudition I have admired since he
was a student at the Harvard Divinity School. I hope that he may be
gratified to note that the sources I have used in writing this paper are
contained almost exclusively in the magnificent set of the *Corpus Scriptorum Historiae Byzantinae*, richly bound in exquisite full morocco in a
variety of handsome colors, and decorated with gold leaf, which he most
graciously sold me a generation ago at his cost price.

Him I now salute in the Byzantine manner:

Chorus: πολλά, πολλά, πολλά ('Many, many, many').
People: πολλὰ ἔτη εἰς πολλά ('Many years, for many years').
Chorus: πολλοί σου χρόνοι ('Many years to thee').

I. *Introduction*

Unlike the Hellenistic rulers and the later Roman emperors, who
had been deemed to be gods and received cult as such, the rulers
of Byzantium were regarded, not as gods, but as God's vicegerents.
They were not themselves divine but were chosen by God to rule
the terrestrial world in his name.[1] This view of divine election,

---

[1] *Important note*: In what follows, I give the original Greek only when it
is necessary to support my argument. I do not reproduce the whole of the
Greek text I have translated but only the words on which I rely to prove
vox populi (vel tyranni) voluntas Dei, and coronation by the hand of God.
I am deeply indebted to my student, Mr. John R. Johnson, for valuable
advice and assistance.

In preparing this paper, I have read through several volumes of the
Corpus Scriptorum Historiae Byzantinae (cited below as CSHB) and a host
of other sources. But I have also profited greatly from the penetrating
analysis of these materials by Professor (Mrs.) Aikaterine Christophilopulu
in her important book on the *Election, acclamation, and coronation of the
Byzantine Emperor*: Ἐκλογή, ἀναγόρευσις καὶ στέψις τοῦ Βυζαντινοῦ Αὐτο-
κράτορος (Πραγματεῖαι τῆς Ἀκαδημίας Ἀθηνῶν, 22, 2 [Athens, 1956]).

On the translation of pagan political theory into Christian terms, see

which persisted from the fourth century to May 29, 1453, when the Byzantine Empire came to an end, is well attested by a host of documents from every period.

No text gives explicit details concerning the process by which the divine will manifested itself or was communicated. But an analysis of the ceremony of coronation indicates that the Byzantines had two principal ways of determining whom God had chosen to be emperor.

In the first place, as the evidence to be summarized below will show, they regarded the divine appointment as having been made in response to, or as a result of, the election of the emperor by the Senate, the army, and the people, who looked upon their decision in this matter as an indication, reflection, or equivalent, if not the actual cause, of what they took to be the will of God. Epigrammatically, perhaps, we might summarize this method of ascertaining the will of God as *vox populi voluntas Dei*.[2]

Until recently, it had been thought that selection of the emperor by the Senate, the army, and the people was a 'constitutional requirement.'[3] Now, however, it has been argued, these three electors did not always function together, and sometimes one of the

---

Francis Dvornik, *Early Christian and Byzantine political philosophy*, 2 vols. (*Dumbarton Oaks Studies*, 9 [Washington, D.C., 1966]), with literature there cited; Otto Treitinger, *Die oströmische Kaiser- und Reichsidee nach ihrer Gestaltung im höfischen Zeremoniell*, 2d ed. with additional chapter (Darmstadt, 1956); Johannes A. Straub, *Vom Herrscherideal in der Spätantike* (*Forschungen zur Kirchen- und Geistesgeschichte*, 18 [Stuttgart, 1939, reprinted Stuttgart, 1964]). Cf. my 'Political theory in the lives of the Slavic saints Constantine and Methodius,' *Harvard Slavic Studies*, 2 (1954), 11-38.

[2] The ancient form of the expression is *vox populi vox Dei*. The *voluntas Dei* is my contribution. See George Boas, *Vox populi, essays in the history of an idea* (Baltimore, 1969), 8, 22f.; S. A. Gallacher, 'Vox populi vox Dei,' *Philological Quarterly*, 24 (1945), 12-19. In a letter to Charlemagne dated ca. 798, Alcuin warns against those who claim that the "voice of the people is the voice of God"; for, he says, 'the unruliness of the common herd is always akin to madness' (Nec audiendi qui solent dicere: "Vox populi, vox Dei," cum tumultuositas vulgi semper insanie proxima sit): *Epistolae Karolini aevi*, 2, ed. E. Duemmler (*Monumenta Germaniae Historica* = MGH below), *Epistolarum*, 4 [Berlin, 1895], Ep. 132, ix, p. 199.25-27. Cf. Hans Walther, *Proverbia, sententiaeque Latinitatis Medii Aevi, Lateinische Sprichwörter und Sentenzen des Mittelalters in alphabetischer Anordnung* (*Carmina medii aevi posterioris latina*, 2, 5 [Göttingen, 1967]), no. 34182, p. 919.

[3] J. B. Bury, 'The constitution of the Later Roman Empire' (The Creighton Lecture, University College, London, November 12, 1909, Cambridge University Press, 1910), reprinted in *Selected essays of J. B. Bury*, ed. Harold Temperley (Cambridge, England, 1930), 99-125.

three or a group of two was sufficient to choose the emperor.[4] This hypothesis seems to be borne out by the sources, although it is not impossible that this impression arises because of gaps in the evidence.[5] Nevertheless, it cannot be denied that the view that all three electors had to agree on the choice of the ruler rests on an assumption which is not supported by any explicit texts, although it is significant that the historian and polymath Michael Psellus (fl. 1070), in discussing the election of the emperor, remarks that the 'security of the emperors depended upon three groups, the common people, the senatorial order, and the army.'[6]

But even when all three of these are mentioned as having participated in an election, it is clear that they did not all play an equal part and that sometimes one or the other of the three took the initiative or was primarily responsible for the final decision. An election became necessary when an emperor died without leaving an heir who could succeed him or appoint someone to do so. This is the situation with which I propose to deal in Part II of this article.

In the second type considered, there was no need for an election since the succession was settled entirely by the reigning monarch himself or his widow. Even under these circumstances, usually—or at least often—there was a ratification of the selection thus made by one or more of the three electors. The sources are laconic and by no means consistent in recording what actually happened on these occasions.

---

[4] Hans G. Beck, *Senat und Volk von Konstantinopel, Probleme der byzantinischen Verfassungsgeschichte (Sitzungsberichte, Bayerische Akademie der Wissenschaften*, philosophisch-hist. Kl. [Munich, 1967], Heft 6). Mrs. Christophilopulu had already examined and discussed many aspects of this problem in her book, *op. cit.* (note 1 above).

[5] I hope someday to prepare an index or tabular summary of all the references in the sources to election, acclamation, and coronation. Most of the elements for such a survey are to be found in the works of Christophilopulu and Beck cited above (notes 1 and 4).

[6] *Chronographia*, 7, 1 [on Michael VI Stratiotikos], ed. Constantine Sathas (London, 1899), 188.25-27: ἐν τρισὶ δὲ τούτοις τῆς φυλακῆς αὐτοῖς [= the emperors] ἱσταμένης, δημοτικῷ πλήθει, καὶ συγκλητικῇ τάξει, καὶ συντάγματι στρατιωτικῷ ... Michael Psellus, *Chronographie*, 2, ed. Émile Renauld (Paris, 1928), 83.10ff.; *The Chronographia* of Michael Psellus, translated by E. R. A. Sewter (New Haven, 1953), 209 (a much criticized but eminently readable translation). Cf. Hans G. Beck, 'Kirche und Klerus im staatlichen Leben von Byzanz,' *Revue des études byzantines*, 24 (= *Mélanges Venance Grumel*, 1) (1966), 1. Cf. Eduard Eichmann, *Die Kaiserkrönung im Abendland*, 1 (Würzburg, 1942), 12-23.

184

But whether or not there was a subsequent confirmation by one or more of the three electors, the decisive step had been taken before the acclamation.[7] That is, the actual choice had already been made previous to any action on the part of the electors, either by the emperor himself (in choosing a successor before his death) or by the late emperor's heir or widow or some influential person like Aspar (see p. 193 below). This method of revealing God's pleasure in the choice of an emperor by the unilateral action of a single individual (to be examined in Part III below) I term *Vox tyranni voluntas Dei*.

II. *Vox populi voluntas Dei and the election of Justin I in 518*

The first of these types can be illustrated by the elevation of the Emperor Justin (518-27) to the throne in 518. On this occasion, we learn from the ἔκθεσις τῆς βασιλείου τάξεως (commonly known by its Latin title, *De cerimoniis aulae Byzantinae*, and entitled the *Book of Ceremonies* in English) compiled by the Emperor Constantine Porphyrogennetos (913-59) in all likelihood from the work of Peter Patricius (fl. ca. 530), a disturbance took place because there was no emperor or empress to choose a successor for Anastasius I (491-518), who had died suddenly during the night.

When it became known that the throne had become vacant, the *silentiarii* (officials who served as ushers for the imperial Consistorium, so called because at least originally they were to impose silence and keep order) notified Celer, the Magistros (the Greek form for *Magister officiorum*, the chief officer of the bureaux of the civil service, who was responsible for the conduct of court

---

[7] It is usually, and correctly, stated that the emperor was regarded as what we should call 'duly elected' when he had been acclaimed Augustus: Eichmann, *op. cit.*, 12ff.; Straub, *op. cit.* (note 1 above), 20-22; Christophilopulu, *op. cit.* (note 1 above), 22 (at note 6), 33 (last sentence); Treitinger, *op. cit.* (note 1 above), 27f.; *idem, Byzantinische Zeitschrift* (cited below as BZ), 39 (1939), 196ff. But these elections or acclamations were normally controlled by some one person (or a few persons) who had already decided who the new emperor was to be, had dictated his choice, and were thus in actuality the moving force behind the acclamations which followed.

This generalization applies only to elections. More normally, the emperor was chosen and crowned by the senior emperor. He probably was recognized immediately thereafter. Whether or not an acclamation was then 'constitutionally' requisite cannot now be determined because of the inconsistency of the sources, which are often silent or ambiguous on this matter. Even if there were such a confirmation, it was only a formality, since the coronation by the emperor had already settled the matter.

ceremonies) and Justin, the *comes* (i.e., the commander) of the *excubitores* (crack troops, the chief palace guards), who was eventually elected emperor. As soon as they arrived at the palace in response to these tidings, Celer ordered the *candidati* (special palace troops whose name was derived from the fact that their uniforms were white) and the rest of the *scholarii* (originally an elite military corps but now parade-ground soldiers) to assemble, and Justin made what seems to have been a formal announcement: "Our Lord [*Despotes*: Emperor], being mortal, has died. We must all therefore take counsel together and choose an emperor pleasing to God and suitable for the Empire." [8] Celer made a similar statement to the *candidati* and the officers of the *scholarii*.

Then at dawn, the chief imperial officials (ἄρχοντες) met [presumably in the palace]. At the same time, the people (ὁ δῆμος) congregated in the hippodrome and called upon the Senate to elect "an emperor chosen by God" (ἐκ Θεοῦ: literally "from God"). Thereupon, the high imperial officials and the Archbishop of Constantinople set up benches in the portico in front of the great triclinium (the *Megas Triklinos*, the great state dining room of the imperial palace with 19 accubita [i.e., couches], each of which had capacity for twelve guests reclining in the ancient manner) and there launched into a bitter discussion of candidates for the succession.[9] As time passed without result, Celer urged that they make up their minds quickly, arguing that if they named a new emperor without delay, they would win popular favor and restore tranquillity. But if they procrastinated, he warned, they would not only soon lose the opportunity of making the selection themselves but also be compelled to yield to the judgment of others.

---

[8] *De cerimoniis*, 1, 93, CSHB, Constantine Porphyrogennetos [abbreviated below CP], 1 (Bonn, 1829), 426ff.; section translated 426.15-18: ὁ δεσπότης ἡμῶν, ὡς ἄνθρωπος, ἐτελεύτησεν· δεῖ οὖν ἡμᾶς πάντας κοινῇ βουλεύσασθαι, καὶ τὸν τῷ Θεῷ ἀρέσκοντα καὶ τῇ πολιτείᾳ συμφέροντα ἐπιλέξασθαι. On the *Book of Ceremonies*, see Gyula Moravcsik, *Byzantinoturcica*, 1, 2d ed. (*Berliner Byzantinistische Arbeiten*, 10 [Berlin, 1958]), 380-84, with bibliography. On Justin, see Alexander A. Vasiliev, *Justin the First* (*Dumbarton Oaks Studies*, 1 [Cambridge, Mass., 1950]), 69-72.

[9] *Op. cit.*, 1, 426.18-427.4. On ἄρχοντες, see note 23 below. On the 'Great Triclinium,' see Rodolphe Guilland, *Études de topographie de Constantinople byzantine*, 1 (*Berliner byzantinistische Arbeiten*, 37 [Berlin-Amsterdam, 1969]), 71-75, 79, reprinted from *Annuaire de l'Institut de Philologie et d'Histoire Orientales et Slaves*, 10 (1950), 293-306 (*Mélanges Henri Grégoire*, 2); R. Janin, *Constantinople Byzantine*, 2d ed. (*Archives de l'Orient Chrétien*, 4a [Paris, 1964]), 112.

Despite this plea, the wrangling continued, and the *excubitores* in the hippodrome chose a certain tribune named John, one of Justin's associates (who later became bishop of Heraclea). But the Blues (one of the four 'demes' or factions of the people) were so displeased by this choice that they threw stones at the *excubitores*, and suffered a number of casualties when the latter retaliated with bows and arrows.[10]

At this juncture, the *scholarii* rushed into action and were about to acclaim a certain unnamed patrician. Before they could do so, however, the *excubitores* laid hold of him and would have murdered him, had he not been rescued by the future emperor, Justinian I, who was at that time serving in the ranks of the *candidati*. Next, the *excubitores* tried to compel Justinian to assume the purple, but he refused. Many other candidates were named and then rejected, one after the other, by the *cubicularii* (eunuchs who were custodians of the royal wardrobe, and apparently had the right to withhold the garments for coronation until they were satisfied that a real choice had been made in the proper way).

At length, the Senate united upon Justin and prevailed upon him to accept. At first, he was opposed by some of the *scholarii*, one of whom punched him in the face and cut his lip. Finally, however, the army and the people gave their assent, Justin was escorted to the hippodrome, the Blues and the Greens (two of the factions of the people) signified approval, and the *cubicularii* sent the royal attire that was required for the coronation.[11]

---

[10] *Op. cit.*, 1, 427.4-19. For the bibliography on the demes and popular factions, see Speros Vryonis, "Byzantine Δημοκρατία and the guilds in the eleventh century," *Dumbarton Oaks Papers*, 17 (1963), 287-314. Cf. also Beck, *op. cit.* (note 4 above), 44f., 75; Gheorghe Cronţ, 'Les dèmes et les partis politiques dans l'Empire byzantin aux Ve-VIIe siècles,' *Revue des études sud-est européennes*, 7 (1969), 671-74; Ewa Wipszycka, 'Les factions du cirque et les biens ecclésiastiques dans un papyrus égyptien,' *Byzantion*, 39 (1969), 180-98; J. V. A. Fine, Jr., 'Two contributions on the demes and factions in Byzantium in the sixth and seventh century,' *Zbornik Radova Vizantološkog Instituta*, 10 (1967), 29-37; Stylianos Spyridakis, 'Circus factions in sixth-century Crete,' *Greek, Roman, and Byzantine Studies*, 8 (1967), 249f.

On the various officials named see A. H. M. Jones, *The Later Roman Empire, 284-602*, 1 (Norman, 1964), *scholarii* (284, 613f., 634, 643, 647f., 657, 681, 1253, 1272, 1280), *silentiarii* (127, 548, 571f.), *excubitores* (267, 658f., 1273), *magistros* (*magister officiorum*: 103, 368f., 490, 498, 575-84, 1144f.), *cubicularii* (49, 346, 490, 566-70). Cf. also Robert Grosse, *Römische Militärgeschichte von Gallienus bis zum Beginn der byzantinischen Themenverfassung* (Berlin, 1920), 93-96 (on *scholarii*), 96f. (*candidati*), 270f. (*excubitores*).

[11] *Op. cit.*, 1, 427.19-428.18.

Having thus prevailed in the election, Justin was led up to the
imperial box in the hippodrome and raised on a shield in the traditional manner. At this point, the battle flags, which had been
lying on the ground, were lifted up, and Justin was vested behind
the protecting shields of his troops. Then, upon being crowned by
Archbishop John of Constantinople, he invoked divine providence,
having ascended the throne, as he put it, "by the decree of Almighty
God and the vote of you all." [12] To this and other pronouncements
made by Justin in a similar vein the people responded (in part), "O
Son of God, have mercy upon him [i.e., Justin]. Thou hast chosen
him." [13]

It is clear from this summary of the proceedings that the Senate,
the army, and the people are said to have produced a joint decision,
which was then hailed as having been made by God. Since it was
the Senate which took the initiative here, perhaps the rubric for
the second part of this article should be *vox Senatus voluntas Dei*.
But in view of the participation of many elements of the population
and Justin's acknowledgment that he had gained the throne by
the will of God *and the vote of all* (quoted in note 12 above), it
might perhaps in some way be justifiable to look upon his election
as having been brought about by the voice of *all* classes of the
people, high and low, military and civilian—i.e. of all of the electors
together, upon 'nomination' by the Senate.

Unfortunately, however, the record is marred in two respects.
In the first place, the suspicion of bribery is raised by two chroniclers (John Malalas and Marcellinus Comes, both of whom flourished in the latter part of the sixth century). According to them,
Amantius, the *praepositus sacri cubiculi* (i.e., the Grand Chamberlain, a powerful official at court, but as a eunuch not qualified to
ascend the throne himself) furnished money to Justin so as to influence the troops to vote for a certain Theocritus. Despite this,
the chroniclers report, in the spirit of that conventional, solipsistic
piety of the Byzantines, who looked upon whatever they did, however selfish, perverse, or subversive of the public welfare, as the
implementation of a divine mandate, the army and the people
refused 'by the will of God' to accept Theocritus and chose Justin

---

[12] *Ibid.* 427.19ff., n.b. 429.18-20: τῇ τοῦ παντοδυνάμου Θεοῦ κρίσει, τῇ τε
ὑμετέρᾳ κοινῇ ἐκλογῇ πρὸς τὴν βασιλείαν χωρήσαντες, τὴν οὐράνιον πρόνοιαν
ἐπικαλούμεθα.

[13] *Ibid.*, 430.6f.: υἱὲ Θεοῦ, σὺ αὐτὸν ἐλέησον· σὺ αὐτὸν ἐπελέξω.

instead.[14] Of course, cynics might well take this to mean that Justin had misappropriated the money given him by Amantius and used it to bribe the electors in his favor.

In the second place, however this lugubrious tale is to be interpreted, no one will make the mistake of supposing that Justin's election was in any way comparable to the kind with which we are familiar in modern democratic society. To say nothing of bribery and corruption, οἱ ἄρχοντες (the high government officials), the Senate, and the detachments of the army stationed in Constantinople were always in a position to intimidate the rest of the population. The common people were very rarely [15] able to offer any kind of meaningful resistance.

Moreover, only the very few who lived in or near Constantinople could ever hope to participate in the final choice or in the acclamations in the hippodrome. Most of the army and of the people would not even learn of the results until long after the election had taken place. Finally, since the only expression of choice that is ever mentioned was oral, it is obvious that the whole operation was easily dominated and controlled by intimidation and skillful use of propaganda. The average person, it must be assumed, would hardly have known who the possible candidates were, nor would many have been able to give any rational reason for preferring any one of them to another. Indeed, it is difficult to avoid the conclusion that when the emperors were not exposed to the public eye, they were somewhat lacking in enthusiasm for ordinary folk, if not openly scornful of them. Whether this be a just appraisal of the imperial attitude or not, it is at least interesting that, when Justin notified Pope Hormisdas of Rome of his accession to the throne, he ascribes his election to divine favor, the high officials, the Senate, and the army but is silent about the role of the people.[16]

---

[14] *Chronographia*, 17, CSHB, 410.4f.: κελεύσει Θεοῦ (of Justin's election by the *excubitores*); 410.8-411.3: ... ὁ στρατὸς οὖν καὶ ὁ δῆμος λαβὼν οὐχ εἵλατο Θεόκριτον, ἀλλὰ θελήσει θεοῦ ἐποίησαν Ἰουστῖνον βασιλέα. Cf. Marcellinus Comes, *Chronicon*, s. anno 519, MGH, *Auctores antiquissimi* = AA below, 11, ed. Theodor Mommsen (Berlin, 1894, reprinted Berlin, 1961), 101.10-22. See A. H. M. Jones, *op. cit.* (note 10 above), 267f.; Vasiliev, *op. cit.* (note 8 above), 81f.

[15] See below on the Empress Theodora in 1042, when at least some of the people sought to put her on the throne as sole empress; Vryonis, *loc. cit.* (note 10 above).

[16] Epistulae imperatorum pontificum aliorum inde ab a. CCCLXVII usque ad a. DLIII datae, Avellana quae dicitur collectio, ed. O. Guenther

III. *Vox tyranni vel imperatoris vel Augustae voluntas Dei*

At the very least, despite all the rancor and violence, the election of Justin was a few degrees freer and more open than the procedure by which emperors were normally chosen in Byzantium. Usually, what appeared to be a free vote of one or more of the electors was only the ratification of a decision that had already been dictated by someone else—in most cases by the emperor himself in naming an heir or by an emperor's widow. In such instances, the vote by the army, Senate, and the people, or even any one of these three, was illusory and merely served as a formal public salutation of a ruler whom no one could reject.

An excellent example of this kind of election occurred in 457, when Leo I (457-74) was chosen to succeed the Emperor Marcian. What happened on this occasion is set forth by the Emperor Constantine VII in the *Book of Ceremonies*.[17] After the election of Leo by the Senate, Constantine says, 'All assembled in the field, including the high officials, the imperial guards, the soldiers, Anatolius, Archbishop of Constantinople, and Martial, the Magistros (presumably the *Magister officiorum*, the chief of the imperial bureaux; cf. Celer at the coronation of Justin I). And after the labara [military flags bearing the Christogram] and the standards were laid on the ground, the entire assemblage began to cry out as follows: "Hear, O God, we beseech thee. Hear, O God. [Long] life to Leo, hear, O God. Leo shall reign. O merciful God, the Empire demands Leo as Emperor. The army demands Leo as Emperor. The laws

---

(*Corpus scriptorum ecclesiasticorum latinorum*, 35, 2 [Vienna, 1898]), Ep. 141, p. 586.2-9: proinde sanctitati uestrae per has sacras declaramus epistolas, quod primum quidem inseparabilis Trinitatis fauore, deinde amplissimorum procerum sacri nostri palatii et sanctissimi senatus nec non electione firmissimi exercitus ad imperium nos licet nolentes ac recusantes electos fuisse atque firmatos; quoted by Beck, *op. cit.* (note 3 above), 17f. But, n.b., Malalas, *loc. cit.* (note 14 above), credits both the army and the people with Justin's election.

[17] *De cerimoniis*, 1, 91, CSHB, CP, 1, 410-17. It was the army (and the high officials) which acclaimed Leo in the hippodrome, maintains Christophilopulu rightly, *op. cit.* (note 1 above), 30-34, against O. Treitinger, who in BZ, 39 (1939), 194-202, n.b. 196f., had argued that Leo had been acclaimed (and elected) by all three of the electors. On Leo's election, see Jones, *op. cit.* (note 10 above), 322, 325, 338; Ernest Stein, *Histoire du Bas-Empire*, French translation by Jean R. Palanque, 1 (n.p., 1959), 353f.; 2, 588f.; J. B. Bury, *History of the Later Roman Empire from the death of Theodosius I to the death of Justinian*, 1 (London, 1923), 314-16; Otto Seeck, *Geschichte des Untergangs der antiken Welt*, 6 (Stuttgart, 1920), 356f., 485.

await Leo. The palace awaits Leo. This is the prayer of the palace. This is the desire of the troops. This is the prayer of the Senate. This is the prayer of the people. The universe awaits Leo. The army awaits Leo. Let Leo, who is the adornment of all, come. Leo, the common good, shall reign. Hear, o God, we beseech thee."[18] As soon as they had finished these acclamations, Leo was brought in. He then mounted to the tribunal, and Busalgus, a *campiductor* (a regimental drill instructor), placed the military chain (μανιάκιν, *torques* in Latin) on his head, and another was placed upon his right hand by Olympius, who also held the rank of *campiductor*.[19] At this moment, the labara were raised, and all cried out "Leo Augustus, thou conquerest. Thou art pious, thou art august. God has given thee. God shall protect thee. Worship Christ, and you always conquer. Many years shall Leo reign. God will watch over the Christian Empire." [20]

Then, hidden from view in the tribunal by the *candidati*, drawn up with overlapping shields, Leo dons the royal garments and diadem, appears before the people, and receives the obeisance of all the high officials in the order of their rank. Thereafter, grasping shield and lance, he is acclaimed by all in the following terms, "Mighty one, Conqueror and Augustus, hail to thee, hail to thee. Many years shalt thou reign, Leo Augustus. God will preserve this Empire. God will preserve the Christian Empire.[21] In acknowledging

---

[18] *Op. cit.*, I, 410.6-411.3; n.b. 410.13-411.3: εἰσάκουσον, ὁ Θεός, σὲ παρακαλοῦμεν. ἐπάκουσον, ὁ Θεός· Λέοντι ζωή. εἰσάκουσον, ὁ Θεός· Λέων βασιλεύσει. Θεὲ φιλάνθρωπε, Λέοντα βασιλέα τὸ πρᾶγμα τὸ δημόσιον αἰτεῖ· ὁ στρατὸς Λέοντα βασιλέα αἰτεῖ· Λέοντα οἱ νόμοι ἐκδέχονται· Λέοντα τὸ παλάτιον ἐκδέχεται· αὗται εὐχαὶ τοῦ παλατίου· αὗται ἐντεύξεις τοῦ στρατοπέδου· αὗται εὐχαὶ τῆς συγκλήτου· αὗται εὐχαὶ τοῦ λαοῦ· Λέοντα ὁ κόσμος ἀναμένει· Λέοντα ὁ στρατὸς ἐκδέχεται· τὸ κοινὸν καλόν, Λέων, ἐλθέτω· τὸ κοινὸν ἀγαθόν, Λέων, βασιλεύσει· εἰσάκουσον, ὁ Θεός, σὲ παρακαλοῦμεν.

[19] *Ibid.*, 411.3-8. On *campiductor*, see Jones, *op. cit.* (note 10 above), 634, 675; Ernest Stein, 'Ordinarii et campidoctores,' *Byzantion*, 8 (1933), 379-87, with literature there cited. On the *torques*, Wilhelm Ensslin, 'Zur Torqueskrönung und Schilderhebung bei der Kaiserwahl,' *Klio*, 35 (1942), 268-98, 288ff. on *campiductor*; Grosse, *op. cit.* (note 10 above), 126f., 225f.; Philip Grierson, *Catalogue of the Byzantine Coins in the Dumbarton Oaks Collection and in the Whittemore Collection*, 3, *Leo III to Nicephorus III, 717-1081, Part I, Leo III to Michael III, 717-867* (Washington, D.C., 1973), 123. On the *labara*, see *ibid.*, 134-40.

[20] *Op. cit.*, I, 411.9-13: Λέων αὔγουστε, σὺ νικᾷς, σὺ εὐσεβής, σὺ σεβαστός· ὁ Θεός σε ἔδωκεν, ὁ Θεός σε φυλάξει· τὸν Χριστὸν σεβόμενος ἀεὶ νικᾷς· πολλοὺς χρόνους Λέων βασιλεύσει· χριστιανὸν βασίλειον ὁ Θεὸς περιφρουρήσει.

[21] *Ibid.*, 411.13-21.

these words, Leo said, ". . . almighty God and your suffrages, most mighty comrades, have under good omens chosen me to be ruler of the Roman Empire."

To which all cried out, "Leo Augustus, thou conquerest. He who chose thee shall guard thee. God will watch over his choice. God will protect the pious Empire. Pious [art thou] and mighty." Then Leo replied, "You will have me as your ruler and commander, who was your comrade in the struggles which I learned to undergo when I campaigned with you." Then all cried out, "Hail. The army wants you to be emperor, o conqueror; the army wants you to be emperor, o fortunate one. We all want you." [22]

It is possibly of some interest to remark that in the above quoted statement by Leo, the compound subject is used with a singular verb (see Greek in note 22 below): "Almighty God and your suffrages *has* elected me emperor." This may be only an accident (since plural subjects are often found with a singular verb) or, perhaps, a scribal or editorial error. But it may also have been deliberate as an indication of the identity of the popular will and God's.

Quite literally, this passage as a whole demonstrates, the electors call upon God to note the results of their election and, in effect, to adopt their choice as his own. In one very important respect, however, this vote, which gives the appearance of expressing the unanimous approval of the Senate, the army, and the people, was grossly misrepresented. For, although the Senate was said to have voted for Leo (as Constantine had stated at the beginning of the text quoted), it was only the army which took part in acclaiming him. The reference at the beginning (see the text at note 18 above) to "high officials" might perhaps suggest that leaders of the Senate were in fact present among those who took part in the ceremony. For the word ἄρχοντες, which I have rendered here by 'high officials' can mean either leaders of the Senate or the chief officers of the

---

[22] *Ibid.*, 411.22-412.9: "ὁ Θεὸς ὁ παντοδύναμος καὶ ἡ κρίσις ἡ ὑμετέρα, ἰσχυρώτατοι συστρατιῶται, αὐτοκράτορά με τῶν τῶν Ῥωμαίων δημοσίων πραγμάτων εὐτυχῶς ἐξελέξατο." παρὰ πάντων ἐκράγη· "Λέων αὔγουστε, σὺ νικᾷς· ὁ σὲ ἐκλεξάμενος σε διαφυλάξει· τὴν ἐκλογὴν ἑαυτοῦ ὁ Θεὸς περιφρουρήσει. εὐσεβὲς βασίλειον ὁ Θεὸς φυλάξει. καὶ εὐσεβὴς καὶ δυνατός." ἀπόκρισις. αὐτοκράτωρ Καῖσαρ αὔγουστος "ἕξεταί με ἐξουσιαστὴν ἄρχοντα τῶν κόπων συστρατιώτην, ὧν μεθ' ὑμῶν ἔτι στρατευόμενος ἔμαθον ὑπομένειν." παρὰ πάντων ἐβοήθη· "εὐτυχῶς· ὁ στρατός σε βασιλεύοντα, νικητά· ὁ στρατός σε βασιλεύοντα, εὐτυχῆ· σὲ ποθοῦμεν πάντες."

192

civil bureaucracy.[23] But Leo's remarks addressed to "most mighty comrades" and his allusion to the travails he had shared with them show that the whole demonstration described above involved only members of the armed forces along with the chief officers of the civil bureaucracy and the patriarch, who are mentioned at the beginning of the passage.

Under these circumstances, we must conclude that, on this occasion, only the troops garrisoned in Constantinople were permitted (or expected) to acclaim the new emperor. They obviously had been authorized to speak for the Senate. But we can only guess as to their warrant for claiming to represent the views of the people. The fact that they took it upon themselves to be the spokesmen for both the Senate and the people is another proof of the kind of autocratic control which was exercised over the entire proceedings, including both the election itself and the acclamations.

The question then arises as to how this apparent 'unanimity' was achieved and who the moving force behind it was. Constantine Porphyrogennetos is the only authority who mentions all three of the electors (in the acclamations). Marcellinus Comes (in the latter part of the sixth century) says Leo was raised to the throne by the army,[24] and Malalas (ca. 491-578) has it that he was crowned by the Senate,[25] whereas Nicephorus Callistus (ca. 1300) maintains that he was acclaimed by the 'common' [=unanimous] vote of the Senate and crowned by the Patriarch Anatolius,[26] while Theophanes (ca. 813) mentions only the coronation by Anatolius, Archbishop of Constantinople,[27] to which, it must be carefully noted, Constantine does not refer. If Theophanes and N. Callistus (both presumably relying here upon Theodore Lector of the sixth century) are to be believed, and the Patriarch *did* crown Leo, he must have done so *after* the ceremony which we have been examining and, therefore, *subsequent* to the acclamation of Leo as emperor. This would mean that the patriarchal rite was purely religious in purpose, that it did

---

[23] Christophilopulu, Ἡ σύγκλητος εἰς τὸ Βυζαντινὸν Κράτος, Ἐπετηρὶς τοῦ Ἀρχείου τῆς Ἱστορίας τοῦ Ἑλληνικοῦ δικαίου τῆς Ἀκαδημίας Ἀθηνῶν, 33; *eadem, op. cit.* (note 1 above), 31.

[24] *Chronicon*, s. anno 457, MGH, AA, 11 (Berlin, 1894), 87.1-5 (Greek version).

[25] *Chronographia*, 14, CSHB, 369.1f.; ἐστέφθη ὑπὸ τῆς συγκλήτου.

[26] *Ecclesiastical History*, 15, 15, Migne, *Patrologia Graeca*, 147, 48B.

[27] Ed. de Boor, 1, 110.19-21; Theodore Lector, 2, 65, PG, 86, 216A.

not have any effect on Leo's election, and could not possibly have
had any constitutional significance.[28]

None of these authorities gives further details concerning Leo's
election or refers to the other electors. Actually, however, the preferred candidate for the succession to Marcian, we learn, was Aspar,
an Alan, who held a high military command and was known to be
an Arian.[29] But, a Latin authority indicates, he himself refused to
accept the throne when it was offered by the Senate in order to
avoid establishing a precedent.[30] This text does not specify what

---

[28] This is consistent with the present consensus of opinion: Beck, *op. cit.*
(note 4 above), 4f.; Christophilopulu, *op. cit.* (note 1), 28-34, 171, 173f.,
230; J. Karayannopulos, BZ, 50 (1957), 488 n. 2; Anton Michel, *Die Kaiser-
macht in der Ostkirche* (Darmstadt, 1959), 156ff., reprinted from *Ostkirchliche
Studien*, 4 (1955), 221-60; Bernhard Sinogowitz, in *Zeitschrift der Savigny-
Stiftung für Rechtsgeschichte, Romanistische Abteilung*, 74 (1957), 489-95;
Franz Dölger, BZ, 43 (1950), 146f.; 38 (1938), 240; Wilhelm Ensslin, *Zur
Frage nach der ersten Kaiserkrönung durch den Patriarchen und zur Bedeutung
dieses Aktes im Wahlzeremoniell* (Würzburg, [?1947]), partly published in
BZ, 42 (1943-49), 101-15, 369-72; Otto Treitinger, BZ, 39 (1939), 200-202;
A. E. R. Boak, 'Imperial coronation ceremonies of the fifth and sixth cen-
turies,' *Harvard Studies in Classical Philology*, 30 (1919), 37-47; W. Sickel,
'Das byzantinische Krönungsrecht bis zum 10. Jahrhundert,' BZ, 7 (1898),
511-57. See note 7 (above) and note on p. 207 (below).
    For the contrary view, that the act of coronation by the patriarch was
constitutionally indispensable and a manifestation of ecclesiastical approval
of the choice of the emperor, see Vasiliev, *op. cit.* (note 8 above), 75-80;
George Ostrogorsky, *History of the Byzantine State*, revised edition (New
Brunswick, 1969), 61; *idem*, BZ, 41 (1941), 211-23; Peter Charanis, 'Coronation and its constitutional significance in the Later Roman Empire,' *Byzantion*, 15 (1940-41), 49-66; *idem*, 'The imperial crown modiolus and its constitutional significance,' *ibid.*, 12 (1937), 189-95; *idem*, 'The crown modiolus
once more,' *ibid.*, 13 (1938), 377-81.
    On coronation in general, see also I. Goschew, 'Zur Frage der Krönungs-
zeremonien und zeremonielle Gewandung der byzantinischen und der bulga-
rischen Herrscher im Mittelalter,' *Byzantino-bulgarica*, 2 (1966), 145-68
(with 18 illustrations); Hermann Fillitz, 'Die Krönungsgewänder des Heiligen Römischen Reiches und ihr Verhältnis zu Byzanz,' *Jahrbuch des österreichischen byzantinischen Gesellschaft*, 4 (1955), 123-34; H. L. del Medico,
'Le couronnement d'un empereur byzantin vu par un juif de Constantinople,'
Byzantino-Slavica, 16 (1955), 43-75; Eichmann, *op. cit.* (note 6 above), 12-23;
Georg Ostrogorsky and Ernst Stein, 'Die Krönungsurkunden des Zeremo-
nienbuches,' *Byzantion*, 7 (1932), 185-233; reviewed by Franz Dölger, BZ,
36 (1936), 145-57; F. E. Brightman, 'Byzantine imperial coronations,'
Journal of Theological Studies, 2 (1900-1), 359-92.
[29] Theophanes, *Chronographia*, A.M. 5961, ed. de Boor, 1, 116, 6-9. Zonaras, *Epitome historiarum*, 13, 25, 31-34; cf. 14, 1, 1-5; CSHB, 3, ed. T. Büttner-Wobst (Bonn, 1897), 121.6-123.1.
[30] See the *Anagnosticum regis* of a council which met in Rome in 501:
MGH, AA, 12, ed. T. Mommsen (Berlin, 1894): Aliquando Aspari a senatu

kind of precedent Aspar had in mind. But, as an Arian, he could not have failed to have been aware of the strong Byzantine prejudice against Arianism.[31] He must therefore have deemed it prudent to defer to the popular feelings in this matter, and rule the Empire through a puppet rather than in his own name. For this reason he and his son Ardaburius chose Leo, a tribune of soldiers, who had managed their property, with the expectation that they would be the real rulers of the Empire.[32]

Though it is clear from these texts (notes 31f. below) that Aspar was responsible for Leo's elevation to the throne, we are ignorant of the procedure by which he secured Leo's election. We know only that, as the event proved, he was able by his influence with the Senate and the army to persuade or compel them to vote for Leo, so as to attain the apparent unanimity described by Constantine Porphyrogennetos. Indeed so successful were these maneuvres that in 471 Leo apparently had no difficulty in executing both Aspar and Ardaburius, to whom he owned his throne, when he decided to rid himself of them.[33] It is somewhat ironical also that it was Aspar's decision, which, by wiles, stratagems, threats, and coercion unchronicled, he transformed into what the armed forces represented as the unanimous vote of the three electors and thus, in the manner described above, into what the Byzantines took to be the voice of God, that in the end encompassed his own death.

In effect, therefore, the 'unanimity' expressed in the acclamations for Leo was nothing more than a fairly transparent mask for the will and determination of a single individual. In other words, we have here another piece of evidence for the unrelieved and un-

---

dicebatur, ut ipse fieret imperator: qui tale refertur dedisse responsum: 'timeo, ne per me consuetudo in regno nascatur.'

[31] According to Zonaras, *loc. cit.* (in note 29 above), Aspar would have been chosen emperor had not the people of Constantinople objected to him because he was an Arian and authorized (or suffered) him to choose Leo. Cf. Theophanes, *loc. cit.* (note 29 above).

[32] Theophanes, *Chronographia*, A.M. 5961, ed. de Boor, 1, 116.6-9; n.b. the last words: αὐτοὶ προσδοκῶντες διοικεῖν τὸ βασίλειον. Cf. Jordanes, *De summa temporum vel origine actibusque gentis Romanorum*, 335, ed. Theodor Mommsen, MGH, AA, 5, 1 (Berlin, 1882, repr. 1961), 43.16f.: Leo . . . Asparis patricii potentia ex tribuno militum factus est imperator.

[33] Zonaras, *Epitome historiarum*, 14, 1, 8, *ed. cit.*, 3, 123.5-7. George Cedrenus, *Compendium historiarum*, CSHB, 1, 607.14f., probably exaggerates in attributing their murder to their being Arians.

In what follows I cite Cedrenus and Zonaras by name only, without mention of titles.

mitigated absolutism of the Byzantine state. The election, if it can
be so called, was only the device by which Aspar had hoped to
establish himself as the real sovereign. Once Leo attained the throne,
however, and was officially recognized as emperor, he was invested
with the Byzantine mystique surrounding the 'elect of God' and
no one could prevent him from dealing as he wished with threats
to his throne from whatever quarter they might come.

A very similar equation between the vote of the electors and the
will of God is to be found in the account of the election of Anastasius I in 491 as successor to Zeno. Here, however, the sponsor was
not an Arian upstart like Aspar, but Ariadne, the widow of the
legitimate emperor Zeno (474-91). In their acclamation of Ariadne,
the multitudes (including the chief imperial officials, many soldiers,
the Archbishop Euphemius, and the people) cried out, "Many years
to the Empress; Ariadne Augusta, thou conquerest, . . . Kyrie
eléëson, Heavenly King, grant us an emperor on earth who will not
be avaricious [and shall rule] the world." [34] In response, Ariadne
announced that, "in order to hold an election that is unsullied and
pleasing to the Lord God, we have commanded the most noble
officials and the sacred Senate, acting with the concurrence of
the very honorable armed forces, to make the choice [of an emperor],
in the presence of the Holy Gospels and the most venerable and
most holy patriarch of this royal city . . . ." [35]

As soon as the balloting began, however, it became clear that
the electors were sharply divided in their views. Accordingly, Urbicius, the *praepositus sacri cubiculi* (the Grand Chamberlain, a digni-

---

[34] Constantine Porphyrogennetos, *op. cit.*, 1, 92, CSHB, 1, 417.14-425.21;
n.b. 419.15f.: Κύριε, ἐλέησον. βασιλεῦ οὐράνιε, δὸς ἡμῖν ἐπίγειον ἀφιλάργυρον
βασιλέα τῇ οἰκουμένῃ. On Anastasius's election, see Evagrius, *Ecclesiastical
history*, 3, 29, edd. J. Bidez and L. Parmentier (London, 1898), 125.10ff.;
Theophanes, *Chronographia*, A.M. 5983, ed. de Boor, 1, 136.3-5; George
Cedrenus, *ed. cit.*, 625.20-24; Zonaras, *op. cit.*, 14, 3, 1, *ed. cit.*, 3, 133.6ff.;
Carmelo Capizzi, *L'imperatore Anastasio I (491-518)* (*Orientalia Christiana
Analecta*, 184 [Rome, 1969]), 71-86; Peter Charanis, *Church and State in the
Later Roman Empire, the religious policy of Anastasius the First, 491-518*
(*University of Wisconsin Studies in the Social Sciences and History*, 26 [Madi-
son, 1939]), 10f.
[35] *Op. cit.*, 1, 419.16-420.2: ἀπόκρισις· "ὥστε δὲ καθαρὰν καὶ τῷ· δεσπότῃ
Θεῷ ἀρέσκουσαν τὴν κρίσιν γενέσθαι, ἐκελεύσαμεν τοὺς ἐνδοξοτάτους ἄρχοντας καὶ
τὴν ἱερὰν σύγκλητον, συντρεχούσης καὶ τῆς τῶν γενναιοτάτων ἐξερκίτων ψήφου,
προκειμένων καὶ τῶν ἁγίων εὐαγγελίων, παρόντος τοῦ ὁσιωτάτου καὶ ἁγιωτάτου
τῆς βασιλίδος ταύτης πόλεως πατριάρχου, καὶ προκειμένων, ὡς εἴρηται, τῶν
ἁγίων λογίων, γενέσθαι τὴν ἐπιλογήν . . . Cf. *ibid.*, 421.6-13.

tary of the highest rank, who wielded enormous influence, though a eunuch), suggested that it would be better to let the Empress select whomever she wished. Accordingly, the Senate sent the patriarch to ask her to do so; and, when she named Anastasius the Silentiarius, they assented at once.[36]

In the ensuing exchange of greetings between the various groups assembled in the hippodrome, Anastasius, the new emperor, responded in part, "It is clear that human power depends upon the will of the supreme glory." [37] He then acknowledged his election by Ariadne, the chief officers of the state, the Senate, the army, and the people "under the leadership of the Holy Trinity." [38]

To this all reply, "Kyrie eléëson. O Son of God, have mercy upon him [i.e., Anastasius]. Anastasius Augustus, mayest thou conquer. God will protect the pious Emperor. God has given thee. God will protect thee ... Worthy art thou of the Empire, worthy of the Trinity, worthy of the city ..." [39] Then, at the conclusion of the ceremony all cry out, "Anastasius Augustus, thou conquerest. Ariadne Augusta, thou conquerest. God has given you [n.b. plural]. God will protect you [plural]." [40]

Here again, we see, as in the election of Leo, which was traceable to one person (Aspar), that the three electors have in effect done nothing but accede to the wishes of Zeno's widow, Ariadne. Nevertheless, here, as before, all of those responsible for the choice of the Emperor attribute the final result to God—Ariadne (note 35), Anastasius (note 38), and the people (notes 39f.).

The pattern established by Ariadne and the Byzantine court set a precedent for future generations. That is, when the emperor died without issue, his widow chose his successor, usually for both the throne and her bed. Thus, upon the death (or rather murder) of

---

[36] *Ibid.*, 421.17-422.4. On Urbicius, see Jones, *op. cit.* (note 10 above), 230, 338; E. Honigmann, 'Le cubiculaire Urbicius,' *Revue des études byzantines*, 7 (1949-50), 47-50; *idem*, Pauly-Wissowa-Kroll, *Realencyclopädie*, Zweite Reihe, 9A, 1 = 17. Halbband (Stuttgart, 1961), 992.13-994.17.

[37] *Op. cit.*, I, 423.22-424.2: δῆλόν ἐστιν τὸ ἀνθρώπινον κράτος τῆς ἀνωτάτω δόξης τῷ νεύματι ἀπαρτίζειν.

[38] *Ibid.*, 424.4-11. Next to the last line for προηγουμένως I read προηγουμένης.

[39] *Ibid.*, 424.11-14, 16f.: Κύριε, ἐλέησον· υἱὲ Θεοῦ, σὺ αὐτὸν ἐλέησον. Ἀναστάσιε αὔγουστε, τούμβηκας· εὐσεβῆ βασιλέα ὁ Θεὸς φυλάξει· ὁ Θεός σε ἔδωκεν, ὁ Θεός σε φυλάξει... ἄξιε τῆς βασιλείας, ἄξιε τῆς τριάδος, ἄξιε τῆς πόλεως ...

[40] CP, 425.11-13: Ἀναστάσιε αὔγουστε, σὺ νικᾷς· Ἀριάδνη αὐγούστα, σὺ νικᾷς· ὁ Θεὸς ὑμᾶς δέδωκεν, ὁ Θεὸς ὑμᾶς φυλάξει.

the Emperor Romanos III Argyros in 1034, Zoe, his widow, the
second daughter of Constantine VIII (1025-28), who had settled
the succession to his throne by marrying her to Romanos,[41] not
only picked Michael IV (1034-41) to be both husband and emperor,
but also crowned him with her own hand, personally set him on
the throne, and bade all to acclaim him and pay homage to him.[42]
Upon his death, Zoe was persuaded by her brothers-in-law (led by
John Orphanotrophos) to allow Michael V Calaphates (her nephew
through Michael IV) to assume the purple.[43]

When Michael V proved unsuitable, he was dethroned by an insurrection of the people, some of whom turned away from Zoe and
would have preferred to make her sister, Theodora, Constantine
VIII's youngest daughter, sole empress, with the result that the
Senate, the people, and some of the clergy actually acclaimed her
as empress in the Church of Hagia Sophia. In the meantime, however, Zoe had returned to the imperial palace and finally overcame
her reluctance to share the throne with Theodora either by her own
volition (as Psellus says) or at the behest of the Senate (as Zonaras
reports) or because of the insistence of the people (as Cedrenus
maintains).[44]

But after three months of their joint reign, fearing that Theodora
might become sole empress or perhaps, Zonaras suggests, because
she had wearied of celibacy and wished to resume marital life, Zoe
ousted Theodora from the throne and bestowed herself upon Constantine (IX) Monomachus, whom she made both emperor and
consort.[45] Despite her removal from the seat of power by the accession of Constantine IX in 1042, after Zoe's death in 1050 [46] and

[41] Psellus, 2, 10, ed. Sathas, 24.22-25.15; ed. Renauld, 1, 30.16-31.28:
Cedrenus, 2, 484.15-485.18; Zonaras, *Epitome*, 17, 10, 17-24, *ed. cit.*, 3, 572.6-
573.14. On the events discussed (at notes 41-48), see, besides, Ostrogorsky,
History of the Byzantine State, 320-38; *Selected essays of J. B. Bury*, ed. Harold
Temperley (Cambridge, England, 1930), 143-200. Cf. also the old classic,
Gustave Schlumberger, *L'épopée byzantine à la fin du dixième siècle* 3, *Les
Porphyrogénètes Zoe et Théodora* (Paris, 1905), 54ff., 156ff., 159ff., 323-28,
355-78, 385ff., 393-400, 749-67.
[42] Psellus, 4, 2, ed. Sathas, 42.24-43.16; ed. Renauld, 1, 53.18-54.24;
Cedrenus, 2, 505.14-506.6; Zonaras, 17, 14, 1-6, *ed. cit.*, 3, 585.11-586.10.
[43] Psellus, 5, 3-5, ed. Sathas, 69.22-70.24; ed. Renauld, 87.17-88.10; Cedrenus, 2, 534.5-535.1; Zonaras, 17, 18, 1-8, *ed. cit.*, 3, 605.5-606.9.
[44] Psellus, 5, 26-33, 34-37, 46, 51, ed. Sathas, 81-87, 90, 92f.; ed. Renauld,
102-16; Cedrenus, 2, 537.5-539.20; Zonaras, 17, 19, 5-28, *ed. cit.*, 3, 610.1-
613.13.
[45] Psellus, 6, 11, 18-21, ed. Sathas, 97.9-22, 100.19-101.21; ed. Renauld,

198

Constantine's in 1055 Theodora was restored to the throne (1055-56); and near the end of her life, after a reign of about a year and and nine months, she was persuaded to crown Michael VI (1056-57) as her successor.[47]

Although the sources do not record public statements in which the electors equated their will with that of God in these elections (i.e., from 1034-56), it must be assumed that they did in point of fact do so. For the historian Michael Psellus, who covers the years 976-1078 in his *Chronographia* and was acquainted at first hand with the imperial elections summarized above, unambiguously states that 'the emperor receives his crown neither from men nor through men but, in accordance with nature, from above.' [48]

This concept was a commonplace in Byzantium, even when there was no election and the imperial power was transmitted directly by the emperor to a successor he had himself chosen. In 578, for example, the Emperor Justin II said after acclaiming Tiberius II as emperor, "Behold, it is God who exalts you; it is God who confers this dignity on you, not I." [49]

The general view in all contexts was that the emperor received his crown from God. Thus the Emperor Leo III (717-41) in the pro-oimion to the *Ecloga*, the code of law which he promulgated in 726, refers to himself as having been crowned by the hand of

---

1, 122.8ff.; 1, 126.11-127.7; Cedrenus, 2, 540.22-542.19; Zonaras, 17, 20, 4-21, 1, *ed. cit.*, 3, 614.4-616.16.

[46] Psellus, 6, 160; ed. Sathas, 162.20-32; ed. Renauld, 2, 50.1-13; Cedrenus, 2, 610.2-23; Zonaras, 17, 28, 1f., *ed. cit.*, 3, 647.15-648.3.

[47] Psellus, *Theodora*, 1-21, ed. Sathas, 180-88; ed. Renauld, 2, 72-82; Cedrenus, 2, 610.23-612.14; Zonaras, 17, 29, 1-10, *ed. cit.*, 3, 651.9-653.11.

[48] Ep. 207, ed. K. N. Sathas, *Bibliotheca graeca medii aevi* (Μεσαιωνική βιβλιοθήκη), 5 (Paris-Venice, 1876), 508f.: ... βασιλεύς, ᾧ τὸ στέφος οὐκ ἐξ ἀνθρώπων, οὐδὲ δι' ἀνθρώπων, ἀλλ' ἄνωθεν ἐνήρμοσται προσφυῶς. This letter does not reappear among the texts edited by E. Kurtz and F. Drexl, *Michaelis Pselli scripta minora*, 2 vols. (Milan, 1936-41). Cf. *Idem, Chronographia*, 6, 18 (where Zoe's choice of Constantine IX seemed to her advisers to be θεοκίνη-τος — 'inspired by God'), ed. Sathas, 100.29f.; ed. Renauld, 1, 126.11f. Note also BC, 1, 7, CP, 1, 54.10f.: σὺ οὖν δοξάσας τῷ στέφει, Θεέ, δεσπότας παλάμῃ σου, φύλαττε ... *Ibid.*, 1, 9, CP, 1, 59.10 and 60.1f., 14f. (θεόστεπτοι). Note additional examples cited by Vasiliev, *op. cit.* (note 8 above), 78-80.

[49] Theophylactus Simocatta, *Historiae*, 3, 11, 8, ed. C. de Boor (Leipzig, 1887), 132.26f.: ἴδε, ὁ θεὸς ὁ ἀγαθύνων σε. Τοῦτο τὸ σχῆμα ὁ θεός σοι δίδωσιν, οὐκ ἐγώ. This text is repeated almost verbatim by Theophanes, A.M. 6070, ed. C. de Boor, 1 (Leipzig, 1883), 248.18f. For a different interpretation see Peter Charanis, 'Coronation and its constitutional significance in the Later Roman Empire,' *Byzantion*, 15 (1940-41), 55.

God.[50] In his *Parainesis* (a collection of moral exhortations), the Emperor Basil I (867-886) reminds his son, Leo VI (886-912), to whom this work was addressed, that, "You received your crown from God through my hand," and urges him to "honor greatly thy mother, the Church, which nurtured you in the Holy Spirit and, with me, through Christ in God, placed the crown on your head." [51] Some one hundred years later, John Mauropus (metropolitan of Euchaïta, often called John Euchaïta, fl. ca. 1050) in a poem addressed to an icon wrote, "Thy mighty hand, O Christ, hath crowned the mighty monarchs and given them power." [52]

This conception of God as crowning the emperor by his own hand is a prominent feature of the services of coronation for the emperor, the empress, and the emperor's heir or personally chosen successor, whether the actual crowning was performed by the patriarch or by the emperor himself. Since the prescribed liturgies in their present form are not later than the Emperor Constantine VII (913-59), there is no reference to the kind of situation which developed in the period between 1034 and 1042 (as sketched above; see notes 41-47), when Zoe controlled the succession to the throne. But since her three favorites (as well as Michael VI, whom Theodora had co-opted) were eventually crowned by the patriarch, it cannot be doubted that they, too, were thought to have been 'God-crowned.' (See texts at note 48 above.)

In what follows I quote a few relevant portions from the ceremony of coronation as recorded by Constantine VII in the *Book of Ceremonies*. In the text as it now stands, special emphasis is laid

---

[50] *Ecloga legum*, edd. J. and P. Zepos, *Jus graecoromanum*, 2 (Athens, 1931), 13: Πιστεύομεν ... καὶ οὕτως ... ὑπὸ τῆς αὐτοῦ [= θεοῦ] παντοδυνάμου χειρὸς στεφανοῦσθαι ἡμᾶς τοῦ περικειμένου διαδήματος ... Translated by Edwin H. Freshfield, *A manual of Roman law, the Ecloga* (Cambridge, England, 1926), 67. For the date, see Ostrogorsky, *History*, 152; Georgios Petropulos, Ἱστορικὴ εἰσαγωγὴ εἰς τὰς πηγὰς τοῦ Ἑλληνικοῦ Δικαίου (Athens, 1961), 76. Some prefer 741; see Bernhard Sinogowitz, *Studien zum Strafrecht der Ekloge* (Πραγματεῖαι τῆς Ἀκαδημίας Ἀθηνῶν, 21 [Athens, 1956]), 1.

[51] PG, 107, xxxiiB: Στέφανον ἐκ Θεοῦ διὰ τῆς ἐμῆς ἐδέξω χειρός. Cf. *ibid.*, xxiv A: ... τίμα περισσῶς τὴν μητέρα σου, τὴν Ἐκκλησίαν, ἥτις ἐν ἁγίῳ πνεύματί σε ἐτιθηνήσατο, καὶ σὺν ἐμοὶ διὰ Χριστοῦ ἐν Θεῷ τῇ κεφαλῇ σου τὸ στέφος ἐπέθηκεν.

[52] Ed. Paul de Lagarde, *Iohannis Euchaitorum Metropolitae quae in Codice Vaticano Graeco 676 supersunt* (Göttingen, 1882), No. 80.1f., p. 39, reprinted from *Abhandlungen der königlichen Gesellschaft der Wissenschaften*, 28 (Göttingen, 1881):
Σὴ χεὶρ κραταιὰ τοὺς κραταιοὺς δεσπότας
ἔστεψε, Χριστέ, καὶ παρέσχε τὸ κράτος.

upon the senior emperor's bestowal of the crown upon 'the newly elected emperor.' (This is indubitably a generalized formula and must be presumed to have been intended to apply to whomever the senior emperor had designated as his successor—whether it was his son or some favorite.) First, Constantine says, the patriarch prays over the crowns and "with his own hand crowns the senior emperor. Then he gives the crown to the emperor, and the emperor crowns the newly-elected emperor." [53] These acts of coronation are followed by acclamations made in the presence of the Senate and the people:

Chorus: "Glory be to God, who crowned thy head" (repeated by the people). Chorus: "Glory be to God, who revealed thee to be emperor" (repeated by the people). Chorus: "Glory be to God who exalted thee in this way" (repeated by the people). Chorus: "But he who crowned thee, so and so, emperor with his own hand" (repeated by the people). Chorus: "Will preserve thee for many years in the purple" (repeated by the people). Chorus: "For the glory and exaltation of the Romans" (repeated by the people) . . . Chorus: "Many years to you, so and so and so and so, emperors of the Romans." The people: "Many years to you." . . . Chorus: "Many years to you, so and so and so and so, Empresses of the Romans." The people: "Many years to you." . . . Chorus: "Many years to thee, so and so, Emperor of the Romans." The people: "Many years to thee." Chorus: "Many years to thee, God-crowned so and so." The people: "Many years to thee." Chorus: "Many years to you, o Lords [= Emperors], together with the Empresses and your children born in the purple." The people: "Many years to you." Chorus: "But the Creator and Lord of the universe" (repeated by the people). Chorus: "Who crowned you [plural] by his own hand" (repeated by the people). Chorus: "Gives you length of days along

---

[53] *De cerimoniis*, 1, 38, CP, 1, 194.10-14, cf. 193.1-3; ed. Albert Vogt, *Le livre des cérémonies*, 2 (Paris, 1939), 3.11-14, cf. 2.7-10. It is not clear whether the text refers to one crown, or presumably, two, one for each of the emperors. I have translated the Greek exactly as it is.

Pseudo-Codinus (of the fourteenth century), *De officialibus Palatii Constantinopolitani*, 17, CSHB, 90.19-22, says the emperor and the patriarch jointly place the crown on the head of the emperor's son. Cf. the commentary of Gretser and Goar *ad loc.*, *ibid.*, 359f.; Christophilopulu, *op. cit.* (note 1 above), 44. According to the rites printed by Jacobos Goar, Εὐχολόγιον sive *Rituale Graecorum* (Paris, 1647), 926, 8 and 16; 2d ed. (Venice, 1730), 727, 8 and 16; the emperor, not the patriarch, crowns the emperor's son, daughter, or wife.

with the Empresses and your children born in the purple" (repeated by the people).[54]

The same ideology recurs in the rites performed at the marriage of the emperor to the empress and at the latter's coronation. In the former of these, she is addressed as both "elected by God" and "Augusta [= empress] appointed by God." [55] The chorus then declares, "Thou wert selected by divine decree [literally 'vote'] for the security and exaltation of the universe; thou wert joined to the purple by God's will. Almighty God has blessed thee and crowned thee with his own hand. But he who has called thee to this rank and joined thee to so and so, the Lord [Emperor[, gives thee length of days in the purple." [56]

At the coronation of the empress, the patriarch prays over the crown, which he gives to the emperor, who places it on the head of the empress.[57] Having been duly crowned in this way, the empress is greeted by the customary traditional acclamations:

---

[54] Op. cit., 1, 38, CP, 1, 194.14-196.16; ed. Vogt, 2, 3.14-5.5; n.b. 4.3ff. I have translated 195.8-196.16 with a few excisions; n.b. the following: οἱ κράκται· "δόξα Θεῷ τῷ στέψαντι τὴν κορυφήν σου." ὁ λαὸς ὁμοίως. οἱ κράκται· "δόξα Θεῷ τῷ ἀναδείξαντί σε βασιλέα." ὁ λαὸς ὁμοίως. οἱ κράκται· "δοξα Θεῷ τῷ δοξάσαντί σε οὕτως." ὁ λαὸς ὁμοίως. οἱ κράκται· "δοξα Θεῷ τῷ εὐδοκήσαντι οὕτως. ὁ λαὸς ὁμοίως. οἱ κράκται· "ἀλλ' ὁ στέψας σε, ὁ δεῖνα βασιλέα, αὐτοχείρως." ὁ λαὸς ὁμοίως . . . οἱ κράκται· "πολλοί σου χρόνοι, θεόστεπτε ὁ δεῖνα." ὁ λαὸς· "πολλοί σου χρόνοι.". . . οἱ κράκται· "ἀλλ' ὁ πάντων ποιητὴς καὶ δεσπότης." ὁ λαὸς ὁμοίως. οἱ κράκται· "ὁ στέψας ὑμᾶς τῇ αὐτοῦ παλάμῃ." ὁ λαὸς ὁμοίως. οἱ κράκται· "τοὺς χρόνους ὑμῶν πληθύνει σὺν ταῖς αὐγούσταις καὶ τοῖς πορφυρογεννήτοις.". . . The basic ideas of this passage are repeated with only minor changes ibid., 1, 40 (on the coronation of the empress), CP, 1, 207.5-9. These acclamations have a certain rhythm but are, perhaps, less formally constructed than those discussed by Paul Maas, 'Metrische Akklamationen der Byzantiner,' BZ, 21 (1912), 28-51. Cf. on the election and crowning of the emperor by God: Goar, op. cit. (note 53 above), 1647 ed., 925, 6f.; 2d ed., 726, 6f. I reproduce only part of the relevant Greek text; see note 1 above.

For the actual crowns, see Percy E. Schramm, Herrschaftszeichen und Staatssymbolik, 2 (Schriften der Monumenta Germaniae Historica, 13, 2 Stuttgart, 1955), 379-84; Josef Deér, ibid., 418-22, 426-41, 445-49; idem, Die heilige Krone Ungarns (Österreichische Akademie der Wissenschaften, philosophisch-hist. Kl., Denkschriften, 91 [Vienna, 1966]).

[55] Op. cit., 1, 39, CP, 1, 198.11 (θεοεπίλεκτε), 200.10 (θεοπρόβλητε); ed. Vogt, 2, 7.21, 9.6f.

[56] Ibid., 198.17-22: σὺ ἐκ θείας ψήφου προεχειρίσθης εἰς σύστασιν καὶ ἀνέγερσιν τοῦ κόσμου, σὺ ἐνυμφεύθης ἐκ Θεοῦ τῇ πορφύρᾳ, σὲ εὐλόγησεν ὁ Θεὸς ὁ παντοκράτωρ, στεφανώσας σε τῇ αὐτοῦ παλάμῃ· ἀλλ' ὁ εἰς ταύτην καλέσας σε τὴν ἀξίαν καὶ συζεύξας σε ὁ δεῖνα τῷ δεσπότῃ τοὺς χρόνους σου πληθύνει ἐν τῇ πορφύρᾳ. These words are repeated antiphonally with a few minor variations by the chorus and the people ibid., 200.15-23; ed. Vogt, 2, 7.28-32, cf. 9.11ff.

[57] Ibid., 1, 40, CP, 1, 203.4-7; ed. Vogt, 2, 11.23-12.1.

Chorus: "Glory to God who revealed thee to be empress" (repeated thrice by the people). Chorus: "Glory to God who crowned thy head" (repeated thrice by the people). Chorus: "Glory to God who hath thus shown [thee] his favor" (repeated thrice by the people). Chorus: "But he who has crowned thee, so and so, by his own hand" (repeated thrice by the people). Chorus :"Will preserve thee many years in the purple" (repeated thrice by the people). Chorus: "for the glory and exaltation of the Romans" (repeated thrice by the people). Chorus: "God will hear your people" (repeated thrice by the people).[58]

In the ceremony for the coronation of the Caesar, after a prayer, the patriarch lifts up the so-called καισαρίκια, the crown intended for the Caesar, kisses it, passes it on to the emperor, who kisses it, has the Caesar kiss it, makes the sign of the cross over the Caesar's head, while repeating the words, "In the name of the Father and of the Son and of the Holy Spirit," and then sets the crown on the head of the person who is to be made Caesar. Whereupon begin the acclamations, which undoubtedly included the words on God's crowning the Caesar with his own hand that occur in the ceremonies for the coronation of the emperor and of the empress.[59]

IV. *Archaeological evidence*

The Byzantine conception of the divine origin of the imperial authority conferred upon the Byzantine emperor, as analyzed above can be fully documented from Byzantine works of art, which represent monarchs being crowned by Christ, the Virgin Mary, an

---

[58] *Ibid.*, 206.6-15: οἱ κράκται· "δόξα Θεῷ τῷ ἀναδείξαντί σε βασίλισσαν." ὁ λαὸς ὁμοίως ἐκ τρίτου. οἱ κράκται· "δόξα Θεῷ τῷ στέψαντι τὴν κορυφήν σου." ὁ λαὸς ὁμοίως ἐκ τρίτου. οἱ κράκται· "δόξα Θεῷ τῷ εὐδοκήσαντι οὕτως." ὁ λαὸς ὁμοίως ἐκ τρίτου. οἱ κράκται· "ἀλλ' ὁ στέψας σε ὁ δεῖνα αὐτοχείρως." ὁ λαὸς ἐκ τρίτου ὁμοίως. οἱ κράκται· "φυλάξει σε εἰς πλήθη χρόνων ἐν τῇ πορφύρᾳ." ὁ λαὸς ἐκ τρίτου ὁμοίως. οἱ κράκται· "εἰς δόξαν καὶ ἀνέγερσιν τῶν 'Ρωμαίων." ὁ λαὸς ὁμοίως ἐκ γ'. οἱ κράκται· "εἰσακούσει ὁ Θεὸς τοῦ λαοῦ ὑμῶν." ὁ λαὸς ὁμοίως ἐκ τρίτου. Ed. Vogt, 2, 14.15-24.

[59] *Ibid.*, 1, 43, CP, 1, 217.18-225.13. This time, however, the texts are not given in full but in abbreviated form with an indication of the *incipit* (225.7: "πολλὰ τὰ ἔτη" καὶ τὰ ἑξῆς) and the *explicit* (225.8f.: ἐν δὲ τῷ τελευτᾶν· "πολλὰ τὰ ἔτη τοῦ εὐτυχεστάτου Καίσαρος"); ed. Vogt, 2, 26-32, n.b. 32.8-10. But, *mutatis mutandis*, these are precisely the words that introduce and terminate the acclamations above translated (note 54, cf. 54 *ad fin.*), which include the references to coronation by the hand of God (195.19ff. and 196.15; 206.17ff. and 207.1of.).

angel, or a saint. Of the large numbers of these monuments in many different media (mosaics, miniatures, enamels, ivories, coins, etc.),[60] it will be sufficient for the present argument to draw attention to only a few of the more striking examples.

Before examining these, however, two preliminary observations must be made. In the first place, it should be remembered that figures of God the Father are exceedingly rare in Byzantine art. The very few extant examples [61] can be explained by the ignorance of the artists, who did not realize that Byzantine theologians had defined God the Father and the divine essence in general to be uncircumscribable (ἀπερίγραφος). The divine, they maintained, is always inaccessible to the human eye: it is invisible and cannot be represented. Both iconoclasts and their opponents agreed, there-

---

[60] See André Grabar, *L'empereur dans l'art byzantin* (*Publications de la Faculté des Lettres de l'Université de Strassbourg*, 75 [Paris, 1936]), pl. 19, 2; 23, 1; 24, 1 and 2; 25, 1 and 2; 26, 1; 28, 5 and 6; pp. 112-22 (with several examples of coronation not discussed above).

The first full length scene of a coronation to appear on a coin was struck for the Emperor Alexander (912-13). On this issue the emperor is represented flanked on his left by a saint (presumably Alexander), who crowns the emperor with his right hand. See Philip Grierson, *Catalogue of the Byzantine coins in the Dumbarton Oaks collection and in the Whittemore collection*, 3, *Leo III to Nicephorus III, 717-1081*, part 2, *Basil I to Nicephorus III, 867-1081* (Washington, D.C., 1973), 523-25, pl. 35, № 2.1, 2.2. For other scenes of coronation see *idem*, 544f., pl. 36, № 5.1, 5.2, 6.1, 6.2 (Romanos I crowned by Christ: both standing figures); 589ff., pl. 42, № 1a, 1b, 1c, 2.1, 3.2, 3.3, 3.7, 4b, 5a, 6a.3, 6b, 6c, (John I Tzimisces crowned by the Virgin: both busts); 711ff., pl. 56, № 1a.2, 1b.2, 1b.3, 1b.9, etc. (8 coins: Romanos III crowned by the Virgin Mary: both full length standing figures); 754ff., pl. 62, № 1a.1, 1a.2, 1b.3 (Michael VI crowned by the Virgin Mary: both nearly full-length standing figures); 764ff., pl. 64, № 2.1, 2.4 (Constantine X Ducas crowned by the Virgin Mary, both full length standing figures); 785ff., pl. 65, № 1.1, 1.2, 2.1, 2.4 (Christ standing on suppedium between Romanos IV and Eudocia and crowning them). On some of these coins, it is difficult to determine whether Christ is crowning the emperor and empress respectively, or whether he is joining them in marriage, since crowning (στεφάνωμα) was also a prominent feature of the latter: Constantine Porphyrogennetos, *Book of Ceremonies*, 1, 39, 41, CSHB, 1, 196.17-202.3, 207.13-216.3. See also Cécile Morrison, *Catalogue des monnaies byzantines de la Bibliothèque Nationale*, 2 (Paris, 1970): scenes of coronation: pl. 80, 84, 88, 89, 96, 99, 100, 102.

[61] Most of the examples cited are illusory. But n.b. Henri Omont, *Évangiles avec peintures byzantines du xie siècle, reproduction des 361 miniatures du manuscrit grec 74 de la Bibliothèque Nationale*, (Paris, n.d.), pl. 1 (f. 1 recto): the Ancient of Days (ὁ παλαιὸς ἡμερῶν); 2 (n.d.), pl. 142 (f. 167 recto: with another representation of the same subject). For discussion and additional examples, see E. Lucchesi Palli, s.v. Christus-Alter der Tage, *Lexikon der christlichen Ikonographie*, 1 (Freiburg im Br., 1968), 394-96; Karl Künstle, *Ikonographie der christlichen Kunst*, 1 (Freiburg im Br., 1928), 233-35.

fore, that it was impossible to make an image of God and that any attempt to do so was blasphemous.

Nevertheless, the Seventh Oecumenical Council, which met in Nicaea in 787 ('the Second Council of Nicaea'),[62] ruled that the Jesus Christ, whose life on earth is described in the New Testament, can be portrayed in paintings, mosaics, embroideries, and many other media. Such representations, the Council held, exhibit Christ's true humanity and lift the mind of the observer so that he may in his mind contemplate Christ's divinity (i.e., the divine Logos or his divine nature), which is uncircumscribable and cannot be the subject of artistic representation.

Secondly, it is important to note, in these icons Jesus Christ is the surrogate for God the Father, who, being uncircumscribable and invisible,[63] can be made accessible to mortal eyes only in the form of his Son. Thus, when Christ (or Mary, an angel, or a saint) is represented as bestowing the crown in scenes of coronation, it should be understood that it is God who is in reality conferring the crown through an agent who is circumscribable. According to the doctrine of 787, true worship (λατρεία) is paid only to God; images are not worshipped but are accorded pious salutation and reverence (ἀσπασμός and προσκύνησις).

Apparently the first scene of coronation occurs in *Parisinus Graecus* 510 (dating from ca. 880), a famous manuscript which contains the homilies of Gregory of Nazianzus. Here, on folio 100 verso, is a miniature of three standing figures; the Emperor Basil I (867-86), flanked on his right by the Prophet Elijah and on his left by

---

[62] On the subject as a whole, see my 'Iconoclasm and imperial rule, 717-842,' *Cambridge Medieval History*, 4, 1 (Cambridge, England, 1966), n.b. 85ff., bibliography, 835-48; Edward J. Martin, *A history of the iconoclastic controversy* (London, n.d., ?1930).

[63] The West, it should be added, never understood the Byzantine doctrine of images and, although Charlemagne denounced the Byzantines as idolaters, representations of God occur frequently in the Western art of the later Middle Ages and the Renaissance. Theologically, such figures are a desecration.

The representations of the Trinity which sometimes adorn the frontispiece of Byzantine liturgical books probably reflect Latin influence since many modern editions still carry on the tradition of the early service books, which were printed in Venice. But, strictly speaking, these Trinitarian groups, which represent God the Father as an elderly gentleman, Jesus Christ in somewhat younger guise sitting to his Father's left, with the Holy Spirit in the form of a dove swooping down upon them from above like a dive bomber, are a theological abomination.

the Archangel Gabriel, who is shown placing a crown on his head. The manuscript has suffered a great deal of flaking. But the subject is recognizable, and along the four sides, forming a frame for the miniature as a whole, is an inscription, the last two lines of which explain that [in this painting] 'Gabriel brings tidings of joy, [Lord] Basil, and crowns thee ruler of the universe.' [64]

About one hundred years later, the Emperor Constantine VII (913-59), whose *Book of Ceremonies* provides the best evidence for the Byzantine rites of coronation, as we have seen, is represented on an ivory (now in the Moscow State Museum of Fine Arts) inclining his head to his left and extending his hands towards Christ in an attitude of submission, as the latter, standing on a one-stepped podium, places a crown on his head. This famous work was apparently produced in 945 to commemorate Constantine's reestablishment on the throne as sole ruler of Byzantium.[65]

During the reign of Constantine VII's son, Romanos II (959-63), or, according to some authorities, Romanos IV (1068-71), in a modification of this iconographic type on an ivory plaque in the Cabinet des Médailles of the Bibliothèque Nationale, Christ is depicted standing between, and slightly higher than, the Emperor Romanos II and his wife, the Empress Eudocia, crowning the former with his right hand and the latter with his left.[66]

Even more explicit than these two very literal translations of the above-quoted texts on the coronation is the inscription on a Georgian enamel of the eleventh century which forms a part of the

---

[64] Henri Omont, *Miniatures des plus anciens manuscrits grecs de la Bibliothèque Nationale du VIe au XIVe siècle* (Paris, 1929), p. 13, pl. 19; cf. pl. 6 (Par. gr. 139, f. 6 verso, of the tenth century: The Psalmist David, raised on a shield and crowned by an angel; H. Buchthal, *The miniatures of the Paris Psalter* (*Studies of the Warburg Inst.*, 2 [1938], pl. 6). The text:
ὁ Γαβριὴλ δὲ τὴν χαρὰν προμηνύων,
Βασίλειε, στέφει σε κόσμου προστάτην.
[65] A. Banck, *Byzantine art in the collections of the USSR* (Leningrad-Moscow, 1966), pls. 124f., pp. 299, 353; Kurt Weitzmann, 'The Mandylion and Constantine Porphyrogennetos,' in *idem, Studies in classical and Byzantine manuscript illumination* (Chicago-London, 1971), 242-45, reprinted from *Cahiers archéologiques*, 11 (1960), 163ff.; David T. Rice, *Kunst aus Byzanz* (Munich, 1959), pl. 96; Philipp Schweinfurth, *Die byzantinische Form, ihr Wesen und ihre Wirkung*, 2d ed. (Mainz, 1954), pl. 65, p. 168.
[66] Rice, *op. cit.*, pl. 97, p. 63; John Beckwith, *The art of Constantinople, an introduction to Byzantine art, 330-1453*, 2d ed. (London-New York, 1968), fig. 101, pp. 81f.; Hayford Peirce and Royall Tyler, 'An ivory of the tenth century,' *Three Byzantine works of art* (*Dumbarton Oaks Papers*, 2 [Cambridge, 1941]), 15 (with references to other literature), pl. 8.

Khakhuli Triptych in the Museum of Fine Arts in Tiflis. Here, the bust of Christ, posed frontally against a blue field sown with small yellow stars, is shown poised above and between the Emperor Michael VII Parapinakes (1071-78) and his wife, the Empress Mary, both of whom he is represented as crowning, Michael with his right hand and Mary with his left. Lower down, under the Christ and somewhat below the Emperor's left hand there is an inscription: "I crown Michael and Mary with my hands." [67]

After Michael VII's abdication and retirement to a monastery, his wife Mary married his successor, the Emperor Nicephorus III Botaneiates (1078-81), a splendid portrait of whose coronation by Christ has been preserved in a manuscript of the homilies of John Chrysostom (*Coislinianus Graecus*, 79 of the Bibliothèque Nationale, f. 1 verso). In this miniature, which dates from the last quarter of the eleventh century, Christ crowns the two monarchs as in the Khakhuli Triptych. But here he floats against the gold background and is represented at about two-thirds length, a figure cut off just above the knees, and set about on a level with the heads of Nicephorus and Mary, who are represented nearly four times taller than he. Christ's head is angled to his right, and he lays his right hand on Nicephorus's crown and his left on Mary's. The inscription, which runs above the frame of the picture, contains a prayer in a slightly irregular form of the ancient iambic trimeter:

"May Christ crown and protect thee,
Lord of Rome,
Together with [thy] altogether
most noble Empress." [68]

The texts and monuments of art discussed above, along with a great many others of similar purport that could be cited, reflect the traditional ideology which the Byzantines always cherished even when the Empire had shrunk to an area barely extending

---

[67] Chalva Amiranachvili, *Les émaux de Géorgie*, translated by François Hirsch (Paris, 1962), 99-101 (with colored plate). Cf. Grabar, *op. cit.* (in note 60 above), 118. The inscription: στέφω Μιχαὴλ σὺν Μαριὰμ χερσί μου (with rectifications).

[68] Omont, *op. cit.*, p. 33, pl. 62; Viktor Lazarev, *Storia della pittura bizantina* (Turin, 1967), p. 190, pl. 232.
The inscription runs: σκέποι τε Χριστὸς εὐλογῶν, Ῥώμης ἄναξ, σὺν βασιλίδι τῇ πανευγενεστάτῃ. The verb σκέπω involves a pun since it means both to 'cover' literally (here 'crown') and to shelter or protect.

beyond the city of Constantinople. Despite all the evidence to the contrary, they always professed to believe that the Byzantine emperor had been chosen and crowned by God to rule over the whole of the inhabited world. This unwavering commitment to both political and metaphysical absolutism is one of the chief characteristics of the 'Byzantine mind' and probably helps to explain why Byzantium never experienced any great cultural, political, scientific, or theological revolutions. For some twelve centuries the Byzantines were the principal custodians of the heritage of ancient Greece. But for them this never proved to be the liberating force that the Renaissance in the West found it to be.

Addition to note 28 above.

Constantine Porphyrogennetos does not discuss or allude to any coronation of the Emperor Leo I by the Patriarch in the *Book of Ceremonies*, and the crown (στέφανος) to which reference is made (*op. cit.*, 413.10, 14, 16-414.1, 415, 3, 11) must have been identical with the diadem assumed by Leo after his acclamation (411.15; see BZ, 39 [1939], 197). It is nevertheless important to emphasize that mention four pages later of the bishop (presumably the Patriarch) as laying the crown upon the head of the emperor (415.11: ἐπιτιθέντος αὐτῷ τὸν στέφανον τοῦ ἐπισκόπου) when the latter was preparing to leave Hagia Sophia for the imperial palace does not in any sense imply that the Patriarch was now performing a service of coronation. For Leo had already become emperor upon being acclaimed and vested with the *torques* (pp. 189ff. above).

Moreover, he had not only already donned the royal garments, along with the diadem (i.e., the crown), received acclamations for the second time, and made a formal statement in which he referred to his elevation to the throne but also had formally begun his reign in the traditional manner by distributing the customary donative to the troops in gratitude for his ascent to the royal power (412.12ff.: ὑπὲρ ἐντεύξεως τῆς ἁγίας καὶ εὐτυχοῦς βασιλείας μου). After his accession to the throne had been thus fully consummated, he is described as making his rounds through the city, stopping at various churches to offer prayer and donations (413.9ff., 14ff.; 415.3, 11), putting down his crown briefly (before praying, e.g.) and then taking it up again. It is only on the last of these occasions, in Hagia Sophia, that, after having deposited his crown on the altar, he received it back from the Patriarch, who placed it upon his head, not by any means in order to confer or bestow it formally upon him for the first time, since the official crowning had taken place previously, but only to return it to him so that he might continue on his way. In other words, what the Patriarch did at this juncture was merely incidental to Leo's first participation *qua* emperor in the liturgy of the Church, and one of the consequences of the coronation.

IV

JUSTINIAN'S DESPOTIC CONTROL OVER THE CHURCH AS ILLUSTRATED BY HIS EDICTS ON THE THEOPASCHITE FORMULA AND HIS LETTER TO POPE JOHN II IN 533.[1]

In paying homage to Professor Ostrogorsky on this occasion as friend and scholar, I venture, with due deference, to treat one of the many subjects[2] on which he is a most distinguished authority.

---

[1] This is a revised version of a portion of my chapter on Justinian in my forthcoming book, *The Mind of Byzantium*, in which I list the major publications on the enormous subject involved. In the meantime, see the bibliographies compiled by Giovanni Pilati, *Chiesa e stato nei primi quindici secoli* (Rome-Paris, 1961), 61 f. (note the references to Alivisatos); and Biondo Biondi, *op cit.* (notes 3 and 6 below). Especially noteworthy are: Franz Dölger, „Justinianos I," *Lexikon für Theologie und Kirche*, 5, 2nd ed. (Freiburg im Br., 1960), 1227—29; I have not seen M. A. Cassetti, *Giustiniano e la sua legislazione in materia ecclesiastica* (Rome, 1958); Attanasio Mozzillo, „Dei rapporti tra gli imperatori ed i concili ecumenici da Costantino a Giustiniano," *Archivio giuridico* „Filippo Serafini," 6th S., 16 (1954), 105—28; *Das Konzil von Chalkedon*, edd. Aloys Grillmeier and Heinrich Bacht, 3 vols. (Würzburg, 1951—54); Karl Bihlmeyer — Hermann Tüchle, *Kirchengeschichte*, 12th ed. (Paderborn, 1951), § 58; Ernest Stein, *Histoire du Bas-Empire*, 2, ed. Jean R. Palanque (Paris-Brussels, 1949), 369—417, 623—90; Louis Bréhier in A. Fliche and V. Martin, *Histoire de l'église*, 4 (Paris, 1945), 437—82; Eduard Schwartz, „Zur Kirchenpolitik Iustinians," *Sitzungsberichte d. bayer. Ak. d. Wiss.*, philos. — hist. Abt., 2 (Munich, 1940); Erich Caspar, *Geschichte des Papsttums: von den Anfängen bis zur Höhe der Weltherrschaft*, 2, *Das Papsttum unter byzantinischer Herrschaft* (Tübingen, 1933), 193—305 *passim;* L. Duchesne, *L'église au VIe siècle* (Paris, 1925), 43 ff., 78 ff., and *passim;* J. B. Bury, *History of the Later Roman Empire, from the death of Theodosius I to the death of Justinian*, 2 (London, 1923). Cf. Otto Treitinger, *Die oströmische Kaiser- und Reichsidee nach ihrer Gestaltung im höfischen Zeremoniell*, 2nd ed. (Darmstadt, 1956). I acknowledge gratefully the suggestions made by my young colleague, William B. Thurman, in the course of our frequent discussions of Justinian's legislative policy, and the memorable kindness of my dear friend, the late Professor Eberhard Bruck of the Harvard Law School.

I have used the following abbreviations: ACO = *Acta conciliorum oecumenicorum*, ed. Eduard Schwartz; COD = *Conciliorum oecumenicorum decreta,*. edd. J. Alberigo, P. P. Joannou, C. Leonardi, P. Prodi, H. Jedin, 2nd ed. (Freiburg im Br., 1962); Cod. = *Codex Iustinianus*, ed. Paul Krueger, *Corpus Iuris Civilis*, 2 (any edition); DTC = *Dictionnaire de théologie catholique* (Paris); Mansi = *Sacrorum conciliorum nova et amplissima collectio;* PG = J. B. Migne, *Patrologia graeca*.

[2] „Автократор и Самодржац." Глас, С. К. А., 164, Други разред, Филос. — филол., друш. и историске науке, 84 (1935), 95—187; „Das Verhältnis von Staat

Few historians have failed to recognize that the Emperor Justinian I ruled the Byzantine Church with an iron hand. But, it has often been argued, despite his autocratic manner and the unlimited power he wielded in the administration of ecclesiastical affairs in general, he never failed to manifest respect for the See of Rome and its bishops. Numerous texts[3] can be cited in proof of this proposition.

But this attitude of deference to Rome and to the clergy of the Christian Church as a whole, it has not yet been fully understood, was only one facet of his policy. As a pious and orthodox emperor, „the elect of God"[4], he deemed it his function to legislate on ecclesiastical matters on his own responsibility altogether, almost invariably without seeking clerical assent. In dealing with theology, however, he made an effort to respect the traditional framework of the Church, and usually, though not always, sought some kind of episcopal, patriarchal, or even conciliar approval for his legislation. But, as many have failed to realize, he always succeeded in obtaining whatever ecclesiastical confirmation he wished and, more significantly, *could not have failed to do so.*

He professed devotion to the first four oecumenical councils and conformity with the creeds they enunciated. He even (Novel 131; cf. Cod. 1. 3. 44 [45]) invested the canons of these councils with the force of law. Nevertheless, he felt free to interpret Christian dogma as he saw fit, and in fact was personally responsible for a radical revision of Christology (see below), which would have scandalized the bishops who formulated the Creed of 451.

Moreover, he issued his dogmatic decrees whenever he chose, and did not concern himself about securing the signatures of bishops and patriarchs until his decree was drafted. Then, after it was officially promulgated, he set about to procure whatever ecclesiastical sanction he saw fit, which on the part of the clergy amounted to no more than the purely administrative act of announcing the Emperor's theological decisions to the churches within their jurisdiction. In every instance, the priests, when asked to give their approbation to an imperial theological decree, were confronted with a *fait accompli,* and were powerless to resist, or to suggest changes.

As his contemporaries were aware[5], Justinian took particular delight in theology, and especially relished the role of judge (i. e., of final ar-

---

und Kirche in Byzanz" (in Russian, with German résumé), SK, 4 (1931), 121—34; and the many valuable discussions in his indispensable *History of the Byzantine state.*

[3] Collected and studied, e.g., by Biondo Biondi, *Giustiniano Primo, principe e legislatore cattolico (Pubblicazioni della Università Cattolica del Sacro Cuore,* Ser. 2, scienze giuridiche, 48 [Milan, 1936]), 117—48. Cf. Martin Jugie, *Le schisme byzantin* (Paris, 1941), 74—76; *idem,* „Justinien Ier," DTC, 8, 2 (1925), 2277—90.

[4] The major texts are listed by Biondi, *op. cit.,* 65 ff., 14 ff. On the subject in general see Treitinger, *op. cit.* (note 1 above), 7 ff., 124·ff. and *passim.*

[5] E.g., Liberatus (Archdeacon of the Church of Carthage, ca. 560—66), *Breviarium,* 23, 162: annuit imperator facillime [sc. to condemn Origen and his works], gaudens se de talibus causis iudicium ferre; *ibid.,* 24, 168 f. (on the *Three Chapters*); ed. Eduard Schwartz, ACO, 2, 5 (1936), 140. 3 ff., 140. 31—141 .1.

biter) in settling doctrinal disputes. He devoted the first title of the first Book of the *Codex Iustinianus* (Cod. 1. 1. 1 – 8) to a detailed summary of his theological position, which is announced bluntly as *De summa trinitate et de fide catholica et ut nemo de ea publice contendere audeat*. These unambiguous words and the texts which follow made it clear that the *fides catholica* was what he defined it to be, and that, as a matter of law, there was no room for question or disagreement. In accordance with this interpretation of his role in the Church, Justinian[6] issued a number of Novels, as well as numerous decrees, constitutions, and edicts which dealt with ecclesiastical questions of every sort – dogma, administration, ethics, marriage, divorce, discipline, the monastic life, and so on. There was no phase of the life of the Church in which he did not regard himself as the highest authority.

A thorough study of Justinian's legislation in this sphere has not yet been undertaken, and this essay on the laws by which he inserted the „Theopaschite" formula into the oecumenical creed is only a preliminary introduction to a large and complicated subject.

Justinian was learned in theology, but he consulted frequently with his clerical acquaintances[7], and may from time to time have been influenced by their judgment, though we should probably exercize more caution than has been customary hitherto in evaluating the testimony of his contemporaries on this subject. Nevertheless, from the point of view of his control over the Church, it makes no difference whether his views on doctrinal questions were based upon his own study and reasoning, as indeed they often were, or whether he reached his conclusions on the advice of his ecclesiastical favorites and counsellors. What is important is that, however he arrived at his dogmatic formulations, he himself in the end made the final decisions and translated them into law.

Actually, as I hope to show[8], Justinian may not have been so much the creature of whim, and the victim of his advisers, as some of his critics believe he was. His dogmatic pronouncements were consistent with his Cyrillian exegesis of the Creed of Chalcedon. What he set out to do, and succeeded in accomplishing, was to re-interpret the Christology of the Church in the light of Cyril's Third letter to Nestorius, with its *Twelve anathemas*. This document had not[9] been accorded oecumenical re-

---

[6] Outlined and discussed, with full bibliography by Biondo Biondi, *Il diritto romano cristiano*, 3 vols. (Milan, 1952—54). Cf. Hans G. Beck. *Kirche und theologische Literatur im byzantinischen Reich (Handbuch der Altertumswissenschaft*, 12, 2, 1 [Munich, 1959]), 285 f., 377 f.

[7] E. g., Sabas allegedly urged him to condemn Origen: *Life of Sabas* by Cyril of Scythopolis 72, ed. Eduard Schwartz, *Kyrillos von Skythopolis (Texte und Untersuchungen*, 4. R., 4, 2 = 49, 2 [Leipzig, 1939]), 175.19 ff.; so did Pelagius, apocrisiarius (i. e. ambassador) from Rome, and the Patriarch Menas of Constantinople: Liberatus, *Breviarium*, 23, ACO, 2, 5 (1936), 140.3 ff.; Theodore Ascidas pressed for action against the *Three Chapters, idem*, 24, *ibid.*, 140.13 ff., etc.

[8] In my forthcoming book, *The Mind of Byzantium*.

[9] See my „Nestorius was orthodox," *Dumbarton Oaks Papers*, 16 (1962), 123, note 8. For the literature on the *Twelve anathemas*, see Johannes Quasten, Patrology, 3, *The golden age of Greek patristic literature from the Council of Nicaea to the Council of*

4

cognition as a criterion of faith at Ephesus in 431 or at Chalcedon in 451. The Emperor Zeno had given it legal validity in the *Henotikon* of 482[10], which had been the ultimate cause of the Acacian schism (484—519). In effecting reconciliation with Rome in 519, the Emperor Justin and Justinian, however, annulled[11] the *Henotikon* both by the more conventional *professio fidei* to which they then gave utterance, and by consenting to the anathematization of both its author and its sponsor (the Patriarch Acacius and the Emperor Zeno), together with their principal followers.

But in successive stages, culminating in his *Edictum ... rectae fidei confessionem continens* of 551[12], and in the theological decrees of the Fifth Oecumenical Council (553)[13], which were taken almost verbatim from the anathemas he had set forth in the *Edictum*, Justinian incorporated the principal theological propositions of the *Henotikon* into the oecumenical dogma of the Church. This was one of the most extraordinary manifestations of the celebrated Byzantine guile, all the more significant in that it has still to be recognized fully in all of its implications. The reinterpretation of the Chalcedonian doctrine in these terms has often been described as Neo-chalcedonianism.[14] It might perhaps better be known as

---

Chalcedon (Utrecht-Antwerp-Westminster, 1960), 134. For the Greek text of Cyril's *Third letter to Nestorius* and the anathemas, see ACO, 1, 1, 1, 33—42; PG, 77, 105—21; T. Herbert Bindley, *The oecumenical documents of the faith*, 4th ed. by F. W. Green (London, 1950), 106—37, 212—19 (with English translation).

[10] Ed. Eduard Schwartz, *Codex Vaticanus gr. 1431, eine antichalkedonische Sammlung aus der Zeit Kaiser Zenos (Abhandlungen d. bayer. Ak. d. Wiss.*, philosoph. — philolog. u. hist. Kl., 32, 6 [Munich, 1927]), 52—54 (Greek), 54—56 (Latin version from Liberatus, *Breviarium*, 17, 113—117, as also in ACO, 2,5 [1936], 127—29); Evagrius, *Ecclesiastical history*, 3, 14, edd. J. Bidez and L. Parmentier (London, 1898), 111. 1—114. 5: Greek text; or see any edition of C. Kirch, *Enchiridion fontium historiae ecclesiasticae antiquae*, Nos. 958 f.
On the *Henotikon* and its significance see Fritz Hofmann, „Der Kampf der Päpste um Konzil und Dogma von Chalkedon ... (451—519)," *Das Konzil von Chalkedon* (note 1 above), 2 (1953), 43 ff.; Rhaban Haacke, „Die kaiserliche Politik in den Auseinandersetzungen um Chalkedon (451—553)," *ibid.*, 117 ff.; A. A. Vasiliev, *Justin the First (Dumbarton Oaks Studies*, 1 [Cambridge, 1950]), 132—253, *passim*; Stein, *op. cit.* (note 1 above), 2, 20 ff., 182 ff., 189 ff., 223—28; G. Bardy and Louis Bréhier, respectively, in A. Fliche and V. Martin, *Histoire de l'église*, 4 (Paris, 1945), 284—320, 423—34; Caspar, *op. cit.* (note 1 above), 2, 10—192, *passim*; Duchesne, *op. cit.* (note 1 above), 43 ff.; Sévérien Salaville, „L'affaire de l'Hénotique," *Échos d'Orient*, 18 (1916—19), 255—65, 389—97; 19 (1920), 49—68, 415—33; *idem*, „Hénotique," DTC, 6, 2, 2153—78.

[11] *Epistulae imperatorum pontificum aliorum ... Avellana quae dicitur collectio*, ed. Otto Guenther, 2 *(Corpus scriptorum ecclesiasticorum Latinorum*, 35,2 [Vienna-Leipzig, 1898]), Epp. 116 b (Hormisdas's *libellus*), 159 (Patriarch John I's version thereof), 160—65, 167, and 223; pp. 520—22, 607—16, 618—21, 683 f., 800 f. (Berlin version).

[12] Ed. Eduard Schwartz, *Drei dogmatische Schriften Iustinians (Abhandlungen d. bayer. Ak. d. Wiss.*, philos. — hist. Abt., N. F. 18 [Munich, 1939]), 71—111: Greek and Latin texts.

[13] Mansi, 9, 376—88; COD, 90—98.

[14] Paul Galtier, „L'occident et le néo-chalcédonisme," *Gregorianum*, 40 (1959), 54—74; Aloys Grillmeier, „Der Neu-Chalkedonismus," *Historisches Jahrbuch*, 77 (1958), 151—66; *idem*, „Vorbereitung des Mittelalters," *Das Konzil von Chalkedon* (note 1 above), 2 (1953), 791—839; Charles Moeller, „Le chalcédonisme et le néo-chalcédonisme en Orient de 451 à la fin du VIᵉ siècle," *ibid.*, 1, 637—720; Marcel Richard, „Le néo-chalcédo-

Justinianism, since it was Justinian who brought about its final triumph
and oecumenical validation.

One of the first steps Justinian took to put this theological program
into effect was his promulgation in 527 or 528 of an edict (Cod. 1. 1.
1. 5), in which he made the Theopaschite formula an essential part of the orthodox Creed. In its simplest form, as it was set forth in the *Henotikon,*
the Theopaschite[15] formula merely stated that the „Trinity remained a
trinity [or we should say 'three in number'] even after the incarnation
of God the Logos, who was one of the Trinity" (μεμένηκε γὰρ Τριὰς ἡ
Τριὰς καὶ σαρκωθέντος τοῦ ἑνὸς τῆς Τριάδος Θεοῦ Λόγου).[16] This is the version Justinian took over into the *Codex Iustinianus* (1. 1. 5. 2), in which
it occurs in conjunction (1. 1. 5. 1) with the same text that precedes it
in the *Henotikon* (ἑνὸς καὶ τοῦ αὐτοῦ τά τε θαύματα καὶ τὰ πάθη ἅπερ ἑκουσίως ὑπέμεινεν σαρκί).[17]

No one could object to the original formula itself. The difficulty
was that its radical proponents, like the Scythian monks, insisted that it
be carried one step further so as to include reference to the passion
and crucifixion. Here, in his first edict on this subject, however, Justinian adopted the simple formula without additions. In promulgating this
law, he made no effort to seek the adhesion of the clergy, to whom he
assigned no rôle except that of disseminating his ruling in their communities (Cod. 1. 1. 5. 4).

Justinian's use of the Theopaschite formula was only one indication
of his revolutionary dogmatic policy, the chief characteristic of which was
his marked partiality for the extreme Cyrillian position. His fondness for
the theology of Cyril and the latter's followers manifested itself most na-
kedly in his avoidance in 1.1.5 and 6 (but see page 8 below) of any
reference to the two natures in Christ or to the Council of Chalcedon.
Similarly, like Cyril once more, he insists (1.1.5.3) that the Virgin
Mary was κυρίως καὶ κατὰ ἀλήθειαν ... Θεοτόκον („properly and truly

---

nisme," *Mélanges de science religieuse,* 3 (1946), 156—61. Cf. Robert Hespel, *Le florilège
cyrillien réfuté par Sévère d'Antioche (Bibliothèque du Muséon,* 37 [Louvain, 1955]):
Greek text and study of an important Neo-chalcedonian document.

[15] On the Theopaschite controversy, see Altaner, *Patrologie* §§ 72.3, 96.4, 97.4
(c), 102.3; *idem,* „Zum Schrifttum der 'skythischen' (gotischen) Mönche," *Historisches
Jahrbuch,* 72 (1953), 568—81; Werner Elert, *Der Ausgang der altkirchlichen Christologie,*
edd. Wilhelm Maurer and Elisabeth Bergsträsser (Berlin, 1957), 93 f., 106 ff., 111—32,
and index s.v. *theopaschitisch;* Muus Feitsma, *Het Theopaschitisme een dogmahistorische
studie over de ontwikkeling van het theopaschitisch denken* (Kempen, 1956); *Das Konzil
von Chalkedon,* 1 (note 1 above), 193—95 (Grillmeier), 676 ff. (Moeller), 737 f. (Marcel
Richard); see index, vol. 3, s.v.; Stein-Palanque, *op. cit.,* (note 1 above), 2, 228—30,
335, 378 ff.; É. Amann, „Théopaschite (controverse)," DTC, 15, 1 (1946), 505—12;
Viktor Schurr, *Die Trinitätslehre des Boethius im Lichte der „skythischen Kontroversen"
(Forschungen zur christlichen Literatur- und Dogmengeschichte,* 18, 1 [Paderborn, 1935]),
136—97; Duchesne, *op. cit.* (note 1 above), 87 ff.; Vasiliev, *op. cit.* (note 10 above),
197, erroneously states that Justinian issued his first Theopaschite edict in 523.

[16] Ed. Schwartz (note 10 above), 54.8 f.; anathema 5 of the Council of 553
(Mansi, 9, 380 C); cf. anathema 4 (*ibid.,* 377 D); COD, 92. 24 ff., cf. 91.23 ff.

[17] Ed. Schwartz, 54.4—6; anathema 3 of 553 (Mansi, 9, 377 B); COD, 90.31 ff.

Mother of God")[18], although the Creed of Chalcedon, in authorizing Θεοτόκος as an epithet of Mary, had merely stated that Christ had been born of Mary the Virgin Theotokos according to the "manhood". In other respects, Justinian cleaved to the traditional doctrine as set forth in the first four oecumenical councils. But the indubitably orthodox phrases to which he had recourse did not diminish the effect of his unambiguous adoption of extr me Cyrillianism.

Five years later, on March 15, 533, he published another and fuller law (Cod. 1. 1. 6) on the same topic, which he addressed to the residents of Constantinople, Ephesus, Caesarea, and a number of other cities, and was, at his request, signed by the Patriarch Epiphanius and the clergy of Constantinople (Cod. 1. 1. 7. 11). According to the *Chronicon Paschale*[20], after publication in Constantinople, this law was sent to the other four patriarchs, as well as to some other bishops, who then proclaimed it in their churches. There is no evidence that the clergy played an active or substantive part in the discussion of the Emperor's theology. As in Cod. 1. 1. 5. 4 (referred to above in connection with the edict of 527, or 528), the bishops had nothing to do with the edict except to make it known to their communities.

In the full form of the Theopaschite formula as he now promulgated it, „Jesus Christ, the Son of God and our God, who was incarnate, became man, and was crucified, was one of the holy and. consubstantial Trinity" (Cod. 1. 1. 6. 7).[21] The strict Chalcedonians and the Nestorians objected[22] to this form of expression because it seemed to imply that

---

[18] This was adopted by the Council of 553 in its sixth anathema: Mansi, 9, 380 D; COD, 93.1 ff.

[19] The text is to be found in ACO, 2, 1, 2, 129 [325] f.; Mansi, 7, 116 ABC; COD, 62.30 f., etc.

[20] The *Chronicon Paschale*, ed. L. Dindorf, 1,CSHB (Bonn, 1832), 630.1—633.16, gives the Greek text very much as it is in Cod. 1. 1. 6, with a preface stating that „the Emperor Justinian issued a sacred edict in Constantinople, and sent it to Rome, Jerusalem, Antioch, Alexandria, Thessalonike, and Ephesus." After transcribing the text of the edict (633.15 ff.), the author notes that „all the bishops received copies of this [document] in their cities, and published it in their churches."

A good example of the method used by Justinian is to be found in the edict against Origen of 542: ACO, 3, 207. 26—208.25, 213.11—214.9, in which it can be seen (n.b. 208.13 ff., 18 ff., 22—25, and 213.11—214.9) that the clergy were in effect *commanded* to sign, and had no practicable alternative.

In a notable new book, Joseph Hajjar, *Le synode permanent dans l'église byzantine, des origines au XIᵉ siècle (Orientalia Christiana Analecta*, 164 [Rome, 1962]), 87 f., states that this e.ict (Cod. 1.1.6) was signed by the members of *synodos endemusa* (the bishops and archimandrites of the Constantinopolitan area), who, he says, thus gave it authority among the faithful and guaranteed the truth of the dogma it set forth. But he does not mention the first edict, which was not signed in this way (Cod. 1.1.5). Nor does Cod. 1.1.7.11 (the passage which refers to the signing of Cod. 1.1.6) give any indication of the sequence of promulgation, signing, etc. I take the position set forth in the text on the basis of Cod. 1.1.5, the edict against Origen, and the passage from the *Chronicon Paschale* cited above. On the edict against Origen, see Schwartz (note 1 above), SB, Munich (1940), 51 f.; *Life of Sabas* 86, in *idem*, ed., *Kyrillos* (note 7 above), 192. 12 ff.

[21] Anathema 10 of 553, Mansi, 9, 384 A; COD, 94.37 ff.

[22] See examples cited in the works listed in note 15.

God was mortal and could die, and that death could affect the Trinity Justinian, like Cyril, justified it as a consequence of the *communicatio idiomatum*[23], since, as he says, God the Word and the human Christ were one and the same (Cod. 1. 1. 6. 5 f.), and it was the same person who performed the miracles and willingly underwent the passion in the flesh, the same who was both God the Word and Jesus Christ, consubstantial with God the Father according to the Godhead, and the same consubstantial with us according to the manhood.

A few days thereafter, on March 26, Justinian addressed a letter (Cod. 1. 1. 7) to the Patriarch Epiphanius of Constantinople, in which he repeats the principal theses set forth in the two previous documents with some significant changes. The chief purpose of these alterations was to emphasize the orthodoxy of Justinian's theology, which he holds to be in every way consonant with the results of the four oecumenical councils. Above all, he was anxious to insist that the Theopaschite formula, originally set forth in the *Tomus ad Armenios* by Bishop Proclus[24] of

---

[23] This phaenomenon, the transfer or exchange of attributes, as defined by the Council of Chalcedon, notably in the Tome of Bishop Leo I (440—61) of Rome, is exhibited by the two natures of Jesus Christ (the divine and the human). According to orthodox doctrine, these natures are united „without confusion, change, separation, or division," and retain all of their properties, which in the union of God and man are distinct from each other but not separate. The difference between the natures had given rise to two appellations of Jesus Christ, who, on account of his divine nature, is Son of God (the divine Logos) and also, at the same time, by virtue of his human nature, the Son of man (Jesus). Whatever the designation, reference is always to one and the same person, Jesus Christ. Strictly speaking, the divine characteristics are attributable to the divine nature and the human to the human. Nevertheless, as a result of the union of the two in one person, it is deemed possible to ascribe the experiences of Jesus Christ in respect of his divine nature to the Son of man, and those which Jesus Christ underwent because of his human nature to the Son of God. Consequently, it was theologically permissible to teach that the „Son of God" underwent death, to which the divine nature was not subject, and that the „Son of man" received worship, which is accorded only to God. See my „Nestorius was orthodox," DOP, 16 (1962), 135 ff. For the text of the Tome of Leo (Ep. 28), see ACO, 2, 2, 1, 24—33 (Latin); 2, 1, 1, 10—20 (Greek version); C. Silva-Tarouca, *S. Leonis Magni Tomus ad Flavianum Episc. Constantinopolitanum (Textus et documenta*, Series theologica, 9 [Rome, 1932]). For exegesis, etc., see Hugo Rahner, „Leo der Grosse, der Papst des Konzils," *Das Konzil von Chalkedon*, 1 (see note 1), 323—39; Paul Galtier, „Saint Cyrille d'Alexandrie et Saint Léon le Grand à Chalcédoine," *ibid.*, 1, 345—87; Trevor Jalland, *The Life and Times of St. Leo the Great* (London, 1941), 451 ff., the best general book on Leo. Cf. Altaner, *Patrologie*, § 78, 11 for further bibliography.

[24] ACO, 4, 2 (1914), 192.7: ὁμολογοῦντες τὸν θεὸν Λόγον, τὸν ἕνα τῆς Τριάδος, σεσαρκῶσθαι. On the *Tomus ad Armenios*, see literature cited in note 15 above. N. b. Elert, *op. cit.* (note 15 above), 111—17; Aloys Grillmeier, „Die theologische und sprachliche Vorbereitung der christologischen Formel von Chalkedon," *Das Konzil von Chalkedon* (note 1 above), 1 (1951), 193 ff.; Marcel Richard, „Acace de Mélitène, Proclus de Constantinople et la grande Arménie," *Mémorial Louis Petit* (Bucharest, 1948), 393—412; *idem*, „Proclus de Constantinople et le Théophaschisme," *Revue d'histoire ecclésiastique*, 38 (1942), 303—31; Schurr, *op. cit.* (note 15 above), 181—97; Eduard Schwartz, *Konzilstudien (Schriften der wissenschaftlichen Gesellschaft in Strassburg*, 20 [1914]), 18—53. Richard (RHE, 38 [1942]) argues that the text quoted in the next note from an alleged letter of Proclus to John of Antioch is falsely so ascribed. Contra are Stein-Palanque, *Histoire du Bas-Empire*, 2, 229 f. Proclus's *Tomus ad Armenios* was declared by the Council of Chalcedon to be one of its principal patristic authorities, along with Atha-

Constantinope in 435, had been specifically approved by the Council of
Chalcedon. He lays stress on this point and on the identity of his doctrine with that of Chalcedon (1. 1. 7. 11, 12, 15, 17—21), which he had
not even mentioned in either of the two previous decrees (1. 1. 5 and
6). Moreover, this time, he takes special pains to insist that Jesus
Christ was „passible in the flesh and the same impassible in divinity" (παθητὸν σαρκί, τὸν αὐτὸν ἀπαθῆ θεότητι). He repeats these phrases
thrice (Cod. 1. 1. 7. 4, 7 f.), in order to eliminate suspicion that he deemed
the Godhead itself capable of suffering or death. Previously, he had not
gone beyond declaring that the Son of God, „who was God of God,"
underwent the passion voluntarily in the flesh (τὰ πάθη ἅπερ ἑκουσίως
ὑπέμεινε σαρκί : Cod. 1. 1. 5. 1; 1. 1. 6. 5). This terminology, which laid
stress upon ἐν σαρκί, was derived from the twelfth anathema of Cyril
against Nestorius and was, on this account, suspect in the eyes of strict
Chalcedonians. In time, of course, Justinian invested Cyril's Twelve anathemas with oecumenical sanction (see notes 12 f. above). But, at this
stage of the proceedings, since he was anxious to make it clear that he
was not himself guilty of the sacrilege of imputing passibility to the
Trinity itself, he found it expedient to express himself more unambiguously than in Cod. 1. 1. 5 f.

Also worthy of note is his preface to this edict, in which he addresses the Patriarch Epiphanius, and says[25], „Wishing Your Holiness to
have knowledge of all matters that pertain to the Church, we have
deemed it necessary to make use of this sacred letter in order to. inform
you of what has been going on . . ." The wording of this proemium is
an indication of the Emperor's own estimate of his dominant position in
the Church. He reports to the Patriarch what he has been doing on his
own initiative to curb what he took to be a recrudescence of activity on
the part of the refractory Nestorians and Monophysites. Had the Patriarch been the highest authority in the Church, or even an autonomous
power, the roles would have been reversed, and he would have felt
obliged to make a statement to the Emperor concerning the situation in
the Church and the measures he was taking to deal with it.

Then, on May 28, 533, Justinian addressed a similar letter on the
same topic to Pope John II of Rome (Cod. 1. 1. 8. 7 ff.). In this document, which is usually cited as proof that he had resigned supremacy in
the Church to the papacy, Justinian begins by stating that, because of
the prestige of the see of Rome, „the head of all the churches" (caput . . .
omnium sanctarum ecclesiarum : Cod. 1. 1. 8. 11), he never fails to keep the
pope informed of all matters concerning the Church. This he does, he

---

nasius and Cyril: ACO, 2, 1, 3, 113 [472]. 15—17, but no portion of the text was
quoted. In his Breviarium, 10, 45 f., Liberatus notes that the Tomus was endorsed by
Chalcedon and then gives his summary of what he took to be Proclus's chief argument:
ACO, 2, 5 (1936), 111. 5—20: et unum ex trinitate secundum carnem crucifixum fa-
temur et diuinitatem passibilem minime blasphemamus.

[25] Γινώσκειν βουλόμενοι τὴν σὴν ἁγιωσύνην πάντα τὰ εἰς ἐκκλησιαστικὴν ὁρῶντα
κατάστασιν ἀναγκαῖον ἡγησάμεθα ταύταις πρὸς αὐτὴν χρήσασθαι ταῖς θείαις συλλαβαῖς
καὶ δι' αὐτῶν δῆλα αὐτῇ καταστῆσαι τὰ κινηθέντα, ἅπερ καὶ αὐτὴν εἰδέναι πεπείσμεθα.

says, to preserve unity with Rome and peace in the Church. For the same reason, also, he instructs the clergy of the Eastern Church to bow in submission to Rome.

Up to this point, his tone has been obsequious and he even adds that the patriarch of Constantinople „exerts himself in all things to follow the apostolic see of Your Beatitude" [i. e., the Pope]. But then he asks papal confirmation for the Theopaschite formula, and goes on to say (Cod. 1. 1. 8. 23)[26] :

„For in this way [i. e., by your approval] the affection that all bear you [grows], [and] the authority of your see increases. And the unity of the holy churches with you will be preserved undamaged, as soon as all the most blessed bishops learn from you the purity of Your Sanctity's doctrine in the matter [i. e., the Theopaschite formula] which I have referred to you." Beneath these compliments and expressions of humility, there is an unmistakable and only thinly veiled threat: bow to my wishes or else harmony will be broken, the prestige of Rome will decline, and the rest of the churches will follow my command anyway.

As Justinian undoubtedly realized, Pope John had no intention of offering resistance, and on March 25, 534 (Cod. 1. 1. 8. 1 ff., 25 ff.) complied most graciously in every respect with the demands that had been made upon him. He not only approved the Emperor's dogmatic statement *in toto*, down to the last detail (Cod. 1. 1. 8. 25)[27], but also went so far as to pronounce it to be the doctrine established by Christ and taught by the Roman Church without change from the beginning to his own day (Cod. 1. 1. 8. 28—30).[28]

In addition, he reported that he condemned Cyrus and his followers because they had rejected the Theopaschite formula. This group of

---

[26] Plus enim ita et circa vos omnium amor et vestrae sedis crescit auctoritas et quae ad vos est unitas sanctarum ecclesiarum inturbata servabitur, quando per vos didicerint omnes beatissimi episcopi eorum, quae ad vos relata sunt, sinceram vestrae sanctitatis doctrinam.

[27] Liquet igitur, gloriosissime imperator, ut lectionis tenor et legatorum vestrorum relatio patefecit, vos apostolicis eruditionibus studere, cum de religionis catholicae fide ea sapitis, ea scripsistis, ea populis fidelibus publicastis, quae, sicut diximus, et sedes apostolica docet et patrum veneranda decrevit auctoritas et nos confirmavimus in omnibus.

[28] See previous note and Cod. 1. 1. 8. 28—30: Neque enim quisquam est, in quo Christi caritas fervet, qui tam rectae, tam verae confessionis vestrae fidei refragator existat, cum impietatem evidenter Nestorii Eutychiique et omnium haereticorum damnantes, unam veram catholicam fidem domini et dei nostri salvatoris Ihesu Christi magisterio institutam et propheticis apostolicisque praedicationibus ubique diffusam et sanctorum per totum orbem confessionibus roboratam, patrum atque doctorum sententiis adunatam et nostrae doctrinae consentaneam inconcusse atque inviolabiliter devota deo et pia mente servatis. Soli etenim vestris professionibus adversantur, de quibus divina scriptura loquitur dicens: 'posuerunt mendacium spem suam et mendacio operiri speraverunt': et iterum qui secundum prophetam dicunt domino: 'recede a nobis, vias tuas scire nolumus', propter quos Salomon dicit: 'semitas propriae culturae erraverunt, colligunt autem manibus infructuosa'. Haec est igitur vestra vera fides, haec certa religio, hoc beatae recordationis, ut diximus, patres omnes praesulesque Romanae ecclesiae, quos in omnibus sequimur, hoc sedes apostolica praedicavit hactenus et inconvulse custodivit: huic confessioni, huic fidei quisquis contradictor exstiterit, alienum a sancta communione, alienum se ipse ab ecclesia iudicavit esse catholica.

dissidents consisted of the monks from the monastery of the Akoimetoi[29] („the sleepless ones") in Constantinople, who were strict Chalcedonians and had gone to Rome in the hope that they might win over the Pope in their struggle against Justinian's theology. The Pope disallowed their plea, and refused to admit them to the churches of Rome unless they recanted (Cod. 1. 1. 8. 31—33). But he urged the Emperor to be reconciled with them if they should repent of their error.

Even more striking proof of Pope John's complete capitulation before the Emperor was the reply[30] he made to a request for a formal opinion on three questions of theology. In his answer, Pope John once more gave his *imprimatur* to the Emperor's *professio fidei* and then in his own words, or in quotations from Greek (in a Latin translation) and Latin patristic authorities, unequivocally adopted as his own the Emperor's Theopaschite formula and the dogma that the *uirginem Mariam et proprie et ueraciter dei genetricem matremque dei uerbi ex ea incarnati [fuisse].*

Similarly, three years later, in 536, Pope Agapetus (535—36)[31] endorsed the doctrine expounded by Justinian in the letter that had been sent to Pope John II, (as above), not, he says, because he recognized the authority of laymen in questions of dogma *(non quia laicis auctoritatem praedicationis admittimus)*[32] but because he found Justinian's theology to be in accord with „all the rules of our fathers and with the dogma of the Apostolic See" *(fidem omnibus patrum nostrorum regulis conuenire et apostolicae sedis concordare dogmatibus).*[33] To this statement he appends[34] the full text of Justinian's letter to Pope John, together with the sting in its tail (see note 26 above), as John himself had done (Cod. 1. 1. 8. 7—24). Like John, also, he declares not only that the Emperor's profession of faith was fully orthodox and in harmony with the teaching of Rome, but also threatens to excommunicate anyone who deviates from it.[35]

Thus, by 533, Justinian had made substantial progress towards overturning the agreement of 519, which, at the time, had seemed to involve significant concessions to Rome. In 521[36], Pope Hormisdas had

[29] On the *Akoimetoi*, see H. Bacht, „Akoimeten," *Lexikon für Theologie und Kirche*, 2nd ed., 1 (Freiburg im Br., 1957), 244 f.; S. Vailhé, „Acémètes," *Dictionnaire d'histoire et de géographie ecclésiastiques*, 1 (Paris, 1912), 274—82; J. Pargoire, „Acémètes," *Dictionnaire d'archéologie chrétienne et de liturgie*, 1, 1 (1907), 307—21.

[30] ACO, 4, 2 (1914), 206—210. He sumarizes his position on this point by affirming unambiguously (208.7 ff.) that: unus igitur ex trinitate crucifixus est carne qua factus est, non tamen deitate qua unitus est patri et spiritui sancto, perpessus est, ne et illos crucifixos pariter asseramus; 209.3 f.: Impassibilis deus non dedignatus est homo esse passibilis et immortalis mortis legibus subiacere. Quotation in text: 209.7 f.

[31] *Collectio Avellana* (note 11 above), Ep. 91, CSEL, 35, 1, 342—47.

[32] *Ibid.*, 343.4 ff., n. b. 13 ff.

[33] *Ibid.*, 343. 20 ff., cf. 14 ff.

[34] *Ibid.*, 344—47.

[35] *Ibid.*, 343.18 ff., 22—26.

[36] *Collectio Avellana* (note 11 above), Epp. 236—37, CSEL, 35, 2, 716—33; Johannes Maxentius, *Adversus Hormisdae Epistulam*, 10, 18 f., 41 [40], ACO, 4, 2 (1914), 48. 13—19, 50. 28 ff., 56. 38—41. Cf. Rhaban Haacke, „Hormisdas," *Lexikon für Theologie und Kirche*, 5 (Freiburg im Br. 1960), 483 f.; *idem, ut vid.*, but title page has: Walter Haacke, *Die Glaubensformel des Papstes Hormisdas im Acacianischen Schisma*

withheld ratification of the Theopaschite formula as an orthodox and necessary corollary of the Creed of 451. But barely ten years later, his successors were compelled to ignore the precedent he had established.

These circumstances indicate that, although Justinian declared the Church of Rome to be the *caput omnium ecclesiarum*, he was at the same time determined to assert control over the popes whenever it pleased him to do so. This policy had already begun to manifest itself in 520, when he first suggested that Hormisdas ought to accede to the Theopaschite formula.[37] The Byzantines were not then ready to insist upon this point. But by 533 the popes were no longer able to hold out against their imperial masters, and the Oecumenical Council of 553, with the assent of Pope Vigilius[38], which in the end he was forced to grant, completed the theological revision of the Council of Chalcedon along the lines laid down by the Emperor in his Edictum of 551.

Not all of his successors were so intransigent as Justinian, nor were many of them interested in making doctrinal innovations. But, so far as they wished, and so long as their military position in Italy permitted, i. e., until 751[39], when they lost Ravenna, they kept the Roman pope under subjection. This they did in accordance with their conception of the divine origin and authorization of their rule (see note 4 above). By the middle of the eighth century, the popes succeeded in liberating themselves from bondage to the emperors of Byzantium, and their authority in Italy was greatly strengthened after the defeat of the Byzantines at Bari in 1071. The patriarchs of Constantinople, on the other hand, never won or actively sought independence from the emperor. But national pride and devotion to the Byzantine form of Orthodoxy on the part of the great majority of the people made it impossible for the emperors, despite numerous strenuous attempts, to establish a lasting union with the Roman Church. This passion for autonomy did not affect the patriarchs of Constantinople[40], who were appointed and removed at the pleasure of the emperor, and were therefore always constrained to do his bidding.

Dumbarton Oaks

(*Analecta Gregoriana*, 20 [Rome, 1939]); Caspar, *op. cit.*, 2 (note 1 above), 177—79; E. Amann, „Hormisdas," DTC, 7, 1, 174 f. N. b. ACO, 4, 2, pp. VII—XI.

[37] *Collectio Avellana*, Ep. 235, CSEL, 35, 2, 715 f.

[38] *Ibid.*, Ep. 92 (dated 540), CSEL, 35, 1, 348—54; n. b. §§ 4, 6—8, pp. 349. 15 ff., 350.10—351.10.

[39] See Ostrogorsky, *History of the Byzantine state*, 151.

[40] On the arbitrariness of the emperors in choosing patriarchs, see Vitalien Laurent, „Le rituel de l'investiture du patriarche byzantin au début du XVe siècle," *Bulletin de la section historique de l'Académie Roumaine*, 28 (1947), 218—32; and Franz Dölger, BZ, 31 (1931), 449 f., with both of whom I agree against Louis Bréhier, „Le recrutement des patriarches de Constantinople pendant la période byzantine,", *Actes du VIe Congrés international des études byzantines*, 1 (Paris, 1950), 221—27; *idem*, „L'investiture des patriarches de Constantinople au Moyen Age," *Miscellanea Giovanni Mercati*, 3 (*Studi e Testi*, 123 [Vatican City, 1946]), 368—72. P. P. Sokolow, *The election of patriarchs in Byzantium from the middle of the ninth to the middle of the fifteenth century* (843—1453) (in Russian) (St. Petersburg, 1907), which I have not seen, gives a general survey of canonical regulations, etc.

V

POLITICAL THEORY IN THE LIVES OF
THE SLAVIC SAINTS CONSTANTINE
AND METHODIUS

I. INTRODUCTION

Φραγκίσκου πολλὰ τὰ ἔτη.

In offering this paper in honor of Professor Dvornik's twelfth lustrum, I have a welcome opportunity to express in part something of the gratification, pride, and personal satisfaction all of us at Dumbarton Oaks, and I in particular, feel on this occasion.

While he has been busily engaged turning out a host of significant contributions to Photian and Slavic studies and to the relations between Byzantium and the Slavs which have won him great fame, he has been at the same time preparing a monumental work on Byzantine political theory, which he traces from its earliest beginnings in Semitic and Hellenistic culture down through the age of Justinian I. For this reason, perhaps, the present sketch [1] of the attitude of the Slavic biographers of Constantine-Cyril (to whom I shall refer below as Constantine) and Methodius [2] towards the Byzantine emperor may be of some interest to him as an illustration of the subsequent

---

[1] I am grateful for assistance of various kinds that I have received from my Harvard colleagues, Professor Roman Jakobson, Professor Harry A. Wolfson, and Dr. Svatava Pírková Jakobson, and from Professor Patrick Skehan of the Catholic University of America.

[2] Throughout my researches on this topic, I have relied heavily upon Dvornik's epoch-making *Les légendes de Constantin et de Méthode vues de Byzance (Byzantinoslavica Supplementa*, 1 [Prague, 1933]), to which I refer as Dvornik; in addition, I have used František Pastrnek, *Dějiny Slovanských Apoštolů Cyrilla a Methoda, s Rozborem a Otiskem Hlavních Pramenů (Spisův Poctěných Jubilejní Cenou*, Číslo 14 [Prague, 1902]), which I cite as Pastrnek; F. Grivec, *Vitae Constantini et Methodii versio Latina, notis*

history of the doctrines whose origin and earlier development he is setting forth in his book on this subject.

The conception of the Byzantine emperor as the vicegerent of God on earth, designated to rule over the universe and to promote the welfare of the State, the Church, and all mankind, has its roots deep in pagan antiquity.[3] These ancient theories were expurgated and Christianized by a number of early Christian writers, but chiefly by the ecclesiastical historian, Eusebius of Caesarea, in two important panegyrics on the life of the Emperor Constantine I (306–37): the εἰς τὸν Βίον Κωνσταντίνου βασιλέως (which is better known by its Latin title, *Vita Constantini,* and is either by, or based upon, Eusebius) and the εἰς Κωνσταντῖνον Τριακονταετηρικός (which was written by Eusebius to celebrate Constantine's thirtieth anniversary

dissertationibusque de fontibus ac de theologia SS. Cyrilli et Methodii illustrata (*Acta Academiae Velehradensis,* 17 [1941]), referred to below as Grivec. Cf. also *Idem,* "Quaestiones Cyrillo-Methodianae," *Orientalia Christiana Periodica,* 18 (1952), 113–34 (with references to recent literature); *Idem, Žitja Konstantina in Metodija: Viri, Žitje Konstantina, Žitje Metodija, Pohvala CM, Italska Legenda, Frizinški Spomeniki* (Ljublani, 1951); *Idem, Die heiligen Slavenapostel Cyrillus und Methodius* (Olmütz-Mainz, 1928); Josef Vajs, *Spisy a Projevy Josefa Dobrovského, Svazek XII, Cyril a Metod, Apoštolové Slovanšti* (Prague, 1948). For the latest bibliography on this ever-flourishing subject, see *idem, Byzantinoslavica,* 11 (1950), 138–51.

I usually cite the *Vita Constantini* (VC) and the *Vita Methodii* (VM) by section numbers (Roman numerals) only, which agree in all editions.

[3] Norman H. Baynes, *The Hellenistic civilization and East Rome* (London, 1946); *Idem,* "Eusebius and the Christian Empire," *Annuaire de l'Institut de philologie et d'histoire orientales,* 2 [Mélanges Bidez], 1934, 13–18; Louis Delatte, *Les traités de la Royauté d'Ecphante, Diotogène et Sthénidas* (*Bibliothèque de la Faculté de Philosophie et Lettres de l'Université de Liége,* Fasc. 97 [Liége, 1942]); Johannes A. Straub, *Vom Herrscherideal in der Spätantike* (*Forschungen zur Kirchen- und Geistesgeschichte,* 18 [Stuttgart, 1939]); Andreas Alföldi, "Die Ausgestaltung des monarchischen Zeremoniells am römischen Kaiserhofe," *Mitteilungen des Deutschen Archaeologischen Instituts, Roemische Abt.,* 49 (1934), 1–118; *Idem,* "Insignien und Tracht d. römischen Kaiser," *ibid.,* 50 (1935), 1–171; Erik Peterson, *Der Monotheismus als politisches Problem* (Leipzig, 1935); Erwin R. Goodenough, "The Political Philosophy of Hellenistic Kingship," *Yale Classical Studies,* 1 (1928), 55–102. Cf. Hendrik Berkhof, *Kirche und Kaiser* (Zürich, 1947); Ernst Kantorowicz, "Kaiser Friedrich II. und das Königsbild des Hellenismus," *Varia Variorum, Festgabe für Karl Reinhardt* (Münster-Köln, 1952), 169–93; *Synesii Cyrenensis opuscula,* ed. N. Terzaghi (Rome, 1944), 18ff., 55–57; Christian Lacombrade, *Le discours sur la royauté de Synésios de Cyrène à l'empereur Arcadios* (Paris, 1951), 42–44, 71f.; Harry A. Wolfson, *Philo, Foundations of Religious Philosophy in Judaism, Christianity, and Islam,* 2 (Cambridge, Mass., 1947), 322–438.

as emperor).[4] The emperor was supreme on earth, and few Byzantine rulers would tolerate resistance even in ecclesiastical matters. They convoked oecumenical councils, often participated directly therein, enforced conciliar decisions by royal authority, and, whenever it seemed necessary, took upon themselves the responsibility for the appointment and dismissal of patriarchs, bishops, and abbots. From time to time, of course, churchmen of strong will opposed what they took to be imperial usurpation of ecclesiastical functions, but in general the emperors prevailed even in the formulation of dogma.[5]

[4] For the latest bibliography on Constantine I and the question of the authorship of the *Vita* see Glanville Downey, "The Builder of the Original Church of the Apostles at Constantinople, a Contribution to the Criticism of the *Vita Constantini* Attributed to Eusebius," *Dumbarton Oaks Papers*, no. 6 (Cambridge, Mass., 1951), 53–80; Paul Petit, "Libanius et la *Vita Constantini*," *Historia*, 1, Heft 4 (1950), 562–82.

See now, above all, Paul Orgels, "A propos des erreurs historiques de la *Vita Constantini*," *Annuaire de l'Institut de philologie et d'histoire orientales et slaves*, 12 [Mélanges Henri Grégoire, 4] (1953), 575–611, who announces a detailed examination of the whole problem in the next number of *Byzantion*.

[5] An excellent survey of recent (1938–50) publications on Byzantine political theory is given by Franz Dölger in Franz Dölger, A. M. Schneider, *Byzanz (Wissenschaftliche Forschungsberichte, Geisteswissenschaftliche Reihe*, ed. Karl Hönn, 5 [Bern, 1952]), 93–100. See also Francis Dvornik, "Emperors, Popes, and General Councils," *Dumbarton Oaks Papers*, no. 6 (Cambridge, Mass., 1951), 1–23; George H. Williams, "Christology and Church-State Relations in the Fourth Century," *Church History*, 20 (1951), no. 3, 3–33; no. 4, 3–26; Louis Bréhier, *Les institutions de l'Empire byzantin* (*Le monde byzantin*, 2 [Paris, 1949]), 1–88, 430–46; W. Ensslin, *Zur Frage nach d. ersten Kaiserkrönung durch den Patriarchen und zur Bedeutung dieses Aktes im Wahlzeremoniell* (Würzburg, n.d. [1943?]); Kenneth M. Setton, *Christian Attitude Towards the Emperor in the Fourth Century* (N. Y., 1941); Peter Charanis, *Church and State in the Later Roman Empire, the Religious Policy of Anastasius the First, 491–518* (Madison, Wisconsin, 1939); Gerhard Kittel, *Christus und Imperator* (Stuttgart-Berlin, 1939); Otto Treitinger, *Die oströmische Kaiser- und Reichsidee nach ihrer Gestaltung im höfischen Zeremoniell* (Jena, 1938); Hans Lietzmann, "Der Glaube Konstantins des Grossen," *SB. d. Preussischen Ak. d. Wiss.*, Philos.-hist. Kl. (1937), 263–75; cf. *idem*, "Die Anfänge des Problems Kirche und Staat," *ibid.* (1938), xxxvii–xlvi (undocumented); André Grabar, *L'empereur dans l'art byzantin* (Paris, 1936); Kaarlo Jäntere, *Die römische Weltreichsidee und die Entstehung d. weltlichen Macht des Papstes* (*Annales Universitatis Turkuensis*, Series B, Tom. 21 [Turku, 1936]); Karl Voigt, *Staat und Kirche von Konstantin dem Grossen bis zum Ende d. Karolingerzeit* (Stuttgart, 1936); Max Vogelstein, *Kaiseridee-Romidee und das Verhältnis von Staat und Kirche seit Konstantin* (Breslau, 1930); Valerian Şesan, *Kirche und Staat im römisch-byzantinischen Reiche seit Konstantin dem Grossen, und bis zum Falle Konstantinopels*, 1 (Czernwitz, 1911), of which only the first volume, *Die Religionspolitik d. christlich-röm. Kaiser*, covering the period between 313 and

2. PROVERBS 21:1

The authors of the extant lives of Constantine and Methodius (for which I shall use the conventional abbreviations, VC and VM) accepted the traditional Byzantine notions of the imperial office without question. The author of the VM even goes so far as to say (XIII) that the "heart of the emperor is always in the hand of God." [6] This is a quotation of a part of Proverbs 21:1 ("the king's heart is in the hand of God as the watercourses: He turneth it whithersoever he will"), which, however, apart from the omission of approximately half of the verse, differs slightly from the Biblical text by the addition of the adverb "always." Philologically, perhaps, this emendation is not of particular significance, although it appears in neither the original Hebrew text nor the Septuagint, Aramaic, Latin, Syriac, or Slavonic versions of the Old Testament, nor in any of the medieval citations of this passage known to me.

This is of some interest because Proverbs 21:1 occurs frequently in Byzantine and Latin writers,[7] who often use it in describing the role of the emperor. Of these perhaps the most relevant from the point of view of the VM is Gregory of Nazianzus, whose works Con-

---

380, was ever published; Heinrich Gelzer, "Das Verhältnis von Staat und Kirche in Byzanz," *Historische Zeitschrift*, 86, N.F. 50 (1901), 193ff., reprinted in Gelzer's *Ausgewählte kleine Schriften* (Leipzig, 1907), 57–141; Am. Gasquet, *De l'autorité impériale en matière religieuse à Byzance* (Paris, 1879). As every Byzantinist knows, the literature on this important subject is inadequate. I have given only the most important titles, omitting lesser works like: Adolfo Giobbio, *Chiesa e Stato nei primi secoli del Cristianesimo, 40–476* (Milan, 1914); Caspar Riffel, *Geschichtliche Darstellung des Verhältnisses zwischen Kirche und Staat von d. Gründung des Christenthums bis auf Justinian I.* (Mainz, 1836). Cf. Frank Gavin, *Seven Centuries of the Problem of Church and State* (Princeton, N. J., 1938); Hans v. Schubert, *Der Kampf des geistlichen und weltlichen Rechts* (SB., Heidelberg, Philos.-hist. Kl., 1926–27, 2.Abh.). Much valuable information is to be found in the pertinent volumes of the *Histoire de l'Église*, ed. A. Fliche and V. Martin; K. Bihlmeyer-H. Tüchle, *Kirchengeschichte;* and other general works.

[6] Dvornik, 390f. All the versions have "always": Pastrnek, 234; *Vita Sancti Methodii*, ed. Fr. Miklosich (Vienna, 1870), 20f.; *Fontes rerum bohemicarum*, Tom. 1, *Vitae sanctorum et aliorum quorundam pietate insignium*, ed. Josef Emler (Prameny dějin Českých, vydávané z Nadání Palackého [Prague, 1873]), 50.

[7] On Proverbs 21:1 note, *inter plurimos*, Irenaeus, *Adv. haereses*, 5, 24, 1, ed. W. W. Harvey, 2 (Cambridge, England, 1857), 388; Adamantius, *Dialogus*,

stantine esteemed so highly that he was said by his biographer
(VC III) to have memorized them all.[8] In addressing the emperors,
Gregory said,

Emperors, revere the purple, . . . understand how much has been
entrusted to you, and with what great awe you are surrounded. The whole
world is beneath your hand, ruled by a small crown and a short garment.
The universe above belongs to God alone; but the world beneath belongs
also to you. Be gods to your subjects, if I may use a bold phrase. We
both say and believe that "the heart of the emperor is in the hand of God."
Here let your power be, not in gold and armies. . . .[9]

At approximately the same time Proverbs 21:1 was quoted in three
orations of the pagan rhetor, Themistius, whom the Emperor
Theodosius I (379–95) admired so greatly that he conferred upon
him a succession of high imperial dignities. Themistius praises these
words from the "Assyrian writings," as he calls the Old Testament,
and uses them to prove that the emperor must devote himself to good
deeds, justice, humanity, and godlike behavior, or forfeit divine
protection.[10]

1, 20, ed. W. H. van de Sande Bakhuyzen, GCS (= *Die griechischen christlichen
Schriftsteller*), 4 (Leipzig, 1901), 40.14; John Chrysostom, *In Salomonis
Proverbia commentariorum reliquiae*, MPG, 64, 725B; Procopius of Gaza,
Comment. in Prov., MPG, 87.1, 1429C; ACO (= *Acta conciliorum oecumeni-
corum*), ed. Eduard Schwartz, 1.1.3, 89.146; 1.2, 26.176, 99.19; 1.4.2, 60.34,
77.19; 2.5, 42.7, 44.33, 97.22; 3, 32.22.

This text occurs frequently in Latin authors also; e.g.: Cyprian, *Testimonia*,
3, 80, CSEL (= *Corpus scriptorum ecclesiasticorum Latinorum*), 3.1, 173.10;
Ambrose, *Expositio Ps. CXVIII*, 14, 30, CSEL, 62, 318.15; Augustine, Ep. 105,
7 and 12, CSEL, 34, 600.4, 603.17f.; *Idem, Contra litteras Petiliani*, 2, 86,
190, CSEL, 52, 117.29; *Idem, Contra Gaudentium*, 1, 39, 53, CSEL, 53, 253.12ff.;
cf. *Idem, De gratia Christi*, CSEL, 42, 144.5; Jerome, *In Hieremiam Prophetam*,
3, 81, CSEL, 59, 218.9, cf. *ibid.*, 1, 74, p. 55. 9f.; *Epistulae (Collectio Avellana)*,
58, 84, CSEL, 35.1, 133.1f., 321.17f.; Eugippius, *Excerpta ex operibus S. Aug.*,
CSEL, 9, 914.10ff.

Proverbs 21:1 does not appear among the Old Testament lections in the
Greek liturgy: it is not cited by Alfred Rahlfs in the index of his "Die alttesta-
mentlichen Lektionen d. griechischen Kirche," *Nachrichten von d. königl.
Gesellschaft d. Wiss. zu Göttingen*, Philol.-hist. Kl., 1915, 28–136.

[8] Dvornik, 78, 109f.; Grivec, 12f., 56ff., 168–170, who reports that Gnidovec,
a pupil of his, has demonstrated in detail that the VM follows closely the model
of Gregory Nazianzen's homily in honor of Athanasius.

[9] *Oratio* 36 (*De seipso*, εἰς ἑαυτόν), 11, MPG, 36, 277C.

[10] *Themistii orationes ex codice Mediolanensi emendatae a Guilielmo Dindorfio*
(Leipzig, 1832), *Orat.* 7, 107.11ff. [= 89d]; *Orat.* 11, 175.17ff. [= 147 bc];
Orat. 19, 278.28ff. [= 229a]. In the first of these Themistius gives the text as

This text occurs also in the *Collectio Avellana*, in a letter which was written by Pope John II of Rome (533–35) to the Emperor Justinian I (527–65) and later inserted by Justinian into the *Codex Justinianus*, whence it passed into the *Basilica*, the law code begun during the reign of the Emperor Basil I (867–86), under whom both Constantine (d. 869) and Methodius (d. 885) were active. Somewhat before this, John of Damascus (d. 749), an author apparently known to our hagiographer, cites Proverbs 21:1 in the section of the *Sacra Parallela* devoted to "the good king who hates evil" (περὶ βασιλέως χρηστοῦ καὶ μισοπονήρου). John reproduces our passage twice, once by itself, and once together with Gregory's comment thereon, partially translated above.[11]

The author of the VM cites Proverbs 21:1 to explain how the Emperor Basil I was inspired by God to frustrate the machinations of the enemies of Methodius by recalling him to Constantinople. His insertion of the adverb "always" (*prisno*) into the Biblical quotation shows that he was so thoroughly imbued with the Byzantine conception of the divine attributes of the kingship that, consciously or subconsciously, he intensified the meaning of the original and broadened the sanction of imperial authority suggested thereby into something like a doctrine of universal imperial infallibility. The addition of this word, though possibly inadvertent, betrays complete and unreserved endorsement of the traditional Byzantine notion of the intimate relation between God and his vicegerent, the emperor.

This is borne out by other references to the emperor in both the VC and the VM. Even the Chazars, who in the middle of the ninth century were allies of Byzantium, believed the Byzantine kingship

---

ὁ νοῦς τοῦ βασιλέως ἐν τῇ τοῦ θεοῦ παλάμῃ δορυφορεῖται. In the other two he substitutes καρδία for νοῦς; the Septuagint has ὥσπερ ὁρμὴ ὕδατος, οὕτως καρδία βασιλέως ἐν χειρὶ θεοῦ. On Themistius see Willy Stegemann, Pauly-Wissowa-Kroll-Mittelhaus, *Real-Encyclopädie d. klassischen Altertumswiss.*, Zw. Reihe [R-2], 5 (Stuttgart, 1934), 1642–80. A critical text and translation of the orations is now being prepared by my colleague, Professor Glanville Downey.

[11] *Corpus Iuris Civilis*, 2, ed. Paul Krueger, 10th ed. (Berlin, 1929), 10; *Epistulae (Collectio Avellana)*, 84, CSEL, 35.1, 321.17f.; *Basilicorum libri LX*, 1, 1, 8, edd. G. E. Heimbach et C. G. E. Heimbach, 1 (Leipzig, 1833), 9.5f.; Βασιλικά, ed. J. D. Zepos, 1 (Athens, 1896), 11; John of Damascus, *op. cit.*, Tit. 9, MPG, 95, 1288D (where the editor of Migne incorrectly cites Proverbs 21:1 as 21:4), 1289 CD. On the biographers' knowledge of John of Damascus, see Dvornik, 78; Grivec, 173.

to be of divine origin. In asking (VC VIII) the emperor for a
learned missionary to combat the arguments of the Jews and Arabs
and so to lead them to accept the Christian faith, the Chazars said,

> Since you are a great nation and hold your Empire from God, we ask
> your counsel and pray you to send us a man of letters in order that we
> may be converted to your faith, if he refutes [the arguments] of the
> Hebrews and the Saracens.[12]

In VC XI one of the Saracens, convinced by Constantine's arguments
against the Jews and Muslims, remarks, with the approval of Constantine and his own people, that "God gave the Christian emperor
power over all people and the greatest of wisdom."

3. DANIEL 2

One of the most interesting and impressive statements of the
heavenly descent of the Byzantine Empire is to be found in VC X,
in connection with the exegesis of the second chapter of Daniel, which
contains Daniel's interpretation of the dream of Nabuchodonosor
(*vulgo*: Nebuchadnezzar). In the words of Daniel (2:31–35, cf. 45),

> Thou, O king, sawest, and, behold, a great image. This image, which was
> mighty, and whose brightness was excellent, stood before thee; and the
> aspect thereof was terrible. As for this image, its head was of fine gold,
> its breast and its arms of silver, its belly and its thighs of brass, its legs
> of iron, its feet part of iron, and part of clay. Thou sawest till that a stone
> was cut out without hands, which smote the image upon its feet that were
> of iron and clay, and brake them in pieces . . . and the stone that smote
> the image became a great mountain, and filled the whole earth.

In discussing this dream of Nabuchodonosor of a mighty image
destroyed by a great stone, which then filled the whole earth, the
Jews and Constantine agreed that the image (or, more properly, as
we learn from Daniel 2:41 and the medieval commentators, the feet
and toes of the image) represented the Roman Empire, and that the
great stone "cut out without hands" was the Anointed One. If all this
is so, the Jews ask, and if the Anointed One (= the Messiah,
Christ) has really come, how is it that the Roman Empire still
exists? To this Constantine replies,

[12] Dvornik, 358.

It [the Roman Empire] no longer exists but has passed away like all the rest, according to the image; our Empire is not that of Rome but that of Christ, as the prophet said, "God shall set up a kingdom which shall never be destroyed, nor shall the sovereignty thereof be left to another people; but it shall break in pieces and consume all these kingdoms, and it shall stand for ever" (Daniel 2:44). Is not the Christian kingdom [which exists] now called by the name of Christ? The Romans worshipped idols. But the others [the Christians], whether of one nation or another, or of one race or another, govern in the name of Christ. . . .[13]

Thus Constantine in this passage accepts the Byzantine Empire as the kingdom of Christ, the fulfilment of prophecy. Grivec in his note *ad locum* points out that in VC VI Constantine describes the Byzantine Empire as a continuation of the Roman Empire, and explains Constantine's remarks here as an exaggeration ascribable to his ardent Byzantine patriotism. Actually, however, what the biographer has Constantine say about the Roman Empire's already having come to an end and its having been superseded by the rule of Christ, though at first glance somewhat startling, is nothing more than one would expect of a devout missionary in the latter part of the ninth century. Archbishop Arethas of Caesarea (*ca.* 895), a disciple of the Patriarch Photius, and a contemporary of the hagiographer who wrote the VC, distinguishes carefully between the pagan Roman rule from Augustus to Diocletian, which had been destroyed, and the Christian Roman rule that began with Constantine. This he does in his commentary on the New Testament Book of Revelation, as Andrew, his source (*ca.* 563–614) and predecessor in the archepiscopal see of Caesarea, whom he reproduces almost verbatim, had done before him.[14] Likewise, the biographer of Constantine makes it very clear in the portion of his work translated above that the Roman Empire he regards as having perished was that in which the worship of idols prevailed, whereas the new régimes were Christian, as he says, and governed in the name of Christ.

[13] Dvornik, 365; Pastrnek, 185f.; Grivec, 74f. The question asked of Constantine by the Jews occurs also in the so-called Dialogue of Adamantius (περὶ τῆς εἰς θεὸν ὀρθῆς πίστεως), ed. W. H. van de Sande Bakhuyzen, GCS, 4, 48–51. Here, too, the Christian (Adamantius) is asked to interpret Daniel 2:34f., which, however, he interprets as applying to the Second Coming.

[14] Andrew, *Commentarius in Apocalypsin*, 54, MPG, 106, 380D–381A: μετὰ δὲ τούτους, ἐν τῇ πρεσβυτέρᾳ Ῥώμῃ τὴν τῶν Ῥωμαίων ἰσχύν, ἐπὶ μὲν Αὐγούστου Καίσαρος . . . ὑπὸ δὲ ἀσεβῶν μέχρι Κωνσταντίνου τοῦ Μεγάλου κατασχεθεῖσαν· ὧν μετὰ τὴν κατάλυσιν, εἰς τὴν νέαν Ῥώμην, τὰ τῶν φιλοχρίστων βασιλέων

But these observations do not completely account for the interpretation of Daniel here involved. To do justice to this aspect of the question, we must survey briefly the medieval treatment of this subject. As we shall see, the statements made by the author of the VC reflect not only the Byzantine exegesis of the Book of Daniel, especially in the form current in Latin writers of the eighth and ninth centuries, but also traditional Byzantine theory on the character of the kingship, on the relation of the emperor to God and Christ, and on the nature of the kingdom of God.

Christian writers like Irenaeus, Tertullian, Origen,[15] Hippolytus,[16]

μετηνέχθη βασίλεια. Cf. *ibid.*, 53, 376A: ἡ γὰρ παλαιὰ 'Ρώμη ἐκ πολλοῦ τὸ τῆς βασιλείας κράτος ἀπέβαλεν. Arethas, *ibid.*, 54, 721B; cf. *ibid.*, 36, 673B (*ad fin.*): ἢ τὴν 'Ρωμαίων ἀρχὴν ἀπολλυμένην διὰ τῆς εἰς πολλὰ διαιρέσεως σφαγῆς τρόπον νομισθῆναι (cf. *ibid.*, 672C).

The more common belief, before the end of the eighth century at least, was that the Roman Empire would last until the end of time — until the Second Coming. This is the notion prevailing in the authors cited in notes 15–30 below. See also the late apocalyptic texts published by Athanasius Vassiliev, *Anecdota Graeco-Byzantina* (Moscow, 1893), 35; Methodius of Patara, περὶ τῆς βασιλείας τῶν ἐθνῶν καὶ εἰς τοὺς ἐσχάτους καιροὺς ἀκριβὴς ἀπόδειξις, ed. V. Istrin, *Revelation of Methodius of Patara and Apocryphal Visions of Daniel* (Čtenija v imperatorskom obščestve istorii i drevnostej Rossijskix pri Moskovskom Universitete [Moscow, 1897], Pt. 4), 23.12ff., 24.7ff., 45f., 64.15ff., 82.9ff. Cf. Helmut Werner, *op. cit.* (n. 54 below).

[15] Irenaeus, *Adv. haereses*, 5, 26, 1f., ed. W. W. Harvey, 2 (Cambridge, England, 1857), 394f. Cf. *ibid.*, 118 (3, 26, 2), 222 (4, 34, 10); John Lawson, *The Biblical Theology of St. Irenaeus* (London, 1948), 280; Tertullian, *Adv. Marcionem*, 3, 7, CSEL, 47, 386.2off.; Origen, *In Genesim*, 4, MPG, 12, 60 AB.

Daniel 2:31–36, 44f. is read in the Greek Liturgy on Christmas Day: A. Rahlfs, *op. cit.* (in n. 7 above), cf. 62, but perhaps no exegetical conclusion should be drawn from this fact, since Isaiah 11:1–10, a famous text on the glories of the Messianic kingdom, is also one of the lections for this occasion.

On the Book of Daniel in general, see Robert H. Pfeiffer, *Introduction to the Old Testament* (2d ed., N. Y., 1942), 748–81, 875; J. A. Montgomery, *A Critical and Exegetical Commentary on the Book of Daniel* (N. Y., 1927); R. H. Charles, *Critical and Exegetical Commentary on the Book of Daniel* (Oxford, 1929).

For the medieval exegesis, see Josef Adamek, *Vom römischen Endreich d. mittelalterlichen Bibelerklärung* (Würzburg, 1938), an excellent work; Leroy E. Froom, *The Prophetic Faith of our Fathers*, 1 (Washington, D. C., 1950), a book of over 1,000 pages, the first installment of a monumental history of the interpretation of Biblical prophecies in four volumes, which, though apologetic in purpose and occasionally homiletical in tone, provides a valuable survey of a great mass of material; L. Bigot, "Daniel," *Dictionnaire de théologie catholique*, 4.1 (Paris, 1939), 63–103, brief but important; Edm. Kocken, *De Theorie van de vier Wereldrijken en van de Overdracht der Wereldheerschappij tot op Innocentius III* (Nijmegen, 1935); Max Hackelsperger, *Bibel und mittelalterlicher*

Eusebius,[17] Aphraates,[18] John Chrysostom,[19] Jerome,[20] Sulpicius Severus,[21] and Theodoretus [22] believed that Daniel had understood the vision of Nabuchodonosor to refer to the empires of Babylonia,

---

Reichsgedanke, Studien und Beiträge zum Gebrauch d. Bibel im Streit zwischen Kaiser und Papsttum zur Zeit d. Salier (Munich diss., Bottrop i. W., 1934). Cf. also Ed. Hertlein, *Der Daniel d. Römerzeit* (Leipzig, 1908); Conrad Trieber, "Die Idee d. vier Weltreiche," *Hermes*, 27 (1892), 321–44. I have not been able to obtain Franz X. Düsterwald, *Die Weltreiche und das Gottesreich nach den Weissagungen des Propheten Daniel* (Freiburg i. Br., 1890).

[16] *In Danielem*, 2, 1–13; 4, 7f., ed. G. N. Bonwetsch and Hans Achelis, GCS, 1, 1, 46ff., 200ff.; 1, 2, 14ff. (*De Antichristo*). See also the edition, with introduction by Gustave Bardy, ed. and transl. by Maurice Lefèvre in the *Sources chrétiennes* (Paris, 1947), 128ff., 274ff. Adolf Hamel, *Kirche bei Hippolyt von Rom* (Gütersloh, 1951), gives a complete bibliography; cf. Karl J. Neumann, *Hippolytus von Rom in seiner Stellung zu Staat und Welt* (Leipzig, 1902), 67ff.

[17] *Demonstratio Evangelica*, 15, frag. 1, ed. I. A. Heikel, *Eusebius Werke*, 6, GCS, 23, 493f.

[18] *Demonstratio*, 5, 11–14 (on Daniel 2), 15ff. (on Daniel 7), *Patrologia Syriaca*, 1, 1 (Paris, 1894), 206ff.

[19] *In Danielem*, 2, MPG, 56, 199–210, espec. 206ff. Pseudo-Chrysostom identifies the fourth empire as that of Rome, but he does not associate the vision of Daniel in chapter two with the Second Coming and the Last Judgment. On the contrary, he suggests that, although it is probably improper when dealing with human affairs to assume that any empire could be everlasting, it is nevertheless possible that there may be some such empire (209.2ff.). Similarly, he says that the monarchs mentioned in Daniel 2:44 ("In the days of those kings shall the God of heaven set up a kingdom which shall never be destroyed") were the Roman emperors (208 *ad fin.*, 209.6f.: ἐν ταῖς ἡμέραις τῶν βασιλέων ἐκείνων, τῶν Ῥωμαίων δηλονότι), and that the prophecy of Daniel could be interpreted as applying to the present (209.23ff.: εἰ δὲ βούλοιτό τις καὶ ἐν τῷ παρόντι καιρῷ λαμβάνειν τὴν προφητείαν, οὐκ ἂν ἁμαρτήσεται. Καὶ γὰρ καὶ νῦν συνέτριψε (*sc.* ὁ θεὸς) τὰς βασιλείας, τὸν τῦφον Μακεδόνων [καὶ] τὸ κῦρος [τῶν Ῥωμαίων]. The words added in brackets here have been suggested by the editor in a footnote, and may have originally stood in the text. If we accept this plausible emendation, the last sentence in the above quotation could then be translated, "For God has destroyed empires even in our own day — the pride of Macedon and the might of Rome." Under this hypothesis, pseudo-Chrysostom would become an early witness, and possible source, for the exegesis discussed below in connection with Andrew, Arethas, Autpertus, and their followers. It is not impossible that such ideas were circulating in Greek and that the author of the VC had had access to them. The author of this commentary has not been identified; see Chrysostomus Baur, *Der heilige Johannes Chrysostomus und seine Zeit*, 1 (Munich, 1929), 238. Chrysostom himself believed that the Roman Empire was the last of the four kingdoms and would survive until the appearance of the Antichrist: Hartung, *op. cit.* (n. 53 below), who quotes Chrysostom on II Thessalonians 2, Homilia 4 (MPG, 62, 485ff.).

[20] *In Danielem*, 2, MPL, 25, 503Cff.; cf. Victorinus, *In Apocalypsin*, ed. J. Haussleiter, CSEL, 49, 150.

[21] *Chronica*, 2, 3, CSEL, 1, 58f. Sulpicius Severus awaits the eternal kingdom

Persia, Greece, and Rome, and had prophesied that the last of these (stated by them to be the Roman Empire) would be destroyed and would be succeeded by the Last Judgment and the inception of the heavenly kingdom, ushered in by Christ in his Second Coming. The four beasts in the vision of Daniel 7 were explained in very similar terms.

But, Theodoretus notes, another school of commentators, whom he does not name, had a different theory, and saw in the last of the kingdoms a reference to the Greek empire of Alexander the Great and his successors — Macedonians, Ptolemies, Seleucids, and Antigonids. In designating the fourth kingdom as the Roman Empire, Theodoretus argues that verses 44 and 45 of the second chapter of Daniel (pp. 17 and 24) presaged the Second Advent of Christ, the end of mortal existence, and the coming of the kingdom of heaven. Since nothing human is everlasting, he says, and no kingdom of men endures forever, the eternal kingdom predicted by Daniel could not have been an earthly one. Moreover, he contends, it is improper to assume, as some did, that Daniel had here prophesied Christ's first appearance on earth, for the Roman Empire did not disappear to make way for the heavenly kingdom, as he believes Daniel's words meant that it would.[23]

Apparently the chief early exponent of the exegesis reprehended by Theodoretus was Ephraem Syrus, the famous Syrian theologian and scholar of the fourth century (d. 373), whose works exerted a profound influence on Byzantine religious thought. This theory of interpretation was not altogether original with Ephraem, who probably borrowed some elements of it from the famous but no longer extant polemic, *Contra Christianos*, of the Syrian Neoplatonist, Porphyry (d. *ca.* 304), which we know only from the fragments preserved in the writings of his Christian opponents.

---

of Christ in the future, but he regards that part of the prophecy which applies in his judgment to the division of the Roman Empire as already fulfilled. He thus provides a transition to the theories of Andrew, Arethas, and Autpertus presented below.

[22] *In Danielem*, 2, MPG, 81, 1296C–1309C.

[23] MPG, 81, 1305C–1309B. For the sake of simplicity I shall not discuss. Daniel 7, for the exegesis of which see the literature cited in n. 15 above. Cf. Nikolaus Reitter, *Der Glaube an die Fortdauer des römischen Reiches im Abendlande während des 5. und 6. Jahrhunderts dargestellt nach den Stimmen d. Zeit* (Diss., Münster, 1900).

V

The chief innovation derived by Ephraem from Porphyry, whose
pagan and pro-Jewish ideas he of course completely rejected, seems
to have been the repudiation of the traditional Byzantine view that
it was the Roman Empire that had been represented by Daniel as
the last of the four kingdoms. According to Ephraem, the four kingdoms were Babylonia, Media, Persia, and that of Alexander, the
last of which overcame the world but finally, during the reign of
ten kings (symbolized by the toes of the feet of the image: Daniel
2:33, 41–43) who were never able to attain unity, gave way to the
eternal kingdom founded by God. This analysis differs essentially
from Porphyry's view that the third and fourth kingdoms were
respectively that of Alexander the Great and that of his successors
down through Antiochus Epiphanes. Still, the elimination of Rome
from the vision and the prophecy of doom may have been a reflection
of Porphyry. The everlasting kingdom envisaged by Daniel, Ephraem
says, was not that of the Jews (as we know Porphyry had maintained
it to be) but that which came into being in the time of Christ, who
in the vision is prefigured by the stone cut from the mountain without
hands, as the Virgin Mary is by the mountain. He sees in the
mountain that filled the whole earth a symbol of the spread of the
Gospel throughout the world.

In his section on Daniel 7 Ephraem states that the prophecy of
the four beasts and the four empires which they symbolized foretold
the Second Coming of Christ and the Last Judgment, but he does
not take Daniel 2 in this sense. For him the prophecies of the second
chapter of Daniel had been completely fulfilled by the birth of
Christ. Of course, like all other Christians, Ephraem looked forward
to a final apocalyptic termination of human history, but he did not
associate these eschatological anticipations with the second chapter
of Daniel.[24]

A trace of the influence of Porphyry is preserved by another Syrian
Greek, Polychronius, Bishop of Apamea (d. ca. 430). In one section
of his commentary on Daniel, Polychronius, who was the brother
of the famous theologian, Theodore of Mopsuestia, describes the
third and fourth empires exactly as Porphyry had done, although

[24] *Sancti patris nostri Ephraem Syri opera omnia*, edd. S. E. Assemani,
Petrus Benedictus, 2 (*Syriace et Latine*, Rome, 1740), 204–206 (espec. 205F–
206F) on Daniel 2, 213–216 on Daniel 7; Georg Moesinger, *Evangelii concor-*

at another point he speaks of Alexander as the ruler of the fourth empire.[25]

In the middle of the sixth century the views of Ephraem were adopted and expounded by Cosmas Indicopleustes, who, through Mar Aba (known in Greek as Patricius, Catholicos of Persia, 540–52) and Thomas of Edessa, had been exposed to Syrian theological principles. Cosmas refers the visions in both Daniel 2 and 7 to the birth and earthly career of Christ and the propagation of the Gospel. He does not link these texts with eschatology,[26] although Ephraem himself had done so in his annotations on Daniel 7. On the Advent of Christ, Cosmas says, the four empires (of the Babylonians, the Medes, the Persians, and the Macedonians, together with the successors of Alexander of Macedon) had all ceased to be; and at this moment the eternal and indissoluble kingdom of Christ began.[27] According to Cosmas, the last of the empires — that of the Macedonians — extended down through the Diadochi, who had inherited the realm of Alexander, as far as Antiochus Epiphanes,[28] but did not include the Roman Empire, since the latter was, he says, neither a part of the succession of the empire of Nabuchodonosor nor of that

---

dantis expositio facta a Sancto Ephraemo doctore Syro (Venice, 1876), 22, 193. An invaluable index to the Biblical citations of Ephraem is provided by James Hamlyn Hill, *A Dissertation on the Gospel Commentary of S. Ephraem the Syrian with a Scriptural Index to his Works* (Edinburgh, 1896), 121–69, *q.v.* On Porphyry, see Adolf von Harnack, *Porphyrius, "Gegen die Christen," 15 Bücher, Zeugnisse, Fragmente und Referate* (*Abhandlungen d. königl. Preussischen Ak. d. Wiss.*, Philos.-hist. Kl. [Berlin, 1916], 1.Abh.), frag. 43, p. 67ff., espec. 67f., which is to be found also in MPL 25 in Jerome's refutation. Cf. Pierre de Labriolle, *La réaction païenne* (Paris, 1934), 267.

[25] Angelo Mai, ed., *Scriptorum veterum nova collectio*, 1 (Rome, 1825–31), third pagination, 3f. (on Dan. 2), 11 (Dan. 7.7); cf. *Timothy's Apology for Christianity* (dated *ca.* 781), ed. and transl. A. Mingana, *Woodbrooke Studies*, 2 (Cambridge, England, 1928), 38f., where the Medes and the Persians are said to represent the second and third kingdoms in Dan. 2 and 7.

[26] *The Christian Topography of Cosmas Indicopleustes*, ed. E. O. Winstedt (Cambridge, England, 1909), 78.20–81.23, 198.5–21. See my articles in *Dumbarton Oaks Papers*, No. 3 (Cambridge, Mass., 1946), 76f., 80; and No. 6 (*ibid.*, 1951), 156. Cf. Jacob of Sarug (d. 521), *Homiliae selectae Mar-Jacobi Sarugensis*, ed. Paul Bedjan, 4 (Paris-Leipzig, 1908), 491ff.

[27] Winstedt, 78. 32–79.7, 8–17, 79.30–80.21.

[28] Winstedt, 77.18–78.19. Cosmas here distinguishes the Macedonian Empire (that of Alexander) from that of the latter's successors, as Porphyry had done, but on the following page (Winstedt, 79.2–7) he shows that he really groups them together as a single entity.

of the Macedonians.[29] On the contrary, Cosmas goes on, when Daniel (2:44) said,

And in the days of those kings shall the God of heaven set up a kingdom which shall never be destroyed, nor shall the sovereignty thereof be left to another people; but it shall break in pieces and consume all these kingdoms and it shall stand for ever,

he had reference primarily to the Lord Christ, but symbolically also (αἰνιγματωδῶς) to the Roman Empire, which came into being contemporaneously with Christ. Thus, since Christ condescended to be recorded in the census of the Roman Empire and to pay taxes thereto, the Roman Empire shares in the merits (τῶν ἀξιωμάτων) of the kingdom of Christ, and, surpassing all others, so far as is possible in this life, will remain unconquered until the consummation of the world (συντελείας).[30]

The Syrian exegesis of Daniel 2 occurs also in a theological dialogue attributed to a certain Anastasius (d. 599) but actually composed, according to its editor, Athanasius Vassiliev (not the late Alex. A. Vasiliev), sometime in the eighth or ninth century and soon thereafter translated from the original Greek into Church-Slavonic. This work contains the elements above summarized, in the context of a dispute among pagans, Jews, and Christians, in the course of which the Christians, relying on Daniel 2 and other Biblical prophecies, maintain that the Messiah had indeed come, and his kingdom had been established.[31]

Almost contemporaneously with the appearance in Arethas of the doctrine that the Roman Empire, viewed as the rule of the pagan

[29] Winstedt, 79.23–25, 80.2–7.

[30] Winstedt, 80.7–26.

[31] *Anecdota Graeco-Byzantina*, ed. Athanasius Vassiliev (Moscow, 1893), 108ff., 119ff. Vassiliev prints two versions of the text entitled respectively: Ἀντιβολὴ γεναμένη ἐν Περσίδι μεταξὺ ἑλλήνων, ἰουδαίων τε καὶ χριστιανῶν περὶ Χριστοῦ τοῦ ἀληθινοῦ θεοῦ ἡμῶν and τὰ λεγόμενα περσικά, ἀναγινωσκόμενα εἰς τὴν τράπεζαν τῇ τῆς Χριστοῦ γεννήσεως ἡμέρᾳ καὶ ἐπὶ τὴν αὔριον. Ἀναστασίου Θεουπόλεως ἐξήγησις περὶ τῶν ἐν Περσίδι πραχθέντων. On the date, see *ibid.*, xxvii–xxxii. Noncommittal as to the precise time of the origin of Christ's kingdom is Peter of Argos (*ca.* 850–920), *In conceptionem S. Annae Oratio*, 11, MPG, 104, 1361A; A. Mai, *Nova patrum bibliotheca*, 9,3 (Rome, 1888), 27. On Peter, see A. A. Vasiliev, "The Life of Peter of Argos and its Historical Significance," *Traditio*, 5 (1947), 163–190.

Cf. also Wilhelm Bousset, *The Antichrist Legend*, trans. A. H. Keane (London, 1896), 41, 50f., 56, 125, 265, and *passim*.

emperors, had been destroyed, the two types of Byzantine exegesis we have been examining were combined in the West in a new and original synthesis. This seems to have been the achievement of Ambrosius Autpertus of Beneventum (d. 781), an older contemporary of Alcuin, the famous Carolingian scholar (*ca.* 730–804), who quickly adopted Autpertus's exegetical scheme and gave it the seal of his approval.[32] These Carolingian exegetes and their associates agreed with the school of Biblical interpretation represented by Irenaeus, Hippolytus, Origen, Jerome, and Theodoretus in fixing upon the Roman Empire as the fourth and last of the earthly kingdoms to which they believed the prophecy of doom in Daniel 2 had reference. Unlike the proponents of this theory, however, the Carolingians did not regard the destruction of the fourth empire as the signal for the Second Coming of Christ and the Last Judgment. Instead, in the manner of Ephraem Syrus, Cosmas Indicopleustes, and possibly, as we have seen, the Pseudo-Chrysostom on Daniel (see n. 19 above), they believed that the fourth empire had already passed away. But they disagreed with Ephraem and Cosmas by holding that this fourth empire was that of Rome. Autpertus and Alcuin apparently felt that the fall of Rome coincided with the incarnation of Christ and the inception of Christ's kingdom. Others (see Berengaudus in n. 36) seem to have put the collapse of the Roman Empire somewhat later.

What led them to suppose that the Roman Empire had already perished is fairly clear. They may, some contend,[33] have come to this

---

[32] *In Apocalypsin*, 4, 7, MPL, 100, 1129 AD, Alcuin does not quite say in so many words that the fourth empire had been destroyed, but this is the inevitable consequence of his interpretation of the feet of the statue in Daniel 2 as symbolizing the Roman Empire, and of his statement that the "stone cut out without hands" is Jesus Christ, who smashed the statue and destroyed it: "Unde et Nabuchodonosor lapidem de monte praecisum sine manibus praefatam statuam percussisse vidit in pedibus ferreis, et comminuisse. Per quem Dominus Jesus Christus designatur de stirpe Judaica sine maritali opere procreatus, qui in pedibus statuam percussit, et cecidit, quia verbi praedicatione extremitatem regni Romanorum tetigit, et praefata saeculi regna salubriter erigenda convertit." This is borne out by Alcuin's reference to Rome in one of his poems as "only a ruin": "Roma, caput mundi, mundi decus, aurea Roma, / Nunc remanet tantum saeva ruina tibi," *Carmen* 9.37f., MGH, *Poetae Latini Aevi Carolini*, ed. H. Duemmler, 1 (Berlin, 1881), 230. Cf. *Libri Carolini*, 2, 19, MPG, 98, 1083; MGH, *Legum Sectio III, Concilia*, II Suppl., ed. H. Bastgen (Hannover-Leipzig, 1924), 77f., which discuss the four kingdoms of Daniel 2 and 7 but identify only three of them, without mentioning the Roman Empire at all.

[33] Josef Adamek, *Vom römischen Endreich d. mittelalterlichen Bibeler-*

conclusion because of what is said to have been the melancholy state of the world at the end of the eighth century, which had had to endure the aggressiveness of the Lombards, the Arab invasions, and such an evil portent as the rule of a woman, the Empress Irene (797–802) in Byzantium — a grievous thing in itself, to be sure, and one of the factors that prompted Charlemagne to claim the imperial title for himself. It is by no means improbable that these circumstances weighed so heavily in the minds of contemporaries as to be regarded as signs of the fall of the Roman Empire. It may be that men thought, like Andrew and Arethas, that the Roman Empire, as a pagan institution, had already ended and had given way to the Christian Empire, as the VC indicates in the section translated above, or that the unity of the Roman Empire had been shattered to such an extent, as Arethas suggests (MPG, 106, 672C; see nn. 14, 36), by the multiplicity of rulers who then held sway over what had once been the domain of Rome that the Empire itself had ceased to exist. It is hardly likely, however, that in the ninth century there was much conscious reminiscence or serious influence of the vague and amorphous but once widely held notion that the world had been scheduled by divine providence to come to an end in the year 6000, which, in the Byzantine reckoning, would have occurred approximately in the year 492.[34]

---

klärung (Würzburg, 1938), 66f.; Hackelsperger (*op. cit.*, n. 15 above), 10f.; Carl Erdmann, *Forschungen zur politischen Ideenwelt des Frühmittelalters* (Berlin, 1951), 21. Cf. Gerhard von Zezschwitz, *Das mittelalterliche Drama vom Ende des römischen Kaisertums deutscher Nation* (Leipzig, 1877).

On Carolingian political theory in general, see the valuable article by Franz Dölger, "Europas Gestaltung im Spiegel d. fränkisch-byzantinischen Auseinandersetzung des 9. Jahrhunderts," reprinted with additions in his *Byzanz und die europäische Staatenwelt* (Ettal, 1953), 282–369, from *Der Vertrag von Verdun 843*, ed. Theodor Mayer (Leipzig, 1943), 203–273. Note the use of the legend, *Christiana religio*, on the reverse of Carolingian coins: Hans Hermann Völckers, "Die Christiana religio-Gepräge, ein Beitrag zur Karolingerforschung," *Hamburger Beiträge zur Numismatik, N.F. d. Veröffentlichungen des Vereins d. Münzfreunde in Hamburg E.V.*, Heft 6/7, vol. 2 (1952–53), 9–54. Dvornik has made an important contribution on the Carolingian conception of the Roman Empire in his book, *The Making of Central and Eastern Europe* (London, 1949), 41–47, and *passim*. I have not seen Gaston Hocquard, "Quelques reflexions sur les idées politico-religieuses d'Alcuin," *Bulletin des Facultés Catholiques de Lyon*, 1952, 13–30.

[34] A. A. Vasiliev, "Medieval Ideas of the End of the World: East and West," *Byzantion*, 16 (1942–43), 462–502; Adamek, *op. cit.*, 44f.

None of the writers discussed in this paper alludes, in the passages I have cited, to the so-called traditional date of the fall of the Western Roman Empire in 476. The Byzantines, it is well-known, to the very end clung to the view that they and their sovereigns were Romans, and that their realm was the lineal descendant of the Roman Empire of Augustus Caesar, which had been transmitted legitimately to them in direct and unbroken succession. But the Carolingians, mindful of the dissolution of Roman and Byzantine dominion in Italy, of Byzantium's loss of Ravenna, and of the crowning of Charlemagne in 800, emphasized the break in the continuity of Roman imperial rule in Italy, as in the words of Frechulf quoted in n. 38. There can be no doubt that the conviction that the old Roman Empire had somehow come to an end was an important factor in the development of Carolingian political theory.

Whatever be the origin of this idea, there is no doubt that Autpertus's interpretation of the second chapter of Daniel[35] was widely accepted in the Latin West, in part, perhaps, because Autpertus had behind him the prestige and authority of Alcuin's endorsement. Autpertus's medium for the dissemination of his doctrine that the Roman Empire had already fallen was a commentary on the New Testament Book of Revelation (the Apocalypse of John), which he had dedicated to Pope Stephen III (767–72). It is not surprising, therefore, that this theory recurs in other Biblical

---

[35] *In Apocalypsim Ioannis Apostoli*, 4 (on Rev. 7.2f.), *Maxima Bibliotheca veterum patrum et antiquorum scriptorum ecclesiasticorum*, ed. M. de la Bigne, 13 (Lugduni, 1677), 488 CDA: "Hoc etiam modo Daniel Propheta sanctissimus, in statua quae Nabuchodonosor nocturna apparuit, saeculi regnum a praeciso de monte sine manibus lapide confractum, regnumque mediatoris nostri totum orbem repleuisse narrauit. . . . Qui [= Christus] videlicet in pedibus statuam percussit, et cecidit: quia verbi praedicatione extremitatem regni Romanorum tetigit, et praefata saeculi regna, quae vnius continebantur tunc regno, salubriter erigenda contriuit. Hinc iam creuit lapis [= Christus] et factus est mons magnus, et impleuit orbem terrarum: quia, illis [= the four empires] ruentibus, regnum eius excreuit, sicut idem Daniel perhibet, dicens [Daniel 2:44]: In diebus autem regum illorum, suscitabit Deus caeli regnum quod in aeternum non dissipabitur, et imperium eius populo alteri non tradetur." A portion of this passage was lifted by Alcuin (see n. 32 above) without change except for the substitution of *convertit* (which occurs in Autpertus a few lines above the extract here reproduced) for the more appropriate *contrivit*, which is retained in another plagiarism of this passage (MPL, 117, 1035A: see n. 37). Cf. Adamek, *op. cit.*, 75; Igino Cecchetti, "Autperto, Ambrogio," *Enciclopedia Cattolica*, 2 (Vatican City, 1949), 499f.

28

commentaries, such as that of Berengaudus (ninth or eleventh century)[36] and those attributed to a certain Haymo of Halberstadt (d. 853), or to Haymo or Remigius of Auxerre (d. 908).[37]

Autpertus wrote his treatise on the Apocalypse considerably before the fateful coronation of Charlemagne on Christmas Day in the year 800, which Charlemagne and his contemporaries regarded as marking the *renovatio imperii*. This belief in the renewal of the Roman Empire at the beginning of the ninth century can be seen in many Carolingian works, including royal documents, a letter of Frechulf of Lisieux (*ca.* 829), and the *De gestis Karoli Imperatoris*, attributed to Notker Balbulus (d. 912). In the last-named text, the shattered image of Nabuchodonosor's dream in the second chapter of Daniel is viewed as a symbol of the end of the Roman Empire, which was succeeded by a new régime inaugurated by Charlemagne.[38]

What is notable in Autpertus and his followers, besides the reiteration of the doctrine that the empire of the Romans, the

[36] *Expositio in Apocalypsin*, PL, 17, 999D–1000B. Cf. Adamek, *op. cit.*, 73; on Berengaudus, see Antonino Romeo, "Berengaudo," *Enciclopedia Cattolica*, 2 (Vatican City, 1949), 1377.

[37] Haymo, *Expositio in Apocalypsin*, 2, 7, MPL, 117, 1034D–1035A; *idem*, *In Epistulam II ad Thessalonicenses*, 2, *ibid.*, 780 BC, cf. 781; *idem*, *Enarratio in Abdiam prophetam*, 1, MPL, 117, 126A: "Romanis, quorum regnum destructum est imperio Christi"; *idem*, *In Isaiam prophetam*, 2, 20 and 51, MPL, 116, 814f., 981C. Cf. Paulus Alvarus of Corduba (*ca.* 800), *Indiculus luminosus*, 21, MPL, 121, 535–536. See Igino Cecchetti, "Aimone di Halberstadt," *Enciclopedia Cattolica*, 1 (Vatican City, 1948), 602–5; W. Neuss, "Remigius v. Auxerre," *Lexikon für Theologie und Kirche*, 8 (Freiburg i. Br., 1936), 815–16.

[38] Frechulf, MGH, *Epistulae*, 5, 319.24ff.: "deficientibus Romanorum imperatoribus seu iudicibus ab Italia, et Gallis, Gothorum quoque regibus, qui successerant, ab eis etiam depulsis"; Notker Balbulus, MGH, *Scriptores*, 2, 731.3ff.: "omnipotens rerum dispositor ordinatorque regnorum et temporum, cum illius admirandae statuae pedes ferreos vel testaceos comminuisset in Romanis, alterius non minus admirabilis statuae caput aureum per illustrem Carolum erexit in Francis." I owe both of these texts to Max Hackelsperger, *op. cit.* (n. 15 above), 11. On Notker, see L. Gulli, *Enciclopedia Cattolica*, 8 (Vatican City, 1952), 1961f.; J. Beckmann, *Lexikon für Theologie und Kirche*, 7 (Freiburg i. Br., 1935), 633f. Cf. Carl Erdmann, *op. cit.* (n. 33 above), 22–24, on Aachen as the Second Rome in place of Byzantium.

On the *renovatio imperii*, see Percy E. Schramm, *Die Anerkennung Karls des Grossen als Kaiser, ein Kapitel aus d. Geschichte d. mittelalterlichen "Staatssymbolik"* (Munich, 1952), 47ff.; *Idem*, *Kaiser, Rom und Renovatio, Studien und Texte zur Geschichte des römischen Erneuerungsgedankens vom Ende des karolingischen Reiches bis zum Investiturstreit*, 1 (*Studien d. Bibliothek Warburg*, 17 [Leipzig-Berlin, 1929]), 38–43.

fourth kingdom of Daniel, had already been destroyed, is the description of the result of Christ's Advent as the kingdom (*imperium*) of Christ.[39]

As a result of this review of the evidence, it can be seen that the assertion of the author of the VC that the Roman Empire had already passed away and had been succeeded by that of Christ may stem in part from Latin sources, which themselves must have been dependent upon several strands of Byzantine exegetical tradition. Nevertheless, though it is possible that the VC on this point may have had some contact with Latin currents of thought, it is obvious that behind Andrew, Arethas, Autpertus, and their imitators in this regard lay a number of axioms of Byzantine political theory, which, when logically applied, abundantly sanctioned the description of the Byzantine Empire as the kingdom of Christ.

4. THE BYZANTINE CONCEPT OF THE KINGSHIP

The empire itself was Christian and eternal;[40] and the emperor was described not only as divine, most Christian, most beloved of God, and perpetual Augustus,[41] but also as the elect one, chosen by

---

[39] See n. 37; cf. also Haymo, *Exp. in Apoc.*, 2, 7, MPL, 117, 1035A, where, after repeating the words of Alcuin quoted in n. 32 above with a few variations, he then adds: "Lapis autem [the stone of Daniel 2, usually taken by the commentators, as we have seen (n. 32 above) to mean Christ] crevit, et suscitatus est in regnum, quod in aeternum non dissipabitur."

[40] ACO (= *Acta conciliorum oecumenicorum*), ed. Eduard Schwartz, 2.3.2, 385.13, 17, 29f.: "Christianissimum et pium uestrum imperium, Christianissima uestra potentia"; *ibid.*, 381.5-7: "orationes offerre domino nostro Christo pro diuturnitate aeterni uestri imperii, qui et inuisibiliter sua bona uoluntate uobis donauit imperium, diui Augusti"; 2.3.3, 505.16f.: "pro aeterna uestra potestate"; 2.3.1, 42.11f.: "incessanter offeramus deo preces pro uestro aeterno imperio, sacratissimi imperatores." Cf. Adamek, *op. cit.* (n. 33 above), 14ff., 60f., 62f.

[41] ACO, 2.1.2, 312.24: θειότατοι αὔγουστοι; 2.2.1, 58.14f.: "sacratissimi imperatoris"; 46.34: "diuino culmine" = θείας κορυφῆς; 47.20: "Christo amabilis" = φιλόχριστος; 43.33, 44.12f., 47.35, 58.1, 59.14, 61.37: "Christianissimi" = φιλόχριστοι; 2.3.2, 435.4: "digni fide, digni Christo"; 435.9: "divinissimus et piissimus noster Dominus"; 380.8, 380.26f.: "petimus diuinitatem uestram"; 1.1.3, 3.4f., 10.27f., 28.22f., 63.24f., 65.5f., et saepe: τοῖς εὐσεβεστάτοις καὶ θεοφιλεστάτοις Θεοδοσίῳ καὶ Οὐαλεντινιάνῳ νικηταῖς τροπαιούχοις ἀεὶ αὐγούστοις. See 1.1.8, 45f., and 2.4, 189f., for an excellent list of imperial titles (Christianissimus, θεοφιλέστατος, etc.). Cf. Louis Bréhier, "L'origine des titres impériaux à Byzance," *Byzantinische Zeitschrift*, 15 (1906), 161-78.

30

God to be his collaborator and messenger,[42] the friend of the Logos-Christ (or of God),[43] who had bestowed upon him sovereignty and power.[44] The rule of the emperor on earth was thus a copy of the eternal heavenly kingdom of God.

For the Emperor, loved by God [as Eusebius says of Constantine], receives from and through Christ the image of supreme sovereignty and is the helmsman who directs the government of all on earth in imitation of God. . . . Adorned with a semblance of heavenly sovereignty, he directs his gaze above, and frames his earthly government according to the pattern of that divine original, finding strength in his imitation of the monarchy of God.[45]

Having received his empire from God, the author of all monarchy,[46] Constantine, conscious of his divine mission, prayed to God to "be merciful and gracious to thy eastern nations" [or people]; and

[42] Eusebius, *Triakontaeterikos*, 9, 14; 10, 7, ed. I. A. Heikel, *Eusebius Werke*, 1, GCS, 7, 220.30–32, 223.15f.; *Idem, Vita*, 2, 41; 2, 73; 3, 10, *ibid.*, 65.26, 71.23, 81.23f.

[43] *Idem, Triakontaeterikos*, 2, 3f., *ibid.*, 199.12–25.

[44] ACO, 2.1.2, 312.22–24; 2.3.2, 381.5–7, cited in n. 40 above; cf. 2.3.3, 504.28ff.: "Deus uobis imperium, ut omnes gubernetis, ad salutem orbis terrarum et pacem sanctarum ecclesiarum iuste donauit"; Eusebius, *Vita*, 4, 29, 4, *loc. cit.*, 129.9–12; cf. *Idem, Triakontaeterikos*, 3,6, *ibid.*, 202.14–18; Otto Schilling, *Naturrecht und Staat nach der Lehre d. alten Kirche* (*Görres-Gesellschaft zur Pflege d. Wiss. im katholischen Deutschland. Veröffentlichungen d. Sektion für Rechts- und Sozialwiss.*, 24. Heft [Paderborn, 1914]), 67f., 116, 131, 153, 167, 215; R. W. and A. J. Carlyle, *A History of Mediaeval Political Theory in the West*, 1, *The Second Century to the Ninth* (Edinburgh-London, 1950), 147–60, 210–18.

[45] Eusebius, *Triakontaeterikos*, 1, 6, *loc. cit.*, 199.1–3; *ibid.*, 3, 5, *loc. cit.*, 201.19–21. Cf. *ibid.*, 5, 2, 203.25–27. On Eusebius's portrayal of the divine character of Constantine's imperial office, see H. Berkhof, *Die Theologie des Eusebius von Caesarea* (Amsterdam, 1939), 53–59; H. G. Opitz, "Euseb von Caesarea als Theologe," *Zeitschrift für die neutestamentliche Wissenschaft*, 34 (1935), 1–19. Cf. Franz Dölger, "Die Kaiserurkunde d. Byzantiner als Ausdruck ihrer politischen Anschauungen," *Byzanz* (cf. n. 33 above), 9–33; F. E. Cranz, "Kingdom and Polity in Eusebius," *Harvard Theological Review*, 45 (1952), 47–66.

[46] See n. 44 above, and Otto Treitinger, *Die oströmische Kaiser- und Reichsidee nach ihrer Gestaltung im höfischen Zeremoniell* (Jena, 1938), 33–39; *Idem*, "Vom oströmischen Staats- und Reichsgedanken," *Leipziger Vierteljahrsschrift für Südosteuropa*, 4 (1940), 1–26; Rodolphe Guilland, "Le droit divin à Byzance," *Eos*, 42 (1947), 142–68; Wilhelm Ensslin, "Das Gottesgnadentum des autokratischen Kaisertums d. frühbyzantinischen Zeit," *Atti del V Congresso internazionale di Studi Bizantini*, 1936, 1 (*Studi Bizantini e Neoellenici*, 5[1939]), 154–66; F. J. Dölger, "Zur antiken und frühchristlichen Auffassung d. Herrschergewalt von Gottes Gnaden," *Antike und Christentum*, 3 (1932), 117–27;

the imperial troops at his direction used in their Sunday prayers to
God a formula in which they said,

> We acknowledge thee the only God; we own thee as our King, and
> implore thy aid. By thy favor have we won the victory; through thee have
> we proved mightier than our enemies. We render thanks for thy past
> benefits and put our faith in thee for future blessings.[47]

This is one of the innumerable texts in which God or Christ is
spoken of as king. In his commentary upon Revelation Arethas
repeats the description of Jesus as the ruler of the kings of the earth
(ἄρχων δὲ τῶν βασιλέων τῆς γῆς), which occurs in Revelation 1:5, and
connects it with Daniel's observation to Nabuchodonosor (Daniel
5:21, in the recension of Theodotion) that the most high God rules
the kingdom of men (κυριεύει ὁ θεὸς ὁ ὕψιστος τῆς βασιλείας τῶν
ἀνθρώπων). Christ is King, Arethas says, over both the spiritual and
the material world.[48]

Of interest, also, on the kingship of Christ is an inscription of the
seventh century from Hauran (Deir-Eyub) in Syria, which dates
a lintel over a church door as having been erected on the 25th day
of July, in the 536th year of the kingship of Lord Christ, which
Waddington says is based on the era of Bostra, and places in the year
641. He explains the clause, κυρίου Ἰησοῦ Χριστοῦ βασιλεύοντος, as a
temporary but innocuous substitute for the Byzantine chronology by

---

idem, "Herrschergewalt hat Gottesmacht," *ibid.,* 128–31; cf. Fritz Kern, *Gottesgnadentum und Widerstandsrecht im früheren Mittelalter (Mittelalterliche
Studien,* 1, 2 [Leipzig, 1914]), 2ff.

[47] Eusebius, *Vita,* 2, 55, 1; 4, 20, *loc. cit.,* 63.24f. (τοῖς σοῖς ἀνατολικοῖς),
125.7ff. Here, and in part of the last sentence quoted in n. 45, I have used the
English translation by Ernest C. Richardson, *A Select Library of Nicene and
Post-Nicene Fathers of the Christian Church,* New Series, 1 (N.Y.C., 1890).

[48] *Comment in Apoc.,* 1 (on Rev. 1:5), 10 (on Rev. 4:7), 43 (on Rev.
14:14), MPG, 106, 508AC, 572B, 693A (ὁ στέφανος τὸν Κύριον Ἰησοῦν βασιλέα
αἰνίττεται. Βασιλεὺς γὰρ τῶν νοητῶν τε καὶ αἰσθητῶν ὁ Χριστός). Cf. Cyril of
Jerusalem, MPG, 33, 1168A (θεῷ τῷ παμβασιλεῖ), 464A (Christ ἔχει τὸ βασιλικὸν
ἀξίωμα . . . τῷ πατρὶ συμβασιλεύων), *et saepissime.* For an interesting descrip-
tion of Christ as king of all the universe, visible and invisible, see Nicephorus
(Patriarch of Constantinople, 806–815), *Antirrheticus III adv. Constantinum
Copr.,* MPG, 100, 397AB, 393B–400A. Cf. Josef Andreas Jungmann, *Die Stellung
Christi im liturgischen Gebet (Liturgiegeschichtliche Forschungen,* Heft 7–8
[Münster in Westf., 1925]), 30, 142 n. 70, 198f.; Adolf von Harnack, *Militia
Christi, die christliche Religion und d. Soldatenstand in den ersten drei Jahr-
hunderten* (Tübingen, 1905), 41, and following n.

imperial regnal years, which, though meaningless during the Arab occupation, the Christians expected soon to be able to resume after what they confidently hoped would be the speedy restoration of Syria to the Byzantine Empire.[49]

The connection between the terrestrial empire and its emperor on the one hand and the heavenly kingdom of God on the other was felt to be so close and intimate that the emperor was regarded as sharing his throne with Christ, and as reigning jointly with God.[50] Similarly, in close conformity with ancient pagan practice, the emperor's person, his possessions and palace, the proceedings of his government, and the royal officers were normally designated as holy, sacred, or divine (ἅγιος, ἱερός, θεῖος, etc.).[51]

Even in the early centuries of the Christian era, during the persecutions, before Christianity became the official religion of the Roman Empire, Christ was offered prayers for the welfare and good fortune of the emperors and the state.[52] At the same time Christian writers, impressed by the rapid spread of Christianity, came to look upon the Roman Empire as the instrument of God's will, especially designed to promote the propagation of the Gospel. Jerome in his commentary on the prophet Micah speaks of the *imperium Christi,* and possibly also of *unius Dei singulare imperium,* as closely bound up with the unity of the Roman Empire.[53]

Many, though convinced that the true end of Christian polity was

[49] Edd. Philippe Le Bas et W. H. Waddington, *Voyage Archéologique, Explication des inscriptions grecques et latines recueillies en Grèce et en Asie Mineure,* Partie 6, Syrie, p. 552, No. 2413 a. Cf. V. Gardthausen, *Griechische Palaeographie,* 2 (2d ed., Leipzig, 1913), 451; Erik Peterson, ΕΙΣ ΘΕΟΣ (*Forschungen zur Religion und Literatur des Alten und Neuen Testaments,* N.F., 24 [Göttingen, 1926]), 162f., 226 n. 1, 315; Ernst Kantorowicz, "Deus Per Naturam, Deus Per Gratiam, a Note on Mediaeval Political Theory," *Harvard Theological Review,* 45 (1952), 253–77.

[50] Treitinger, *Die oströmische Kaiser- und Reichsidee,* 33f., 39f.

[51] *Ibid.,* 41f.

[52] Ludwig Biehl, *Das liturgische Gebet für Kaiser und Reich, ein Beitrag zur Geschichte des Verhältnisses von Kirche und Staat* (*Görres-Gesellschaft,* etc. as in n. 44 above, 75. Heft [Paderborn, 1937]); Gerd Tellenbach, *Römischer und christlicher Reichsgedanke in d. Liturgie des frühen Mittelalters* (*SB. d. Heidelberger Ak. d. Wiss., Philos.-hist. Kl.,* 1934–35, 1. Abh.), 9ff.; Cecil John Cadoux, *The Early Church and the World* (Edinburgh, 1925), 257 n. 9, 386f., 551; (Guilelmus) Wilhelm Mangold, *De ecclesia primaeva pro Caesaribus ac magistratibus Romanis preces fundente* (Bonn, n.d.), is now obsolete.

[53] See besides the texts collected by Tellenbach, *op. cit.,* 9f., Cosmas Indi-

the attainment of the divine, everlasting kingdom of God, which man could not hope for on earth, nevertheless equated the Church so closely with the kingdom of God that the mundane, terrestrial Church, or company of true believers, came to be looked upon as a counterpart or actual, visible, earthly embodiment of the supracelestial kingdom of God. Here, many felt, in the piety and devotion of the faithful, was to be found the kingdom of God on earth. This doctrine is clearly enunciated by Origen, who connected it with Luke 17:21 ("for lo, the kingdom of God is within you"), and also, despite many apparent contradictions, by Augustine in the *De Civitate Dei* (*ecclesia regnum Christi est regnumque caelorum*). Some such conception,[54] especially in its Greek form, may well have counted among the sources for the idea of the author of the VC that the kingdom of Christ had already arrived.

---

copleustes, *Christian Topography*, 2 (edition cited in n. 26 above), 80.7–81.23; Cadoux, *op. cit.*, 386, 561f. Tellenbach cites but misquotes Jerome, *In Michaeam*, 1, 4, MPL, 25, 1188A: "Postquam autem ad imperium Christi singulare imperium Roma sortita est, [et] Apostolorum itineri pervius factus est orbis, et apertae sunt eis portae urbium ad praedicationem, unius Dei singulare imperium constitutum est." The text in Migne is unreadable; but the meaning becomes clear if after *est* we add *et*, the omission of which by haplography is easily understood, and put a comma either before *unius Dei* (so as to give the sense suggested above) or thereafter (to give a somewhat different but equally plausible interpretation). Cf. Adamek, *op. cit.* (n. 33 above), 13 n. 24. Johannes Hartung, *Die Lehre von d. Weltherrschaft im Mittelalter, ihr Werden und ihre Begründung* (Inaug. Diss., Halle a. S., 1909), 22ff.

[54] See Origen, *De oratione*, 25.1, ed. Paul Koetschau, *Origenes Werke*, 2, GCS, 3, 356.26ff. The history of the exegesis of this text, on which I have collected some materials, cannot be discussed here; J. A. Cramer does not print any relevant passages in his *Catenae Graecorum patrum in Novum Testamentum*, 2 (Oxford, 1844), in the section on Luke. Augustine, *De Civitate Dei*, 20, 9, CSEL, 40.2, 450.6f.

Cf. Robert Frick, *Die Geschichte des Reich-Gottes-Gedankens in d. alten Kirche bis zu Origenes und Augustin* (*Beihefte zur Zeitschrift für die neutestamentliche Wissenschaft*, 6 [Giessen, 1928]), 100ff., 138ff.; Elizabeth Pfeil, *Die fränkische und deutsche Romidee des frühen Mittelalters* (*Forschungen zur mittelalterlichen und neueren Geschichte*, herausg. von Albert Brackmann, Fritz Hartung, etc., 3 [Munich, 1929]), 32–42; Cadoux, *op. cit.*, 227f.; Otto Schilling, *Die Staats und Soziallehre des hl. Augustins* (Freiburg im Breisgau, 1910); Étienne Gilson, *Introduction à l'étude de Saint Augustin* (*Études de philosophie médiévale*, 11 [3rd ed., Paris, 1949]), 125–42; Viktor Stegemann, *Augustins Gottes-Staat* (*Heidelberger Abhandlungen zur Philosophie und ihrer Geschichte*, 15 [1928]), 26, 29, 31, et passim; Hans Leisegang, "Der Ursprung d. Lehre Augustins von d. Civitas Dei," *Archiv für Kulturgeschichte*, 16 (1925), 127–58; Sägmüller, "Die Idee von d. Kirche als *imperium Romanum* im kanonischen

34

That the empire and its government were universally recognized as belonging to God (or Christ: see n. 59 below) is proved also by a hymn sung on Easter Monday by the people to the emperor on his way back from the Church of the Apostles to the palace. On this occasion, according to an undated text in the *Book of Ceremonies*, compiled and edited by the Emperor Constantine VII Porphyrogennetus (913–59), the people prayed that "the Godhead may grant you a hundred years to rule its empire" (σὲ ἡ θεότης ἐπὶ χρόνους ἑκατὸν ἀξιώσῃ τὴν ἑαυτοῦ διέπειν πολιτείαν). The *Book of Ceremonies* itself is described in its title as a "treatise . . . truly worthy of the imperial efforts and of the Emperor Constantine, the friend of Christ, and the son, in Christ, the Eternal King, of the most wise Emperor Leo of everlasting memory." [55]

5. I PETER 2:17

When the Emperor Michael III (842–67) asked Constantine and Methodius to undertake the mission to Moravia in response to the request of King Rastislav (VM V), the hagiographer points out, they did as the Emperor wished, for "they obviously could not refuse God and the Empire, since St. Peter (I Peter 2:17) had said, 'Fear God and honor the Emperor.' " [56] The author of the VM quotes only this

---

Recht," *Theologische Quartalschrift*, 80 (1898), 50–80; Helmut Werner, *Der Untergang Roms* (*Forschungen zur Kirchen- und Geistesgeschichte*, 17 [Stuttgart, 1939]), 142ff.; Ernst Staehelin, *Die Verkündigung des Reiches Gottes in d. Kirche Jesu Christi*, 1 (Basel, 1951), contains patristic excerpts on the kingdom of God in German translation.

[55] *De Ceremoniis*, 1, 5, ed., transl. Albert Vogt, *Constantin VII Porphyrogénète, Le livre des cérémonies*, 1 (Paris, 1935), 43.14ff.; 1.1ff.; ed. Reiske, 1, 49.17ff.; 3.2ff.: Κωνσταντίνου τοῦ φιλοχρίστου καὶ ἐν αὐτῷ τῷ Χριστῷ τῷ αἰωνίῳ βασιλεῖ βασιλέως υἱοῦ Λέοντος τοῦ σοφωτάτου καὶ ἀειμνήστου βασιλέως σύνταγμά τι καὶ βασιλείου σπουδῆς ὄντως ἄξιον ποίημα.

[56] Among many quotations of I Peter 2:13–17 note: *Martyrium Polycarpi*, 10, 2; Clemens Romanus, *I Epistula ad Corinthios*, 61, 1, *Patrum apostolicorum opera*, edd. Gebhardt, Harnack, Zahn, 1, 1 (2d ed., Leipzig, 1876), 103f. (with references); Theophilus, *Ad Autolycum*, 1, 11, MPG, 6, 1040f.; Tertullian, *Scorpiace*, 14, CSEL, 20, 177.21ff.; Origen, *Contra Celsum*, 8, 68, *Origenes Werke*, 2, GCS, 3, 285.15; Didymus Alexandrinus, *In Epistolam I S. Petri*, MPG, 39, 1765D–1767B; Augustine, *Speculum*, 44; *Idem, De divinis scripturis sive Speculum*, 94, CSEL, 12, 263.1ff., 614.5ff.; Fulgentius of Ruspe, *Ad Trasimundum*, 1, 2, MPL, 65, 226C; Facundus of Hermiane, *Pro defensione trium capitulorum*, 2, 1, MPL, 67, 559B; M. Aurelius Cassiodorus, *Complexiones canonicarum*

verse, which is derived from Proverbs 24:21 ("My son, fear thou God and the King"), although the passage as a whole (I Peter 2:13–17) is relevant:

> Be subject to every ordinance of man for the Lord's sake: whether to the king, as supreme; or unto governors, as sent by him for vengeance on evil doers and for praise to them that do well. For so is the will of God, that by well-doing ye should put to silence the ignorance of foolish men: as free, and not using your freedom for a cloak of wickedness, but as bond-servants of God. Honor all men. Love the brotherhood. Fear God. Honor the king.

In the patristic exegesis, this portion of the First Epistle of Peter, like Proverbs 21:1 and the second chapter of Daniel, was used to justify the Byzantine imperial government as a part of the divine plan for the universe. According to a commentary thereon attributed to John Chrysostom,[57] Christians must subject themselves to the officials appointed by the emperors, but are released from the obligation of obedience if ordered to violate God's will.[58] This might almost seem to open the way to indiscriminate and wilful resistance to the emperor and his royal officers, but Chrysostom's next words effectively dispose of this possibility and, buttressed by a quotation from Romans 13, which is the most notable chapter in the New Testament that enjoins submission to the higher powers, pronounce resistance to the government as tantamount to opposition to the commandment of God (Romans 13:2: "Therefore he that resisteth the power withstandeth the ordinance of God").

Obedience to human rulers, Chrysostom says, is not inconsistent with piety, since he who yields to the emperor and his agents is not obeying the officials but God. Furthermore, he adds, in expounding upon verse 15 of this same chapter ("by doing good ye put to silence

---

epistularum septem, 6, MPL, 70, 1365 AB; Gregory the Great, *In primum regum expositiones*, 4, 42, MPL, 79, 312C; Eligius Noviomensis, *Homilia* 1, MPL, 87, 595D; Oecumenius of Tricca, *In I Petrum*, 4, MPL, 119, 537A–540D, who comments also on Chrysostom's treatment of this passage, which is discussed below; Photius, *Epistulae*, 1, 14, MPG, 102, 764C; cf. *Idem, Ad Amphilochium*, 179, MPG, 101, 881–883. Note how Fulgentius and Facundus attempt to interpret I Peter 2:17 as a justification for their attack on Justinian's theology.

[57] J. A. Cramer, *Catenae Graecorum Patrum in Novum Testamentum*, 8 (Oxford, 1844), 54–56.

[58] *Ibid.*, 55.1–5.

36

the ignorance of senseless men"), it is not true, as some slanderers
assert, that Christ came to overthrow the government and to teach
contempt for all earthly institutions. Therefore, when these calumnia-
tors see Christians submissive to the civil authorities, they are silenced
and realize that it was wrong of them to disparage the government of
Christ.[59]

All this Chrysostom writes by way of annotation upon I Peter
2:13–15. On verses 16–17 he adds:

whatever the rulers do justly and legally, they do without being called
to task; but when they act unjustly, illegally, and tyrannically, to overthrow justice, they are destroyed, because the righteous judgment of God
reaches all men alike. Therefore, government on earth was established by
God for the welfare of mankind, not, as some say, by the devil, in order
that men, in fear of it, might abstain from devouring each other like fish.
By the imposition of laws the manifold injustice of men is checked.
Accordingly, "the powers that be are ordained of God" (Romans 13:1)
and are the servants of God, as Paul says. It is therefore obvious that the
devil lied when he said, "It [authority] hath been delivered unto me; and
to whomsoever I will I give it" (Luke 4:6). For kings are not ordained
by his command. Some are appointed for the improvement and benefit of
their subjects, and for the preservation of justice; others, to frighten,
punish, correct, and rebuke them, or because of their mockery, insolence,
and excessive pride, according to their deserts before the righteous judgment
of God, as we have said above. Disobedience and lack of submission to the
rulers is wicked. . . .[60]

The admonition of I Peter 2:17 was used also in a later day by
Patriarch Anthony IV of Constantinople (1391–97) in a reply to
the Grand Duke Basil I Dimitrevich (1371–1425) of Moscow. Confronted by the collapse of Byzantine power at the end of the fourteenth century (ca. 1394–97), Basil reaffirmed his loyalty to the
Byzantine Church, but expressed unwillingness to continue to recognize the supremacy of the emperor of Constantinople. Anthony quotes
I Peter 2:17 to prove that there was only one emperor in the world

[59] *Ibid.*, 55.8ff.
[60] *Ibid.*, 55.27ff. For similar expressions on the obligations of Christians to
their rulers, cf. Carlyle (op. cit., n. 44 above), 89–98, 128–131, 161–174, 210–
218; and *The Norman Anonymous of 1100 A.D.*, ed. George H. Williams (Harvard Theological Studies, 18 [1951]), 198f.
    See also Karl Hermann Schelkle, "Staat und Kirche in d. patristischen Ausle-
gung von Rm 13.1–7," *Zeitschrift für die neutestamentliche Wissenschaft*, 44
(1952–53), 223–36.

and that all save the emperor of Constantinople were usurpers and totally unworthy of regard.[61]

6. CONCLUSION

The possibility that Latin influences may be discernible in the VC, alongside of the strictly Byzantine, should occasion no surprize in view of the sojourn of Constantine and Methodius both in Rome and in regions like Moravia and Bulgaria, in which emissaries of the popes and of the Franks had long been active. Indubitable traces of a Western environment have already been noted by Dvornik, as for example in the use of the term *apostolicus* as an epithet for the pope [62] and in the prominence given Sylvester and other Roman pontiffs in the enumeration of the first six oecumenical councils.[63] On the other hand, the unqualified acceptance in the VC and VM of the Byzantine doctrine of the kingship give evidence of a close dependence upon the Constantinopolitan court.

This circumstance may perhaps have some bearing on the much discussed question of the relationship of the two Slavic apostles to the Patriarch Photius (858–67, 877–86). Dvornik maintains that they were his active partisans and allies.[64] But Grivec, because of what appears to be a deep emotional hostility to Photius, whose rehabilitation by Dvornik as orthodox even from the Roman point of view he cannot be induced wholly to accept, insists that they must have been at least neutral in the contest between Photius and the papacy, if not actually supporters of the latter and of Photius's rival, Ignatius (Patriarch, 847–58, 867–77).[65]

Since, however, both Constantine and Methodius seem always to have enjoyed the favor of the Byzantine emperors (Michael III,

---

[61] *Acta et diplomata graeca medii aevi sacra et profana*, 2 (*Acta Patriarchatus Constantinopolitani, MCCCXV–MCCCCII*), edd. F. Miklosich et I. Müller (Vienna, 1862), 191f. For the date, see Georg Ostrogorsky, *Geschichte des byzantinischen Staates* (2d ed., Munich, 1952), 439.

[62] Dvornik, 1, 295–300, 378, 380, 386–390.

[63] *Ibid.*, 300, 383f. (VM I).

[64] *Ibid.*, 33, 52, 44f., 66, 68, 79f., 146f., 313–330; *Idem, The Photian Schism, History and Legend* (Cambridge, England, 1948), 33, 52.

[65] "De ss. Cyrilli et Methodii amicitia dubia cum Photio," *Orientalia Christiana Periodica*, 17 (1951), 192–203; V. Grumel, "Byzance et Photius dans les légendes slavonnes des saints Cyrille et Méthode," *Échos d'Orient*, 33 (1934), 353.

842–67, and Basil I, 867–86) and frequently to have performed missions on their behalf, it is not logical to suppose, in the absence of a single direct statement to this effect in the sources, that they could have withheld their support from the patriarch whom the emperor himself had chosen and championed, at least in the two periods of Photius's incumbency, 858–67 and 877–86, the former of which extends almost to the death of Constantine, who died in 869, and the latter of which goes one year beyond the life of Methodius, who died in 885.

BYZANTINE THEOLOGY

VI

Dedicated to the memory of my mother, Stella Anastos, who
died on January 26, 1962.

Αἰωνία ἡ μνήμη

VI

NESTORIUS WAS ORTHODOX

1. PREFATORY REMARKS ON NESTORIUS AND CYRIL[1]

JUST as all thinking people are said to be either Platonists or Aristotelians, most theologians favor either Nestorius or Cyril. Both have their admirers, who usually assume, with championship of one of the two, an intense dislike for the other. Tradition and the Church (except, of course, for the Nestorians) have handed down a judgment adverse to Nestorius. This is unfortunate, not because Nestorius was always right, as he was not, but rather because both he and Cyril, when measured by the standard of the Fourth Oecumenical Council (held at Chalcedon in 451) and its Creed, which is the major criterion of Christological orthodoxy, have similar—or reciprocal defects.

It should be noted carefully that my dogmatic definitions and the case for Nestorius are based upon the Chalcedonian Symbol and Cyril's *Second Letter to Nestorius*. Except for a brief reference (at note 66 *infra*), I do not discuss the question of the relationship between Nestorius' Christology and that of Cyril's *Third Letter* (with its *Twelve Anathemas*), which did not achieve oecu-

---

[1] I had completed this article before reading Aloys Grillmeier's admirable paper (see *infra*), with which I am in essential agreement. The major difference between us is that I take Nestorius to have been *completely* orthodox, whether judged on the criterion of the Chalcedonian Symbol or from the point of view of speculative theology, whereas he has some reservations. Excellent also is the book (see *infra*) of R. V. Sellers, who argues that Nestorius and Cyril were in reality seeking the same theological goals. His results are very similar to mine except that my method and purpose differ from his.

For the earlier bibliography on Nestorius, see Johannes Quasten, *Patrology*, 3, *The Golden Age of Greek Patristic Literature from the Council of Nicaea to the Council of Chalcedon* (Utrecht-Antwerp-Westminster, 1960), 514–19; Berthold Altaner, *Patrologie*, 5th ed. (Freiburg im Breisgau, 1958), § 72; Eng. transl., Hilda C. Graef (*ibid.*, 1960). See especially Aloys Grillmeier, "Das Scandalum oecumenicum des Nestorius in kirchlich-dogmatischer und theologiegeschichtlicher Sicht," *Scholastik*, 36 (1961), 321–56; Helmut Ristow, "Der Begriff πρόσωπον in der Theologie des Nestorius," *Aus der byzantinistischen Arbeit der deutschen demokratischen Republik (Berliner byzantinistische Arbeiten*, 5 [Berlin, 1957]), 218–36, who makes little use of the *Bazaar*; Luigi I. Scipioni, *Ricerche sulla Cristologia del "Libro di Eraclide" di Nestorio (Paradosis*, 11 [Freiburg, Switzerland, 1956]), is ecclesiastically committed to the traditional condemnation of N., though his approach to N.'s "metaphysics" is fresh and original; Chrysostomus Baur, "Drei unedierte Festpredigten aus der Zeit der nestorianischen Streitigkeiten," *Traditio*, 9 (1953), 101–26: texts with an "Antiochene" Christology; Thomas Camelot, "De Nestorius à Eutyches," *Das Konzil von Chalkedon*, edd. Aloys Grillmeier and Heinrich Bacht, 1 (Würzburg, 1951), 213–42; Henry Chadwick, "Eucharist and Christology in the Nestorian Controversy," *Journal of Theological Studies*, N.S. 2 (1951), 145–64; Aubrey R. Vine, *An Approach to Christology* (London, 1948); G. L. Prestige, *Fathers and Heretics* (London, 1940), 120–79; R. V. Sellers, *Two Ancient Christologies* (London, 1940); É. Amann, "Nestorius," *Dictionnaire de théologie catholique*, 11, 1 (Paris, 1931), 76–157; Friedrich Loofs, *Nestorius and His Place in the History of Christian Doctrine* (Cambridge, 1914); J. F. Bethune-Baker, *Nestorius and His Teaching* (Cambridge, 1908). On the philosophical implications of "Nestorianism," see Harry A. Wolfson, *The Philosophy of the Church Fathers*, 1 (Cambridge, Mass., 1956), 451–63. See special note at the bottom of p. 140.

The sources on which this paper is based are: Paul Bedjan, ed., *Nestorius, Le Livre d'Héraclide de Damas* (Leipzig-Paris, 1910), a critical edition of the Syriac version, against which I have verified the principal texts quoted *infra*; all of the English translations have been taken verbatim from G. R. Driver and Leonard Hodgson, *Nestorius, the Bazaar of Heracleides, newly translated from the Syriac* (Oxford, 1925). Cf. F. Nau, *Nestorius d'après les sources orientales* (Paris, 1911); Friedrich Loofs, *Nestoriana, Die Fragmente des Nestorius* (Halle a. S., 1905); and the immensely learned, extremely detailed, but massively unusable work of Ignaz Rucker, *Studien zum Concilium Ephesinum*, A. *Orientierende Quellenkunde*; B. *Zur Dogmengeschichte nach dem syrischen Liber Heraclidis*, ed. Bedjan, 1910 (1930–35), outlined by the author in B, IV, a, b, c, *Das Dogma von der Persönlichkeit Christi* (Oxenbronn bei Günzburg a. D., 1934), and *idem*, A, III, *Ephesinische Konzilsakten in syrischer Überlieferung (ibid.*, 1935).

120

menical sanction until 553 (see note 8 *infra*), and is therefore irrelevant to the subject of this paper.

Nestorius was condemned at Chalcedon (as also in 431 at Ephesus by the Third Oecumenical Council) for dividing Christ into two separate persons, although he always claimed that he was not guilty of making such a division, and continually affirmed his belief in the oneness of Christ. On the other hand, Cyril, who was enthusiastically acclaimed at both Ephesus and Chalcedon, formulated a Christology which many deem to be in direct conflict with that of 451. He repeatedly declares Christ to have been both divine and human, God and man. But his critics complain that, in his advocacy of the "hypostatic union" and the Apollinarian Christological formula, μία φύσις τοῦ Θεοῦ Λόγου σεσαρκωμένη ("one incarnate nature of God the Word"), which he mistakenly took to be Athanasian in origin, he lost sight of Christ's human nature. Curiously, in the appraisal of Nestorius and Cyril, it can be shown that the case for each rests mainly upon his understanding and use of a single word, to which he assigned contradictory meanings. The decisive term for Nestorius was πρόσωπον (person), which he used in two different senses; and Cyril[2] had similar difficulty with φύσις (nature).

Both were guilty of flagrant inconsistency. But both obviously meant to be what we call orthodox; and the more this question is studied, the more it appears that the conflict between them was not primarily theological in character, but largely personal, ecclesiastico-political, and terminological. If Nestorius and Cyril could have been compelled to discuss their differences calmly and to define their terms with precision, under the supervision of a strict and impartial arbiter who could have kept them under control until they had explained themselves clearly, there is little doubt that they would have found themselves in substantial agreement theologically, though separated *toto caelo* as far as the prestige of their respective archiepiscopal sees was concerned. Being Archbishop of Constantinople (428–31) and champion of the theological tradition of the city of Antioch, in which he had begun his career, Nestorius resented the intervention of Cyril, the Archbishop of Alexandria (412–44), who had determined to humble the clergy of the capital city and gain dominion over the entire Eastern Church.

In discussing Nestorius, I have for obvious reasons disregarded almost entirely the remarks attributed to him by his opponents, and have relied heavily upon his own book, the so-called *Bazaar of Heracleides*, which he

---

[2] For the bibliography on Cyril, see A. Spindeler, "Kyrillos," *Lexikon für Theologie und Kirche*, 6, 2nd ed. by Josef Höfer and Karl Rahner (Freiburg im Br., 1961), 706–9; Quasten, *Patrology*, 3, 116–42; Altaner, *Patrologie*, § 56. In my forthcoming book, *The Mind of Byzantium*, I discuss Cyril's position and the Emperor Justinian I's espousal of the Cyrillian theology in separate chapters. For the Apollinarian origin of Cyril's Christological formula, see Hans Lietzmann, *Apollinaris von Laodicea und seine Schule*, 1 (Tübingen, 1904), 108 ff., 133 f., 185 ff., 251.1 ff.; *Contra fraudes Apollinaristarum*, P.G., 86, 2, 1948–76 (authorship unknown). Cf. Joseph van den Dries, *The Formula of Saint Cyril of Alexandria, mia physis tu Theu Logu sesarkomene* (Rome, 1939). In 532, Hypatius of Ephesus, a strict Chalcedonian, denounced the Apollinarian forgeries. He refused to believe that the highly revered Cyril could ever have been duped by them and preferred to regard the frequent appearance of the Apollinarian formula in Cyril's works as the result of interpolation by heretics: *Acta conciliorum oecumenicorum*, ed. Eduard Schwartz (cited *infra* as *ACO*), 4, 2 (Berlin, 1914), 171.40–173.2, 179.38–180.3; cf. note 8 *infra*.

completed in exile *ca.* 451. Unfortunately, the Greek text of this work has disappeared, but there is a Syriac translation dating from the sixth century which seems to be reliable, notwithstanding an initial error of the translator, who misunderstood the word πραγματεία ("treatise") in the original title, and incorrectly rendered it by *Bazaar*. The Heracleides in question was a man of high repute, whose name Nestorius deliberately substituted for his own, as we learn from the preface to the Syriac version, in order to attract readers, since, he feared, the pious would have been repelled by that of a notoriously heretical author.

It may be, as some object, that the *Bazaar* represents a Nestorius who had had twenty years since his condemnation in 431 to repent of his errors and make essential emendations. Even if this be true, it remains legitimate to allow him to be judged by his own latest and most mature efforts.

2. NESTORIUS GETS INTO TROUBLE

Theodore of Mopsuestia,[3] the leading theologian of the School of Antioch, vigorously attacked the Apollinarian formula, *one incarnate nature of God the Word*; and his antipathy for this description of the relation of the two natures in Jesus Christ was shared by Nestorius, who had been transferred to Constantinople in 428, the year of Theodore's death. Nestorius first provoked[4] the ire of conservative theologians when he espoused the view of a Constantinopolitan presbyter by the name of Anastasius that Mary the Virgin should not be described as Θεοτόκος ("she who bore God" or "Mother of God"). It was proper to speak of Mary as Χριστοτόκος ("Mother of Christ"), or, with the appropriate reservations, as Ἀνθρωποτόκος ("Mother of man"), or even possibly as Θεοδόχος ("God-receiving"), Nestorius said, but impious to suggest that a mortal woman could have been the Mother of God.

The designation Theotokos for Mary had been current at least since the beginning of the fourth century,[5] and meant that Mary, the mother of Jesus

---

[3] On Theodore of Mopsuestia, see the works cited in notes 1 f. *supra*, s.v. In my paper, "The Immutability of Christ, and Justinian's Condemnation of Theodore of Mopsuestia," *Dumbarton Oaks Papers*, 6 (1951), 125–60, I show that Theodore's Christology was heretical because of his misuse of the term τρεπτός as defined by the First Council of Nicaea in 325. This seems to me to be a simpler and more decisive solution of the problem of Theodore's Christology than the erudite but complicated analyses to be found in the numerous books and monographs that have been written on this subject. The literature is collected by Luise Abramowski, "Zur Theologie Theodors von Mopsuestia," *Zeitschrift für Kirchengeschichte*, 4.F. 10 = 72 (1961), 263–93; Quasten, Altaner, etc., *op. cit.*, s.v.

[4] Socrates, *H. E.*, 7, 32, P.G., 67, 808 ff.; cf. note 6 *infra*.

[5] First occurence, ed. Hans-Georg Opitz, *Athanasius Werke*, 3, 1, 1 (Berlin-Leipzig, 1934), 28.15 f. (P. G. 18, 568C): a letter written in 324 by Bishop Alexander of Alexandria to the homonymous bishop of Thessalonike. Socrates, *H. E.*, 7, 32, 17, says that Origen wrote a long dissertation on the suitability of this designation for Mary in his *Commentary on Romans*, but the term cannot be found in the extant text or in the other early authors who are often cited (see works listed *infra*).

On the Virgin Mary, see Georges Jouassard, "Marie à travers la patristique," ed. Hubert du Manoir, *Maria, études sur la sainte Vierge*, 1 (Paris, 1949), 70 ff., n.b. 85 ff.; Antoine Wenger, "Foi et piété mariales à Byzance," *ibid.*, 5 (1958), 923–81; *idem, L'assomption de la T. S. Vierge dans la tradition byzantine du vi^e au xe siècle* (Paris, 1955); Carlo Cecchelli, *Mater Christi*, 4 vols. (Rome, 1946–54); Mauricius Gordillo, *Mariologia orientalis (Orientalia Christiana Analecta*, 141 [Rome, 1954]); Martin Jugie, *L'immaculée conception dans l'Écriture Sainte et dans la tradition orientale* (Rome, 1952); *idem, La mort et l'assomption de la Sainte Vierge* (Studi e Testi, 114 [Vatican City, 1944]); V. Schweitzer,

Christ, was in a strict sense the mother of the humanity of Jesus, which had been united in her womb with the divine nature of the eternal Logos. No one ever suggested that Mary was the mother of the divine nature, but only that the divine Logos had joined himself to the human nature of Jesus at the moment of conception, and that, by reason of the closeness of the union between the divine and human natures in Christ (the *communicatio idiomatum*, on which see notes 56-70 *infra*), she might then be *called* the Mother of God (see note 65 *infra*). For, all agreed, the flesh to which she gave birth was that of the divine Logos, and the Jesus Christ she bore was God as well as man.

Nestorius concedes that the epithet Theotokos was innocuous if properly explained in this fashion.[6] But, with rare exceptions, he refuses to use it by itself, as Cyril constantly did, without adequate qualification. Even apart from his strictures on this term, however, which was sanctioned by the universal Church at the Fourth Oecumenical Council in 451 (see note 9 *infra*), Nestorius was accused of other theological irregularities, and stands officially condemned as a heretic.

But he still has his champions.[7] The Christians of Persia, who seceded from the Byzantine imperial Church in 424, before the Nestorian question had arisen, and their descendants, the "Nestorians" of later times, revere his authority. In addition, a host of modern writers have taken up the cudgels in his defence.

"Alter des Titels θεοτόκος," *Der Katholik*, Ser. 3, 27 (1903), 97–113. Cf. also Georges Jouassard, "Deux chefs de file en théologie mariale dans la seconde moitié du ivème siècle: saint Epiphane et saint Ambroise," *Gregorianum*, 42 (1961), 5–36; Daniel Stiernon, "Bulletin de théologie mariale byzantine," *Revue des études byzantines*, 17 (1959), 201–50; *Lexikon der Marienkunde*, edd. Konrad Algermissen, Ludwig Böer, Georg Engelhardt, Michael Schmaus, Julius Tyciak (Regensburg, 1957-); René Laurentin, *Court traité de théologie mariale*, 4th ed. (Paris, 1959); Sergius S. Fedyniak, *Mariologia apud pp. orientales* (*Basilium M., Gregorium Naz., Gregorium Nys.*) (Rome, 1958).

[6] My references to the *Bazaar of Heracleides* are to the pages of the translation of Driver and Hodgson. See on this point pp. 99f., 148ff., 185, 193f., 293f., 295ff., 387 (fr. 271); Loofs, *Nestoriana*, index C, s.vv. ἀνθρωποτόκος, χριστοτόκος, Maria (p. 402), θεοδόχος. N. b. 177.11f., 263.12, 276.3-5, 277.20; Nestorius' *Second homily on the temptations of Jesus*, ed. F. Nau, *op. cit.* (note 1 *supra*), 345.7f., in which he uses θεοτόκος without exegesis; cf. Loofs, *op. cit.*, 191.6, 19f., 272.13-273.1.

[7] See especially in note 1 *supra*: Grillmeier, Vine, Sellers, Loofs, Bethune-Baker, *op. cit.* Of these, Sellers is the most favorable to Nestorius. On the Persian Council of 424, see J. B. Chabot, *Synodicon orientale ou recueil de synodes nestoriens* (*Notices et extraits des manuscrits de la Bibliothèque Nationale et autres bibliothèques*, 37 [Paris, 1902]), 43-53, 285-98. Cf. Ignacio Ortiz de Urbina, "Storia e cause dello scisma della Chiesa di Persia," *Orientalia Christiana Periodica*, 3 (1937), 456-85; J. Labourt, *Le christianisme dans l'empire perse sous la dynastie sassanide, 224-632* (Paris, 1904), 121-25.

On the Nestorians, see J. Joseph, *The Nestorians and their Muslim Neighbors* (Princeton, 1961) (modern only); Bertold Spuler, "Die nestorianische Kirche," *Handbuch der Orientalistik*, 1. Abt., Bd. 8, Abschn. 2 (Leiden, 1961), 120-69; Raymond Janin, *Les églises orientales et les rites orientaux*, 4th ed. (Paris, 1955), 409-29; Wilhelm de Vries, *Der Kirchenbegriff der von Rom getrennten Syrer* (*Orientalia Christiana Analecta*, 145 [Rome, 1955]); *idem*, *Sakramententheologie bei den Nestorianern* (*Orientalia Christiana Analecta*, 133 [Rome, 1947]); A. C. Moule, *Nestorians in China* (London, 1940); Aubrey R. Vine, *The Nestorian Churches, a Concise History of Nestorian Christianity from the Persian Schism to the Modern Assyrians* (London, 1937): a popular survey; Martin Jugie, *Theologia dogmatica christianorum orientalium ab ecclesia catholica dissidentium*, 5 (Paris, 1935), 9-347; E. Tisserant, "L'église nestorienne," *Dictionnaire de théologie catholique*, 11, 1 (Paris, 1931), 157-323; Konrad Lübeck, *Die altpersische Missionskirche* (*Abhandlungen aus Missionskunde und Missionsgeschichte*, 15 [Aachen, 1919]): has references to sources. Cf. also Juan Mateos, *Lelya-Ṣapra, essai d'interprétation des matines chaldéennes* (*Orientalia Christiana Analecta*, 156 [Rome, 1959]); Henri Bernard, *La découverte de nestoriens mongols aux Ordos et l'histoire ancienne du Christianisme en Extrême-Orient* (Tientsin, 1935); George P. Badger, *The Nestorians and Their Rituals*, 2 vols. (London, 1852): erudite travelogue with translations from the liturgy.

Some argue that the action of the Council of Ephesus in 431 was ambiguous and cannot be regarded as a valid oecumenical condemnation of Nestorius. They point out, also, that the Letter of Cyril (the Third) most damaging to Nestorius, was not approved by the Church until 553.[8] Others contend, in a variety of ways, that Nestorius has been misrepresented or misunderstood and never was guilty of the dogmatic lapses that have been attributed to him.

But in general not even the most favorably disposed among his defenders have said much more in his behalf than that he was almost or nearly orthodox. In dogmatic theology, however, such an apologia is meaningless, and is very much like saying of an egg that "it is partly fresh" or that "parts of it are excellent." A doctrine is either heretical or it is not, and only a slight defect, no larger than the letter iota, which was all that separated the orthodox from the heretics in the matter of ὁμοούσιος, is sufficient to invalidate an entire system.

My own thesis is that Nestorius was not only thoroughly and indubitably orthodox, but also in many respects the profoundest and most brilliant theologian of the fifth century. It must be admitted that his style is often turgid and confusing. The repetitiousness of his great theological treatise, the *Bazaar of Heracleides*, is frustrating, wearisome, and painful. It would have been vastly more effective if some expert rhetorician had pruned it of tautology, eliminated contradictions, added the necessary logical definitions, which Nestorius unhappily eschewed, and reduced its length by a half or three quarters. Still, even in a morass of verbiage, the *Bazaar* is a document that merits careful consideration. The first book, which is devoted to a metaphysical analysis of Nestorius' first principles, is altogether unique, and constitutes the subtlest and most penetrating study of the mystery of the incarnation in the whole of patristic literature.

3. TERMINOLOGICAL COMPLEXITIES AND AMBIGUITIES

Nestorius fell into disrepute primarily because of his theory of the elements that made up the person of Jesus Christ, who was both perfect God and perfect man. The view authorized at Chalcedon in 451 was that in Jesus Christ there

[8] Cf. note 2 *supra*. The Council of Ephesus deliberately, it seems, withheld approval from Cyril's *Third Letter to Nestorius*: *ACO* (see note 2 *supra*), 1, 1, 1 (Berlin-Leipzig, 1927-30), 33-42; *ibid.*, 1, 2 (*ibid.*, 1925-26), 45-51; 1, 3 (*ibid.*, 1929), 26-35; P.G., 77, 105 ff. As Joseph Hefele-H. Leclercq, *Histoire des conciles*, 2, 1 (Paris, 1908), 301 note 2, say, there is no record that the letter was acclaimed or approved at Ephesus. According to *ACO*, 1, 2, 51.34, it was merely incorporated into the *Acta*. Bishop Hypatius of Ephesus pointed out at a conference held in Constantinople in 532, that the Council of Chalcedon had expressly withheld approval from Cyril's *Twelve anathemas* (which form an appendix to the *Third Letter*): *ACO*, 4, 2, 169-84; n.b. 173.18 ff., 21-29; 175.33-38; 177.10-17. On Hypatius, see Charles Moeller, "Le chalcédonisme et le néo-chalcédonisme en Orient de 451 à la fin du vi^e siècle," *Das Konzil von Chalkedon*, 1 (cited in note 1 *supra*), 661; Marcel Richard, "Le néo-chalcédonisme," *Mélanges de science religieuse*, 3 (1946), 158 f. For the literature on the twelve anathemas, see Quasten, *Patrology*, 3, 134. Jean Gouillard, "Hypatios d'Éphèse ou du Pseudo-Denys à Théodore Studite," *Revue des études byzantines*, 19 (*Mélanges Raymond Janin*) (Paris, 1961), 63-75, and the literature there cited deal with other aspects of Hypatius' activity, not with the problem at issue here.

Diepen, *Douze dialogues* (see note 66 *infra*), 49-126, makes a valiant but unsuccessful attempt to prove, against just about all of the major authorities, that the *Twelve Anathemas* (and Cyril's *Third Letter to Nestorius* as a whole) had received oecumenical endorsement at Ephesus and Chalcedon. He has found no evidence prior to 553 which indicates that these texts were used as oecumenically valid criteria of Christological orthodoxy.

VI

124

were two natures, one divine and one human, which together formed one hypostasis or person (prosopon).[9] Nestorius granted that there were two natures in Christ. But he held that each nature (physis) implied an οὐσία (substance or essence), an ὑπόστασις (hypostasis),[10] and a prosopon, so that there were in Christ two natures, two substances (or essences), two hypostases (which he often omits), and two prosopa.[11] Cyril and his school admitted that each nature involved a substance, for these terms were synonymous in the Christological usage of the fifth century;[12] and they agreed that each nature had an hypostasis and a prosopon.

[9] The text of the Creed of 451 is to be found in *ACO*, 2, 1, 2, 129 [325]f.; J. B. Mansi, *Sacrorum conciliorum nova et amplissima collectio*, 7 (Florence, 1762), 116ABC, or in any of the numerous editions of H. Denzinger-I. B. Umberg, *Enchiridion symbolorum*, e.g., ed. 28 (Freiburg im Br., 1947), no. 148, p. 70f.; T. Herbert Bindley, *The Oecumenical Documents of the Faith*, 4th ed. by F. W. Green (London, 1950), 183–99, with introduction, translation, and notes. For commentary, see J. N. D. Kelly, *Early Christian doctrines*, 2nd ed. (London, 1960), 338–43; R. V. Sellers, *The Council of Chalcedon* (London, 1953); Aloys Grillmeier, "Die theologische und sprachliche Vorbereitung der christologischen Formel von Chalkedon," *Das Konzil von Chalkedon*, 1 (cited in note 1 *supra*), 1, 5–202; Ignacio Ortiz de Urbina, "Das Symbol von Chalkedon, sein Text, sein Werden, seine dogmatische Bedeutung," *ibid.*, 1, 389–418; Wilhelm de Vries, "Die syrisch-nestorianische Haltung zu Chalkedon," *ibid.*, 1, 603–35. In the text which follows I reproduce Schwartz's edition, *loc. cit.*, except that after the second ὁμοούσιον I read τὸν αὐτὸν ἡμῖν instead of ἡμῖν τὸν αὐτόν.

Ἑπόμενοι τοίνυν τοῖς ἁγίοις πατράσιν ἕνα καὶ τὸν αὐτὸν ὁμολογεῖν υἱὸν τὸν κύριον ἡμῶν Ἰησοῦν Χριστὸν συμφώνως ἅπαντες ἐκδιδάσκομεν, τέλειον τὸν αὐτὸν ἐν θεότητι καὶ τέλειον τὸν αὐτὸν ἐν ἀνθρωπότητι, θεὸν ἀληθῶς καὶ ἄνθρωπον ἀληθῶς τὸν αὐτόν, ἐκ ψυχῆς λογικῆς καὶ σώματος, ὁμοούσιον τῷ πατρὶ κατὰ τὴν θεότητα, καὶ ὁμοούσιον τὸν αὐτὸν ἡμῖν κατὰ τὴν ἀνθρωπότητα, κατὰ πάντα ὅμοιον ἡμῖν χωρὶς ἁμαρτίας· πρὸ αἰώνων μὲν ἐκ τοῦ πατρὸς γεννηθέντα κατὰ τὴν θεότητα, ἐπ' ἐσχάτων δὲ τῶν ἡμερῶν τὸν αὐτὸν δι' ἡμᾶς καὶ διὰ τὴν ἡμετέραν σωτηρίαν ἐκ Μαρίας τῆς παρθένου τῆς θεοτόκου κατὰ τὴν ἀνθρωπότητα,ἕνα καὶ τὸν αὐτὸν Χριστόν, υἱόν, κύριον, μονογενῆ, ἐν δύο φύσεσιν, ἀσυγχύτως, ἀτρέπτως, ἀδιαιρέτως, ἀχωρίστως γνωριζόμενον· οὐδαμοῦ τῆς τῶν φύσεων διαφορᾶς ἀνῃρημένης διὰ τὴν ἕνωσιν, σῳζομένης δὲ μᾶλλον τῆς ἰδιότητος ἑκατέρας φύσεως καὶ εἰς ἓν πρόσωπον καὶ μίαν ὑπόστασιν συντρεχούσης, οὐκ εἰς δύο πρόσωπα μεριζόμενον ἢ διαιρούμενον, ἀλλ' ἕνα καὶ τὸν αὐτὸν υἱὸν μονογενῆ θεὸν λόγον κύριον Ἰησοῦν Χριστόν, καθάπερ ἄνωθεν οἱ προφῆται περὶ αὐτοῦ καὶ αὐτὸς ἡμᾶς Ἰησοῦς Χριστὸς ἐξεπαίδευσεν καὶ τὸ τῶν πατέρων ἡμῖν παραδέδωκε σύμβολον.

[10] Nestorius uses this term less frequently than he does the others, but he links it with them: *Bazaar*, 163, 208, 218f., 228.

[11] *Ibid.*, 163, 170, 218f., 262.

[12] On the history and development of this technical vocabulary, see Ernst Hammerschmidt, "Ursprung philosophisch-theologischer Termini und deren Übernahme in die altkirchliche Theologie," *Ostkirchliche Studien*, 8 (1959), 202–20; *idem*, "Eine Definition von 'Hypostasis' und 'Ousia' während des 7. allgemeinen Konzils: Nikaia II 787," *ibid.*, 5 (1956), 52–55; *idem*, "Hypostasis und verwandte Begriffe in den Bekenntnisschriften des Gennadios II. von Konstantinopel und des Metrophanes Kritopulos," *Oriens Christianus*, 40 = 4. S. 4 (1956), 78–93; *idem*, "Die Begriffsentwicklung in der altkirchlichen Theologie zwischen dem ersten allgemeinen Konzil von Nizäa (325) und dem zweiten allgemeinen Konzil von Konstantinopel (381)," *Theologische Revue*, 51 (1955), 145–54; *idem*, "Einige philosophisch-theologische Grundbegriffe bei Leontios von Byzanz, Johannes von Damaskus und Theodor Abû Qurra," *Ostkirchliche Studien*, 4 (1955), 78–93; Heinrich Dörrie, *Hypostasis, Wort- und Bedeutungsgeschichte, Nachrichten*, Göttingen, 1, Philologisch-hist. Kl. (1955), Nr. 3: concentrates on ancient, but does not neglect Christian, usage; contains references to texts but not to literature; G. L. Prestige, *God in Patristic Thought*, 2nd ed. (London, 1952), see index; Juan L. Oreja, "Terminología patrística de la Encarnación," *Helmantica*, 2 (Salamanca, 1951), 129–60; M. Nédoncelle, "Prosopon et persona dans l'antiquité classique," *Revue des sciences religieuses*, 22 (1948), 277–99; Marcel Richard, "L'introduction du mot 'hypostase' dans la théologie de l'incarnation," *Mélanges de science religieuse*, 2 (1945), 5–32, 243–70; A. Grandsire, "Nature et hypostases divines dans saint Basile," *Recherches de science religieuse*, 13 (1923), 130–52; A. Michel, "Hypostase," *Dictionnaire de théologie catholique*, 7, 1 (Paris, 1921), 369–437; Louis Rougier, "Le sens des termes οὐσία, ὑπόστασις et πρόσωπον dans les controverses trinitaires post-nicéennes," *Revue de l'histoire des religions*, 74 (1916), 48–63; 133–89; J. Tixeront, "Essais et notices: des concepts de 'nature' et de 'personne' dans les Pères et les écrivains ecclésiastiques des vᵉ et viᵉ siècles," *Revue d'histoire et de littérature religieuses*, 8 (1903), 582–92; T. B. Strong, "The History of the Theological Term 'Substance'," *Journal of Theological Studies*, 2 (1901), 224–35; 3 (1902), 22–40; 4 (1903), 28–45.
On the Latin use of these terms, cf. my "Some Aspects of Byzantine Influence on Latin Thought," *Twelfth Century Europe and the Foundations of Modern Society*, edd. Marshall Clagett, Gaines Post, and Robert H. Reynolds (Madison, 1961), 133, 165 note 11, 182 note 97.

But they differed radically from Nestorius in the Christological formula to which this logic led them, and attacked him because they thought that, when he spoke of two natures, he divided Christ into two, and was accordingly making the monstrous error of introducing a fourth member into the Trinity. Therefore, they felt bound to deny, not without equivocation, that there were two natures in Jesus Christ, and taught that there was "only one incarnate nature [or hypostasis] of God the Word." In so doing, they were making physis the equivalent of what the Chalcedonian Symbol called a prosopon or hypostasis, and alleged that this "one *incarnate* nature of God the Word" necessarily implied the two natures. Nestorius was puzzled by this terminology for many reasons, but in part because he himself followed the fathers of the Nicene period, who had treated hypostasis, usia, and physis as synonyms.

4. NESTORIUS' METAPHYSICAL AND CHRISTOLOGICAL PRESUPPOSITIONS

As stated *supra*, Nestorius' Christology appears to be diametrically opposed to Cyril's. But we shall not be able to evaluate it without determining carefully what Nestorius meant by the terminology he used. It should be noted at the outset that, in the first Book of the *Bazaar*, and frequently thereafter, he denounces the Jews, the Manichaeans, the Arians, the Sabellians, and the Apollinarians. In addition, he expressly condemns Paul of Samosata and the notion that there were two sons.

He based his theological system on the hypothesis that every independently existing object, thing, animal, or person, including man and God the Logos, has a substance or essence (usia)[13] of its own, as the indispensable underlying factor, from which it derives life or existence. The usia, which is invisible, is what the object is in itself, in its inmost being, apart from being perceived. Each usia, in turn, he thought, has a distinctive nature (physis), i.e., the totality of qualities, features, attributes, and peculiarities (both positive and negative) which give it its individual stamp or character. Every nature is founded upon its own usia; there is no nature without an usia; and no usia without a nature. Thus, usia and nature are correlative terms, each of which implies and requires the other.

But neither the usia nor the nature is fully present or effective without a third equally indispensable element, the prosopon. None of the three can be

---

[13] For the definition of these terms, see *Bazaar*, 10–86. I am greatly indebted to A. R. Vine's *An Approach to Christology* and to Luigi I. Scipioni's *Ricerche* (cited in note 1 *supra*) for valuable assistance in the study of Nestorius' terminology. The latter is prevented on ecclesiastical grounds from rehabilitating Nestorius. The former comes closer to my position, although he is convinced that Nestorius was not really orthodox. Vine would have exerted a greater influence ·had it not been for the occasional austerity of his style in passages like (p. 171): "The quasi-prosopon of the syntax in the case of a voluntary syntactic unity which includes a dominating animate nature is necessarily identical with the allogenous prosopon of that dominating animate nature. In the case of the syntax Jesus Christ the dominating animate nature is God the Word. Jesus Christ, then, is the allogenous prosopon of God the Word, and holds a place in the continuity of His durative prosopon. Indeed, during the duration of the syntax Jesus Christ, God the Word remained continuously in that syntax, so that for that entire period His prosopon was an allogenous prosopon, the quasi-prosopon of the syntax Jesus Christ. Jesus Christ, therefore, may be regarded as a syntax with a quasi-prosopon, or as the allogenous prosopon of God the Word during a certain period. Anything or anyone of which God the Word made use as an allogenous prosopon would similarly be a syntax with a quasi-prosopon which was also the allogenous prosopon of the God the Word ...."

separated from the other two, nor can the usia and the nature be recognized externally apart from the prosopon (see § 5 *infra*), which reveals them.[14] No ordinary entity or individual being has more than one each of these three components, nor does any one of the three have more than one each of the other two.

From this metaphysical structure, which may have been influenced in part by Stoicism, presumably via the Cappadocian fathers,[15] Nestorius derives his fundamental presupposition that the substance of God the Word and that of the manhood of Christ were both complete in themselves. They were "whole" natures, because the human could have become man by the creative power of God, without union with the divinity, and the latter was altogether independent of the former. On this account, he rejects Cyril's comparison of the union of God and man in Christ with that of body and soul in man. For soul and body are brought together in man, Nestorius says, by constraint, by an act of divine creation, whereas God and man in Christ joined in a union that was voluntary on the part of both participants. On the other hand, when body and soul are united, each is complemented by the other, since "the body has need of the soul that it may live, for it lives not of itself, and the soul has need of the body that it may perceive."[16]

It is not improbable, of course, that the tension between Nestorius and Cyril affected the former's attitude in this matter to some extent. Nevertheless, Nestorius' definition of usia and physis lay at the foundation of his Christological theorem that neither God the Word nor the human nature of Christ was combined with the other in its own nature or usia. They were mutually exclusive, or "alien to one another,"[17] so that neither could have served as the basis of union for the other. Hence, it was impossible for them to be joined together except through a third medium, the prosopon. For, according to him, this was the only vehicle of union[18] that was capable of preserving the properties of the two usiai and natures of Christ inviolate. This was for him essential, since otherwise Christ could not have been both perfect God and perfect man.

His proof of the unsuitability of the two natures (or usiai) as centers for the union illustrates the theory that lay behind his doctrine of the prosopic union. Natures (or usiai) cannot be combined, or changed in any way, he claims, without serious damage[19] to one or the other of them. For, either the one will be

---

[14] *Bazaar*, 158. There is no external prosopon which lacks an usia and a nature of its own: *ibid.*,208f., 220, 245–247, 228, 231; cf. 163, 170, 174, 216, 218f., 261f., 309, 322.

[15] Grillmeier, "Das Scandalum," cited in note 1 *supra*, 339ff., would trace the Stoic elements in Nestorius' metaphysics to the Cappadocians. See also Scipioni, *Ricerche* (note 1 *supra*), 15–24, 31–44, 98–109, 133–37; Endre Ivánka, *Hellenisches und christliches im frühbyzantinischen Geistesleben* (Vienna, 1948), 84ff.; R. Arnou, "Nestorianisme et néoplatonisme," *Gregorianum*, 17 (1936), 116–31.

[16] *Bazaar*, 304, 161. On the union between the divine and human as voluntary, see *ibid.*, 37f., 47, 85, 90f., 163, 179, 182, 184, 304. For Cyril's comparison of the incarnation to the union of body and soul in man, see P.G., 77, 225 B; cf. Hubert du Manoir de Juaye, *Dogme et spiritualité chez saint Cyrille d'Alexandrie* (Paris, 1944), 138ff.

[17] *Bazaar*, 298f.

[18] *Ibid.*, 23, 53f., 89, 143f., 145. 17f., 147, 157–59, 160f., 166f., 170, 174, 189–91, 196, 206f., 214–16, 219–20, 231, 240f., 246f., 262, 299, 308f., 310f., 313f., 319–20. Cf. 33ff., 37–39.

[19] *Ibid.*, 27.6–8, 28–36.

VI

absorbed by the other, or the result of their combination will be some third nature that is different from both of them.

If, for example, God should take flesh into his own usia, he would not truly become man because he is "not of the nature of men."[20] Still worse, since the Godhead is characterized by lack of body or flesh, if God were to admit flesh or body into his usia, he would cease to be God.[21] Similarly, if Christ's manhood were to take God into its usia, there would be no incarnation of God,[22] but rather the obliteration of the human nature, the deification of man, and the addition of alien matter to the Trinity. That is, as he puts it, things which are changed from their original usia possess only the nature into which they have been changed, and cease to be what they formerly had been.[23] He enunciates this principle also in dealing with Moses' miracle of changing the water of the Nile into blood. In that case, he was of the opinion that the Nile had become blood in usia for the Egyptians, but had been changed back into water for the Hebrews when they used it.[24]

Normally, however, and especially with regard to the divine and the human usiai in Christ, he took such changes of usia to be impossible since "there are no means whereby the usia which was should cease to be, nor whereby that which was made should become unmade, ... nor again whereby a nature which was not should come into being, nor whereby that which is not eternal should become eternal either by a change of nature or by confusion or by mixture; or whereby from the usia of the eternal should come into being that which is not eternal."[25] Therefore, he concludes, the uncreated God the Word, who is eternal, cannot be transformed into that which is created (body), nor can the human body of Christ be changed into the usia of God the Word. On these premises, also, he rejects Cyril's formula of a "natural union" or "hypostatic union" in Christ, both of which, in his estimation, involved a mixture and confusion of natures or hypostases, and consequently an impairment of their integrity that would have been fatal to both the divine and human natures of Christ (cf. notes 19ff., 46f.).

5. THE PROSOPIC UNION

So, when he says that God the Word became man, he means that the manhood of Jesus formed a distinct usia alongside the usia of God, and that the two were joined together in the prosopon.[26] But he never even suggested that there were two persons in Christ, as his enemies allege, and, hence, four (a quaternity) in what tradition called a Trinity. This charge he spiritedly repudiates, and reiterates many times that

[20] Ibid., 20–23.
[21] Ibid., 14.
[22] Ibid., 23–26; cf. note 25 infra.
[23] Ibid., 17f.
[24] Ibid., 18f.
[25] Ibid., 26f., 36f., 80f., 182, 220.
[26] Ibid., 1, 1, 27 and 29, cf. 18, pp. 20, 21f., 22f., 15; 55, 166, 210, 233, 236, 247.

"no one else than he who was in the bosom of his Father came and became
flesh and dwelt among us; and he is in the bosom of his Father and with
us, in that he is what the Father is, and he has expounded unto us what he
is in the bosom of his Father...."[27]

Such texts abound and, he confesses, in conformity with the Creed of 451,

"in one Christ two natures without confusion. By one nature on the one
hand, that is [by that] of the divinity, he was born of God the Father; by
the other, on the other hand, that is, [by that] of the humanity, [he was
born] of the holy virgin."[28]

In view of these express and unambiguous declarations, there can be no
doubt that Nestorius firmly believed "that there is of the divinity and of the
humanity one Christ and one Lord and one Son ...," and that "there both
exists and is named one Christ, the two of them [i.e., the natures] being united,
he who was born of the Father in the divinity, and of the holy virgin in the
humanity, for there was a union of the two natures."[29]

He frequently refers to this union of the two natures[30] in the one prosopon of
Jesus Christ, and denies that it should be described as a union of prosopa.[31]
Most significantly of all, he envisaged this union in impeccably orthodox fashion.
What he says[32] is that the human Jesus "received his prosopon as something
created, in such wise as not originally to be man but at the same time Man-God
by the incarnation [ἐνανθρώπησις] of God ...." This is an extremely subtle
description of the oneness of Jesus Christ, and shows that Nestorius conceived
the Man-God to have been the divine Logos, plus what would have become the
separate individual man Jesus, if the Logos had not been united with him from
the moment of conception. For the child born of the Virgin was at no time,
Nestorius states, a separate man but "at the same time Man-God."

In addition, in the very next sentence he adds, "He [i.e., the Man-God] indeed
was the Maker of all, the law-giver, ... the glory, the honour and the power; he
was also the second man [the 'New Adam,' as in Romans 5:14ff.; I Cor. 15:22
and 45, i.e., Jesus] with qualities complete and whole, so that God was his
prosopon while he was in God." This is a favorite subject with him, and he
repeatedly gives utterance to his conviction that in Jesus Christ God and
man were one (cf. notes 27f., 34, 41, 43), as when he argues that the "child [the
human Jesus] and the Lord of the child [the divine Logos] are the same."[33]

---

[27] Ibid., 50; cf. 53, 192f.

[28] Ibid., 296.

[29] Ibid., 295f. Nestorius' meaning is more clearly expressed in the translation by F. Nau, op. cit.,
note 1 supra, 262: "Il y a et on reconnaît un seul Christ, les deux (natures) étant unies, lequel est né du
Père selon la divinité et de la Vierge sainte selon l'humanité, car il y a eu union des deux natures."

[30] Ibid., 58, 79f., 89, 143, 148, 156f., 161, 163, 172, 182, 295ff., 300–302, 308, 310, 314f.

[31] Ibid., 156, 172, 224.

[32] Ibid., 1, 1, 64, p. 60; cf. 92.1f., 237, 304. Although Nestorius frequently refers to what seems to
be the assumptus homo (as ibid., 237f.), the texts cited show that he understood by the "man assumed"
nothing more than the human nature of Christ. See also following note.

[33] Ibid., 230ff. N. b. 45 ("he who judges and is judged is the judge .... Who is it who has accepted
the offering for all men, when it is he who accepts and he who is offered?"); 200 ("he who descended is
the same whom the Father has sanctified and sent into the world"); 207 (the "taker" and the "taken"

Such texts are re-inforced by his statement, "We say not one and another, for there is one prosopon of both natures," by which Nestorius gives sanction to the orthodox doctrine that the divine and human in Jesus Christ should not be taken to be masculine in gender, ἄλλος καὶ ἄλλος, or ἕτερος καὶ ἕτερος, or *alius* and *alius*, as of two separate persons, but neuter, ἄλλο and ἄλλο, or *aliud* and *aliud*, of the two separate "things," i.e., natures or usiai, which were united in Jesus Christ.

Had his critics taken these passages into account, they could not have persisted in denouncing him as a heretic, especially in the face of his oft-repeated and passionate denial[34] that there were two Sons or Lords or Christs. Nor could they have accused him of having been committed to the doctrine that the human prosopon assumed by the divine Logos constituted a separate man, the *assumptus homo*, who lived by the side of the Logos during the incarnation—and therefore amounted to a second Son and a "fourth member of the Trinity."

Nevertheless, in order to do full justice to both sides, let us examine the objections that have been made against Nestorius, even if they must be regarded as deprived of all substance not only by the text quoted above but also by the emphasis he lays upon the union of the two natures and the oneness of Jesus Christ, as at notes 27-29 above and elsewhere.

Hostility towards Nestorius arises because, although he describes the union as taking place only in the prosopon, which he defines innumerable times as one in number (see note 43), he also makes reference to two prosopa (that of the divine nature and that of the human) and occasionally also to a "union of the prosopa."[35] Even when he does so, however, he immediately explains, in the same context, that the latter "took place for the prosopon" and that there was only "one prosopon of the two natures."

Such explanations demonstrate both that Nestorius did not conceive of the two prosopa which he mentions as in any way compromising the unity or oneness of Jesus Christ, and that he uses the word prosopon in two different senses. According to one usage (*sense A*), prosopon—i.e., what may be called the natural or external prosopon, means the exterior aspect or appearance of a thing, not opposed to its genuine character, but, in the words of a modern critic, "as an objectively real element in its being..., without which, or if it were other than it is, the thing would not be what it is."[36] This is the more general significance of the word (see notes 12 and 14 *supra*). When applied to the two natures in Jesus Christ it indicates, not that each nature had a separate,

are one, not two); 233. Nestorius' denial that there were in Christ "one and another" (masculine) is to be found *ibid.*, 200-201 (n.b. the Greek text Nestorius had in mind in quoting these words), 209, 224, 237. On the orthodox affirmation of the same principle, see Eduard Weigl, *Christologie vom Tode des Athanasius bis zum Ausbruch des nestorianischen Streites, 373-429* (*Münchener Studien zur historischen Theologie*, 4 [Munich, 1925]), 45, 47, 57f., 108f., 112, 152; J. N. D. Kelly, *Early Christian doctrines*, 297; Sellers, *Two Ancient Christologies*, 72f.; cf. my "Some aspects of Byzantine influence on Latin thought," *Twelfth Century Europe* (see note 12 *supra*), 161f.

[34] *Bazaar*, 47-50, 146, 160, 189-91, 196, 209f., 215, 224f., 227, 237f., 295-302, 314, 317.
[35] *Ibid.*, 218-20; cf. 163, 246, 252, 261f., 302, 309; and note 40 *infra*.
[36] *Ibid.*, 414-16. Cf. the texts cited in notes 11 and 14 *supra*.

independent existence (as a person), but that each had a substantive reality, recognizable in its distinctive qualities, which remained undiminished after the union. Hence, prosopon in *sense A* is to be understood as nothing but another aspect of physis or usia, to which, as we have seen (notes 12–14 *supra*), it is inextricably bound.

The other kind of prosopon (*sense B*) is an approximate equivalent of our word "person" and occurs in the *Bazaar of Heracleides* as the designation for Jesus Christ, "the common prosopon of the two natures."[37]

Let us now see how Nestorius applies these definitions to the union. "Man," he says, taking prosopon in *sense A* as above defined, "is known by the human prosopon, that is, by the *schema* [outward form] of the body and by the likeness, but God by the name which is more excellent than all names, and by the adoration of all creation and by the confession [of him] as God."[38] That is, every individual man is identified as such and distinguished from his fellows by the physical characteristics of his appearance. These constitute his prosopon (*sense A*). But the prosopon (*sense A*) of God, who is invisible, is recognized in a different way—by his glorious name and by the fact that he is acknowledged to be God. More specifically, to refer to one of the most significant paragraphs in the *Bazaar* (see note 32 *supra*), the prosopon of the divine nature (*sense A*) was God the Logos himself.

On the basis of these definitions, Nestorius maintains that, as a result of the union, a transfer of attributes (*communicatio idiomatum*: see § 6 *infra*) took place. God the Logos (understood as the prosopon in *sense A* of the divine nature) became the prosopon of Jesus Christ's human nature (note 32 *supra*). Nestorius sets forth the same idea somewhat differently when he says, citing Philippians 2: 9–11, that the divine Word of God gave the human nature of Jesus Christ his name so that, "at the name of Jesus every knee should bow which is in heaven and on the earth, and every tongue should confess that Jesus is the Lord."[39] Likewise as a consequence of the union, the Logos united with his divine nature the flesh—the body and appearance (i.e., the prosopon in *sense A* of the human nature). Or, to adopt one of Nestorius' favorite expressions, "the divinity makes use of the prosopon of the humanity, and the humanity of that of the divinity."[40]

These two prosopa (*sense A*), which, it will be remembered, were intimately connected, but not identical, with the two natures themselves, fulfilled the functions assigned them by Nestorius (see notes 14 and 36 *supra*). For they were the characteristic or visible elements by which the divine and human natures, respectively, were made apparent to the observer in all of their aspects. Hence, Nestorius was enabled to define the union of the two natures in the one prosopon (*sense B*) of Jesus Christ, the incarnate divine Logos,

[37] *Ibid.*, 319, 58, 148, 166, 170f., 220.
[38] *Ibid.*, 1, 1, 66, p. 61; *ibid.*, 64f., 67, pp. 60–62. Cf. pp. 55, 58f., 70, 89, 165–67, 246–49, 312–15. Hodgson, *ibid.*, 415f., ingeniously explains that the union of the prosopa is of two natures and usiai, "which nevertheless are identical in appearance," so that the "appearances overlap." But this would be an illusion, not the true union which Nestorius had in mind.
[39] *Ibid.*, 1, 1, 65, p. 61.
[40] *Ibid.*, 58, 207, 220, 240f. (quotation).

in terms of their external revelation through their prosopa (*sense A*). In addition, the two prosopa (*sense A*) served as media for the *communicatio idiomatum*. But in no respect did they connote a division or bifurcation into two separate persons. For Nestorius carefully adds (see note 40) so as to avoid "Nestorian" implications: "and thus we say one prosopon [i.e., in *sense B*] in both of them. Thus God appears whole, since his nature is not damaged in aught owing to the union; and thus, too, man [is] whole, falling short of naught of the activity and of the sufferings of his own nature owing to the union."

The last sentence indicates that Nestorius had not fallen into the error of supposing that the union of God and man in Jesus Christ, the *one* common prosopon (in *sense B*), which unites the two usiai and natures, was in any way illusory or involved a diminution of the fullness and perfection of either the divine or the human nature. This is a point to which he frequently returns, as when he says[41] of Jesus Christ, "He is truly God, ... in naught falling short of the nature of the Father; and we confess that the man is truly man, completely in his nature, in naught falling short of the nature of men, neither in body nor in soul nor in intelligence ...." Likewise, he adds elsewhere, "God indeed remained God and was made man, and man remained man and was made God; for they took the prosopon of one another, and not the natures."

Similarly (cf. notes 27-32 *supra*), in the language of the Creed of 325 Nestorius unequivocally identifies the one Lord Jesus Christ, "the only-begotten Son of God, that is, from the ousia of God the Father. God from God and Light of Light, Very God of Very God, born and not made, consubstantial with the Father, by whom all that is in heaven and in earth was made," with the same one Lord Jesus Christ, who "on account of us men and on account of our salvation came down and was made flesh of the Holy Spirit and of the Virgin Mary, who also was made man..., suffered and rose on the third day and ascended into heaven and will come to judge the living and the dead"—he who is "consubstantial with the Father" and "consubstantial with the mother, one Lord Jesus Christ."

At the same time, the quotations at notes 32-34, 37-40 show that Nestorius kept well within the permissible limits of orthodox theology in describing the difference between the two natures in Christ. The incarnation is a mystery, and cannot be made comprehensible in purely logical terms. But it would be difficult to conceive of a description that is, under the circumstances, more explicit or more orthodox than Nestorius'.

This point can best be proved by a brief review of his analysis of the unity of the two natures and usiai in one prosopon, the prosopon of union (*sense B*), Jesus Christ,[42] to the oneness of which he testifies uncompromisingly.[43] The prosopon of the human nature (*sense A*) was the visible manhood of Jesus, not merely his outward physical features, and signified the whole of his human individuality, with all the qualities that go to make up a perfect man. The

41 *Ibid.*, 233, 220. For Nestorius' treatment of the Nicene Creed, see *ibid.*, 144f.; cf. note 70 *infra*.
42 *Ibid.*, 23, 53, 55, 58, 64, 66, 89, 143, 145-49, 156-59, 161, 164f., 166f., 174, 182f., 189, 196, 201f., 207, 214, 216, 220, 227, 230ff., 235f., 246f., 252ff., 258, 260ff., 299, 301, 308ff., 313f., 315, 318. 319.
43 *Ibid.*, 58, 148, 166, 170f., 220, 236, 240, 246, 252, 310, 319.

prosopon of the manhood, thus understood, revealed by Christ's miracles the invisible divine nature of the eternal God the Word, who has neither physical form nor shape, but was fully present in the common prosopon (*sense B*) Jesus Christ, and manifested himself behind the cloak of flesh through his prosopon (in *sense A*), by the exertion of divine power.

Consequently, in Nestorius' system, the prosopon (*sense A*) of the divine nature, which was actually God the Logos himself, as we have seen, was recognized by the performance of divine acts and the manifestation of omnipotence, as we should say, or as he himself expresses it (note 38 f.), by the name of God, "the adoration of all creation," and "confession of him as God." This language was intended, it would seem, to emphasize the immateriality of God and to explain how the divine Logos could be united with the humanity of Jesus without any objection able duality of person. But, it must be emphasized, this is only Nestorius' way of defining the indefinable prosopon of God the Logos in Christ, whom he represents consistently (see *supra*, notes 27-29, 41, *infra*, 51 ff.) as no mere external power or spirit, but truly the divine, eternal Logos, who descended from heaven and was joined with the human nature in the womb of the Virgin.

Thus, to the one prosopon,[44] the "common prosopon of our Lord Jesus Christ, the only-begotten Son of God," Nestorius referred "all the [properties] of God the Word whose nature is impassible and is immortal and eternal, and all the [properties] of the humanity, which are a nature mortal and passible and created, and those of the union and of the incarnation. ..." For[45] in Jesus Christ "the earthly and the heavenly, the visible and the invisible, the limited and the unlimitable are the same." These formulations, which vie with the Oecumenical Creeds in lucidity and exactitude, can apply only to what we should call a single person, the God-Man Jesus Christ, who is simultaneously perfect God and perfect man—the divine Logos, who became man and was known on earth through the prosopa (*sense A*) described *supra*.

According to Nestorius, therefore, Jesus Christ was the divine Logos incarnate, the Son of God in the flesh,[45a] the Lord whom his disciples knew as a man but recognized to be God. The unity of his "personality" was further guaranteed by the fact that it was the Logos who both "gave" his prosopon (*sense A*) to the human nature and "took" that of the human for his own. Moreover, the human will of Christ (see notes 51–55a *infra*) was always obedient to the divine, so that there never was any conflict or division between the two.

This analysis is a legitimate summary of Nestorius' Christology, which he himself, however, never presents systematically. Nor does he ever differentiate the "common prosopon" of Jesus Christ from the two prosopa (*sense A*), except by his constant emphasis upon its oneness or indivisibility and upon its having been the vehicle of the union of the two natures or the "common prosopon of the two natures" (*supra*, notes 30 f., 37, 42 f.). He obviously felt that

---

[44] *Ibid.*, 171.

[45] *Ibid.*, 230 f.

[45a] *Ibid.*, 60 f., 191, 193, 196–8, 200–1, 237. On the Logos' "giving" and "taking," see *ibid.*, 55, 61, 69, 165, 225.

these distinctions were in themselves decisive, and he would have been as-tounded by the hypersubtlety of the scholars (cf. note 13 *supra*) who have tried to speak for him in this matter—in language that he would have found utterly incomprehensible.

It is hardly necessary to add that his failure to attempt a more fully artic-ulated metaphysical analysis of the "common prosopon of Jesus Christ" (*sense B*) is neither surprising nor in the slightest degree heretical. The Chal-cedonian Symbol (see note 9 *supra*) merely affirms the oneness of the prosopon or hypostasis and denies that it was divided into two. Nestorius is far more explicit than his contemporaries, none of whom expounds the incarnation so fully as he does, or lays greater stress upon the oneness and unity of Jesus Christ.

Nestorius' deep personal commitment to the unity of Christ is demonstrated also by his acceptance of the Cyrillian idea of the hypostatic union, if hypostasis be defined as a synonym for prosopon and not for usia.[46] On this basis he could indorse the Cappadocian Trinitarian formula, one usia in three hypostases, although he himself preferred to speak of one usia in three prosopa.[47]

In addition, the quotation at note 32 above constitutes a powerful refutation of the Cyrillian taunt that Nestorius had an inadequate conception of the union of the two natures in Christ, and separated the one from the other spatially. Scorning Nestorius' specific denials that he ever divided or isolated the natures from each other, Cyril attacks him for saying, "I separate the natures but unite the adoration,"[48] as if Nestorius meant that, notwithstanding the absence of a real union of the natures, the separate man Jesus deserved to be worshipped because of his close association with the Logos. The verb "separate" (χωρίζω), which Cyril finds offensive, was banned at Chalcedon. But Nestorius replies that he intended it to refer to the distinction between the two natures, since one was divine and the other human, not to any physical or spatial sepa-ration between them. Never, Nestorius protests, did he distinguish God the Word from "him that is visible,"[49] i.e., he never made a division in Jesus Christ as if between the Logos and the man Jesus. Nor did he say that there were two adorations, as if the divine Logos and the human nature of Jesus formed separate persons, and each received worship of his own. On the contrary,[50] he contends, the adoration in question, like the prosopon of Jesus Christ, was singular in number, though it was quite proper to conceive of the human nature (not a separate man) as being adored together with the divine, with which it was joined in the one prosopon of Jesus Christ.

It was the unity of Christ, furthermore, which made it possible for Nestorius to understand how it was that the will and purpose of Jesus Christ's human

[46] *Ibid.*, 156f. but cf. 208, 218.
[47] *Ibid.*, 247.
[48] *Ibid.*, 311 ff. See also the texts cited in notes 49–55 *infra*. Cf. Sellers, *op. cit.* (note 1 *supra*), 91–95, 190–200.
[49] *Ibid.*, 314.
[50] *Ibid.*, 188 f., 196, 202, 207, 227, 237 f., 314. For proof of the orthodoxy of Nestorius' doctrine of the adoration of the human nature of Jesus together with the Word, see Paul Galtier, *De incarnatione et redemptione* (Paris, 1947), §§ 288 ff.

nature were identical with those of God the Word.[51] This identity might have led to the "Nestorian" or adoptionist interpretation that the divinity of Jesus Christ consisted of nothing but his extraordinary submission to the divine will, which won for him the title of Son of God by way of reward or honor, and that the divine in Christ was comparable to the indwelling of God in Moses, the prophets, and the saints.

But Nestorius was not attracted by these notions, and insists that the union in Christ was not merely "moral" but truly metaphysical (see note 55). He does not fail on this account, however, to record the human traits[52] of Christ as recorded in the Gospels: his birth, low estate, swaddling clothes, "increase in stature and in wisdom with God and with men," suffering, death, and resurrection. Throughout, stress is laid on the Son's obedience, despite travail and temptation, and on his freedom of the will.[53] But Nestorius refrains from drawing "Nestorian" conclusions therefrom, rejects the notion that Christ achieved Sonship "as a consequence of moral progress" or by degrees (by adoption after proving his merit)[54] and traces the identity between the will of Christ's humanity and that of God the Logos to the union of their natures, that is, as he expressly states, to the very moment of Christ's conception.[55]

These pronouncements of Nestorius deserve close scrutiny. He understood by the identity of the divine and human wills in Christ, it should be noted, that the two were in complete harmony with each other, not that the two natures had only a single will between them or that the one had absorbed or obliterated the other. There were two wills, but they made identical decisions. The human will, despite its independence of the divine will, was always actively and deliberately obedient to it, through every trial and vicissitude. Nestorius argues (whether rightly or wrongly it is not my purpose to determine in this paper) that Cyril's treatment of this topic was unsatisfactory. The latter does not, of course, deny that the humanity of Jesus Christ was perfect, and included a human rational faculty, which was endowed with freedom of the will. But, Nestorius charges,[55a] Cyril ascribes Christ's moral and spiritual victories to the activity and power of the divine Logos, rather than to the free exercize of his human volition. Unless his human will had faced a real moral choice, Nestorius holds, and had responded thereto in genuinely human fashion, Christ could not have had a truly human nature. Nor could his humanity have otherwise been the model, vehicle, and assurance of immortality for all mankind. This conception was basic for Nestorius' soteri-

[51] On identity of the wills: *Bazaar*, 57 (end), 59, 62–68, 70, 163; God was *truly* in Christ, not just as in the saints: 44–46, 203–6, 227; cf. notes 48–55, especially note 50.

[52] *Ibid.*, 91 ff., 205 f., and *passim*.

[53] *Ibid.*, 62–66, 93 f.

[54] *Ibid.*, 57 (end) f., 59 f., 72, 252 f., cf. 314.

[55] *Ibid.*, 60.3 ff., 314; cf. 72 (end) and note 50 *supra*.

[55a] *Ibid.*, 91 ff., 210–12, 240, 247 f. For the argument of Cyril reprehended by Nestorius, see *Sancti Patris Nostri Cyrilli Archiepiscopi Alexandrini in D. Joannis Evangelium*, ed. Philip E. Pusey, 1 (Oxford, 1872), 487. 16–23 (on John 6:38 f.); *ibid.*, 2 (Oxford, 1872), 316–8–317.7, 320.13–23 (on John 12:27 f.); P. G., 73, 532 AB; P. G. 74, 88D–89A, 92D. Cf. Sellers, *op. cit.* (note 1 *supra*), 104 ff. The latter of these texts is deemed not to have been written by Cyril: Liébaert, *op. cit.* (note 66 *infra*), 131–37.

ology. It also serves to illustrate his understanding of the unity of Christ's personality, which, according to him, never experienced dissension or discord since the human will always followed the divine.

6. THEOTOKOS AND THE *Communicatio Idiomatum*

On the basis of the foregoing analysis, we are justified in clearing Nestorius of the charge of "Nestorianism," and can pronounce his theology to be unobjectionable when measured by Chalcedonian criteria. But, some urge, his unwillingness to designate Mary the Virgin as Theotokos without qualification indicates that he failed to comprehend fully the implications of the *communicatio idiomatum* (ἀντίδοσις τῶν Ιδιωμάτων or ὀνομάτων).

This phenomenon, the transfer or exchange of attributes, as defined by the Council of Chalcedon, notably in the Tome of Bishop Leo I (440-61) of Rome (see note 71 *infra*), is exhibited by the two natures of Jesus Christ (the divine and the human). According to orthodox doctrine, these natures are united "without confusion, change, separation, or division" (see note 9 *supra*), and retain all of their properties, which in the union of God and man are distinct from each other but not separate. The difference between the natures had given rise to two appellations of Jesus Christ, who, on account of his divine nature, is Son of God (the divine Logos) and also, at the same time, by virtue of his human nature, the Son of man (Jesus). Whatever the designation, reference is always to one and the same person, Jesus Christ. Strictly speaking, the divine characteristics are attributable to the divine nature and the human to the human. Nevertheless, as a result of the union of the two in one person, it is deemed possible to ascribe the experiences of Jesus Christ in respect of his divine nature to the Son of man, and those which Jesus Christ underwent because of his human nature to the Son of God. Consequently, it was theologically permissible to teach that the "Son of God" (see note 65f. *infra* for further extension of this idea) underwent death, to which the divine nature was not subject, and that the "Son of man" received worship, which is accorded only to God.

Neither the Council of Chalcedon nor Bishop Leo of Rome was less ambiguous or more positive about this doctrine than Nestorius. Like them, he says,[56] "we name the man God indeed on account of the union of the divinity but man in nature; yet similarly once more also God the Word is God indeed in nature, but we call God man by reason of the union of the prosopon of the humanity."

In support of this proposition, he cites Athanasius[57] approvingly to the same effect: "Now that the Word has become man and has made the properties of the flesh his own, the same are no longer imputed to the body because the Word has come to be in it." From this, like Athanasius, he concludes that in the union the Logos acquired the characteristics of man, and the human in Christ, in turn,

[56] *Ibid.*, 248; cf. 180, 228, 233.
[57] *Ibid.*, 221.

those of God. He specifically states[58] that he agrees with the orthodox who assign "the [properties] of the humanity to the divinity and those of the divinity to the humanity, and this is said of the one and that of the other, as concerning natures whole and united, united indeed without confusion and making use of the prosopa of one another."

He does not mean of course that such an exchange was actually effected between the two natures, but rather between God the Logos and the human in Christ, through their prosopa. His formula for this transfer is the sentence, "the divinity makes use of the prosopon of the humanity and the humanity of that of the divinity," which recurs repeatedly in the *Bazaar*, in one form or another, and must be ranked high among patristic attempts to define this central mystery of the incarnation.

This was his way of safeguarding the divinity and integrity of the divine nature of the Logos. For it enabled him to attach Jesus Christ's human experiences and agony, which God the Word assumed,[59] not to the divine nature, but to the human prosopon (*sense A*) which the Logos "used." Hence, in the kenosis[60] (the "emptying" by which God humiliated himself and took on human form: Philippians 2:6–11), the Logos endured "death upon the cross, in that he made use of the prosopon of him who died and was crucified as his own prosopon, and [i.e., as a consequence] in his own prosopon he made use of the things which appertained unto him who died and was crucified and was exalted."

Accordingly, he does not question the validity of such traditional affirmations as "God suffered" and "God died," if correctly understood as applying to the human prosopon the divine Logos took, not to his nature. Thus, he recognizes Jesus Christ's two generations (note 28f. *supra*) and confesses[61] of the Logos that "nothing is his own apart from the human humiliation; but while remaining God in all things, [he is] that which the man was by his nature in sufferings, even in impassibility." Or, in other words, the Logos "is impassible in a passible body"[62] and "truly...came to be in the body and was not distinguished from the body."

He was, however, far more persistent than Cyril in pointing out that God the Logos did not undergo the human process in his own nature. For, he shows,[63] in the New Testament death and suffering are never associated with God but only with Christ, the Son, or the Lord, since these names are "indicative of two natures

---

[58] *Ibid.*, 240f.; see also 81, 174, 182f., 191, 233. For Nestorius' formula for the *communicatio idiomatum*, see *ibid.*, 240, 190, 207, 219f., 233 ("the one is the other and the other the one"), 238; cf. 66, 69, 81, 159, 163, 167, 172, 183, 252, 261, 320.

[59] *Ibid.*, 174.

[60] *Ibid.*, 58; cf. 138 ("the Only-begotten Son of God created and was created; the Son of God suffered and suffered not, the same but not in the same [*ousia*]; for [some] of these things are in the nature of the divinity and [others] of them in the nature of the humanity. He suffered all human things in the humanity, and all divine things in the divinity ...."), 165, 170, 179, 191, 193, 221. On the kenosis, see Paul Henry, "Kénose," *Dictionnaire de la Bible, Supplément*, 5 (Paris, 1957), 7–161.

N. b. that Nestorius' analysis on this point (cf. note 63 *infra*) was accepted by Cyril and the Council of Chalcedon (note 72a *infra*).

[61] *Bazaar*, 70.

[62] *Ibid.*, 237.

[63] *Ibid.*, 256f.

and indicate sometimes the divinity, but sometimes the humanity and sometimes both of them." Cyril was to be censured, therefore, he felt,[64] for failing
to appreciate adequately the impassibility of the divine nature.

Basically, as Nestorius in part understood, Cyril really was in agreement with
him on this point. In his *Second Letter to Nestorius*,[65] for example, which
received oecumenical indorsement at the Councils of Ephesus and Chalcedon,
Cyril declared that the Logos, though begotten of the Father before the ages
and in no need of a second birth, is *said* (λέγεται) to have been born in the flesh
(σαρκικῶς) because he had united himself with human nature. In this sense, the
Virgin Mary, who was in no wise, Cyril concedes, the mother or source of God
the Word himself or his divine nature, could be regarded as Theotokos, since
she gave birth to the flesh to which the Logos was joined in hypostatic union.
Likewise, the Logos, who is in his own nature incorporeal, impassible, incorruptible, and immortal, is *said* to have suffered, died, and risen from the dead,
because of his union with a human body which underwent these experiences.
By this process of reasoning, Cyril evolved a formula,[66] according to which the
Logos submitted to birth, suffering, and death *in the flesh* (σαρκί) or according to
the flesh (κατὰ σάρκα). His treatment of the Word's relation to passibility is
eminently reasonable, and closely resembles what Nestorius has to say on this
subject (see note 72ᵃ *infra*).

Unhappily, the latter, out of the same contrariety which led Cyril to contradict him at every turn, repudiates[67] Cyril's solution of the problem, and objects[68]
that Cyril referred the qualities of both the human and the divine natures to
the eternal Logos but failed to attribute those of God the Word to Christ's manhood. As a consequence, he complains, Cyril was guilty of the Manichaean error
of reducing Christ's flesh to an illusion. This is not the place to analyze Cyril's
position on these matters. But Nestorius' animadversions, however unjustified,
prove once again that he thoroughly understood the *communicatio idiomatum*,
and realized that there could have been no true union of the divine Logos and

---

[64] *Ibid.*, 91–94, 136 ff., 141–51, 174, 176, 181 ff., 188, 191–206, 247, 252–62, 295 ff., 323, 362, 364 ff.,
367 f.
[65] Nestorius insists that Cyril at times agrees with him on the impassibility of the divine nature:
ibid., 145, 150, 174, 191, 195, 221 f., 232 252, 260, 262, 265 f., 296 f. For the text of Cyril's Second Letter
to Nestorius, see *ACO*, I, I, I, 25. 23–28. 26; P.G., 77, 44 ff.; Bindley, *op. cit.* (note 9 *supra*), 94 ff.,
209 ff.
[66] See previous note and Cyril's *Third Letter to Nestorius*, *ACO*, I, I, I, 33–42; P.G., 77, 105–21; ed.
and trans. with commentary by Bindley, *op. cit.*, (note 9 *supra*), 106–37, 212–19; n.b. 111.149, 165 f.;
113.253–70, and the twelfth anathema in this letter. On Cyril's view of the *communicatio idiomatum*,
see Georges Jouassard, "Impassibilité du Logos et impassibilité de l'âme humaine chez saint Cyrille
d'Alexandrie," *Recherches de science religieuse*, 45 (1957), 209–44, and other articles by him, listed in
Quasten, *Patrology*, 3, 141. A warm and erudite defense of Cyril, along with an attack on the theology
of the *assumptus homo*, is made by H. M. Diepen, *Douze dialogues de christologie ancienne* (Rome, 1960);
idem, *La théologie de l'Emmanuel* (n. p., 1960); *idem*, *Aux origines de l'anthropologie de saint Cyrille
d'Alexandrie* (n. p., 1957), who directs his fire mostly against Déodat de Basly (see my "Immutability"
[note 3 *supra*], 138, note 52). Cf. Paul Galtier, "Saint Cyrille et Apollinaire," *Gregorianum*, 37 (1956),
584–609; Jouassard, *loc. cit.*; and Jacques Liébaert, *La doctrine christologique de saint Cyrille d'Alexandrie
avant la querelle nestorienne* (*Mémoires et travaux publiés par les professeurs des facultés catholiques de
Lille*, 58 [Lille, 1951]), with all three of whom I agree against Diepen. A precise summary of Cyril's position
is to be found in Hubert du Manoir de Juaye, *op. cit.* (note 16 *supra*), 145–50.
[67] *Bazaar*, 150 f.
[68] *Ibid.*, 146, 219, 225, 239, 240 f., 245–48, 260.

138

the human nature in Jesus Christ unless the qualities of the one were deemed applicable to the other and *vice versa*.

Actually, the fundamental difference between Nestorius and Cyril in interpreting the results of the *communicatio idiomatum* stems from their disagreement concerning the subject of the God-man's career and experience. Cyril, as Nestorius remarks,[69] preferred to begin with the divine Logos ("the maker of the natures"), and habitually speaks of the Logos as saying, doing, suffering, dying, and rising from the dead. Nestorius, on the other hand, associates all these activities with "the prosopon of the union" (the Jesus Christ of the Gospels). In defence of his position, he appeals to the New Testament (see note 63 *supra*) and the Creed of Nicaea.[70] The latter, he contends, in a rebuttal of Cyril, ascribes the incarnation, death, and resurrection to Jesus Christ, not to the divine Logos. It should be added, also, that the Symbol of Chalcedon follows the same pattern (see note 9 *supra*), and qualifies the terrestrial generation of Jesus Christ exactly as Nestorius does, stating that he "was born of Mary the Virgin Theotokos, *according to the manhood*." We cannot censure him for expressing himself with similar circumspection, and there is no doubt that he would have subscribed unreservedly to this Creed and to the Tome of Leo, as one of his followers claims.[71]

[69] *Ibid.*, 143–146, 153 and *passim*.

[70] *Ibid.*, 141 ff., 144 ff., and *passim*. For the text of the Creed of 325, see *ACO*, 2, 1, 2, 79 [275]. 16 ff. Other versions and the so-called Creed of 381: *ACO*, 1, 1, 1, 12.32–13.5, 35.1–11; *ACO*, 1, 1, 2, 12.29–13.7; *ACO*, 1, 1, 3, 39.1–11; *ACO*, 1, 1, 7, 65 f.; *ACO*, 2, 1, 1, 90.30 ff.; *ACO*, 2, 1, 2, 127 [323] f.; *ACO*, 3, 4.24–5.11; Mansi, *op. cit.* (note 9 *supra*), 7, 110–12. Apart from minor variants in punctuation, I reproduce the text of *ACO*, 2, 1, 2, 79.16, except for ἢ κτιστὸν in the last sentence, which occurs in Athanasius' recension and seems to be an essential element of the Creed: *De decretis Nicaenae Synodi*, 37, 2, ed. Hans-Georg Opitz, *Athanasius Werke*, 2, 1 (Berlin-Leipzig, 1935), 36.33–37.2. For the formation and meaning of the Creed, see J. N. D. Kelly, *Early Christian Creeds* (London, 1951), 215 ff., and the literature set forth in *Dumbarton Oaks Papers*, 6 (1951), 141 note 60.

πιστεύομεν εἰς ἕνα θεὸν πατέρα παντοκράτορα, πάντων ὁρατῶν τε καὶ ἀοράτων ποιητήν. καὶ εἰς ἕνα κύριον Ἰησοῦν Χριστόν, τὸν υἱὸν τοῦ θεοῦ, γεννηθέντα ἐκ τοῦ πατρὸς μονογενῆ, τουτέστιν ἐκ τῆς οὐσίας τοῦ πατρός, θεὸν ἐκ θεοῦ, φῶς ἐκ φωτός, θεὸν ἀληθινὸν ἐκ θεοῦ ἀληθινοῦ, γεννηθέντα οὐ ποιηθέντα, ὁμοούσιον τῷ πατρί· δι᾽ οὗ τὰ πάντα ἐγένετο, τά τε ἐν τῷ οὐρανῷ καὶ τὰ ἐν τῇ γῇ, τὸν δι᾽ ἡμᾶς τοὺς ἀνθρώπους καὶ διὰ τὴν ἡμετέραν σωτηρίαν κατελθόντα καὶ σαρκωθέντα καὶ ἐνανθρωπήσαντα, παθόντα καὶ ἀναστάντα τῇ τρίτῃ ἡμέρᾳ, ἀνελθόντα εἰς τοὺς οὐρανούς, καὶ ἐρχόμενον κρῖναι ζῶντας καὶ νεκρούς. καὶ εἰς τὸ ἅγιον πνεῦμα. τοὺς δὲ λέγοντας, ἦν ποτε ὅτε οὐκ ἦν, καὶ πρὶν γεννηθῆναι οὐκ ἦν, καὶ ὅτι ἐξ οὐκ ὄντων ἐγένετο, ἢ ἐξ ἑτέρας ὑποστάσεως ἢ οὐσίας φάσκοντας εἶναι, ἢ κτιστὸν ἢ τρεπτὸν ἢ ἀλλοιωτὸν τὸν υἱὸν τοῦ θεοῦ [τούτους] ἀναθεματίζει ἡ καθολικὴ καὶ ἀποστολικὴ ἐκκλησία.

The so-called Creed of 381, which first appears as such in the Acts of the Council of Chalcedon is taken from *ACO*, 2, 1, 2, 80 [276]:

Πιστεύομεν εἰς ἕνα θεὸν πατέρα παντοκράτορα, ποιητὴν οὐρανοῦ καὶ γῆς, ὁρατῶν τε πάντων καὶ ἀοράτων. καὶ εἰς ἕνα κύριον Ἰησοῦν Χριστόν, τὸν υἱὸν τοῦ θεοῦ τὸν μονογενῆ, τὸν ἐκ τοῦ πατρὸς γεννηθέντα πρὸ πάντων τῶν αἰώνων, φῶς ἐκ φωτός, θεὸν ἀληθινὸν ἐκ θεοῦ ἀληθινοῦ, γεννηθέντα οὐ ποιηθέντα, ὁμοούσιον τῷ πατρί, δι᾽ οὗ τὰ πάντα ἐγένετο, τὸν δι᾽ ἡμᾶς τοὺς ἀνθρώπους καὶ διὰ τὴν ἡμετέραν σωτηρίαν κατελθόντα ἐκ τῶν οὐρανῶν καὶ σαρκωθέντα ἐκ πνεύματος ἁγίου καὶ Μαρίας τῆς παρθένου καὶ ἐνανθρωπήσαντα, σταυρωθέντα τε ὑπὲρ ἡμῶν ἐπὶ Ποντίου Πιλάτου, καὶ παθόντα καὶ ταφέντα, καὶ ἀναστάντα τῇ τρίτῃ ἡμέρᾳ κατὰ τὰς γραφάς, καὶ ἀνελθόντα εἰς τοὺς οὐρανούς, καὶ καθεζόμενον ἐν δεξιᾷ τοῦ πατρός, καὶ πάλιν ἐρχόμενον μετὰ δόξης κρῖναι ζῶντας καὶ νεκρούς· οὗ τῆς βασιλείας οὐκ ἔσται τέλος. καὶ εἰς τὸ πνεῦμα τὸ ἅγιον, τὸ κύριον καὶ ζωοποιόν, τὸ ἐκ τοῦ πατρὸς ἐκπορευόμενον, τὸ σὺν πατρὶ καὶ υἱῷ συμπροσκυνούμενον καὶ συνδοξαζόμενον, τὸ λαλῆσαν διὰ τῶν προφητῶν· εἰς μίαν ἁγίαν καθολικὴν καὶ ἀποστολικὴν ἐκκλησίαν. ὁμολογοῦμεν ἓν βάπτισμα εἰς ἄφεσιν ἁμαρτιῶν· προσδοκῶμεν ἀνάστασιν νεκρῶν καὶ ζωὴν τοῦ μέλλοντος αἰῶνος.

[71] *Bazaar*, frag. 308, p. 388 f., cf. *ibid.*, ix f., xxix f., 241, 369 ff., 374 f., 378. For the text of the Tome of Leo (Ep. 28), see *ACO*, 2, 2, 1, 24–33 (Latin); 2, 1, 1, 10–20 (Greek version); C. Silva-Tarouca, *S. Leonis Magni Tomus ad Flavianum Episc. Constantinopolitanum* (*Textus et documenta*, Series theologica, 9 [Rome, 1932]). For exegesis, etc.: Hugo Rahner, "Leo der Grosse, der Papst des Konzils," *Das Konzil von Chalkedon*, 1 (see note 1), 323–39; Paul Galtier, "Saint Cyrille d'Alexandrie et Saint Léon le

Still, since Cyril is universally esteemed in the Church as a Chalcedonian before Chalcedon, the Christology of Nestorius, if orthodox, should be reconcilable, notwithstanding angry denials on both sides, with Cyril's. In truth, it must be admitted, the line which separates them on this, as on all other issues, is either very thin or nonexistent. Both agreed that the qualities of the two natures were referable to the one person, Jesus Christ. They defined this entity somewhat differently, but it is obvious that Cyril's "one prosopon, ... the one incarnate hypostasis of God the Logos,"[72] and Nestorius' "one prosopon of Jesus Christ" (notes 37, 42 f.) were both intended to define the Jesus Christ of the Gospels. Moreover, Cyril's characteristic notion that "the Logos suffered in the flesh" is theologically the exact equivalent of Nestorius' dogma that the Logos suffered in the prosopon of the manhood which he took for his own. For, as we have seen (note 38 ff.), the prosopon of the manhood is the *schema* or the flesh and body of Jesus Christ.

Nevertheless, Nestorius was always offended by Cyril's constant preoccupation with the paradox that God the Logos suffered, died, and was raised from the dead—*in the flesh*—although he recognized (notes 57-62) the validity of the proposition stated in this form. His unwillingness to do so without the necessary restrictions, however, and his insistence that the human experiences should in a strict sense be attributed to Jesus Christ, or to his human nature (or, as he preferred to put it, to the human prosopon [*sense A*] which the Logos appropriated for himself), rather than to the divine nature of the Logos, are by no means to be regarded as idiosyncrasies of "Nestorianism." On the contrary, Cyril himself made similar qualifications, as in his letter to John of Antioch, in which he quotes with approval the compromise Creed of 433. A passage in this document, whose orthodoxy received oecumenical confirmation at the Council of Chalcedon in 451, corresponds exactly with what Nestorius had to say on the same topic (see quotations in notes 60 and 63 *supra*): "With regard to the evangelical and apostolic texts concerning the Lord, we know that the theologians make some common as referring to one person, and distinguish others, as referring to two natures, assigning those appropriate to God to the divinity of Christ, and the humble ones to his humanity."[72a]

At the same time, granting Nestorius to have been technically correct on all these matters, we can be sure that the Chalcedonians would have been bewildered by his strange view[73] that God only "passed through the holy virgin, the

Grand à Chalcédoine," *ibid.*, 1, 345-87; Trevor Jalland, *The Life and Times of St. Leo the Great* (London, 1941), 451 ff., the best general book on Leo. Cf. Altaner, *Patrologie*, § 78,11 for further bibliography.

[72] *ACO*, 1, 1, 1, 38.21 ff.; Bindley, *op. cit.*, (note 9 *supra*), 112.205-7; P.G., 77, 116 C: ἐνὶ τοιγαροῦν προσώπῳ τὰς ἐν τοῖς εὐαγγελίοις πάσας ἀναθετέον φωνάς, ὑποστάσει μιᾷ τῇ τοῦ Λόγου σεσαρκωμένῃ. Κύριος γὰρ εἷς Ἰησοῦς Χριστός, κατὰ τὰς γραφάς. Cf. du Manoir de Juaye, *loc. cit.* (note 66 *supra*).

[72a] *ACO*, 1, 1, 4, 17. 17-20; P.G., 77, 177 AB: Bindley, *op. cit.* (note 9 *supra*), 142.61 ff.: τὰς δὲ εὐαγγελικὰς καὶ ἀποστολικὰς περὶ τοῦ Κυρίου φωνάς, ἴσμεν τοὺς θεολόγους ἄνδρας, τὰς μὲν κοινοποιοῦντας, ὡς ἐφ' ἑνὸς προσώπου, τὰς δὲ διαιροῦντας, ὡς ἐπὶ δύο φύσεων· καὶ τὰς μὲν θεοπρεπεῖς κατὰ τὴν θεότητα τοῦ Χριστοῦ, τὰς δὲ ταπεινὰς κατὰ τὴν ἀνθρωπότητα παραδιδόντας.

Approval by Chalcedon: *ACO*, 2, 1, 2, 81 [277]. 1-13. When the Illyrian and Palestinian bishops expressed doubts as to the orthodoxy of expressions of this sort, other passages were quoted from Cyril's writings to the same effect: *ibid.*, 82 [278]. 4-36; Mansi, 6, 972D. See Galtier, *loc. cit.* (note 50 *supra*), 355 f.; Sellers, *op. cit.* (note 1 *supra*), 90-95; Nestorius, *Bazaar*, 314 ff.

[73] *Bazaar*, 296. Gregory of Nazianzus had opposed this view: P.G., 37, 177Cf.

'mother of Christ'," but was not born of her. They agreed with him that God did not derive the origin of his being from Mary, but they expressed this idea differently (see the Creed of 451 in note 9 *supra*). In strict justice, Nestorius can be vindicated on this point also, and he definitely avoided the Gnostic and Manichaean implications of this peculiar description of the relation of the Godhead to Mary. For the Gnostic doctrine that "Jesus passed through Mary like water through a pipe"[74] was directed against Christ's assumption of a truly human nature, which Nestorius always championed.

It is not correct, however, to say, as many do, that he was primarily concerned with the human nature of Jesus. He does, of course, lay great stress upon Christ's manhood. But he by no means neglects the divine nature. Indeed, his theory that neither of the two usiai could be mixed with the other or combined with it in its own usia was intended, among other things, to preserve the impassibility of the divine nature (see notes 59-64 *supra*). Actually, Nestorius' Christology is not characterized by preoccupation with either one of the two natures to the exclusion or detriment of the other, but rather by uncompromising insistence upon the union of both of them in Christ, in their full totality, and unimpaired.

He was the dyophysite *par excellence*, and, more than any other theologian, except possibly Theodoret of Cyrus (d. 466),[75] his friend and ally, devoted his energies to demonstrating that Jesus Christ was equally and in full measure both God and man, both human and divine. No one else championed this principle more vigorously than he, or was more forceful in denouncing the slightest deviation from it.

In view of the great merit of his theological ideas, it is all the more regrettable that he was not able to present them more skilfully. The obscurity and prolixity of his style are major defects, from which he cannot be exculpated, and explain in part why he failed to hold the favor of Emperor Theodosius II (408-50), and spent the last years of his life (from 431–*ca*. 451)[76] in agonizing exile.

---

[74] Irenaeus, *Against Heresies*, 3, 11, 8, ed. W. W. Harvey, *Sancti Irenaei episcopi lugdunensis libros quinque adversus haereses*, 2 (Cambridge, 1857), 42.

[75] On Theodoret, see Quasten, *Patrology*, 3, 536–54; Altaner, *Patrologie*, § 73.

[76] For the chronology, see, in addition to the works cited in note 1 *supra*, B. J. Kidd, *A History of the Church to A.D. 461*, 3 (Oxford, 1922), 267f.; J. F. Bethune-Baker, "The Date of the Death of Nestorius," *Journal of Theological Studies*, 9 (1907-8), 601–5: Nestorius was alive at the time of the Council of Chalcedon.

Note: Special tribute should be paid to G. R. Driver, Leonard Hodgson, and François Nau (see note 1 *supra*) for their meticulous translations of the *Bazaar*, without which this essay would never have been undertaken. In my quotations therefrom, I have used square brackets to indicate words added by the translators or my own exegesis of the text.

VII

THE IMMUTABILITY OF CHRIST AND JUSTINIAN'S CONDEMNATION OF THEODORE OF MOPSUESTIA

Milton V. Anastos

JUSTINIAN condemned Theodore of Mopsuestia because he was
convinced that Theodore had divided the Logos-Christ into two persons, one human and one divine, and that Theodore's Christ was no
more than a mere man. Opinions of the orthodoxy of Theodore's Christology
have differed widely in medieval and modern times, but a thorough appraisal
of Justinian's theological writings and his judgment of Theodore has yet to be
made. The present article,[1] which will deal with only one phase of this question, is devoted to an examination of the meaning of the terms τρεπτός (mutable), ἀλλοιωτός (subject to change, changeable), τρεπτότης (mutability),
ἄτρεπτος (immutable), ἀτρεπτότης or ἀτρεψία (immutability), ἀναλλοίωτος
(unchangeable), and the like in the Christological controversies of the
fourth, fifth, and sixth centuries.

The signification of these epithets will be made clear by the texts cited
in the course of this paper, but a few preliminary definitions may be of
service. They refer in the first instance to the eternity and unchangeableness
of the divine essence of the Logos, which is to be regarded as having united
itself with human nature at the incarnation without change. The Logos became flesh by union with human nature in the womb of the Virgin, not by
transformation into flesh. These words are used frequently in this sense; and
a whole treatise of Theodoretus, entitled Ἄτρεπτος, expounds this conception
in great detail.[2] The reverse is also possible, and we often find denials that
the human nature was changed into the divine after the incarnation.[3] The
Chalcedonian Symbol of 451 in its formula, ἕνα καὶ τὸν αὐτὸν Χριστόν, υἱόν,
κύριον, μονογενῆ, ἐν δύο φύσεσιν ἀσυγχύτως, ἀτρέπτως, ἀδιαιρέτως, ἀχωρίστως
γνωριζόμενον, expressly rejected the view of Eutyches and the Monophysites
that after the incarnation the human nature was absorbed by the divine.[4]

[1] This is a preliminary draft of a part of my book on the theology of the Emperor
Justinian I.

[2] MPG, 83, 31–106.

[3] E.g., Justinian, Confessio rectae fidei, ed. Eduard Schwartz, Drei dogmatische Schriften
Iustinians (Abhandlungen d. Bayerischen Akademie d. Wissenschaften, Philosophisch-historische Abt., N. F., Heft 18 [1939]), 74.21–24; MPG, 86.1, 997A, quoted in n. 16 below.

[4] Ed. Eduard Schwartz, Acta conciliorum oecumenicorum (abbreviated below as ACO),
2.1.2, [325], 129.30 f.; J. D. Mansi, Sacrorum conciliorum nova et amplissima collectio, 7
(Paris-Leipzig, 1901), 116B. On the reading ἐν δύο φύσεσιν, which Schwartz adopts on the
authority of the best manuscripts instead of ἐκ δύο φύσεων, see J. Hefele–H. Leclercq, Histoire
des conciles, 2.2 (Paris, 1908), 723 ff.; H. Denzinger, Enchiridion symbolorum (26th ed.,
Freiburg im Breisgau, 1947), no. 148, pp. 70 f.; Philip Schaff, The Creeds of Christendom,
2 (New York, 1877), 62 ff. Justinian in his Contra Monophysitas reads ἐν δυσὶ φύσεσιν: ed.
Schwartz, Drei dogmatische Schriften Iustinians (abbreviated below as Ed. Schwartz), 31.23;

This is the doctrine denounced in the so-called Athanasianum (*Quicunque vult*), attributed to Athanasius but probably a work of the end of the fifth century, in the clauses:

Qui licet deus sit et homo, non duo tamen, sed unus est Christus. Unus autem, non conversione divinitatis in carnem, sed assumptione humanitatis in deum. Unus omnino, non confusione substantiae sed unitate personae.[5]

These connotations will be fully illustrated below.

A somewhat different interpretation is put upon these terms in the works of Arius [6] and Theodore of Mopsuestia, as also in some of the writings of Justinian that discuss Theodore's conception of the ἀτρεπτότης of Christ, and in the twelfth anathema of the Fifth Oecumenical Council.[7] Here τρεπτός refers to mutability of soul, which is glorified and divinized after the resurrection to immutability (ἀτρεπτότης). Arius and Theodore apparently sought in this way to preserve Christ's human freedom of will. In combating the Apollinarians with their doctrine of a Jesus Christ who had perfect humanity except for the νοῦς or reasonable soul (ψυχὴ λογική), which was supplied by the divine Logos, Theodore wished to emphasize the perfect humanity of Christ. He was careful to insist that Christ was without blemish, but he deemed it essential for the salvation of mankind that Christ should have been free to choose evil and to sin had he wished to do so. Arius taught that Christ was a perfect created being of God, immutable and unchangeable by the exercise of his will, and that, by exerting his will, Christ remained good as long as he wished, since he was of a mutable nature.[8]

Actually, however, as Athanasius had the acumen to realize, all these conceptions merge into one. There is no question of the freedom of the will here, but the more basic one of the essence of the Logos. Dealing in this way

MPG, 86.1, 1133D. Severus of Antioch, the Monophysite, believed that the Creed had ἐκ δύο φύσεων: ed. A. Sanda, *Severi Philalethes* (Beirut, 1928), c. 62, p. 116. On the pre-Chalcedonian form of this phrase, see Andreas Schmid, *Die Christologie Isidors von Pelusium* (n. 104 below), 52 ff.

[5] Mansi, 2, 1355B; Denzinger, *Enchiridion symbolorum*, no. 39 f., pp. 17 f.; Schaff, *Creeds*, 2, 66 ff. On the various authors proposed, see Berthold Altaner, *Patrologie* (2d ed., Freiburg im Breisgau, 1950), 235 f. G. D. W. Ommanney, *A Critical Dissertation on the Athanasian Creed* (Oxford, 1897), ascribes it to Vincent of Lerins at the first half of the fifth century.

[6] See Henry M. Gwatkin, *Studies of Arianism* (2d ed., Cambridge, England, 1900), 22, 24 f., 44, 120–122; G. Bardy, *Recherches sur Saint Lucien d'Antioche* (Paris, 1936), 235 ff.; J. N. D. Kelly, *Early Christian Creeds* (London, 1950), 231 ff., 242. It is curious that, despite their insistence on freedom of the will in Christ, the Arians believed, as did Apollinarius later on, that the place of the rational soul in Christ was taken by the divine Logos.

[7] See n. 10 below.

[8] Quoted by Athanasius in *De synodis*, 16, MPG, 26, 709A: ἰδίῳ θελήματι ἄτρεπτον καὶ ἀναλλοίωτον κτίσμα τοῦ θεοῦ τέλειον. See Gwatkin, 25, n. 3. See texts cited in nn. 70 f. below.

with the problem raised by the Arian view of the τρεπτότης of Christ, Athanasius made a brilliant and highly original contribution to Christian thought. His solution was accepted by the church and lies behind much of the Christology, not only of Cyril, Justinian, and the Council of 553, but also of the Sixth Oecumenical Council (680–681), which definitely settled the question of the relation in Christ between the human and divine wills. Although the formula of 681 [9] advances beyond that of Athanasius, it reaches fundamentally the same conclusion and is based upon the same premises. In what follows we shall see that Justinian was completely justified in anathematizing Theodore's doctrine of Christ as τρεπτός until after the resurrection, and that in so doing he was merely following the sacrosanct tradition of Nicaea and applying a necessary corrective to a Christology which violated the fundamental tenets of Christian doctrine.

The best brief summary of Justinian's criticism of Theodore is to be found in the twelfth anathema of the Fifth Oecumenical Council (held in Constantinople in 553).[10]

[9] Denzinger, *Enchiridion symbolorum*, nos. 289–293, pp. 135 ff.; Schaff, *Creeds*, 2, 72 f.

By the ninth century the phrase ἄτρεπτος καὶ ἀναλλοίωτος had become so much a part of the language of scholars that Photius could use it of literary style in a discussion of the authenticity of certain orations of Demosthenes: *Bibliotheca*, cod. 265, MPG, 104, 176C.

[10] Printed in Charles Joseph Hefele–H. Leclercq, *Histoire des conciles*, 3.1 (Paris, 1909), 123 ff., which is taken from Mansi, 9 (Paris–Leipzig, 1902), 384 f.: Εἴ τις ἀντιποιεῖται Θεοδώρου τοῦ ἀσεβοῦς, τοῦ Μοψουεστίας, τοῦ εἰπόντος ἄλλον εἶναι τὸν θεὸν λόγον, καὶ ἄλλον τὸν Χριστὸν ὑπὸ παθῶν ψυχῆς καὶ τῶν τῆς σαρκὸς ἐπιθυμιῶν ἐνοχλούμενον, καὶ τῶν χειρόνων κατὰ μικρὸν χωριζόμενον, καὶ οὕτως ἐκ προκοπῆς ἔργων βελτιωθέντα, καὶ ἐκ πολιτείας ἄμωμον καταστάντα, ὡς ψιλὸν ἄνθρωπον βαπτισθῆναι εἰς ὄνομα πατρὸς καὶ υἱοῦ καὶ ἁγίου πνεύματος, καὶ διὰ τοῦ βαπτίσματος τὴν χάριν τοῦ ἁγίου πνεύματος λαβεῖν, καὶ υἱοθεσίας ἀξιωθῆναι· καὶ κατ' ἰσότητα βασιλικῆς εἰκόνος εἰς πρόσωπον τοῦ θεοῦ λόγου προσκυνεῖσθαι, καὶ μετὰ τὴν ἀνάστασιν ἄτρεπτον ταῖς ἐννοίαις, καὶ ἀναμάρτητον παντελῶς γενέσθαι· καὶ πάλιν εἰρηκότος τοῦ αὐτοῦ ἀσεβοῦς Θεοδώρου τὴν ἕνωσιν τοῦ θεοῦ λόγου πρὸς τὸν Χριστὸν τοιαύτην γεγενῆσθαι οἵαν ὁ ἀπόστολος ἐπὶ ἀνδρὸς καὶ γυναικός· ἔσονται οἱ δύο εἰς σάρκα μίαν· καὶ πρὸς ταῖς ἄλλαις ἀναριθμήτοις αὐτοῦ βλασφημίαις τολμήσαντος εἰπεῖν ὅτι μετὰ τὴν ἀνάστασιν ἐμφυσήσας ὁ κύριος τοῖς μαθηταῖς, καὶ εἰπών· λάβετε πνεῦμα ἅγιον, οὐ δέδωκεν αὐτοῖς πνεῦμα ἅγιον, ἀλλὰ σχήματι μόνον ἐνεφύσησεν. οὗτος δὲ καὶ τὴν ὁμολογίαν Θωμᾶ τὴν ἐπὶ τῇ ψηλαφήσει τῶν χειρῶν καὶ τῆς πλευρᾶς τοῦ κυρίου μετὰ τὴν ἀνάστασιν, τό· ὁ κύριός μου καὶ ὁ θεός μου, εἶπε, μὴ εἰρῆσθαι περὶ τοῦ Χριστοῦ παρὰ τοῦ Θωμᾶ, ἀλλ' ἐπὶ τῷ παραδόξῳ τῆς ἀναστάσεως ἐκπλαγέντα τὸν Θωμᾶν ὑμνῆσαι τὸν θεόν, τὸν ἐγείραντα τὸν Χριστόν. τὸ δὲ χεῖρον, καὶ ἐν τῇ τῶν πράξεων τῶν ἀποστόλων γενομένῃ παρ' αὐτοῦ δῆθεν ἑρμηνείᾳ συγκρίνων ὁ αὐτὸς Θεόδωρος τὸν Χριστὸν Πλάτωνι καὶ Μανιχαίῳ καὶ Ἐπικούρῳ καὶ Μαρκίωνι λέγει ὅτι, ὥσπερ ἐκείνων ἕκαστος εὑράμενος οἰκεῖον δόγμα τοὺς αὐτῷ μαθητεύσαντας πεποίηκε καλεῖσθαι Πλατωνικοὺς καὶ Μανιχαίους καὶ Ἐπικουρείους καὶ Μαρκιωνιστάς, τὸν ὅμοιον τρόπον καὶ τοῦ Χριστοῦ εὑραμένου δόγμα ἐξ αὐτοῦ Χριστιανοὺς καλεῖσθαι· εἴ τις τοίνυν ἀντιποιεῖται τοῦ εἰρημένου ἀσεβεστάτου Θεοδώρου καὶ τῶν ἀσεβῶν αὐτοῦ συγγραμμάτων, ἐν οἷς τάς τε εἰρημένας καὶ ἄλλας ἀναριθμήτους βλασφημίας ἐξέχεε κατὰ τοῦ μεγάλου θεοῦ καὶ σωτῆρος ἡμῶν Ἰησοῦ Χριστοῦ, ἀλλὰ μὴ ἀναθεματίζει αὐτὸν καὶ τὰ ἀσεβῆ αὐτοῦ συγγράμματα καὶ πάντας τοὺς δεχομένους ἢ καὶ ἐκδικοῦντας αὐτὸν ἢ λέγοντας ὀρθοδόξως αὐτὸν ἐκθέσθαι, καὶ τοὺς γράψαντας ὑπὲρ αὐτοῦ καὶ τῶν ἀσεβῶν αὐτοῦ συγγραμμάτων, καὶ τοὺς τὰ ὅμοια φρονοῦντας ἢ φρονήσαντας πώποτε καὶ μέχρι τέλους ἐμμείναντας τῇ τοιαύτῃ αἱρέσει, ἀνάθεμα ἔστω.

If anyone defends the impious Theodore of Mopsuestia, who said that one is the
God Logos and another is the Christ, who was harassed by anxieties of the soul and
the desires of the flesh, and was gradually liberated from the baser passions, and in this
way was elevated because of progress in his deeds and became blameless in his life; that
he was baptized as a mere man in the name of the Father, Son, and Holy Spirit; that
by reason of the baptism he received the grace of the Holy Spirit and was considered
worthy of adoption; and that in the manner of a royal image he was worshipped in the
person of the God Logos, and after the resurrection became immutable in his thoughts
and completely sinless. And [if anyone defends] the same impious Theodore, who taught
also that the union between the God Logos and Christ was the same as that which the
apostle describes between a man and a woman: "The two shall be one flesh," and who,
in addition to his other innumerable blasphemies, dared to assert that when the Lord
blew upon the disciples after the resurrection and said, "Receive ye the holy spirit"
(John 20.22), he did not give them the Holy Spirit but only blew upon them symbolically. And this fellow declared that the confession of Thomas, "My Lord and my God,"
when he touched the hands and the side of the Lord after the resurrection (John 20.28),
was not uttered by Thomas with regard to Christ but that Thomas, overwhelmed by
the miracle of the resurrection, was with these words paying homage to God, who had
raised Christ. And, still worse, in his commentary on the Acts of the Apostles the same
Theodore compares Christ to Plato, Manichaeus, Epicurus, and Marcion, and maintains
that, as each of these discovered his own system and was thereby responsible for his followers' being called Platonists, Manichaeans, Epicureans, and Marcionites, so also
Christ discovered a system, and the Christians are named after him. If anyone, therefore, defends the said most impious Theodore and his impious writings in which he
poured forth against the great God and our savior Jesus Christ the blasphemies described and innumerable others, and does not anathematize him, his sacrilegious works,
and all who accept or justify him or hold that his views are orthodox, together with
those who have written to defend him or his books, and those whose views resemble,
or have ever resembled, his, and who have persevered until death in this heresy, let
him be anathema.

Leclercq [11] has documented these charges in some detail from the writings of Theodore, but he quotes no text to support Justinian's reference to
Theodore's view of Christ as τρεπτός before the resurrection; and no modern
scholar has ever before discussed the significance of this aspect of Justinian's
theology. Accordingly, in the analysis which follows we shall for the most
part ignore the other objections of Justinian and concentrate upon his interpretation of Christ's τρεπτότης. Actually, as we shall see, many of the major
errors of Theodore's Christology arise from the doctrine of the Person of
Christ presupposed by the theory that Christ did not attain ἀτρεπτότητα until
after the resurrection.

The twelfth anathema of the Fifth Oecumenical Council translated
above reproduces with minor alterations the eleventh anathema, published

[11] Hefele–Leclercq, *loc. cit.*

by the Emperor at the end of his *Confessio rectae fidei*.[12] He repeats the
same charge also in a memorandum he sent to the Council of 553 to inform
them of the importance he attached to the condemnation of the Three
Chapters.[13] In this brief document of a little more than three columns of
Migne, called the Τύπος τοῦ Βασιλέως Ἰουστινιανοῦ πρὸς τὴν ἁγίαν σύνοδον
περὶ Θεοδώρου τοῦ Μοψουεστίας καὶ τῶν λοιπῶν, the Emperor states the defects
of Theodore's system in very much the same language that is to be found in
his other two pronouncements on this subject. The chief difference in the
portion of the text that has to do with ἄτρεπτος is the addition of πρὸς τὰ
κρείττονα to balance τῶν χειρόνων (thus strengthening the idea of a change
in Christ from a state that was worse or lower to one that was better
or higher), and of the adjective ἀρίστῃ to modify πολιτείᾳ (which adds the
connotation that Christ became blameless by the perfection of his way of
life).[14] These variations do not of course affect Justinian's judgment of
Theodore in any way. In the same work Justinian expounds the relation of
the two natures in Christ, by saying that

According to the flesh . . . he was born of the holy Virgin; but since God the Logos descended from heaven and emptied himself, taking the form of a servant, he was called
son of man although he remained what he was, that is God. For he is immutable and
unchangeable by nature.[15]

[12] Ed. Schwartz, 92.26–94.13; MPG, 86.1, 1017 ABC.

[13] By the "Three Chapters" (τρία κεφάλαια) are meant (a) the person and works of
Theodore of Mopsuestia, (b) the letter of Ibas, Bishop of Edessa (d. 457), to Maris, Bishop
of Hardaschir (in Persia), and (c) the polemic of Theodoret against the twelve anti-
Nestorian anathemas of Cyril and the Council of Ephesus, and in defence of Theodore and
Nestorius. See É. Amann, *s.v.* Trois-chapitres (affaire des), *Dictionnaire de théologie
catholique*, 15 (1947), 1868–1924.

[14] MPG, 86.1, 1039D–1041A: πρὸς γὰρ ταῖς ἄλλαις ἀναριθμήτοις αὐτοῦ δυσφημίαις εἰς Χριστὸν
τὸν θεὸν ἡμῶν γενομέναις, ἄλλον εἶναι τὸν θεὸν λόγον καὶ ἄλλον τὸν Χριστὸν ἀπὸ τῶν τῆς ψυχῆς
παθῶν, καὶ τῶν τῆς σαρκὸς ἐπιθυμιῶν ἐνοχλούμενον, καὶ τῶν χειρόνων κατὰ μικρὸν ἀφιστάμενον πρὸς
τὰ κρείττονα τῇ προκοπῇ τῶν ἔργων ἐληλυθέναι, καὶ τῇ ἀρίστῃ πολιτείᾳ γενόμενον ἄμωμον. καὶ ὡς
ψιλὸν ἄνθρωπον ἐν ὀνόματι πατρός, καὶ υἱοῦ, καὶ ἁγίου πνεύματος βαπτισθῆναι, καὶ διὰ τοῦ βαπτίσματος
τὴν χάριν τοῦ ἁγίου πνεύματος εἰληφέναι καὶ υἱοθεσίας ἠξιῶσθαι, καὶ καθ' ὁμοίωσιν βασιλικῆς εἰκόνος
εἰς πρόσωπον τοῦ θεοῦ λόγου τὸν Χριστὸν προσκυνεῖσθαι, καὶ μετὰ τὴν ἀνάστασιν ἄτρεπτον ταῖς
ἐννοίαις καὶ ἀναμάρτητον γεγενῆσθαι. καὶ πρὸς τούτοις εἶπε τοιαύτην γεγενῆσθαι τὴν ἕνωσιν τοῦ θεοῦ
λόγου πρὸς τὸν Χριστὸν ὁποίαν ὁ ἀπόστολος ἔφη περὶ τοῦ ἀνδρὸς καὶ τῆς γυναικός· ἔσονται οἱ δύο
εἰς σάρκα μίαν.

[15] *Ibid.*, 1037C–1039A: καίτοι γεγέννηται κατὰ σάρκα, ὡς εἴρηται, ἐκ τῆς ἁγίας παρθένου, ἐπειδὴ
δὲ ὁ ἄνωθεν ἐξ οὐρανοῦ καταφοιτήσας θεὸς λόγος κεκένωκεν ἑαυτόν, μορφὴν δούλου λαβών, καὶ
κεχρημάτικεν ἀνθρώπου υἱὸς μετὰ τοῦ μεῖναι ὃ ἦν, τουτέστι θεός· ἄτρεπτος γὰρ καὶ ἀναλλοίωτος κατὰ
φύσιν ἐστίν· ὡς εἰς ἤδη νοούμενος μετὰ τῆς ἰδίας σαρκός, ἐξ οὐρανοῦ λέγεται κατελθεῖν, ὠνόμασται δὲ
καὶ ἄνθρωπος ἐξ οὐρανοῦ, τέλειος ὢν ἐν θεότητι, καὶ τέλειος ὁ αὐτὸς ἐν ἀνθρωπότητι, καὶ ὡς ἐν ἑνὶ
προσώπῳ νοούμενος. εἰς γὰρ κύριος Ἰησοῦς Χριστός, κἂν ἡ τῶν φύσεων διαφορὰ μὴ ἀγνοῆται, ἐξ ὧν
τὴν ἀπόρρητον ἕνωσίν φαμεν πεπρᾶχθαι. τοιγαροῦν ὁμολογοῦμεν τὸν μονογενῆ υἱὸν τοῦ θεοῦ λόγον,
θεὸν τέλειον, καὶ ἄνθρωπον τέλειον, ἐκ ψυχῆς λογικῆς καὶ σώματος, πρὸ αἰώνων μὲν ἐκ τοῦ πατρὸς

The God Logos, Justinian says, became flesh and became man without change and without being transformed into flesh,[16] remaining always the only begotten Logos of God the Father, the Son begotten before the ages. On this point he cites pseudo-Augustine to prove that the child of Mary was not just a man but God, who chose to be born a humble man in order to show by this humility his own greatness.[17]

But we must not infer from Christ's suffering and humiliation, the Emperor warns, that the divine essence underwent change, for the ancient fathers teach that the glorification and the abasement are both to be ascribed to the one only begotten God Logos, who took flesh and became man.[18] Christ, Justinian remarks on the authority of a sermon on the Virgin Mary delivered by Proclus of Constantinople (d. *ca.* 446), was not a man who had been deified, or one who had become God by reason of the progress he had made, but God who took flesh, who was impassible by nature and became passible out of pity for mankind.[19] Those, however, like Nestorius

γεννηθέντα κατὰ τὴν θεότητα, ἐπ' ἐσχάτων δὲ τῶν ἡμερῶν τὸν αὐτὸν δι' ἡμᾶς καὶ διὰ τὴν ἡμετέραν σωτηρίαν ἐκ Μαρίας τῆς παρθένου κατὰ τὴν ἀνθρωπότητα· ὁμοούσιον τῷ πατρὶ τὸν αὐτὸν κατὰ τὴν θεότητα, καὶ ὁμοούσιον ἡμῖν κατὰ τὴν ἀνθρωπότητα.

[16] Ed. Schwartz, 74.21 f., 76.2 ff., 88.12 f.; MPG, 86.1, 997A: οὔτε γὰρ ἡ θεία φύσις εἰς τὴν ἀνθρωπίνην μετεβλήθη, οὔτε δὲ ἡ ἀνθρωπίνη φύσις εἰς τὴν θείαν ἐτράπη. 997C–999A: ὁ γὰρ υἱὸς τοῦ θεοῦ υἱὸς ἀνθρώπου γέγονεν καὶ μείνας ὅπερ ἦν, οὐ μετέβαλεν ὅπερ γέγονεν. ὅθεν καὶ δύο γεννήσεις τοῦ αὐτοῦ μονογενοῦς θεοῦ λόγου ὁμολογοῦμεν, τὴν μὲν πρὸ αἰώνων ἐκ τοῦ πατρὸς ἀσωμάτως, τὴν δὲ ἐπ' ἐσχάτων τῶν ἡμερῶν τοῦ αὐτοῦ ἐκ τῆς ἁγίας ἐνδόξου θεοτόκου καὶ ἀειπαρθένου Μαρίας σαρκωθέντος, καὶ ἐνανθρωπήσαντος. ὁ γὰρ ἐκ πατρὸς ἐκλάμψας ὑπὲρ ἔννοιαν ἐκ μητρὸς ἀνέτειλεν ὑπὲρ λόγον, καὶ ὢν θεὸς ἀληθὴς ἄνθρωπος γέγονεν ἀληθῶς. διὰ τοῦτο κυρίως καὶ κατ' ἀλήθειαν θεοτόκον τὴν ἁγίαν, ἔνδοξον, καὶ ἀειπάρθενον Μαρίαν ὁμολογοῦμεν, οὐχ ὡς τοῦ θεοῦ λόγου τὴν ἀρχὴν ἐξ αὐτῆς λαβόντος, ἀλλ' ὅτι ἐπ' ἐσχάτων τῶν ἡμερῶν ὁ πρὸ τῶν αἰώνων μονογενὴς θεὸς λόγος σαρκωθεὶς ἐξ αὐτῆς ἀτρέπτως ἐνηνθρώπησεν. καὶ ἀόρατος ὢν ἐν τοῖς ἑαυτοῦ ὁρατὸς γέγονεν ἐν τοῖς παρ' ἡμῖν, καὶ ἀπαθὴς ὢν ὡς θεὸς οὐκ ἀπηξίωσε παθητὸς εἶναι ἄνθρωπος καὶ ὁ ἀθάνατος νόμοις ὑποκεῖσθαι θανάτου. 1011B: ὅθεν αὐτὸν τὸν θεὸν λόγον ἀτρέπτως ἄνθρωπον γεγενῆσθαι ὁμολογοῦμεν καὶ οὐκ εἰς ἄνθρωπόν τινα αὐτὸν ἐληλυθέναι . . . So also ed. Schwartz, 63.26–9 = 1079D. Opposite the Greek text Schwartz prints the text of a contemporary Latin translation, which bears the title (ed. Schwartz, p. 73): *Edictum piissimi imperatoris Ivstiniani rectae fidei confessionem continens et refvtationem heresium qvae adversantvr Catholicae Dei Ecclesiae.* A marginal note in one Greek manuscript labels it πρόγραμμα ἤτοι διδασκαλία καὶ ἔκδοσις ἀκριβὴς περὶ τῆς ἀμωμίτου καὶ ὀρθοδόξου πίστεως ἡμῶν τῶν χριστιανῶν. Other authorities call it ἴδικτον τοῦ εὐσεβεστάτου βασιλέως ἰουστινιανοῦ τὴν τῆς ὀρθῆς πίστεως περιέχον ὁμολογίαν καὶ ἀνασκευὴν τῶν μαχομένων αἱρέσεων τῇ καθολικῇ τοῦ θεοῦ ἐκκλησία.

[17] Ed. Schwartz, 54.37 ff.; MPG, 86.1, 1059D: ἐκεῖνο θαύμασον μᾶλλον ὅτι ὁ λόγος ἔλαβεν σάρκα καὶ οὐκ ἐτράπη εἰς σάρκα, ὅτι μένων θεὸς γέγονεν ἄνθρωπος . . . οὕτως ἠβουλήθη ὁ ὕψιστος γεννηθῆναι ταπεινός, ἵνα ἐν αὐτῇ τῇ ταπεινώσει ἐπιδείξηται τὴν μεγαλειότητα.

[18] Ed. Schwartz, 59.20–23; MPG, 86.1, 1071A: οὐδὲ γὰρ διὰ τὰ ταπεινὰ τροπὴν λέγουσιν τῆς τοῦ υἱοῦ θεάτητος, οὐδὲ διὰ τὰ ὑψηλὰ διαιροῦσι τὴν ἀνθρωπότητα τῆς θεότητος, ἀλλὰ τοῦ ἑνὸς καὶ τοῦ αὐτοῦ μονογενοῦς θεοῦ λόγου σεσαρκωμένου καὶ ἐνανθρωπήσαντος καὶ τὰ ὑψηλὰ καὶ τὰ ταπεινὰ εἶναι παραδιδόασιν.

[19] Ed. Schwartz, 54.26–28; MPG, 86.1, 1059C: ὁ ὢν κατὰ φύσιν ἀπαθὴς γέγονε δι' οἶκτον πολυπαθής· οὐκ ἐκ προκοπῆς γέγονε θεὸς ὁ Χριστός, μὴ γένοιτο, ἀλλὰ δι' οἶκτον γέγονεν ἄνθρωπος ὁ θεὸς ᾧ πιστεύομεν· οὐκ ἄνθρωπον ἀποθεωθέντα κηρύττομεν, ἀλλὰ θεὸν σαρκωθέντα ὁμολογοῦμεν. On

and his teacher Theodore, who do not confess that the God Logos became man, clearly make Christ a mere man, who was called Son of God by grace. In point of fact, Justinian says, the Logos is by nature the true Son of God, and men are sons of God only by grace.[20] Biblical texts like Psalms 8.5 ("For thou hast made him a little lower than the angels, and hast crowned him with glory and honor"), 2 Corinthians 8.9 ("For ye know the grace of our Lord Jesus Christ, that, though he was rich, yet for your sakes he became poor, that ye through his poverty might be rich"), Hebrews 2.9 ("But we see Jesus, who was made a little lower than the angels for the suffering of death, crowned with glory and honor"), and John 14.28 ("My father is greater than I") have reference only to the incarnation of the Logos. They show that it was the divine Logos who humbled himself and became man for the sake of mankind, and not a man who was later elevated to glory and honor. To assume that Christ was promoted in this way, as Theodore does in his exegesis of the eighth Psalm, Justinian says, is to divide Christ in two, to introduce the false doctrine of the glorification of Christ for merit, and to assume that he who was thus glorified was previously alien to the sphere to which he had been raised.[21]

Although Justinian appeals often to individual authorities like Athanasius, Gregory of Nazianzus, and Cyril, he seems in condemning Theodore and the Three Chapters as a whole to have put his chief reliance on the four oecumenical councils preceding that of 553, which he himself had convoked. In the Τύπος (see n. 14 above) to the Fifth Council he devotes most of his space to an enumeration of the first four universal councils and to a summary of their dogmatic decisions. He makes much, too, of the imperial precedents, and notes with obvious relish the role of his predecessors, Constantine, Theodosius I, Theodosius II, and Marcian, in formulating the orthodox faith and securing the condemnation of the heretics.[22] In introducing his

---

the doctrine of Proclus in the controversy over the Three Chapters, see Franz Xaver Bauer, *Proklos von Konstantinopel, ein Beitrag zur Kirchen- u. Dogmengeschichte des 5. Jahrhunderts* (*Veröffentlichungen aus dem Kirchenhistorischen Seminar München*, IV, 8 [Munich, 1919]), 64–95.

[20] Ed. Schwartz, 49.7–9; MPG, 86.1, 1047C: οἱ δὲ αὐτὸν τὸν θεὸν λόγον ἐνανθρωπῆσαι μὴ ὁμολογοῦντες φανεροί εἰσι τὸν Χριστὸν ψιλὸν ἄνθρωπον εἶναι καὶ κατὰ χάριν υἱὸν θεοῦ ὀνομάζεσθαι λέγοντες, ὡς ἡ κακοδοξία Νεστορίου καὶ Θεοδώρου τοῦ διδασκάλου αὐτοῦ λέγει. Cf. ed. Schwartz, 76.16 ff.; MPG, 86.1, 999AB.

[21] Ed. Schwartz, 74.24–76.12 (Philippians 2.6 f.), 55.21–59.13; MPG, 86.1, 997B–999A, 1061C–1069D.

Biblical references, unless otherwise indicated, are to the King James version (occasionally with minor changes).

For the history of the exegesis of Philippians 2.5 ff., see P. Henry, *s. v.* kénose, *Dictionnaire de la Bible, Supplément*, 5 (1950), 7–161.

[22] MPG, 86.1, 1035B–1039D.

denunciation of Theodore, which follows immediately after his summary of the great conciliar decisions, he notes that the Nestorians had taken advantage of the opportunity offered by Theodore of Mopsuestia, "whose blasphemies are much grosser than those of his disciple Nestorius," to circumvent "these four councils." [23] He reinforces his argument in the Τύπος by a long extract from the letter written by Cyril after the Council of Ephesus to Theodosius II in which Cyril had declared Christ to be immutable and unchangeable by nature.[24]

In all such matters, Justinian says, the chief authority is the Nicene Creed drafted by the 318 fathers in 325, which he received at baptism and faithfully observes, and which was accepted as the touchstone of the faith by the "150 fathers" (i.e., the Second Oecumenical Council at Constantinople in 381), the Third Council (Ephesus, 431), and the Fourth (Chalcedon, 451). He asserts vigorously and lays great emphasis upon the fact that the fathers of each of the three oecumenical councils that were subsequent to Nicaea remained faithful to the Symbol of 325 in all respects, and that the councils of 431 and 451 expressly rejected all creeds except that of 325. It is not surprising, therefore, that he places his own anathemas, which he subjoins immediately after this discussion, within the same Nicene tradition,[25] and that he censures Theodore for misinterpreting the Creed of the 318 fathers.[26]

In keeping with this principle also is the prominence that he gives in his system to Nicene terms like ὁμοούσιος, and his insistence that Christ was the eternal Logos of God the Father, of the same essence as the Father, and in no wise a created being.[27]

THEODORE OF MOPSUESTIA

Modern opinions on the Christology of Theodore differ widely. The older critics acquiesced easily in his condemnation by Justinian and the Council of 553; and Mai, in rejecting Theodore, repudiated those who attempted to force an orthodox interpretation upon his works.[28] Neander and

[23] *Ibid.*, 1039D–1041D.
[24] *Ibid.*, 1037D.
[25] Ed. Schwartz, 88.34–90.15; MPG, 86.1, 1013ABC.
[26] Ed. Schwartz, 100.30 ff.; MPG, 86.1, 1025AB. The creed mentioned here by Justinian as condemned at Ephesus and Chalcedon was first associated directly with Theodore's name by Marius Mercator; see n. 59 below.
[27] Ed. Schwartz, 72.29–74.16, 76.21 ff., 59.16 ff.; MPG, 86.1, 995C–997A, 999B, 1035C, 1071A. For other passages in Justinian on Christ's immutability, see 27.3 ff., 31.15, 36.21 ff., 53.32 ff.
[28] Le Nain de Tillemont, *Mémoires pour servir à l'histoire ecclésiastique des six premiers siècles*, 8 (2d ed., Paris, 1713), 565–568; Leo Allatius, *Diatriba de Theodoris*, reprinted in

THE IMMUTABILITY OF CHRIST 133

Dorner,[29] on the other hand, in their attempt to give an objective account, make no clear pronouncement on the question of his orthodoxy. The older view is repeated also in the preface to the edition of Theodore's *Commentary on the Minor Epistles of St. Paul* by H. B. Swete, who, however, remarks that Theodore was "far from being a wilful heretic" and erred largely because of his zeal in combating Apollinarianism.[30]

This judgment prevailed [31] until the recent publication of a considerable body of new texts of Theodore's works, both in the original Greek and in Syriac translation, necessitated a reëxamination and reappraisal of Theodore's theological position. The chief of these is Theodore's renowned commentary on the Psalms, mostly in Greek but partly in Latin, edited with great skill and learning by Monsignor Robert Devreesse,[32] who had published previously a valuable critical edition of the work of the Roman deacon Pelagius, *In defensione Trium Capitulorum*.[33] Devreesse has now terminated some twenty years of fruitful research on Theodore with an important book of over four hundred pages, modestly entitled *Essai sur Théodore de Mopsueste*,[34] which contains the results of his studies and one hundred pages of the Greek remains of Theodore's Commentary on the Gospel of St. John, patiently extricated from the *catenae* and a host of manuscripts that often conceal the words now identified as Theodore's under the name of other authors. Significant contributions have been made also by A. Mingana, the modern initiator of the new interest in this subject, who produced the Syriac

---

MPG, 66, 80C *et passim*; Angelo Mai, *Scriptorum veterum nova collectio*, 6 (Rome, 1832), v f.; Otto Fridolin Fritzsche in his *De Theodori Mopsuesteni vita et scriptis commentatio historica theologica* (Halle, 1836, as reprinted in MPG, 66, 24B, 59-60).

[29] Augustus Neander, *General History of the Christian Religion and Church*, transl. by Joseph Torrey, 4 (London, 1851), 108 ff., 409 ff., 430 ff.; J. A. Dorner, *History of the Development of the Doctrine of the Person of Christ*, Div. II, vol. I (transl. by D. W. Simon, Edinburgh, 1869), 25 ff., 380 ff.

[30] *Theodori Episcopi Mopsuesteni in Epistolas B. Pauli Commentarii*, ed. H. B. Swete, 1 (Cambridge, England, 1880), lxxix-lxxxvii.

[31] So Bardenhewer, Harnack, Schwane, Seeberg, and Tixeront. The question is still discussed on the old premises, without use of the newly published material, in the fifth edition of Friedrich Loofs, *Leitfaden zum Studium d. Dogmengeschichte*, ed. Kurt Aland (Halle-Saale, 1950), 217-227.

[32] *Studi e Testi*, 93 (Vatican City, 1939). Other important new texts have been published by Karl Staab, *Pauluskommentare aus d. Griechischen Kirche* (*Neutestamentliche Abhandlungen*, 15 [Münster, i. W., 1933]), 113-212. In the same series appeared J. Reuss, *Matthäus-, Markus-, u. Johannes-Katenen* (1941), but this I have not yet been able to obtain. See also Johannes Quasten, "Theodore of Mopsuestia on the Exorcism of the Cilicium," *Harvard Theological Review*, 35 (1942), 209-219; *idem*, ed., Francis J. Reine, *The Eucharistic Doctrine and Liturgy of the Mystagogical Catecheses of Theodore of Mopsuestia* (*Catholic University of America Studies in Christian Antiquity*, 2 [Washington, D. C., 1942]).

[33] *Studi e Testi*, 57 (Vatican City, 1932).

[34] *Ibid.*, 141 (*ibid.*, 1948).

of Theodore's catechetical homilies together with an English rendering (On the Nicene Creed, On the Lord's Prayer, On Baptism, On the Eucharist and Liturgy, and a brief Catechism, that purports to give a synopsis of Christian doctrine); [35] by J. M. Vosté, who edited and translated into Latin (from the Syriac) Theodore's *Commentary on the Gospel of St. John*, and has written a number of notable articles on Theodore; [36] and by Raymond Tonneau, who, working in collaboration with Devreesse, has put out a photographic reproduction of *Ms. Mingana Syr. 561* with a French version of the same catechetical orations that Mingana had rendered into English in *Woodbrooke Studies*.[37] In bringing out this corpus, though not unmindful of the great services of Mingana and the accuracy of his scholarship, Tonneau sought to reproduce Theodore's ideas with even greater fidelity, in order to do Theodore full justice and spare him criticism arising from infelicities of style or misinterpretation of key doctrinal passages.

Devreesse summarizes all that is known of Theodore and gives a well-documented exposition of Theodore's theological system. As a result of his textual researches he concludes that, when it is possible to control them by the genuine body of Theodore's writings, the fragments represented by the Council of 553 as excerpts from his works "se présentent tronqués, falsifiés, dénaturés de toute manière"; and that, wherever passages exist only in the conciliar acts and cannot be found in context in the indubitable works of the author himself, they should be regarded as in conflict with Theodore's position ("là où la pierre de touche fait défaut nécessité est de reconnaître qu'ils contredisent l'enseignement de Théodore").[38] Believing that no one today would condemn Origen as Justinian did, he requests the same indulgence for Theodore. One can detect omissions and exaggerations in Theodore's treatises, Devreesse says, but we should not on this account impute to him errors of which he was not guilty or reproach him for the date of his birth.[39]

---

[35] *Woodbrooke Studies*, 5–6 (Cambridge, England, 1932–33); *Bulletin of the John Rylands Library*, 5 (Manchester, 1919), 296–316.

[36] *Theodori Mopsuesteni Commentarius in Evangelium Iohannis Apostoli* (*Corpus Scriptorum Christianorum Orientalium, Scriptores Syri*, Series Quarta, Tomus III, Textus, No. 115 [Paris, 1940], Versio, No. 116 [Louvain, 1940]); "Théodore de Mopsueste sur les Psaumes," *Angelicum*, 19 (1942), 179–198; "L'oeuvre exégétique de Théodore de Mopsueste au ii° concile de Constantinople," *Revue Biblique*, 38 (1929), 382–395, 542–554; *idem*, "Le Commentaire de Théodore de Mopsueste sur St. Jean, d'après la version Syriaque," *ibid.*, 32 (1923), 522–551. See also Berthold Altaner, *Patrologie* (2d ed., Freiburg im Breisgau, 1950), 277 f.; L. Patterson, *Theodore of Mopsuestia and Modern Thought* (London, 1926).

[37] *Les homélies catéchétiques de Théodore de Mopsueste, reproduction phototypique du Ms. Mingana Syr. 561* (*Selly Oak Colleges' Library, Birmingham*), *traduction, introduction, index* (*Studi e Testi*, 145, Vatican City, 1949).

[38] *Essai*, 283.

[39] *Ibid.*, 285.

Actually, Devreesse finds little to reprehend in Theodore and, in his final summary, presents Theodore's Christology in eminently orthodox terms: At the appointed time, he says, the Son of God condescended to dwell among men; and the Logos took flesh, being God, like his Father, from whom he is inseparable, and also perfect man, like us mortal men, assuming and assumed, two natures, one person.[40]

In this exposition Devreesse makes no attempt to collate Theodore's theories with orthodox dogma. He does not point to their Nestorian character or attempt to justify or explain them on dogmatic grounds. Thus, he presents without historical comment or exegesis Theodore's notion, which surely smacks of Nestorianism, that the man assumed by the Logos was brought back to life by Him and by Him made immortal, impassible, incorruptible, and absolutely immutable, and placed at the right hand of the Father as judge of the universe.[41] Apparently, in the numerous other passages in which Theodore seems to have divided Christ sharply into two persons (one human and one divine), Devreesse feels that these views are tolerable dogmatically because the subjects they treat had not yet been formulated in precise terms by an oecumenical council. Moreover, he would probably argue, Theodore constantly appeals to the traditional language and insists that the two natures, the human and the divine, are united in the one Jesus Christ. Amann gave a very similar interpretation in the critique he wrote to salute the appearance of Mingana's *Woodbrooke Studies*, as also in a more recent article.[42]

Both Amann and Devreesse seem to have been so impressed by the originality and sound instincts of Theodore in Biblical exegesis,[43] and by the vigor with which he attacked Docetism and Apollinarianism, that they criticize him only with the greatest reluctance and many qualifications. Neither Martin Jugie nor Wilhelm de Vries felt any such qualms, and repudiate Theodore unequivocally as a heretic. Jugie calls him "le vrai père de la doctrine condamnée par l'Église sous le nom de nestorianisme," and finds his sacramental doctrine also defective for teaching that the consecrated

[40] *Ibid.*, 279: "Au temps marqué dans le plan divin, le Fils de Dieu condescend à habiter parmi les hommes. C'est le Verbe qui prend chair: Dieu, comme son Père, dont il est inséparable; homme parfait, comme un mortel d'entre nous. Assumant et assumé, deux natures, une personne — le Christ historique, d'un mot. L'Esprit — Saint forme son temple, le conduit au désert, le ressuscite. C'est lui, cet Homme-Dieu, qui est glorifié; c'est lui qui viendra juger le monde."

[41] *Ibid.*, 117 f.

[42] "La doctrine christologique de Théodore de Mopsueste (à propos d'une publication récente)," *Revue des sciences religieuses*, 14 (1934), 161–190; *s.v.* Théodore de Mopsueste, *Dictionnaire de théologie catholique*, 15 (1943), 235–279.

[43] Devreesse, *Essai*, 5–42, 53–93, gives the necessary bibliography.

VII

136

elements in the Eucharist are only figuratively the real body and blood of Christ.[44]

In the same vein, but more thorough and more detailed is the judgment of Wilhelm de Vries, who finds Theodore's dogmatic position unsatisfactory on several counts.[45] He is of the opinion that the chief error of Theodore is his denial of the true incarnation of the Son of God, his refusal to recognize that God truly became man in Christ and that God and man in Christ are one. In distinguishing between him who assumes and him who is assumed, and in stating categorically that these two are not the same, Theodore, according to de Vries, imperils the whole doctrine of salvation and of the sacraments.[46] Moreover, he says, Theodore in the περὶ τῆς ἐνανθρωπήσεως,[47] asserts that since no φύσις (nature) can exist without an hypostasis and no hypostasis, without a πρόσωπον, and since the two natures of the person are both complete, there must be in Jesus Christ two πρόσωπα, one of the Logos and another of the humanity.[48] Thus, Theodore lacked a true conception of the communicatio idiomatum, actually taught that there were two persons in Christ, denied original sin and its consequences, and, by refusing to recognize that Christ is truly God (since God only dwells in him), made a mere man, and not God, the cause of our salvation. This means, he believes, that the participation of mankind in the humanity of Jesus Christ, who, according to Theodore, is only the adoptive Son of God, gives us no consortium divinae naturae. Theodore's ideas on the sacraments follow the same pattern and in effect contravene the teaching of the Church that we become united with Christ in this world through baptism, or that there is a Real Presence of the Body and Blood of Christ in the Eucharist, or that the sacraments in general have more than symbolic value. De Vries admits that Theodore constantly made use of acceptable language

[44] "Le 'Liber ad baptizandos' de Théodore de Mopsueste," Échos d'Orient, 34 (1935), 257–271 (by "Liber ad baptizandos" Jugie means the various catechetical orations published by Mingana and Tonneau); Theologia dogmatica christianorum orientalium ab ecclesia catholica dissidentium, 5 (Paris, 1935), 90–91, 296–299, 308–311, 318 f.

[45] "Der 'Nestorianismus' Theodors von Mopsuestia in seiner Sakramentenlehre," Orientalia Christiana Periodica (abbreviated below as OCP), 7 (1941), 91–148; Sakramententheologie bei den Nestorianern (Orientalia Christiana Analecta, 133 [Rome, 1947]), index, s.v.

[46] OCP, loc. cit., 92 f.; Mingana, Woodbrooke Studies, 5, 198, 82; cf. 142, 38; 208, 91; 206, 90.

[47] Many of the criticisms made against Theodore stand the test of modern critical methods. But the passage on which de Vries relies here, taken from Leontius of Byzantium, does Theodore a great injustice, as is brilliantly demonstrated by Marcel Richard, "La tradition des fragments du traité περὶ τῆς ἐνανθρωπήσεως de Théodore de Mopsueste," Le Muséon, 56 (1943), 64 f.; idem, "L'introduction du mot 'hypostase' dans la théologie de l'incarnation," Mélanges de Science Religieuse, 2 (1945), 21–29.

[48] OCP, 93 f.

VII

THE IMMUTABILITY OF CHRIST 137

in expounding Christology and the sacraments, but claims that, despite this fact, he always abandons the teaching of the Church for the rationalistic and heretical exegesis of the Antiochene School, of which he was the foremost spokesman.[49]

From the strictly theological standpoint de Vries's strictures have great merit. The flaw in his argument, however, is that he oversimplifies the historical situation here and fails to demonstrate at any given point that the theories of Theodore which he reprehends as heretical could have been recognized as such by Theodore or his contemporaries. He offers no proof that during Theodore's lifetime the doctrine of the Person of Christ, of the relation between $\phi\acute{v}\sigma\iota\varsigma$, $\acute{v}\pi\acute{o}\sigma\tau\alpha\sigma\iota\varsigma$, and $\pi\rho\acute{o}\sigma\omega\pi o\nu$, had been formulated in any juridical or oecumenical way. Theodore died in 428, and therefore can hardly be criticized for not following the mandate of the Third Oecumenical Council of Ephesus (431), even if it were possible to determine what, if any, truly oecumenical decisions were reached at that time, in view of the bifurcation of the Council into two sections, one consisting of the partisans of Cyril of Alexandria and the other of the Antiochene group led by John of Antioch and Nestorius.[50] Likewise, it would be improper to condemn Theodore for failure to adhere to the Compromise Formula of 433, to which both John of Antioch and Cyril found it possible to subscribe, or to the Christological Symbol of the Fourth Oecumenical Council of 451.

Thus, we are faced with the problem as to whether Justinian and the Fifth Council of 553 were guilty of the same kind of anachronistic mistake. Unlike the Council of Chalcedon, which gave its oecumenical sanction to only two of Cyril's writings (the *Epistula dogmatica ad Nestorium* and the *Epistula ad orientales*),[51] Justinian's theologians in 553 endorsed also Cyril's *Twelve Anathemas* against Nestorius (the so-called *Epistula Synodica*), which clearly and unambiguously rejected the doctrine of the *assumptus homo*[52] and the premises underlying the Antiochene Christology. It is

---

[49] OCP, 94, 96, 99 f., 102–106, 108, 111, 123 f., 127, 132, 136–138.

De Vries occasionally refers (OCP, 97 f., 100, 104 f., 106–108) to Theodore's statements on the immortality, incorruptibility, and immutability of Christ, but without analysis, historical interpretation, or discussion of their true significance.

[50] Adhémar d'Alès, *Le dogme d'Éphèse* (Paris, 1931), 155 ff.; Friedrich Loofs, *Nestorius and His Place in the History of Christian Doctrine* (Cambridge, England, 1914), 53 f., 94 f.

[51] The two documents of Cyril approved at Chalcedon (*Epistolae* 4 and 39) are to be found in MPG, 77, 44–49, 173–81; Eduard Schwartz, ACO, 1.1.1, 25–28; 1.1.4, 15–20; 1.2, 37–39, 104–107; 1.5, 49–51, 334–340. Cf. Mansi, 6, 960AB, 973C; 7, 113BC; 8, 821E–822E. See Hubert du Manoir de Juaye, *Dogme et spiritualité chez Saint Cyrille d'Alexandrie* (Paris, 1944), 515 f.; Loofs, *op. cit.*, 97 f.

[52] Justinian and the Fifth Oecumenical Council expressly rejected the view set forth repeatedly by Theodore that the Logos joined himself to, or assumed, a man: Ed. Schwartz,

138

often said that Justinian's condemnation of the *Three Chapters* was intended to mollify the Monophysites and to win their loyalty to the Empire. This is a large question and will be treated *in extenso* in the book of which the present paper is an excerpt. As far as the anathematization of the works of Theodore is concerned, however, there can be no doubt that Justinian was addressing himself to a purely theological matter that had no specifically political implications.

Theodore's soteriology was closely bound up with his view of Christ as achieving immortality at the resurrection. God, he says, pronounced judgment against Satan, while

He raised Christ our Lord from the dead, and made Him immortal and immutable, and took Him up to heaven. And He vouchsafed to all the (human) race, while still on the earth, the joy of (His) gifts so that no room might be left to Satan from which to inflict injuries on us.[53]

This is a commonplace in Theodore and occurs countless times.

He [Jesus Christ] was also baptised so that He might perform the Economy of the Gospel according to order, and in this (Economy) He died and abolished death. It was easy and not difficult for God to have made Him at once immortal, incorruptible and immutable as He became after His resurrection, but because it was not He alone whom He wished to make immortal and immutable, but us also who are partakers of His nature, He rightly, and on account of this association, did not so make the firstfruits of us all in order that, as the blessed Paul said, "He might have the pre-eminence in all things" [Col. 1.18]. In this way, because of the communion that we have with Him in this world, we will, with justice, be partakers with Him of the future good things. . .

74.32–35, 88.3–7; MPG, 86.1, 997C, 1011B; n.b. anathemas 2, 3, 14: Mansi, 9, 377AB, 385D–388B; Hefele-Leclercq, *Histoire des conciles*, 3.1, 107 ff., 128 ff.

The attempts of modern theologians like F. Déodat de Basly (*La Christiade Française* [2 vols., Paris, 1927], supported by a series of learned and ingenious but unconvincing articles in *La France Franciscaine*, 11 [1928], 265–313; 12 [1929], 125–160; 17 [1934], 418–473, etc., which were analyzed at length by Auguste Gaudel, *Revue des sciences religieuses*, 17 [1937], 64–90, 214–234; 18 [1938], 45–71, 201–217) and Léon Seiller (*La psychologie humaine du Christ et l'unicité de personne* [Paris, 1949], published also in *Franziskanische Studien*, 1949, and reviewed adversely by P. Galtier, *Gregorianum*, 31 [1950], 457 f.) to prove that the Orthodox Church, East and West, has always endorsed the patently Nestorian doctrine of the *assumptus homo* are quite unsuccessful, as I hope to show on another occasion. H. Diepen, "De Assumptus-Homo-theologie. Een onderzoek naar de Christologie van R. P. Déodat de Basly, O.F.M.," 1948, I know only from the note in *Ephemerides Theologicae Lovanienses*, 25 (1949), 481.

[53] Translated from the Syriac by Mingana, *Woodbrooke Studies*, 6, 29; Tonneau, *Homélies*, 355: "et (Dieu) . . . condamna l'usurpateur (τύραννος) en raison de la volonté perverse qu'il avait montré contre lui (le Christ) et contre toute notre race, et il émit contre lui une sentence. Il ressuscita alors d'entre les morts Notre-Seigneur le Christ, le fit immortel et immuable et le fit monter au ciel. Dès lors il proposa pour tout le genre (humain, γένος) la jouissance des dons, en sorte qu'il ne restât plus au démon même la moindre occasion de nous nuire."

We also when we are baptised show (in ourselves) the symbol of the world to come; we die with Him in baptism, and we rise symbolically with Him, and we endeavour to live according to His law in the hope of the future good things which we expect to share with Him at the resurrection from the dead. If Christ our Lord had immediately after his rising from the dead, raised also all men who had previously died, and had bestowed upon them new life fully and immediately, we should have been in no need of doing anything; as, however, He actually performed only on Himself the renewal which is to come and through which He rose from the dead and His body became immortal and His soul immutable, it became necessary that this decrepit and mortal world should last further in order that mankind might believe in Him and receive the hope of communion (with Him) and future life.[54]

In these words the importance for human salvation of the immortality, incorruptibility, and immutability conferred upon Christ by the resurrection is strongly emphasized. A few more texts are of interest, both to confirm those already cited and to illustrate Theodore's sharp division between the Logos and the human Jesus Christ, which, it must be said, gives the impression of a Jesus Christ consisting of two persons. In his treatment of the sacrament of baptism, Theodore says:

The things that the ancients held as figures and shadows came now into reality when our Lord Jesus Christ, who was assumed from us and for us, died according to the human law, and through His resurrection became immortal, incorruptible and for ever immutable, and as such ascended into heaven, as by His union with our nature He became to us an earnest of our own participation in the event. In saying: "If Christ rose from the dead, how say some among you that there is no resurrection of the dead [1 Cor. 15, 12]," (the Apostle) clearly showed that it was necessary for all to believe that there is a resurrection, and in believing in it we had also to believe that we will equally clearly participate in it. As we have a firm belief that things that have already happened will happen to us, so [the things that happened at the resurrection of our Lord] we believe that they will happen to us.[55]

Theodore seems completely to have lost sight here of the presence of the Logos in the person of Christ. His Jesus Christ seems hardly more than a man, ψιλὸς ἄνθρωπος. Similarly, further along, Theodore adds:

And He [the man assumed from us] became for ever immune from death, and immortal and incorruptible by nature. And as such He ascended into heaven and became for ever beyond the reach of the harm and injury of Satan, who was thus unable to do any harm to a man who was immortal, incorruptible and immutable, and who dwelt in heaven and possessed a close union with the Divine nature.[56]

---

[54] *Woodbrooke Studies*, 5, 69 f.; Tonneau, *Homélies*, 151–153.
[55] *Woodbrooke Studies*, 6, 19 f.; Tonneau, *Homélies*, 331.
[56] *Woodbrooke Studies*, 6, 22; Tonneau, *Homélies*, 337.

140

At one point, in comparing the sacrament of baptism to the death (during the baptism itself and immersion into the water) and resurrection (in rising out of the water) of the Lord, he goes so far as to say that

you have been born and have become a new man; you are no more part of Adam who was mutable and burdened and made wretched by sin, but of Christ who was completely freed from sin through resurrection, while even before it He never drew nigh unto it. It was congruous that (this sinless state) should have had its beginning in Him before (His resurrection), and that at His resurrection He should fully receive an immutable nature. In this way He confirmed to us the resurrection from the dead and our participation in incorruptibility.[57]

Otherwise, he no doubt felt, Christ could not have been a complete and perfect man, and could not have held out to all men the hope of eternal life.

Several attempts have been made to reconstruct from the extant Syriac the original text of the Nicene Creed [58] that Theodore expounded in his catechetical orations. All of these differ slightly from each other but all agree that Theodore's Creed, not to be confused with the *Symbolum fidei* ascribed to him by the Fifth Council,[59] bore closer resemblance to the so-called Symbol of 381 than to that of 325, and lacked the anathemas in which the fathers of 325 denounced the Arian doctrine that Christ was τρεπτός. The Creed of 325 is so frequently cited in the early centuries of the church together with

[57] *Woodbrooke Studies*, 6, 67; Tonneau, *Homélies*, 455: "Tu es né et devenu complètement autre; tu n'es plus dès lors partie de (cet) Adam, qui est changeant, — parce que accablé de péchés et malheureux, — mais (tu es partie) du Christ, qui fut absolument exempt (de l'atteinte) du péché par la résurrection, n'en ayant même fait aucun depuis le commencement, parce qu'il convenait que cela aussi fût aussi en lui à titre primordial; mais, par la résurrection, c'est complètement qu'il reçoit la nature immuable. Par conséquent, pour nous aussi, il confirme la résurrection d'entre les morts et la participation à l'incorruptibilité."

[58] Devreesse, *Essai*, 103, n. 3; *idem*, "Les instructions catéchétiques de Théodore de Mopsueste," *Revue des sciences religieuses*, 13 (1933), 425–427; J. Lebon, "Les anciens symboles dans la définition de Chalcédoine," *Revue d'histoire ecclésiastique*, 32 (1936), 835–840. A. Rücker, *Ritus Baptismi et Missae, quem descripsit Theodorus Ep. Mopsuestenus in sermonibus catecheticis* (*Opuscula et Textus historiam ecclesiae eiusque vitam atque doctrinam illustrantia, Series liturgica*, edd. R. Stapper et A. Rücker, [Münster, 1933]), 43 f. See also J. N. D. Kelly, *Early Christian Creeds*, 187 f.

[59] *Essai*, 256 f.; see index, *s.v. symbole*. Devreesse accepts as Theodore's no *symbolum fidei* except that included in the commentary on the Nicene Creed. He denies the authenticity of the creed attributed to Theodore by Marius Mercator and condemned as Theodore's by Justinian, the Fifth Council, and Leontius, and believes that it is improper to associate this latter document with Theodore in any way whatsoever. W. de Vries, *loc. cit.*, on the other hand, while uncertain whether it was actually penned by Theodore himself, is of the opinion that the theological notions it contains may properly be traced back to him. Kelly, *loc. cit.* (in previous note), rightly draws attention to the striking resemblance between the creed rejected by Devreesse and the Nestorian symbol reconstructed by C. P. Caspari, *Ungedruckte, unbeachtete u. wenig beachtete Quellen zur Geschichte des Taufsymbols u. d. Glaubensregeln*, 1 (Christiania, 1866), 116 ff.; G. Ludwig Hahn, *Bibliothek der Symbole u. Glaubensregeln d. alten kirche*, (3rd ed., Breslau, 1897), no. 132 (pp. 144–146).

its anathemas that it is difficult to understand why Theodore was unaware
of the unacceptability of his doctrine of ἄτρεπτος, although the Creed does
occur occasionally without the anathemas. It is of some interest that Nestorius apparently meant by the "Nicene Creed" a formula like the so-called
Niceno-Constantinopolitan Creed, which, with the exception of the hybrid
symbol given by Epiphanius in his *Panarion,* regularly omits the anathemas.[60] None of Theodore's modern critics has noted the relevance of the
Nicene anathemas to a true appraisal of Theodore's Christology. But Justinian, whose talents in this field have often been misunderstood, depreci-
ated, and scorned, was too acute a theologian to miss so obvious a point.
What he was doing was to judge Theodore by the criterion of the *Symbolum
fidei* to which all churchmen professed allegiance, and which was by universal assent the infallible criterion of orthodoxy, always cited by all sides.

The Council of 325 intended by its anathema of those who regarded
Christ as τρεπτός to condemn the view that Jesus Christ like a man made a
choice between good and evil by virtue of his freedom of the will, and
could even have chosen sin and error had he willed to do so. This can be
proved by the pronouncement made earlier in 325 when the Council of fifty-
six bishops from Asia Minor, Syria, and Palestine that met at Antioch to appoint a successor to Philogonius took it upon itself to formulate an anti-Arian
creed rejecting such a conception.[61] Since this material was first published

---

[60] Kelly, *Early Christian Creeds,* 318 f.; Francis J. Badcock, *History of the Creeds* (2d ed.,
London, 1938), 195 f., 209; cf. P. T. Camelot, "'Symbole de Nicée,'" OCP, 13 (1947), 425 ff.
   Eduard Schwartz, "Das Nicaenum u. das Constantinopolitanum auf der Synode von
Chalkedon," *Zeitschrift für die neutestamentliche Wissenschaft,* 25 (1926), 38–88; J. Lebon,
"Les anciens symboles dans la définition de Chalcédoine," *Revue d'histoire ecclésiastique,*
32 (1936), 809–876; *idem,* "Nicée-Constantinople, les premiers symboles de foi," *ibid.,* 537–
547; A. d'Alès, "Nicée. Constantinople, les premiers symboles de foi," *Recherches de science
religieuse,* 26 (1936), 85–92. Cf. Ignacio Ortiz de Urbina, *El Símbolo Niceno* (Madrid, 1947);
idem, "Textus Symboli Nicaeni," OCP, 2 (1936), 330–350.
   For rare instances of the omission of the anathemas from the Nicene Creed, see the Latin
version quoted by Pope Leo I in his letter to the Emperor Leo I (*Ep.* 165), ed. Schwartz,
ACO, 2.4, 114.18 ff.; MPL, 54, 1159B (Latin), 1160B (Greek); Cuthbert H. Turner,
*Ecclesiae occidentalis monumenta iuris antiquissima, canonum et conciliorum Graecorum
interpretationes Latinae,* 1.2.1 (Oxford, 1913), 306. But cf. (with anathemas) *ibid.,* 298 f.,
304–305, 307, 309–320. Note also *ibid.,* 300, where one manuscript omits the *et mutabilem
uel conuertibilem esse Filium Dei,* and 308, a copy of the Creed taken from Cyril, *Epistola* 1,
in which Cyril fails to give the anathemas: MPG, 77, 16C; Mansi, 5, 479 f.; Schwartz, ACO,
1.1.1, 12.32–13.5; 1.3, 6.4–11. Cyril gives the anathemas in *Epp.* 4 and 55, for which see nn. 51
and 106. Other quotations of the Creed with anathemas can be found in Schwartz, ACO, 1.1.4,
51.19–29; 1.3, 28.12–22, 60.31–61.5, 120.38–121.10.
   [61] Erich Seeberg, *Die Synode von Antiochien im Jahre 324/25. Ein Beitrag zur Geschichte
des Konzils von Nicäa* (*Neue Studien zur Geschichte d. Theologie u. d. Kirche,* 16 [Berlin,
1913]), gives a review of the evidence and of the controversy. H. G. Opitz has now fixed the
date definitely as 325: "Die Zeitfolge des Arianischen Streites von den Anfängen bis zum
Jahre 328," *Zeitschrift für die neutestamentliche Wissenschaft,* 33 (1934), 151.

VII

142

by Schwartz in 1905 its authenticity has been doubted, principally by Harnack and Nau, but authorities now agree that the Syriac texts which are our sole extant authorities for this pre-Nicene Synod, are genuine and reliable.[62] In any case, the text itself is clearly anterior to the Nicene Creed (which is a much crisper and more formal document) and undoubtedly represents the theological ideas of early opponents of Arius. The anathemas of this Antiochene formulary do not deviate substantially from those of Nicaea but they are slightly fuller in form and, hence, give added precision to the condemnation of the use of $\tau\rho\epsilon\pi\tau\acute{o}\varsigma$ for Christ. At Nicaea the fathers wrote:

those who say, there was when when he was not, and, he did not exist before he was made, and that he was created out of nothing, or who assert that the Son of God is of a different substance or essence, or is created or mutable or changeable – these the Catholic and Apostolic Church anathematizes.[63]

But the Antiochene anathema of the use of $\tau\rho\epsilon\pi\tau\acute{o}\varsigma$ as a description of Christ is much more explicit:

In addition [we anathematize] those who hold that he is immutable by reason of his free will, and likewise those who derive his birth from nothing and claim that He is not immutable by nature like the Father. For our Savior has been taught to be the image of the Father in all respects, but especially in this.[64]

The bishops at Antioch indubitably meant to repudiate the Arian contention that Christ could conceivably have chosen the wrong path if he had wished to do so.

Obviously the same interpretation is valid in the exegesis of $\tau\rho\epsilon\pi\tau\acute{o}\varsigma$ in the Nicene Symbol. Schwartz maintains that Constantine I, knowing of the work of the Council of Antioch of 325, purposely forced a verdict at Nicaea that

[62] Kelly, *Early Christian Creeds*, 208 f.; Monald Goemans, *Het algemeen concilie in de vierde eeuw* (Nijmegen-Utrecht, 1945), 26 f.

[63] See n. 68; cf. C. H. Turner, *History and Use of Creeds and Anathemas* (London, 1906).

[64] The Greek version was prepared by E. Schwartz on the basis of the Syriac, "Zur Geschichte des Athanasius VI," *Nachrichten von d. königl. Gesellschaft d. Wissenschaften zu Göttingen*, Philologisch-historische Kl. (1905), 277.8 ff.; reprinted by Hans Georg Opitz, *Athanasius Werke*, 3.1.1 (Berlin–Leipzig, 1934), 39.16–40.2: . . . ἀναθεματίζοντες ἐκείνους, οἳ λέγουσιν ἢ νομίζουσιν ἢ κηρύττουσιν τὸν υἱὸν τοῦ θεοῦ κτίσμα ἢ γενητὸν ἢ ποιητὸν καὶ οὐκ ἀληθῶς γέννημα εἶναι ἢ ὅτι ἦν ὅτε οὐκ ἦν· ἡμεῖς γάρ, ὅτι ἦν καὶ ἔστιν καὶ ὅτι φῶς ἐστιν, πιστεύομεν· προσέτι δὲ κἀκείνους οἳ τῇ αὐτεξουσίῳ θελήσει αὐτοῦ ἄτρεπτον εἶναι αὐτὸν ἡγοῦνται, ὥσπερ καὶ οἱ ἐκ τοῦ μὴ ὄντος παράγοντες τὴν γέννησιν, καὶ μὴ φύσει ἄτρεπτον κατὰ τὸν πατέρα. εἰκὼν γὰρ ὡς ἐν πᾶσιν, οὕτως καὶ μάλιστα ἐν τῷδε τοῦ πατρὸς ἐκηρύχθη ὁ σωτὴρ ἡμῶν. Cf. also *ibid.*, 3 ff.: ἀλλὰ κυρίως καὶ ἀληθῶς υἱὸν λέγουσιν αὐτὸν αἱ γραφαὶ γεννηθέντα, ὥστε καὶ πιστεύομεν ἄτρεπτον εἶναι καὶ ἀναλλοίωτον αὐτὸν οὐδὲ θελήσει ἢ θέσει γεννηθῆναι ἢ γενέσθαι, ὥστε ἐκ τοῦ μὴ ὄντος αὐτὸν εἶναι φαίνεσθαι, ἀλλὰ καθὸ γεννηθῆναι αὐτὸν εἰκός, οὐδ' ὅπερ οὐ θέμις ἐννοεῖν καθ' ὁμοίωσιν ἢ φύσιν ἢ μῖξιν οὐδενὸς τῶν δι' αὐτοῦ γενομένων . . .

would be independent of the episcopal decision made at Antioch, and show the superiority of the imperial to the episcopal or even conciliar authority.[65] Actually, apart from the lack of the Nicene ὁμοούσιος in the Antiochene decree and ạ few other minor variations, the two creeds do not differ radically. In any case, the anathemas of both are very similar, and in the condemnation of τρεπτός the Nicene version departs from its predecessor only by being more terse.

That τρεπτός is to be understood in the same sense in both formulae is demonstrated by incontestable contemporary evidence. Earliest in point of time is the Ἐπιστολὴ τῆς ἐν Νικαίᾳ συνόδου κατὰ Ἀρείου καὶ τῶν σὺν αὐτῷ, copies of which are preserved by Athanasius in his De decretis Nicaenae synodi,[66] as well as by the ecclesiastical historians, Gelasius, Socrates, and Theodoretus.[67] According to Athanasius the Council of Nicaea anathematized the view that the Son of God was free by exercise of his will to choose either evil or virtue.[68] Neither τρεπτός nor ἄτρεπτος is mentioned at this

[65] Eduard Schwartz, "Zur Geschichte des Athanasius VII," Nachrichten von d. königl. Gesellschaft d. Wissenschaften zu Göttingen, Philologisch-historische Kl. (1908), 370 ff.
[66] Opitz, Athanasius Werke, 2.1.3 (Berlin–Leipzig, 1935), 35.8–37.2.
[67] Socrates, H.E., 1.9.1, MPG, 67, 77C; Gelasius, H.E., 2, 34, 4, edd. Gerhard Loeschke et Margret Heinemann (Leipzig, 1918), 121.5–11; cf. Theodoretus, H.E., 1, 9, 4, ed. Léon Parmentier (Leipzig, 1911), 39.2–7; MPG, 82, 928C.
[68] De decretis Nicaenae synodi, 36, 3, ed. Opitz, op. cit., 2.1.3, 35.18 ff.: καὶ παμψηφὶ ἔδοξεν ἀναθεματισθῆναι τὴν ἀσεβῆ αὐτοῦ [sc. Ἀρείου] δόξαν καὶ τὰ ῥήματα καὶ τὰ ὀνόματα τὰ βλάσφημα, οἷς ἐκέχρητο βλασφημῶν τὸν υἱὸν τοῦ θεοῦ, λέγων 'ἐξ οὐκ ὄντων εἶναι' καὶ 'πρὶν γεννηθῆναι μὴ εἶναι' καὶ 'εἶναί ποτε ὅτε οὐκ ἦν,' καὶ αὐτεξουσιότητι κακίας καὶ ἀρετῆς δεκτικὸν τὸν υἱὸν τοῦ θεοῦ λέγοντος καὶ κτίσμα ὀνομάζοντος καὶ ποίημα. Comparison with the actual anathemas in the Nicene Creed itself, as quoted by Athanasius a few lines farther on (op. cit., 36.40 ff.), show that the intention in the last clause here is to anathematize the Arian use of τρεπτός. τοὺς δὲ λέγοντας 'ἦν ποτε ὅτε οὐκ ἦν' ἢ 'οὐκ ἦν πρὶν γεννηθῇ' ἢ 'ἐξ οὐκ ὄντων ἐγένετο' ἢ ἐξ ἑτέρας ὑποστάσεως ἢ οὐσίας φάσκοντας εἶναι ἢ κτιστὸν ἢ τρεπτὸν ἢ ἀλλοιωτὸν τὸν υἱὸν τοῦ θεοῦ τοὺς τοιούτους ἀναθεματίζει ἡ καθολικὴ καὶ ἀποστολικὴ ἐκκλησία.
This version of the anathemas differs only very slightly from the usually accepted oecumenical version. The Creed itself with anathemas runs as follows (ed. Schwartz, ACO, 1.1.7, 65.15–26; Schwartz gives the Latin form of the same in ACO, 1.3, 120.38–121.10):
πιστεύομεν εἰς ἕνα θεὸν πατέρα παντοκράτορα, πάντων ὁρατῶν τε καὶ ἀοράτων ποιητήν· καὶ εἰς ἕνα κύριον Ἰησοῦν Χριστὸν τὸν υἱὸν τοῦ θεοῦ, γεννηθέντα ἐκ τοῦ πατρὸς μονογενῆ, τουτέστιν ἐκ τῆς οὐσίας τοῦ πατρός, θεὸν ἐκ θεοῦ, φῶς ἐκ φωτός, θεὸν ἀληθινὸν ἐκ θεοῦ ἀληθινοῦ, γεννηθέντα, οὐ ποιηθέντα, ὁμοούσιον τῷ πατρί, δι' οὗ τὰ πάντα ἐγένετο, τά τε ἐν τῷ οὐρανῷ, καὶ τὰ ἐν τῇ γῇ, τὸν δι' ἡμᾶς τοὺς ἀνθρώπους καὶ διὰ τὴν ἡμετέραν σωτηρίαν κατελθόντα καὶ σαρκωθέντα, ἐνανθρωπήσαντα, παθόντα καὶ ἀναστάντα τῇ τρίτῃ ἡμέρᾳ, ἀνελθόντα εἰς οὐρανούς, ἐρχόμενον κρῖναι ζῶντας καὶ νεκρούς. καὶ εἰς τὸ ἅγιον πνεῦμα.
τοὺς δὲ λέγοντας· ἦν ποτε ὅτε οὐκ ἦν, καὶ πρὶν γεννηθῆναι οὐκ ἦν, καὶ ὅτι ἐξ οὐκ ὄντων ἐγένετο, ἢ ἐξ ἑτέρας ὑποστάσεως ἢ οὐσίας φάσκοντας εἶναι ἢ τρεπτὸν ἢ ἀλλοιωτὸν τὸν υἱὸν τοῦ θεοῦ, τούτους ἀναθεματίζει ἡ ἀποστολικὴ καὶ καθολικὴ ἐκκλησία.
See also the expanded version of the Creed prepared by Athanasius to solemnize his conviction that the Holy Spirit is of the same essence as the Father and the Son: ACO, 1.1.7, 66. 10–34; MPG, 26, 1232 ABC.

juncture, but the context makes it perfectly clear that it is the τρεπτός of the Nicene anathema to which these authors have reference.

ATHANASIUS

For Athanasius, as for the Nicene party in general, this was a vital question. They did not of course deny that Jesus Christ as τέλειος ἄνθρωπος was endowed with a free will, nor had they the slightest intention of imposing any limitations upon the Godhead. What they would not tolerate was the hypothesis that Christ might conceivably have failed in any way to be what he was, or might possibly have made any choice at variance with those recorded in the Gospels. Hence, they fought strenuously against the Arian notion that Christ's sinlessness was the result of the exercise of his will. This, Athanasius said, would be to make Christ's divinity and resurrection a reward for proper discipline and would in effect do away with his eternal divinity, his Sonship, and his unity with God:

It is obvious that all men [have become sons of God] through him and he before all, or rather, that he is the sole true Son, who alone is true God of true God, having this rank, not as a reward of virtue, nor as one who is alien to it, but being divine by nature, by essence. For he is the Son begotten of the essence of the Father, so that none may doubt that, like the immutable Father, the Logos also is immutable. . . . For he was not advanced from a lower state to a higher one, but rather, being God, took the form of a Servant (cf. Isaiah 53, Philippians 2.5 ff.), and in taking it was not elevated but humbled himself. Where then in all this is there a reward for virtue, or what progress or improvement is there in humiliation? [69]

[69] *Oratio I contra Arianos*, 39 f., MPG, 26, 93ABC: δῆλον ὅτι δι' αὐτοῦ μὲν οἱ πάντες, αὐτὸς δὲ πρὸ πάντων, μᾶλλον δὲ μόνον αὐτὸς ἀληθινὸς υἱός, καὶ μόνος ἐκ τοῦ ἀληθινοῦ θεοῦ θεὸς ἀληθινός ἐστιν, οὐ μισθὸν ἀρετῆς ταῦτα λαβών, οὐδὲ ἄλλος ὢν παρὰ ταῦτα, ἀλλὰ φύσει, κατ' οὐσίαν ὢν ταῦτα. γέννημα γὰρ τῆς τοῦ πατρὸς οὐσίας ὑπάρχει, ὥστε μηδένα ἀμφιβάλλειν, ὅτι καθ' ὁμοιότητα τοῦ ἀτρέπτου πατρὸς ἄτρεπτός ἐστι καὶ ὁ λόγος . . . οὐ γὰρ ἐξ ἐλαττόνων βελτίων γέγονεν· ἀλλὰ μᾶλλον θεὸς ὑπάρχων τὴν δούλου μορφὴν ἔλαβε, καὶ ἐν τῷ λαβεῖν οὐκ ἐβελτιώθη, ἀλλ' ἐταπείνωσεν ἑαυτόν. ποῦ τοίνυν ἐν τούτοις μισθὸς τῆς ἀρετῆς, ἢ ποία προκοπὴ καὶ βελτίωσις ἐν ταπεινώσει;

In the references that follow, the *Oratio I contra Arianos* will be abbreviated by the letters C.A. The first number thereafter indicates the section, the succeeding ones, the columns in MPG, 26.

Most instructive as sources of Athanasian theology are the letters of Bishop Alexander of Alexandria (313–328), approximately seventy of which were known to Epiphanius (*Panarion*, 69, 4, 3 [ed. Karl Holl, 3, 155.25 ff.]). Of the few that have been preserved in the works of other writers, perhaps the most notable is the one addressed to Bishop Alexander of Thessalonike [so designated by Opitz; otherwise spoken of as Alexander of Constantinople], which contains in brief outline most of what Athanasius has to say about the immutability of Christ: Theodoretus, *H.E.*, 1, 4, 1–61, ed. Parmentier, 8 ff.; MPG, 82, 888B–909B; ed. Opitz, *op. cit.*, 3.1.1, Urk. 14, 19–29; n.b., for the immutability of Christ and Athanasius's treatment of this subject in the *Oratio I contra Arianos* and the *De decretis Nicaenae synodi*: 21.11–22, 24.11–24, 25.1–5, 27.1 f., 13 f. Cf. Alexander's letter to all the bishops of the church, *ibid.*, Urk. 4b, 8.2 f., 7–10; 9.7 ff.; Socrates, *H.E.*, 1, 6, MPG, 67, 44A–52A; Gelasius, *H.E.*, 2, 3, 1–21, edd. Loeschke and Heinemann, 34.22–40.18.

THE IMMUTABILITY OF CHRIST 145

This passage epitomizes Athanasius's argument against the Arian doctrine of the mutability of Christ. But in view of the high importance he himself attached to this polemic, which occupies the greater part of his first *Oratio contra Arianos*, and in view of the fact that his theory of the ἀτρεπτότης of Christ became normative for the Byzantine Church, it will be instructive to analyze his treatment of this subject with some care.

Unless Christ is to be likened to wood or a stone, the Arians contended, he must be mutable and have freedom to choose either good or evil, as he wishes. This proposition Athanasius attacked in the first instance because it rested on the Arian thesis, abominated by him and the Orthodox Church, that Christ was a created being (κτιστόν). If, he asks, the Logos were mutable and changeable, when would he come to rest, and when would he cease to progress? And how could the mutable be like the immutable? Were the Logos mutable, and his will undependable, he would be constantly changing, and could not be the image of the Father. Nor would Christ ever have said, "He that hath seen me hath seen the Father" (John 14.9), unless he were, like the Father, immutable and changeless. Moreover, if he were mutable and if he made progress daily, he would not be perfect.

But, how could he not be perfect [exclaims Athanasius], who is equal to God? Or how could he not be immutable who is one with God and the true Son of his essence? Since the essence of the Father is immutable, immutable also would he be who is the truly begotten of his Father's essence,[70] . . . even as the entire Trinity is perfect, immutable, and unchangeable.[71]

For a harsh judgment on the theology of Athanasius, see Marcel Richard, "Saint Athanase et la psychologie du Christ selon les Ariens," *Mélanges de science religieuse*, 4 (1947), 5–54, who argues that Athanasius made no provision for the human soul in Christ, and never realized the inadequacies of a Christology that did not so provide. Louis Bouyer, *L'Incarnation et l'église — corps du Christ dans la théologie de Saint Athanase* (Paris, 1943), 102 ff., tries to show that Athanasius does not deny Christ a human soul.

[70] C.A., 35, 84A–85B: 'αὐτεξούσιός ἐστιν ἢ οὐκ ἔστι; προαιρέσει κατὰ τὸ αὐτεξούσιον καλός ἐστι, καὶ δύναται, ἐὰν θελήσῃ, τραπῆναι, τρεπτῆς ὢν φύσεως· ἢ ὡς λίθος καὶ ξύλον οὐκ ἔχει τὴν προαίρεσιν ἐλευθέραν εἰς τὸ κινεῖσθαι καὶ ῥέπειν εἰς ἑκάτερα;' . . . εἰ γὰρ τρεπτὸς καὶ ἀλλοιούμενός ἐστιν ὁ λόγος, ποῖ ἄρα στήσεται, καὶ ποῖον αὐτοῦ τὸ τέλος ἔσται τῆς ἐπιδόσεως; ἢ πῶς ὅμοιος τῷ ἀτρέπτῳ ὁ τρεπτὸς εἶναι δυνήσεται; πῶς δὲ ὁ τὸν τρεπτὸν ἑωρακὼς ἑωρακέναι τὸν ἄτρεπτον νομίσειεν; ἐν ποίᾳ δὲ ἄρα ἐὰν γένηται καταστάσει, δυνήσεταί τις τὸν πατέρα ἐν αὐτῷ βλέπειν; δῆλον γὰρ ὡς οὐκ ἀεί τις ὄψεται ἐν αὐτῷ τὸν πατέρα, διὰ τὸ ἀεὶ τρέπεσθαι τὸν υἱόν, καὶ ἀλλοιουμένης αὐτὸν εἶναι φύσεως· ὁ μὲν γὰρ πατὴρ ἄτρεπτος καὶ ἀναλλοίωτος, καὶ ἀεὶ καὶ ὡσαύτως ἔχει, καὶ ὁ αὐτός ἐστιν· ὁ δὲ υἱὸς εἰ κατ' ἐκείνους τρεπτός, καὶ οὐκ ἀεὶ ὁ αὐτός, ἀλλ' ἀεὶ ἀλλοιουμένης φύσεώς ἐστι, πῶς ὁ τοιοῦτος εἰκὼν τοῦ πατρὸς εἶναι δύναται, οὐκ ἔχων τὸ ὅμοιον τῆς ἀτρεψίας; πῶς δὲ καὶ ὅλως ἐν τῷ πατρί ἐστιν, ἀμφίβολον ἔχων τὴν προαίρεσιν; τάχα δὲ καὶ τρεπτὸς ὤν, καὶ καθ' ἡμέραν προκόπτων, οὔπω τέλειός ἐστιν· ἀλλ' ἡ μὲν τοιαύτη τῶν Ἀρειανῶν οἰχέσθω μανία, ἡ δὲ ἀλήθεια λαμπέτω, καὶ δεικνύτω τούτους παραφρονοῦντας. πῶς γὰρ οὐ τέλειος, ὁ ἴσος θεῷ; ἢ πῶς οὐκ ἄτρεπτος, ὁ μετὰ τοῦ πατρὸς ἓν ὤν, καὶ τῆς οὐσίας ἴδιος ὢν υἱὸς αὐτοῦ; τῆς δὲ οὐσίας τοῦ πατρὸς οὔσης ἀτρέπτου, ἄτρεπτον ἂν εἴη καὶ τὸ ἐξ αὐτῆς ἴδιον γέννημα. εἰ δὲ τούτου οὕτως ὄντος, τοῦ λόγου τροπὴν καταψεύδονται, μανθανέτωσαν ποῦ τούτων ὁ λόγος κινδυνεύει· ἐκ γὰρ τοῦ καρποῦ καὶ τὸ δένδρον ἐπιγινώσκεται· διὰ τοῦτο καὶ ὁ ἑωρακὼς

VII

146

The Son is unvarying like the Father, Athanasius argues,[72] even after his incarnation, and discloses his changelessness and immutability to those who might think that he was altered by his union with flesh and had become something different from what he had always been. Created beings arise out of nothing, have no existence before creation, and are unstable by nature. But the Son is the eternal Wisdom; the cause of change in creation, he himself remains immutable.[73]

He then goes on to grapple with the Arian exegesis of Biblical texts that deal with the exaltation of Christ. The Arians took Philippians 2.9 ("Wherefore God also hath highly exalted him and given him a name which is above every name") and Psalm 45.7 ("Therefore God, thy God, hath anointed thee with the oil of gladness above thy fellows") to mean that Christ received grace, was exalted and anointed as a reward for the wise use he had made of his freedom, and was thus proved to have been of a mutable nature.[74] But, it is objected, this would mean that Christ, having won his Sonship by virtue and progress, could not have been the true God or genuine Son of God, since those who are called sons by reason of virtue and grace are not really sons by nature or being and can forfeit their sonship by misbehavior.[75] Christ then could not have been the Son of God according to the essence, but only by the grace imparted to him, whereby the Father is his creator, as he is of all the rest of the universe.[76] He could not, therefore, have been Son of God from the beginning, but only from the time of his incarnation, when he showed obedience even unto death. According to this interpretation, it would not be the Son who glorified human flesh but the flesh which glorified him. This reasoning, however, contradicts the Scriptures

---

τὸν υἱὸν ἑώρακε τὸν πατέρα, καὶ ἡ τοῦ υἱοῦ γνῶσις γνῶσίς ἐστι τοῦ πατρός. Cf. C.A., 40 and 35, 93B, 85A; MPG, 26, 292B (Or. c. A., 2, 68), 709A (De synodis, 16); MPG, 25, 205A, 449C, 456CD.

[71] C.A., 18, 49B, 1097A (Contra Apollinarium, 1, 3). Cf. Epistola ad Episcopos Aegypti et Libyae, 12, MPG, 25, 564BC: 'καὶ ὅτι τῇ μὲν φύσει τρεπτός ἐστι, τῷ δὲ ἰδίῳ αὐτεξουσίῳ, ὡς βούλεται, μένει καλός· ὅτε μέντοι θέλει, δύναται τρέπεσθαι καὶ αὐτὸς ὥσπερ καὶ τὰ πάντα. διὰ τοῦτο γὰρ ὁ θεός, προγινώσκων ἔσεσθαι καλὸν αὐτόν, προλαβὼν ταύτην αὐτῷ τὴν δόξαν δέδωκεν, ἣν ἂν καὶ ἐκ τῆς ἀρετῆς ἔσχε μετὰ ταῦτα. ὥστε ἐξ ἔργων αὐτοῦ, ὧν προέγνω ὁ θεός, τοιοῦτον αὐτὸν νῦν γεγονέναι.' 565 B: οὐ γάρ ἐστι τοῦ πατρὸς ἴδιον καὶ φύσει γέννημα ὁ λόγος, ἀλλὰ καὶ αὐτὸς χάριτι γέγονεν. Cf. ibid., 13, ibid., 568BC.

[72] On the basis of Hebrews 13.8, Malachi 3.6, Deuteronomy 32.39, Psalm 102.26–28.

[73] C.A., 36, 85BC–88A: [ὁ υἱὸς] γενόμενος ἄνθρωπος δείκνυσι τὴν ταυτότητα καὶ τὸ ἄτρεπτον ἑαυτοῦ τοῖς νομίζουσι διὰ τὴν σάρκα ἠλλοιῶσθαι αὐτόν, καὶ ἕτερόν τι γεγενῆσθαι . . . ὁ δὲ υἱός, ἐκ τοῦ πατρὸς ὤν, καὶ τῆς οὐσίας αὐτοῦ ἴδιος, ἀναλλοίωτος καὶ ἄτρεπτός ἐστιν, ὡς αὐτὸς ὁ πατήρ. οὐ γὰρ θέμις εἰπεῖν ἐκ τῆς οὐσίας τῆς ἀτρέπτου τρεπτὸν γεννᾶσθαι λόγον καὶ ἀλλοιουμένην σοφίαν.

[74] C.A., 37, 88BC: εἰ διὰ τοῦτο ὑψώθη, καὶ χάριν ἔλαβε, καὶ διὰ τοῦτο κέχρισται, μισθὸν τῆς προαιρέσεως ἔλαβε. προαιρέσει δὲ πράξας, τρεπτῆς ἐστι πάντως φύσεως.

[75] C.A., 37, 89A.

[76] C.A., 38, 89B.

and would make of Christ either something distinct from the Son, God, and Logos, or else a mere man.[77]

For, [says Athanasius], if Christ did not exist [before the incarnation], or if he did exist but afterwards improved, how were all things created through him, or how did the Father delight in him if he were not perfect? . . . Or if he first received adoration after his death, how is it that Abraham worshipped him in his tent (Gen. 18) and Moses in the bush (Exod. 3)? And how did Daniel see ten thousand myriads and thousands upon thousands ministering unto him (Dan. 7.10)? And if, according to them, he gained dignity recently, how is it that the Son referred to the heavenly glory he had before the foundation of the universe when he said, "And now, O Father, glorify thou me with thine own self with the glory which I had with thee before the world was" (John 17.5)? And if he were now exalted for the first time, as they say, how can it be that before this he "Bowed the heavens also, and came down" (Psalm 18.9) . . . If, therefore, the Son had his glory before the creation of the universe and was Lord of glory and the Most High, and descended from heaven, and is ever to be worshipped, then he was not glorified after his descent, but rather himself glorified what stood in need of glorification. And if he descended to improve our lot, he did not receive the titles of Son and God as a reward, but rather himself made us the sons of his Father and by becoming a man himself made men gods.[78]

Next, Christ is shown by further citation of the Scriptures [79] to have been God first and then man.[80] Moreover, we are told, St. Paul in Philippians 2.5–11 teaches that Christ in the incarnation did not advance from an inferior position to a higher one, but rather, as God, took the form of a servant, through which he was not exalted but humbled. This precludes the possibility of Christ's having received any kind of promotion thereby; being from eternity in the Father, he was plainly incapable of further advancement or exaltation.[81] The texts, contrariwise, like Philippians 2.9 (quoted above) according to which "God hath highly exalted him and given him a name which is above every name," refer not to Christ's divinity, but to his humanity, which he glorified and made immortal, and in so doing destroyed the power of death over mankind.[82]

For, just as Christ died and was exalted as a man, so also as a man he is said to receive what he always had as God, in order that the grace thus given might be vouchsafed also to us. For the Logos was not impaired when he took a body, so as to seek to

[77] C.A., 38, 89CD: φαίνεται γὰρ μηδὲν βελτιώσας αὐτὸς τὴν σάρκα, ἀλλὰ μᾶλλον αὐτὸς δι' αὐτῆς βελτιωθείς, εἴ γε κατὰ τὴν κακόνοιαν αὐτῶν τότε ὑψώθη καὶ υἱὸς ἐλέχθη, ὅτε γέγονεν ἄνθρωπος.
[78] Ibid., 92AB.
[79] John 1.3, Colossians 1.15–17.
[80] C.A., 39, 92C.
[81] C.A., 40, 93B–96B.
[82] C.A., 41–43, 96B–101B. Similar exegesis is to be found for Proverbs 8.22, Acts 2.36, and Hebrews 3.1–4 in sections 53–64.

obtain grace, but instead even deified what he had put on and conferred this great benefit upon the human race. Being Logos and existing in the form of God, he has always received adoration. Likewise, remaining unchanged, even after becoming man and being called Jesus, he none the less has dominion over all creation, which bends the knee to him in this name, and confesses that the incarnation of the Logos and his submission to death in the flesh in no way discredit his divinity but increase the glory of God the Father.[83]

Athanasius applies the same method of interpretation to the unction mentioned in Psalm 45.7 ("Thou hast loved righteousness and hated iniquity. Therefore, God, thy God, hath anointed thee with the oil of gladness") and to the benefits of Christ's baptism, both of which he ascribes, not to him who was already God and Son and King and Logos, but to the humanity that was joined to him in the incarnation and was thus ennobled, freed from sin, and made immortal by the Logos without a transformation of his nature.[84]

Jesus Christ, [he says, citing Hebrews 13.8], is the same yesterday, today, and forever, and remains immutable. It is the same who gives and who receives, giving as the Logos of God, and receiving as man. For it is not the Logos, as Logos, who is the beneficiary of improvement, since he has had everything from all eternity, but mankind, who in him and through him have the source of all gifts.[85]

The first half of the above-cited seventh verse of Psalm 45 ("Thou hast loved righteousness and hated iniquity") was taken by the Arians as proof of Christ's mutability. But, replies Athanasius, this passage really proves the contrary and demonstrates that Christ was not subject to change. It is true of men, he says, that some have transgressed and some have disobeyed. They are so inconstant that often a man who had been good or just at one time might at another be bad or unjust. Accordingly, there was need for one who was invariable, so that men might then have before them the unvarying exemplar of the justice of the Logos as a spur to virtue. Since the first Adam erred and with his sin brought death into the world, it was needful that the second Adam be immutable and thus empower mankind to gain the same victory over sin that he had won by reason of his immutability and invariability.

Very properly, therefore, the Lord, who is from eternity immutable by nature and a lover of justice and a hater of evil, was anointed and himself sent so that, being unchangeable and remaining so, he might take mutable flesh, condemn the sin in it, make

[83] C.A., 42, 97C–100A.
[84] C.A., 46–49, 105B–116A: αὐτὸς δὲ ὁ αὐτός ἐστι· καὶ οὐκ ἐπειδὴ γέγονεν ἄνθρωπος . . . ἐτράπη (112B).
[85] C.A., 48, 112C.

it free, and enable men in the future to fulfil the justice of the law in it, and thus be able to say, "We are no longer in the flesh but in the spirit, if the spirit of God dwelleth within us" (Romans 8.9).[86]

Athanàsius repudiates the Arian Biblical exegesis in general because it fails to recognize that the Logos has all that the Father has, including the Father's immutability and unchangeableness.

It is not as subject to the laws and to inclination in either direction that he [sc. Christ] loves one thing and hates another, as if in fear of falling from grace, should he choose what he ought not and in other ways be shown to be mutable. But since he is God and the Logos of the Father, he is a just judge, who loves virtue, or rather, is the bestower of virtue. Being just and holy by nature, he is therefore said to love justice and hate injustice; or, in other words, he loves and embraces the virtuous and rejects and hates the unrighteous.[87]

Furthermore, Athanasius adds, there are similar texts (Psalm 10.7; 5.6; 86.2; Malachi 1.2 f.; Isaiah 61.8) that describe God the Father as loving justice and hating iniquity, not because God would just as easily choose either alternative, for that is the characteristic of created beings, but because as judge he favors the just over the wicked. So, in this also, the Son is the image of the Father.[88]

This is the way Athanasius presents his argument in the *Oratio I contra Arianos*. In the *De decretis Nicaenae synodi*, he is more concerned to prove that Christ is of the same essence as the Father, (ὁμοούσιος τῷ πατρί) and is begotten of the essence of the Father (τουτέστιν ἐκ τῆς οὐσίας τοῦ πατρός), as the Nicene Creed plainly declares.[89] He is therefore unlike all κτίσματα (creatures) and by nature ἄτρεπτος.[90] He had no need to win or achieve by good works what he already was. He was righteous, virtuous, and blameless, not by effort but by nature. The fathers at Nicaea, Athanasius wrote, in refuting Arianism, declared

[86] C.A., 51, 117B–120A.
[87] C.A., 52, 120AB: ὁ λόγος γὰρ ὁ τοῦ θεοῦ ἄτρεπτός ἐστι, καὶ ἀεὶ καὶ ὡσαύτως ἔχει, οὐχ ἁπλῶς, ἀλλ' ὡς ὁ πατήρ . . . ἢ πῶς πάντα τὰ τοῦ πατρὸς τοῦ υἱοῦ ἐστιν, εἰ μὴ καὶ τὸ ἄτρεπτον καὶ τὸ ἀναλλοίωτον τοῦ πατρὸς ἔχει; οὐχ ὡς ὑποκείμενος δὲ νόμοις, καὶ τὴν ἐπὶ θάτερα ῥοπὴν ἔχων, τὸ μὲν ἀγαπᾷ, τὸ δὲ μισεῖ, ἵνα μή, φόβῳ τοῦ ἐκπεσεῖν, τὸ ἕτερον προσλαμβάνῃ, καὶ ἄλλως πάλιν τρεπτὸς εἰσάγηται· ἀλλ' ὡς θεὸς ὢν καὶ λόγος τοῦ πατρός, κριτής ἐστι δίκαιος καὶ φιλάρετος, μᾶλλον δὲ καὶ χορηγὸς ἀρετῆς· δίκαιος οὖν φύσει καὶ ὅσιος ὤν, διὰ τοῦτο ἀγαπᾶν λέγεται δικαιοσύνην καὶ μισεῖν ἀδικίαν . . .
[88] *Ibid.*, 120B–121A. The references are to the Septuagint.
[89] See the Creed as published by Denzinger, *Enchiridion*, and n. 68 above. The recent and most learned work of Ignacio Ortiz de Urbina, *El Símbolo Niceno* (Madrid, 1947), does not deal with the problem of Christ's mutability.
[90] *De decretis Nicaenae synodi*, 19, 2–20, 2, ed. Opitz, *op. cit.*, 2.1.3, 16.4–37; cf. *ibid.*, 5.23–30 (6, 1); 33.12–17 (35, 14); 30.3 f., 28–36 (33, 8, 12 f.).

150

the Son to be of the same essence as the Father, so that they might indicate that the Son is of the Father, not only like him but the same in likeness, and so that they might show that the immutability of the Son and his resemblance [to his Father] differ from what we call imitation [of the divine], which we attain by virtue and by keeping the commandments. The bodies of men that are similar to each other can differ in certain respects and be far from each other, as in the relation between the sons of men and their fathers, as it is written of Adam and Seth, the son he begot, who was like his father "after his image" (Genesis 5.3). But the begetting of the Son by the Father is far above human nature, and the Son is not only like, but indivisible from, the Father's essence, and the Son and the Father are one (John 10.30), as he himself said; and the Logos is always in the Father and the Father in the Logos (John 14.10), as the reflection is in the light, for that is what the word means. Accordingly, with this in mind, the Council rightly wrote "of the same essence," in order to overturn the malevolence of the heretics and show that the Logos differs from creatures. Moreover, after writing "of the essence," they at once added, "the holy catholic church anathematizes those who say that the Son of God was *ex nihilo* or created or mutable or a creature or of a different essence." In this way they showed clearly that the words, "of the essence" and "of the same essence," do away with the foolish expressions of impiety, like "created being" and "creature" and "made" and "mutable" and "he did not exist before he was begotten." [91]

The Nicene fathers, Athanasius argues a few pages farther along in the *De decretis*, thought it amounted to the same thing whether they said the Logos "was from God" or from "the essence of God," since they took the word God to mean the essence of his being (cf. Exodus 3.14, where God says of himself Ἐγώ εἰμι ὁ ὤν). But, they believed, if the Logos were not from God, as a true son would be by nature from his father, but is only said to be of God like created beings in general because of having been created by God, then he would not be of the essence of God, nor would he be Son by essence but by reason of his virtue, just as men are called the children of God by grace. Hence, they concluded that, being the true and sole Son of God, he is of the essence of God, the effulgence of God, inseparable from his essence, and thus immutable and invariable.[92] This being so, he suffers no change at any time, either in his sojourn on earth in the body, or in his experience of hunger, thirst, and fatigue, or in the crucifixion and passion.[93]

This is not the place for a history of the enormous influence that Athana-

[91] *De decretis Nicaenae synodi*, 20, 3–6, ed. Opitz, *op. cit.*, 2.1.3, 17.5–25; MPG, 25, 452BCD: ἀλλ' οἱ ἐπίσκοποι. . . ἠναγκάσθησαν. . . εἰπεῖν καὶ γράψαι, ὁμοούσιον εἶναι τῷ πατρὶ τὸν υἱόν, ἵνα μὴ μόνον ὅμοιον τὸν υἱόν, ἀλλὰ ταὐτὸν τῇ ὁμοιώσει ἐκ τοῦ πατρὸς εἶναι σημαίνωσι καὶ ἄλλην οὖσαν τὴν τοῦ υἱοῦ ὁμοίωσιν καὶ ἀτρεψίαν δείξωσι παρὰ τὴν ἐν ἡμῖν λεγομένην μίμησιν, ἣν ἐξ ἀρετῆς διὰ τὴν τῶν ἐντολῶν τήρησιν ἡμεῖς προσλαμβάνομεν·

[92] *De decretis Nicaenae synodi*, 22, 4–23, 2, ed. Opitz, *op. cit.*, 2.1.3, 19.2–17; MPG, 25, 456BCD. Cf. Opitz, 21.1–32, 26.29 ff., 30.32–35.

[93] *Epistola ad Epictetum*, 5, MPG, 26, 1060A. So also pseudo-Athanasius, *Contra Apollinarium, ibid.*, 1096A, 1112C, 1136A, 1161AB.

sius exerted upon patristic literature. But a few texts will be cited to illustrate the continuity of the tradition between the Creed of Nicaea, as expounded and championed by Athanasius, and the dogmatic decrees of the Emperor Justinian. The immutability of Christ and the unchangeability of his divine essence were axiomatic.

Basil the Great (d. 379) twice quotes the Nicene Creed with its anathemas,[94] frequently expresses great respect for the Council of 325, and says that not a word should be set aside in its Creed, which he esteemed more highly than any of its successors.[95] Christ was, according to him, of the same nature and essence as the Father,[96] and the true Son of the Father by nature (φύσει), not by adoption.[97] With obvious reference to the Arian arguments rebutted by Athanasius in the *Oratio I contra Arianos* he interprets John 5.19 ("The Son can do nothing of himself") to mean that, unlike creatures, the Son, who was very justice itself, always did what he wished, and was not the pawn of haphazard decisions made by creatures of unstable and varying constitution.[98] In all this, however, his principal concern is to rebut the Macedonians, who maintained that the Holy Spirit was a creature of a different essence from that of the Father. In dealing with this contention, Basil assumes the results of Nicaea and goes on to prove that the Holy Spirit was of the same essence as the Father and the Son. Thus, in *Epistola 8*, he denies that the Holy Spirit had a mutable nature (τρεπτὴν οὐσίαν), and insists that it was consubstantial with the Father and the Son (ὁμοούσιον πατρὶ καὶ υἱῷ . . . τῆς αὐτῆς φύσεως τῷ πατρὶ καὶ υἱῷ).[99] A few years later, and with the same objective, Epiphanius, in his *Panarion*, likewise taught that all three members of the Trinity were immutable.[100]

Gregory of Nazianzus declares that the Son has all that the Father has

[94] *Epistola* 125, 2; 140, 2: MPG, 32, 548CD, 588CD–589A.

[95] *Ep.* 114, MPG, 32, 529A (μηδεμίαν τῶν ἐκεῖ λέξεων ἀθετεῖν); *Ep.* 81, *ibid.*, 457A; *Ep.* 125, 1, *ibid.*, 545BC–548B; *Ep.* 159, 1, *ibid.*, 620B.

[96] *Ep.* 52, 1 ff., *ibid.*, 391C–396A; *Ep.* 159, 1, *ibid.*, 620BC.

[97] *Adversus Eunomium*, 4, MPG, 29, 672A, 689B–692B.

[98] *Ep.* 8, 9, MPG, 32, 261B: ἀλλὰ καὶ τό, οὐ δύναται ὁ υἱὸς ποιεῖν ἀφ᾽ ἑαυτοῦ οὐδέν, λαμβάνουσιν οἱ θεομάχοι ἐπὶ καταστροφῇ τῶν ἀκουόντων. ἐμοὶ δὲ καὶ τοῦτο τὸ ῥητὸν μάλιστα καταγγέλλει τῆς αὐτῆς φύσεως εἶναι τὸν υἱὸν τῷ πατρί. εἰ γὰρ ἕκαστον τῶν λογικῶν κτισμάτων δύναταί τι ποιεῖν ἀφ᾽ ἑαυτοῦ, αὐτεξούσιον ἔχον τὴν ἐπὶ τὸ χεῖρόν τε καὶ κρεῖττον ῥοπήν, ὁ δὲ υἱὸς οὐ δύναταί τι ποιεῖν ἀφ᾽ ἑαυτοῦ· οὐ κτίσμα ὁ υἱός. εἰ δὲ μὴ κτίσμα, ὁμοούσιος τῷ πατρί. καὶ πάλιν, οὐδὲν τῶν κτισμάτων τὰ ὅσα βούλεται δύναται. ὁ δὲ υἱὸς ἐν τῷ οὐρανῷ καὶ ἐπὶ τῆς γῆς πάντα ὅσα ἠθέλησεν ἐποίησεν· οὐκ ἄρα κτίσμα ὁ υἱός. καὶ πάλιν, πάντα τὰ κτίσματα ἢ ἐκ τῶν ἐναντίων συνέστηκεν, ἢ τῶν ἐναντίων ἐστὶ δεκτικά. ὁ δὲ υἱὸς αὐτοδικαιοσύνη, καὶ ἄϋλός ἐστιν· οὐκ ἄρα κτίσμα ὁ υἱός. εἰ δὲ μὴ τοῦτο, ὁμοούσιος τῷ πατρί.

[99] *Ep.* 8, 10 f., MPG, 32, 262C–265B.

[100] *Panarion Haer.*, 69, 26, 4, ed. Karl Holl, 3 (Leipzig, 1933), 176.19 f.; cf. *ibid.*, 157.13, 158.5–10, 159.8 (statements of the Arian view).

152

(John 16.15), that he is of the Father, consubstantial with him, and immutable. Amphilochius of Iconium, the follower and friend of the Cappadocians, writes in the same vein,[101] while, according to an anonymous homily on the *Hypapante*, once attributed to Cyril of Jerusalem, Christ had his Father's essence, and was not subject to change (ἀναλλοίωτος).[102] Didymus the Blind, the famous scholar of Alexandria, who died at the end of the fourth century, describes the ἐνανθρώπησις as ἀτρεπτοτάτη, and says that the Logos became man without change (ἀτρέπτως).[103] Isidore, an ascetic priest from Pelusium, the provincial capital of Augustamnica Prima, also maintains that the Logos remained immutable despite the incarnation. Similarly, Theodotus, Bishop of Ancyra, a contemporary and ally of Cyril in the struggle against Nestorius, in his Ἑρμηνεία εἰς τὸ Σύμβολον, repeats the Nicene anathemas, and denies that the Logos suffered change at the incarnation.[104]

CYRIL OF ALEXANDRIA

Of greater interest and importance are the works of Isidore's great fellow African, Cyril of Alexandria. Like his predecessors, Cyril stands firmly on the Creed of Nicaea, not one word or letter of which, he says, could be altered, and makes it the basis of the two works from his hand that were endorsed officially by the Council of Chalcedon in 451. He would not tolerate any additions to this Creed, and declares that his own doctrines are in complete harmony with it.[105] He even wrote out a copy of the Creed, with its anathemas, including the one that condemns the Arian use of τρεπτός or ἀλλοιωτός for Christ, and sent it, together with a detailed commentary, to a group of monks, whom he warned that Christ himself had sat with the fathers of Nicaea and had presided over their deliberations.[106] In all three of these documents he maintains that Christ was immutable, that he was not changed into flesh or a man at the incarnation, and that he never ceased to

[101] *Oratio* 30, 11, 20; 39, 13: MPG, 36, 116C, 128D, 349A. Karl Holl, *Amphilochius von Ikonium in seinem Verhältnis zu den grossen Kappadoziern* (Tübingen-Leipzig, 1904), 192, 232, 240, 248, 250.

[102] MPG, 33, 1196AB, 1197B.

[103] *De Trinitate*, 1, 26; 3, 1, 3, 4, 10, 18, 21: MPG, 39, 389A, 780B, 821BC, 829D, 857C, 884D, 900A; *In Psalmos*, 15, 8; *ibid.*, 1232B–D. Cf. Eduard Weigl, *Christologie vom Tode des Athanasius bis zum Ausbruch des Nestorianischen Streites*, 373–429 (*Münchener Studien zur historischen Theologie*, 4 [Munich, 1925]), 104 f.

[104] For Isidore see Andreas Schmid, *Die Christologie Isidors von Pelusium* (*Paradosis: Beiträge zur Geschichte d. altchristlichen Literatur u. Theologie*, 2 [Freiburg in d. Schweiz, 1948]), 42, 48, 78, 88. For Theodotus see MPG, 77, 1316C, 1317AD, 1325B, 1336C, 1341A.

[105] See n. 51 above; *Ep.* 39, MPG, 77 180D–181A, 176C–177B; *Ep.* 4, *ibid.*, 45B, 48D.

[106] *Ep.* 55, MPG, 77, 289D–320A, n.b. 293A; Schwartz, ACO, 1.1.4, 49–61; 1.5, 343–53; cf. Mansi, 9, 246C–247B.

be God.[107] Near the beginning of his *Apologeticus contra Theodoretum pro xii capitibus* (his defence of his twelve anathemas against Nestorius), in which he says the God Logos was superior to change (τροπῆς ἀμείνων), he expressly mentions and approves the relevant Nicene anathema.[108]

In his commentary on the Creed, Cyril adds that Christ is of the same essence as the Father (ὁμοούσιος), God begotten of God, and that the Son is in the Father and the Father in the Son.[109] He was God first and man afterwards, not a man who was elevated to be God. Nor did he join a man to himself, share glory and honor with him, and prepare him thus for the cross, resurrection, ascent into heaven, and *sessio* at the right hand of God. In humbling himself and taking the form of a servant, as Philippians 2.5 ff. shows, though remaining God, he became man and submitted to humiliation.[110]

In his annotations on the Gospel of John, Cyril carries the argument a step further and advances beyond Athanasius. From the negative point of view, Athanasius denies that Christ was mutable or led a life of rectitude and nobility by exercise of his freedom of the will. Positively, he insists on Christ's being of the same essence as the Father. But he never follows his reasoning to its logical conclusion, and never states in so many words that Christ did what he did because he was what he was, although the implication is obvious. Cyril states explicitly what Athanasius left unsaid. His point of departure is John 8.28: "I do nothing of myself; but as my Father hath taught me, I speak these things." Basil had dealt with a similar text, which was popular among those who wished to deny the full divinity of Christ, but his exegesis is far from brilliant.[111] Cyril is more successful. Christ spoke these words, he says, because he often pretended as a man not to know what he actually knew as God, as for example in the incident of the raising of Lazarus, when he asked, "Where have you laid him?" (John 11.34), although as God he had even foretold Lazarus's death.[112] What he knew as God he says he learned from the Father.

Christ never acted separately or apart from the Father; but, being identical with the Father in essence, his thoughts, wishes, and acts were always

---

[107] MPG, 77, 45B, 180A, 304ABC. For other passages in Cyril on this subject, see MPG, 76, 16CD, 44A, 49A, 52AD, 53D–56A, 179A, 320AB, 321B, 328B, 397AB, 413B, 420CD, 421B, 424B, 440D.

[108] MPG, 76, 396BC.

[109] MPG, 77, 297CD, 305B, 300AB.

[110] *Ep.* 55, MPG, 77, 304BC, 301BC, 312BC.

[111] N. 98 above.

[112] *In S. Joannem*, 5.5, *Cyrilli Archiepiscopi Alexandrini in D. Joannis Evangelium*, ed. Philip E. Pusey, 2 (Oxford, 1872), 50.13–51.14; MPG, 73, 845C–848B.

154

the same as the Father's in all respects.[113] It is absurd, therefore, says Cyril, to claim, as did the Arians, that Christ was inferior to the Father and had to receive aid from him. For that would be the same as saying that God the Father provided his own power with power or made his own wisdom wiser, since Christ is the strength and wisdom of the Father. Similarly, it is ridiculous to think of progress and improvement on the part of Christ, who is God by nature, and has all the attributes of divinity.[114]

That the Son does everything according to the will of the Father does not make him the servant or disciple of the Father but demonstrates the identity of their essence.[115] The good always adheres to the divine nature.[116]

Created beings, it is argued, can choose evil and often fall from better to worse. So far as they are concerned, therefore, the good is the result of piety and virtue. But this is not true of the divine essence. In the absence of change and mutation, the good can be explained from the nature of the essence itself, like heat in fire or cold in snow. Fire, for example, exerts the force peculiar to it, not by will but by reason of its nature and substance, and can be nothing but what it is. Jesus Christ, likewise, is not subject to change and fluctuation. He does not, in the manner of men, choose a certain course of action because of a desire to please God, but because, by the laws of his nature, he neither thinks or does anything that is out of harmony with the wishes of the Father. The consubstantial Godhead is never at variance with itself.[117]

[113] Pusey, loc. cit., 38.21 ff.; MPG, 73, 833B: μαθήσεσθε γὰρ ὅταν ἴδητε κατὰ φύσιν ὄντα θεὸν καὶ υἱόν, ὡς εἰμὶ μὲν ἰδιογνώμων οὐδαμῶς, συνεθελητὴς δὲ ἀεὶ τῷ θεῷ καὶ πατρί, καὶ ὅσαπερ ἂν ἐργάζοιτο ταῦτα καὶ αὐτὸς ποιεῖν οὐκ ὀκνῶν, λαλῶν δὲ πάλιν ὅσα καὶ αὐτὸν οἶδα λέγοντα. τῆς γὰρ αὐτῆς οὐσίας εἰμὶ τῷ γεννήσαντι. ἐθεράπευον μὲν γὰρ τῷ σαββάτῳ τὸν πάρετον . . . ἀλλ' ἐνεργὸν ὑμῖν ὑπέδειξα τὸν πατέρα καὶ ἐν σαββάτῳ. (Christ is represented speaking here in the first person.)
N.b.: Pusey, loc. cit., 51.29–52.4; MPG, 73, 848C: οὐκ ἄρα διὰ τὸ ἡττῆσθαι τῆς πατρῴας ἀρετῆς, οὐδὲ διὰ τὸ μὴ δύνασθαί τι κατορθοῦν ἐξ ἰδίας ἰσχύος, οὐδὲν ἀφ' ἑαυτοῦ ποιεῖν ἐν τούτοις διισχυρίσατο, ἀλλ' ἐπείπερ ἰσογνώμων ἐστὶ καὶ συνεθελητὴς ἀεὶ τῷ γεννήσαντι πρὸς πᾶν ὁτιοῦν, καὶ οὐδὲν μελετήσας κατὰ μόνας ὥσπερ καὶ διῃρημένως ἐπιτελεῖν.
[114] Pusey, loc. cit., 40.5–41.4; MPG, 73, 836 ABC: . . . κατὰ τίνα τρόπον, λέγε μοι, πάλιν ὁ θεὸς καὶ πατὴρ τῇ ἰδίᾳ δυνάμει χορηγήσει τὸ δύνασθαι, ἢ πῶς ἂν τὴν ἑαυτοῦ σοφίαν σοφωτέραν ἐργάσαιτο; ἢ γὰρ ἀνάγκη λέγειν ὡς ἐπί τι μεῖζον ἄνεισιν ἀεί, καὶ προκόπτει κατὰ βραχὺ πρὸς τὸ δύνασθαί τι καὶ πλέον τῆς ἐνούσης ἰσχύος αὐτῷ· ὅπερ ἐστὶν εὔηθές τε καὶ ἀδύνατον παντελῶς . . . πῶς ἂν ἔτι καὶ τῶν δυνάμεων ὀνομάζοιτο κύριος ὁ υἱός, ἢ πῶς ἂν ἔτι νοοῖτο σοφία καὶ δύναμις, δυναμούμενος καθ' ὑμᾶς καὶ σοφούμενος παρ' ἑτέρου; . . . ἤγουν εἰ πιστεύετε κατὰ φύσιν εἶναι θεόν, δότε δὴ δότε τελείως ἔχειν αὐτῷ τὰ τῆς θεότητος ἴδια. ἴδιον δὲ τῆς κατὰ φύσιν ἰδιότητος τὸ μήτε περὶ μηδὲν ἀσθενεῖν, μήτε μὴν τῆς ἀνωτάτω σοφίας ἀπολιμπάνεσθαι, μᾶλλον δὲ αὐτὸ κατὰ φύσιν εἶναι σοφίαν καὶ δύναμιν.
[115] Pusey, loc. cit., 44.18–45.7; 46.10–47.13; MPG, 73, 840BC, 841B–844A.
[116] Pusey, loc. cit., 39.27 f.: MPG, 73, 833D: δεῖν γε οἶμαι τῷ γε ὄντι κατὰ φύσιν θεῷ πάντα τελείως προσεῖναι τὰ ἀγαθά.
[117] Pusey, loc. cit., 52.3–26, 53.21–54.9; Liber vi, ibid., 102.16–23, MPG, 73, 848C–849A, 849CD, 901D–904A.

THE IMMUTABILITY OF CHRIST 155

SOUNDNESS OF JUSTINIAN'S VIEWS

For a just evaluation of Justinian's attitude towards Theodore, it will be necessary to survey briefly the dogmatic situation at the middle of the sixth century.[118] Zeno's *Henoticon* (482), having served only to exacerbate tempers and multiply the grounds for dissent on all sides, had proved a complete failure. The Chalcedonian symbol still preserved its official position, but the Monophysites attacked it openly, and it left many problems unsolved. Perhaps the most serious of these, so far as the present paper is concerned, is that of the *communicatio idiomatum* (κοινωνία ἰδιωμάτων).[119] The question is whether it was possible after the Chalcedonian definition of 451 to describe Jesus Christ, *qua* man, as mutable in his soul like mankind in general. This would seem to have been ruled out by both the symbol and the two letters of Cyril endorsed by the Council in 451.[120] Yet the Tome of Leo, which the Council of Chalcedon had pronounced valid,[121] despite the distinction it made between the human and the divine in Christ, decreed that the union between the two in Christ was so close as to permit one to say of the Logos that he had suffered or of Jesus that he had performed the miracles, although in a strict sense the human nature of Christ was the subject of the passion and the glorification, while the Logos was responsible for the miracles.[122] If the venerable Tome could sanction such language, and could even go so far as to endorse the doctrine of the *assumptus homo*, would it not, in like manner, authorize followers of Theodore to say of Christ that he was mutable and did not obtain his immortality, incorruptibility, and immutability until after the resurrection? Juridically, perhaps, these alternatives were possible, but they opened the way for a

[118] The latest book on this period, Ernest Stein, *Histoire du Bas Empire*, II, 476–565 (Brussels, 1949), is not very satisfactory for ecclesiastical or intellectual history in general, but has good bibliographies. See above all Marcel Richard, "Le Néo-chalcédonisme," *Mélanges de Science Religieuse*, 3 (1946), 156–161, and the literature there cited.

A detailed analysis of Justinian's estimate of Theodore will be found in my book. Here I confine myself to Theodore's doctrine of the τρεπτότης of Christ.

[119] On the meaning of this term see Adhémar d'Alès, *De verbo incarnato* (Paris, 1930), 135–141. Eduard Weigl, *op. cit.* (n. 103 above), 187–192 and index *s.v.*; Bethune-Baker, *op. cit.* (n. 122 below), 293 f.

[120] See n. 51 above.

[121] Mansi, 6, 972AB; 7, 113C–116A. See the edition of the Tome by C. Silva-Tarouca, S. *Leonis Magni Tomus ad Flavianum Episc. Constantinopolitanum* (*Ep.* 28), (Rome, 1932), and introduction, pp. 1–19. Cf. Trevor Jalland, *Life and Times of Pope St. Leo the Great* (London, 1941).

On Leo's espousal of the *assumptus homo*, see the Tome, *ed. cit.*, 26 n. 93, 28 n. 122; and P. Galtier, *De incarnatione ac redemptione* (*ed. nova*, Paris, 1947), 82 f. Cf. n. 52 above.

[122] For a good summary of this doctrine, see J. F. Bethune-Baker, *An Introduction to the Early History of Christian Doctrine* (4th ed., London, 1929), 288 ff.

156

Christology that contravened the Definition of 451 and even imperiled the Creed of Nicaea.

Because of the paucity of extant texts in Greek written from the Antiochene point of view, it is difficult to gauge the strength of this movement within the boundaries of the Byzantine Empire. But we know that two Nestorians, Mar Aba (Catholicos of Persia, 540–52) and Thomas of Edessa, had found a receptive audience of Greeks in Alexandria, the very stronghold of the Monophysites, and that the *Christian Topography* of their disciple, Cosmas Indicopleustes,[123] reproduced many of the leading ideas of this school, including Theodore's teaching that Christ did not receive his immortality, incorruptibility, and immutability until after the resurrection.[124] There were others, too, within the Empire, who clung to Nestorianism, and the Emperor had even felt constrained to issue an edict forbidding Nestorians the right to build or acquire churches.[125] Moreover, Theodore of Mopsuestia, the *fons et origo malorum*, had somehow escaped oecumenical censure, partly, because of his death (in 428) before Nestorianism had been assailed seriously, and partly, no doubt, because he was overshadowed by the dramatic figure of Nestorius.

Justinian, therefore, must have thought that the time had come to put an end officially to the type of Christology that Theodore represented, and protect the dogma of the orthodox church from further distortion of this sort. The history of the doctrine of the immutability of Christ, as summarized above, abundantly vindicates Justinian's anathematization of the term τρεπτός as applied to Christ. Actually, error on this point inevitably leads to heretical views on other major premises of Christian theology. It lies behind Theodore's extreme bifurcation of the person of Christ and is primarily responsible for the basic defects of his system. For if Jesus Christ be denied immutability until after the resurrection, it will be difficult to invest the Christ of the Gospels with the proper attributes of his divinity, and to avoid the impression that he was only a mere man (ψιλὸς ἄνθρωπος).

Devreesse and Amann [126] are inclined to believe that Theodore was orthodox in essentials, and guilty of only a few slight exaggerations. But in the history of dogma, where everything depends on precision and accuracy of a high order, what appear to be minor aberrations often have grave con-

[123] *Dumbarton Oaks Papers*, No. 3 (Cambridge, Massachusetts, 1946), 76 f.

[124] Ed. E. O. Winstedt (Cambridge, England, 1909), 86.14–18. I will discuss the Christology of Cosmas at greater length in my book.

[125] *Novella*, 131, 14, 2, edd. R. Schoell et W. Kroll, *Corpus Iuris Civilis*, 3 (5th ed., Berlin, 1928), 663.15 ff. Cf. *ibid.*, 115, 3, 14, pp. 541.24 ff., 543 (restrictions on wills of Nestorians and Acephali).

[126] Nn. 40, 42 above.

sequences. The theologians denounced as heterodox have rarely departed radically from the dogmatic decrees enacted by the oecumenical councils. Thus, in the fourth century the addition of a single iota, the smallest letter in the alphabet, ,to the word ὁμοούσιος of the Nicene Creed occasioned great scandals and was sharply repudiated,[127] although the difference between ὁμοούσιος (of the same nature) and ὁμοιούσιος (of like nature) would not ordinarily be accounted of great moment. Similarly, the distinction between orthodoxy and what the Church denounced as Nestorianism, significant as it is in the history of doctrine, arose solely because of the desire of Theodore and his group, perfectly innocuous in itself, to stress the humanity of Jesus against the Apollinarians, who in their turn sought to correct what they took to be an exaggerated insistence upon the human nature of Jesus Christ.

As far as Theodore is concerned, his deviation from orthodoxy can be measured by a single letter, an alpha privative. This is perhaps trivial philologically — actually it amounts to the difference between yes and no — but it makes Theodore an opponent of the most venerated creed of Christendom, and seems to have been of greater significance than has been previously realized.

CONCLUSION

It is not the purpose of this paper to prove that in every instance Justinian's criticism of Theodore rested on a solid basis. When, for example, he accused Theodore of having taught that there was no nature (φύσις) without an hypostasis and no hypostasis without a person (πρόσωπον),[128] he had before him a text quoted by Leontius of Byzantium, but recently proved, on the basis of a comparison with the Syriac version,[129] to have been reasonably free of error. Similarly, in his criticism of Theodore's exegesis of Psalm 8, Justinian, like Vigilius,[130] makes Theodore speak of the human and the divine in Christ as ἕτερος and ἕτερος (Vigilius says alius et alius); another form of the same excerpt from Theodore, however, is a little more cautious in posit-

[127] Gwatkin, op. cit. (in n. 6 above), 121, 133, 161, 169 f., 177, 178, 181 f., 183 ff., 231, and passim.
[128] Against the Three Chapters, ed. Schwartz, 60.20 ff.; MPG, 86.1, 1073AB. For Justinian's definitions of these basic Christological terms, see Contra Monophysitas, ed. Schwartz, 37.14–40.2; MPG, 86.1, 1137 D ff.
[129] Marcel Richard, loc. cit. (n. 47 above).
[130] Ed. Schwartz, 55.21–56.13; MPG, 86.1, 1062C–1063B; Le commentaire de Théodore de Mopsueste sur les Psaumes (I–LXXX), ed. Robert Devreesse, Studi e Testi, 93 (Vatican City, 1939), 46 f.
For Pope Vigilius's rejection of mutability in Christ, see his Constitutum de tribus capitulis, c. 11, ed. O. Guenther, Corpus scriptorum ecclesiasticorum latinorum, 35.1 (Vienna, 1895), 247.4 ff.

158

ing a division between the two, and is perhaps somewhat less obviously unorthodox. Nevertheless, for every passage in which Theodore makes use of unobjectionable terminology, there is another that is clearly heretical. A number of the latter that were cited by the Fifth Council were taken from Theodore's Catechetical Orations and are indubitably heterodox either in attributing mutability to Christ (pp. 132ff. above), or in dividing Jesus Christ into two persons, one human and one divine.[131] Despite Theodore's good intentions, therefore, he could not permanently escape condemnation, and the anathematization of his system as a whole was inevitable.

Justinian's authorities for taking this step have already been indicated in general terms, but it will be necessary to illustrate his method briefly here by a few examples. As we know, he appeals frequently to the Nicene Creed of 325 and to the decisions of the first four oecumenical councils.[132] In addition he leans heavily on the major patristic writers, and especially on Athanasius and Cyril.

In his treatise *Against the Three Chapters*, Justinian quotes from the *Oratio I contra Arianos* three bits of Athanasius's exegesis of Philippians 2.6 f., according to which "[Christ] did not advance from a lower to higher estate, but, being God, took the form of a servant and in so doing was not exalted but humbled." [133] This, it will be recalled, was an integral part of Athanasius's argument against the Arian conception of the mutability of Christ. In his *Contra Monophysitas* he reproduces *in toto* the letter of Athanasius to the Emperor Jovian in which Athanasius expounds the Nicene

---

[131] Mingana identifies the sections from the Catechetical Orations that were cited by the Fifth Oecumenical Council: *Woodbrooke Studies*, 5, 8 ff.; 6, xxiii.

For Theodore's endorsement of the doctrine of two sons in the Logos-Christ, cf. *ibid.*, 6, 66 f.: "There was also the Son [i.e., of God] in the One who was baptised [i.e., Jesus Christ], and by His [i.e., the Son's] proximity to Him [Jesus Christ] and by His union with the one who was assumed [Jesus Christ], He was confirming the adoption of children." *Woodbrooke Studies*, 5, 60: "Our blessed Fathers said that He became incarnate so that you might understand that He assumed a complete man, who was a man not only in appearance but a man in a true human nature, and that you might believe that He assumed not only the body but the whole man who is composed of a body and an immortal and rational soul. It is such a man that he assumed for our salvation and it is through Him that He effected salvation for our life . . ." Tonneau, *Homélies*, 453, 127; expressions of this sort abound in the Catechetical Orations.

[132] *Codex Iustinianus*, 1, 1, 2, 1 f., 3, 3; 7, 11 ff., ed. P. Kreuger, *Corpus Iuris Civilis*, 2 (10th ed., Berlin, 1929), 5 f., 9 f.; *Novella*, 42, pr.; 115, 3, 14; 131, 1, edd. R. Schoell et W. Kroll, *Corpus Iuris Civilis*, 3 (5th ed., Berlin, 1928), 264, 541, 654 f. (Praedictarum enim quattuor synodorum dogmata sicut sanctas scripturas accipimus et regulas sicut leges servamus.)

Drei dogmatische Schriften, ed. Schwartz, 43.18 ff., 63.20–64.11, 64.36 ff., 88.38 ff., 100.30 ff., 102.29 ff.; MPG, 86.1, 1144D–1145C, 1079C–1081C, 1083B, 1013B, 1025AB, 1027AB. Cf. Mansi 9, 370C, 375ACD.

[133] Ed. Schwartz, 58.32 ff.; MPG, 86.1, 1069BC; MPG, 26, 93C, quoted in n. 69 above.

Creed of 325 with its anathemas as of divine and apostolic authority, and
three times cites the condemnation of the Arian view of the mutability of
Christ. The Arians, Athanasius writes, said that the Son of God was created
out of nothing, and did not exist from all eternity but was mutable and a
creature. For this reason they had been anathematized by the fathers of the
Church, who believed the Son to be not only like the Father or like God, but
truly God of God, of the same essence as the Father, and the true and legitimate Son of him, who was his Father by nature.[134] Farther along in the same
treatise, Justinian takes over from the *Contra Apollinarium* a passage in
which the pseudo-Athanasius affirms the immutability and ineffableness of
the Logos.[135] There are many other points of contact, as for example in the
use of the Bible, discussion of which lies beyond the scope of the present
investigation.

Of even greater importance was Cyril, Justinian's favorite author. The
Emperor makes use of Cyril's letter to Theodosius II and its reference to
Christ's immutability, as we have seen,[136] and in the *Contra Monophysitas*
quotes from Cyril's Commentary of the Gospel of St. John to prove that the
Logos could suffer no change or passion.[137] He relies also on three other
works of Cyril to support his refutation of Theodore's contention that
Hebrews 2.9, Philippians 2.5 ff., and II Corinthians 8.9 refer to the man
Christ joined to himself in the incarnation. These texts have been misinter-
preted by Theodore, Justinian says, and actually prove that the Logos
descended from heaven and took flesh for our salvation.[138]

These are just a few of the many references Justinian makes to Cyril in
the course of reinterpreting the Christological problem in Cyrillian terms.
He could not openly reject the Tome of Leo, which had been sanctioned by
the Council of Chalcedon, but in expounding the Chalcedonian symbol he
secured oecumenical validity for Cyril's Twelve Anathemas against Nestorius,[139] and himself constantly used and defended Cyril's Apollinarian formula, μία φύσις τοῦ θεοῦ λόγου σεσαρκωμένη (one incarnate nature of the
God Logos), which, like Cyril, he falsely attributed to Athanasius.[140]

[134] Ed. Schwartz, 21.23 ff., espec. 21.29 f., 36 f.; 22.23 ff.; 23.1 f.; MPG, 26, 813A ff.
[135] Ed. Schwartz, 30.26 f.; MPG, 26, 1164B. For a brief review of critical opinion on the
authenticity of this work see Louis Bouyer, *op. cit.* (n. 69 above), 155.
[136] N. 24 above.
[137] Ed. Schwartz, 29.29 ff.; 31.5 f.; MPG, 73, 161B, 581A.
[138] Ed. Schwartz, 57.29–58.23; MPG, 86.1, 1067A–1069A.
[139] Mansi, 9, 374A, 376AB, 385C–388B; Hefele-Leclercq, *Histoire des conciles*, 3.1, 128 ff.
On the anathemas, see Hubert du Manoir de Juaye, *op. cit.* (n. 51 above), 491 ff.; J. Mahé,
"Les anathématismes de Saint Cyrille d'Alexandrie," *Revue d'histoire ecclésiastique*, 7 (1906),
505–542.
[140] Ed. Schwartz, 17.30 ff.; 33.13 ff.; 52.17 ff.; 78.8 ff.; MPG, 86.1, 1055B, 1001A.

In following Cyril here, however, in insisting on the immutability of
Christ, and in rejecting the doctrine of the *assumptus homo*,[141] favored by
Theodore, Justinian was not completely consistent. Theodore had said that
Christ won his immortality, incorruptibility, and immutability at the resurrection; but the Fifth Council condemned only one third of this theory, and
passed over in silence the question of whether Christ had been immortal
and incorruptible before the resurrection. It was probably felt that to include
these other two attributes in the condemnation of the mutability of Christ
would be to deprive Christ of his full humanity. Logically, except for the
Nicene anathemas, it might have been possible to consider all three of these
epithets on the same level, and either reject or approve all of them together.
Justinian himself at the end of his long reign became convinced that the body
of Christ was always incorruptible.[142] Though discussion of this notion,
known as aphthartodocetism, must be reserved for another occasion, there
is little doubt that Justinian was led to espouse it for the sake of consistency
with the doctrine of Christ's immutability, which he had accepted on the
authority of the Nicene Creed and of its principal patristic exegetes.

[141] See nn. 52 and 121 above.

[142] See Martin Jugie, "L'empereur Justinien a-t-il été aphthartodocète?" *Échos d'Orient*, 31
(1932), 399–402. The best work on the theological principles involved is that of René Draguet,
*Julien d'Halicarnasse et sa controverse avec Sévère d'Antioche sur l'incorruptibilité du corps
du Christ* (Louvain, 1924). Cf. also on an important aspect of the theology of Justinian not
treated in this paper É. Amann, "Théopaschite (Controverse)," *Dictionnaire de théologie
catholique*, 15 (Paris, 1946), 505–512.

VIII

LEO III's EDICT AGAINST THE IMAGES IN THE YEAR 726-27 AND ITALO-BYZANTINE RELATIONS BETWEEN 726 AND 730 [1]

In paying tribute to my illustrious friend Professor Franz Dölger on his seventy-fifth birthday, and to his towering position in Byzantine studies for more than a generation, I hope to prove that the *Life of Pope Gregory II* (715-31) in the *Liber Pontificalis* provides clear and incontrovertible evidence that in the year 726-27 the Emperor Leo III (717-41) issued an edict which forbade the possession of images of saints, martyrs, and angels (see n.4 below). This prohibition extended also, *a fortiori*, it would appear, to representations of Christ and Mary (since the word *sanctus* here probably refers to holy persons in general), as the entire history of iconoclasm (see n. 30 below) shows.

The biography of Gregory II in which these data are to be found was virtually completed before his death, and even the second re-

[1] I had the privilege of discussing this article in 1956 with Professor Georg Ostrogorsky and, as can be seen from my references to his works, I have profited enormously from his valuable contributions to the history of the iconoclastic controversy. I regret deeply that he did not continue with his project of writing a full-length book on this subject, for which he had made admirable preparations with his papers: 'Die Chronologie des Theophanes im 7. und 8. Jahrhundert,' *Byzantinisch-Neugriechische Jahrbücher*, 7 (1930), 1–56; 'Les débuts de la querelle des images,' *Mélanges Charles Diehl*, 1 (Paris, 1930), 235–55; 'Über die vermeintliche Reformtätigkeit der Isaurier,' BZ, 30 (1929–30), 394–400; *Studien zur Geschichte des byzantinischen Bilderstreites (Historische Untersuchungen*, 5 [Breslau, 1929]; "Die erkenntnistheoretischen Grundlagen des byzantinischen Bilderstreites" (in Russian with German summary), *Seminarium Kondakovianum*, 2 (1928), 47–52; etc. If he had not been occupied with other projects, he would undoubtedly have carried the problem discussed in this paper to its final solution. I am indebted also for valuable counsel to Professors Francis Dvornik, Romilly J. H. Jenkins, Gerhard Ladner, Cyril Mango, and Speros Vryonis. What follows provides additional documentation for my chapter on the iconoclastic period in the *Cambridge Medieval History*, 4, 2d ed., Part 1 (1966), 61–104, 835–48.

6

cension was finished shortly after 737–39.[2] Accordingly, this portion of the *Liber Pontificalis* is the source that is most nearly contemporaneous with the event under review and antedates all of the other major authorities for this period: the *Chronography* of Theophanes (which was written between 810 and 814), the Ἱστορία σύντομος (the so-called *Breviarium* of the Patriarch Nicephorus, which cannot be earlier than 775 or later than 829, the year of the author's death), and the *Life of Stephen the Younger* by Stephen the Deacon (dating from 808), which is of only minimal usefulness for the present investigation.

The *Liber Pontificalis* is therefore completely decisive on the question at issue and is supported by Paul the Deacon's *Historia Langobardorum*, a derivative work, which, though completely dependent upon the *Liber Pontificalis* for the years 726–27, has the advantage of its early date (between ca. 783 and 799). Nevertheless, a distinguished series[3] of Byzantinists have ignored the meaning of a crucial passage in the *Liber Pontificalis* and have consequently denied that Leo really did

[2] See Louis Duchesne in his edition of the *Liber Pontificalis*, I (=LP below), (Paris, 1886), ccxx-ccxxiii, ccxxxiii; Gyula Moravcsik, *Byzantinoturcica*, I, 2nd ed. (*Berliner ¡Byzantinistische Arbeiten*, 10 [Berlin, 1958]), 456–59 and 531. On account of the lack of evidence on this matter, neither Moravcsik nor Krumbacher ventures a date for the composition of Nicephorus's *Breviarium*, which covers the period between 602 and 769. Paul Alexander, *The Patriarch Nicephorus of Constantinople* (Oxford, 1958), 162, merely guesses. See also Joseph Gill, 'The Life of Stephen the Younger by Stephen the Deacon,' *Orientalia Christiana Periodica*, 6 (1940), 114–39, n.b. 128; and, for Paul the Deacon, Max Manitius, *Geschichte der lateinischen Literatur des Mittelalters* (Iwan von Müller and Walter Otto, *Handbuch der Altertumswissenschaft*, 9.2.1 [Munich, 1911]), 258 f., 267 ff.; Levison-Loewe, *op. cit.* (n. 16 below), 221–24.

[3] The chief arguments for this position are set forth by Ostrogorsky in his valuable paper, 'Les débuts de la querelle des images,' *Mélanges Charles Diehl*, I, as in n. 1 above, favorably reviewed by Franz Dölger in BZ, 31 (1931), 458. Cf. I. D. Andreev, *Germani Tarasii, patriarchi konstantinopolskie* (Sergiev Posad, 1907), as quoted by Ostrogorsky, *loc. cit.*, 236, 239. Other supporters of this view are listed by Ostrogorsky, *Geschichte des byzantinischen Staates* (*Byzantinisches Handbuch*, I. 2, 3rd ed. [Munich, 1963]), 136, n. 1; they include Louis Bréhier, Johannes Haller, and P. Alexander. See also André Grabar, *Le dossier iconographique d'iconoclasme* (Paris, 1957), 133, but cf. 94; Leopold Breyer, *Bilderstreit und Arabersturm in Byzanz* (*Byzantinische Geschichtsschreiber*, ed. Endre v. Ivánka, 6 [Graz, 1957]), 186; Demosthenes Savramis, 'Die Kirchenpolitik Leons III.', *Südost-Forschungen*, 20 (1961), 1–22.

initiate legislation against the icons in 726–27.

But the *Liber Pontificalis* is altogether unambiguous and resolves all doubts:[4]

> In orders dispatched subsequently [i.e., after the events described in the previous paragraphs,] the Emperor had issued a decree [decreverat] forbidding the possession of an image of any saint, martyr, or angel; for he declared them all to be accursed. If the Pope did as he was bidden [with regard to the images, he was told,] he would gain the Emperor's favor; [but] if he were obstructive, he would be dethroned. Contemptuous of the Emperor's impious command, the Pope armed himself against the Emperor as against an enemy, condemned the Emperor's heresy, and wrote far and wide [warning] Christians to beware because impiety had arisen.

In the face of the clear and unimpeachable testimony of this practically contemporary source, there can be no doubt whatsoever that Leo did formulate a legal document of some sort against the icons in 726–27. Moreover, as we shall see, the situation in Italy immediately following the receipt of the Emperor's *iussio* as above described and all the other relevant mediaeval authorities re-inforce and confirm this conclusion.

Before examining the texts which bear on this subject, however, it will be necessary to review the arguments that have been urged against the above outlined interpretation of the facts. Before 1907,[5]

[4] LP, 404. 9–17: Iussionibus itaque postmodum missis decreverat imperator ut nulla imago cuiuslibet sancti aut martyris aut angeli haberetur: maledicta enim omnia asserebat. Et si adquiesceret pontifex, gratiam imperatoris haberet; si et hoc fieri praepediret, a suo gradu decederet. Despiciens ergo vir profanam principis iussionem, iam contra imperatorem quasi contra hostem se armavit, renuens heresem eius, scribens ubique caveri se christianos quod orta fuisset impietas. For the continuation of this text, see nn. 42–52 below. Cf. Dölger, *Regesten*, 1, nos. 289, 291, 298. On Gregory, see n. 50 below.

[5] The dissenting voice in 1907 was that of Andreev, *op. cit.* (n. 3 above). The major authorities in favor of the view that Leo issued an edict against the images in 726–27 are: Franz Dölger, *Corpus der griechischen Urkunden des Mittelalters und der neueren Zeit*, Reihe A, Abt. 1, *Regesten der Kaiserurkunden des oströmischen Reiches von 565–1453*, 1 (Munich, 1924), 35; Charles Diehl, 'Leo III and

8

it should be added, historians had assumed that the iconoclastic decree of 730 had been preceded by an earlier one in 725 or in 726. The scholars who made this assumption appealed to a passage in the chronicle of Theophanes for the *annus mundi* 6217 (September 1, 724, to August 31, 725), which Ostrogorsky has convincingly demonstrated to be the equivalent of the year 726-27. Theophanes says:[6]

the Isaurian dynasty,' *Cambridge Medieval History*, 4 (1927), 9; *idem* and Georges Marçais, *Histoire du moyen âge*, 3, *Le monde oriental de 395 à 1081*, 2d ed. (Paris, 1944), 264 (but with no references to texts); Karl Schwarzlose, *Der Bilderstreit* (Gotha, 1890), 51 ff.; Joseph Hefele, H. Leclercq, *Histoire des conciles*, 3.2 (Paris, 1910), 632; cf. P. Lajolo, 'L'editto di Bisanzio del 725, trattamento della Sicilia durante la persecuzione iconoclasta,' *Archivio storico per la Sicilia orientale*, 19 (1922-23), 155-66. Without arguing the point or citing the pertinent literature, François Masai, in his provocative study, 'La politique des Isauriens et la naissance de l'Europe,' *Byzantion*, 33 (1963), 191-221, assumes (p. 198) that there was a decree against the icons in 726.

[6] *Theophanis Chronographia*, ed. C. de Boor, 1 (Leipzig, 1883), 404.3 ff.:

Τούτῳ τῷ ἔτει ἤρξατο ὁ δυσσεβὴς βασιλεὺς Λέων τῆς κατὰ τῶν ἁγίων καὶ σεπτῶν εἰκόνων καθαιρέσεως λόγον ποιεῖσθαι. καὶ μαθὼν τοῦτο Γρηγόριος, ὁ πάπας Ῥώμης, τοὺς φόρους τῆς Ἰταλίας καὶ Ῥώμης ἐκώλυσε γράψας πρὸς Λέοντα ἐπιστολὴν δογματικήν, μὴ δεῖν βασιλέα περὶ πίστεως λόγον ποιεῖσθαι καὶ καινοτομεῖν τὰ ἀρχαῖα δόγματα τῆς ἐκκλησίας, τὰ ὑπὸ τῶν ἁγίων πατέρων δογματισθέντα.

A German translation of the passages quoted in this paper from Theophanes can be found in L. Breyer, *op. cit.* (n. 3 above).

For the date, see Ostrogorsky, 'Die Chronologie' (n. 1 above), 51; 'Les débuts' (n. 1 above), 238. I have taken λόγος here as 'rule, principle, law,' as in Henry G. Liddell and Robert Scott, ed. Henry S. Jones and Roderick McKenzie, *A Greek English Lexicon*, 2 (Oxford, 1940), 1057, III, 2, d. E. J. Martin, *A history of the iconoclastic controversy* (London, n.d. = 1930), 26, translates λόγον ποιεῖσθαι in Theophanes by 'to make a public declaration of policy on a question,' and he is probably right. But Anastasius Bibliothecarius (ca. 817-79) in his version renders the sentence very literally: Quo videlicet anno coepit impius imperator Leo depositionis contra sanctas et venerabiles imagines facere verbum: *Theophanis Chronographia*, ed. C. de Boor, 2 (Leipzig, 1885), 260.35 f. On Anastasius see the general summary and bibliography by L. Ueding, *Lexikon für Theologie und Kirche*, 1, 2d ed. (Freiburg im Br., 1957), 493 f.; A. Noyon, *Dictionnaire d'histoire et de géographie ecclésiastiques*, 2 (Paris, 1914), 1477-79. Ulla Westerbergh, *Anastasius Bibliothecarius, Sermo Theodori Studitae de Sancto Bartholomeo Apostolo* (*Studia Latina Stockholmiensia*, 9 [Stockholm, 1963]), confines herself to a special problem, unconnected with the subject under discussion, as does Claudio Leonardi, 'Anastasio Bibliotecario e l'ottavo concilio ecumenico,' *Studi medievali*, S. 3, 8, 1 (1967), 59-192.

In this year the impious Emperor Leo began to frame [or, perhaps: 'began to issue' or 'first issued'] regulations [or 'formulated a policy calling,' if not 'issued a decree calling'] for the destruction of the holy and revered icons. As soon as Pope Gregory learned of this, he withheld the taxes of Italy and Rome, and wrote a dogmatic letter to Leo [in which he protested] that the Emperor had no right to legislate concerning the faith or to make innovations affecting the ancient dogmas of the church, which had been established by the holy fathers.

Schwarzlose took this as proof that in 726 (or 725) Leo began to promulgate an edict against the images. But Andreev[7] expressed dissatisfaction with this interpretation, and it is now maintained by many that Theophanes meant only that Leo in the year named had begun to *speak* of the destruction of the images.[8] This view is confirmed, it is argued, by the words of the Patriarch Nicephorus, who, in recording the same event in his ἱστορία σύντομος, had written: ἐκδιδάσκειν δὲ τὸν λαὸν τὸ οἰκεῖον ἐπεχείρει δόγμα ('the Emperor undertook to expound his theory to the people').[9] These words refer, it is alleged, to an attempt by Leo to persuade his subjects to repudiate the icons by argument alone, without publishing a law on the subject.

Further corroboration for this view has been found in the *Life of Stephen the Younger* (d. 764) by Stephen the Deacon, according to whom Leo, at a public gathering he had summoned in 726, denounced the images as idolatrous, but quickly changed the subject, when he saw that his proposal was violently opposed.[10] This passage indicates,

[7] Quoted by Ostrogorsky, *loc. cit.* (in n. 2), 239.

[8] *Ibid.*: 'En cette année l'impie empereur Léon commença à parler de la destruction des saintes et vénérées images.'

[9] *Nicephori archiepiscopi Constantinopolitani opuscula historica*, ed. C. de Boor (Leipzig, 1880), 57, 26 f. As a curiosity cf. *Abrégé de l'histoire byzantine de S. Nicéphore, Patriarche de Constantinople, Traduite du Grec par le Sieur Moret* (Paris, 1684).

[10] MPG, 100, 1084 BC. In many a serio-comic passage, the text reveals the bitterness of the iconoclasts towards Leo (for Greek text see n. 26 below): 'Having summoned a meeting of his subjects, the wild beast, who is called Leo, roared like a lion in the midst of the assemblage and belched forth from his wrathful heart that wretched voice of his, like fire and sulphur from Mt.

the above-named experts hold, that in 726 Leo took no legal steps against the images. It must be noted, however, that the words οὐ δεῖ ταύτας προσκυνεῖν ('they [i.e., the images] must not be worshipped'), which occur at the same point in the narrative,[11] being pronounced without qualification by an autocratic, absolutistic emperor, accustomed to obedience, might well indicate some legal measure, and should in all probability be translated, 'the worship of images is forbidden.' Moreover, the *Life of Stephen* has little bearing, for it does not contravene the text above cited from the *Liber Pontificalis*, the meaning of which cannot be doubted.

However these passages are to be interpreted, it is agreed on all sides that Leo was impelled, as Nicephorus says,[12] to move against the images by the great submarine earthquake of the summer of 726, which was regarded in iconoclastic circles as a sign of divine disapproval of the use of icons. Ostrogorsky prefers to follow Nicephorus on this point rather than Theophanes, who represents the volcanic eruption as subsequent to Leo's first attack on the images and as requiring an intensification of the campaign against them.[13] Actually, there is little to choose between the two accounts; and no one doubts that Leo did proceed against the icons 'par une manifestation préliminaire,' which resulted in 726 or at the beginning of the following year in the destruction or possibly removal of the representation of Christ over the Bronze Gate of the imperial palace.[14]

Aetna. "Since the manufacture of images is an idolatrous art," he said, "their worship is forbidden." But when the orthodox people, devoted to Christ, groaned and cried out [against him] as soon as he had spoken, the sinner immediately became silent and started to give utterance to a contrary view.' For bibliography see F. Halkin, *Bibliotheca hagiographica graeca*, 3rd ed., 2 (*Subsidia hagiographica*, no. 8a [Brussels, 1957]), 253; Joseph Gill, 'The Life of Stephen the Younger by Stephen the Deacon,' cited in n. 2 above.

[11] MPG, 100, 1084C; see n. 26 below.

[12] *Op. cit.*, 57.5–26.

[13] *Op. cit.*, 1, 404.18–405.2 (n.b. the last sentence): ὃς τὴν κατ' αὐτοῦ θείαν ὀργὴν ὑπὲρ ἑαυτοῦ λογισάμενος ἀναιδέστερον κατὰ τῶν ἁγίων καὶ σεπτῶν εἰκόνων ἤγειρε πόλεμον....

[1] For references to sources, see following notes. It cannot be determined with certainty whether the image in question was a painted panel of wood, a mosaic, or a piece of sculpture; the second seems to be the most probable, the last the

The extant sources on this incident differ in several particulars, but the errors can be eliminated, and the principal facts ascertained. Neither the *Liber Pontificalis* nor Nicephorus records the desecration or destruction of an image or images in 726-27, although this may conceivably be inferred from the statement of the former (n. 4 above) that the ownership of images was prohibited. The leading authority on this famous episode is Theophanes, who relates that imperial officers removed or destroyed (καθελόντας can mean either) the image of Jesus Christ which stood over the Bronze Gate of the Royal Palace, and that, while they were thus engaged, they were attacked and slain by a mob of iconophiles, the most prominent of whom were subsequently punished by mutilation, flogging, exile, and fines.[15]

The destruction of the image is mentioned also by Paul the Deacon (ca. 720-783), who says in his *Historia Langobardorum* that Emperor Leo not only had the images taken down and burned but also thereupon ordered Pope Gregory II to follow his example if he wished to retain imperial favor.[16] Paul's testimony has no independent value

least. On the image itself, see André Grabar, *L'iconoclasme byzantin, dossier archéologique* (Paris, 1957), 124, 130 et s. vv. Constantinople, Palais impériaux, Porte de Chalcé (de Bronze); and, above all, Cyril Mango, *The Brazen House, a study of the Vestibule of the Imperial Palace of Constantinople* (*Arkaeologisk-kunsthistoriske Meddelelser udgivet af Det Kongelige Danske Videnskabernes Selskab*, 4, 4, [Copenhagen, 1959]), 112 ff., 170 ff. Cf. Ernst Kitzinger, 'The cult of images in the age before iconoclasm,' *Dumbarton Oaks Papers*, 8 (1954), 102; Franciscus Combefis, *Historia haeresis Monothelitarum, Auctarium novum*, 2 (Paris, 1648), 612-48. N.b. Manolis Chatzidakes, 'An encaustic icon of Christ at Sinai,' *Art Bulletin*, 49 (1967), 197-208; cf. A. Frolow, 'Le Christ de la Chalcé,' *Byzantion*, 33 (1963), 107-20.

[15] *Op. cit.*, I, 405.5-14:

οἱ δὲ κατὰ τὴν βασιλίδα πόλιν ὄχλοι σφόδρα λυπούμενοι ἐπὶ ταῖς καιναῖς διδασκαλίαις αὐτῷ τε ἐμελέτων ἐπελθεῖν καί τινας βασιλικοὺς ἀνθρώπους ἀνεῖλον καθελόντας τὴν τοῦ κυρίου εἰκόνα τὴν ἐπὶ τῆς μεγάλης Χαλκῆς πύλης, ὡς πολλοὺς αὐτῶν ὑπὲρ τῆς εὐσεβείας τιμωρηθῆναι μελῶν ἐκκοπαῖς καὶ μάστιξι καὶ ἐξορίαις καὶ ζημίαις, μάλιστα δὲ τοὺς εὐγενείᾳ καὶ λόγῳ διαφανεῖς· ὥστε καὶ τὰ παιδευτήρια σβεσθῆναι καὶ τὴν εὐσεβῆ παίδευσιν τὴν ἀπὸ τοῦ ἐν ἁγίοις Κωνσταντίνου τοῦ μεγάλου καὶ μέχρι νῦν κρατήσασαν, ἧς καὶ μετὰ ἄλλων πολλῶν καλῶν καθαιρέτης ὁ σαρακηνόφρων οὗτος Λέων γέγονεν.

[16] Paul the Deacon, *Historia Langobardorum*, ed. G. Waitz, 6, 49, *Scriptores*

but is interesting as a paraphrase of the *Liber Pontificalis*. Paul reproduces therefrom in essence the section on the edict of 726–27, which, however, he conflates with what he found in the same source concerning Leo's iconoclastic policy of 730 (see n. 30 below). Hence, for 726–27 he reports not only Leo's iconoclastic edict (as recorded in the *Liber Pontificalis*) but also the removal and burning of images (*imagines depositas incendit*), which the papal book associates with the year 730, but not with 726–27. Since Paul was not, of course, acquainted with Theophanes, who wrote in the following century, and did not in all likelihood go beyond the *Liber Pontificalis* in his researches on this point, it appears that, by inadvertence, he produced a fairly correct summary of the events of 726–27.

rerum langobardicarum et italicarum saec. vi-ix (Hanover, 1878), 181.22–24; also ed. *idem, Scriptores rerum germanicarum in usum scholarum ex Monumentis Germaniae Historicis recusi* (Hanover, 1878), 234: Hac tempestate Leo imperator aput Constantinopolim sanctorum imagines depositas incendit Romanoque pontifici similia facere, si imperialem gratiam habere vellet, mandavit.

The incorrect dating of the first iconoclastic removal or profanation of images (i.e., 730) is to be found in the *Life of Stephen the Younger* (MPG, 100, 1084) and elsewhere, as in *Acta sanctorum martyrum Constantinopolitanorum*, 2, 13, *Acta Sanctorum*, August, vol. 2 (Antwerp, 1735), 441 (August 9). But these *Acta* are a meaningless mélange of Theophanes and the *Life of Stephen the Younger*, composed in the latter half of the ninth century. Cyril Mango, *op. cit.* (n. 14 above), 170–74, discusses the possibility of placing the destruction of the image over the Bronze Gate in 730 rather than in 726–27 and reviews the evidence for both dates without committing himself in favor of either. But since we have now proved (see n. 4) that Leo did legislate against the icons in 726–27, the conclusion is inescapable that the incident described by Theophanes under this year (726–27) actually took place when he said it did. For it is inconceivable that, after issuing his edict, the Emperor would have failed to take action against so prominent an image, which decorated one of the principal entrances to the royal palace.

On Paul the Deacon, see Wilhelm Levison and Heinz Löwe, *Wattenbach-Levison, Deutschlands Geschichtsquellen im Mittelalter, Vorzeit und Karolinger*, II (Weimar, 1953), 203 ff., especially 221–24; Pier S. Leicht, 'Paolo Diacono e gli altri scrittori delle vicende d'Italia nell' età carolingia,' *Atti del 2º Congresso internazionale di studi sull' alto medioevo* (Spoleto, 1953), 54–74; Paolo Lamma, 'Il mondo bizantino in Paolo Diacono,' *ibid.*, 199–215; and the volume in general; A. Pontoni, *Introduzione agli studi su Paolo diacono* (Naples, 1946); cf. the papers on Paul the Deacon by Dante Bianchi, Roberto Cessi, etc. in *Memorie storiche forogiuliesi*, 8 (1929).

A host of other Latin chronicles[17] of later date reproduce Paul the Deacon's summary of Leo's iconoclastic measures (by direct, though unacknowledged, quotation or paraphrase), and some make use of Theophanes in the Latin translation of Anastasius Bibliothecarius or texts dependent thereon. Since they are not primary witnesses, it is profitless to list or quote them here. But special mention should be made of the *Chronica* of Sigebert[18] of Gembloux (ca. 1030–

---

[17] See, e.g., *Monumenta Germaniae Historica, Scriptores rerum langobardicarum et italicarum saec. vi-ix* (Hanover, 1878), 207.20 ff., 422.21 ff.; MGH, *Scriptores*, 1 (Hanover, 1826), 553 b; *ibid.*, later vols., *passim*, especially vol. 24 (see index s.v. *Leo III imperator*); *Historia Miscella*, 21, MPL, 95, 1082C–1083B.

[18] MGH, *Scriptores*, 6 (Hanover, 1844), 330. (I cite only the portion of the text that is relevant):

(725) Leo imperator a quodam Beser refuga fidei seductus, contra imagines Christi et sanctorum eius bellum indicit, easque ubique deponi et incendi edicit.

(727) Constantinopolitani contra Leonem imperatorem pro depositione imaginum Dei tumultuantur; aliqui etiam pro hoc martyrizantur.

(729) Gregorius papa, quia Leonem imperatorem incorrigibilem vidit, Romam et Italiam et Hesperiam totam ab eius iure descire facit, et vectigalia interdicit.

(730) Sanctus Germanus Leoni imperatori pro impietate sua aversus, a sede episcopali est deiectus.

(731) Gregorius 85us Romanae aecclesiae presidet; qui et ipse Leonem imperatorem erroris redarguit, et populum Romanum et vectigalia Hesperiae ab eo avertit.

It is of some interest to note that Hermannus Contractus (so-called because he was a paralytic mute), otherwise known as Herman of Reichenau (i.e., H. Augiensis), a great scholar, computist, and chronicler of the eleventh century (1013–54), apparently made no use of Theophanes directly or indirectly, and ignored what the LP says on the edict of 726. He was poorly informed about Byzantium and makes no mention of the iconoclastic controversy, except for an enigmatic entry for the year 794: Pseudosinodus Grecorum pro adorandis imaginibus habita, ab episcopis damnata est. See MGH, SS, 5, ed. G. H. Pertz (Hanover, 1844), 98–100. In Sigebert's *Chronica*, on the other hand, which shows some contact at second hand (see his entries for 725, 727, and 729; cf. n. 57 below), at least, with Anastasius Bibliothecarius's Latin translation of Theophanes's *Chronographia*, Leo's accession (717) and length of reign (24 years) are correctly calculated (Herman has it that Leo ruled for only nine years), and the great Arab siege of Constantinople in 717-718 (see n. 44 below) is summarized tolerably well, although under the year 720 (*op. cit.*, 330). It is obvious, then, from these data (including the texts quoted at the beginning

1112), who has the merit of providing a better, or at least more conventional, chronology than that of our principal early authorities.

Neither the *Liber Pontificalis*, nor Paul the Deacon, nor Theophanes[19] gives dates of the Christian era according to our present system. But Sigebert, like many of the later Latin chroniclers, set himself the goal of assigning specific years of our era to the events he records. Thus, he puts Leo's first edict against the icons under the year 725 (instead of 726–27), assigns to 727 (correctly, it seems) the riot provoked by the removal of the icons (he uses the plural), reports that in 729 (on this point see n. 57 below) Pope Gregory II not only removed Rome, Italy, and the entire West from Leo's jurisdiction, but also refused to submit to Byzantine taxation, and is on

of this note), not only that Sigebert had access to far better sources than were available to Herman, whom he neither knew nor needed, but also that he was far more diligent and more competent a historian than most of his contemporaries. Cf. on these authors Max Manitius, *Geschichte der lateinischen Literatur des Mittelalters*, 2 (Iwan von Müller and Walter Otto, *Handbuch der Altertumswissenschaft*, 9.2.2 [Munich, 1923]), 757, 759–62; *idem, ibid.*, 3=9.2.3 (1931), 344 f., with the introductions by G. H. Pertz in MGH, SS, 5, 67–74; and L. C. Bethmann, MGH, SS, 6, 268–99; Anna Dorothee v. den Brincken, *Studien zur lateinischen Weltchronistik bis in das Zeitalter Ottos von Freising* (Düsseldorf, 1957), 154 f., 182–85.

[19] Theophanes, 1, 391.4, puts Emperor Leo III's accession, e.g., in ψθ′ (i.e., 709) of the 'years of the holy incarnation' (τῆς θείας σαρκώσεως ἔτη), i.e., of the Christian era according to our current reckoning. For Theophanes's errors in the computation of these dates, see F. K. Ginzel, *Handbuch der mathematischen und technischen Chronologie*, 3 (Leipzig, 1914), 290 f. Theophanes does not, however, note the 'years of the holy incarnation' annually, but usually only at the beginning of each reign. For the successive years thereafter he contents himself with the *Annus Mundi*. Sigebert, on the other hand, dispenses with the latter entirely, and works out what Theophanes designated as the 'years of the holy incarnation' for every one of his annual entries.

On the problem of the eras used by the Byzantines, see V. Grumel, *La chronologie (Traité d'études byzantines*, 1, ed. Paul Lemerle [Paris, 1958]), 95–128. Grumel has shown, *loc. cit.*, and in other works ('L'année du monde dans l'ère byzantine,' *Échos d'Orient*, 34 [1935], 319–26; and 'L'année du monde dans la Chronographie de Théophane,' *ibid.*, 33 [1934], 396–408) that the year of the Christian era in Theophanes is computed by subtracting 5492 from the *Annus Mundi* as he gives it (from March 25 to December 31) or 5491 (from January 1 to March 24), not by subtracting 5492 (from January 1 to August 31) or 5493 (from September 1 to December 31), as had previously been believed.

firm ground once again when he notes that Germanos was removed by Leo from the patriarchal throne in 730.

The dates he gives throughout his chronicle constitute one of his major contributions to historiography, since they represent the results of a truly prodigious effort on his part to sift the evidence available to him in historical and hagiographic sources, resolve the conflicts among them, and work out on this basis, with the occasional assistance also of archival documents, a consistent system of chronology. The chronological details concerning the iconoclastic controversy itself probably rest upon a consensus among his predecessors, who had already evolved a fairly satisfactory arrangement of the dates for these events. But the substantive information he records on this subject, apart from the dates, is a web woven out of data he had gleaned from the *Liber Pontificalis*, Paul the Deacon's *Historia Langobardorum*, and either the *Chronographia* of Theophanes itself (in the Latin translation of Anastasius Bibliothecarius) or one of its Latin derivatives. The Latin tradition of chronography is supported, it should be added, by Michael the Syrian (d. 1199), who, though not invariably unimpeachable, expressly states that Leo did put forth an iconoclastic edict in 725.[20]

Andreev's followers, on the other hand, who do not deal with these Latin chronicles, except insufficiently with the *Liber Pontificalis*, the full significance of which they ignore, surmise that the violence of the pro-image outbreak at the time of the affront done to the image over the Bronze Gate as recorded in Theophanes (n. 15 above) convinced Emperor Leo that he would have to prepare the ground more carefully before he could advance further with his iconoclastic program. Accordingly, they conclude, the first legal steps against the icons were not taken until 730 at the time of the deposition of the Patriarch Germanos.

To bolster the arguments of his predecessors on this point, Louis

---

[20] *Chronique de Michel le Syrien*, 11, 19 f., 456 f., ed. and transl. J. B. Chabot, 2 (Paris, 1901), 491, 538 (date 725): "A cette époque, l'empereur des Romains, Léon, ordonna lui aussi, à l'exemple du roi des Taiyayê [Arabes], d'arracher les images des parois, et il fit abattre les images qui étaient dans les églises et les maisons: celles des saints aussi bien que celles des empereurs ou d'autres."

It was a mistake on Michael's part to include imperial along with religious images. But this error does not vitiate the text as a whole.

Bréhier[21] draws attention to the fact that, prior to his removal from the patriarchal throne, the Patriarch Germanos begged the Emperor not to prohibit the images. Germanos would hardly have expressed himself in these terms, Bréhier maintains, had Leo already issued a law proscribing the images.

Bréhier presents his case adroitly, as always, but his inference is not so obvious as at first it would appear. Let us consider the passage in Theophanes to which he alludes. In pursuit of his nefarious designs against the orthodox faith, Theophanes says, Leo set out to win over Germanos by flattery. It was because of these favorable circumstances, we may suppose, that the Patriarch seized the opportunity of speaking freely about the images:[22]

[21] 'Sur un texte relatif au début de la querelle iconoclaste,' *Échos d'Orient*, 37 (1938), 17–22; *Histoire de l'Église*, edd. A. Fliche and V. Martin, 5 (Paris, 1938), *Grégoire le Grand, les états barbares, et la conquête arabe* (590–757), 448 ff.

[22] Theophanes, I, 407.15–29 (A.M. 6221):

Τῷ δ' αὐτῷ ἔτει ἀπομανεὶς Λέων, ὁ παράνομος βασιλεύς, κατὰ τῆς ὀρθῆς πίστεως καὶ ἐνέγκας τὸν μακάριον Γερμανὸν ἤρξατο αὐτὸν θωπευτικοῖς λόγοις δελεάζειν. ὁ δὲ μακάριος ἀρχιερεὺς ἔφη πρὸς αὐτόν· "τὴν μὲν καθαίρεσιν τῶν ἁγίων καὶ σεπτῶν εἰκόνων ἀκούομεν ἔσεσθαι, ἀλλ' οὐκ ἐπὶ τῆς σῆς βασιλείας." τούτου δὲ ἐπαναγκάσαντος εἰπεῖν ἐπὶ τίνος βασιλείας; ἔφη· "ἐπὶ Κόνωνος." ὁ δὲ ἔφη· "τὸ βαπτιστικόν μου ὄνομα ἐν ἀληθείᾳ Κόνων ἐστίν." ὁ δὲ πατριάρχης ἔφη "μὴ γένοιτο, δέσποτα, διὰ τῆς σῆς βασιλείας τὸ κακὸν τοῦτο τελεσθῆναι· 'Αντιχρίστου γάρ ἐστι πρόδρομος ὁ τοῦτο πληρῶν καὶ τῆς ἐνσάρκου θείας οἰκονομίας ἀνατροπεύς." ἐπὶ τούτοις χαλεπήνας ὁ τύραννος ἐνεῖχε τῷ μακαρίῳ, ὡς Ἡρώδης ποτὲ τῷ προδρόμῳ. ἀνέμνησε δὲ αὐτὸν ὁ πατριάρχης καὶ τῶν πρὸ τῆς αὐτοκρατορίας αὐτοῦ συνθηκῶν, ὅπως αὐτῷ θεὸν ἐγγυητὴν δέδωκεν ἐν μηδενὶ σαλεῦσαι τὴν ἐκκλησίαν τοῦ θεοῦ τῶν αὐτῆς ἀποστολικῶν καὶ θεοπαραδότων θεσμῶν. ἀλλ' οὐδ' οὕτως ᾐσχύνθη ὁ ἄθλιος.

George Monachus in his *Chronicon* (composed *after* 867), ed. C. de Boor, 2 (Leipzig, 1904), 738.10–741.20, puts an expanded version of this dialogue at the very beginning of Leo's reign. But his opinion is valueless, and the text itself is a fabric woven out of bits from Theophanes, the *Life of Stephen*, etc. (see de Boor's notes). On Conon, see William Fischer, 'Leo der Isaurier-Konon?' BZ, 8 (1899), 718.

On Germanos, see Wolfgang Lackner, 'Ein hagiographisches Zeugnis für den Antapodotikos des Patriarchen Germanos I. von Konstantinopel,' *Byzantion*, 38 (1968), 42–104; K. Baus, 'Germanos I.,' *Lexikon für Theologie und Kirche*, 2d ed., 4 (Freiburg im Breisgau, 1960), 754; V. Grumel, *op. cit.* (n. 25 below), 1–8; Franz Drexl, 'Das Traumbuch des Patriarchen Germanos,' Λαογραφία, 7 (1923), 428–48 (*not* by G.).

'We hear that the holy and venerable icons will be condemned,' the blessed Patriarch said, 'but not during your reign.'
When the Emperor insisted that he be told in whose reign
this would take place, Germanos answered, 'In Conon's.' To
which the Emperor rejoined, 'My baptismal name is really
Conon.' Whereupon, the Patriarch replied, 'Heaven forbid,
my Lord, that this evil be accomplished by Your Majesty.
For whoever does this is the forerunner of Antichrist and the
subverter of the divine, incarnate dispensation.'[23] Angered
by these words, the tyrant threatened the Patriarch, as Herod
once had threatened the Forerunner [i.e., John the Baptist].
But the Patriarch reminded Leo [that] before his accession
[he had made] agreements in which he had sworn by God
that he would in no way interfere with the apostolic and God-
given rules of the Church of God. Despite this, however, the
wicked Emperor remained adamant.

It should be strongly emphasized that, if the participants in this
colloquy seem to be unaware of any existing iconoclastic ordinance,
as Bréhier contends, *they also ignore the fact that a famous image of
Christ had actually been destroyed or removed in 726-27,* as Theophanes
had already indicated two pages previously.[24] Moreover, the destruction
of an image [or images] in 726-27 is conceded by all. Hence, whatever
else Theophanes may have had in mind here, his words no more prove
that Leo did not legislate against the icons in 726-27 than that an
icon or icons were not desecrated in that year.

How, then, are we to interpret the conversation between Patriarch
and Emperor? The answer depends upon the interpretation of the
fact that none of our authorities makes the slightest allusion to further
attacks of Leo upon the images between the original onslaught of
726-27 and the renewed attack of 730. No contemporary explanation
is offered for this lull, and it is perhaps idle to speculate about it,
although it would seem reasonable to infer that Leo suspended opera-

[23] What Germanos means is that the iconoclasts, by rejecting representations
of the Jesus Christ of the Gospels, who walked, talked, and ate as a man with
his disciples, in effect denied the incarnation.

[24] Theophanes, *op. cit.*, I, 405.5–8 (see text in n. 15 above).

tions for a time in the hope of securing an indorsement of his iconoclastic schemes from the patriarch. Whether this is what he had in mind or not, it is obvious that in 729 Leo made a serious effort to conciliate Germanos, as Theophanes reports, and there is no reason to doubt that Leo's attempts to ingratiate himself with Germanos were intended to overcome the latter's opposition to iconoclasm, as Theophanes says they were. Leo's failure to continue with the iconoclastic policy of 726-27 and the friendly overtures he was making probably encouraged Germanos to feel that the time had come for him to persuade the Emperor to give up his hostility to the images. Germanos might well have hoped, as he had apparently written to Pope Gregory,[25] that Emperor Leo could be, or even had been, converted, and Gregory himself shared this opinion, even in the midst of the open warfare that had broken out between Rome and Constantinople over this issue (see n. 42 below).

It is conceivable also that the condemnation of the images Germanos dreaded and sought to avert was one which, as in 730, would receive the sanction of the Church and the patriarch, who had previously escaped involvement in the emperor's earlier iconoclastic schemes. Under these circumstances, unless we are to make utter nonsense out of Theophanes (and Paul the Deacon, to say nothing of the *Liber*

[25] The letter in which Germanos is believed by modern scholars to have expressed hope that Emperor Leo could be persuaded to abandon iconoclasm has been lost. But his optimism with regard to this possibility has been inferred from a letter addressed to him by Pope Gregory II in which the latter congratulates him for winning a great victory for the faith over a powerful, presumably imperial foe: Mansi, *Sacrorum conciliorum nova et amplissima collectio*, 13, 92–100, n.b. 92E, 94AB, 97DE. See V. Grumel, *Le patriarcat byzantin*, Série 1, *Les regestes des actes du patriarcat de Constantinople*, vol. 1, *Les actes des patriarches*, fasc. 2, *Les regestes de 715 à 1043* (n.p., 1936), pp. 2 f., no. 327; Erich Caspar, 'Papst Gregor II. und der Bilderstreit,' *Zeitschrift für Kirchengeschichte*, 3.F., 3 = 52 (1933), 29–89, n.b. 31 ff.; Ostrogorsky, 'Les débuts' (*loc. cit.*, n. 1), 243.

In an exhaustive and penetrating analysis, Jean Gouillard ('Aux origines de l'iconoclasme: le témoignage de Grégoire II?' *Centre de recherche d'histoire et civilisation byzantines, Travaux et Mémoires*, 3 [Paris, 1968], 243–307, n.b. 244–53) has convincingly demonstrated that the letter in question can no longer be attributed to Pope Gregory II. He believes that it was probably written by Germanos to a now unidentifiable bishop and that, for a number of reasons, it has little value as a historical document except, possibly, as a source for the theology of the iconophiles at an early stage in its development.

Pontificalis), we cannot assume, as Bréhier did, that Germanos was treating with Leo as if the question of images had not yet arisen. Admittedly, the conversation between Patriarch and Emperor is enigmatic, if not legendary, and can be interpreted in more than one way. But it by no means precludes the issuance of a decree in 726–27.

Furthermore, attention should be drawn to the fact that Symeon Metaphrastes's version of the episode in question differs at two material points from that which is to be found in the *Life of Stephen the Younger*.[26] According to the Metaphrast, in the tenth year of his reign

[26] On the faithfulness of Symeon to his sources, see J. Gill, 'A note on the Life of St. Stephen the Younger, by Symeon Metaphrastes,' BZ, 39 (1939), 382–86, in which the Greek text of Symeon, which was unavailable previously, except for modern Latin translations, is now published for the first time:

Stephen the Deacon,
PG. 100: 1084 B, C:

Μετὰ δὲ δέκατον χρόνον τῆς αὐτοῦ κατάρξεως, ὁ νέος οὗτος Βαλτάσαρ αἵρεσιν ἐμπνεῖ τῇ ἐκκλησίᾳ Μανιχαϊκήν, τάχα, ἵν᾿ εἴπω τι, καὶ τῶν Ἀφθαρτοδοκητῶν ἐφάμιλλον. Καὶ τὸν ὑπ᾿ αὐτοῦ λαὸν ἐκκλησιάσας, μέσον πάντων λεοντοειδῶς βρύξας ὁ ἀνήμερος θὴρ καὶ λεοντώνυμος, ἐκ τῆς ὀργίλου αὐτοῦ καρδίας ὡς ἐξ ὄρους Αἰτναίου πῦρ καὶ θέαφον ἠρεύξατο τὴν ἐλεεινὴν ἐκείνην φωνήν, καὶ εἶπεν· "Εἰδωλικῆς τεχνουργίας ὑπαρχούσης τῆς τῶν εἰκόνων ἀνατυπώσεως, οὐ δεῖ ταύτας προσκυνεῖν". Τοῦ φιλοχρίστου καὶ ὀρθοδόξου λαοῦ θορυβηθέντος ἅμα τῇ φωνῇ καὶ στενάξαντος, ὁ ἀλιτήριος παρευθὺ τὸ ἑξῆς ἐσιώπησε, καὶ πρὸς ἑτερογνωμίαν τὸν λόγον μετήγαγεν. Ὄντως, τάφος ἀνεῳγμένος ὁ λάρυγξ αὐτοῦ καὶ τοῖχος κεκονισμένος ἡ τούτου καρδία.

Symeon Metaphrastes,
Cod. Vat. gr. 806.

Ἐπεὶ δὲ χρόνος ἤδη δέκατος αὐτῷ τῆς βασιλείας ἠνύετο, μηκέτι στέγειν οἷός τε ὤν, ἐκρήσσει τὸ πονηρὸν κύημα, καὶ συγκαλέσας τοὺς τῆς συγκλήτου βουλῆς, τὸ βλάσφημον ἐκεῖνο καὶ ἀπηχὲς ἐξηρεύξατο, εἰδωλικήν τινα τύπον ἀποσώζειν, λέγων τὰς τῶν εἰκόνων γραφὰς καὶ ὅτι ,,μὴ δεῖ ταύταις τὴν προσκύνησιν ἀπονέμειν, ἵνα μὴ λάθωμεν'', φησίν, ,,εἰδώλοις προσκυνοῦντες ἀντὶ Θεοῦ''. Εὐθὺς οὖν θροῦς ἄφατος ἤρθη παρὰ τοῦ πλήθους καὶ κατηφείας νέφος τὴν ὀρθόδοξον ἐκάλυπτεν ἐκκλησίαν, ὅπερ ὁ σκολιὸς ἐκεῖνος αἰσθόμενος, εὐθὺς τὸν τοῦ Γύγου δακτύλιον στρέφων, λανθάνειν ἠγάπα, οὐχὶ λέοντος ἐλευθερίαν ζηλῶν, ἀλλὰ πολλὰς κατὰ τοὺς χαμαιλέοντας μᾶλλον τὰς μορφὰς ἐξαλλάττων, καὶ ὅτι ,,μὴ παντελῆ τὴν καθαίρησιν'', λέγων, ,,κατεψηφισάμην αὐτῶν — μὴ τοῦτο εἴη —, ἀλλ᾿ ἐκεῖνο δήπου φημί, τὸ μετεωρότερον ταύτας ἱστᾶν, ὥστε μὴ τῷ στόματι θιγεῖν αὐτῶν καὶ οὕτω τρόπον τινὰ τὰ τίμια καθυβρίζεσθαι." Τί τοῦτο λέγων ἐκεῖνος καὶ τί μηχανώμενος; Ἵνα τῷ μακρὰν ἡμῶν τιθέναι ταύτας καὶ οἱονεὶ πόρρω βάλλειν τῶν ὀφθαλμῶν, ὡς μήτε ῥᾳδίως ὁρᾶν ἔχειν μήτε προσφαύειν, ὅπερ δὴ πολλάκις κἂν ἄλλοις τοῖς φιλου-

(i.e., in 726–27), after convoking the Senate, Leo condemned images as idols, and said they should not be worshipped (μὴ δεῖ ταύταις τὴν προσκύνησιν ἀπονέμειν), lest it seem that worship was directed to idols rather than to God. When he saw his words were not well received, Leo changed his appearance, and more in the manner of a chameleon than a lion, the author remarks in a popular pun on Leo's name, explained that, when he condemned (κατεψηφισάμην) the images, he had not decreed that they be destroyed (καθαίρησιν) altogether, but rather that they be raised up out of the reach of those who by kissing them would profane what was worthy of respect. The hagiographer comments, that, under guise of protecting the images from desecration, Leo's real purpose was to elevate them beyond the range of vision, so that they might eventually be forgotten.

The Metaphrastic account raises many problems, principally concerning the convocation of the senate and the proposed elevation of the images, neither of which is mentioned by Stephen the Deacon. The tendency would be to favor the latter's version of the affair, since it was written in 808, some two centuries earlier than the time of Symeon Metaphrastes. Nevertheless, it is significant that Symeon faithfully reproduces the narrative as set forth by Stephen the Deacon in all significant particulars except for the two details noted. Occasionally, he somewhat embroiders, or fills out, Stephen the Deacon, but only here does he introduce changes of substance. Further, his introduction of what he gives as direct quotations from Leo by the conjunction ὅτι may indicate that he was transcribing an actual source in which these words were recorded. We cannot now determine whether Symeon is worthy of credence here, and for this reason no weight should be placed on this text. But, if he can be relied upon, the verb κατεψηφισάμην ('I condemned'), a legal term signifying the act of sentencing, which he quotes from Leo's discourse on this occasion, further strengthens the evidence supporting the proposition set forth in this paper.

This conclusion is in harmony with that of Erich Caspar,[27] who

> μένοις πάσχομεν, ἐν λήθῃ τε κατ᾽ ὀλίγον
> γενώμεθα καὶ τὸν πρὸς αὐτὰς ἀπομάθωμεν
> πόθον· εἶτα καὶ τὸ μὴ προσκυνεῖν ἐκείνας
> μηδὲ τιμᾶν ὁμαλῶς οὕτω καὶ ἀθορύβως
> παραδεξώμεθα.

[27] Loc. cit. n. 25 above.

was convinced that Leo actually did issue an edict against the images in 726. He draws attention to the fact that, in the sentence in which Pope Gregory is described by Theophanes as objecting μὴ δεῖν βασιλέα περὶ πίστεως λόγον ποιεῖσθαι, the last two words, λόγον ποιεῖσθαι, cannot be translated 'discuss' (as the school of Andreev would have it), and the clause as a whole must be understood as signifying that the Pope denied the Emperor jurisdiction in the ecclesiastical realm.[28] Caspar bases his case on the life of Pope Gregory II (715–31) in the *Liber Pontificalis*, in which he finds reference to two iconoclastic decrees by Leo, the first in 726, set forth in the letters (or 'orders') in which Leo had prohibited images of saints, martyrs, and angels,[29] and the second in 730.[30]

Against this interpretation, it has been urged that *iussio* (which, with its Greek equivalent κέλευσις, is regularly used in the *Corpus Iuris Civilis* to designate imperial edicts) was not to be understood in the Latin of the eighth and ninth centuries as a decree or law but merely as a letter of some kind.[31] Actually, however, in his Latin

[28] Theophanes, 1, 404.6 f.

[29] See the excerpt from the LP in n. 4 above, and the paraphrase by Paul the Deacon in n. 16.

[30] LP, 409.4–14: Nam post paucos dies claruit malitia imperatoris pro qua persequebatur pontificem, ita ut conpelleret omnes Constantinopolim habitantes, tam virtute quamque blandimentis, et deponeret ubicumque haberentur imagines tam Salvatoris quamque eius sanctae genetricis vel omnium sanctorum, eas in medio civitatis, quod dicere crudele est, incenderet. Et quia plerique ex eiusdem civitatis populo tale scelus fieri praepedibant, aliquanti capite truncati, alii partem corporis, poenam pertulerunt. (Note continuation of this text in n. 56 below.)

The second redactor improves the syntax of the first by emending the text to read: *easque in medio civitatis, quod dicere crudele est, igne cremaret* and then adds, upon what authority it is impossible to determine, that the walls of churches adorned with images were white-washed (*et omnes dealbaret depictas ecclesias*).

[31] On this, see Georg Ostrogorsky, *Geschichte des byzantinischen Staates*, 3rd ed. (*Byzantinisches Handbuch*, 1.2 [Munich, 1963]), 136. For the law codes, see *Codex Iustinianus*, 1.3.35; 1.3.42.2, etc., with a multitude of references in Robert Mayr and M. San Nicolò, *Vocabularium Codicis Iustiniani*, 2 vols. (Prague, 1923-25), s.vv.; n.b. vol. 2, 231 (θεία κέλευσις). See also J. F. Niermeyer, *Mediae Latinitatis Lexicon Minus*, fasc. 6 (Leiden, 1958), s.v. *iussio* (pp. 568 f.), who lists no authority for *iussio* as 'letter' but refers to numerous texts, two of which stem from our period, for the meaning 'order, command, ordinance.'

version of the Acts of the Second Council of Nicaea (787), Anastasius
Bibliothecarius (ca. 817–79) translates the Greek τῇ …κελεύσει τοῦ…
πατριάρχου πειθαρχοῦντες by *iussioni… patriarchae… parentes* (i.e.,
'obeying the patriarch's order').[32] Of course, κέλευσις is often used as

In other passages, *iussio* has legal significance of a somewhat different nature
(like last will and testament, etc.). Similar definitions (with no examples of
iussio as 'letter') are to be found in Albert Blaise and Henri Chirat, *Dictionnaire
latin-français des auteurs chrétiens* (Strasburg, 1954), 480.

During the seventh century, it may be, *iussio* did not always signify an
imperial command. In the *Exemplar divinae jussionis Justiniani Augusti,
directae ad Joannem papam urbis Romae* (dated 687), for example, *iussio* is
not to be taken strictly in the sense of 'order', although the context may possibly
indicate that this meaning is not far below the surface. Justinian here announces
to the pope that he had summoned a meeting of imperial officials and high ecclesia-
stics (including the papal *apocrisiarius*), in order to protect the integrity of the text
of the Acts of the Sixth Oecumenical Council (680–81), which he had bidden them,
after diligent examination, to authenticate by affixing their signatures thereto.

The documents were then turned over to him, he says, so that he might
preserve them intact, and prevent anyone from changing, or tampering with,
them in any way. After remarking that he hoped to be able to safeguard them
against alteration in his lifetime, he concludes that for this reason he was in-
forming the pope of what he had done:

> … nos speramus… quia usque dum noster spiritus statutus est ex
> Deo esse in nobis, ipsas chartas illibatas & incommutabiles semper
> conservabimus. Ad insinuandum itaque vestrae paternae beatitudini
> hujusmodi capituli motiones, praevidimus & earum scientiam notam
> fecisse beatitudini vestrae. (Mansi, *Sacrorum conciliorum nova et amplis-
> sima collectio*, 11 (Florence, 1765), 737f.; PL, 96, 425–28).

The *Liber Pontificalis* (1, 368. 17) cites this same dispatch as *divalem iussionem*,
but immediately thereafter (*ibid.*, 369. 1 f.) *iussio* is twice used for an imperial
order (as also *ibid.*, 373. 10). Either, therefore, the above summarized *iussio*
of Justinian is to be understood exceptionally as merely an imperial letter or
more normally, as a command in the form of an imperial re-confirmation of
the Sixth Council, with an implied warning against any attempts to question
or subvert the theology there enunciated.

Even if *iussio* in the later medieval period does occasionally designate a
letter which does not necessarily involve an imperial command, the argument
of this paper is not affected thereby, since the evidence quoted in n. 4 above
(*decreverat*) and n. 34 below proves decisively that the Emperor Leo III did
issue an edict against the icons in 726. On the text quoted, see Caspar, *Geschichte des Papsttums*, 2, 631 f.

[32] J. D. Mansi, *Sacrorum conciliorum nova et amplissima collectio*, 13 (Florence,
1767), 3-4C.

a technical term for a letter dispatched by the emperor to his officials throughout the world. But these documents are so designated because they usually contained, or in effect amounted to, orders or commands.

This understanding of the term is borne out by the *De administrando imperio* of the Emperor Constantine VII (913–59),[33] in some sections of which κέλευσις signifies nothing more than 'order' or 'command.' In others, it obviously must be taken to mean 'imperial letter.' But the context in this latter category indicates that the 'imperial letter' or rather 'imperial mandate' (as Professor Jenkins renders it) was one which carried official instructions and orders. What is even more conclusive, the author of the *Liber Pontificalis* himself understood *iussio* in this sense, as can be seen from his use of the word in passages occurring in close proximity to the one under review, according to which a spatharius had been sent out with orders to depose the Pope, and the Pope along with the Italians is described as scorning the Emperor's *iussiones* and looking upon them as provocation to war.[34]

Paul the Deacon interprets *iussionem* of the *Liber Pontificalis* without qualification by *talibus iussis* ('such commands'),[35] and the *Liber Pontificalis* clearly uses *rescriptis* (a legal synonym for 'edict') as an alternative for *iussio*.[36] Most significantly of all, the argument that there was no iconoclastic edict in 726–27 disregards the main verb in the sentence, *decreverat* (see note 4 above), which is the *terminus technicus* for 'decreed, ruled, determined,' and the like, and consequently furnishes irrefutable proof that the writer was summarizing or paraphrasing a decree or edict.

This is the plain, indisputable meaning of what the *Liber Pontificalis*

[33] Gyula Moravcsik and Romilly J. H. Jenkins, *Constantine Porphyrogenitus, De administrando imperio*, 2d ed., 43.62, 50.29, 53.131 f. (*Corpus fontium historiae byzantinae*, 1 [Washington, D.C., 1967]), 190 f., 232 f., 264 f., and *passim*.

[34] LP, *ed. cit.*, 1, 404.1 ff., 13 ff.: spatharius cum iussionibus missus est alter, ut pontifex a sua sede amoveretur. See the texts quoted in notes 36, 39, 42, below.

[35] LP, 1, 404.18 f. (as in n. 42 below): contra imperatoris iussionem restiterunt; Paulus Diaconus, *op. cit.* (n. 16 above), 234: talibus iussis uno animo restiterunt.

[36] LP, 1, 406.15 f.: Qui rescriptis detestandam viri [*sc.* imperatoris] dolositatem dispicientes. Cf. *ibid.*, 404.13 f.: Despiciens ergo vir [*sc.* Gregorius Papa] profanam principis iussionem. The identity in the meaning of the two words is obvious to anyone who will read pp. 404.13–406.16 through.

has to say about the action taken by Leo against the icons in 726–27, as can be seen from the full text and translation of the original Latin (reproduced at n. 4 above) and in the paraphrases of subsequent chroniclers.

Hence, there is every reason to accept, as Caspar does, Duchesne's explanation that there were two iconoclastic edicts, which differ in that the first (in 726) was issued by Leo alone without the collaboration of the patriarchal authorities and that the second (in 730) had the sanction of the Church.[37] Perhaps, also, if the *Liber Pontificalis* can be relied upon, the first merely forebade the use of images in general terms as 'accursed' (see text in note 4 above), while the second, besides outlawing images formally, like the first, not only provided specifically for their removal and destruction (by fire) but also prescribed punishment by death or maiming for all who interfered with the enforcement of the Emperor's wishes in this matter (n. 30 above).

It would be tempting to draw attention also to the fact that Theophanes says Pope Gregory II responded to Leo's original denunciation of the images by withholding the taxes of Rome.[38] But the *Liber Pontificalis* puts Pope Gregory's rebellion against the imperial tax gatherers before[39] the arrival in Rome of the Emperor's decree against the images, and is probably more dependable for the history of Italian affairs than the Byzantine chroniclers. The word of Theophanes should not therefore prevail on this matter. Nor is the precise sequence of these two events relevant to the point of issue. Whether Leo's edict preceded or followed Gregory's stand against the Emperor's tax collectors, the *Liber Pontificalis* and the entire Latin historiographic tradition demonstrate that Leo did promulgate a law against

[37] LP, i, 412, n. 25.

[38] A. M. 6217, ed. de Boor, i, 404.4 ff., as quoted in n. 6 above.
Cf. Thomas Hodgkin, *Italy and her invaders*, vol. 6, 2d ed. (Oxford, 1916), 415 ff., for a list of Theophanes's major inaccuracies concerning the West.

[39] LP, i, 403.20 ff.: (other attempts having failed), illis diebus imperatorum iussione Paulus patricius qui exarchus fuerat eundem pontificem conabatur interficere, eo quod censum in provincia ponere praepediebat et suis opibus ecclesias denudare, sicut in ceteris actum est locis, atque alium in eius ordinare locum. Then comes i, 404.9 ff. (concerning the decree against images, quoted in n. 4 above). See Dölger, *Regesten*, i, 287, 289. Hubert, *loc. cit.* (n. 42 below), 7 f., incorrectly dates Gregory's rebellion against taxation. His theory of a double indiction should be repudiated.

the icons ca. 726 and before 730.

Also before 730, according to Nicephorus,[40] and possibly Theophanes also, the theme of Hellas and the Cyclades rose up against Leo on account of Leo's hostility to the images. Obviously, the rebels would not have been provoked to insurrection on dogmatic grounds, and the great seismic disturbances of 726 could not have impelled Leo to intensify his attack upon the images, as Theophanes claims they did (n. 13 above), if Leo had done no more at first, in 726-27, than initiate public discussion on the subject.

2. Iconoclasm and Italo-Byzantine relations, 726-30.

Furthermore, we learn from the *Liber Pontificalis* that Byzantine iconoclasm was one of the factors (ca. 726-29 and before 730) in the dangerous revolt in Italy that was consequent upon the attempt of the Exarch Paul of Ravenna (726-27) and his immediate successor, Eutychius, who was the last to hold this post, to punish Pope Gregory II

---

[40] Nicephorus, *op. cit.* (n. 9 above), 57.21-58.3:

Ταῦτά φασιν ἀκούσαντα τὸν βασιλέα ὑπολαμβάνειν θείας ὀργῆς εἶναι μηνύματα, καὶ ἥτις αἰτία ταῦτα κεκίνηκε διασκέπτεσθαι. ἐντεῦθεν λοιπὸν κατὰ τῆς εὐσεβείας ἵσταται καὶ τῶν ἱερῶν εἰκονισμάτων μελετᾷ τὴν καθαίρεσιν ὡς ἐκ τῆς τούτων ἱδρύσεώς τε καὶ προσκυνήσεως γεγονέναι οἰόμενος τὸ τεράστιον, κακῶς εἰδώς. ἐκδιδάσκειν δὲ τὸν λαὸν τὸ οἰκεῖον ἐπεχείρει δόγμα. πολλοὶ γοῦν τὴν ὕβριν τῆς ἐκκλησίας ἀπωλοφύροντο. διὸ δὴ καὶ οἱ τὴν Ἑλλάδα καὶ τὰς Κυκλάδας νήσους οἰκοῦντες οὐ προσιέμενοι τὸ δυσσέβημα πρὸς τὸν βασιλέα διαστασιάζουσι, καὶ πλεῖστον στόλον ἀθροίσαντες Κοσμᾶν τοὔνομα ἐφ' ἑαυτοῖς βασιλεύουσι.

Nicephorus describes the uprising as an expression of disapproval of the Emperor's impiety. Theophanes (1,405.14 ff.) does not make this connection specific, and merely remarks that the rebels were inspired by 'divine zeal' (θείῳ κινούμενοι ζήλῳ στασιάζουσι), which is somewhat ambiguous.

On the theme of Hellas see: Peter Charanis, 'Hellas in the Greek sources of the sixth, seventh, and eighth centuries,' *Late classical and mediaeval studies in honor of Albert Mathias Friend, Jr.* (Princeton, 1955), 171; idem, 'The term *Helladikoi* in Byzantine texts of the sixth, seventh, and eighth centuries,' Ἐπετηρὶς Ἑταιρείας Βυζαντινῶν Σπουδῶν, 23 (1953), 615-620; Georg Ostrogorsky, 'Postanak tema Helada i Pelponez' (on the origin of the themes of Hellas and the Peloponnesus), *Zbornik radova*, 21, Vizantoloshki Institut, 1 (Belgrade, 1952), 64-77; A. Pertusi, *Costantino Porfirogenito, De thematibus (Studi e testi*, 160 [Vatican City, 1952]), XVII, 22 f., 25, 27, 29 (pp. 83, 154 f.); Western division, 5.1 ff. (pp. 89 f., 170-72); 9.31 (p. 94); J. B. Bury, 'The Helladikoi,' *English historical review*, 7 (1892), 80 f.

for interfering with the collection of imperial taxes (see texts in nn. 39 above and nn. 42–51 below).

For although, as we have seen (n. 39 above), the author of the sketch of Gregory in the *Liber Pontificalis* represents Leo's edict against the images in 726–27 as subsequent to the papal resistance to the new imperial taxes (and not the first grievance which provoked the Pope into opposition), he likewise makes it clear that the Italian insurrection entered a new phase after Leo's iconoclastic outburst. The Emperor's plunge into heresy outraged the Pope to the extent that he was willing to go to war against the Byzantine Empire (note 4 above: *iam contra imperatorem quasi contra hostem se armavit*), in order to oppose the Emperor's doctrinal innovations. But he did not[41] for this reason convoke a Roman synod in defence of the icons in 727, as some believe he did, or at any other time during his pontificate.

The religious issue injected into the situation by Leo's edict obviously accounted for much of the hostility to Byzantium manifested by the Italians,[42] notably at first (before the insurrection affected

---

[41] The most decisive argument against such a Roman synod in favor of the icons ca. 727 is the silence of the LP, which, however, does mention a Roman council of this kind (1, 416.5–17) during the pontificate of Gregory III (731–41). See also Edward J. Martin, *A history of the iconoclastic controversy* (London, n. d. [1930]), 75 f.; Ostrogorsky, 'Les débuts' (n. 1 above), 255 n. 1.

[42] LP 1, 404.17–406.20. N.b. 404.17–405.3: Igitur permoti omnes Pentapolenses atque Venetiarum exercita contra imperatoris iussionem restiterunt, numquam se in eiusdem pontificis condescendere necem, sed pro eius magis defensione viriliter decertarent, ita ut anathemate Paulum exarchum vel qui eum direxerat eiusque consentaneos summitterent; spernentes ordinationem exarchi, sibi omnes ubique in Italia duces elegerunt; atque sic de pontificis deque sua immunitate cuncti studebant. Cognita vero imperatoris nequitia, omnis Italia consilium iniit ut sibi eligerent imperatorem et ducerent Constantinopolim; sed compescuit tale consilium pontifex, sperans conversionem principis.

Masai, *loc. cit.* (n. 5 above), 198 n. and *passim*, comments sagely on this text and the papal attitude towards Leo III, which he would interpret very much as I do.

On the situation in Italy during this period, see Ottorino Bertolini, 'I papi e le relazioni politiche di Roma con i ducati longobardi di Spoleto e di Benevento, 3, Il secolo VIII: da Giovanni VI (701–705) a Gregorio II (715–731),' *Rivista di storia della chiesa in Italia*, 9 (1955), 1–57, n. b. 13 ff., 33 ff.; idem, *Roma di fronte a Bisanzio e ai Longobardi* (*Storia di Roma*, 9 [Bologna, 1941]), 423–52, 768 f., with 787–91 (bibliography on the papal *patrimonium*); G. Romano and A. Solmi, *Le dominazioni barbariche in Italia, 395–888*, 3rd ed. (Milan,

the whole of northern Italy except for Naples) by the inhabitants of the Pentapolis and the 'hosts of Venice,' who vowed that they would never suffer the Pope to be put to death, but would exert themselves with all their might in his defence. Accordingly, they anathematized simultaneously the Byzantine Exarch Paul, the Emperor, and all who agreed with him. Here and frequently (§§ xiv, xv, xvi, xvii, xviii, xix), in the *Life of Gregory* reference is made to imperial orders that had been given for the execution of the Pope. But it is extremely improbable that the Emperor sought any more than Gregory's removal from the papal throne, and the same source itself observes (§ xvi) that this is what Leo had in mind (see text in n. 34; cf. n. 39 above). Under similar

1940), 401–8, 417 f.; Gian P. Bognetti, 'Longobardi e Romani,' *Studi di storia e diritto in onore di Enrico Besta*, 4 (Milan, 1939), 351–410; Emerich Schaffran, *Geschichte der Langobarden* (Leipzig, 1938): superficial; Erich Caspar, *Geschichte des Papsttums*, 2 (Tübingen, 1933), 639–64; Ludo M. Hartmann, *Geschichte Italiens im Mittelalter*, 2, 2 (*Allgemeine Staatengeschichte*, 1, *Geschichte der europäischen Staaten*, 32 [Gotha, 1903]), 85–111, 118–21; *idem, Untersuchungen zur Geschichte der byzantinischen Verwaltung in Italien, 540–750* (Leipzig, 1889), 16, 21–24, and *passim*; Michele Rosi, *Longobardi e Chiesa Romana al tempo del Re Luitprando* (Catania, 1890): n.b. 46–54. J. B. Bury, *A history of the Later Roman Empire from Arcadius to Irene, 395 A.D. to 800 A. D.* (London-N.Y., 1889), 432, 440–45; Hugo Cohn, *Die Stellung der byzantinischen Statthalter in Ober- und Mittelitalien, 540–751* (Berlin, 1889); Charles Diehl, *Études sur l'administration byzantine dans l'Exarchat de Ravenne, 568–751* (*Bibliothèque des Écoles françaises d'Athènes et de Rome*, 53 [Paris, 1888]), 331 f., 335 f., 343 f., 355, 363–67, 376–80, 395, 410 f.; A. Gasquet, *Études byzantines, l'Empire byzantin et la monarchie franque* (Paris, 1888), 228–31; Henri Hubert, 'Étude sur la formation des états de l'Église, les papes Grégoire II, Grégoire III, Zacharie et Étienne II et leurs relations avec les empereurs iconoclastes,' *Revue historique*, 69 (1899), 1–40, 241–72, n. b. 1–18; Wilhelm Martens, *Politische Geschichte des Langobardenreichs unter König Liutprand, 712–744* (Heidelberg, 1880). Giuseppe Pochettino, *I Langobardi nell'Italia meridionale, 570–1080* (Naples, n.d.), has little to offer, except a lengthy bibliography, which, though occasionally inaccurate, has some value. Antiquated but not without interest remains Ferdinand Gregorovius, *Geschichte der Stadt Rom im Mittelalter*, 1 (1859, used in the edition of Fritz Schillmann, Dresden, 1926), 413–28. C. Calisse, 'Il governo dei Bisantini in Italia,' *Rivista storica italiana*, 2 (1885), 265–335; and Amédée Gasquet, 'Le Royaume Lombard, ses relations avec l'empire grec et avec les Francs,' *Revue historique*, 33 (1887), 58–92, have lost their savour. But see Roberto Cessi, 'La crisi dell' esarcato ravennate agli inizi dell' iconoclastia,' *Reale Istituto Veneto di Scienze, Lettere ed Arti, Atti*, 93, P. II. (1933–34), 1671–85.

circumstances,[43] it will be remembered, Emperor Justinian I in 537 had banished Pope Silverius, whom he replaced with Vigilius, just as Emperor Constans II in 653 had Pope Martin I arrested and carried off from Rome.

These precedents might have indicated that Pope Gregory's life was not really in immediate danger. None the less, his allies, who were both incensed and alarmed, refused to recognize the Exarch's authority, chose leaders for themselves throughout Italy, and in this way made provision for their own protection and that of the Pope. 'When the wickedness of the Emperor became known,' the *Liber Pontificalis* puts it, 'the whole of Italy made plans to choose a new emperor and lead him to Constantinople. But the Pope vetoed this scheme, and hoped for the Emperor's conversion.'[44]

Some might, perhaps, be puzzled by these simple words, and wonder why the Pope should not have encouraged his compatriots to carry

---

[43] On these precedents, see Erich Caspar, *Geschichte des Papsttums*, 2, 230–32, 568 ff. (cf. 245 ff. on the arrest and removal from Rome of Pope Vigilius in 545).

[44] LP, 1, 404.25–405.3, quoted in n. 42 above. On the campaign of 717–18, see Ostrogorsky, *Geschichte*, 130 f.; Rodolphe Guilland, 'L'expédition de Maslama contre Constantinople (717–718),' *Études byzantines* (Paris, 1959), 109–33; Marius Canard, 'Les expéditions des arabes contre Constantinople dans l'histoire et dans la légende,' *Journal Asiatique*, 208 (1926), 61–121, n.b. 80 ff. For the texts on the Arab siege and the attempted usurpations, see Theophanes, 1, 395.13–399.19, 398.7–399.4, 400.18–401.3, 405.14–24; Nicephorus, *op. cit.* (n. 9 above), 53.10–55.19, 54.20–55.12, 55.19–56.27, 57.27–58.10 (for the last text see n. 40 above); Dölger, *Regesten*, 1, nos. 281–85. Hartmann, *op. cit.* (n. 42 above), 88 (cf. 85 f.), suggests the possibility of Gregory's involvement in the Sicilian uprising and in the insurrection centering around Artemius (Anastasius II). He finds support for this conjecture in the fact that the LP mentions an imperial plot to murder the Pope even before referring to Gregory's opposition to the imperial taxes. I doubt, however, as I argue throughout this paper, that Gregory would have been so reckless as to imperil himself and the papacy in this way. It has recently been demonstrated that the battle of Poitiers took place in 733, not in 732, as it had previously been believed: M. Baudot, 'Localisation et datation de la première victoire remportée par Charles-Martel contre les Musulmans,' *Mémoires et documents publiés par la Société de l'École des Chartes*, 12 (1955), 93–105; G. E. von Grunebaum, *Der Islam im Mittelalter* (Zürich-Stuttgart, 1963), 15, 443. Cf. Ekkehard Eickhoff, *Seekrieg und Seepolitik zwischen Islam und Abendland, das Mittelmeer unter byzantinischer und arabischer Hegemonie (650–1040)*, (Berlin, 1966), 32 ff.

out their project of electing a new emperor and installing him in Constantinople, as they wished. But such doubts about Gregory's motives do him a grave injustice, and fail to recognize that he was too shrewd to involve himself in a conspiracy of such far-reaching proportions, which would have involved an enormous expeditionary force, to say nothing of a direct assault upon the impregnable walls of Constantinople. Besides, he was indubitably acquainted with the terrible fate which had overtaken the Arabs who were so temerarious as to attack Byzantium in 717–718, for his biography (§ xii), which (see n. 2 above) was written during his lifetime, refers to the siege of 717–718 and to the annihilation of most of the attacking forces (*maxima illic eorum parte fame ac bello interempta confusi recesserunt, Leone principe*).

Gregory probably did not know that, of the huge armada of 2,560 ships and of the army of 180,000 men the Arabs had mustered on this occasion, only five of the former and 30,000 of the latter ever reached home, since these statistics, which surely exaggerate the magnitude of Leo's victory, are to be found only in chronicles that were not accessible to the author of the *Liber Pontificalis*. Nor would he have been aware, as modern historians were the first to perceive, that this was one of the decisive battles of history, comparable with, and probably more significant than, Charles Martel's triumph over the Muslims at Poitiers in 733. Likewise he could not have foreseen that the Arabs were so profoundly impressed by this defeat that they never dared attack the capital city again. But he did realize that the Arabs had suffered an appalling disaster, and that, however feeble or inept the Byzantines might appear on Italian soil, the Emperor himself could not be challenged in his home territory.

In addition, the papal intelligence services would surely have received word of Leo's ruthlessness and unvarying success in crushing the rivals who had had the hardihood to rebel against him. For the reasons set forth in the course of this article it is not reasonable to suppose that Gregory himself was a party to any of these. But he certainly would have been informed about the ignominious failure of three attempts at usurpation: one of which (in 718) was led by the Pro- tospatharios Sergios, who had set up a rival emperor named Tiberius (orginally Basil) in Sicily; the second of which (in 719–20) was command- ed by the former Emperor Anastasius II (713–15), known as Artemius;

and the third of which (in 728) was under the leadership of a usurper
named Cosmas, who stood at the head of the themes of the Helladikoi
and the Cyclades and was easily overcome by the Byzantine navy in
the waters near the capital. Artemius and Cosmas had got up to the
walls of Constantinople, but both failed to gain admission to the
capital city itself. All of the usurpers lost their heads, as did most
of their leading accomplices, including (in the second episode) even
the Archbishop of Thessalonike.

In the face of such a record, no man of prudence would take the
risk of provoking what by every indication must have seemed to
be the inevitable Leonine retaliation from Constantinople. Instead,
Gregory, who was one of the most astute diplomats ever to occupy
the papal throne, preferred to exploit the confused situation in Italy
on a less grandiose scale than that of emperor-making. But the benefits
he secured for the Roman See in this way were both more satisfying
and more permanent than those enjoyed for a limited time by the
usurpers and their sponsors.

The hour of final humiliation for Byzantium in Northern Italy,
which followed upon the loss of Ravenna in 751, had not yet arrived.
But Gregory was quick to seize the opportunities that now became
his, and exploited them to the full without committing himself to
hazardous enterprizes of doubtful outcome, or goading Leo beyond
the limits of endurance. Fortunately for him, Leo failed to send
reinforcements, which might have altered the balance of power
greatly. Nor was the Emperor able by any of the means available to
him to exact obedience from the Italians, who after 726–27 had been
largely alienated from whatever loyalty they may ever have felt
for Byzantium.

As a result, the Roman militia, who favored the Pope, not only
slew[45] the Roman Duke Exhilaratus, together with the latter's son
Hadrian, for conspiring with the Emperor against the Pope, but
also blinded another duke, Peter by name, presumably for the same
reason. Simultaneously, during a sanguinary outbreak in Ravenna the
Byzantine Exarch Paul[46] was put to death by the Pope's partisans.

On the other hand, the Pope personally intervened to save the life

[45] LP, 1, 405.5–11.

[46] LP, 1, 405.12–15.

of the legate whom Exarch Eutychius had dispatched from Naples to Rome with orders to execute a number of Roman nobles, including the Pope himself.[47] At the same time, the papal allies anathematized Eutychius, and swore an oath to defend the Pope, whom they pronounced to be the 'champion of the Christian faith and defender of the churches' (*pontificem christianae fidei zelotem et ecclesiarum defensorem*).[48]

Similarly, they frustrated the plot by which Eutychius sought, with the offer of huge bribes, to persuade Liutprand (King of the Lombards, 712-44) to make common cause with Byzantium against the Pope. Instead of succumbing to the Emperor's wiles, the Lombards joined forces with the Romans, together with whom they not only scorned the imperial rescripts but also bound themselves as brothers by a chain of faith to fight to the death in defence of the Pope in the war he was waging for the true faith and the welfare of the Christians (*pro fide vera et christianorum certantem salutem* [sic for *salute*]).[49]

The passion of the Italians for the Pope and their eagerness to die for him may perhaps have been exaggerated by the papal annalist, as some critics suggest. But there is no doubt that a crisis had arisen which made of the Pope a rallying point for the disaffected and a national champion against the foreign invaders.

In the resulting conflicts, hostility for Byzantium was compounded of many elements – local, financial, political, and nationalistic, as well as theological. Nationalism was clearly involved, and undoubtedly played a role in Gregory's elevation to the papal throne, since he was only the second[50] out of the 13 popes between 678 and 752 who was

[47] LP, 1, 405.19-406.7.

[48] LP, 1, 406.7-12.

[49] LP, 1, 406.12-20. Cf. Ottorino Bertolini, 'Le relazioni politiche di Roma con i ducati di Spoleto e di Benevento nel periodo del dominio longobardo,' *Atti del primo Congresso internazionale di studi longobardi* (Spoleto, 1952), 37-49.

[50] LP, 1, 396.1: natione Romanus, ex patre Marcello. On Gregory II, see P. Jaffé, *Regesta pontificum romanorum ab condita ecclesia ad annum post Christum natum MCXCVIII*, 2d ed. by W. [Gulielmus] Wattenbach, etc., 1 (Leipzig, 1885), 249-57. Cf. A. Schäfer, *Die Bedeutung der Päpste Gregor II.*

a Roman (the other was Benedict II, 684–85). All the rest were Greeks, Syrians, or Sicilians (who had, of course, long been Hellenic or, at least, in great degree Hellenized).

Nevertheless, for the papacy theology was always a primary consideration; and Pope Gregory was more concerned, as we have already seen, with purity of dogma, the traditions of his Church, and the security of the Roman See rather than with breaking away from Byzantium or setting up a rival emperor in Italy. For this reason, as well as for others to be considered below, in the midst of the turmoil consequent upon Eutychius's attempt to alienate the Lombards from Rome, he exhorted the people to remain fast in the faith but not to fail in devotion or loyalty to the Roman Empire.

During these troubled times, his biographer comments, Gregory managed by acts of charity, constant exhortation, and serenity of temper (fortified by prayer and fasting) to comfort his people and restrain them from the rash undertakings they were contemplating.[51] Moreover, the power of his personality was so great, and he was so gifted a negotiator, that he was able to prevail over his enemies even when they had overcome him by force of arms. The best example of his diplomatic virtuosity is the way he turned to his advantage what must at first have appeared to be a catastrophic defeat at the hands of the Byzantine Exarch Eutychius and the Lombard King Liutprand.[52] When Eutychius first sought to organize a Byzantino-Lombard entente, it will be remembered (n. 49 above), he had failed miserably and succeeded only in provoking the Lombards to ally

(715–731) und Gregor III. (731–741) für die Gründung des Kirchenstaates (Münster i. W., 1913); J. Dahmen, Das Pontifikat Gregors II. nach den Quellen bearbeitet (Düsseldorf, 1888). N.b. Jules Gay, 'Quelques remarques sur les papes grecs et syriens avant la querelle des iconoclastes (678–715),' Mélanges offerts à M. Gustave Schlumberger, 1 (Paris, 1924), 40–54. See the list of the relevant popes by A. Pietro Frutaz, 'Papa,' Enciclopedia Cattolica, 9 (1952), 760. Cf. L. Spätling, 'Gregor II.,' Lexikon für Theologie und Kirche, 2d ed., 4 (Freiburg im Breisgau, 1960), 1181.

[51] LP, 1, 406.21–407.5; n.b. the last two sentences: blando omnes sermone ut bonis in Deum proficerent actibus et in fide persisterent rogabat, sed ne desisterent ab amore vel fide Romani imperii ammonebat. Sic totorum corda molliebat et dolores continuos mitigabat.

[52] LP, 1, 407.19–408.12 (note both versions).

themselves with the Romans against Byzantium. In the following year, however (ca. 728), Eutychius at last won over Liutprand and appeared with him in the midst of a sizable army on the *campus Neronis*, that is, on the plain lying between the Vatican hill, Monte Mario, and the Tiber River. But at the very moment in which Byzantine diplomacy was thus about to achieve a brilliant victory over Pope Gregory, the latter, alert as always to the exigencies of the hour, sallied forth to meet his putative conquerors and, though unarmed, deprived them of the fruits of their successful campaign. Unfortunately, we have no transcript of the words which passed between the Pope and his adversaries. But whatever was said, Liutprand was so deeply moved that he fell down in homage at the Pope's feet, swore to do him no injury, laid his arms and accoutrements of royalty at the grave of St. Peter, and meekly departed.[53] In so doing, he abandoned the plans he had concerted with the Exarch for carrying out the Emperor's orders. The *Liber Pontificalis* does not specify what these were, but we may assume that they involved the Pope's execution or, more probably (see nn. 34 & 39 above), his expulsion from the papal throne.

The later recension of the *Liber Pontificalis* adds that, before leaving the scene, Liutprand arranged a reconciliation between Gregory and Eutychius, and that the latter then established himself in Rome.[54] There is no reason to doubt that the two antagonists were able to come to terms, even though the Exarch must have been apprehensive when he began to wonder how he was going to justify his conduct to his imperial master.

To make matters worse, at this very moment a new problem arose in the form of a certain Petasius, who had managed to raise the banner of revolt and had got himself proclaimed emperor under the name of Tiberius. Eutychius was greatly alarmed by this new development. But Pope Gregory once more roused himself to meet the challenge,

[53] LP, 1, 407.22 ff. The later and more legendary recension specifies (408.4–8) that Liutprand divested himself of his mantum (cape), armilausiam (military cloak), balteum (belt), spatam atque ensem deauratos (*sic*) (golden sword and dagger) necnon coronam auream et crucem argenteam (gold crown and silver cross). Both versions include *ante corpus apostoli*.

[54] LP, 1, 408.8 ff.: Post oratione facta obsecravit pontificem ut memoratum exarchum ad pacis concordiam suscipere dignaretur: quod et factum est. Et sic recessit, rege declinante a malis quibus inerat consiliis cum exarcho.

and provided the army by which the usurper was captured and slain. There is no doubt that he was delighted to be in a position to confer a favor on the hapless Exarch, whose complaisance had served him well, especially since he was thus enabled to offer substantial proof of his loyalty to the Byzantine Empire and at the same time to rid himself of an unwelcome local emperor. It must, therefore have been with considerable satisfaction that he had Petasius's head removed and dispatched to Constantinople. But he was disappointed, his biographer plaintively remarks, when the Emperor failed to express gratitude for this act of fealty.[55]

Disinterested observers, however, will understand why the Byzantine government felt disinclined to exchange amenities with the Pope so long as he blocked the flow of revenue from Italy to Constantinople, encouraged rebellion against imperial authority, and fulminated against the Emperor's iconoclastic decree. Indeed, if he were fully apprized of what was going on in Italy at this time, Leo might well have been exasperated to learn that, in spite of the allied 'victory' over the Pope, which had cost much more than it was worth, the only tangible results were (1) that the fierce and undoubtedly dearly bought Liutprand had proved to be a broken reed, (2) that the imperial Exarch had become little more than a papal tool, and (3) that the Pope, who had been defeated, emerged as the victor, and not only remained secure in the possession of the papal throne, but also unrepentantly continued to flout the imperial *iussiones*.

Gregory was greatly incensed when Germanos was compelled to yield the patriarchal throne to Anastasius in 730 and urged the Emperor to return to orthodoxy.[56] But it is extremely improbable

---

[55] LP, 1, 408.13–409.3: n.b. last sentence: Et nec sic plenam Romanis gratiam largitus est imperator.

[56] LP, 1, 409.4–14 (quoted in n. 30 above), plus 409.15–24: Eodem tempore Germanus patriarcha a propria expulsus est sede imperatoris nequitia, sibique complicem Anastasium presbiterum in eius loco constituit. Qui missa synodica dum talius (corrected in the later recension to *talis*) erroris eum consentientem apostolicus repperiret vir, non censuit fratrem aut consacerdotem, sed scriptis commonitoriis, nisi ad catholicam convinceret fidem, etiam extorrem a sacerdotali officio esse mandavit. Imperatori quoque suadens salutaria ut a tali execrabili miseria declinaret scriptis commonuit. Theophanes, 1, 408.31–409.18 (A. M. 6221). See on computation n. 19 above.

that he then in retaliation severed 'Rome, Italy, and the whole of the West from political and ecclesiastical obedience to Leo and his imperial government,' as the Byzantine chroniclers and their Latin imitators say he did.[57] For to have done so would have been to expose himself

[57] Theophanes, 1, 408.21–25:
ἐν δὲ τῇ πρεσβυτέρᾳ 'Ρώμῃ Γρηγόριος, ὁ πανίερος ἀποστολικὸς ἀνὴρ καὶ Πέτρου τοῦ κορυφαίου σύνθρονος, λόγῳ καὶ πράξει διαλάμπων, ὃς ἀπέστησε 'Ρώμην τε καὶ Ἰταλίαν καὶ πάντα τὰ ἑσπέρια τῆς τε πολιτικῆς καὶ ἐκκλησιαστικῆς ὑπακοῆς Λέοντος καὶ τῆς ὑπ' αὐτὸν βασιλείας.
So also ibid., 409.14–18, 410.4 f. Somewhat similarly, George Monachus, op. cit. (n. 22 above), 2, 744.4–10, says:
διὰ ταῦτα οὖν καὶ ὁ τῆς μεγάλης 'Ρώμης πρόεδρος Γρηγόριος τὴν τῆς αὐτοῦ βασιλείας ὑποταγὴν ἐκτιναξάμενος τὸ αἱρετικὸν αἶσχος ἀποδιδράσκει σπονδὰς εἰρηνικὰς εἰς τὴν τῶν Φράγγων ὑποταγὴν εἰσδεξάμενος σὺν πάσῃ τῇ Ἰταλίᾳ, καὶ τοὺς φόρους εὐθὺς κωλύσας τὸν Ἀναστάσιον καὶ τοὺς σὺν αὐτῷ ἀνεθεμάτισεν.
(i.e., 'For this reason, therefore, Gregory, the head of the great [Church] of Rome, renounced allegiance to [Leo's] government, and avoided the shame of heresy by concluding, along with the whole of Italy, a treaty of peace with the Franks, which provided for submission to Frankish sovereignty. At the same time, he prevented [the Byzantines] from [collecting] taxes, and anathematized Anastasius [i.e., the iconoclastic patriarch appointed by Leo on January 22, 730], together with his followers.'). George Cedrenus, Historiarum Compendium, ed. Immanuel Bekker, 1, CSHB (Bonn, 1838), 799.2–9, 800.11–13, differs only slightly from George Monachus:
ἐν δὲ τῇ πρεσβυτέρᾳ 'Ρώμῃ Γρηγόριος ἀποστολικὸς ἀνὴρ καὶ Πέτρου τοῦ κορυφαίου σύνθρονος, ὃς διὰ τὰ ὑπ' αὐτοῦ γινόμενα θεῖα πονήματα Διάλογος ἐκλήθη. οὗτος ὁ ἅγιος διὰ τὰς ἀνοσιουργίας Λέοντος ἀφηνίασε, καὶ πρὸς τὸν Φράγγον σπονδὴν εἰρηνικὴν ποιησάμενος τούς τε φόρους ἐκώλυσε καὶ Ἀναστάσιον καὶ τοὺς σὺν αὐτῷ ἀνεθεμάτισε. τὸν δὲ βασιλέα δι' ἐπιστολῶν αὐτοῦ πολλῶν πολλοῖς ἐγνωσμένων ἀριδήλως ἐλέγχει. ... ὁ δὲ βασιλεὺς ἐμαίνετο κατὰ τοῦ πάπα καὶ τῆς ἀποστάσεως 'Ρώμης καὶ Ἰταλίας, καὶ ἐξοπλίσας στόλον μέγαν ἀπέστειλε κατ' αὐτῶν.
(The reference to Dialogus [Pope Gregory I, 590–604] is erroneous.) Comparable data recur in Michael Glycas, Annales, 4, ed. Immanuel Bekker, CSHB (Bonn, 1836), 522.2–5: ἀλλὰ τὸν Αἰθίοπα σμῆξαι μὴ δυνηθεὶς τοὺς φόρους τῆς Ἰταλίας καὶ 'Ρώμης ἐκώλυσε τελεῖσθαι πρὸς τὸν βασιλέα, καὶ τὴν ὅλην δὲ χώραν αὐτῶν τῆς ἐξουσίας ταύτης ἀπέστησε.
A similar account is given by Zonaras, Epitomae historiarum, 15, 4, 1 and 8, ed. Theodor Büttner-Wobst, 3, CSHB (Bonn, 1897), 261.6–11, 262.15–263,1, who, however, says nothing about Gregory's involving Rome and Italy in his act of treason. These authors were mistaken in putting the papal alliance with the Franks, which was not concluded until 754, under Gregory II: (Hubert, loc. cit., n. 42 above, 3, apparently accepts these texts without question.)

and the papacy to the dangers reviewed above. Furthermore, as Gregory had been quick to see, in the anomalous situation which then prevailed in Italy, he had all the advantages of having taken this momentous step without thrusting his head into the lion's mouth by actually taking it. So long as he obstructed the collection of imperial taxes, and had the support of the people, he maintained *de facto* control in Central Italy, and was able, *more suo*, with the best Italo-Byzantine guile, to manipulate friend and foe alike as his puppets. Under these circumstances, there would have been no need for Gregory to jeopardize his position by treasonably slicing off a piece of the Empire and thereby openly defying the Emperor.

It is difficult to fix the exact chronology of these events (nn. 42–55), but they are all securely dated as occurring prior to 730 because the author of this section of the *Liber Pontificalis* places them before the second wave of iconoclasm under Leo, which coincided with the forced abdication of Patriarch Germanos of Constantinople on January 7, 730 (n. 56 above). Thereafter (n. 30, cf. nn. 56 f. above), images were removed and burned, churches were white-washed (presumably to cover the vacant areas on the walls and to conceal mosaics or icons that could not otherwise be effaced), and iconophiles were punished by death or mutilation.

Summary

At first sight, it might appear that Pope Gregory was pursuing contradictory ends in first opposing the Byzantine *iussiones* and then

N.b. the *Chronica* of Sigebert (see his entry for 729 in n. 18 above), who derived his version of this affair from a source that was dependent upon Anastasius Bibliothecarius's Latin translation of the *Chronographia* of Theophanes. But he did not use Anastasius directly on this point as a comparison of the two texts shows: Theophanes, ed. de Boor, 2, 264.23–27: in seniori vero Roma Gregorius, sacratissimus vir apostolicus et Petri verticis apostolorum consessor, verbo et actu coruscans, qui removit Romam et Italiam nec non et omnia tam rei publicae quam ecclesiasticae iura in Hesperiis ab oboedientia Leonis et imperii sub ipso constituti. See also *Historia Miscella*, 21, MPL, 95, 1086A. Cf. Charles Diehl, *Études sur l'administration byzantine* (n. 42 above), 376 f., with whom I agree on the whole, although he does not make use of the Latin chronicles, which, erroneously I believe, support Theophanes on this point.

reversing himself by interfering in the Emperor's behalf. But both patterns of behavior can be explained as parts of a thoroughly consistent policy. The Pope resisted the Emperor with regard to the images both because he was an iconophile himself and because he felt, as Theophanes reports, that the Emperor had no right to interfere in dogmatic and ecclesiastical questions, which according to him belonged exclusively to the domain of the Church (n. 6 above).

Likewise, he opposed the collection of new taxes because they were, we may well suspect, levied principally upon the properties owned by the papacy itself, that is, upon the patrimonies of the Roman Church, which by the eighth century were considerable in extent, and a portion of which (those in Sicily and Calabria) in 732–33 yielded the Pope an annual revenue of three and a half talents.[58] This, it seems, is what is meant by the reference to Gregory's interference with taxes that in his judgment would deprive the churches of their substance.[59] For the Romans, like the Pope, were convinced that Eutychius and the imperial legates were attempting 'to violate the churches of Christ, ruin everyone, and carry off the wealth of all.'[60]

These passages, taken with the designation of Gregory as the *ecclesiarum defensor*[61] (see n. 48 above) give a hint that one of Gregory's

[58] Theophanes, 1, 410.11–14 (A. M. 6224). On the patrimonies see Karl Bihlmeyer and Hermann Tüchle, *Kirchengeschichte*, 2, 17th ed. (Paderborn, 1962), 40 ff. (with bibliography) and nn. 42 above and 61f. below; Paul Fabre, *De patrimoniis Romanae ecclesiae usque ad aetatem Carolinorum* (Paris, 1892), 59 ff., 65 f.; Karl Schwarzlose, 'Die Verwaltung und die finanzielle Bedeutung der Patrimonien der römischen Kirche bis zur Gründung des Kirchenstaates', *Zeitschrift für Kirchengeschichte*, 11 (1889–90, title page: 1890), 62–100; Masai, *loc. cit.* (n. 5 above), 198 ff.

[59] LP, 1, 403.20–25, quoted in n. 39 above.

[60] LP, 1, 405.23 ff.: claruit cunctis pessimum consilium quia Christi violare conabantur ecclesias et perdere cunctos atque diripere omnium bona.

[61] On the *defensor ecclesiae*, see Balthasar Fischer, 'Defensor ecclesiae', *Reallexikon für Antike und Christentum*, 3 (Stuttgart, 1957), 656–58; *idem*, 'Die Entwicklung des Instituts der Defensoren in der römischen Kirche,' *Ephemerides liturgicae*, 48, N.S. 8 (1934), 443–54; Annibale Bugnini, 'Defensor Ecclesiae', *Enciclopedia cattolica*, 4 (Vatican City, 1950), 1301 f.; F. Martroye, 'Les "defensores Ecclesiae" au Ve et VIe siècle', *Revue historique de droit français et étranger*, S. 4, 2 (1923), 597–622 (a great part of the article concerns Pope Gregory I [590–604] and his use of the *defensores*, on which cf. F. Homes Dudden,

principal objectives in taking up arms against the Emperor was the protection of the papal patrimonies and their revenues. For in the eighth century the *defensores ecclesiae* were officials appointed by the pope to administer the patrimonies of the Roman Church and to watch over papal interests there. Pope Gregory I (590–604) occasionally assigned the *defensores ecclesiae* other missions, but one of their chief functions was to watch over the patrimonies; and they often wielded great power themselves as well as through their chief officer, the *primicerius defensorum*, who was an important official at the papal court.

By the beginning of the eighth century the properties thus entrusted by the pope to administration by the *defensores ecclesiae* had grown to considerable size, and were distributed throughout the western part of the Empire. They must have seemed tempting morsels, ripe for plucking, to the Emperor in need of new revenues, as he must have been after the exhausting wars and revolutions which had taxed the resources of Byzantium in the early years of his reign (see n. 44). Under these circumstances, the new imperial taxes would have appeared particularly ominous to Gregory, who could not have failed to realize that what the Emperor taxed he might also confiscate. Gregory's anxiety on this score was fully justified, as his successor, Gregory III (731-41), learned to his dismay in the year 732–33, when Leo increased the capitation tax of Sicily and Calabria by one third and confiscated the papal patrimonies in Sicily and Calabria,[62] the former

Gregory the Great, 1 [London, 1905], 300–7); Paul Fabre, *op. cit.* (n. 58 above), 46 ff. Cf. also Amedeo Crivellucci, 'Le chiese cattoliche e i Longobardi ariani in Italia', *Studi storici*, 6 (Torino-Livorno, 1897), 592 ff.; Schwarzlose, *loc. cit.*, n. 58 above, 68 ff.

Paolo L. Zovatto, 'Il "defensor ecclesiae" e le iscrizioni musive di Trieste', *Rivista di storia della chiesa in Italia*, 20 (1966), 1–8, discusses four recently discovered mosaic inscriptions containing names of *defensores*.

[62] Theophanes, 1, 410.9 ff.; Theophanes does not identify the papal patrimonies confiscated by Leo, but they are listed in the letter which Pope Nicholas I (858–67) wrote to request Emperor Michael III (842–67) to restore to the papacy the patrimonies of Sicily and Calabria: MGH, *Epistolarum*, 6, *Epistolae Karolini Aevi*, 4, ed. E. Perels (Berlin, 1925), 438.25–439.11; reproduced also by C. Silva-Tarouca, *Epistularum romanorum pontificum ad vicarios per Illyricum aliosque episcopos Collectio Thessalonicensis* (*Pontificia Universitas Gregoriana, Textus et documenta*, 22, *Series theologica*, 23 [Rome, 1937]), v (23 on the wrap-

of which included some of the pope's richest possessions.

Thus, in going to the extremes noted by the *Liber Pontificalis* and summarized above, Gregory was fighting not only to defend Christian dogma, over which the Church claimed exclusive jurisdiction, but also to secure the papal patrimonies against encroachment and confiscation. His rebellion against Leo's *iussiones*, dogmatic and fiscal, are therefore to be understood as resistance to measures that threatened the autonomy of the Church of Rome, which it was his responsibility to safeguard at all costs.

But resolute as he was in opposing imperial invasions of papal sovereignty in the realm of theology and in the administration of the papal patrimonies, he had no desire to throw off the Byzantine yoke altogether. Indeed, there is every reason to believe that, while he welcomed support from all quarters against Byzantine iconoclasm and financial exactions, he was equally determined not to substitute an Italian ruler or imperial power on *Italian soil* for the remote control that was only ineffectually exerted over Italy and the Roman Church by the Byzantine emperor, who lived half a world away. It was in the best interests of the papacy to submit to political supervision stemming from distant Constantinople rather than cope with an Italian despot or Italian imperial court, which would know well how to govern Italy directly in its own interest without regard for the wishes of the Roman pontiff.

The loose and largely ineffective suzerainty of the Byzantine emperor, who sent exarchs with commands but no troops,[63] gave the popes great freedom of action in dealing with the separate secular entities in Italy. For, in the ambiguous political circumstances which

per, 22 on the title page). For the literature on the date of this sequestration, see my article, 'The transfer of Illyricum, Calabria, and Sicily to the jurisdiction of the patriarchate of Constantinople in 732–733', *Studi bizantini e neoellenici*, 9 (*Silloge byzantina in onore di Silvio Giuseppe Mercati* [Rome, 1957]), 14–31. My conclusions have been accepted by Werner Ohnsorge in *Vierteljahrsschrift für Sozial- und Wirtschaftsgeschichte*, 51 (Wiesbaden 1964), 503.

See also the interesting materials collected by Masai, *loc. cit.* (n. 5 above), 198–203, who, however, does not examine the critical problem of the date on which Leo instituted these jurisdictional changes.

[63] Cf., e.g., besides the cases of this kind already cited from the LP, LP, 1, 442.6 ff., 452.11–453.10; Louis Halphen, *Charlemagne et l'empire carolingien*, 2d ed. (Paris, 1949), 25 f., 34, 42 f.

VIII

40

then prevailed, it enabled them to offer ostensible loyalty to the Byzantine Empire at the same time that they reserved the right, in practice, to defy imperial decrees whenever they chose. Nevertheless, despite not a few instances of insubordination, which sorely vexed the Byzantine administration, and which a stronger central government would not have tolerated, the papacy hid behind the imperial authority of Byzantium, if necessity required, as a shield against the waxing Lombard power and the Italian cities, both of which it was skilled in manipulating to its own advantage.

It was by astute diplomacy and subtle management of the numerous conflicts of interest among these mutually antagonistic forces that the popes succeeded a generation later (754–56) in creating the papal state.[64] Thus it came about that a dispute over a basic point of theology

---

[64] Of the vast literature on the early history of the papal state, in addition to the bibliography in nn. 42, 58, 61 f., above, see above all Louis Duchesne, *Les premiers temps de l'état pontifical*, 3rd ed. (Paris, 1911): the best general treatment. Cf. Ottorino Bertolini, 'Le chiese longobarde dopo la conversione al cattolicesimo ed i loro rapporti con il papato,' *Settimane di studio del centro italiano di studi sull' alto medioevo*, 7, 1 (*Le Chiese nei regni dell'Europa occidentale e i loro rapporti con Roma sino all' 800* [Spoleto, 1960]), 455–92; *idem*, 'Il problema delle origini del potere temporale dei papi nei suoi presupposti teoretici iniziali', *Miscellanea Pio Paschini*, 1 (*Lateranum*, N.S., A. 14 [Rome, 1948]), 103–71; Amedeo Crivellucci, *Le origini dello stato della chiesa* (Pisa, 1909); Johannes Haller, *Die Quellen zur Geschichte der Entstehung des Kirchenstaates* (Leipzig-Berlin, 1907); G. Romano, *L'origine del potere civile e della signoria territoriale dei Papi* (Pavia, 1905): unavailable to me; Julius Jung, 'Organisationen Italiens von Augustus bis auf Karl d. Gr. (zugleich ein Beitrag zur Vorgeschichte des Kirchenstaates)', *Mittheilungen des Instituts für oesterreichische Geschichtsforschung*, 5. Ergänzungsband (Innsbruck, 1896–1903), 1–51; Heinrich Hamel, *Untersuchungen zur älteren Territorialgeschichte des Kirchenstaates* (Göttingen, 1899); Gustav Schnürer, *Die Entstehung des Kirchenstaates* (Cologne, 1894), translated into Italian by Angelo Mercati as *L'origine dello stato della chiesa* (Siena, 1899); Paul Fabre, *De patrimoniis Romanae ecclesiae usque ad aetatem Carolinorum* (cited in n. 58 above); Carl Schwarzlose, *Die Patrimonien der römischen Kirche bis zur Gründung des Kirchenstaates* (Berlin, 1887). Cf. also Walter Ullmann, *The growth of papal government in the Middle Ages*, 2d ed. (London, 1962), 52 ff., 91 ff.; Johannes Haller, *Das Papsttum*, 1, 2d ed. (Urach-Stuttgart, 1950), 412–65, 553–59; Louis Halphen, *Charlemagne et l'empire carolingien*, 2d ed. (Paris, 1949), 29–34, 38–47, 106–119, 234–36, 254–58, and *passim*; René Aigrain, in Fliche et Martin, *Histoire de l'Église*, 5, 428 f.; Hermann Tüchle, 'Kirchenstaat', *Lexikon für Theologie und Kirche*, 2d ed., 6 (1961), 260–65.

was an important factor in the foundation of the political power of the Roman Church.

This evidence for the issuance of a decree against the icons in 726–27 could be reinforced by the two letters in which Pope Gregory censures Leo for attacking the images, if the authenticity of these documents were established. Many scholars have branded them as forgeries, but Ostrogorsky and Caspar accept them as genuine, except for some interpolations.[65] Now, however, in the introduction to his exemplary critical edition of these two letters, which appeared more than two years after this article was completed (*loc. cit.*, n. 25 above, 253–76), Gouillard has thoroughly demolished the case which had once been made in their favor. Some parts of the second, he argues, may have issued from the pen of Gregory, but the first is indubitably a falsification, as is most, if not all, of the second. His new text completely replaces all previous versions, and his conclusions are irrefutable. Nevertheless, it is of some relevance to the problem here under discussion to note that the historical situation which their author envisaged falls between 726 (for the desecration of the image of Christ over the Bronze Gate of the Imperial Palace in Constantinople is mentioned) and 730 (for nothing is said about the Patriarch Germanos's abdication, which took place in January of that year).

Ottorino Bertolini, 'Quale fu il vero obbiettivo assegnato in Italia da Leone III "Isaurico" all' armata di Manes, stratego dei Cibyrreoti?' *Byzantinische Forschungen*, 2 (1967), 15-49, which was published long after the completion of my article, would probably agree (p. 20 n. 18 *ad fin.*) with my conclusions (n. 62 below) about the date of the transfer of jurisdiction but does not deal with the problem of the edict of 726-27.

After the completion of this paper, Haller, *Quellen*, was superseded by Horst Fuhrmann, *Quellen zur Entstehung des Kirchenstaates (Historische Texte, Mittelalter*, 7 [Göttingen, 1968]). Note that Karl (n. 58 above) and Carl Schwarzlose are the same. Rarely if ever cited, but of great interest is Hermann Proehl, *Beiträge zur Geschichte der Entstehung des Kirchenstaates* (Halle a. S., 1914).

[65] See Ostrogorsky, 'Les débuts,' 244–55 and *Geschichte des byzantinischen Staates*, 3rd ed., 126, 136, for bibliography and discussion.

COMPLEMENTARY NOTE

H.G.Beck (BZ, 65 (1972), 173) rejects the unambiguous statement of the Liber Pontificalis that there was a decree against the images in 726 as tendentious. But Stephen Gero, Byzantine Iconoclasm during the Reign of Leo III (Corpus Scriptorum Christianorum Orientalium, Subsidia, 41) (Louvain,1973), 106, n.55, admits that I have made "a very strong case for the early Latin sources witnessing an edict in 726" and reasons that Theophanes may have suppressed mention of an edict in 726 "in order to avoid presenting Germanus as acquiescing in, and collaborating with, an official, albeit temporizing, iconoclastic policy between 726 and 730...." According to Gero, it is Theophanes's account that is tendentious.

Concerning my suggestion (p.9) that logon poieisthai can mean something like "frame regulations" or "formulate a policy" if not actually "issue a decree", or, as we say, "give the word" (for the destruction of the icons), see my references on p.8, n.6, and Stephanus, Thesaurus Graecae Linguae, 6 (reprinted, Graz, 1954), 368A (on logos meaning "order"); G.W.H.Lampe, A Patristic Greek Lexicon (Oxford, 1964), fasc.3, 807, s.v. logos, I,A,3, ("command"); cf. 808, B,b. Naturally, I do not believe that logon poieisthai means more than "formulate a policy" here. But the examples cited are interesting; and, whatever Theophanes meant in this passage, the Liber Pontificalis is altogether unambiguous (p.7) and cannot be undermined.

IX

THE TRANSFER OF ILLYRICUM, CALABRIA AND SICILY TO THE JURISDICTION OF THE PATRIARCHATE OF CONSTANTINOPLE IN 732-33 [1]

The brevity of the present article is not to be taken as a measure of my devotion to Professor Mercati, who is esteemed throughout the world for his vast erudition, generous disposition, and unfailingly jovial temperament.   In paying tribute to him here, I wish to express my gratitude for the many friendly and ungrudging services of which I, like countless others, have been the beneficiary.

It has long been believed that the Emperor Leo III transferred Illyricum, Calabria, and Sicily from the ecclesiastical jurisdiction of the Roman papacy to that of the patriarchate of Constantinople in 732-33 [2] in reprisal for

[1] I should like also to acknowledge here my great indebtedness to the *Commissione Americana per gli Scambi culturali con l'Italia* for the award of a Fulbright fellowship (1954-1955), and to the John Simon Guggenheim Memorial Foundation for a similar grant, which has enabled me to pursue my studies outside of Italy.

This paper owes much to His Eminence, Cardinal Giovanni Mercati, and the Reverend Prefect Anselmo Albareda, O. S. B., of the Vatican Library, to the Reverend Professor A. Raes, S. J., of the Pontificium Institutum Orientalium Studiorum, and to the Reverend Drs. August Schuchert and Ludwig Völkl of the Campo Santo Teutonico, all of whom have generously made available to me the treasures of the libraries of which they are the custodians.

[2] Georg OSTROGORSKY, *Geschichte des byzantinischen Staates*, 2 d ed. (Munich, 1952), 132; Louis BRÉHIER, *Le monde byzantin*, 1 (*Vie et mort de Byzance* [Paris, 1947]), 80; Franz DÖLGER, *Regesten der Kaiserurkunden des oströmischen Reiches*, 1 (Munich-Berlin, 1924), n. 301; J. HERGENRÖTHER, *Photius, Patriarch von Constantinopel*, 1 (Regensburg, 1866), 236 f., 455 f. For the chronology of Theophanes, see OSTRO-GORSKY, *Die Chronologie des Theophanes im 7. und 8. Jahrhundert. Byzantinisch-Neugriechische Jahrbücher*, 7 (1928-1929), 1-56.

The Illyricum intended is the *praefectura Illyrici*, one of the four principal divisions of the Empire instituted by Diocletian, comprising the dioceses of Macedonia and Dacia and their provinces, of which the former was made up of six (Achaia, Macedonia, Creta, Thessalia, Epirus vetus, Epirus nova, pars Macedoniae salutaris), and the latter of five (Dacia mediterranea, Dacia ripensis, Moesia prima, Dardania, Praevalitana, pars Macedoniae salutaris). Cf. Otto SEECK, *Notitia dignitatum* (Berlin, 1876), 8-10; C. SILVA-TAROUCA, *Epistularum Romanorum pontificum ad vicarios per Illyricum aliosque episcopos, Collectio Thessalonicensis* (Pontificia Universitas Gregoriana, Textus et documenta, Series theologica, 23 [Roma, 1937]), v-vii.   This is what is known as " eastern Illyricum ", and in view of the detailed list of provinces given by Nicholas (p. 25 below) seems to have been the region affected by Leo's punitive

Pope Gregory II's resistance to the iconoclastic decree of 726 (¹).   Illyricum
itself had been under the civil rule of the emperor of Constantinople ever
since the end of 395 or the beginning of 396, although it had been subject to
Rome ecclesiastically with only a few brief interruptions (in 421 and, perhaps to some extent, during the Acacian schism, 484-519) (²).

---

action of 732-3. My colleague, Francis DVORNIK, however, has adduced some interesting evidence of Byzantine control exercized over churches in *western* Illyricum; see
his *La lutte entre Byzance et Rome à propos de l'Illyricum au IXᵉ siècle, Mélanges Charles
Diehl*, 1 (Paris, 1930), 68; reprinted with some changes in IDEM, *Les légendes de Constantin et de Methode vues de Byzance, Byzantinoslavica Supplementa*, 1 (Prague, 1933),
262 f., 264 f., 268 f., 282.

On the evidence for including Calabria and Sicily along with Illyricum, see
pp. 17, 21, 25 below.

(¹) I offer what I take to be conclusive proof that there was actually an iconoclastic decree in 726 in, *Leo III's Edict against the Images in the Year 726-7 and Italo-
Byzantine Relations between 726 and 730, Polychordia. Festschrift Franz Dölger*,
III (Amsterdam, 1968). OSTROGORSKY, *op. cit.*, 130 f. denies the existence of any
formal legislation on this subject before 730.

(²) On the partition of Illyricum, see: Émilienne DEMOUGEOT, *À propos des
partages d'Illyricum en 386-395, Actes du VIᵉ Congrès international d'études byzantines*,
1 (Paris, 1950), 87-92; EADEM, *Note sur la politique orientale de Stilicon, de 405 à 407,
Byzantion*, 20 (1950), 27-37; EADEM, *Les partages de l'Illyricum à la fin du IVᵉ siècle
à propos d'un livre récent, Revue historique*, 198 (1947), 16-31; EADEM, *De l'unité à la
division de l'empire romain, 395-410* (Paris, 1951); Louis DUCHESNE, *L'Illyricum
ecclésiastique*, BZ, 1 (1892), 531-550; Francis DVORNIK, *La lutte entre Byzance et Rome
à propos de l'Illyricum au IXᵉ siècle, Mélanges Charles Diehl*, 1 (Paris, 1930), 61-80
etc., as cited in n. 2 above; S. FRIEDRICH, *Über die Sammlung der Kirche von Thessalonich und das päpstliche Vicariat für Illyricum, Sitzungsberichte der philosophisch-
philologischen und historischen Classe der k. bayerischen Ak. der Wiss.* (Munich, 1891),
771-887; S. L. GREENSLADE, *The Illyrian churches and the vicariate of Thessalonica,
378-95, Journal of theological studies*, 46 (1945), 17-30; V. GRUMEL, *L'annexion de
l'Illyricum oriental, de la Sicile et de la Calabre au patriarcat de Constantinople. Le
témoignage de Théophane le chronographe, Recherches de science religieuse*, 40, *Mélanges
Jules Lebreton*, 2 (1951-1952), 191-200; IDEM, *Cause et date de l'annexion de l'Illyricum
oriental, de la Sicile et de la Calabre au patriarcat byzantin, Studi bizantini e neoellenici*,
7 (1953), 376; IDEM, *L'Illyricum, de la mort de Valentinien Iᵉʳ (375) à la mort de Stilicon
(408), Revue des études byzantines*, 9 (1951), 5-46; IDEM, *Le vicariat de Thessalonique
et le premier rattachement de l'Illyricum oriental au Patriarcat de Constantinople, Annuaire de l'école des législations religieuses.* Institut Catholique de Paris, 1950-1951,
(1952), 49-63; V. LAURENT, *L'érection de la métropole d'Athènes et le statut ecclésiastique
de l'Illyricum au VIIIᵉ siècle, Études byzantines*, 1 (1943), 58-72; P. LEPORSKI, *Istoriia
Fessalonikskago Exzarkhata do vremeni priscedinenie ego k Konstantinopolskomu pa-
triarkhatu* (St. Petersburg, 1901); Athanasius MATANIĆ, *De origine tituli Dalmatiae
ac totius Croatiae primas* (Rome-Subiaco, 1952); A. Ch. MPUTURAS, Περὶ τοῦ πάλαι
πατριαρχικοῦ ἀξιώματος τοῦ μητροπολίτου Θεσσαλονίκης, Γρηγόριος ὁ
Παλαμᾶς, 4 (1920), 43-50; IDEM, Περὶ τῆς ἐπωνυμίας 'παναγιώτατος' τοῦ
μητροπολίτου Θεσσαλονίκης, ibid., 2 (1918), 405-410; 4 (1920), 199; Robert
VON NOSTITZ-RIENECK, *Die päpstlichen Urkunden für Thessalonike und deren Kritik
durch Prof Friedrich, Zeitschrift für katholische Theologie*, 21 (1897), 1-50; J. R.

But Venance Grümel, whose *Regestes* are recognized universally as an indispensable tool of research, and whose opinion always commands respect, now advances the hypothesis that the change in ecclesiastical jurisdiction took place between 752 and 757, during the pontificate of Stephen II, rather than in 731 or 733 (¹). He is preparing a large and greatly needed monograph on Illyricum, which will be welcomed by all, and in this paper I propose to remind him, for possible consideration in his book, of the grounds, which still seem to be compelling, for accepting the earlier date.

Before considering Grumel's theory and the texts which in my judgment invalidate it, we shall have to examine the testimony of Theophanes the Confessor, our chief authority for this period (d. 818). He does not mention the alienation from Rome of any of its ecclesiastical dependencies, but merely says that, when Pope Gregory II of Rome (715-731) learned of Leo's legislation against the icons (726), he prevented the collection of taxes in Italy and Rome and wrote Leo that the Emperor had no right to intervene in matters of faith or to make innovations in dogma (²). Later, in describing the Pope's attitude towards Leo's dismissal of the iconophile Patriarch Germanus (730) in favor of the iconoclast, Anastasius, Theophanes says that Gregory severed Rome, Italy, and all of the West from the political and ecclesiastical domain of Leo and his government (³). In order to punish the pope for this insub-

---

PALANQUE, *Collégialité et partages dans l'empire romain aux IVe et Ve siècles, Revue des études anciennes*, 46 (1944), 47-64, 280-298; IDEM, *La préfecture du prétoire de l'Illyricum au IVe siècle, Byzantion*, 21 (1951), 5-14; Louis PETIT, *Les évêques de Thessalonique*, EO, 4 (1900-1901), 136-145, 212-221; 5 (1901-1902), 26-33, 90-97, 150-156, 212-224; 6 (1903), 292-298; Josip POSEDEL, *Pitanje dalmatinskog temata u prvoj polovici ix stoljeća, Historijski Zbornik*, 3 (1950), 217-220; C. SILVA-TAROUCA, *Epistularum Romanorum pontificum ad vicarios per Illyricum aliosque episcopos, Collectio Thessalonicensis, Textus et documenta, series Theologica* (Rome, 1937); Ernst STEIN, *Untersuchungen zur spätrömischen Verwaltungsgeschichte*, I. *Die Teilungen von Illyricum in den Jahren 379 und 395, Rheinisches Museum*, 74 (1925), 347-354; Fritz STREICHHAN, *Die Anfänge des Vikariates von Thessalonich, Zeitschrift der Savigny-Stiftung für Rechtsgeschichte*, 43, Kan. Abt. 12, (1922), 330-84; Siméon VAILHÉ, *Annexion de l'Illyricum au patriarcat oecuménique*, EO, 14 (1911), 29-36; VULIĆ, *PWK*, 9 (1916), 1085-1088.

(¹) *Studi bizantini e neoellenici*, 7 (1953), 376; RSR, 40 (1951-1952), 191-200.

(²) *A. m.* 6217, ed. C. DE BOOR, I, 404. 3-9: τούτῳ τῷ ἔτει ἤρξατο ὁ δυσσεβὴς βασιλεὺς Λέων τῆς κατὰ τῶν ἁγίων καὶ σεπτῶν εἰκόνων καθαιρέσεως λόγον ποιεῖσθαι. Καὶ μαθὼν τοῦτο Γρηγόριος, ὁ πάπας Ῥώμης, τοὺς φόρους τῆς Ἰταλίας καὶ Ῥώμης ἐκώλυσε γράψας πρὸς Λέοντα ἐπιστολὴν δογματικήν, μὴ δεῖν βασιλέα περὶ πίστεως λόγον ποιεῖσθαι καὶ καινοτομεῖν τὰ ἀρχαῖα δόγματα τῆς ἐκκλησίας, τὰ ὑπὸ τῶν ἁγίων πατέρων δογματισθέντα. On the reasons for dating this in 726 rather than 725 see Georg OSTROGORSKY, *Les débuts de la querelle des images, Mélanges Charles Diehl*, I, 240.

(³) THEOPHANES, *a. m.* 6221, ed. DE BOOR, I, 408. 23-25, 409, 17 f.: ἀπέστησε Ῥώμην τε καὶ Ἰταλίαν καὶ πάντα τὰ ἑσπέρια τῆς τε πολιτικῆς καὶ ἐκκλησιαστικῆς ὑπακοῆς Λέοντος καὶ τῆς ὑπ' αὐτὸν βασιλείας... καὶ τὴν Ῥώμην σὺν πάσῃ τῇ Ἰταλίᾳ τῆς βασιλείας αὐτοῦ ἀπέστησεν.

ordination, Leo sent out a fleet under Manes, general of the Cibyrrhaeot theme; and after the destruction of Manes's fleet in the Adriatic, the Emperor (in 732-33) increased the capitation tax of Sicily and Calabria by one third, confiscated the papal patrimonies in Sicily and Calabria, which amounted annually to three and a half talents, and ordered the registration of all male children ([1]). In summarizing the events of Leo's reign, Theophanes ascribes the measures taken with regard to Sicily, Calabria, and Crete (which now appears for the first time in this context) to Leo's avarice and desire for money ([2]).

Nowhere, Grumel points out, does Theophanes allude to bishoprics forfeited by Rome. As far as Rome was concerned, he contends, none of Leo's retaliatory measures as described by Theophanes had any weight except the confiscation of the papal patrimonies, no small loss for the papacy, though a slight thing compared with the apostasy of all of Italy, which Theophanes says the Empire suffered as a consequence of Leo's hostility to the icons. For the new taxes levied upon Sicily and Calabria, which formed part of Byzantine territory in the West, could not in any way affect the popes, who were in no position to dispute such questions with the emperors.

Actually, Grumel maintains, Theophanes's reference to papal disaffection is based upon a misunderstanding. What happened, he argues, relying upon the *Liber Pontificalis*, was that Pope Gregory II stood in the way of the imperial tax-collectors (presumably to safeguard the revenues of his own see and to protect the Italian churches from what he deemed excessive taxation), *before* Leo's decree against the icons ([3]). On the other hand, as Theo-

---

([1]) THEOPHANES, *a. m.* 6224, I, 410. 4-16: ὁ δὲ βασιλεὺς ἐμαίνετο κατὰ τοῦ πάπα καὶ τῆς ἀποστάσεως Ῥώμης καὶ Ἰταλίας, καὶ ἐξοπλίσας στόλον μέγαν ἀπέστειλε κατ' αὐτῶν Μάνην, τὸν στρατηγὸν τῶν Κιβυραιωτῶν, κεφαλὴν ποιήσας εἰς αὐτούς. ᾐσχύνθη δὲ ὁ μάταιος ναυαγήσαντος τοῦ στόλου εἰς τὸ Ἀδριακὸν πέλαγος. Τότε ὁ θεομάχος ἐπὶ πλεῖον ἐκμανεὶς Ἀραβικῷ τε φρονήματι κρατυνόμενος φόρους κεφαλικοὺς τῷ τρίτῳ μέρει Σικελίας καὶ Καλαβρίας τοῦ λαοῦ ἐπέθηκεν. τὰ δὲ λεγόμενα πατριμόνια τῶν ἁγίων καὶ κορυφαίων ἀποστόλων, τῶν ἐν τῇ πρεσβυτέρᾳ Ῥώμῃ τιμωμένων, ταῖς ἐκκλησίαις ἔκπαλαι τελούμενα χρυσίου τάλαντα τρία ἥμισυ τῷ δημοσίῳ λόγῳ τελεῖσθαι προσέταξεν, ἐποπτεύειν τε καὶ ἀναγράφεσθαι τὰ τικτόμενα κελεύσας ἄρρενα βρέφη, ὡς Φαραώ ποτε τὰ τῶν Ἑβραίων.

Theophanes does not specifically state that the *patrimonia* involved were located in Sicily and Calabria, but this is made clear by Pope Nicholas I (858-867), who in a letter to Emperor Michael III (842-867) criticizing the ejection of Patriarch Ignatius and the elevation of Photius requests the retrocession to Rome of the ecclesiastical dioceses and the patrimonies of Calabria and Sicily, which the Byzantine government had seized. See p. 25 below; cf. Paul FABRE, *De patrimoniis Romanae ecclesiae usque ad aetatem Carolinorum* (Paris, 1892).

([2]) *A. m.* 6232, THEOPHANES, I, 413. 4-7: καὶ ὅσα μὲν ἐπὶ Λέοντος τοῦ ἀσεβοῦς κακὰ Χριστιανοῖς συνέβη περί τε τὴν ὀρθόδοξον πίστιν καὶ περὶ τῶν πολιτικῶν διοικήσεων αἰσχροῦ κέρδους καὶ φιλαργυρίας ἐπινοίᾳ κατά τε Σικελίαν καὶ Καλαβρίαν καὶ Κρήτην....

([3]) *Liber Pontificalis*, ed. L. DUCHESNE, I (Paris, 1886), 403. 20-25: Illis diebus imperatorum iussione Paulus patricius qui exarchus fuerat eundem pontificem cona-

phanes suggests, Leo's financial exactions were purely fiscal in scope and were not punitive in origin ([1]). It was Theophanes, Grumel believes, who erroneously linked all these measures and presents them in the sequence: 1) Leo's iconoclastic decree of 726, 2) Gregory's interference with the collection of the imperial taxes, 3) Leo's ill-starred naval expedition, and 4) the confiscation of the papal patrimonies along with the imposition of new taxes in Sicily, Calabria, and elsewhere.

Grumel reinforces his argument by showing that Theophanes, who was strongly prejudiced against Leo, blames the latter for the falling away of Italy from the Byzantine Empire, although in point of fact this did not take place until a generation later. Moreover, he claims, it is incorrect to assume that Gregory was really hostile to the Byzantine Empire. For, despite his opposition to the Emperor's theological position, Gregory hoped for Leo's conversion; and, when the Italians were proposing to choose a new emperor and lead him to Constantinople, Gregory urged them to remain loyal to the Byzantine Empire ([2]). Later, Gregory not only resumed friendly relations with Eutychius, the last Byzantine Exarch of Ravenna, who had been dispatched by the Emperor, according to the Latin sources, to assassinate him ([3]), and had plotted with Liutprand against Rome ([4]), but even helped Eutychius suppress the attempted insurrection of a usurper named Petasius, who (ca. 730) sought the imperial throne under the name of Tiberius and was executed by Eutychius with the Pope's aid ([5]).

Furthermore, Grumel remarks, Pope Gregory III (731-741) continued the conciliatory policy of his predecessor by inducing Duke Trasimond to return the fortress Gallese to Byzantine suzerainty ([6]), and persuading the Venetians, with whom the Exarch Eutychius had taken refuge after the capture of Ravenna by the Lombards, to reconquer Ravenna (sometime before 735, it would seem), restore it to Byzantium, and convey Eutychius to his capital ([7]). Pope Zachariah (741-752) followed in the same path, and

---

batur interficere, eo quod censum in provincia ponere praepediebat et suis opibus ecclesias denudare, sicut in ceteris actum est locis, atque alium in eius ordinare locum. 404. 9-11: Iussionibus itaque postmodum missis decreverat imperator ut nulla imago cuiuslibet sancti aut martyris aut angeli haberetur: maledicta enim omnia asserebat.

([1]) THEOPHANES, a. m. 6232, I, 413. 5ff., quoted in n. 2 p. 17.

([2]) Liber Pontificalis, I, 404. 25-405. 3; cf. ibid., I, 407. 2f.

([3]) Ibid., I, 405.19-406.7; PAULUS DIACONUS, Historia Langobardorum, Monumenta Germaniae Historica, Scriptores rerum Langobardicarum et Italicarum saec. VI-IX, edd. L. BETHMANN, G. WAITZ (Hannover, 1878), Book 6, 49, p. 181.

([4]) Liber Pontificalis, I, 407.19-408.12.

([5]) Ibid., I, 408.13-409.3

([6]) Ibid., I, 420.13-421.1, with DUCHESNE's note 32, ibid., 424.

([7]) Charles DIEHL, Études sur l'administration byzantine dans l'Exarchat de Ravenne (568-751), Bibliothèque des Écoles françaises d'Athènes et de Rome, 53 (Paris, 1888), 377 n. 5, 388. It was probably out of gratitude for papal assistance of this

in 742 recovered for Byzantium the cities of Ameria, Horta, Polimartium, and Blera, which had been seized by Liutprand in 739 ([1]). Later on, he prevailed upon Liutprand to lift the siege of Ravenna, and yield back Cesenate, together with the part of the city of Ravenna itself which he had captured, to the exarchate (743-44) ([2]). Finally, in 749 he dissuaded Ratchis, who had become King of the Lombards in the fall of 744 after the brief reign of Hildebrand, Liutprand's immediate successor, from continuing with the siege of Perusa ([3]). In addition, Gregory III was a Syrian and Zachariah was a Greek, and had been raised to the papacy, Grumel conjectures, in a conscious effort to placate the Byzantines. In view of all these circumstances, Grumel prefers to put the transfer of Illyricum from Roman to Constantinopolitan jurisdiction in 752-757, at the time in which Byzantium really was forced to abandon all of Italy and the West except for Sicily, Calabria, Naples, and Venice ([4]).

Grumel might even have cited the ninth century *Notitia Basilii*, according to which the bishoprics of the prefecture of Illyricum became subject to the patriarch of Constantinople at a time when the pope of Rome was under barbarian domination ([5]). This would accord well with Grumel's date of *ca*. 752-757, which marked the expulsion of the Byzantines from Ravenna and the triumph in Italy of the Franks, whom the Byzantines might readily have described as barbarians. A much earlier date for this papal reorientation, however, is suggested by Georgius Monachus, Cedrenus, and Zonaras, who say that it was Pope Gregory (presumably Gregory II) who cut himself off from Byzantium and formed an alliance with the Franks. This may be an exaggeration, but we know that between 739 and 740 Gregory III appealed to Charles Martel for aid against the Lombards, and the Life of Stephen II (752-757) in the *Liber Pontificalis* records the tradition that Stephen's three predecessors (Gregory II, Gregory III, and Zachariah) all sought Frankish intervention against the Lombards. This may or may not indicate that the

---

sort that Eutychius presented six splendid and richly ornamented onyx columns to the Church of St. Peter: *Liber Pontificalis*, I, 417.5-9.

([1]) *Liber Pontificalis*, I, 426.6-429.8, 436 (n. 4), 437 (n. 22).

([2]) *Ibid.*, I, 429.8-431.10.

([3]) *Ibid.*, I, 433.20-434.3.

([4]) On the loss of the exarchate of Ravenna, see Charles DIEHL, *op. cit.*

([5]) Τάξις προκαθεδρίας τῶν ὁσιωτάτων πατριαρχῶν, ed. H. GELZER, *Georgii Cyprii descriptio orbis Romani; accedit Leonis imperatoris diatyposis genuina adhuc inedita* (Leipzig, 1890), xiv f. (on the date of composition), 27.520 ff.: εἰσὶ δὲ καὶ οἱ ἀποσπασθέντες ἐκ τῆς Ῥωμαϊκῆς διοικήσεως, νῦν δὲ τελοῦντες ὑπὸ τὸν θρόνον Κωνσταντινουπόλεως μητροπολῖται καὶ ὑφ' ἑαυτοὺς ὄντες ἐπίσκοποι· α. ὁ Θεσσαλονίκης. β. ὁ Συρακούσης. γ. ὁ Κρήτης. δ. ὁ Κορίνθου. ε. ὁ τοῦ Ῥηγίου. ϛ. ὁ Νικοπόλεως. ζ. ὁ Ἀθηνῶν. η. ὁ Πατρῶν. οὗτοι προσετέθησαν τῇ συνόδῳ Κωνσταντινουπόλεως διὰ τὸ ὑπὸ τῶν ἐθνῶν κατέχεσθαι τὸν πάπαν τῆς πρεσβυτέρας Ῥώμης. ὡσαύτως καὶ ἀπὸ τῆς ἀνατολικῆς διοικήσεως ἀποσπασθεὶς ὁ Σελευκείας Ἰσαυρίας καὶ αὐτὸς τελεῖ ὑπὸ τὸν Κωνσταντινουπόλεως μετὰ τῶν ὑπ' αὐτὸν ὄντων κδ' ἐπισκόπων.

popes had decided to abandon Byzantium long before the pontificate of Stephen II, who actually took this step; and there are many errors, omissions, and inaccuracies in the extant accounts of what actually happened in these years. But there is no doubt that Gregory III thrice sought aid from Charles Martel (¹); and this fact, distorted and magnified, would have been enough to convince the Greek chroniclers that the Pope was then, as the *Notitia Basilii* says, in the hands of the barbarians.

Theophanes's conclusion that Gregory II put an end to Byzantine rule in Italy is consistent with what Georgius Monachus, Cedrenus, and Zonaras say on this subject, despite his failure to mention Gregory's diplomatic negotiations with the Franks. It should be added, also, that, given Theophanes's preoccupation with the veneration of images, it may very well have seemed to him that Leo's iconoclasm was the chief cause of the defection of the papacy and the subsequent alienation of Italy, even if the rupture did not take place until 755-756. We now know that the falling away of the West from Byzantine allegiance cannot be traced entirely, or even primarily, to theological origins, and that other factors, such as the deep-seated cultural antagonism between Greece and Rome, the political and territorial aspirations of the popes

---

(¹) GEORGIUS MONACHUS, *Chronicon*, ed. C. DE BOOR, 2 (Leipzig, 1904), 744.4 ff· (636): διὰ ταῦτα οὖν καὶ ὁ τῆς μεγάλης Ῥώμης πρόεδρος Γρηγόριος τὴν τῆς αὐτοῦ βασιλείας ὑποταγὴν ἐκτιναξάμενος τὸ αἱρετικὸν αἶσχος ἀποδιδράσκει σπονδὰς εἰρηνικὰς εἰς τὴν τῶν Φράγγων ὑποταγὴν εἰσδεξάμενος σὺν πάσῃ τῇ Ἰταλίᾳ, καὶ τοὺς φόρους εὐθὺς κωλύσας τὸν Ἀναστάσιον καὶ τοὺς σὺν αὐτῷ ἀνεθεμάτισεν. Cedrenus, 1.799.5-9: οὖτος ὁ ἅγιος διὰ τὰς ἀνοσιουργίας Λέοντος ἀφηνίασε, καὶ πρὸς τὸν Φράγγον σπονδὴν εἰρηνικὴν ποιησάμενος τούς τε φόρους ἐκώλυσε καὶ Ἀναστάσιον καὶ τοὺς σὺν αὐτῷ ἀνεθεμάτισε. τὸν δὲ βασιλέα δι' ἐπιστολῶν αὐτοῦ πολλῶν πολλοῖς ἐγνωσμένων ἀριδήλως ἐλέγχει. Zonaras, 15, 4, 1 and 8: Διὰ ταῦτα ὁ τῆς πρεσβυτέρας Ῥώμης τότε τὴν ἐκκλησίαν ἰθύνων Γρηγόριος τῆς πρὸς τὸν τῆς νέας Ῥώμης προεδρεύοντα καὶ τοὺς ἐκείνῳ ὁμόφρονας ἀποστὰς κοινωνίας, ἐκείνους μὲν σὺν τῷ βασιλεῖ συνοδικῷ καθυπέβαλεν ἀναθέματι, τοὺς δὲ μέχρι τότε τῇ βασιλείᾳ κομιζομένους ἐκεῖθεν φόρους ἐπέσχε, τοῖς Φράγγοις σπεισάμενος... ἀποστατήσας οὖν, ὡς εἴρηται, τῆς τοῦ βασιλέως ὑπακοῆς ὁ πάπας Γρηγόριος διὰ τὴν ἐκείνου κακοδοξίαν τοῖς Φράγγοις ἐσπείσατο, πρότερον πολλάκις σπεύσας διὰ γραμμάτων τὸν Λέοντα τῆς μισοθεΐας μετενεγκεῖν καὶ μεταπεῖσαι τὰς ἱερὰς εἰκόνας σεβάζεσθαι... On this point these three chroniclers are independent of Theophanes, who does not allude to papal negotiations with the Franks, but nevertheless was of the opinion, as we have seen, that Gregory II had withdrawn Italy and the West from the Byzantine Empire and that Leo was responsible for this grievous blow to the Empire (THEOPHANES, *a. m.* 6221, 1, 408.23-25, 409.14-18; *a. m.* 6232, 1.413.4-8).

See also *Codex Carolinus*, epp. 1 and 2, ed. W. GUNDL, MGH, *Epistolarum 3, Merovingici et Carolini Aevi* 1 (Berlin, 1892), 476-79; *Liber Pontificalis*, ed. Louis DUCHESNE, 1, ccxxiii, 420.16-21, 424 (n. 34), 444.6 ff., 457 (n. 17); cf. Henri HUBERT, *Étude sur la formation des états de l'Église. Les Papes Grégoire II, Grégoire III, Zacharie, Étienne II et leurs relations avec les empereurs iconoclastes (726-757)*, *Revue historique*, 69 (1899), 27-30, with citations of the pertinent western chroniclers; Thomas HODGKIN, *Italy and her invaders*, 6 (Oxford, 1895), 476-479; *ibid.*, 7 (1899), 58 f.; Erich CASPAR, *Geschichte des Papsttums*, 2 (Tübingen, 1933), 730.

and of the rising western nationalities, and the inability of the Byzantine
Empire to send adequate military forces to protect their holdings in the West,
contributed greatly to the final cleavage. Still, Leo's iconoclastic decrees
did provoke the break in the first instance, and from this point of view Theophanes can be justified for charging Leo with responsibility for what he calls
the ἀπόστασις of Italy, Rome, and the West.

But even if we repudiate these Byzantine authorities and their notion
of the significance of the pontificate of Gregory II, there remain serious and,
in my judgment, insuperable objections to the acceptance of Grumel's
theory. What Grumel says about the silence of Theophanes concerning the
bishoprics of Illyricum is perhaps correct. Nevertheless, there is, conceivably, one slight clew that Theophanes may have been at least partially
aware of the realignment of 732-33 and actually alludes to it. This is to be
found in his summary of the damage done the Empire by Leo, in which he
descants upon " the evils suffered by the Christians with regard to the faith
and in the political administration, inspired by avarice and desire for wicked
gain, of Sicily, Calabria, and Crete " (¹). The second half of this passage

---

(¹) THEOPHANES, 1, 413.4 ff., reproduced in n. 2 p. 17. Cf. also the treatise
on the five patriarchates written in Sicily in 1142-1143 by NILOS DOXAPATRES (ed.
Franz Nikolaus FINCK, Des Nilos Doxapatres τάξις τῶν πατριαρχικῶν θρόνων ar-
menisch und griechisch [1902]; M P G, 132, 1083 ff.), according to whom the ecclesiastical administration of Sicily, Calabria, and at least parts of Illyricum (he specifies
Sicily, Calabria, Crete, and, possibly also in the same context, Thessalonike and Corinth),
which, like Crete, belonged to the diocese of Macedonia (see p. 1 above), was taken
over from Rome by Constantinople at the time of the capture of Rome by the Goths,
when the pope had been made a prisoner. These privileges were retained by Constantinople, Nilos asserts, until the coming of the Franks. This is a weird jumble, valueless
for dating, but worthy of mention here as an example of the errors into which a careless, though erudite, compiler might fall. Cf. V. LAURENT, L'œuvre géographique
du moine sicilien Nil Doxapatris, EO, 36 (1937), 5-30. Doxapatres becomes slightly
more intelligible if we take his Φράγκοι as a reference, not to the Carolingian Franks,
but to the Normans. If we could assume that by Gothic tribes (ἔθνη Γοτθικά) he
meant the Franks, his estimate of the situation would not differ greatly from that
of the works quoted in notes 5 p. 19 and 1 p. 20. The pertinent passages follow:
FINCK, 24.1 ff.; MPG, 132, 1100 CD: ἰδοὺ γὰρ προφανῶς ὁ κανὼν οὗτος τῆς ἁγίας
συνόδου φησὶ διὰ τὸ εἶναι τὴν Ῥώμην βασίλισσαν, ἔχειν τὴν προτίμησιν· μέχρι γὰρ τότε
καὶ ἐπὶ πολλοῖς χρόνοις βασιλεὺς ἐκεῖσε ἀπὸ τοῦ Κωνσταντινουπόλεως βασιλέως ἐπέμπετο.
ἐπεὶ δὲ ἐπαύθη τὸ εἶναι βασίλισσα διὰ τὸ ὑπὸ ἀλλοφύλων αἰχμαλωτισθῆναι καὶ βαρβάρων
ἐθνῶν Γοτθικῶν, καὶ νῦν ὑπ' ἐκείνων κατέχεσθαι, δῆθεν ὡς ἐκπεσοῦσα τῆς βασιλείας ἐκεί-
νης ἐκπίπτει καὶ τῶν πρωτείων ... FINCK, 24,20 ff.; MPG, 132, 1100 D f.: ἐπεὶ οὖν ἡ
Ῥώμη ἐξέπεσε τῆς οἰκείας βασιλείας δι' ἣν καὶ προετιμᾶτο, καὶ νῦν ὑπὸ βαρβάρους τελεῖ,
ἐκπέπτωκε πάντως καὶ τῶν πρωτείων. ὡς γὰρ βασιλεύουσα ταῦτα εἶχε καὶ ἔμεινε πρῶτος ὁ
τῆς ἀληθῶς βασιλευούσης Κωνσταντινουπόλεως θρόνος, ὡς τοῦ πρώτου παυθέντος βασιλεύειν
μᾶλλον δὲ καὶ ἀποσχισθέντος τῶν λοιπῶν θρόνων.
FINCK, 26.24 ff.; MPG, 132, 1104 AB: πάλιν ἀπὸ τῆς δυτικῆς διοικήσεως δύο ἔξαρ-
χοι ὁμοίως ὑπέκυψαν τότε τῷ Κωνσταντινουπόλεως προέχοντες τῶν λοιπῶν μητροπολιτῶν

may apply exclusively to the tax imposed by Leo after the destruction of
Manes's fleet; but the exact meaning of these words defies exegesis, and the
inclusion of Crete (¹) in this category may possibly be, by a kind of geographical metonymy, a faint shadow or reminiscence of Leo's innovation with
regard to the prefecture of Illyricum, to which Crete belonged as one of the
six constituent provinces of the diocese of Macedonia (see page 14 above).
Similarly, Theophanes' statement that Pope Gregory " severed Rome, Italy,
and all the West from the political and ecclesiastical jurisdiction of Leo and
his government » (²) may in effect be a corollary of the new administrative
system established by Leo for the churches in the prefecture of Illyricum:
if Italy and the West were cut off from the civil and ecclesiastical rule of the
Byzantine Empire, the inference is that the reverse was true in the East,
and that the churches in the eastern provinces were under the dominion of
the patriarch of Constantinople.

This reasoning, though admittedly tortuous, seems to be borne out by
the facts. But even if we grant that Theophanes knew and recorded nothing
about Leo's new ecclesiastical administration of Illyricum, Calabria, and

---

τῶν ὑπὸ τὴν αὐτῶν διοίκησιν, ὁ Θεσσαλονίκης καὶ ὁ Κορίνθου, καὶ ἠκολούθησαν τούτοις
καὶ οἱ ὑπ' αὐτοὺς μητροπολῖται καὶ ἀρχιεπίσκοποι. καὶ οὗτοι ὑπὸ τὸν Κωνσταντινουπόλεως...
ἀλλὰ καὶ ἡ Σικελία μετὰ ταῦτα καὶ ἡ Καλαβρία γέγονεν ὑπὸ τὸν Κωνσταντινουπόλεως καὶ
ἡ Ἁγία Σεβερίνη ἡ καὶ Νικόπολις καλουμένη...

FINCK, 27.23 ff.: MPG, 132, 1104 CD: προσετέθησαν γοῦν καὶ ὁ τῆς Σικελίας θρόνος καὶ ὁ τῆς Καλαβρίας καὶ ὁ τῆς Ἁγίας Σεβερίνης τῷ Κωνσταντινουπόλεως, ἀποσπασθέντες τῆς Ῥώμης, ὅτε βάρβαροι κατέσχον τὸν πάπαν, καὶ τὴν Ῥώμην ᾐχμαλώτησαν καὶ
ἰδιοποιήσαντο. ὥσπερ καὶ ἡ Κρήτη ὑπὸ τὴν Ῥώμην οὖσα ὑπὸ τὸν Κωνσταντινουπόλεως γέγονε. πλὴν πρὸ τούτων ὁ πάπας εὑρίσκεται κατέχων μέρη τινὰ εὐτελῆ καὶ ἐπισκοπὰς ἐκ
μέρους τινὰς ἐν Σικελίᾳ καὶ Καλαβρίᾳ. τὰς γὰρ μητροπόλεις καὶ τοὺς ἐν αὐταῖς ἐξ ὁλοκλή-
ρου κατεῖχεν ὁ Κωνσταντινουπόλεως μέχρι τῆς τῶν Φράγκων ἐλεύσεως.

FINCK, 28,9 ff.; MPG, 132, 1104 D f.: ἐπεὶ γὰρ τὸ δουκάτον πάσης Λογγιβαρδίας,
τῆς παλαιᾶς Ἑλλάδος οὔσης, ἣν ὑπὸ τὸν βασιλέα Κωνσταντινουπόλεως, ὁ δὲ πάπας κεχω-
ρισμένος ἦν καὶ ὑπὸ ἕτερα ἔθνη δῆθεν, διὰ τοῦτο καὶ ὁ πατριάρχης εἶχε τὰς ἐκκλησίας...
μεθ' ὃ δὲ ὡς Φράγκοι ἀφείλοντο τὸ τοιοῦτον δουκάτον, τότε ὁ Ῥώμης ἐχειροτόνησε ἐν πά-
σαις ταῖς τοιαύταις ἐκκλησίαις. ὅσην γὰρ χώραν κατεῖχεν ὁ βασιλεὺς Κωνσταντινουπόλεως
ἢ μετὰ ταῦτα ἀπὸ ἐθνῶν ἐξεκίνησεν, εἰκότως καὶ ὁ πατριάρχης Κωνσταντινουπόλεως ἐχει-
ροτόνει ἐκεῖ, ὡς τῆς Ῥώμης ἀλλοτριωθείσης παντελῶς τῆς Κωνσταντινουπόλεως καὶ ὑπὸ
ἄλλους γεγονυίας.

FINCK, 28.28 ff.; MPG, 132, 1105 AB: περὶ δὲ τοῦ ἀνὰ μέρος κατέχειν τὸν πάπαν
τινὰ ἐν Σικελίᾳ πρότερον, δῆλον ἀπὸ τοῦ βίου τοῦ ἁγίου Γρηγορίου τοῦ ἐπισκόπου Ἀκρα-
γάντων... ἀλλὰ τότε οὔπω ἡ Ῥώμη ἐχωρίσθη τελείως τῆς Κωνσταντινουπόλεως. κατεῖχεν
οὖν ἡ Κωνσταντινούπολις πρὸ πολλοῦ ἀνὰ μέρος καὶ Σικελίαν καὶ Καλαβρίαν, καὶ ὁ πάπας
ὀλιγοστά τινα, ὥσπερ καὶ ἐν Λογγιβαρδίᾳ ἕως τῆς ἀλλοτριώσεως τοῦ πάπα. τότε γὰρ ἠλλο-
τριώθη καὶ τῶν τοιούτων χωρῶν ὁ πάπας, ἕως τῆς τῶν Φράγκων ἐλεύσεως...

(¹) Cf. NILOS DOXAPATRES (ed. FINCK, 27.23-30; MPG, 132, 1104 CD), quoted
in the previous note, where Sicily, Calabria, and Crete are also discussed together.
This collocation may be of some significance.

(²) THEOPHANES, 1, 408.23-25, quoted in note 3 p. 16.

Sicily, we have decisive evidence from another quarter, which unambiguously
puts the change of jurisdiction in 732-33. This is to be found in the letters
of Popes Hadrian I (772-795) and Nicholas I (858-867). Hadrian's letter,
in which Hadrian expounds to Charlemagne a defence of the theological
definition in favor of images formulated at the Second Council of Nicaea,
was written sometime after 787 (when the Council of Nicaea concluded its
deliberations) and either shortly before or after the Council of Frank-
fort (794) (¹).

Whatever its exact date, Hadrian's letter has great importance for the
chronology of Illyricum. Hadrian says that at the time he wrote to Constantine VI and Irene in behalf of the images he also requested the restoration
to the Roman See of the bishoprics and archbishoprics which the first iconoclastic emperors had removed from Roman control (²).

When we appealed to them [i. e., to Constantine VI and Irene] on a previous
occasion [Hadrian writes] to restore the holy images, we likewise referred
to the archbishoprics and bishoprics of the Holy Catholic and Apostolic
Roman Church and requested the restitution to the same Holy Catholic and
Apostolic Roman Church of the [rights and privileges appertaining to these
ecclesiastical units] of which they had deprived us *at the same time that they
confiscated our patrimonies and deposed the holy images.* But they have never

---

(¹) Émile AMANN, *L'époque carolingienne* (*Histoire de l'Église depuis les origines
jusqu'à nos jours*, edd. A. FLICHE and V. MARTIN, 6 [Paris, 1947]), 125-127; S. ABEL,
*Papst Hadrian I und die weltliche Herrschaft des römischen Stuhls, Forschungen zur
deutschen Geschichte,* I (1862), 531-532; Karl HAMPE, *Hadrians I. Vertheidigung der
zweiten nicaenischen Synode gegen die Angriffe Karls des Grossen, Neues Archiv der
Gesellschaft für ältere deutsche Geschichtskunde,* 21 (1896), 94-102; Hubert BASTGEN,
Das Capitulare Karls d. Gr. über die Bilder oder die sogenannten Libri Carolini, ibid.,
37 (1912), 490; Wolfram VON DEN STEINEN, *Entstehungsgeschichte der Libri Carolini,
Quellen und Forschungen aus italienischen Archiven und Bibliotheken,* 21 (1929-30),
1-11; Georg OSTROGORSKY, *Rom und Byzanz in Kampe um die Bilderverehrung* (*Papst
Hadrian I. und das VII. ökumenische Konzil von Nikäa*), *Seminarium Kondakovianum,* 6 (1933), 73-87.

(²) MGH, *Epistolarum 5, Epistolae Karolini Aevi,* 3, ed. Karl HAMPE, (Berlin,
1899), 57.5-16; MANSI, 13, 808 D: Dudum quippe, quando eos pro sacris imaginibus
erectione adortavimus, simili modo et de diocesi tam archiepiscoporum, quam et episcoporum sanctae catholice et apostolice Romane ecclesiae, quae tunc cum patrimoniis nostris abstulerunt, quando sacras imagines deposuerunt, commonentes, restituere
eidem sanctae catholicae et apostolicae Romane ecclesiae quaesivimus, et nec responsum qualibet exinde dederunt. Et in hoc nimis palam ostenditur, quia ex uno capitulo
ab errore reversi sunt, ex aliis duobus in eodem permanent errore. Si enim ubique Christianorum ecclesiae canonice intactas suas possident dioceses, quanto amplius sancta
catholica et apostolica Romana ecclesia, que est caput omnium Dei ecclesiarum, sua
diocesi, videlicet archiepiscoporum et episcoporum, immo et patrimonia pro luminariorum concinnatione atque alimoniis pauperum inrefragabili iure et tenere et possidere modis omnibus debetur!

replied to this petition; and thus it is clear that, although they have reformed their ways in one respect [in that they have restored the use of images], in two other regards [in retaining the dioceses and the papal patrimonies] they persist in the same error. For if everywhere the canonical Christian churches keep their dioceses intact, how much more fitting is it for the Holy Catholic Apostolic Roman Church, which is the head of all the churches of God, to hold and possess indisputable authority in its own administrative sphere over its own archbishops and bishops, and, above all, [to retain] its patrimonies, [which are used] for the lighting of candles and the relief of the poor?

Hadrian then goes on to say that, if the Byzantines persist in their refusal to return the archbishoprics, bishoprics, and patrimonies in question, he will condemn them as heretics despite their orthodoxy with regard to the images ([1]).

Hadrian had also made this same demand in a letter to Constantine and Irene (dated October 27, 785). But when his letter was read in Greek translation before the Council of 787, the sections dealing with this problem were omitted together with those in which Hadrian had expressed dissatisfaction over Tarasius's designation of himself as ecumenical patriarch and over the latter's rapid elevation from layman to patriarch ([2]). The original document, however, was accessible to Anastasius Bibliothecarius *ca.* 873, when he was translating the Acts of the Council of 787 from Greek into Latin, and is very similar to the text translated above, except that it omits the clauses concerning the date on which the events described took place ([3]).

([1]) *Ibid.*, 57.16-23: Unde si vestra annuerit a Deo protecta regalis excellentia, eodem adortamur imperatore pro sacris imaginibus in pristino statu erectione gratiam agentes et de diocesi sanctae nostre Romane ecclesie tam archiepiscoporum, quam episcoporum seu de patrimoniis iterum increpantes commonemus, ut, si noluerit ea sanctae nostrae Romane ecclesiae restituere, haereticum eum pro huiusmodi erroris perseverantia esse decernimus. Plus enim cupimus salutem animarum et recte fidei stabilitatem conservare, quam huius ambitum mundi possidere.

([2]) MANSI, 12, 1071-1072; Charles Joseph HEFELE, H. LECLERCQ, *Histoire des conciles*, 3.2 (Paris, 1910), 748, cf. 752 f. (on the letter to Tarasius); K. MANN, *The lives of the popes in the early middle ages*, I, pt. 2 (London, 1902), 447-448, 451-452, 457-458.

([3]) MANSI, 12, 1073 CD: Porro et hoc vestrum a Deo coronatum ac piissimum poscimus imperium: ut si veram et orthodoxam sanctae catholicae ecclesiae Romanae nitimini amplecti fidem, sicut antiquitus ab orthodoxis imperatoribus, seu a ceteris Christianis fidelibus oblata atque concessa sunt patrimonia beati Petri apostolorum principis, fautoris vestri, in integrum nobis restituere dignemini pro luminariorum concinnatoribus eidem Dei ecclesiae, atque alimoniis pauperum. Immo et consecrationes archiepiscoporum, seu episcoporum, sicut olitana constat traditio, nostrae dioecesis existentes penitus canonice sanctae Romane nostrae restituantur ecclesiae, ut nequaquam schisma inter concordiam perseverare valeat sacerdotum, sicut in vestra serenissima iussione exaratum est.

Hadrian's prayer for restitution went unheeded and was repeated on September 25, 860 by Pope Nicholas I (858-867) in a letter to the Emperor Michael III (842-867), chiefly important in the present context because it supplements Hadrian's by specifically identifying the ecclesiastical dioceses which the Roman Church was seeking to repossess ([1]). Nicholas's list, which confines itself to the prefecture of Illyricum, is presumably correct except for what appears to be the accidental omission of Crete and the erroneous addition of the word Illyricum, referring as it would seem, to the diocese of Illyricum in the prefecture of Italy, which was never subject to the bishop of Thessalonike as papal vicar for the administration of this area. Furthermore, he is silent about the dioceses of Sicily and Calabria, although further along he asks for the return of the patrimonies of Sicily and Calabria, and then adds, " Together with these and the abovementioned [privileges], we request that the consecration of the archbishop of Syracuse may depend upon our [i. e., the Roman] see, lest the tradition inaugurated by the apostles be in any way overturned in your reign " ([2]). This sentence makes it clear that the ecclesiastical jurisdiction of Sicily was also involved; and it has always been conceded, even by Grumel, that, whatever its date, and despite the fact that no

---

([1]) MGH, *Epistolarum* 6, *Epistolae Karolini Aevi*, 4, ed. E. PERELS (Berlin, 1925), 438.25-439.11, with bibliographies *ad. loc.*: Oportet enim vestrum imperiale decus, quod in omnibus ecclesiasticis utilitatibus vigere audivimus, ut antiquum morem, quem nostra ecclesia habuit, vestris temporibus restaurare dignemini, quatenus vicem, quam nostra sedes per episcopos vestris in partibus constitutos habuit, videlicet Thessalonicensem, qui Romanae sedis vicem per Eperum veterem Eperumque novum atque Illiricum, Macedoniam, Thessaliam, Achaiam, Daciam riperensem, Daciam mediterraneam, Misiam, Dardaniam et Praevalim (tenebat), beato Petro apostolorum principi contradicere nullus praesumat; quae antecessorum nostrorum temporibus, scilicet Damasi, Siricii, Innocentii, Bonifacii, Caelestini, Xysti, Leonis, Hilari, Simplicii, Felicis atque Hormisdae sanctorum pontificum sacris dispositionibus augebatur. Quorum denique institutiones ab eis illis in partibus destinatas per nostros missos, ut rei veritatem cognoscere queatis, vestrae augustali potentiae dirigere curavimus. Praeterea Calabritanum patrimonium Siculumque, quae nostrae ecclesiae concessa fuerunt et ea possidendo optinuit et disponendo per suos familiares regere studuit, vestris concessionibus reddantur, quoniam irrationabile est, ut ecclesiastica possessio, unde luminaria et concinnationes ecclesiae Dei fieri debent, terrena quavis potestate subtrahantur; sed domui Dei restituta meritum redditoris multiplicent et suscipientes votum spiritalis desiderii lucris exerceatur. Inter ista et superius dicta volumus, ut consecratio Syracusano archiepiscopo nostra a sede impendatur, ut traditio ab apostolis instituta nullatenus vestris temporibus violetur.

I use the text as given by C. SILVA-TAROUCA (so far as it goes), *op. cit.* (n. 2 p. 14), V, and accept his interpretation.

([2]) Last sentence in text in n. 1 above. Cf. Domenico Gaspare LANCIA DI BROLO, *Storia della Chiesa in Sicilia nei primi dieci secoli del Cristianesimo*, 2 (Palermo, 1884), 145; Roccho PIRRO, *Sicilia Sacra disquisitionibus et notitiis illustrata*, 1 (Palermo, 1733), 610-612; Francis DVORNIK, *The Photian schism, history and legend* (Cambridge, England, 1948), 75 f., 91.

text earlier than the *Notitia Basilii* of the ninth century, directly mentions all three of these regions, the transfer of jurisdiction under discussion here concerned the churches of Calabria, Sicily, and Illyricum, all three of which were affected at the same time ([1]). The letter of Nicholas is decisive for Illyricum and Sicily, and the addition of Calabria seems authorized by the *Notitia Basilii*, which groups bishoprics from Illyricum (six in number) with one from Sicily (Syracuse) and one from Calabria (Reggio) ([2]).

In the absence of evidence of other losses suffered by Rome to the patriarchate of Constantinople in the interval between the pontificates of Hadrian I and Nicholas I, the conclusion is inescapable that Hadrian, who obviously knew what the real facts were, associates the removal of these dioceses from papal sovereignty with the forfeiture of the patrimonies to the Byzantine crown at the beginning of the iconoclastic movement. Since the patrimonies were seized by Leo in 732-33, as Theophanes says, there is no doubt that Illyricum, Calabria, and Sicily passed under the control of the Byzantine patriarchate at the same time.

A few years later (*ca.* 871-872) ([3]), Anastasius Bibliothecarius, in his preface to the Acts of the Council of 869, which the West once regarded as the Eighth Oecumenical Council ([4]), although the Byzantine Church recognizes only seven, refers to this jurisdictional dispute and says that, after it lost its empire in the West, the Byzantine government altered the ancient boundaries, subverted the privileges of the Roman See, took away almost all of the administrative rights Rome possessed in this area, and wickedly bestowed them upon the patriarchate of Constantinople ([5]). At first sight these words

---

([1]) Note the titles of Grumel's papers in *Mélanges Lebreton* and *Studi bizantini e neoellenici* (n. 2 p. 15). On Calabria cf. Giovanni MINASI, *Le chiese di Calabria* (Naples, 1896); Jules GAY, *Les diocèses de Calabre à l'époque byzantine d'après un livre récent*, Revue d'histoire et de littérature religieuses, 5 (1900), 233-260; Francesco RUSSO, *La metropolia di S. Severina*, Archivio storico per la Calabria e la Lucania, 16 (1947), 1-20; Ekkehard EICKHOFF, *Tema e ducato di Calabria* (*Per la storia dell'organizzazione dell'Italia meridionale bizantina*), ibid., 21 (1952), 105-118.

([2]) See text quoted in n. 5 p. 19; cf. also the τάξις τῶν πατριαρχικῶν θρόνων of NILOS DOXAPATRES (n. 1 p. 21), 26.24 ff., 26.27-28.2, 28.28-29.9; MPG, 132, 1104-1105.

([3]) Arthur LAPÔTRE, *De Anastasio Bibliothecario sedis apostolicae* (Paris, 1885), 330. See the dedication to Pope Hadrian II (867-872), MANSI, 16, 1 B: Domino sancto et coangelico patri patrum Hadriano summo pontifici et universali papae.

([4]) On this question, see Francis DVORNIK, *Photian schism*, 309-330.

([5]) MANSI, 16, 10 B: Nam tota Dardania, Thessalia, Dacia, et utraque Epirus, atque ceterae regiones juxta Istrum fluvium sitae, apostolicae sedis vestrae moderamine antiquitus praecipue regebantur et disponebantur. Sed postquam imperatores Romanorum, qui nunc Graecorum appellantur, variorum fautores vel incentores effecti errorum, sanctam Christi ecclesiam diversis haeresibus scindere minime formidaverunt; scidit Deus imperium eorum, et in occiduis partibus paulatim regnare, superno decernente judicio, cessaverunt: donec Romanos pontifices suis pravitatibus

seem to corroborate Grumel's theory. But, soon thereafter, Anastasius remarks that the Roman See had never protested the withdrawal of these privileges [1]. This inaccuracy invalidates the whole of what Anastasius has to say on this subject, for it proves that he had either failed to read or to remember the papal letters quoted above. By the time of the pontificate of John VIII (872-882), however, to whom he dedicates (ca. 873) his edition and translation of the Acts of the Second Council of Nicaea (787) [2], Anastasius had increased his acquaintance with the papal archives and was able to rectify at least the error he had made in his preface with regard to the history of papal appeals for the return of these dioceses. For, in the course of his researches, he came upon the passage in which Hadrian I had complained to Constantine VI and Irene about these regions, and which, as Anastasius explains, the Greeks had omitted from the Greek version read before the Council itself [3]. Perhaps his ignorance (ca. 871-872) of these papal requests is proof that he did not participate in the composition of Nicholas's letter of 860, as it had once been believed [4]. In any case, his inexactitude here affords just one more example of his general unreliability [5], and cannot be used to impugn the testimony of Pope Hadrian quoted above.

---

incurvare conantes, nec valentes, ac per hoc multiplicibus poenis afficientes, Hesperiae potestatem jam prorsus amitterent, occidentis etiam amisso imperio, nihilo minus Romanis pontificibus, quia jam jubere nequeunt, suadere nituntur; suis laesis favorem sensibus accommodandum. Sed quia isti cum Petro super petram verae confessionis stantes pestiferam suggestionem audire possunt, obaudire non possunt, mox illi quoniam aliter eos laedere nequeunt, patrios et antiquos terminos transferunt, privilegia sedis apostolicae corrumpunt, et pene omnia jura disponendarum dioeceseon auferunt, atque suis haec fautoribus consentaneis et sectatoribus conferunt: cum quibus etiam jus quod sedes apostolica super praedictas regiones habuit, quia juxta se sitae videbantur, usurpant, et Constantinopolitanae dioecesi, nequiter applicant... sed his nec ipsi diu fruuntur, siquidem jam memorata Vulgarorum gens protinus irruit, et universa circa Danubium occupat...

(1) MANSI, 16, 12 B: super quibus [i. e., the provinces under discussion] recipiendis ideo apostolica sedes nullam reperitur fecisse querelam, quoniam mox has, ut praedictum est, saepe memorata Vulgarorum natio adit, et sibi jure potestatis omnia vindicat.

(2) LAPÔTRE, op. cit., 330; MANSI, 12, 981-982 C: Domino coangelico Joanni pontifici summo et universali pape Anastasius exiguus.

(3) MANSI, 12, 1073-1076: Ab hinc usque ad finem hujus epistolae codex Graecus non habet. Graeci namque, quia eodem tempore ex laicis fuerat Constantinopoli patriarcha factus, ne publice ab Apostolica sede argui videretur, et adversus eum tamquam reprehensione dignum, haereticis repugnandi occasio praeberetur, ac per hoc synodi, cui intererat, utilitas excluderetur: ea quae sive de non facienda laicorum promotione, sive de caeterarum praesumptionum redargutionibus subsequuntur, in synodo hac nec recitari, nec actis inseri passi sunt...

(4) LAPÔTRE, op. cit., 99 ff.; Ernst PERELS, Papst Nikolaus I. und Anastasius Bibliothecarius (Berlin, 1920), 266, 268, 306.

(5) LAPÔTRE, op. cit., 127-207, 254-272, 287 f.; PERELS, op. cit.

Grumel's point about the loyalty of Popes Gregory II and III to the Byzantine Empire is an interesting one. But this bright side of the coin had its reverse. Gregory II did hinder the Byzantine tax collectors [1] and did lead the Italian states to rebellion against Byzantium [2]. According to the *Liber Pontificalis*, " he took arms against the Emperor as against an enemy "[3]; and forces sent by the Exarch Paul from Ravenna were forcibly excluded from Roman territory [4], while the Pope's allies slew a pro-Byzantine official named Exhilaratus, together with the latter's son, Hadrian, in Campania [5], blinded Peter, a pro-Byzantine general, and murdered the Exarch Paul [6]. The Emperor could hardly have been pleased by this turn of events, nor would he have found satisfaction in the stout opposition offered Eutychius, the new (and last Exarch of Ravenna), whom the Romans ana- thematized and whose efforts to carry out the Emperor's orders were stoutly resisted by a Romano-Lombard coalition [7]. Still less would he have rejoiced when Liutprand, the Lombard King, who had set out against Rome as an ally of the Exarch Eutychius, defected to the Pope [8].

It is doubtful also whether the Emperor Leo could have distinguished between dogmatic and political loyalty. Given the traditional Byzantine view of such matters, Leo would have regarded the flouting of his iconoclastic decrees by Popes Gregory II and III as a demonstration of infidelity; and Gregory III's Roman Council of 731, which reaffirmed the Roman position in favor of images and excommunicated all iconoclasts, would have been interpreted in Constantinople as an act of treason. Indeed, Leo's intransigence on this subject was so well known that George the Presbyter, whom Gregory III had sent to Constantinople with a letter urging the re-establishment of the icons, returned to Rome without having dared to present the *commoni- toria scripta* which he had been charged to deliver. Gregory was so incensed by his subordinate's timorousness that he wanted to unfrock him (*ab ordine sacerdotali privare*). But a Roman synod refused to discipline George in this way; instead, the latter was subjected to penance and ordered to set out once again for Constantinople on the same mission that he had failed to carry out on the previous occasion. This time, the imperial government

---

[1] *Liber Pontificalis*, I, 403.20 ff. (quoted in n. 3 p. 17).
[2] *Ibid.*, I, 404.5-8.
[3] *Ibid.*, I, 404.14-16: contra imperatorem quasi contra hostem se armavit. DIEHL, *op. cit.* (see p. 18 above), 377 n. 8, in a note *ad loc.*, attempts, unsuccessfully in my judgment, to explain why these words should not be taken as indicating real hostility on the part of the Pope.
[4] *Liber Pontificalis*, I, 404.1-8.
[5] *Ibid.*, I, 405.5-10.
[6] *Ibid.*, I, 405.10-15.
[7] *Ibid.*, I, 406.1-20.
[8] *Ibid.*, I, 407.19-408.12.

forced George to remain in Sicily, and the emperors would not permit the documents he carried to leave the Sicilian shore. In addition George was exiled for nearly a year. The Roman iconophile Council of 731 then sent a similar set of papers (*alia similiter scripta*) in care of *Constantinus* the *defensor*. But this messenger was likewise threatened and detained in Sicily for almost a year. Next, when the whole province of Italy wrote to Leo, their messages were seized by Sergius Patricius, the commander of Sicily, who imprisoned the bearers for eight months before allowing them to return to Rome. Finally, another packet of letters was addressed to the Patriarch Anastasius and the emperors *via* Peter the *defensor*. The fate of this attempt to dissuade Leo from continuing his iconoclastic policy is unknown. But Leo was clearly displeased by the papal attitude, as his decision to send out a punitive naval expedition under Manes and his subsequent conduct clearly show [2].

It is true the Emperor Constantine V (741-775) bestowed the rich estates of Ninfa and Norma upon Pope Zachariah (741-752) [3] (*ca.* 745) after the former's victory over the usurper Artavasdus, who had made himself emperor with the aid of the pro-image party and had held sway in Constantinople from the midsummer of 742 (after June) to November 2, 743 [4]. But this act of generosity is no doubt to be explained as a Byzantine attempt to placate the West and to influence the Pope and the Italians to support the Byzantine position in Ravenna and elsewhere in Italy that was then gravely menaced by the Lombards. The *Liber Pontificalis*, to be sure, rejected Artavasdus as a traitor [5], but it was obviously written after the conflict between Artavasdus and Constantine V had been fully resolved and had become a matter of history. In point of fact, the Roman See apparently recognized Artavasdus as emperor soon after his usurpation of the throne. Papal documents of 743 and 744 (June 22 and November 5) [6] designate Artavasdus

---

[1] *Liber Pontificalis*, I, 416.5-15.

[2] *Ibid.*, I, 415.15 ff., 416.5, 417.1.

[3] *Ibid.*, I, 433.6-8.

[4] THEOPHANES, I, 414.16-421.6 (a.m. 6233-6235).

[5] *Liber Pontificalis*, I, 432.18-433.4.

[6] P. JAFFÉ, W. WATTENBACH, S. LOEWENFELD, F. KALTENBRUNNER, P. EWALD, *Regesta Pontificum Romanorum*, I (2d ed., Leipzig, 1885), 264 f.: nos. 2270, 2271; MGH, *Legum Sectio* III, *Concilia*, 2, *Concilia aevi Karolini*, I, I (Hannover, 1906), 8; MANSI, 12, 323 A, 325 B, 383 A; MPL, 89, 925 CD, 927 BC, 929; *Die Briefe des heiligen Bonifatius und Lullus*, ed. Michael TANGL, *Epistolae selectae in usum scholarum ex monumentis Germaniae historicis separatim ediiae*, I (Berlin, 1916), ep. 57, 105.18-21: imperante domno piissimo augusto Artavasdo a Deo coronato magno imperatore anno III, post consulatum eius anno III, sed et Niciphoro magno imperatore anno III, indictione X; *ibid.*, ep. 58, 108.10-13: imperante domno piissimo augusto Artauasdo a Deo coronato magno imperatore anno tertio, post consulatum eius anno tertio, sed et Nicapharo magno imperatore eius filio anno tertio, indictione tertia decima. Cf. M. TANGL, *Studien zur Neuausgabe der Bonifatius-Briefe*, *Neues Archiv der Gesellschaft für*

and his son Nicephorus as emperors; and the papal legate who visited Constantinople during the period of Artavasdus's ascendancy probably gave adhesion to him, although the same envoy seems to have found no difficulty in treating with Constantine as emperor immediately upon the latter's reconquest of Constantinople.

In these relations between the papacy and the Byzantine empire, the apparent contradictions between what might seem to be pro-Byzantine and anti-Byzantine policy can be reconciled, if the interests of the papacy and the policy adopted by the Roman See to serve them are properly understood. Occasionally, it is true, the popes opposed the Byzantine emperors for financial or doctrinal reasons. But at the same time Rome came forward in defence of its Constantinopolitan sovereigns. For, while fending off all imperial infringements upon the prerogatives of the Roman See in either the theological or the economic sphere, the popes realized that an emperor safely established at a distance in Constantinople was less likely to threaten papal autonomy and freedom of action than a monarch resident in Italy. Being shrewd administrators, they shifted their tactics to meet changing conditions. Hence, they resisted the Byzantine tax-collectors, fulminated against the iconoclasts, and led the Italian cities against the imperial forces in Italy, but simultaneously repudiated schemes to set up usurpers as emperors, and urged their people to remain loyal to the Empire. When they wrested cities from the Lombards and restored them to the imperial government, they were protecting their own privileges in those cities, imposing salutary limits upon what must have seemed an ominous expansion of Lombard power at the expense of the Byzantine Exarchate of Ravenna, to which they had turned in the past for defence, and safeguarding their indispensable line of communications with Ravenna. In short the popes knew well how to maintain friendly relations with both Byzantium and the latter's foes, and so to weaken the offensive strength of both.

At the conclusion of his article, Grumel asks why Theophanes does not allude to Illyricum if it had really been severed from Rome at this time, since Rome was always jealous of its privileges in this part of the Empire, and mention of it would have been most pertinent at this point. But Theophanes's failure to treat of this matter here is not really significant. He

---

ältere deutsche Geschichtskunde, 40 (1916), 776-782; Erich CASPAR, *Geschichte des Papsttums*, 2 (1933) 739.

I reproduce the text and dates given by Tangl, who, however, mistakenly asserts that the insurrection of Artavasdus began a few days after the accession of Constantine V. Actually, the rebellion did not begin until *ca*. June 27, 742, or slightly more than a year after his ascent of the throne, which had taken place on June 18, 741 (see THEOPHANES, *a. m.* 6232, 6233, 1, 412.26-414.20). I hope to re-examine the chronology of these documents in my book; but the precise date does not, of course, affect the argument.

wrote his chronicle *ca.* 813-815 at a time when this transfer of jurisdiction had long been an accomplished fact, but he does not describe it either under the year 6224 (= 732-33) unless the reference to Crete, as suggested above, is to be understood as an oblique indication of this administrative change, or in his account of the years 752 to 757, where Grumel would put it. The fact is that Theophanes, despite his merits and great importance, has many faults and often, if not usually, ignores or confuses the most vital matters.

In this instance, our information comes from two papal sources which are hardly to be impeached. I am sure that Grumel would not deem them less trustworthy than the ambiguous silence of Theophanes.

Harvard University, Dumbarton Oaks.

X

THE ARGUMENT FOR ICONOCLASM
AS PRESENTED BY THE ICONOCLASTIC COUNCIL OF 754

IN saluting "Sir Boss" on his sixtieth birthday and paying homage to him, not only for his vast erudition, but also for his selfless and devoted labors in behalf of Byzantine studies, Dumbarton Oaks, and all of us, corporately and individually, I present a summary of the proceedings of the iconoclastic Council of 754.[1] I proffer it with apologies to Professor Friend for concentrating on the heterodox views of the iconoclasts, whose theology he does not find congenial, and promise to redress the balance at another time with a similar account of the orthodox refutation. As he himself would agree, it is instructive to examine the extant *Acta* of 754 by themselves with some care as an example of iconoclastic polemics, reasoning, and theology.

The iconoclastic Council of 754, which designated itself as the Seventh Oecumenical Council but was forced to relinquish this high-sounding title in 787 to the Second Council of Nicaea, met in the Palace of Hiereia (on the Asiatic coast of the Sea of Marmora, south of Chalcedon) for a session that lasted from February 10 to August 8. It was attended by 338 bishops, whose deliberations were conducted under the presidency of Bishops Theodosius of Ephesus (the son of the former Emperor Tiberius III [698-705]) and Pastillas of Perga. In what follows, the Council of 754 will be referred to merely as the Council, without further description.

From the Chronicles of Theophanes and Nicephorus[2] we learn little about the Council except the number of bishops who attended, the date and place of meeting, and the names of the presiding officers. Theophanes emphasizes the fact that none of the five patriarchs was present at its deliberations, and that the Emperor Constantine V elevated the monk Constantine to the patriarchal throne of Constantinople at the termination of the Council. On the transactions of the Council itself these chroniclers give no information at all beyond the fact that the iconoclasts condemned images along with Patriarch Germanus I, George of Cyprus, and John of Damascus, three of the foremost champions of the use of images.

[1] The former date of 753 has been discarded; see Georg Ostrogorsky, *Geschichte des byzantinischen Staates*, 2d ed., Munich 1952, p. 139; *idem, Studien zur Geschichte des byzantinischen Bilderstreites*, in *Historische Untersuchungen*, 5, Breslau 1929, 14; Louis Bréhier, "Vie et mort de Byzance," in *Le Monde byzantin*, 1, Paris 1947, 82; V. Grumel, "L'année du monde dans la chronographie de Théophane," *Échos d'Orient*, 37 (1934), 406f.; E. W. Brooks, "The Chronology of Theophanes," BZ, 8 (1899), 85f.; Louis Bréhier and René Aigrain, *Histoire de l'Église depuis les origines jusqu'à nos jours*, ed. by A. Fliche and V. Martin, 5, *Grégoire le Grand, les états barbares, et la conquête arabe (590-757)*, Paris 1947, 468ff., 431ff.; C. Baronius, *Annales ecclesiastici*, 12, ed. A. Theiner, Bar-le-Duc 1867, 582-587.

[2] Theophanes, *Chronographia*, A.M. 6245, ed. C. de Boor, 1, Leipzig 1883, 427f.; Bonn CSHB, 1 (1839), 659f.; Nicephorus, *Breviarium*, ed. C. de Boor (1880), p. 65. Other sources on the Council of 754, like the *Vita Stephani Junioris*, MPG, 100, 1112CD, 1113A, 1120D-1121A, 1124B, 1141D, 1144A, etc., I hope to treat at length in my book on the iconoclastic controversy. For those who advocate the wrong date, cf. C. J. Hefele and H. Leclercq, *Histoire des conciles d'après les documents originaux*, 3.2, Paris 1910, 693-705; Edward James Martin, *A history of the iconoclastic controversy*, London, n.d. (1930), pp. 45ff.; J. Pargoire, *L'église byzantine*, Paris 1905, pp. 256ff.; Alfred Lombard, *Constantin V, Empereur des Romains*, Bibliothèque de la Faculté des Lettres, 16, Paris 1902, 135ff.

Concerning the fact that no patriarch was present, see texts cited by Martin, *op. cit.*, p. 46.

The fullest and best record of the activities of the Council is the transcript of its Definition (ὅρος, *Horos*) reproduced and refuted during the Sixth Session of the Seventh Oecumenical Council,[3] which met in Nicaea in 787. Usually to be sure, the champions of orthodoxy are not the most reliable authorities for the views of their opponents, whom the Church now brands as heretics; and the disentanglement of truth from fiction or distortion in orthodox denunciations or even allegedly disinterested summaries of heretical writings constitutes a well-known hazard for historians. Indeed, this problem is so complex that many scholars seriously doubt that Nestorius, for example, was a Nestorian or that the so-called Monophysites were really Monophysites. This difficulty stems both from the dearth of heterodox sources, very few of which have escaped destruction at the hands of orthodox opponents, and from the undeniable fact, freely admitted by men of good will, that Nestorius and the Monophysites really intended to be orthodox and often expressed themselves unobjectionably. In dealing with iconoclasm, however, we find that the situation is somewhat different. The iconoclasts also aspired to orthodoxy, it is true, and most of their writings have perished. But the account of iconoclastic doctrine presented in the Sixth Session of the Council of 787 is thoroughly reliable and seems not to have been corrupted. No one could ever claim that the iconoclasts were not unequivocally opposed to images, or that they did not hold the views set forth in the document now to be studied. I can find no instance of tampering with this text on the part of the orthodox and there are many signs, as the candid reader will soon see, that it has been transmitted to us with singular fidelity and objectivity.

At the Sixth Session, which met on October 5, 787,[4] the *Horos* of the Council of 754 was read in separate sections of varying length by Gregory, Bishop of Neocaesarea, each of which was followed immediately by a detailed refutation read by Epiphanius,[5] Deacon and Κουβουκλείσιος (the title of a patriarchal dignitary). We shall follow the *Horos* as read by Gregory without taking into account the arguments of Epiphanius, which will be reserved for treatment in a subsequent paper.[6] In this way we shall be able to study the Definition of 754 as it was originally presented without constant interruption by the orthodox spokesman.

The proceedings of the Sixth Session of the Council of 787 are divided into six *Tomoi*. In the first *Tomos*, after a few preliminary words on the holding of the Council in Constantinople by order (θέσπισμα) of the Emperors Constantine V (741-775) and his son, Leo IV (Emperor, 775-780), in the Church of St. Mary of Blachernae,[7] the Council summarizes briefly the story of creation, the fall of Lucifer (Ἑωσφόρος), his corruption of man, whom he seduces into "worshiping the creature more than the Creator" (cf. Rom. 1:25), and of the latter's redemption by Christ.[8] The purpose of

---

[3] J. D. Mansi, *Sacrorum conciliorum nova et amplissima collectio*, 13 (1767, in the anastatic reprint, Paris-Leipzig 1902), 204-364, cited below as M., followed by the number of the column.
[4] M. 204A.   [5] See Martin (*op. cit.* in note 2 above), 46.
[6] This article is a fragment of a chapter in my book on the history of the iconoclastic period.
[7] M. 209CD. The Council of 754 met at Hiereia until August 8, when it was removed to the Church of St. Mary of Blachernae in Constantinople, to witness the Emperor Constantine's announcement of his choice of a new patriarch (Constantine II, 754-766) and to secure imperial confirmation of its *Horos*.
[8] M. 212Bff.

this allusion to the work of Christ is to introduce a reference to the worship of idols (τῆς τῶν εἰδώλων πλάνης τε καὶ λατρείας), from which mankind was liberated by Christ, who taught worship in spirit and in truth (τὴν ἐν πνεύματι καὶ ἀληθείᾳ προσκύνησιν:[9] cf. John 4:24).

The true faith, thus received, Gregory says, was preserved without a blemish by the apostles, Christian teachers, and the six oecumenical councils,[10] until, we are told at the beginning of Tomos 2, the "aforementioned originator of evil" (= Satan: ὁ προλεχθεὶς τῆς κακίας δημιουργός), seeking to enthrall the human race, introduced idolatry under the guise of Christianity (ἐν προσχήματι Χριστιανισμοῦ) and persuaded men to worship (προσκυνεῖν) and reverence (σέβεσθαι) created objects (κτίσιν) and to regard manufactured articles (τὸ ποίημα) bearing the name of Christ as God.[11] Wherefore, Gregory continues, Christ raised up "his servants, the emperors, rivals of the apostles, endowed with the . . . power of the Holy Spirit, not only to perfect and instruct mankind but also to destroy the demonic strongholds raised against the knowledge of God and to refute diabolical . . . heresy." The emperors, roused by the damage done to the churches, summoned a council of bishops to undertake a scriptural examination of the "deceptive art of painting images in color (περὶ τῆς ἀπατηλῆς τῶν ὁμοιωμάτων χρωματουργίας) that has seduced the mind of men from the exalted worship that is fitting for God to a groveling and material worship of creatures," and to set forth under the inspiration of God their own views on this matter.[12]

By way of a preface to its own decrees, the Council reviews briefly the main results of the first six oecumenical councils, in each instance stating the name of the emperor under which the council was held and summarizing the doctrinal questions there determined.[13] On the basis of this survey of the history of dogma they claim that they were led by the Holy Spirit to conclude that the art of painting is unlawful (ἀθέμιτον), trespasses against the dogma of the incarnation of Christ, and subverts the six oecumenical councils.[14] Specifically, the use of images is repugnant to them on Christological grounds. For, in their judgment, it is derived from the Christology of the Nestorians[15] or that of Arius, Dioscorus, Eutyches, and Severus (= Monophysites),[16] and thus does violence (Tomos 3 begins here) to the doctrine of the union of the two natures (the divine and the human) in Christ, in one hypostasis (= one person), which admits of neither separation nor confusion.[17]

They digress slightly to condemn the idea of representing by the graphic arts that

---

[9] M. 216BC.   [10] M. 217AB.   [11] M. 221CD.

[12] M. 225D, 229ADE. The relation between church and state which arises at this point I have discussed in a paper published in Studi in honore di Giorgio La Piana (Ricerche Religiose, Rome, 1955 or 1956).

[13] M. 232E-237D.   [14] M. 240C.   [15] M. 241E.

[16] M. 244D. Arius is placed in this Monophysite company here and at n. 19 below because he anticipated Apollinarius in teaching that in Jesus Christ the place of the νοῦς or the human rational soul was taken by the divine Logos.

Nontheologians should perhaps be reminded that Nestorius was condemned (in 431 and 451) for teaching that Christ had two hypostases and two prosopa (or persons), one for each of his two natures, the divine and the human. The Monophysites, on the other hand, were expelled from the Orthodox Church (451) for having denied that Christ had more than one nature. This is a crude summary, which does not attempt to evaluate the justice of the charges or the merits of the case for the defense.

[17] M. 245DE.

"which is believed by the heart and confessed by the mouth" as a senseless notion, inspired by sordid love of gain.[18] Thereafter, they revert to the two contradictory Christological heresies just mentioned which, they charge, underlie the whole iconophile position. (1) Since the word Christ, they say, denotes both God and man, an icon of Christ would be regarded as an image of both God and man. In the irreverent mind of the man who painted it, such an image either circumscribes the uncircumscribable divinity within the outline of created flesh, or confuses the unconfused union (of the divine and the human in Christ). In either case, both the painter and the worshiper of the image blaspheme against the Godhead, and both are guilty of the same heresy as Arius, Dioscorus, Eutyches, and the Acephali.[19]

(2) Then, the antithetical argument that an image of Christ represents only his flesh which [the disciples] had seen, touched, and lived with[20] is repudiated as Nestorian. The fathers had taught, they contend, that the flesh of Christ was also the flesh of the divine Logos, and could not be conceived of as divided therefrom, since it had been completely united with the divine nature and wholly deified. Similarly, when the divinity of the Son took up the nature of the flesh into his own hypostasis [= "person"], the soul became the mediator between divinity and flesh. Thus, just as the flesh [of the man Jesus Christ] is also the flesh of the divine Logos, his soul is likewise the soul of the Logos. Both the soul and the body [of Christ] were deified, and were inseparable from the divinity even when the soul departed from the body at the time of the passion.[21] It is, therefore, impious to sever the flesh from the divinity and produce an image [of Christ] as if he were only a man. For to do this is to deprive Christ's flesh of its deified character, and to make of it a separate hypostasis, and a fourth person in the Trinity. Under these circumstances, they insist, images were falsely so-called (ψευδωνύμως) and should neither be made nor reverenced.[22]

For the iconoclasts, the only true image was the Eucharist. When Christ, on the eve of the Crucifixion said of the Eucharistic elements, "Take, eat ... This is my body ... This is my blood ... This do in remembrance of me" (cf. Matt. 26:26-28; Mark 14:22-24; Luke 22:17-20; I Cor. 11:23-26), he was in effect indicating that this was the only form or figure he had chosen that could represent his incarnation (ὡς οὐκ ἄλλου εἴδους ἐπιλεχθέντος παρ' αὐτοῦ ἐν τῇ ὑπ' οὐρανόν, ἢ τύπου, εἰκονίσαι τὴν αὐτοῦ σάρκωσιν δυναμένου). Thus, the Eucharist is the image of Christ's lifegiving body (ἡ εἰκὼν τοῦ ζωοποιοῦ σώματος αὐτοῦ), whose purpose it was to reveal the mystery of his incarnation. In order to avoid idolatry, they point out, this Eucharistic icon of Christ did not have the appearance of a man, just as the human nature assumed by Christ at his birth did not constitute a separate person.[23]

[18] M. 248E.
[19] M. 252AB. The terms, circumscribable (περίγραπτος) and uncircumscribable (ἀπερίγραπτος), with their roots, derivatives, and cognates, have a technical meaning in this discussion. That which is circumscribable can be seen by the eye and represented in a painting, mosaic, or picture. Uncircumscribable, on the other hand, is practically a synonym for "invisible." That which is uncircumscribable cannot be seen and, consequently, cannot be depicted by an artist. A man is circumscribable and can be painted or photographed; his soul, like the plans or purposes which he forms in his mind, cannot.
[20] M. 256AB.   [21] M. 256E-257B.   [22] M. 257E-260B: [23] M. 261D-264C.

X

Moving on (in *Tomos* 4) to other grounds for hostility against images, to which it refers abusively once again as "the evil name of icons falsely so-called" (ἡ δὲ τῶν ψευδωνύμων εἰκόνων κακωνυμία), the Council objects that images were not derived from the tradition of Christ, or the apostles, or the fathers, and had no holy prayer of sanctification, whereby they might be transformed from the common to a state of holiness (πρὸς τὸ ἅγιον ἐκ τοῦ κοινοῦ μετενεχθῇ). Consequently, the image remains a common, ordinary thing, without honor (or sanctity), just as it was when the painter completed it.[24] An attack is then made upon those, who, while agreeing with the condemnation of images of Christ for the reason that the two natures united in the one hypostasis of Christ are indivisible and unconfused, nevertheless could not understand why the same prohibition should extend to images of the Virgin Mary, the prophets, apostles, and martyrs, who were mere men, and not a union of the divine and the human in one hypostasis.

This contention receives careful consideration by the iconoclasts. (1) First of all, they reply, since images of Christ are forbidden, there is no need for any other images.[25] (2) Christianity steers a middle course between Judaism and paganism, and follows the new path of piety with a distinctive God-given liturgy of its own that shuns the bloody offerings and holocausts of the Jews, as well as pagan sacrifice, manufacture of idols, and idolatry. The pagans invented "the abominable art of image-making," the iconoclasts say, because they had no belief in resurrection, and consequently attempted by means of idols to present things that were not present as if they were. But the Christian Church, which admits no foreign elements (οὐδὲν τῶν ξένων ἐστὶν ἐν αὐτῇ), could only reject this pagan practice as alien to it and as the invention of men possessed by demons.[26] (3) Moreover, the saints live eternally with God even though they have departed from this world; whoever believes he can set them up again as statues by a dead and hateful art that has never conferred life, but is the vain invention of the pagans, is guilty of blasphemy.[27]

(4) Further, it is impossible to represent in the vulgar art of the pagans the Mother of God, whom the fulness of the Godhead overshadowed, and by whom the unapproachable light shone upon us, since she is more exalted than the heavens and holier than the cherubim. (5) Similarly, it would be degrading to depict in pagan art the saints, who will reign with Christ, join him as judges (συγκαθέδρους) in the judgment of the world, and share in his glory (συμμόρφους τῆς δόξης αὐτοῦ). The world was not worthy of them (Hebr. 11:38). Therefore, Christians, who have the hope of resurrection, are not permitted to follow the customs of the demon-worshiping heathen and to insult with inglorious and lifeless material the saints, who are to shine in glory [in the age to come]. (6) Finally, the analysis of this point ends with another vigorous rejection of pagan rites and a reminder that Christ rebuked the demons who addressed him as God because he scorned testimony about his work from that quarter (cf. Mark 1:25; Luke 4:41).[28]

Thereupon, the *Horos* proceeds to examine the passages in the fathers and in the

[24] M. 268B-269C.   [25] M. 272ABD.   [26] M. 273BCD.   [27] M. 276D.   [28] M. 277CDE.

Scriptures which, it is claimed, support iconoclasm, and which, if properly understood, could not be gainsaid. The Council urges those who do not know these texts to
learn them and lay them to heart (κατεχέτω), since they come from God. The first
citations come from the Gospel of John: "God is a spirit: and they that worship him
must worship him in spirit and in truth" (4:24); "No man hath seen God at any
time" (1:18); "Ye have neither heard his voice . . . nor seen his shape" (5:37);
"blessed [are they] that have not seen, and yet have believed" (20:29).[29] Appeal is then
made to the Old Testament, and first of all to the Second Commandment: "Thou
shalt not make unto thee any graven image, or any likeness of anything that is in
heaven above or that is in the earth beneath. . . ." (Exod. 20:4; Deut. 5:8). For on
the mountain, "out of the midst of the fire: ye heard the voice of the words, but saw
no similitude; only ye heard a voice" (Deut. 14:12).[30] These quotations are followed
by a selection from the Epistles of Paul: "And [they] changed the glory of the uncor-
ruptible God into an image like to corruptible man . . . and worshiped and served
the creature more than the Creator" (Rom. 1:23 and 25b); "Yea, though we have
known Christ after the flesh, yet now henceforth know we him no more . . . For we
walk by faith, not by sight" (II Cor. 5:16 and 7); and "So then faith cometh by hearing,
and hearing by the word of God" (Rom. 10:17).[31]

In *Tomos* 5, the iconoclasts pass on from the Bible to the fathers, beginning with
the warning of Epiphanius,[32] Bishop of Salamis in Cyprus (d. 403), to his people to
hold fast to their traditions, and not to set up images in the churches, in the cemeteries
of the saints, or in private houses, but to remember God continually in their hearts
and eschew flights of fancy brought on by the eyes and the wandering of the imagina-
tion.[33] The same principle, they say, was enunciated by Gregory the Theologian [of
Nazianzus], who maintained that it was shameful (ὕβρις) to put faith in colors, rather
than in the heart, since that [faith] which reposes in colors is easily effaced.[34] Next they
quote from a work attributed to John Chrysostom (d. 407), according to which we
enjoy the presence of the saints in their writings, from which we obtain images, not
of their bodies, but of their souls, since their words are the images of their souls.[35]

Likewise, they continue, St. Basil (of Caesarea in Cappadocia) had declared that the
study of the sacred Scriptures constitutes the best path to the ascertainment of what
is fitting, because they provide a guide for conduct as well as the biographies of

---

[29] M. 280DE.   [30] M. 284C.   [31] M. 285BC.

[32] These words cited as from Epiphanius by the iconoclasts have not been preserved apart from the proceedings of the Council of 754. Nevertheless, they have been accepted as genuine even by Ostrogorsky,
Studien zur Geschichte des byzantinischen Bilderstreites, pp. 67f., 75, 101, 102f., 109-111, who (*op. cit.*, pp.
61-113) criticizes Karl Holl's attempt ("Die Schriften des Epiphanius gegen die Bilderverehrung," *Sitzungsberichte d. pr. Ak. d. Wiss.*, Berlin 1916, pp. 828-868, reprinted in Holl, *Gesammelte Aufsätze zur Kirchengeschichte*, 2, *Der Osten*, Tübingen 1928, 351-387), to authenticate the whole corpus of passages adduced
by the iconoclasts on the authority of Epiphanius, and condemns as spurious all the allegedly Epiphanian
fragments except those reproduced at this point. Franz Dölger, *Göttingische gelehrte Anzeigen*, 191 (1929),
353-372, supports Holl against Ostrogorsky; cf. Hans Barion, "Quellenkritisches zum byzantinischen Bilderstreit," *Römische Quartalschrift*, 38 (1930), 78-90. I will discuss these and other reviews in my book.

[33] M. 292DE; Ostrogorsky, *Studien*, pp. 67f.; Karl Holl, *op. cit.*, p. 363, who gives references to some other
sources.

[34] M. 297A; a paraphrase of Gregory, *Carmina theologica; 2, Poemata moralia*, MPG, 37, 913, lines 39f.
[35] M. 300AB.

blessed men that serve as animate images of a godly life and inspiration for the emulation of godlike deeds.[36] In the next patristic citation, Athanasius (d. 373), whom they describe as the Beacon of Alexandria, commiserates with worshipers of creatures (κτίσματα), because, though endowed with sight and hearing themselves, they pray to that which cannot see or hear, and because a creature cannot be saved by a creature.[37] A similar argument, they note, is to be found in Amphilochius of Iconium, who protested against the representation on tablets of the physical faces of the saints in colors, since, he said, we do not need such things but rather to imitate their way of life by virtuous deeds of our own.[38] Theodotus of Ancyra, an associate of Cyril of Alexandria, is then cited for the doctrine that Christians have been taught to fashion images (ἰδέας) of the saints, not by means of figures of material colors, but by imitating their virtues, which are really living images (οἷόν τινας ἐμψύχους εἰκόνας), with the aid of books in which their exploits are recorded, so as to be stimulated in this way to a zeal like theirs. After rhetorically inquiring of those who favor images what benefit is derived from them, or to what spiritual contemplation reflection on them leads, he concludes that they are fruitless and the invention of diabolical cunning.[39]

Perhaps the most interesting of these references to the fathers are the excerpts from the letter the ecclesiastical historian Eusebius of Caesarea wrote to Constantia, the sister of Constantine the Great and wife of Licinius. Constantia had asked Eusebius to send her an image of Christ. In refusing to grant her request, Eusebius inquires, "What, or of what nature is that which you call an image of Christ? Is it the true and unchangeable image which indicates the characteristics that are his by nature (τὴν ἀληθῆ καὶ ἀμετάλλακτον, καὶ φύσει τοὺς αὐτοῦ χαρακτῆρας φέρουσαν)? Or do you mean that which he assumed for our sake, when he put on the shape (σχῆμα) of the form of a servant (cf. Phil. 2:5ff.)? But I do not believe you are looking for an image of the form of God, since you have learned from him [i.e., Christ] 'that no man hath known the Father, save the Son; neither would any man know the Son himself properly, save the Father who begat Him' (cf. Matt. 11:27). . . . Undoubtedly, therefore, you seek an image of the form of the servant and of the garment of flesh with which he was clothed for our sake. But, we know that this was mixed (ἀνακεκρᾶσθαι) with the glory

---

[36] M. 300AB: Μεγίστη γὰρ ὁδὸς πρὸς τὴν τοῦ καθήκοντος εὕρεσιν, ὁ ἅγιος ἔφη Βασίλειος, ἡ μελέτη τῶν θεοπνεύστων γραφῶν· ἐν ταύταις γὰρ καὶ αἱ τῶν πράξεων ὑποθῆκαι εὑρίσκονται, καὶ οἱ βίοι τῶν μακαρίων ἀνδρῶν ἀνάγραπτοι παραδεδομένοι, οἷόν τινες εἰκόνες ἔμψυχοι τῆς κατὰ θεὸν πολιτείας, τῷ μιμήματι τῶν κατὰ θεὸν ἔργων προκείμενοι. As a sample of the merit of John Mendham, *The Seventh General Council*, London 1850, a translation of the Acts of the Second Council of Nicaea, note (*op. cit.*, 386): "the great Basil observes—'the most effective way to the attainment of that which is fitting to us is diligent application to the inspired Scriptures, for by these are the principles of good actions discovered; and the lives of blessed men being written herein are handed down to us, being, as it were, certain living images of the conversation which is according to God, by their imitation of the works which are according to God.'" On the whole Mendham's work deserves the highest praise. He usually renders the Greek with felicity and skill; and I have occasionally borrowed from him. Still, he is often inaccurate, as in the last clause quoted, and must be used with caution.

[37] M. 300E. With the aid of Guido Müller, *Lexicon Athanasianum*, Berlin 1952, the sources of this quotation can be identified as: Athanasius, *Contra gentes*, 13, Migne, *Pat. Gr.*, 25, 29 A; *idem*, *Epistola ad Adelphium Episcopum*, MPG, 26, 1081C. Both passages are transcribed faithfully from Athanasius except for minor changes.

[38] M. 301D; cf. K. V. Zetterstéen, ed., "Eine homilie des Amphilochius von Ikonium über Basilius von Cäsarea," *Oriens Christianus*, 31 (1934), 68.22ff.

[39] M. 309E-312A.

of the Godhead, and that his 'mortality has been swallowed up of life' (cf. II Cor. 5:4 c). . . . Who, then, would be able to portray (καταχαράξαι) the brilliant, dazzling splendor of such dignity and glory in lifeless, inanimate colors and lines, when even the blessed disciples on the Mount [of Transfiguration] could not look upon him but fell upon their faces and confessed that the sight was more than they could endure (ἀφόρητον)? If, therefore, his incarnate form attained such glory and was transfigured by the Godhead dwelling within it, what must we say of it when, after stripping off mortality and washing away corruption, he transformed the appearance of the form of a servant into the glory of Lord and God—after his victory over death, his ascent into heaven, his *sessio* on the royal throne at the right hand of God the Father, and his coming to rest in the indescribable and ineffable bosom of the Father, being hailed by the heavenly powers as he ascended and was restored thereto with the words, 'Lift up your gates, ye princes, and be ye lifted up ye everlasting doors, and the king of glory shall come in'?" (Ps. 23 [LXX]:7-9).[40] Foregoing further citation of Scriptural and patristic authorities, in order to avoid excessive length, *Tomos* 5 is brought to an end with this passage, and with a prohibition, unanimously enacted, of all images of all materials and colors fashioned by the "evil art of painters."[41]

At the opening of *Tomos* 6, which contains the canons and anathemas of the Council, the iconoclasts sternly forbid the production of images, their worship (προσκυνῆσαι), erection in churches or private homes, or concealment. Bishops, presbyters, and deacons who disregarded this ordinance were to be deposed, while recalcitrant monks or laymen were to be anathematized and subjected to prosecution under the imperial laws as foes of God's commandments and the teaching of the fathers.[42] At the same time, to avoid abuse of this edict, persons in authority over churches and holy places are warned not to use fervor against icons as a pretext for seizing sacred vessels, vestments, and tapestries, or any other consecrated objects which are covered with images,[43] so as to apply them to other purposes. Such transformations, it is provided, could be made only with the approval of the oecumenical patriarch and on the authorization of the emperors. Similarly, nobles and laymen are enjoined from taking over churches and converting them to their own uses, as many had already done.[44]

Following conciliar tradition, the bishops of the Council claim apostolic authority (ἀποστολικῶς εἰπεῖν) and the guidance of the Holy Spirit (πιστεύομεν πνεῦμα Χριστοῦ ἔχειν). Under these auspices, they set forth a series of anathemas,[45] the first seven of which

[40] M. 313A-D. This interesting text is not to be found in the extant corpus of Eusebius' writings, but its authenticity seems to have been admitted even by the orthodox, who, in their refutation (M. 313Dff.), concentrated their fire on the Arianizing tendencies of Eusebius' theology, which they deemed sufficient to invalidate his testimony, and did not attempt to question its authorship.
On the theological problems involved, see George Florovsky, "Origen, Eusebius, and the Iconoclastic Controversy," *Church History*, 19 (1950), 77-96. The Biblical quotation at the end is taken from the Septuagint version, in which Psalm 23 is the equivalent, except for some variants, of Psalm 24 of the English.
[41] M. 324CDE.   [42] M. 328BC.
[43] M. 329DE, 332B. On the acts of vandalism and misuse of ecclesiastical property that had occurred, see Martin, *op. cit.* (in note 2 above), 40, n. 3, 45, n. 6, 51.
[44] M. 332DE.   [45] M. 333BC.

summarize the Trinitarian and Christological doctrine of the Church as formulated at the fifth and sixth oecumenical councils, and in the first, second, and eleventh anathemas of Cyril of Alexandria (d. 444) against Nestorius.[46] They then go on to deal with images. These anathemas, together with the remainder of the *Horos* are given below in full translation.

"8. If anyone endeavors to contemplate the divine form of God the Logos in his incarnation through the medium of material colors, and does not worship him with the whole heart, with the eyes of the mind, as he sits *in excelsis*, more dazzling than the sun, at the right hand of God, on the throne of glory, anathema.[47]

"9. If anyone seeks to circumscribe by material colors in images of human form the uncircumscribable substance and hypostasis of God the Logos because of the incarnation, and does not, on the contrary, teach (θεολογεῖ) that he is nonetheless uncircumscribable even after the incarnation, anathema.[48]

"10. If anyone attempts to portray in an image the inseparable hypostatic union of the nature of the God Logos and [his] flesh, or the One [Person], unconfused and undivided, that arose out of the two [natures], calling it Christ,—since the name Christ signifies both God and man,—and thus monstrously contriving a confusion of the two natures, anathema.[49]

"11. If anyone isolates the flesh united to the hypostasis of the God Logos, considering it by itself in mere thought, and hence sets out to make an image of it, anathema.[50]

"12. If anyone divides the One Christ into two hypostases, separating the Son of God from the son of the Virgin Mary, and does not confess him to be one and the same, but [argues] that the union of the two is a relative one, so that he may portray the son of the Virgin as if he had a separate hypostasis, anathema.[51]

"13. If anyone represents in an image the flesh divinized by union with the divine Logos, as if separating it from the Godhead, which assumed it and deified it, and therefore picturing it as devoid of divinity, anathema.[52]

"14. If anyone tries to depict in lifeless colors God the Logos, who, existing in the form of God, assumed the form of a servant in his own hypostasis and became in all respects like us, except for sin, [regarding him] as if he were a mere man, and seeks to separate him from his inseparable and unchangeable divinity (θεότητος), thus introducing a fourth member (τετράδα) into the holy and life-giving Trinity, anathema.[53]

"15. If anyone does not acknowledge Mary, ever a virgin, to be properly and truly Mother of God (θεοτόκον), and higher than all creation, visible and invisible, and does

---

[46] M. 333E-336D.

[47] M. 336E. In my translation, I have used the indicative mood exclusively in rendering the apodoses of the anathemas. The Greek text presents a mélange of indicatives, subjunctives, and optatives. This syntactical eccentricity must be explained as the result of (a) itacism, (b) carelessness and inconsistency on the part of scribes and correctors, and (c) lack of precision in the use of moods that is by no means uncommon in the eighth century. Perhaps grammatical order may be restored in the critical edition of the *Acta* to be prepared by Professor Johannes Straub of Erlangen, who, however, is still working on the proceedings of the Council of 553.

[48] M. 337C.   [49] M. 340C.   [50] M. 341A.   [51] M. 341CD.   [52] M. 341E.   [53] M. 344C.

not with sincere faith entreat intercession of her, as one who has the privilege of speaking openly (παρρησίαν) to our God, whom she bore, anathema.[54]

"16. If anyone ventures to set up profitless figures of all the saints in lifeless, speechless images made of material colors—for this is a vain invention (ἐπίνοια) and the discovery of diabolical craft—and does not, on the contrary, reproduce their virtues in himself as animate, living images with the aid of what has been revealed about them in books, in order to be stimulated to zeal similar to theirs, as our inspired fathers have said, anathema.[55]

"17. If anyone does not confess that all the saints from the beginning of time until the present day, who pleased God before the law, under the law, and under grace, are honored in His sight both in soul and body, and does not, according to the tradition of the Church, entreat their prayers since they have the παρρησίαν to intercede for the world, anathema.[56]

"18. If anyone does not confess the resurrection of the dead, the judgment, and the reward to each according to his deserts by the righteous scales of God, and [does not confess] that there is no end of punishment or of the heavenly kingdom, which is the enjoyment of God, 'for the kingdom of heaven,' according to the divine apostle (Rom. 14:17), 'is not meat and drink, but righteousness, and peace, and joy in the Holy Spirit,' anathema.[57]

"19. If anyone does not accept this, our holy seventh oecumenical council, but criticizes it in any way, and does not endorse without reserve what it has decreed in accordance with the teaching of divinely inspired Scripture, anathema from the Father, and the Son, and the Holy Spirit, and the seven oecumenical councils.[58]

"20. These things having been determined by us with all precision and unity (ἐμμελείας), we ordain that no one shall be permitted to set forth any doctrine other than this or to write, or contrive, or think, or teach contrary to it; and that any who dare to devise, or bring forward, or teach, or impart a different doctrine to those who

[54] M. 345AB. In my book I shall examine carefully the history of the Emperor Constantine V's allegedly radical teaching about Mary, including his unwillingness to grant her the title Theotokos, etc.; cf. Martin, op. cit. (in note 2 above), pp. 42, 49f.; Ostrogorsky, Studien, pp. 7-45. Concerning the Byzantine doctrine of Mary, see S. Salaville in Maria, Études sur la Sainte Vierge, ed. Hubert du Manoir, 1, Paris 1949, 247-326, cf. 327ff., 428f.; ibid., 2, Paris 1952, 403ff.; Martin Jugie, L'immaculée conception dans l'écriture sainte et dans la tradition orientale, Rome 1952, 114ff. and passim; idem, La mort et l'assomption de la Sainte Vierge Marie, Studi e Testi, 114, Vatican City 1944, 226ff.

[55] M. 345CD. In a learned and provocative paper, "The iconoclastic council of St. Sophia (815) and its definition (ὅρος)," Dumbarton Oaks Papers, 7 (1953), Paul J. Alexander argues that the iconoclasts in 815 did much more than merely copy the arguments of the Council of 754 and actually made important innovations hitherto ignored by historians. He admits that there is nothing particularly striking about their Horos, but maintains that the original note was introduced, more or less surreptitiously, in some of their patristic citations, the burden of which was that the only valid image of the saints was imitation of their virtues by pious Christians. There is no doubt that this concept is to be found in the iconoclastic catena of patristic testimonies published by Ostrogorsky, Studien, as well as in Alexander's fuller and better edition of these same texts. But it cannot be said that this theory of an image was new in 815 either in itself or in the emphasis that was laid upon it. For it occurs not only in the passage here translated but also at several other points in the Horos of 754, in the excerpts quoted from the fathers: see above, nn. 36, 38, 39, cf. nn. 33, 35. Furthermore, if there were anything new or startling about this doctrine in 815, is it not strange that, as Alexander shows, Patriarch Nicephorus's refutation of the theological principles of the Horos of 815 almost completely ignores it?

[56] M. 348DE.   [57] M. 349C.   [58] M. 349DE.

wish to be converted from any heresy whatsoever to the acknowledgment of the truth, or [who dare] to introduce novelty of expression or innovation of language in order to overturn these, our decrees, shall, if bishops or clergy, be deposed, the bishops from their bishopric, the clergy from orders, and shall, if monks or laymen, be anathematized.[59]

"The most divine Emperors Constantine (V) and Leo (IV) said: 'Let the holy oecumenical council declare if the decree that has just been read was proclaimed with the approbation of all the most holy bishops.'

"The holy council cried out: 'We all believe thus; we are all of one mind; we have all signed unanimously and freely; we all hold the orthodox faith; offering our adoration to a spiritual Godhead, we all worship spiritually. This is the faith of the apostles, this is the faith of the fathers, this is the faith of the orthodox. Thus have all who serve God worshiped him. Long live the Emperors! O Lord, grant them a pious life. Eternal be the memory of Constantine and Leo. You are the peace of the world. May your faith preserve you. Honor Christ, and he will watch over you. You have confirmed orthodoxy. O Lord, grant them a pious life. Let there be no envy of your royal authority. God preserve your rule. God give you a peaceful reign. Your life is the life of the orthodox. Heavenly King, protect the kings of the earth. Through you the universal church has gained peace. You are the lights of orthodoxy. O Lord, preserve the lights of the world. Eternal be the memory of Constantine and Leo. Long live the new Constantine, [our] most pious Emperor. Lord preserve him who is orthodox like his family before him (ἀπὸ γένους). Grant him, O Lord, a pious life. Let there be no envy of his royal authority.—Long live the most pious Empress. God preserve the pious and orthodox Empress.—

"Let there by no envy of your royal authority. May God preserve your rule. May God grant you a peaceful reign. You have affirmed the inconfusability [of the natures] in the incarnation of Christ. You have proclaimed more firmly the inseparability of the two natures of Christ. You have confirmed the doctrine of the six holy oecumenical councils. You have destroyed all worship of idols. You have gained a victory over the teachers of this heresy. You have laid the brand of infamy upon all who are contrary-minded.[60]

"You have destroyed the conceit (φρόνημα) of the heretics, Germanus, George, and Mansur [= John of Damascus]. Anathema to the vacillating Germanus, the wood-worshiper. Anathema to George, his fellow-heretic (ὁμόφρονι), the falsifier (φαλσευτῇ) of the teachings of the fathers. Anathema to Mansur, the Saracen-minded, who has a name of ill-omen [i.e., an Arab name]. Anathema to Mansur, the image-worshiper, the writer of falsehoods. Anathema to Mansur, who insults Christ and plots against the Empire. Anathema to Mansur, who teaches impiety and perverts the meaning of the Holy Scripture. The Trinity has deposed these three."[61]

[59] M. 352CD.   [60] M. 352E-353C.
[61] M. 356CD. The champions of orthodoxy specially selected for anathematization by the iconoclasts, besides John of Damascus, the famous theologian (d. 749), who wrote three orations supporting the use of images, to say nothing of the renowned πηγὴ γνώσεως (De fide orthodoxa), were Germanus I, Patriarch of

Detailed analysis and criticism of the iconoclastic *Horos* must be deferred. But attention should be drawn to the anathema directed against John of Damascus, who is described as Σαρακηνόφρων, "Saracen-minded," the term of opprobrium usually applied by the supporters of images to the iconoclasts. It is at least interesting, as I hope to show elsewhere, that John of Damascus, the zealous champion of images, grew up in the Arab court, in close contact with the Muslims. Is it really as obvious as many believe that the Muslim and Semitic scruples against idols gave the impetus to Byzantine iconoclasm? At the very least, it would appear, Arab influence here has been greatly exaggerated.

The principal emphasis in both the iconoclastic attack upon the images and the orthodox rebuttal is upon principles of Christian theology. This is made clear by the above paraphrase and translation, which may now be concluded with a brief summary. The iconoclasts opposed the use of images for four main reasons. In the first place, they regarded the use of images as a mark of idolatry that had been condemned not only in both the Old Testament and the New Testament, but also by the fathers of the Church. They were offended by the material character of images, which, they felt, never ceased to be ordinary physical objects, and always remained devoid of grace or sanctity. Second, they reasoned that, since Christ is both God and man, images of Christ involve either circumscription of the uncircumscribable Godhead and a Monophysite confusion of the two natures or a Nestorian division of the human from the divine in Christ that results in a separate hypostasis of the flesh of Christ and introduces a fourth member into the Trinity. Third, they maintained that the Eucharist was the only true image of Christ. Fourth, in condemning the manufacture and use of images of the saints and the martyrs, they laid stress on a number of texts, according to which the only admissible images of the saints were their virtues, which it was the duty of every Christian to exemplify in himself.

Whatever one's own theological predilections may be, it must be admitted that the iconoclasts presented the best possible case that could be made against the use of images. They omit nothing of importance that could be said on their side, and present their material with force, logic, and energy. The further question of the validity of their argument when tested by comparison with that of their opponents will form the subject of a subsequent paper.

HARVARD UNIVERSITY. DUMBARTON OAKS

WASHINGTON, D.C.

Constantinople (715-730), the author of a number of important letters, who was deposed by the Emperor Leo III because of his unyielding support of the images, and George of Cyprus, who is noted chiefly for his defense of the images in his Νουθεσία γέροντος περὶ τῶν ἁγίων εἰκόνων. For bibliography, see Ostrogorsky, *Geschichte*, pp. 120-123, 131f., 139f.

XI

THE ETHICAL THEORY OF IMAGES FORMULATED BY THE ICONOCLASTS IN 754 AND 815

XI

This essay is a revised version of parts of the two papers on iconoclasm which I read at the Dumbarton Oaks Symposium of 1951.

A T their famous Council of 754, the iconoclasts, as is well known, did not denounce all representations of Christ but only those which attempted in one way or another to simulate his outward form or appearance by means of painting or sculpture. In fact, they specifically endorsed what they called the image of Christ as set forth in the Eucharist.[1] This fact and the orthodox reply thereto, that the Eucharist was actually Christ himself, not merely his image,[2] are familiar to all students of the subject. Many, however, seem not to be aware that the iconoclasts at the same time announced their approval of still another, and, from the ethical point of view, at least, more significant conception of an image, which described the virtues of the saints as living images and called for their imitation. According to this definition of images, one should put reliance, not upon pictorial representations, but upon the scriptures and the biographies of the saints.

This spiritual or ethical interpretation of the image is probably to be understood as a part of the iconoclastic campaign to purify Christian worship of what many took to be superstitious and idolatrous practices. Our knowledge of these iconoclastic efforts in the direction of reform, dating from the so-called First Iconoclastic period (726–787), we owe principally to the text of the ὅρος (Horos, or dogmatic definition) and anathemas pronounced by the iconoclastic Council of 754, which have been preserved to us in their refutation by the orthodox party (which favored the use of images) at the Sixth Session (Tomoi 5 and 6, respectively) of the Seventh Oecumenical Council, held in Nicaea in 787. For reasons I have stated elsewhere,[3] this version of the proceedings of the Council of 754 may be accepted without the slightest reserve as a reliable record of iconoclastic doctrine and belief.

Apart from a brief general introduction and conclusion, the florilegium of 754 consists of eight excerpts from the fathers, of which all but two deal with what I shall, for the sake of brevity, call the ethical theory of the image.

[1] J. D. Mansi, *Sacrorum conciliorum nova et amplissima collectio*, 13 (Florence, 1767, in the anastatic reprint, Paris — Leipzig, 1902, cited below as Mansi, 13), 261 D–264 C. For the large and growing bibliography on the iconoclastic controversy, I must refer to my forthcoming article in the new edition of the fourth volume of the *Cambridge Medieval History*.

[2] Mansi, 13, 264 D–268 A.

[3] "The argument for iconoclasm as presented by the iconoclastic Council of 754," *Late classical and mediaeval studies in honor of Professor Albert Matthias Friend, Jr.* (Princeton, 1954). In what follows I repeat, for the sake of the argument, which would otherwise be difficult to follow, a very small (and revised) portion of my summary of the ὅρος of 754.

In the first of the other two, Athanasius maintains that it is ridiculous for
sentient beings to pray to insensate objects, since salvation cannot be obtained from what is created. In the second, the ecclesiastical historian,
Eusebius of Caesarea, writing to the Empress Constantia, contends that it is
impossible to produce an image of Christ because the presence of the divine
within him at all stages of his existence put him beyond the range of mortal
images. Thus the florilegium lays considerable stress upon the spiritual view
of the image.[4]

The basic principle underlying this concept occurs in the first quotation
in the florilegium, which comes from Epiphanius of Cyprus, who had urged
his people not to set up images in churches, in cemeteries of the saints, or in
private houses, but always to remember God in their hearts.[5] This idea lies
behind the citation of a poem of Gregory of Nazianzus, according to whom
"it is shameful to put trust in colors and not in the heart, for that [faith]
which is in colors is easily washed away, while that which is in the depth
of the mind is dear to me."[6] The florilegium then embraces a passage from
a work attributed to St. John Chrysostom, who is reported as saying, "we
enjoy the presence of the saints in their writings, in which we have images,
not of their bodies, but of their souls, since their words are images of their
souls."[7] The practical consequences of this doctrine are more clearly enunciated by Basil of Caesarea, who maintained, the iconoclasts say, that "the
study of the holy writings constitutes the best path to the ascertainment of
what is proper, because they provide a guide for conduct, together with the

[4] Mansi, 13, 300 E, 313 A–D. Actually, the six passages dealing with the ethical theory of
images occupy 49 lines of space in Mansi as against 45 for Athanasius (6) and Eusebius
(39), and 16 in the conclusion. But their relative importance can be gauged by the fact that
the six passages on the spiritual view of the image are separately refuted by the orthodox
spokesman at great length in approximately 8 full columns of Mansi (ca. 511 lines), while the
other two texts get 5 columns (ca. 317 lines) of refutation.

In this paper, I do not discuss the ultimate sources used by the iconoclasts in formulating
the ethical theory of the image. To this question I hope to return later. Cf. Jean Daniélou,
Origène (Paris, 1948), 48; George Florovsky, "Origen, Eusebius and the Iconoclastic Controversy," Church History, 19 (1950), 91; Paul J. Alexander, loc. cit. (n. 13 below), 50, 56;
Wigbert Hess, "Imago Dei," Benediktinische Zeitschrift, 29 (1953), 370–400, especially 385
ff.

[5] Mansi, 13, 292 DE: προσέχετε ἑαυτοῖς, καὶ κρατεῖτε τὰς παραδόσεις, ἃς παρελάβετε· μὴ
ἐκκλίνητε δεξιά, μηδὲ ἀριστερά . . . καὶ ἐν τούτῳ μνήμην ἔχετε, τέκνα ἀγαπητά, τοῦ μὴ ἀναφέρειν
εἰκόνας ἐπ' ἐκκλησίας, μήτε ἐν τοῖς κοιμητηρίοις τῶν ἁγίων· ἀλλ' ἀεὶ διὰ μνήμης ἔχετε τὸν θεὸν ἐν ταῖς
καρδίαις ὑμῶν· ἀλλ' οὔτε κατ' οἶκον κοινόν.

[6] Mansi, 13, 297 A: ὕβρις πίστιν ἔχειν ἐν χρώμασι, καὶ μὴ ἐν καρδίᾳ. ἡ μὲν γὰρ ἐν χρώμασιν
εὐχερῶς ἐκπλύνεται· ἡ δὲ ἐν τῷ βάθει τοῦ νοός, ἐκείνη ἐμοὶ προσφιλής.

[7] Mansi, 13, 300 A: ἡμεῖς διὰ τῶν γραφῶν τῆς τῶν ἁγίων ἀπολαύομεν παρουσίας, οὐχὶ τῶν
σωμάτων αὐτῶν, ἀλλὰ τῶν ψυχῶν τὰς εἰκόνας ἔχοντες. τὰ γὰρ παρ' αὐτῶν εἰρημένα, τῶν ψυχῶν αὐτῶν
εἰκόνες εἰσί.

biographies of the blessed ones, that serve as living images of a godly life and the inspiration for the emulation of god-like behavior." [8]

Furthermore, the iconoclasts continue, invoking the authority of Amphilochius of Iconium, "there is no point in painting the physical faces of the saints with colors on tablets, since we do not need such things but rather to imitate their way of life by virtuous deeds of our own." [9] A similar argument was made, they add, by Theodotus of Ancyra, the contemporary and theological ally of Cyril of Alexandria, for Theodotus believed that "we have been taught, not to fashion images of the saints by means of material colors, but rather to imitate their virtues, which are really living images, with the aid of what has been recorded about them in books, so that we may be stimulated in this way to a zeal like theirs." [10]

The same thought is latent, though not directly expressed, in the eighth anathema of the Council of 754, which condemns anyone who would contemplate the incarnate Logos "through the medium of material colors, and does not worship him with the whole heart, with the eyes of the mind, as he sits *in excelsis*, more dazzling than the sun, at the right hand of God, on the throne of glory." [11] The whole case in behalf of this type of image is summarized in the sixteenth anathema of the Council as follows:

If anyone ventures to set up profitless figures of all the saints in soul-less, speechless images made of material colors — for this is a vain invention and the discovery of diabolical craft — and does not, on the contrary, reproduce their virtues in himself as actually living images, with the aid of what has been recorded about them in books, in order to be stimulated to zeal like theirs, as our inspired fathers have said, let him be anathema. [12]

This iconoclastic doctrine of the image has much to recommend it, and would undoubtedly have commanded universal assent as an ethical principle,

[8] Mansi, 13, 300 AB: μεγίστη γὰρ ὁδὸς πρὸς τὴν τοῦ καθήκοντος εὕρεσιν . . . ἡ μελέτη τῶν θεοπνεύστων γραφῶν· ἐν ταύταις γὰρ καὶ αἱ τῶν πράξεων ὑποθῆκαι εὑρίσκονται, καὶ οἱ βίοι τῶν μακαρίων ἀνδρῶν ἀνάγραπτοι παραδεδομένοι, οἷόν τινες εἰκόνες ἔμψυχοι τῆς κατὰ θεὸν πολιτείας, τῷ μιμήματι τῶν κατὰ θεὸν ἔργων προκείμενοι.

[9] Mansi, 13, 301 D: οὐ γὰρ τοῖς πίναξι τὰ σαρκικὰ πρόσωπα τῶν ἁγίων διὰ χρωμάτων ἐπιμελὲς ἡμῖν ἐντυποῦν, ὅτι οὐ χρῄζομεν τούτων, ἀλλὰ τὴν πολιτείαν αὐτῶν δι' ἀρετῆς ἐκμιμεῖσθαι.

[10] Mansi, 13, 309 E–312 A: τὰς τῶν ἁγίων ἰδέας οὐκ ἐν εἰκόσιν ἐξ ὑλικῶν χρωμάτων ἀναμορφοῦν παρειλήφαμεν, ἀλλὰ τὰς τούτων ἀρετὰς διὰ τῶν ἐν γραφαῖς περὶ αὐτῶν δηλουμένων οἷόν τινας ἐμψύχους εἰκόνας ἀναμάττεσθαι δεδιδάγμεθα, ἐκ τούτου πρὸς τὸν ὅμοιον αὐτοῖς διεγειρόμενοι ζῆλον.

[11] Mansi, 13, 336 E: εἴ τις τὸν θεῖον τοῦ Θεοῦ λόγου χαρακτῆρα κατὰ τὴν σάρκωσιν δι' ὑλικῶν χρωμάτων ἐπιτηδεύοι κατανοῆσαι, καὶ μὴ ἐξ ὅλης καρδίας προσκυνῇ αὐτὸν ὄμμασι νοεροῖς, ὑπὲρ τὴν λαμπρότητα τοῦ ἡλίου ἐκ δεξιῶν τοῦ Θεοῦ ἐν ὑψίστοις ἐπὶ θρόνου δόξης καθήμενον, ἀνάθεμα.

[12] Mansi, 13, 345 CD: εἴ τις τὰς τῶν ἁπάντων ἁγίων ἰδέας ἐν εἰκόσιν ἀψύχοις καὶ ἀναύδοις ἐξ ὑλικῶν χρωμάτων ἀναστηλοῦν ἐπιτηδεύοι, μηδεμίαν ὄνησιν φερούσας· ματαία γάρ ἐστιν ἡ ἐπίνοια, καὶ διαβολικῆς μεθοδείας εὕρεσις· καὶ οὐχὶ δὴ μᾶλλον τὰς τούτων ἀρετὰς διὰ τῶν ἐν γραφαῖς περὶ αὐτῶν δηλουμένων οἷόν τινας ἐμψύχους εἰκόνας ἐν ἑαυτῷ ἀναζωγραφεῖ, καὶ πρὸς τὸν ὅμοιον αὐτοῖς ἐκ τούτου διεγείρεται ζῆλον, καθὼς οἱ ἔνθεοι ἡμῶν ἔφησαν πατέρες, ἀνάθεμα.

even in orthodox circles, had it not been combined with hostility to other, more conventional kinds of images. It is not surprising, therefore, that it was revived during the second iconoclastic controversy (813–843) and was incorporated in the Acts of the iconoclastic Council of 815 convoked by the iconoclastic Emperor Leo V (813–820).

This time, the theory of the image propounded by the Council of 754 is to be found only in the florilegium of patristic authorities. From what remains of the Acts of the Council of 815, there is no indication that this idea penetrated also into the anathemas of that council, although it is not impossible that it may have appeared in a portion of the proceedings that is no longer extant. In the reconstruction of the florilegium of 815, which we owe to the patient labors of Professor Paul Alexander,[13] it can be seen that the iconoclasts of 815 copied out five of the total of six passages in the florilegium of 754 that were concerned with the view of images here under review, taking over with little or no change the quotations from Epiphanius, Gregory, John Chrysostom, Amphilochius, and Theodotus. Because of their brevity and conciseness, these texts make up what is in some ways the strongest expression of this theory of the image in the entire history of iconoclasm. Indeed, the clearest and fullest of these, that of Theodotus, represents this doctrine of the image in all its facets more precisely and more unambiguously than any of the new passages introduced into the florilegium by the iconoclasts of 815. This can be made clear from the following summary: [14]

A. Texts bearing more or less directly upon the ethical theory of images.

18. Asterius of Amaseia (MPG, 40, 168 B) warns against painting figures of Christ, since it was enough that Christ had humiliated himself

[13] Until recently our knowledge of the proceedings of the Council of 815 was limited to the fragments collected and published by Daniel Serruys, "Les Actes du concile iconoclaste de l'an 815," École Française de Rome, *Mélanges d'archéologie et d'histoire*, 23 (1903), 345–351. This collection of fragments was improved and revised by Georg Ostrogorsky, *Studien zur Geschichte des byzantinischen Bilderstreites*, Historische Untersuchungen, 5 (Breslau, 1929), 48–51. Both of these scholars gleaned their material from the treatise Nicephorus wrote to refute the work of the iconoclasts in 815; both of them confined their search to the ὅρος of 815. Recently, Professor Paul Alexander has carried out further dredging operations in the same stream and has come up with a number of hitherto undiscovered fragments of the ὅρος, plus a considerable portion of the florilegium of 815: "The iconoclastic Council of St. Sophia (815) and its Definition (*Horos*)," *Dumbarton Oaks Papers*, No. 7 (1953), 37–66.

[14] I give brief summaries of the patristic texts assembled by the iconoclasts, restricting myself here to epitomizing the material at hand. Critical questions of authorship, as well as a detailed critique of the florilegium as a whole, I postpone to another time. The numeration of the fragments is that of Alexander, *loc. cit.* On excerpts 29 (Nilus to Olympiodorus) and 30 C (Epiphanius to Theodosius), see Gabriel Millet, "Les iconoclastes et la croix, à propos d'une inscription de Cappadoce," *Bulletin de Correspondance Hellénique*, 34 (1910), 99 f.

once at the time of the incarnation, and urges men to carry the incorporeal Logos spiritually (νοητῶς) in their souls.

19. A certain Leontius, commenting on Luke 9.28, remarks on the difficulty of producing an image (εἰκόνα) of Christ, since he had appeared in many different guises — in the baptism, in the transfiguration, in the crucifixion, in the tomb, and in the resurrection. "If you want a likeness (ὁμοιωσίδιον) of Christ," Leontius says, "lay it in your heart, for the Lord cannot be represented in an image."

20. Theodotus of Ancyra (from 754), here described as Theodotus of Galatia.

21. Basil of Seleuceia: Men should not honor those who have lived virtuous lives by means of pagan colors but should be reminded of them by studying written records and be spurred to imitate their zeal.

22. Amphilochius of Iconium (from 754, with additions emphasizing the value of reading about the saints).

23. Basil of Caesarea (MPG, 44, 273 AB) stresses man's ability to make himself like God and contrasts this with the vanity and futility of images.

25. Gregory of Nazianzus (from 754).

26. Christ should not be depicted by visual means, John Chrysostom objects, since he dwells in heaven, governs the universe, suffers when a soul rejects him, and is nourished only by the salvation of believers.

28. John Chrysostom (from 754).

30 A. Epiphanius (from 754).

30 B. In a long series of excerpts from Epiphanius, in which images are denounced for a number of reasons, the faithful are admonished to emulate the patriarchs and the prophets (p. 63), and, also, as it would seem, although the Greek is a little peculiar (p. 64. 3f.: οὐκοῦν εἰκόνας αὐτῶν τὰς αὐτῶν ἐντολὰς δι᾽ ἀρετῶν στήσωμεν), to regard the commandments of the apostles as models (or images) for imitation.

B. Iconoclastic texts irrelevant to the ethical theory of images.

17. A text from the Apostolic Constitutions warns against the use of unsuitable (i.e., pictorial) decoration (ἄκοσμον κόσμον) in the representation of the cross.

24. According to Gregory of Nyssa one should not worship the form of the Servant, but God the Logos, existing in the glory of the Father and in the form of God.[15]

27. John Chrysostom alludes to a sculptural (?) representation of the

---

[15] I have transferred this text from the relevant list in which Alexander, *loc. cit.*, p. 44, places it, because it seems to me to have nothing to do with the ethical theory of images.

158

story of Genesis 18 (Abraham, Sarah, and the three angels), and rejects this and other similar works of pagan inspiration.

29. Nilus advises Olympiodorus (MPG, 79, 577 D) that, except for an incised cross, the sanctuary should remain free of pictorial adornment.

30 C. In a letter to the Emperor Theodosius I, Epiphanius rejects images on account of the lack of patristic warrant for their use, and urges the Emperor to order, under penalty of a fine, that textiles decorated with images of the apostles or of the prophets or of Christ be used for the burial of the poor, that wall paintings be obliterated, and that mosaics be removed, or at least that no more be laid, since the fathers had authorized no figures except that of the cross.

30 D. Epiphanius relates how he deliberately tore down a hanging because it had a representation of Christ or one of the saints, and suggested that it be used to bury some poor man. In replacing this curtain by a plain one, he asks that no such works (i.e., none decorated with images) be placed in the churches.

From this résumé it can be seen that, of the twelve excerpts added to the florilegium of 754 by the iconoclasts of 815, only six (or seven if we count number 24, which is not really pertinent) are concerned with the ethical theory of the image: a text of Epiphanius (30 B), which is the only one of the new texts that states the full doctrine of the florilegium of 754 as summarized in the sixteenth anathema of its ὅρος (translated above; see n. 12), two others (from Basil of Seleuceia [21] and Basil of Caesarea [23]), which allude to it in one way or another, two more (from Asterius [18] and Leontius [19]), which are cited as witnesses for the slightly less explicit, but closely related, form of the "ethical" definition of the image, i.e., that Christians should carry the image of Christ in their souls, and another from Chrysostom (26), which touches upon salvation. Thus the florilegium of 754, much of which is incorporated within that of 815, as we have seen, was reinforced in 815 by a number of additional patristic citations, which were, however, inspired by those collected in 754, the iconoclasts of 815 having been unable, according to the so-called *Scriptor incertus de Leone*, to find patristic authorities for their hostility to images until they secured the records of the Council of 754, which guided them in their search for appropriate texts.[16] The relationship between the two florilegia described above tends to

[16] P.G., 108, 1025 AB: καὶ δὴ συναγαγόντες πλήθη πολλὰ βιβλίων, ἐποιοῦντο ἐν αὐτοῖς τὴν ἔρευναν, πλὴν οὐδὲν εὕρισκον οἱ ἄφρονες ὧνπερ αὐτοὶ κακούργως ἐπεζήτουν, ἕως οὗ μετὰ χεῖρας ἔλαβον τὸ συνοδικὸν [sic legendum puto] Κωνσταντίνου τοῦ Ἰσαύρου, τοῦ καὶ Καβαλλίνου, καὶ ἐκ τούτου τὰς ἀρχὰς λαβόντες, ἤρξαντο καὶ ἐν τοῖς βιβλίοις εὑρίσκειν τὰς χρήσεις, ἅσπερ αὐτοὶ ἀφρόνως καὶ ἀνοήτως προέφερον, σημάδια βάλλοντες εἰς τοὺς τόπους, ἔνθα ηὕρισκον, βουλόμενοι πεῖσαι τὸν ἄφρονα λαόν, ὅτι Ἐν παλαιοῖς βιβλίοις εὕρομεν τοῦ μὴ προσκυνεῖσθαι τὰς εἰκόνας.

corroborate this statement. Statistics are of little account in such matters, but it is perhaps of some interest to note that some of the material (30 C and 30 D) added to the florilegium of 754 by the iconoclasts is quite long, while 30 B, cited above as supporting the "ethical" theory, extends for forty lines of small type on a quarto page, and is actually made up of eleven quotations, only a very few of which (two or three) are directly concerned with the "ethical" theory. If we count each folio reference in Alexander's edition of the florilegium separately, we find a total of twenty-eight excerpts (five from the florilegium of 754 and twenty-three new ones), of which approximately one half (five repeated from 754, the six discussed above, and perhaps two or at most three more of the component parts of Alexander's fragment 30 B) treat of the "ethical" theory.

As a result of this examination we must conclude that the florilegium of the Council of 815 does not advance beyond the iconoclastic theology of the earlier period. Thus the florilegium of 815, which had been unknown until its fortunate discovery and publication by Alexander, fully justifies the conclusion of previous scholars that its authors made no original contributions, and merely re-used materials or repeated arguments current among the iconoclasts of 754. The most that can be said is that the iconoclasts of 815 added 12 (or 28) patristic references to the florilegium of 754, none of which, however, can be regarded as constituting an innovation or substantial addition to the iconoclastic armory.

The above analysis of the florilegia of 754 and 815 nullifies Professor Alexander's attempt [17] to demonstrate that the iconoclasts of 815 were innovators and were the first to introduce what I have been referring to as the "ethical" theory of the image, or what he calls the doctrine that "the only true image of Christ and of the saints is Man endowed with the Christian virtues" (pp. 44, 50). He does not realize that the "ethical" theory first appeared, and was strongly emphasized, as has been shown above, in 754, although in his edition of the fragments of the florilegium of 815, he four times [18] gives the reference by volume and page to the section of the florilegium of 754, from which the iconoclasts of 815 had copied these particular texts. He even quotes, in a footnote,[19] the sixteenth canon of the ὅρος of 754 (see above), which demolishes the hypothesis that the iconoclasts of 815

[17] Loc. cit., 37, 44, 50 f.

[18] Ibid., 61 (Nos. 20, 22), 62 (Nos. 25, 28); 54 f., nn. 20, 22, 23. But is it not somewhat surprising to say (ibid., p. 55, n. 22) that "fragments 20, 22, and 25 were indeed precious supports for the central thesis of 815," when the fact is that, together with the two other texts transplanted from 754 into the florilegium of 815, they are rather the inspiration, source, and heart of what he calls the "central thesis of 815"?

[19] Ibid., 55, n. 23.

160

were the first to apply the "ethical" theory to the image controversy; and he goes so far as to state that: "The Council of Hiereia [the Council of 754] had expressed, in one of its anathemas, what was to become the central thesis of the Council of St. Sophia" (i.e., that of 815). If he had noticed the close connection between this anathema and the passage from Theodotus included in both the florilegia of 754 and 815, he would never have claimed originality for the Council of 815. Moreover, he confuses the issue when he suggests at the end of note 23 that the Council of 754 is to be distinguished from that of 815 by reason of the former's emphasis upon Christology. For, it should be noted, the ὅρος of the Council of 815 deals with Christology no less emphatically than that of 754, as Alexander would concede,[20] while the Patriarch Nicephorus (806–815) devotes 157 out of a total of 160 folios in his treatise on the Council of 815 to an attack upon its Christology, and only three to its doctrine of the true image.[21] The cardinal fact, which Alexander disregards, is that the florilegium of 815 is based upon, and derived from, that of 754.

Similarly, other features of the Council of 815 which Alexander deems distinctive can be traced back to the proceedings of 754. Thus the description of the saints by the iconoclasts of 815 as τοὺς συμμόρφους αὐτοῦ ἁγίους — "like Christ in form" (fr. 9, 30 B), which is patterned upon Romans 8.29, and the definition of images as "soulless" (fr. 13) — ἀψύχοις εἰκόσι — or "false" (fr. 30 B) — ψευδώνυμοι — occur in 754.[22] Nevertheless, although we are reluctantly compelled to repudiate Alexander's thesis on these points, his edition of the florilegium of 815 is of great interest and value both in itself and as a forerunner of the long-awaited publication of the entire text of Nicephorus's treatise, upon which he has been working for many years.

[20] Ibid., 40 f.

[21] Ibid., 47.

[22] συμμόρφους: Mansi, 13, 277 D; εἰκόσιν ἀψύχοις: ibid., 345 C and cf. 300 AB and 312 A (nn. 8, 10, 12 above); ψευδώνυμοι: ibid., 260 B, 268 BC, and cf., for the use of ψευδής with regard to the iconoclasts, ibid., 204 D, 205 A, 208 D.

XII

SOME ASPECTS OF BYZANTINE INFLUENCE
ON LATIN THOUGHT IN THE TWELFTH CENTURY[I]

After the disaster of 1071 at Bari, as a result of which Byzantine forces
were expelled from Italy,[2] it might have been expected that the influence
of Byzantium on the West would have waned and diminished, especially
since the victory of the Normans in this fateful year had been preceded
by the rupture between the Byzantine and Roman churches, which had
taken place on July 18, 1054,[3] when Cardinal Humbert deposited the
bull of excommunication on the high altar of the Church of Hagia
Sophia. National and ecclesiastical antagonisms, it might have been
thought, would have combined to drive out all memory of the hated
Greeks from the Latin world.

Actually, this animosity found expression in a number of diatribes
entitled *Contra errores Graecorum*,[4] or the like, in which the Latins attacked
the Byzantines for a number of reasons, but not least because of the
refusal of the Byzantine Church to accept the Latin doctrine of the
double procession of the Holy Spirit. Nevertheless, not even those who
despised the Greeks, or disagreed with them, could avoid succumbing
to the allurement of Greek learning, to which the intellectual currents
of the period subsequent to 1071 proved, as it turned out, to be exceedingly favorable. Indeed, so numerous and widespread were the manifestations of the penetration of Hellenic ideas into the life and thought
of the West in this era that the twelfth century must be considered a
turning point in the history of civilization on this account. The present
essay provides only a brief introduction to this vast and complicated, but
fascinating subject.

ROBERT OF MELUN ON THE GREEK LANGUAGE

Among those who looked with suspicion and disfavor upon the study of Greek was Robert of Melun (Robertus de Meleduno or Meledunensis), a distinguished theologian, born in England near the end of the eleventh century, who succeeded Abelard at the *Schola artium* of Mount Ste. Geneviève (*ca.* 1137), and then became successively magister at the school of Melun near Paris, magister of theology at St. Victor in Paris, and finally bishop of Hereford in England from *ca.* 1160 until his death in 1167.[5]

His position with regard to Byzantine theology and Greek philology in general is contradictory and inconsistent, but probably reflects an attitude that was not uncommon in his day. Before going on, therefore, it may be instructive to consider briefly what Robert has to say on this head. He felt so strongly about the sinister consequences of instruction in Greek that he devoted nine pages in the *Prefatio* of his *Sententie* (written *ca.* 1152–60)[6] to an assault upon its advocates. He admitted that it was unsuitable (*culpabile*) to apply the unpolished idiom and style of children (*inani puerorum concinnitate*) to the exposition of the Catholic faith. It was, however, much more reprehensible, he felt, to go to the other extreme, as many of his contemporaries were then doing with great aplomb, and sprinkle quotations in Greek throughout their writings so as to cover their Latin with a shining mantle of Greek[7] and thus win fame for esoteric lore.

He denounces those who used Greek as suffering from one of two complaints. Either, he charges, their minds are so blinded by the tumor of idle pride, that they judge that what is not is, and solemnly assert that what is is not, deeming the good to be useless and deformed, and the ugly beautiful and desirable. Or else, Robert continues in words that reflect the anguish and torment he suffered in the course of his lessons in Greek, they look down upon their hearers as so inept as to consider nothing clear except what is obscure and nothing sweet except "what is compounded of the bitterness of gall."[8]

In attempting to teach theology by way of the Greek language, Robert objects, the professor of Greek not only does not lead the mind of his students to understanding, but creates uncertainty and ambiguity. Although the theologian should concern himself with showing what theological concepts mean, he wastes his time and that of his classes with foreign grammar and vocabulary, thus reducing his pupils to the level of children learning their letters for the first time.[9] Instead of helping him with the understanding of ideas, Robert charges, his teacher compelled him to struggle with Greek words, which could never be adequately translated into Latin anyway, and did not at all promote his comprehension of theology. "Our little Greek master (*greculus preceptor*)," he says, does not seem to have the progress of the pupil very much in mind, but appears instead to be looking for nothing but an opportunity for an ostentatious display of the knowledge of Greek.[10]

"By what principle of faith," Robert asks, "by what fitness of discipline, when a professor intends to expound the unity of the divine substance and explain the distinction of the persons, does he resort to a mixture of languages, and not confine himself to Latin? Why does he say that there are three *hypostases* and one *usia*, and not express this in Latin, or else altogether in Greek?"[11] The adoption of Greek theological terminology, especially of this Trinitarian formula, one *usia* in three *hypostases*, was just about universal in the twelfth century, but Robert stubbornly professes to regard the introduction of Greek terms as an affectation or even as a device deliberately intended to serve as camouflage for error.

He claims that "the lamentable experience of the present time" clearly proves that his attack on Greek studies is well-founded, but it is difficult to tell from this cryptic remark whether Robert was alluding here to his theological opponents, like Gilbert de la Porrée (or, perhaps more properly, Porreta),[12] who drew heavily upon Greek materials in translation, or whether he merely meant that the professors of Greek were more concerned for rhetorical and philological subtleties than for the substance of theology. At any rate, he compared them to the foolish virgins of Matthew 25, since, he says, "they have lamps but no oil," that is, they have "melodious words, full of deceptive color, which vainly caress the ears, but do not illumine the mind. Because [these teachers] lack oil, that is, are empty of meaning, those who listen to them will be excluded from the granary of the Lord of the Harvest, and will be cast like empty, crackling stalks into the fire" (Matt. 13 : 30; Luke 3 : 17). Spurning what he calls the "vain embellishment of words" that gains nothing for the faith but "a damnable contempt," Robert condemns "this method of teaching, which consists of the mixing together of Greek and Latin words, feeds the ears, and delights by sound, but does not penetrate to the soul to inform it by faith."[13]

Robert was not the only one who protested against Greek theology. Hugh of Fouilloy (*ca.* 1160) refused to use "Greek, barbarian, or other unusual terms which confuse simple folk," [14] and Eberhard of Bamberg (sometime before 1169) rejected the Greek authorities to which Gerhoh of Reichersberg had appealed on a point of Christology as *minus authenticum*.[15] An adversary of Abelard (Pseudo-William of St. Thierry) branded Maximus the Confessor (d. 662) as the source of heresy in John Scotus Erigena, and Walter of St. Victor (*ca.* 1178) denounced what he called the "errors and heresies of John of Damascus," to whom he refers disparagingly as *nescio quis Iohannes Damascenus*.[16] Many others expressed dissatisfaction with the introduction of Greek phraseology and methods of analysis, but these voices of dissent and disapproval were soon silenced.

Even the seemingly irreconcilable Robert of Melun was by no means so inflexibly hostile to Greek scholarship as his strictures on this subject in the *Prefatio* to his *Sententie* might have led us to believe. For at the beginning of his career (*ca.* 1137–40), while teaching at the *Schola artium* of Mount Ste. Geneviève, as we learn from his pupil, John of Salisbury, he expounded the *Topica* of Aristotle in his lectures.[17] Later on, he quoted Origen, Eusebius of Caesarea, and John Chrysostom in his *Questiones de epistolis Pauli* (written between 1145 and 1155) and the last named also in his *Questiones de divina pagina* (of *ca.* 1143–47), while a few words from the Pseudo-Dionysius are invoked by him in the first book of his *Sententie*.[18] Furthermore, he not only cites John of Damascus with approval in the second book of the abridged edition of his *Sententie*, but also takes over from John the very word, *hypostasis*, the adoption of which by Latin theologians he had ridiculed in the passage summarized above (n. 11). He even reproduces the word in the Greek form of the genitive plural, *hypostaseon*, which he apparently copied from Peter the Lombard.[19] This abridgment of the *Sententie* seems to have been prepared by his disciples, rather than by Robert himself, but it probably represents his own ideas. It is not likely that the abbreviators interpolated a quotation from John of Damascus which was lacking in the manuscript of the work they were epitomizing.

To judge from the texts he cites, Robert depended exclusively upon Latin translations from the Greek, and had no direct contact with the original. This fact possibly explains in part the apparent inconsistency of his attitude towards Greek: he had no objection to Greek authors if suitably clad in Latin dress, but he would have nothing to do with the language itself.

BYZANTINE INFLUENCE ON LATIN ART

The anti-Hellenic tirades found in the *Prefatio* of Robert's *Sententie* reflect the bitterness engendered by the remorseless conflicts between the Byzantines and the Crusaders. This animosity was, of course, warmly reciprocated by the Greeks, who, as we learn from Anna Comnena and other sources, frequently regarded the Latins as a crude and particularly loathsome breed of barbarians. On the Byzantine side, this resentment of the Latins led, in 1182, to a massacre of the Latin community of Constantinople; and the hatred of the Latins for the Greeks culminated, apart from the outrages perpetrated upon Constantinople in 1204, in the Norman sack of Thessalonike, the second city of the Empire in 1185,[20] in which a great part of the population was put to the sword. "Thus," as Nicetas Choniates, a contemporary Byzantine historian, put it, "between us and them (the Latins) yawns a vast chasm of discord. We have no meeting of minds and stand diametrically opposed, even though we keep up our external contacts and often share the same habitations."[21]

Despite all this friction and rancor, however, the splendor and beauty of the city of Constantinople, with its magnificent palaces, incomparable churches, scintillating mosaics, sparkling marbles, and seemingly boundless treasures of fine stuffs and precious stones of every description, dazzled the Latins[22] and filled them both with envy and with the desire to imitate the works of art they beheld. Merchants and travellers usually carried souvenirs from Constantinople, which they had either bought or stolen, and the Crusaders soon acquired a passion for Byzantine jewelry, richly adorned reliquaries, gold, silver, ivories, enamels, silks, and textiles, which led, in a dark hour, to the wanton looting of Constantinople in 1204.

In the first Crusade, the Latins had pillaged the Greek cities on their line of march;[23] and, during the second Crusade (but, of course, not as a part of it), in 1147, King Roger II of Sicily (1101–54) made off with a treasure of such dimensions, including precious metals and valuable stuffs, from Thebes, then a wealthy city, that the ships on which he loaded his booty rode heavy in the water. He also plundered Corinth and Athens, and carried off from Thebes a number of women skilled in weaving, in order to stimulate the silk industry in Sicily. At the same time, he took with him, it would seem, Byzantine craftsmen who had had experience in designing and producing mosaics. Roger's Admiral, George of Antioch, in all likelihood made a special point of assembling Byzantine mosaicists in

XII

these raids, and the Normans must have taken advantage of other similar opportunities to round up the experts they needed to decorate the cathedral of Cefalù (*ca.* 1131–75), the Cappella Palatina (*ca.* 1140–89), and the Martorana (*ca.* 1143–51) in Palermo, and the Cathedral of Monreale (*ca.* 1172–92). They may well have been enabled to do so by the marriage negotiations with the Constantinopolitan court in 1143 and 1171–72, by the conclusion of peace between William I and Manuel II in 1158, the embassies exchanged in the years 1181–82, or during William II's expedition to the East in 1185, which was marked by the bloody attack on Thessalonike.[24]

Whenever or however the mosaicists were obtained, it is clear that the mosaic decoration of these four great Sicilian monuments is Byzantine in craftsmanship, iconography, and style. Western and Arabic traits can be detected at various points, but the mosaics were indubitably planned by Byzantine artists and set up under their close supervision. The very idea of producing monumental mosaics of this type is also Byzantine in origin, and its adoption by Roger and his successors indicates that they were consciously imitating Byzantine absolutistic rule. For there can be little doubt that Roger connected the great mosaics of Byzantium with Byzantine political theory, and used his own mosaics as symbols of his autocratic power in both state and church. This point is illustrated by the mosaic in the Martorana in Palermo, which represents Roger II arrayed in the royal robes of the Byzantine emperor, receiving his crown from Christ in a typical Byzantine iconographical scheme. Roger used Byzantine law codes, and in negotiating with the Byzantine emperor demanded that he be recognized as the latter's equal in all respects.[25]

In Sicily, as well as in southern Italy, the Greek language and the Byzantine liturgy continued to flourish even after the Byzantine defeat at Bari in 1071. A large number of south Italian churches and Basilian monasteries, many of them in crypts and caves, were decorated in the Byzantine manner, and many illuminations in twelfth-century codices of the Exultet-rolls of South Italy are marked by Byzantine characteristics, as are a number of Latin illuminated manuscripts which were prepared by artists who had had direct contact with Byzantine art either in the Near East or in the West.[26]

Other notable examples of Byzantine influence can be seen in the mosaics of the twelfth century in the Church of San Marco in Venice, in the mosaics of the Basilica Ursiana at Ravenna (1112), possibly in the apsidal mosaics of Santa Maria in Trastevere (*ca.* 1140), in some of the famous bronze doors of Venice, Southern Italy, and Sicily, in the architectural design of a series of churches in the environs of Perigord, notable for domes resting on pendentives, and in the technique of ornamentation found in many Romanesque churches, especially in Languedoc and Provence. It is of some interest to note that the bronze doors and romanesque patterns of decoration often reproduce motifs such as palmettes, stylized acanthus leaves arranged in rinceaux and intricate designs of interlace, and animals framed in medallions, with which the Latins became acquainted through portable objects like textiles, ivory boxes, and illuminated manuscripts.[27]

LITERATURE, PHILOSOPHY, AND THEOLOGY

Less obvious but perhaps more profound and far-reaching was the Byzantine influence on literature, philosophy, and theology. The publication of new texts and studies relating to our period, which in recent years has been accelerating at an extraordinary rate, is not only demonstrating anew that the so-called "Renaissance of the twelfth century," to use the title of Haskins' famous book, was in every sense a great era in the history of thought, but is also proving in a very substantial manner that the use of Greek materials, in Latin dress at least, was far more prevalent than once had been supposed.[28] Actually, apart from the bits of Plato and Aristotle that had been current in Latin since the early centuries, several Byzantine classics had been known in Latin for a long time. Porphyry's *Eisagoge* to the *Categories* of Aristotle, written at the beginning of the Byzantine period, had been translated into Latin not only by Marius Victorinus in the fourth century but also by Boethius (with commentaries) in the sixth, and left its mark on the whole of medieval philosophy. In the ninth century, the same service had been performed for the Pseudo-Dionysius by Hilduin and John Scotus Erigena, the latter of whom discharged a similar function for Maximus the Confessor and Gregory of Nyssa.[29]

These and many more had been accessible in Latin before the beginning of the twelfth century, during which the increased contact with the Greek world through the Crusades and the humanistic court of the Normans in Sicily, to say nothing of other factors, created a new and practically insatiable demand for Greek authors, ancient and medieval. The number of Latins in this period who were competent to make satisfactory translations from the Greek was not great, but a few notable experts achieved considerable success in this field. Henricus Aristippus, who undertook a hazardous study of the eruptions of Etna and, after a distinguished career, died in prison in Palermo (1162), not only rendered into Latin Plato's *Meno* and *Phaedo*, and the fourth book of Aristotle's *Meteorologica*, but also appears at least to have planned to go on to do Diogenes Laertius and Gregory of Nazianz.[30] James of Venice produced a Latin version of Aristotle's so-called *Logica nova*, which comprised the *Analytica Priora* and *Posteriora*, the *Topica*, and the *Sophistici Elenchi*.[31] Admiral Eugenius of Sicily (d. 1202) aided an unknown scholar in making Ptolemy's *Almagest* (or more correctly, *Syntaxis Mathematike*) available in Latin, and seems himself to have been responsible for a revision in Latin of the Greek original of the so-called *Prophecy of the Erythraean Sibyl*.[32]

Another noted linguist, Moses of Bergamo by name, is associated with a Latin paraphrase of the grammar of Theodosius of Alexandria.[33] In addition, Euclid's *Dedomena* (*Data*), *Optica*, and *Catoptrica*, Proclus' so-called *Elementatio philosophica* (or *physica*), and the *Pneumatica* of Hero were turned from Greek into Latin by anonymous hands, as were also the *Kiranides*, a curious collection of materials bearing on the occult powers of animals, plants, and stones.[34]

These translators were concerned primarily with pagan lore. But others, like Burgundio of Pisa, who was one of the most prolific writers and distinguished diplomats of the twelfth century, devoted themselves both to ancient science and to medieval theology. He translated ten works of Galen, some Hippocrates, an extract from the *Geoponica*, and a great number of theological texts, including the *De fide orthodoxa* of John of Damascus, three long treatises of John Chrysostom, the *De natura hominis* of Nemesius (which circulated then under the name of Gregory of Nyssa and had been done into Latin by Bishop Alfano of Salerno in the latter part of the eleventh century), Basil's commentary on Isaiah, and apparently many more.[35] Less productive than he was Hugo Eterianus' brother, Leo Tuscus, who had a career resembling that of Burgundio in diplomacy and Greek scholarship, and left a Latin rendering of the *Liturgy of St. Chrysostom* and of the ninth-century dream book (*Oneirocriticon*) by Achmet.[36] Mention should be made also of the activities of Cerbanus of Hungary, who put some of John of Damascus (*De fide orthodoxa*) and Maximus the Confessor into Latin.[37]

Though many Latins like Robert of Melun resisted the penetration of Byzantine ideas, at least ostensibly, the majority enthusiastically welcomed "the light from the East"—*orientale lumen*, as it was termed by William of St. Thierry, a Cistercian monk (d. 1147), who was attracted to the *De hominis opificio* of Gregory of Nyssa *via* the version made by John Scotus Erigena *ca.* 862–64, which he followed closely in his *De natura corporis et animae*. William was influenced also by Gregory's brother, Basil, by Origen, and by the Pseudo-Dionysius.[38] Even the obdurate and anti-intellectual St. Bernard of Clairvaux succumbed to the same forces and drew heavily upon Origen, Gregory of Nyssa, and Maximus the Confessor.[39] Cyril of Alexandria was often cited in the twelfth century,[40] and the great interest in the theology of Pseudo-Dionysius led John Sarrazin not only to write a commentary on that author's *Celestial Hierarchy* but also, at the instance of John of Salisbury, to revise Erigena's translation of this same work because it was all but unintelligible.[41]

These are only a very few of the large number of writers in the twelfth century who were affected in one way or another by Greek authorities. It was once believed that the appeal to Greek sources, pagan and Christian, on the part of some authors like Peter Abelard, Gilbert de la Porrée, and Joachim of Flore, was an important factor in the heretical teaching of which these men were deemed guilty. But recent studies have thrown doubt upon this once widely held generalization, and it is now being denied that it was Greek theology or learning which had led these men astray, and even that they ever were heretics at all.[42]

The new approach to medieval theology involved in this judgment merits careful investigation for its own sake as well as for its bearing upon the transmission and reception of Greek scholarship, both secular and theological, in the West during the Middle Ages. As a small contribution to the study of this problem, I offer the following analysis of two theological treatises, one of which stresses opposition to Byzantine theology, and the other indebtedness thereto.

In exploring the relationship of Byzantine thought to that of the West, it should be remembered that Byzantine theology constitutes the most striking and most contemporaneously relevant of the Byzantine contributions to civilization. The basic doctrines of the Trinity and the Incarnation, as these were understood not only in the twelfth century but also in all ages from early times until the present day, were formulated and codified by Byzantine theologians at the Seven Oecumenical Councils (325–787) in technical language that still commands all but universal assent in the entire Christian Church. The Roman Church participated in these decisions, it is true, but only through the presence of a very few delegates, and the councils were dominated by the Byzantine emperors, who convoked them and invested their dogmatic decrees with the force of law.[43]

The Byzantine insistence (see the next section) that the Holy Spirit proceeds from the Father alone stems from the so-called Niceno-Constantinopolitan Creed of 381 (now usually, but unfortunately, designated in the Churches as the Nicene Creed, from which it differs markedly). According to the *symbolum fidei* of 381, the Holy Spirit "proceeds from the Father, and is worshipped and glorified together with the Father and the Son." Apparently in 589 the Church of Toledo in Spain added *Filioque* to this Creed and meant to assert thereby that the Holy Spirit "proceeds from the *Father and the Son.*" This addition, which sanctions the "double procession" of the Holy Spirit, was officially endorsed by Rome under Pope Benedict VIII (1012–24), but is rejected by the Byzantine Church because it does not occur in any of the oecumenical formularies.

In the theological discussions which follow in the next two sections, it should be noted carefully that the Trinitarian problem is concerned with the Father, Son, and Holy Spirit, and their relation to the Godhead and to each other, whereas the Christological problem has to do with the relation between the two natures, the human and the divine, within the person of Jesus Christ. After much confusion and misunderstanding, the Greek and Latin terms for the Godhead (the divine substance, essence, or nature common to the three persons) and for the individual, distinct person became standardized in orthodox circles. The former was designated as οὐσία (*substantia* or *essentia* in Latin) or φύσις (*natura*), the latter as πρόσωπον or ὑπόστασις (*persona, hypostasis,* and *subsistentia* in Latin); and it became customary to speak of the Trinity as consisting of one substance in three persons. Peter Lombard and Peter of Poitiers usually referred to the divine substance as *essentia,* but they by no means spurned the synonyms, *substantia* and *natura* or *usia,* the transliteration of οὐσία. To avoid confusion, therefore, in my analysis of Latin theological terminology (pp. 159 ff. and 168 ff. below), I follow the usage of the sources closely, using *essence* for *essentia, substance* for *substantia, nature* for *natura,* etc.

HUGO ETERIANUS ON THE DOUBLE PROCESSION OF THE HOLY SPIRIT

Let us look first at the treatise, *De sancto et immortali Deo,* written between 1176 and 1177 by Hugo Eterianus (otherwise known as Hugo of Pisa), which deals exhaustively with the Byzantine critique of the Roman doctrine of the double procession of the Holy Spirit. Hugo lived approximately fifteen years at Constantinople, from about 1166, if not so early as 1161 or before, until perhaps as late as the beginning of 1182, the year of his death, which took place in Italy sometime between the middle of July and the seventh of December, only a few days or weeks after he had been named cardinal deacon of Sant' Angelo by Pope Lucius III (1181–85). During their sojourn in Constantinople, Hugo and his brother, Leo the Tuscan, who served the Byzantine Emperor Manuel I (1143–80) as interpreter, acquired not only a thorough command of the Greek language, but also a wide acquaintance with the writings of the Byzantine theologians of their own day and of previous times, which they read with great avidity in the libraries of the capital city.[44]

Manuel, as is well known, sought to establish friendly relations with the West, and in his eagerness to restore the unity of the Roman Empire and secure for himself recognition as emperor in the West as well as in the East, was attempting to secure the union of the Greek and Roman churches.[45] In furtherance of this ambition he asked Hugo to prepare a list of patristic authorities that would sanction the Latin doctrine of the double procession.[46] Hugo was pleased to comply with this request, which had been supported also by a similar demand on the part of the three Roman clerics who journeyed to Constantinople about 1168 in order to negotiate with Manuel for the union of the Churches.[47] The Pope (Alexander III, 1159–81) was delighted, and urged Hugo to persuade Manuel to show reverence to Rome and bring about unity in the Church by recognizing the supremacy of the Roman pope.

Hugo set about this task with great enthusiasm and even went so far, he tells us himself,[48] as to prepare a Greek version of his treatise, in order, no doubt, to win converts among the Byzantines to the Latin point of view. Aiming at two targets, he intended both to fortify his co-religionists in their defense of Latin dogma, and to convince the Byzantines that the double procession was consistent with Byzantine theological tradition and could be demonstrated out of the works of impeccable Byzantine theologians like Athanasius, Basil, John Chrysostom, and Cyril. For this reason, he took great pains to ransack Byzantine patrology for evidence proving that distinguished Byzantine authorities taught the procession of the Holy Spirit from the Father and Son. His detailed summaries and his meticulous refutations of the Byzantine objections to the double procession also indicate that he was seriously hoping to be able to persuade the Greeks that they could embrace this Latin doctrine without apprehension, and thus lay the foundation for the reconciliation with Rome toward which the Emperor Manuel aspired.

In spite of his great erudition, however, Hugo does not present an argument that can be reduced to a logical outline. Except for the first part of the third book, he did not attempt to organize his material systematically, nor did he seek to construct a case based upon points which succeed each other in order of importance according to the requirements of logic. Instead, in the manner of compilers of *catenae* and *excerpta*, Hugo piles topic on topic without attempting to subordinate or link one to another. The first and second books and the end of the third are built around the Byzantine syllogisms hostile to the Latin dogma. But in his refutation of each one of these, considered individually, he proceeds in a coherent, orderly manner. In what follows, emphasis will be laid on this part of Hugo's work. The third book, which was devoted to the affirmative defense of the double procession by metaphysical argumentation and the recitation of Biblical and patristic *testimonia*, will be left out of account, except for a summary of the section on the papacy and the oecumenical councils, and a critique of Hugo's citation of the Greek fathers.

After dedicatory epistles to Pope Alexander III and the Latin Patriarch Aimericus of Antioch, and quotations from Plato and Plotinus on the triadic division of the incorporeal universe, not without a reference to Aristotle,[49] Hugo begins by saying that the three persons, Father, Son, and Holy Spirit, are one (*unum, una unitas, una substantia, unum principium*),[50] that the Father begets (*gignit*) the Son and sends forth (*emittit*) the Holy Spirit, and that, since the Father does not differ from the Son, the Holy Spirit proceeds from the Son as well as from the Father. For, he explains, if the Spirit proceeded from only one of these two, it could not belong equally (*commune*) and without difference to both, but only to the one from which it proceeded. Since the Spirit does belong equally and without difference to both, however, it belongs no less to the Son than to the Father, and proceeds from them both.[51]

To this general definition of the Latin doctrine of the double procession, Hugo admits, the Greeks objected that, if the Holy Spirit proceeded from the Father and the Son, the Holy Spirit, being one, would have two causes (*principia*), and duality (or the number two) would be the cause of unity (or the number one). This was manifestly absurd, the Byzantine theologians, Archbishop Nicetas of Nicomedia (fl. 1135) and Bishop

Nicholas of Methone (d. 1165), had protested, since the contrary is true, unity being the constituent element or cause of duality and of all numbers.

Hugo replied first by stating, on the authority of Aristotle, that all terms in syllogisms should be of the same genus. Secondly, he declared it inaccurate of them to designate the Father and the Son as two principles, for they are not two things, substances, principles, or Gods, but, though two persons or hypostases, make up together only one principle as the source of the Holy Spirit.[52] That is, he distinguishes the divinity or the godhead—the essence, *substantia*, *usia*, or nature, which is one and is shared by Father, Son, and Holy Spirit alike—from the three hypostases or persons, who are one in essence, but nevertheless three members of the same Trinity.

Hugo himself might perhaps seem to be guilty of the very logical error he reprehends, since he is content to designate the Holy Spirit as one, that is, one person, but insists that the Father and the Son, two distinct persons (i.e., two in the same sense that the Holy Spirit is one), constitute only one nature. He attempts to extricate himself from this difficulty by comparing the unity of the Father and the Son as sources of the Holy Spirit to the distance from Thebes to Athens. The *ascensio* here is not the *descensio*, he says, or *vice versa;* nevertheless both together form one distance, not two. Similarly, he argues, the Father is not the Son, nor the Son the Father, but both of them form one *principium*, not two, just as both the Father and the Son are creators of the universe, but in the work of creation operate as one cause, creator, and principle, not two.[53]

Hugo's comparison of the Father and the Son to the distance between Athens and Thebes is perhaps ingenious, if somewhat peculiar. In other contexts, however, he imitates the Nicene theologians of the fourth century, in comparing them, more felicitously, to the sun, its rays of light, and its heat, three individualized but inseparable phenomena, which were in medieval times believed to be the same in substance, and therefore affording an excellent example of how three distinct hypostases could be regarded as consubstantial or *homousioi*.

Next, Hugo considers the contention of Nicetas of Byzantium, a disciple of Photius in the second half of the ninth century, that, if the Spirit proceeds from the Son as from the Father, the Spirit must be the son of a son (thus a grandson), and so on *ad infinitum*. For Nicetas took it to be the logical consequence of the Latin doctrine of the double procession, that that out of which the Spirit proceeds has a Son.[54] This is not

XII

only impossible and indemonstrable, Hugo objects, but is based upon the erroneous assumption that the Father as *genitor* is the *emissor* of the Spirit, that is, that the Spirit proceeds from the Father in the Father's capacity as Father of Jesus Christ, whereas, in point of fact, it is *qua cause* or *principium* that he sends forth the Spirit. According to Hugo, the Spirit is not the son of the Father, since the latter has only one son, not two. The Father does not emit the Spirit insofar as he differs from the Son, but insofar as he does not differ from the Son; and the Father differs from the Son only in those functions by which he does not project the Spirit. Or, as we should say, the Father differs from the Son only in that he begets the Son, but emits the Spirit by virtue of those qualities which he and the Son jointly possess.[55] Moreover, he adds, the attributes pertaining to all three persons together indistinguishably because of their being one in nature are far more numerous than those which uniquely and specifically characterize each one of them individually as distinct members of the Trinity.[56]

At another point, Hugo faces the objection raised by Nicetas of Nicomedia on the basis of the principle that the characteristics which are not distinctive of one of the three persons belong to all three alike.. This being so, Nicetas maintained, if the procession of the Spirit is not attributed solely to the Father but also to the Son, the projection of the Spirit will be the joint property of all the three persons, so that the Spirit will then be both the projected and the projector (*emissor simul et emissus*).[57] Here Hugo rejects the major premise (i.e., that the qualities not peculiar to one member of the Trinity are common to all three), and contends that the Father and the Son share some qualities in which the Spirit does not participate.[58]

Following somewhat the same lines as Nicetas of Nicomedia in the last syllogism, Nicholas of Methone attacked the Latins for assuming that, since the Father and the Son are one in nature, the Spirit must proceed from the Son as well as from the Father. If this reasoning be sound, Nicholas had countered, it would be equally true to say that the Son is generated by the Spirit no less than by the Father, since the Father and the Spirit are also of the same nature. Otherwise, Nicholas ironically concluded, the Spirit would not be one in nature with the Father, and the Macedonian view of the inferiority of the Spirit to the Father would be vindicated.[59]

Here again, as in the example previously noted, Hugo in effect repudiates the major premise in Nicholas' syllogism, and argues that the

Latins defend the double procession, not because the Father and the Son are one God, but because the Son is equal to the Father and to the person of the Father. He realizes that his opponents will rejoin that the Spirit is also equal to the person of the Father, and therefore should, like the Father, be regarded as the Father of the Son. This conclusion is untenable, however, in his judgment because "it is nowhere stated that the Son belongs equally to the Father and the Spirit, although all confess that the Spirit belongs equally to the Father and the Son." The Son is always mentioned alongside the Father, he avers, in all gifts of the Spirit, but it is impious to speak of the Spirit as Father or the Son as the son of the Spirit. Hugo then reiterates in several different ways his conviction that the Father's projection is not connected with his character (*proprietas*) as Father.[60]

In the Second Book, after some introductory remarks on the nature of God and the universe, in which he quotes from Aristotle and Pseudo-Dionysius, Hugo turns to grapple with a series of propositions advanced by Nicetas of Byzantium. If, Nicetas had written, the Spirit proceeds from the Son, as from the Father, the procession from the Son must be either the same as that from the Father or different. If it is different, it must be either better or worse. If it is better, the Son will necessarily be proved better than the Father. But if it is worse, the Son could not be of the same nature as the Father. On the other hand, if the procession from the Son is equal to that of the Father, it will be the same as the Father's. Then, the question arises as to whether the procession from the Son completes the existence of the Spirit or not. If it does not, it is pointless, and would violate the principle that nothing about God is in vain (*nihil autem circa Deum frustra*). But if it does actually complete the existence of the Spirit, the procession from the Father would be imperfect.[61]

Scorning all of these alternatives, Hugo insists that neither the Father nor the Son projects the Spirit *ex parte* but both project it completely, perfectly, and equally (*ex toto et perfecte uterque pariter*), for the Son, as the image of the Father, who alone derives his being directly from the Father without any intermediary (*solus enim Filius existit de Patre absque medio*), emits the Spirit as the Father does.[62]

Some Byzantine theologians (note 74 below) who refused to countenance the double procession were, however, inclined to accept a compromise, according to which the Spirit was said to proceed from the Father *through* the Son (*per Filium*, διὰ τοῦ υἱοῦ). But the most irreconcilable, like Nicetas of Nicomedia, refused to make this concession. If, Nicetas said, we hold that the Spirit proceeds from the Father *through* the Son (*ex Patre per Filium*), while the Son issues directly from the Father without intermediary (*sine medio*), the Spirit is inferior to the Son, because that which participates in something through an intermediary is inferior to that which participates in it directly. Hugo overturns Nicetas' major premise (that that which participates in something through an intermediary is inferior to that which participates in it directly) by citing the example of the Word of God, which participates in the human race through the medium of a rational soul, although no one would conclude that the Word of God is on this account inferior to the rational soul or to his Virgin Mother.[63] (See note 144, below.)

Rejecting the double procession because, among other things, it seemed to him to deny the Spirit equality with the Father and the Son, Nicholas of Methone had protested that, if we admit that the Son receives from the Father the power of producing the Spirit, we are bound to conclude that the Spirit lacks this honor since he is not enabled by the Father to be the cause of the Son or of any being like himself.[64] Hugo attacks this difficulty by quoting John 16 : 7: "Unless I go, the Paraclete will not come to you, but if I go I will send him to you," which he takes as proof that the Son produces the Spirit. Then he explains that the Spirit is not the cause of any being similar to himself, lest there be the addition of a fourth member to the Trinity. Moreover, he says, the Son is assigned the function of judging, in which the Spirit does not participate, as in John 5 : 22f.: "The Father judgeth no man but hath committed all judgment unto the Son. That all men should honor the Son, even as they honor the Father." Similarly, the Son receives the function of transmitting the Spirit from the Father, just as he receives life and judgment from the same source. Hugo apparently means, though he does not say so, that the bestowal of the function of judgment on the Son, and not on the Spirit, does not affect the honor or standing of the Spirit. But he does add that, just as the *nascibilitas* of the Son does not prevent him from having the same nature as the Father, so the procession from the Father and the Son does not prevent the Spirit from having the same nature as the Father and the Son.[65]

Hugo comes at length, near the end of the second book, to the great Patriarch Photius (858–67, 877–86), who was the chief author of the Byzantine panoply of arguments against the double procession, and the principal source of subsequent Byzantine writings on this theme. In addition to having fashioned the most devastating of the Byzantine syllogisms on the inadmissibility of *Filioque* to the Creed, Photius specifically raised the question of the juridical validity of the Latin case. Which of our fathers or priests or what oecumenical council, Photius asked, ever taught that the Spirit proceeded from the Son? The Second Council (which met in Constantinople in 381), he argued, declared that the Spirit proceeded from the Father, and this doctrine, as confirmed by five subsequent oecumenical councils, was no longer subject to revision.[66]

Hugo's reply is threefold. In the first place, he asks rhetorically, what synod sanctioned the use of leavened bread (which the Byzantine Church used in the Eucharist) or prescribed that it be cut by a lance? For he interpreted the Last Supper, celebrated by Christ before his Crucifixion, to be the paschal meal of the Jews, which necessarily involved the use of azyma (i.e., of unleavened bread). This he proves by reference to the New Testament (Luke 22 : 15: "With desire have I desired to eat this pascha with you before I suffer," and Matthew 26 : 17: "Where dost thou wish us to prepare the pascha for thee?"), and to John Chrysostom, Cyril, and Epiphanius. He defends the Latins against the charge that, in clinging to unleavened bread, they are judaizers, by pointing out that the Orthodox Church had institutionalized many practices of Jewish origin (such as the use of "temple, altar, oil, water, light, incense, images of the angels," and the custom of not shaving).[67] Then he asks what council authorized the Greeks to prescribe oil in connection with baptism, or hot water in the Eucharist, or the frequent chanting of Κύριε ἐλέησον instead of *Christe eleison*.[68]

Secondly, he admits that the Councils had taught that the Spirit proceeds from the Father and had not mentioned the Son in this connection. But, he adds, "although the Father alone is named, the Son is clearly to be understood also, both because the [Spirit] did not come forth from the Father without an intermediary,"[69] and because the Father never said that he *alone* produced the Spirit, nor did any of the prophets or fathers ever say so. In other words, he insists, John 15.26 merely indicates that "the Spirit proceeds from the Father," and does not specifically state that the Spirit proceeds "from the Father alone."[70]

Thirdly, he argues in Book III that, just as the Second Oecumenical Council in 381 added the clause on the procession of the Holy Spirit to the Nicene Creed of 325, and just as the Council of Chalcedon put out a supplement to the Creed of 381 (i.e., to the Symbol today designated in the Churches as the Creed of Nicea) to combat Nestorius and Eutyches, the Pope of Rome was justified in introducing the phrase *Filioque*. For the Pope had, and always will have, the right to "confirm the brethren, issue decrees, and set forth interpretations" when need arises. Furthermore, he urges, the Chalcedonian prohibition of additions and changes in the Creed was not affected by the insertion of *Filioque* because the latter did not alter the meaning of the Creed.[71] Thus, in the last analysis, here and in the succeeding paragraphs, Hugo vindicates *Filioque* by reason of the primacy of Rome and of the authority of the Pope as the head of all of the churches in Christendom.[72]

Hugo then refutes the criticism that the procession of the Spirit from the Son could not be eternal since the apostles and prophets received the Spirit from Christ in historical time, by alleging that this procession did not begin in time but must be understood as from all eternity, like the generation of the Son.[73] He next rejects the proposal of Nicetas of Maronea, who became archbishop of Thessalonike (fl. 1133), that the Latins give up the addition of *Filioque* to the Creed, and hearken to the teaching of Athanasius, Cyril, and John of Damascus that the Spirit proceeds from the Father *through* (*per*), rather than out of (*ex*), the Son, because he took the preposition *per* (through) with the accusative to be the equivalent of *ex* (from) with the ablative. Hence, he concludes, the Greeks who tolerate the procession *per Filium* must also accept the Latin doctrine of the procession *ex Filio*.[74]

Hugo's chief contribution to Latin theology lay in his conscientious study of Byzantine patristic literature. In the first place, he quoted or summarized the leading Byzantine arguments, and answered them as well as he could. Secondly, he was able to cite Greek authors in behalf of the double procession much more fully than previous Latin writers, like Alcuin (d. 804), Theodulph (d. 821), Aeneas of Paris (d. 870), Ratramnus (d. 868), and Anselm of Aosta (d. 1109), who had dealt with the problem far less thoroughly, and had been able to muster only a few Greek authorities on their side.[75] Having had the advantage of a long sojourn in Constantinople and free access to the great theological libraries of the capital city, Hugo succeeded in finding five Byzantine props for the Latin cause that had been unknown in the West hitherto.

Three were from the *Ancoratus* of Epiphanius (d. 403), according to which God the Spirit belongs to the Father and to the Son, is from the Father and the Son, and is from both.[76] Two others Hugo discovered in Cyril of Alexandria (d. 444), who asserts in one that the Spirit is of the Father and the Son, and proceeds in substance from both, "or rather, from the Father through the Son." But, it should be noted, Hugo disingenuously suppressed the last part of this sentence, which contradicts the point he was trying to make. Nevertheless, he was able to unearth a phrase from Cyril which represents the Spirit as coming from the Son.[77]

In addition, Hugo claims Basil of Caesarea (d. 379) as a proponent of the view that there would be no order in the Trinity unless the Father were the cause of the Son and the Holy Spirit, the Son came from the Father, and the Holy Spirit were deemed to be of both. But these words cannot be found in the extant works of Basil. Nor can it be proved that Basil's treatise, *Adversus Eunomium* (3,1), really contained the clauses which Hugo records, to the effect that the Holy Spirit derives its being from the Son (*ab ipso esse habens, et ab illo accipiens..., et quod omnino de illa causa exeat*). Even if this passage proved Hugo's point, it apparently does not occur in the earliest Greek MSS of Basil, and was repudiated by Byzantine theologians as an interpolation, notwithstanding its acceptance by the Latins and *Latinophrones* like Bessarion (d. 1472).[78]

Hugo attempts, also, to turn John of Damascus into a proponent of Latin dogma by assuming that the latter's words, "we deny that the Spirit is of the Son (*ex Filio*, ἐχ), but call him the Spirit [of the Son]," can be construed as corroborating the double procession. For, he contends, if the Spirit is the Son's, he must also proceed from the Son. Indeed, he takes this perverse exegesis so seriously that he rejects as a later addition an indubitably authentic passage from John's *Homilia in Sabbatum Sanctum*, which was indisputably and irreconcilably hostile to the Latin theory.[79]

These tactics availed him little among his Greek opponents, but his collection of excerpts from Byzantine patrology proved useful to the Latins in later times, and demonstrate a wide and penetrating knowledge of Greek theology. It must be admitted, however, that only four or five of his quotations from the Greek (notes 76 f. above) could possibly be regarded as confirming the double procession. The rest are either completely irrelevant or only very indirectly pertinent.

JOHN OF DAMASCUS AND THE
LIBRI SENTENTIARUM OF PETER THE LOMBARD

Although Hugo Eterianus stressed as strongly as he could the Byzantine authorities in whom he found, or professed to find, support for the Latin dogma of the double procession of the Holy Spirit, his primary goal was to attack a fundamental article of Byzantine theology. He appealed to Greek sources whenever it served his purposes to do so. But his intention was polemical. Despite his ostensibly eirenic goal of winning the Greeks over to the Latin view, his aim was to subvert a long established position of the Byzantine Church. He quoted the Greek fathers not so much for their own sake or to illustrate and expound a doctrinal point as such, but chiefly in order to refute and confound the Byzantine theologians of his own day out of their own theological tradition.

A very different attitude, as we shall see below, marks the reception of the new Latin translations of the great theological encyclopedia of John of Damascus, the ἔκδοσις ἀκριβὴς τῆς ὀρθοδόξου πίστεως, which the Latins usually designated as On the orthodox faith (De fide orthodoxa) and Peter the Lombard cited as De Trinitate, apparently because he thought that the Trinity was its chief topic. John flourished in the eighth century (d. 749), but his summary of orthodox theology, actually only the third division of a larger work entitled The Fountain of Knowledge (πηγὴ γνώσεως), was not rendered into Latin until sometime before 1145, when a Latin version of a portion of the text was produced in Hungary by Cerbanus. A few years later, about 1153–54, the whole of the treatise was translated by Burgundio of Pisa, whose rendition of the Greek not only held the ground until ca. 1235–40, when Robert Grosseteste issued it in a revised form, but also continued to be copied even as late as 1500. Grosseteste's recension seems not to have been transcribed after ca. 1300, and still remains unpublished. But we now have the good fortune of being able to study the methods and achievements of the two translators of the twelfth century in the admirable edition of Eligius M. Buytaert, which forms the basis for all subsequent research on this subject.[80]

The De fide orthodoxa was turned into Latin once again at the end of the medieval period by the Carmelite Johannes Baptista Panetius (d. 1497). But the other two sections of John's Fountain of Knowledge, the Dialectica (or "chapters on philosophy") and a handbook On heresies, were unknown in Latin during the Middle Ages, except for the Dialectica, which was made available by Robert Grosseteste.

Considerable energy has been devoted to these Latin translations, and much progress has been made in identifying passages in the writings of Peter the Lombard, Arno and Gerhoh of Reichersberg, and other writers of the twelfth century who show acquaintance with John of Damascus. But the scholars who have investigated this question have satisfied themselves with the selfless task of editing texts and listing parallel passages, without attempting to evelute the substantive theological use that was made of these materials.[81]

Accordingly it may be of interest to examine the quotations from John of Damascus carefully in order to determine the precise role played by him in the twelfth century. Special interest attaches to the references to John made by Peter the Lombard, whose four *Libri Sententiarum* (*ca.* 1155–57), after some vicissitudes in the twelfth century, received the stamp of orthodoxy in the thirteenth, especially with regard to Trinitarian questions, and exerted a truly enormous influence upon Latin thought in the Middle Ages and even subsequently.[82] There is no doubt that the great popularity of Peter's *Sententiae* and the influence of his example were important factors in the great prestige which the views of John of Damascus acquired in the twelfth century and above all in the thirteenth, when Thomas Aquinas, Albertus Magnus, Robert Grosseteste, Alexander of Hales, Bonaventura,[83] and many others, in no small measure affected by the precedent set by Peter in this regard, relied heavily upon John as a major theological authority. In the twelfth century, writers like Peter of Poitiers (d. 1205),[84] Gandulphus of Bologna (d. *ca.* 1185),[85] an anonymous *Summa Sententiarum*,[86] and Stephen Langton (d. 1228),[87] to name only a few,[88] borrowed extensively from Peter the Lombard, and derived at least some of their citations of John of Damascus from him. Others, like Gerhoh (d. 1169)[89] and Arno (d. 1175) of Reichersberg,[90] Simon of Tournai (d. 1201),[91] Alan of Lille (d. 1202),[92] and William of Auxerre (d. 1247),[93] apparently were independent of Peter in their citation of John.

Peter usually refers to John as Ioannes Damascenus, or simply as Ioannes. Like most of his contemporaries, Peter gives no indication of acquaintance with more than the third book of John's great theological encyclopedia. This circumstance led some scholars to infer that Peter had secured a Latin translation limited to the first three books. But it has recently been argued that he had seen the whole of Burgundio's *De fide orthodoxa*, but did not have the opportunity of studying more than a portion of it at the time that he was composing the *Sententiae*. However this may be, it has been shown that Peter originally used Cerbanus' version, and subsequently corrected it at some points after he had seen Burgundio's.[94]

Passages from John of Damascus frequently occupy a key position in Peter's patristic armory,[95] and are cited to reinforce major points of doctrine. In all but one of these, Peter finds John's treatment of the subject in hand extremely congenial as a principal source and justification of his own views. In this one instance, however, Peter disagrees with

John, and rejects an analogy used by the latter in expounding the relation of the divine essence (*substantia, essentia*) of the Godhead to the three persons of the Trinity.[96] The Cappadocian fathers in the fourth century had explained the paradox of how the Father, the Son, and the Holy Spirit, though three in number and all divine, were nevertheless not three Gods but only one. This they had done in part by comparing the relationship between the divine substance and the three members of the Trinity to that which obtains between men and the human race. John, Peter, and Andrew, for example, are three in number, they had maintained, but only one in nature because, as members of the human race, all three have the same nature.[97]

Following in their footsteps, and faithful to his boast that he was in no sense an innovator but only a recorder of patristic tradition, John of Damascus had said that "that which is general or universal is predicated of the particulars that belong to this category. Hence, (in the Godhead) the substance is the universal, and the hypostasis is the particular—particular not as possessing a portion of the nature, but particular in number, like an individual. For the hypostases are said to differ in number, not in nature."[98] As John had said on another occasion, "substance indicates the common category that embraces hypostases of the same nature, like God or man. But the hypostasis designates the individual, like Father, Son, and Holy Spirit, or Peter and Paul."[99]

After quoting these two texts from John, Peter points out that the doctrine they embody (that God is the universal like man or mankind, and that the Father, Son, and Holy Spirit are individuals like Peter and Paul), contradicts Augustine. In this case, he preferred to follow Augustine's conclusion that three men, though of the same nature, are not only one man but three, and that two men are something more than one man, whereas in the Godhead the Father and the Son together are not greater in essence than the Father alone or the Son alone, since the three persons together are equal to each person individually.[100]

Of course, John of Damascus would not have denied the proposition set forth in the last sentence, and in another context Peter depends upon John as his sole authority for maintaining that: "the Father is not greater than the Son, nor is the Father or the Son greater than the Holy Spirit, nor are two persons [of the Trinity] together greater than one, nor are three together greater than two, nor is the essence greater in three than in two, nor in two rather than one, since the whole is in each." This concept Peter borrowed from John, who, as Peter notes, had said, "We confess the whole nature (*naturam*, φύσιν) of the Godhead to be present in its entirety (*perfecte*, τελείως) in each of its hypostases [or persons]: the whole [of it] in the Father, the whole in the Son, the whole in the Holy Spirit. Therefore, God the Father is perfect, God the Son is perfect, God the Holy Spirit is perfect."[101]

Though Peter disavows John's application of the relation between the universal and the particular to that which obtains between the divine substance and the three persons, he introduces John's words on this subject by remarking that he was one of the great Greek authorities (*inter Graecorum doctores magnus*), whose *De Trinitate* had been translated into Latin at the instance of Pope Eugene III. But he then adds that what John really meant was unobjectionable. For, he says, John applied the terms, universal and particular, to the Trinity and its three persons respectively because of the similarity which he descried between eternal and temporal categories, not because he intended to apply philosophical modes of reasoning to God. Augustine, on the other hand, Peter remarks, felt the difference between the eternal and temporal categories more keenly than such similarity as may have appeared between them, and consequently considers these designations unsuitable for the Trinity.[102]

Peter probably found the passages from Augustine on which he relied in Abelard or Hugh of St. Victor.[103] But this philosophical attitude stemmed from John Scotus Erigena's *De divisione naturae*, I,1, according to which God was neither genus, species, nor accident. Erigena, in turn, who had translated the works of the Pseudo-Dionysius the Areopagite from Greek into Latin, derived from the latter and from Augustine's *De Trinitate*, as he specifically states, the notion that none of the ten Aristotelian categories is applicable to God. The concept itself can be traced back to Philo, Clement of Alexandria, and the Neoplatonists.[104]

In the next *capitulum* of the same *Distinctio*, Peter singles out for special treatment the statement of John quoted in the previous section that the hypostases differ in number, not in nature. He agrees that they do not differ in nature. But he is unwilling to accept John's dictum that they differ in number if the difference envisaged denotes a difference of individuals or particulars (in the way that Socrates, e.g., differs from Plato). On the other hand, he recognizes another kind of numerical difference among things which in enumeration or computation are not added to each other (viz., to form a larger whole, unit, or amount) but are distinguished from each other, as one, two, or three in number. In this latter sense, he concedes, it is possible to say that the Father is one, the

Father and Son are two, and the Father, Son, and Holy Spirit are three, and, similarly, that this person is one, this and that person are two, and this, that, and the other person are three. Even so, he concludes, it is more appropriate that these three persons be distinguished by their properties and in no other way.[105]

Like Peter the Lombard, Peter of Poitiers in his *Sententiae* examines John's doctrine that the divine *substantia* could be defined as the universal and the *hypostasis* as the particular. He agrees with the Lombard both in giving the preference to Augustine in this matter, and in granting that there is an analogy between the philosophical terminology and the relation of the divine substance to the three hypostases.[106] But, unlike the Lombard, he adopts without qualification John's definition of the hypostases as differing from each other in number, not in nature. He omits altogether the objections noted above and merely reproduces faithfully what Peter had said about the kind of numerical difference he would accept with regard to the Trinity. Imitating the Lombard, Peter of Poitiers explains that "One thing is said to differ from another because it is not that or anything which the other is, nor is it contained in the other. Thus, the Father is not said to differ from the Son in number because he is what the Son is and is in the Son. But he is said to differ from him in number because he is counted with him, since it can be said that the Father, Son, and Holy Spirit are three, or (in regard to two of them) are two."[107]

Like the majority of Latin theologians, Peter had taken over the Byzantine Trinitarian formula, μία οὐσία ἐν τρισὶν ὑποστάσεσι, which had been translated into Latin in the form, *una substantia, essentia, natura,* or *usia* and *tres personae, hypostases,* or *subsistentiae*—one substance in three persons. This he found not only in John of Damascus,[108] whom he quotes, but also in Jerome's Epistle to Damasus on the Catholic faith. He does not share the antagonism which marked Robert of Melun's attitude to these Byzantine terms; but, like Jerome, he warns that "poison lurks within the honey," and that the word *hypostasis* should be used as an equivalent for *persona,* not for *usia* or *natura,* with which the heretics deliberately equated it, as if there were three divine natures rather than one.[109]

Peter appeals to the authority of John of Damascus in support of a number of basic theological propositions. Thus, in expounding the dogma that the distinguishing features of the three persons determine the *hypostases* (of the three persons) and not the substance or nature of the

Godhead, he repeats John's exposition of this matter.[110] John had explained that the three hypostases differ from each other, not in their substance, but in the qualities which characterize them as distinct persons. That is, as John put it, the hypostasis (or person) of the Word (i.e., Jesus Christ) is consubstantial (*homousios*) with the Father and has all that the Father has, being distinguished from the Father's hypostasis only by having been begotten, but in no way separated (*secedentem*) from the Father's hypostasis.

This was the method of reasoning by which Athanasius and the Cappadocian fathers in the fourth century had proved that the belief in the Trinity did not compromise monotheism. Insisting that the three persons were one in substance, they made a special effort to demonstrate that the ways in which the Trinity could be regarded as made up of three persons did not destroy the divine unity. Their solution of this problem, which has remained authoritative ever since, was incorporated into the theological encyclopedia of John of Damascus, who summarized the teaching of his predecessors on this topic in the passage quoted here by Peter.[111] We recognize the difference of the hypostases, John had said, in the three characteristics of paternity, sonship, and procession, although the three hypostases are inseparable and undivided. Still, they are united without confusion and remain three, each being perfect and retaining its own characteristics and mode of existence. Thus, they are distinguished but unseparated (*divisas... indistanter*), and, by reason of the unity of substance, they are not divided from the hypostasis of the Father.[112]

Peter then directs this same definition against the School of Gilbert de la Porrée, which had accused him of Sabellianism. Peter maintained that the properties or distinctive attributes of the three persons of the Trinity are in the three persons, and are themselves the persons and the divine essence (*fateamur ergo et proprietates [personarum] esse in tribus personis, et ipsas esse personas atque divinam essentiam*).[113] But the Porretani contended that, if the properties or individual characteristics of the hypostases are in the divine essence or are themselves the divine essence, the three persons of the Trinity would not differ in any respect, since all three are of the same essence. This, they objected, would eliminate the distinction of the persons, and lead to Sabellianism, according to which the Trinity consisted, not of three distinct eternal persons, but only of three temporary manifestations of the divine essence which succeeded each other in time and did not exist simultaneously.[114]

Peter replied by citing John's dictum that the properties of the hypostases determine the hypostases, not the divine nature. According to the Lombard, these words mean that the properties of *Paternitas* (of God the Father) and Sonship (of Jesus Christ), though being in the divine essence, are not present therein to the same extent that they are in the individual hypostases. Hence, he concludes, it is not correct to say that the divine essence both generates (as a Father) and is generated (as a Son). For the property determines the person, so that, by reason of one property, one hypostasis (the Father's) generates, and, by reason of another property, another hypostasis (the Son's) is generated.[115]

Proceeding then in Book III to Christology, Peter Lombard leans upon John of Damascus to demonstrate that what the divine Logos assumed was a complete human nature, including a human body and rational soul, with all their qualities, and that he was perfect God and also perfect man.[116] These citations from John were aimed at the Monophysites, who held that Jesus Christ had only one nature, the divine, after the incarnation, and at the Apollinarians, who taught that the divine Logos at the incarnation assumed only a human body and a human vegetative soul, but not a human rational soul (or mind).

At the end of this *Distinctio*, Peter reproduces from John a famous anti-Apollinarian text, "What was not assumed was not saved." This was derived ultimately from the Cappadocian fathers, who had formulated it in the course of their polemic against the Apollinarian conception that Christ did not have a human rational soul. It summed up admirably the orthodox objection that if the reasoning power in the incarnate Jesus Christ were not truly human, but only the divine Logos which the Son of God had brought down from heaven, redemption would not have been complete, for the human mind, which required salvation as much as human flesh did, would not then have had any part in Christ and therefore could not have been affected by his triumph over sin and death.[117]

In the second *capitulum* of the same *Distinctio*, Peter turns to John for confirmation of the Christological axiom current in the middle of the twelfth century that the Son of God was united to human flesh through the medium of the soul (*mediante anima*). He reproduces only the sentence in which John declared that this union was mediated by the mind (νοῦς). But his analysis shows that he was familiar with the whole paragraph from which this quotation was drawn. He obviously knew that John had declared the mind to be (the loftiest) part of the soul, and he agrees with John that the mediation of the mind was necessary in order to effect a transition between the purity of God and the coarseness of flesh.[118]

Similarly upon John of Damascus Peter bases the doctrine that, before the earthly generation of Jesus Christ, the Holy Spirit purified the Virgin Mary and made her capable both of receiving the deity of the Logos and of conceiving him, so that the Son of God, who was consubstantial with the Father, overshadowed her "like divine semen" (*sicut divinum semen*) and joined to himself of the Virgin real human flesh that had a rational soul. But the incarnation itself involved on the part of the Logos, not an act of insemination, but an act of creation through the Holy Spirit (*non seminans, sed per Spiritum sanctum creans*).[119]

Despite his manhood, which was complete and total in every sense of the word, Lombard demonstrated by quoting from John, Christ remained completely uncircumscribed. Corporeally, he experienced physical limitations, but he continued to be uncircumscribed in his divine nature, since his flesh was not co-extensive with his uncircumscribed divinity. "Thus," as John had said, "Christ was simultaneously in all things, and beyond them, both when he lay in the womb of the Virgin and in the very moment of incarnation."[120]

Peter then addresses himself to the delicate problem of whether it was a person or a nature which, in the human generation of Christ, assumed a person or nature, and whether it was correct to say that the nature of God became incarnate. Peter at the outset pronounces in favor of the proposition that it was not a nature or a person which assumed a person in Jesus Christ, but rather a person who assumed a nature—that is, he means, the person of the divine Logos, who took on human nature in Jesus Christ.[121] But in reviewing the ecclesiastical authorities on this matter (Augustine, the eighth and eleventh councils of Toledo, Hilary of Poitiers, and Jerome), he notes that there is a conflict of opinion, not only, as he says, among the various theologians who had written on this subject, but even within the writings of the same author. In order to eliminate contradictions, he declares himself satisfied with the conclusion that it was both the person of the Son and the divine nature itself which were joined to the human nature in the Son.[122] For, he explains, the fact that the Son alone is said to have taken on the form of a servant excludes the other two persons, the Father and the Holy Spirit, but not the divine nature itself, from the assumption of the form of a servant. Furthermore, he says, the doctrine that the incarnation is associated with what is specifically or characteristically the Son's (*id quod est proprium Filii*), not with what is common to the Trinity (*non quod commune est Trinitati*), must be understood as signifying that it was the divine nature in the hypostasis of the Son (*proprie in hypostasi Filii*), and not as existing in common to the three persons (*non in tribus communiter personis*), which was united with the human nature.[123]

This solution he adopts directly from John of Damascus, who had asserted that "in the incarnation of God the Word, the whole, perfect nature of the divinity became incarnate (i.e., was joined to human nature) in one of its hypostases." In this union, it was not merely a part united with a part, but "the whole nature or substance of the divinity that was joined with the whole of human nature." That is, John says, "it is the same nature which subsists in each of the hypostases, and when we say that the nature of the Word became incarnate, we mean, according to the blessed Athanasius and Cyril, that the divinity was joined to flesh, and we confess one incarnate nature of God the Word. For the Word possesses both that which is common to the (divine) substance and that which is distinctive of the hypostasis or person."[124]

It is of no small significance in the history of the Byzantine influence in the Latin West in the twelfth century that John of Damascus is used to resolve so important a conflict and lead to a conclusion of great significance in Christology. It is somewhat ironical, however, that the ancient Apollinarian trick, which circulated the heretical writings of Apollinarius in the fourth century under the protective mantle of the venerable name of Athanasius, the indefectibly orthodox champion of the Nicene theology, whose authority none would dare to question, not only deceived Cyril of Alexandria in the fifth century, the Emperor Justinian in the sixth, and John of Damascus in the middle of the eighth, but under these distinguished auspices imposed also upon Latin theology, and left its stamp upon both the *Sententiae* of Peter Lombard and the *Summa* of Thomas Aquinas.[125]

Actually, the formula, *una natura Dei Verbi incarnata* (see note 124), one incarnate nature of God the Word, is plainly heretical, and was condemned by the fathers in the fourth century, as well as by the Fourth Oecumenical Council, which met at Chalcedon in 451, because it denied that Christ had two natures—the divine and the human. It was not until the sixth century that the fraud was discovered.[126] But then it was too late, and the orthodox have always defended the formula, explaining that it really implies two natures. Nevertheless, it is from the logical point of view unfortunate that the Apollinarian deception succeeded, both because it enabled the Monophysites to claim the support of Athanasius for their view that Jesus Christ had only one nature, and because it forced Cyril, Justinian, and other defenders of orthodoxy into extremely tortuous paths of argument, which otherwise could have been avoided.

Further on in the third book of the *Sentences*, Peter summarizes at length three different theories of the nature of the "hypostatic union" of God and man in Christ. He marshals excerpts from the fathers in support of each of the three, and notes also what he took to be the weak points of the first and the second, the latter of which was espoused by John of Damascus and represented the position of the Church as a whole. But since he refrains from offering any criticism of the third, it has been conjectured that he himself was one of its advocates, and accordingly believed that the human flesh and soul of Jesus were not combined with the divine nature in order to form a person, but served as the garment (*velut indumento*) of God the Word, so that he might become visible to mortal eyes. The proponents of this view held that God became man *secundum habitum*, i.e., by being clad with the flesh and soul of a man, and were therefore led to deny that Christ, so far as he was a man (*secundum quod homo*), was a substantial reality (*persona* or *aliquid*).[127]

This Christological nihilism, as it has been called, was untenable and was condemned after Peter's death by Pope Alexander III (1159–81). But John of Cornwall in his polemic against it stoutly affirmed that it was only an *opinio* of the school of Abelard put forward by Peter for discussion, not an *assertio* of the latter's own final judgment. Apparently Peter Lombard himself had also disclaimed responsibility for such *opiniones*.[128] Thus we cannot be certain whether Peter favored or opposed the second of these three hypotheses, that of John of Damascus. Whatever Peter's own attitude may have been, he sets forth John's exposition of the hypostatic union in some detail; and the Church, including Thomas Aquinas, has followed John of Damascus on this matter.[129]

John, Peter shows, compensated fully for the ambiguity of the Christological formula (notes 124–26) he had unwittingly taken over from the Apollinarians by his unequivocally dyophysite ("two-natured") description of the two perfect natures—the divinity and the humanity—united in one composite hypostasis (*composita hypostasis*, ὑπόστασις σύνθετος), which had once been the *simplex* (ἁπλῆ) *hypostasis* of the Logos alone but which, after the incarnation, became the vehicle not only for the properties and characteristics of Christ's divine Sonship (*divinae Dei-Verbi filiationis characteristicum et determinativum idioma*, τῆς θείας τοῦ Θεοῦ Λόγου υἱότητος τὸ χαρακτηριστικὸν καὶ ἀφοριστικὸν ἰδίωμα), by which he is distinguished from the Father and the Holy Spirit, but also for the properties and characteristics of the flesh which marked him as an individual man who was different from Mary and other men.

It is regrettable that Peter terminates his quotation here and does not add the next few lines, in which John completes his classical definition of Christ's hypostasis. Still, in his next excerpt from John, Peter makes it clear that John ruled out both Nestorianism and Monophysitism. Nestorianism he eliminates by stressing the fact that the two natures are united without separation or division in one composite hypostasis. He does away with Monophysitism by insisting that, in coming together, the two natures suffer neither confusion, conversion, nor change, and are united in a substantial (οὐσιώδης) union. By this he means that the union is real (ἀληθής), not illusory, and that the two natures do not supplement each other so as to form one composite nature (φύσις σύνθετος), but are truly joined together in one composite hypostasis. Here the difference of the two natures is preserved, the created remaining created, the uncreated uncreated, the mortal mortal, the immortal immortal, the circumscribable circumscribable, and the uncircumscribable uncircumscribable, of which the one, as Leo I (440–61) had said, coruscates with miracles, and the other is subjected to indignities.[130]

The divine continues as it was, John adds in Peter's next selection from the *De fide orthodoxa;* the human is neither transformed into the divine nor eliminated; and the two do not form one composite nature, compounded out of divinity and humanity, since such a nature would be consubstantial (*homousion*) with neither of the natures out of which it was composed, and such a Jesus Christ would be consubstantial neither with God nor with Mary, and could then be called neither God nor man. On the contrary, Christ, John says, is perfect God and perfect man and is confessed to be both of and in two natures.[131] John reinforces this point by attacking the position of the Adoptionists and their followers that Christ was only an ordinary man who by God's grace had been predestined and enabled to become, but had not been eternally, Son of God. Such a Christ, John felt, could not have been truly God from all eternity, as the earliest tradition of the Church declared him to have been. He therefore takes pains to refute Adoptionism with the pronouncement, quoted by Peter, that Jesus Christ was "not a deified man but God, who became man."[132]

It is not clear whether Peter would have agreed with John that this affirmation was essential to safeguard the perfection of Christ's divinity.

But he realized that the corollary of this proposition, which asserted the completeness of Christ's human nature, was altogether indispensable. Christ must have been fully divine, the theologians had taught, in order to make possible the resurrection and redemption of mankind. He had also to have been fully man, in order to guarantee that all mankind might have a share in his redemptive work. If he had not been truly God, he could not have conquered sin and death. Had he not been truly man, mankind could not have benefited from his victory. This reasoning was founded upon the belief that Christ was both the Son of God the Father, as God, and of Mary, as man. Hence, Peter devotes the final *capitulum* of the next *Distinctio* to Christ's double nativity, which affirms this doctrine; and he expounds it on the basis of Augustine and John, according to the latter of whom "we venerate two nativities of Christ: the one [whereby he was begotten] of God before the ages, which is beyond cause, reason, time, and nature; the other, which took place in these latter days, for our sake ... and for our salvation....," when he was born miraculously of the Holy Spirit and the Virgin.[133]

This paragraph from the *De fide orthodoxa*, which was anti-Adoptionist and anti-Monophysite in purpose, is a paraphrase of a part of the Chalcedonian Symbol, as also is the sentence adduced from John on the nature of Christ's humanity, which John had defined (*tradit auctoritas*) as including all human characteristics save sin.[134] Still, Peter says elsewhere, again on the authority of Augustine and John, though the flesh of Christ was perfectly human in all respects, except for sin, it could properly be worshipped, because it was not just ordinary flesh (*nudam carnem*) but flesh in union with deity, since both natures of Christ, the human and the divine, had been brought together in the one hypostasis [i.e., person] of God the Word. Like Cyril of Alexandria, John had compared this relationship of the divine and the human in Christ to a piece of coal (cf. the human nature), which becomes dangerous to touch only when it has been brought into contact with fire (cf. the divine nature).[135]

Finally, it was in the *De fide orthodoxa* that Peter found warrant for interpreting the gender of the adjectives used for the Godhead as a whole and for God and Christ. Following the patristic tradition, John had explained that the neuter adjective (*totum*) applied to the "nature" and the masculine (*totus*) to the hypostasis ("person"). Thus, one could say that "totus Christus est Deus perfectus" and "totus [est] homo perfectus," but not "totum," since Christ is both God and man, not just one or the other. On this account, Peter observes, it is correct to affirm that *totus*

Christus, that is, the whole *person* of Christ, which includes the two natures, the human and divine, is in heaven, in the grave, and everywhere. If the neuter adjective (*totum*) were used, however, the reference would be, not to the person of Jesus Christ, but only to the entirety of *one* of his two natures. For this reason the fathers had believed that *tres unum* [neuter] *sunt* (the three are one *thing*—the divine nature of the Trinity), and hence all equally God, but can be distinguished, *alius* and *alius* [masculine], as distinct persons.[136]

Especially noteworthy is Peter's appeal to John of Damascus as his major authority in elucidating the fundamentals of orthodox Christology, according to which Jesus Christ had two perfect natures, the divine and the human, united in one hypostasis or person, without confusion or change, division or separation. In this respect Peter was followed by Arno of Reichersberg (d. 1175),[137] neither of whom based his analysis of this doctrine upon the dyophysite creed of Chalcedon, which had been promulgated at the Fourth Oecumenical Council in 451, and had remained ever since the orthodox definition of Christology in both the East and the West. Their reliance on John of Damascus rather than on the dogmatic decree of Chalcedon illustrates the exalted position which the name of the former had attained. It is even more significant, perhaps, that the entire twelfth century seems to have been of one mind with them in this respect. For recent researches indicate that the scholars of this era depended heavily upon John of Damascus for an authoritative résumé of the orthodox dyophysite Christology, and usually ignored the symbol of 451.[138]

Equally striking is the somewhat similar neglect of the Nicene Creed, the touchstone of orthodoxy on Trinitarian dogma. It is indeed remarkable that, like the majority of his contemporaries, Peter Lombard refrains from transcribing or summarizing the text of these two important oecumenical formularies. He does, however, reproduce a few words from the article on the Holy Spirit in his defense of the double procession, but he attributes them to the Council of Nicea (325), not realizing that this article did not appear in the Creed until the Council of 381.[139]

The Chalcedonian Creed was quoted in its entirety only once in the twelfth century, by Walter of St. Victor in the *Contra quatuor labyrinthos Franciae*,[140] which he wrote (*ca.* 1178) as an attack upon Peter Abelard, Peter Lombard, Peter of Poitiers, and Gilbert de la Porrée. These four Walter denounces as the four labyrinths, or, by metonymy, the four

Minotaurs, the most abominable monsters of France. Since he condemns John of Damascus along with the "four labyrinths," it is not surprising that he felt obliged to seek out a more congenial authority on Christology. He was probably pleased to be able to refer to the Council of Chalcedon rather than to John of Damascus, whom he repeatedly brands as a heretic. Yet even he was compelled, on occasion, to buttress his argument with theological principles enunciated by John.[141]

John is outranked by Augustine and others in bulk of citation in Peter Lombard's *Libri sententiarum*. But he stands high as a decisive spokesman on basic principles of Christian doctrine; and the Lombard's respectful attitude towards John may be taken as an illustration of the profound indebtedness of the medieval world and of our own era to Byzantine thought. In the twelfth century, the *De fide orthodoxa* was valued both as an authoritative summary of dogmatic theology, and as a key that enabled the Latin West to unlock a great treasury of patristic literature, most of which had been previously unavailable.

IMPORTANCE OF BYZANTIUM IN THE HISTORY OF CIVILIZATION

Even after this brief summary, it should be obvious that the influence of Byzantine art and theology on the West during the twelfth century was extensive, deep, and penetrating. This was only a partial manifestation of the same forces which Byzantium exerted not only upon the Middle Ages and the Renaissance, but also upon the modern world.

This influence extended to many other aspects of life as well. Roman law, for example, as codified by Byzantine jurists under Justinian I, and Byzantine political theory experienced a revival in the twelfth century,[142] and have contemporary relevance—the latter as the prototype of Soviet absolutism, which has its Byzantine aspects, and the former as the foundation of the legal systems of continental Europe, Latin America, and the sovereign state of Louisiana.

Perhaps, in conclusion, it may be of interest to mention one case of the Byzantine transmission of the classics which transformed the whole of modern history and affords an example of the dependence of the empirical sciences on the humanities that may be of some relevance in this age of tragic unawareness on the part of many in high places that the liberal arts are indispensable to our way of life, and must be cultivated intensively if we are to survive.

I refer to the geographical encyclopedia (τὰ Γεωγραφικά) of Strabo, a

Greek who flourished at the end of the first century before Christ. The Latin West knew nothing of Strabo until the Council of Ferrara-Florence (1438–39), when George Gemistus Pletho (*ca.* 1355–1452), a Byzantine philosopher celebrated in both the East and the West as the greatest scholar of his day, made a determined effort to persuade the Latin scientists whom he met to study the Strabonic geography. Strabo, Pletho felt, deserved particular attention because of what he had to say about the circumnavigability of Africa, which Ptolemy had pronounced to be landlocked, and because of his belief in the existence of unknown but habitable lands east of India. Eventually Pletho succeeded, and in 1458 Guarino Guarini completed a Latin translation of the Greek text of τὰ Γεωγραφικά.

This Latin version had an immediate effect upon Renaissance geography and may have affected the Portuguese voyages around Africa. Most important of all, Christopher Columbus frequently cites Strabo, and is said by his son to have counted Strabo among his chief authorities for believing that, by sailing due west along the latitude of Athens, it would be possible to reach new lands lying east of India. Thus, although we should not credit Pletho and Byzantium with a direct share in the discovery of America, we must recognize that, in interesting the scholars of the West in Strabo's *Geography*, Pletho made an important contribution to the development of the geographical theory of the Renaissance, which reached its culmination in the great achievement of Columbus.[143]

NOTES

1   In what follows the word Byzantine has reference to the Greek Medieval Empire, which fringed the Mediterranean and flourished from 284, the year of the accession of the Emperor Diocletian, to May 29, 1453, when the capital city of Constantinople fell to the Ottoman Turks.

I am grateful to my friends, Professors Marshall Clagett, Gaines Post, and Robert L. Reynolds, of the University of Wisconsin for their invitation to write this paper and for the opportunity to visit the vigorous school of medieval and renaissance studies they have established. I am indebted for counsel and friendly encouragement to my colleagues, Professors Harry A. Wolfson, Eberhard F. Bruck, and George H. Williams, and acknowledge with gratitude the assistance of my student, Mr. Robert D. Crouse, who helped me with a number of problems.

I owe the reference to Herrade de Lansberg (n.27 below) to Professor Cyril Mango. N.b.: Albert Siegmund, *Die Überlieferung der griechischen christlichen Literatur in der lateinischen Kirche bis zum zwölften Jahrhundert* (Abhandlungen der Bayerischen Benediktiner-Akademie, 5 [Munich-Pasing, 1949]), does *not* cover the twelfth century.

2 L. Bréhier, *Vie et mort de Byzance* (*Le monde byzantin*, 1 [Paris, 1947], pp. 278 f.,; G. Ostrogorsky, *History of the Byzantine State*, tr. J. Hussey (Oxford, 1956), pp. 305 f.; J. Gay, *L'Italie méridionale et l'empire byzantin* (*Bibliothèque des écoles françaises d'Athènes et de Rome*, 90 [Paris, 1904]), 535–38; F. Chalandon, *Histoire de la domination normande en Italie et en Sicile*, 1 (Paris, 1907), 184–90. See also P. Lamma, *Comneni e Staufer, ricerche sui rapporti fra Bisanzio e l'Occidente nel secolo xii* (2 vols.; *Istituto storico italiano per il medio evo, studi storici*, 14–18, 22–25 [Rome, 1955–57]).

   In the same year, the Byzantine Empire suffered a grievous defeat at Manzikert, in Armenia, north of Lake Van, which put an end to effective Byzantine domination in northern Asia Minor.—Bréhier, *op. cit.*, p. 281; C. Cahen, "La campagne de Manzikert d'après les sources musulmanes," *Byzantion*, 9 (1934), 613–42.

3 S. Runciman, *The Eastern Schism* (Oxford, 1955), maintains that it is not possible to fix upon a precise date for the break between the two Churches.

4 J. de Ghellinck, *Le mouvement théologique du xiie siècle* (*Museum Lessianum, section historique*, 10 [Brussels-Paris, 1948]), pp. 179 n. 1 f., 184 n. 2, 257, 264, 402 f., 406 n. 4, 467 n. 6. Cf. note 44 below.

5 For biographical sketch, see R. M. Martin, ed., *Œuvres de Robert de Melun*, Vol. 1 (*Spicilegium sacrum Lovaniense, Études et documents*, 13 [Louvain, 1932]), vi ff.; Vol. 3, 1, *ibid.*, 21 (1947), 37.14 and note (cf. F. Anders, *Christologie*, cited, note 19 below, p. xiii).

6 Martin, *Œuvres de Robert de Melun*, Vol. 3.1 (*Spicilegium*, 21), 36.22–44.15. On the date see *ibid.*, p. vi.

7 *Ibid.*, 36.25 f.: qui greculum sermonem locutioni lingue latine velut panniculum late splendentem interserunt.

8 *Ibid.*, 37.13: nil dulce sapiant nisi quod est amaritudine fellis confectum.

9 *Ibid.*, 37.29 f.

10 *Ibid.*, 41.10 ff.

11 *Ibid.*, 40.33 ff. Cf. on these words, J. de Ghellinck, "L'entrée d'essentia, substantia, et autres mots apparentés, dans le latin médiéval," *Bulletin du Cange, Archivum latinitatis medii aevi*, 16 (1942), 77–112; *idem*, "L'histoire de 'persona' et d' 'hypostasis' dans un écrit anonyme porrétain du xiie siècle," *Revue néoscolastique de philosophie*, 36 (2nd series, 41, 1934), 111–27; cf. Heinrich Dörrie, "'Υπόστασις. Wort- und Bedeutungsgeschichte," *Nachrichten der Akademie der Wissenschaften, Philol.-Hist. Kl.*, Nr. 3 (Göttingen, 1955), 35–92. Somewhat before 1148, the anonymous author of "A Short Treatise on the Trinity from the School of Thierry of Chartres," ed. N. M. Haring, *Mediaeval Studies*, 18 (1956), 125–34, discusses four Greek synonyms for the Latin *substantia* (pp. 126 f., 129 f.).

12 Martin, *Œuvres de Robert de Melun*, Vol. 1 (*Spicilegium*, 13), viii f. Cf. note 42 below.

13 *Ibid.*, Vol. 3.1 (*Spicilegium*, 21), 43.6 ff.

14   Migne, *Patrologia Latina*, 176, 1131A. On notes 14–16 see M. D. Chenu, *La théologie au douzième siècle* (Paris, 1957), pp. 287 f.

15   Epistle 16, Migne, *P.L.*, 193, 555A.

16   Migne, *P.L.*, 180, 288A; M. D. Chenu, "*Involucrum*, le mythe selon les théologiens médiévaux," *Archives d'histoire doctrinale et littéraire du moyen âge*, 22 (1955), 78; "Le *Contra quatuor labyrinthos Franciae* de Gauthier de Saint-Victor," ed. P. Glorieux, *ibid.*, 19 (1952), 187–335; see p. 335 for list of references to John of Damascus and n. 100 below; cf. *ibid.*, p. 319, in which John's opinion is accepted as authoritative (note 115 below); *idem*, "Mauvaise action et mauvais travail. Le 'Contra quatuor labyrinthos Franciae,'" *Recherches de théologie ancienne et médiévale*, 21 (1954), 179–93.

17   Martin, *Œuvres de Robert de Melun*, Vol. 1 (1932), vii.

18   *Idem*, *ibid.*, Vol. 2 (*Spicilegium*, 18 [1938]), lvii f., 6.1–4, 8.7–9, 13.7 f., 197.19 f., 227.9 f., 257.12 f., 305.1–3, cf. 127.21; *ibid.*, Vol. 1 (1932), li f., 48.6 f., 53.17–20, cf. 18.1 f.

19   *Sententie*, 2, 25, ed. F. Anders, *Die Christologie des Robert von Melun* (*Forschungen zur christlichen Literatur- und Dogmengeschichte*, 15.5 [Paderborn, 1927]), 56.15–17, cf. vi–xv; *De fide orthodoxa*, 3, 6 (Migne, *P.G.*, 94, 1004B); *Petri Lombardi Libri iv Sententiarum studio et cura PP. Collegii S. Bonaventurae*, Vol. 2 (2nd ed.; Ad Claras Aquas, 1916), 3, 5, 1, p. 570 n. 30. Anders' text is taken from the shorter recension of the *Sententie*, which Martin, *Œuvres de Robert de Melun* (Vol. 1 [1932], xiii; *idem*, *Revue d'histoire ecclésiastique*, 28 [1932], 313–29), deems to be an abridgment of Robert's work prepared by his disciples and not by his own hand. The second volume of the *Sententie*, Martin, *Œuvres de Robert de Melun*, Vol. 3.2 (*Spicilegium*, 25 [1952]), edited for publication after Martin's death by R. M. Gallet, has reached only Book 1, part 6.

20   On the Byzantine contempt for the Latins, see the references to sources collected by G. Buckler, *Anna Comnena* (Oxford, 1929), pp. 440–43, 449–52, 458–61, 469–72, 476–78, 539 (*s.v. Crusaders*), and *passim;* and Φ. Κουκουλές, Θεσσαλονίκης Εὐσταθίου τὰ λαογραφικά, 2 ('Εταιρεία Μακεδονικῶν Σπουδῶν. 'Επιστημονικαὶ πραγματεῖαι, σειρὰ φιλολογικὴ καὶ θεολογική, 6 (Athens, 1950), 375–79.

On the massacres of 1182 and 1185, see Bréhier, *Vie et mort de Byzance*, pp. 346 f., 348 f., who gives the necessary bibliographical indications. Cf. H. Hunger, *Die Normannen in Thessalonike, die Eroberung von Th. durch die Normannen in der Augenzeugenschilderung des Bischofs Eustathios* (*Byzantinische Geschichtsschreiber*, ed. Endre v. Ivánka, 3 [Graz, 1955]); O. Tafrali, *Thessalonique des origines au xive siècle* (Paris, 1919), pp. 182–91.

21   *Historia, Corpus scriptorum historiae byzantinae* (Bonn, 1835), pp. 391 f.

22   Cf. J. Ebersolt, *Constantinople byzantine et les voyageurs du Levant* (Paris, 1918), pp. 27 ff.; A. A. Vasiliev, "Quelques remarques sur les voyageurs du moyen âge à Constantinople," *Mélanges Charles Diehl*, 1 (1930), 293–98. See also S. G. Mercati, "Santuari e reliquie Costantinopolitane secondo il codice Ottoboniano Latino 169 prima della conquista Latina (1204)," *Rendiconti della Pontificia Accademia Romana di Archeologia*, 12 (1936), 133–56. On the

booty carried off in 1204, see Comte Riant, *Exuviae sacrae Constantinopolitanae* (2 vols.; Geneva, 1877–78); Vol. 3 by F. de Mély, *La croix des premiers croisés* (Paris, 1904).

23   S. Runciman, *A History of the Crusades*, 1 (Cambridge, Eng., 1951), 122–33, 149–71; cf. F. Duncalf in K. M. Setton, M. H. Baldwin, *A History of the Crusades*, 1 (Philadelphia, 1955), 269, 271 f., 274 f., 279. Cf. P. Rassow, "Zum byzantinisch-normannischen Krieg 1147–1149," *Mitteilungen des Instituts für oesterreichische Geschichtsforschung*, 62 (1954), 213–18.

24   O. Demus, *The Mosaics of Norman Sicily* (London, 1950), pp. 5 ff., 18, 25 ff., 82, 123–48, 372; F. Chalandon, *Histoire de la domination normande en Italie et en Sicile*, 2 (Paris, 1907), 135–37; E. Caspar, *Roger II* (Innsbruck, 1904), pp. 376–84. Cf. U. Monneret de Villard, "La tessitura Palermitana sotto i Normanni e i suoi rapporti con l'arte bizantina," *Miscellanea Giovanni Mercati*, 3 (*Studi e Testi*, 123 [Vatican City, 1946]), 464–89.

25   P. E. Schramm, *Herrschaftszeichen und Staatssymbolik*, 1 (*Schriften der Monumenta Germaniae historica*, 13, 1 [Stuttgart, 1954]), 34 f., 77–80, 85; A. Marongiu, "Lo spirito della monarchia normanna nell' allocuzione di Ruggero II ai suoi grandi," *Atti del congresso. . .*, Verona, 4 (see note 142 below), 313–27; J. Deér, *Der Kaiserornat Friedrichs II.* (*Dissertationes Bernenses*, Ser. 2, 2 [Bern, 1952]), 13–19; Demus, *Mosaics*, pl. 58A; E. Kitzinger, "On the Portrait of Roger II in the Martorana in Palermo," *Proporzioni*, 3 (1950), 30–35; W. Ohnsorge, *Das Zweikaiserproblem im früheren Mittelalter, die Bedeutung des byzantinischen Reiches für die Entwicklung der Staatsidee in Europa* (Hildesheim, 1947), pp. 83–121, 139–41; E. Kantorowicz, *Laudes regiae* (Berkeley-Los Angeles, 1946), pp. 158–60; Sigfried H. Steinberg, "I ritratti dei re normanni di Sicilia," *La Bibliofilia*, 39 (1937), 29–57. Cf. P. K. Enepekides, "Byzantinische Prinzessinen im Hause der Babenberger und die byzantinischen Einflüsse in den österreichischen Ländern des 12. und 13. Jahrhunderts," Πεπραγμένα τοῦ θ′ διεθνοῦς βυζαντινολογικοῦ συνεδρίου, 2 ('Ελληνικά, παράρτημα 9 [Athens, 1956]), 368–74.

In a provocative article, "L'institution monarchique dans les états normands d'Italie," *Cahiers de civilisation médiévale*, x^e–λii^e *siècles*, 2 (1959), 303–31, 445–68, L. R. Ménager argues that the Norman kings were not absolute rulers like the emperors of Byzantium, and did not adopt Byzantine political theory. In another valuable paper, "Notes sur les codifications byzantines et l'occident," *Varia, études de droit romain*, 3 (*Institut de droit romain de l'Université de Paris*, 16 [Paris, 1958]), 239–303, he expresses doubt that the copies of the Byzantine law codes (in Greek) which were produced in the West had any real application in Sicily during the twelfth century, and concludes that they served the requirements of scholars rather than of lawyers. These monographs form part of Ménager's eagerly awaited book, *Études sur le royaume normand d'Italie*, and make an important contribution. At the moment, however, I am sceptical about his conclusions, both of which are directed against the authorities noted in the previous paragraph. Perhaps his book will provide evidence to dispel scepticism.

26   A large number of periodicals published by various Italian cities and com-

munities are crammed with material of interest to students of the influence
of Byzantium on Italy during the twelfth century. Among these, in addition
to the well-known series put out by the learned academies of Venice, Rome,
and Naples, mention should be made of the following: *Archivio storico della
Calabria* (5 vols., 1912–17); *Archivio storico per la Calabria e la Lucania* (1931—);
Archivio storico Pugliese (1948—); *Archivio storico per la Sicilia* (1935—); *Archivio
storico per la Sicilia orientale* (1904—); *Archivio storico Siciliano* (1876—);
Bessarione (36 vols., 1896–1920); *Bollettino della Badia greca di Grottaferrata*
(1947—); *Brutium* (1922—); *Calabria nobilissima* (1947—); *Iapygia* (17 vols.,
1930–46); *Rivista storica Calabrese* (14 vols., 1893–1906); *Roma e l'Oriente*
(21 vols., 1910–21); *Siculorum Gymnasium* (1948—). I will refrain from giving
the entire bibliography in this paper, but hope that I may be able to return
to the subject at another time.

Linguistic matters are discussed in these publications, and especially in
three books by G. Rohlfs: *Historische Grammatik der unteritalienischen Gräzität
(Sitzungsberichte der bayerischen Akademie der Wissenschaften, Philos.-hist. Klasse,*
1949, Heft 4 [Munich, 1950]); *Scavi linguistici nella Magna Grecia* (Halle a. S.-
Rome, 1933); and *Etymologisches Wörterbuch der unteritalienischen Gräzität* (Halle
a. S., 1930), which contain useful bibliographies. Note also G. Alessio,
"L'elemento greco nella toponomastica della Sicilia," *Centro di Studi filologici
e linguistici siciliani, Bollettino,* 1 (1953), 65–106; 3 (1955), 223–61; 4 (1956),
310–56; S. G. Kapsomenos, "Beiträge zur historischen Grammatik der
griechischen Dialekte Unteritaliens," *Byzantinische Zeitschrift,* 46 (1953),
320–48. See also note 145 below.

Inter alia see L. R. Ménager, "Notes et documents sur quelques monastères
de Calabre à l'époque normande," *Byzantinische Zeitschrift,* 50 (1957),
7–30, 321–61; *Atti del primo Congresso storico Calabrese* (1954; published Rome,
1956); F. Russo, "Relazioni culturali tra la Calabria e l'Oriente bizantino
nel M.E.," πεπραγμένα (cited, note 25 above), pp. 592–607; K. M. Setton,
"The Byzantine Background to the Italian Renaissance," *Proceedings of the
American Philosophical Society,* 100 (1956), 1–76; F. Grillo, "Italia antica e
medioevale," *Calabria nobilissima,* 5 (1951), 131–44; 6 (1952), 179–86; 7
(1953), 1–8, 57–65, 165–84; 8 (1954), 1–10; M. Scaduto, *Il monachismo
basiliano nella Sicilia medievale, rinascita e decadenza, secoli xi-xiv* (Rome, 1947);
L. T. White, Jr., *Latin Monasticism in Norman Sicily* (Cambridge, Mass., 1938);
A. de Stefano, *La cultura in Sicilia nel periodo normanno* (Palermo, 1938), which
is too brief, but has a good bibliography; C. Korolevskij, "Basiliens italo-
grecs et espagnols," *Dictionnaire d'histoire et de géographie ecclésiastiques,* 6
(1932), 1180–1236; G. Robinson, *History and Cartulary of the Greek Monastery
of St. Elias and St. Anastasius of Carbone (Orientalia Cristiana,* XI, 5 [No. 44],
XV, 2 [No. 53], XIX, 1 [No. 62], 1928–30); D. L. Raschellà, *Saggio storico sul
monachismo italo-greco in Calabria* (Messina, 1925); A. Vaccari, *La Grecia
nell'Italia meridionale (Orientalia Christiana,* III, 3, No. 13 [Rome, 1925]);
G. Minasi, *Le chiese di Calabria dal quinto al duodecimo secolo* (Naples, 1896);
P. Batiffol, *L'abbaye de Rossano* (Paris, 1891); P. Rodotà, *Dell' origine, progresso
e stato presente del rito greco in Italia* (3 vols.; Rome, 1758–63).

Note the numerous Greek documents issued in Sicily and southern Italy during the twelfth century in S. Cusa, *I diplomi greci ed arabi di Sicilia* (2 vols.; Palermo, 1868–82); F. Trinchera, *Syllabus graecarum membranarum* (Naples, 1865); G. Spata, *Le pergamene greche esistenti nel grande archivio di Palermo* (Palermo, 1862). See the three papers by A. Guillou summarized by F. Dölger, *Byzantinische Zeitschrift*, 49 (1956), 461. Cf. A. Strittmatter, "Liturgical Latinisms in a Twelfth Century Greek Euchology," *Miscellanea G. Mercati*, 3 (note 24 above), 41–64; E. Pontieri, *Tra i Normanni nell' Italia meridionale* (Naples, 1954); S. la Sorsa, *Storia di Puglia*, Vols. 2–3 (Bari, 1953-54). N. D. Evola, *Bibliografia Siciliana* (1938–1953) (Palermo, 1954); and D. Zangari, *Catalogo ragionato della "Collezione Calabra Morano": opere di storia regionale* (Naples, 1922), give long but unclassified bibliographies.

For the latest data, see P. Collura, "Appendice al regesto dei diplomi di Re Ruggero compilato da Erich Caspar," *Atti del convegno internazionale di studi Ruggeriani*, 2 (Palermo, 1955), 545–625; A. Guillou, "Le corpus des actes grecs de Sicile," *ibid.*, 1, 147–53; A. de Stefano and F. Bartolini, *I documenti originali dei re normanni di Sicilia*, 2 fascs., *Archivio paleografico italiano*, 14, 60–61 (Rome-Palermo, 1954). See also note 146 below.

The literature on Byzantine influence in Germany is set forth in Lamma, *Comneni e Staufer*, and Classen, "Konzil von Konstantinopel" (notes 2 and 36; cf. notes 25 and 28, above.) Cf. also the collected papers of W. Ohnsorge, *Abendland und Byzanz* (Darmstadt, 1958); K. J. Heilig, *Ostrom und das deutsche Reich um die Mitte des 12. Jahrhunderts, Kaisertum und Herzogsgewalt im Zeitalter Friedrichs I. (Schriften des Reichsinstituts für ältere deutsche Geschichtskunde [Monumenta Germanicae historica]*, 9 [Leipzig, 1944]), 1–271.

27 On the arts I note here only a few of the major authorities. Besides O. Demus' monumental forthcoming two-volume study of the Church of San Marco in Venice, see H. Buchthal, *Miniature Painting in the Latin Kingdom of Jerusalem, with Liturgical and Palaeographical Chapters by Francis Wormald* (Oxford, 1957); G. Martelli, "Chiese monumentali di Calabria," *Calabria nobilissima*, 10 (1956), 33–40, a bibliographical summary; B. Cappelli, "Chiese rupestri del Materano," *ibid.*, pp. 45–59; G. Galassi, *Roma o Bisanzio* (2 vols., 2nd ed.; Rome, 1953); G. Agnello, *L'architettura bizantina in Sicilia* (Florence, 1952); E. Kitzinger, "The Mosaics of the Cappella Palatina in Palermo," *Art Bulletin*, 31 (1949), 269–92; C. A. Willemsen, *Apulien* (Leipzig, 1944), useful for excellent plates and a bibliography; H. M. Schwarz, "Die Baukunst Kalabriens und Siziliens im Zeitalter der Normannen," *Römisches Jahrbuch für Kunstgeschichte*, 6 (1942–44), 1–112; P. Orsi, *Sicilia bizantina*, 1 (Rome, 1942); *idem, Le chiese basiliane della Calabria* (Florence, 1929); A. Medea, *Gli affreschi delle cripte eremitiche pugliesi* (2 vols.; Rome, 1939); A. Frangipane, *Elenco degli edifici monumentali d'Italia*, Vols. 58–60 (Rome, 1938); *idem, Inventario degli oggetti d'arte d'Italia*, Vol. 2 (Rome, 1933), both of which are devoted to Calabria and were reviewed by B. Cappelli, *Archivio storico per la Calabria e la Lucania*, 4 (1934), 104–72; *ibid.*, 10. (1940), 146–82; G. Gabrieli, *Inventario topografico e bibliografico delle cripte eremitiche*

basiliane di Puglia (Rome, 1936); M. Avery, *The Exultet Rolls of South Italy* (plates but no text; Princeton, 1936); A. Colasanti, *L'art byzantin en Italie* (2 vols.; Paris, 1926); O. M. Dalton, *Byzantine Art and Archaeology* (Oxford, 1911); C. Diehl, *L'art byzantin dans l'Italie méridionale* (Paris, 1894). Note, e.g., É. Bertaux, *L'art dans l'Italie méridionale* (Paris, 1903), pp. 401–508 and *passim;* C. Diehl, *Manuel d'art byzantin*, 2 (2nd ed.; Paris, 1926), 713–34; Demus, *Mosaics*, pp. 371, 388 f.

For the bronze doors, see H. Leisinger, *Romanische Bronzen, Kirchentüren im mittelalterlichen Europa* (Zürich, 1956), with superb plates; A. Boeckler, *Die Bronzetüren des Bonanus von Pisa und des Barisanus von Trani*, ed. R. Hamann, *Die frühmittelalterlichen Bronzetüren*, 4 (Marburg-Lahn-Berlin, 1953); C. Angelillis, *Le porte di bronzo bizantine nelle chiese d'Italia, Le imposte della Basilica di Monte S. Angelo* (Arezzo, 1924); A. K. Porter, "Wreckage from a Tour in Apulia," *Mélanges offerts à M. Gustave Schlumberger*, 2 (Paris, 1924), 408–15. C. A. Willemsen's *Apulien* has come out in a new edition as *Apulia*, ed. D. Odenthal, with English translation by Daphne Woodward (New York, 1959).

One of the most striking examples of Byzantine influence on Latin manuscript illumination is to be found in the *Hortus deliciarum* (an encyclopaedia devoted to the doctrine of salvation), of which at least 344 miniatures were known. The codex itself was destroyed by fire in 1870, but a photographic record, based largely on previous publications, has been issued by Joseph Walter, *Herrade de Landsberg, Abbesse du Mont Sainte-Odile, 1167–1195, Hortus deliciarum* (Strasbourg-Paris, 1952).

28   On the knowledge of Greek in the West during the later Middle Ages, see the following (with bibliographies): B. Bischoff, "Das griechische Element in der abendländischen Bildung des Mittelalters," *Byzantinische Zeitschrift*, 44 (1951), 27–55 (excluding Italy); L. Brou, "Les chants en langue grecque dans les liturgies latines," *Sacris Erudiri*, 1 (1948), 165–80; *ibid.*, 4 (1952), 226–38; E. Wellesz, *Eastern Elements in Western Chant (Monumenta musicae byzantinae*, Subsidia, Vol. 2, No. 1, American series [Oxford, 1947]); A. Allgeier, "Exegetische Beiträge zur Geschichte des Griechischen vor dem Humanismus," *Biblica*, 24 (1943), 261–88; B. Altaner, "Die Kenntnis des Griechischen in den Missionsorden während des 13. und 14. Jahrhunderts," *Zeitschrift für Kirchengeschichte*, 3. Folge, 4, 53 (1934), 436–93, with important bibliography for the earlier period; M. Manitius, *Geschichte der lateinischen Literatur des Mittelalters*, 2, 3 (*Handbuch der Altertumswissenschaft*, 9, 2, 3, ed. W. Otto [Munich, 1931]), *s.v. Griechisch*, etc.; P. Duhem, *Le système du monde*, 3 (Paris, 1915), 163–230; J. E. Sandys, *A History of Classical Scholarship*, 1 (2nd ed.; Cambridge, Eng., 1906), 524–58. See notes 25–27 above, 29 ff. below. Cf. G. Moravcsik's study of the Byzantine origin of the name Katapán, summarized in *Byzantinische Zeitschrift*, 49 (1956), 464 f.

29   See J. T. Muckle, "Greek Works Translated Directly into Latin before 1350," *Mediaeval Studies*, 4 (1942), 33–42; 5 (1943), 102–14; H. D. Saffrey, "Versions latines d'auteurs grecs," *Bulletin Thomiste*, 8 (1947–53), 221–32; M. Cappuyns, *Jean Scot Érigène, sa vie, son œuvre, sa pensée (Universitas Catholica*

Lovaniensis, Dissertationes ad gradum magistri in Facultate Theologica, 2nd series, 26 [Louvain-Paris, 1933]), 128–79; H. F. Dondaine, ed., "Les 'Expositiones super Ierarchiam caelestem' de Jean Scot Érigène," *Archives d'histoire doctrinale et littéraire du moyen âge*, 18 (1950–51), 245–302 (an *editio princeps* of the full text of Erigena's commentary on the work of the Pseudo-Dionysius, based upon a manuscript of the twelfth century); M. Grabmann, *Die Geschichte der scholastischen Methode*, 1 (Freiburg im Breisgau, 1909), 151 ff.; 2 (1911), 59 ff., and *passim*. See also note 147 below.

Cf. also A. Malet, *Personne et amour dans la théologie trinitaire de Saint Thomas d'Aquin (Bibliothèque Thomiste*, 32 [Paris, 1956], pp. 161–80, who lists medieval Latin translations of the Greek fathers. For Hilduin and his version of the Pseudo-Dionysius, see P. G. Théry, *Études dionysiennes*, 1–2 (*Études de philosophie médiévale*, ed. É. Gilson, 16 and 19 [Paris, 1932–37], in which is included the Latin text.

30 For texts and studies on Aristippus see R. Klibansky, V. Kordeuter, C. Labowsky, L. Minio-Paluello, *Corpus philosophorum medii aevi, Corpus Platonicum, Plato Latinus*, 1–3 (London, 1940–53); M. T. Mandalari, "Enrico Aristippo Arcidiacono di Catania nella vita culturale e politica del sec. XII," *Bollettino storico Catanese (R. Deputazione di storia patria per la Sicilia, sezione di Catania)*, 4 (1939), 87–123 f. Cf. R. Klibansky, *The Continuity of the Platonic Tradition During the Middle Ages* (London, 1939), p. 27; L. Metelli, "Sulle due redazioni del Fedone latino di Aristippo," *Atti del Reale Istituto Veneto di scienze, lettere ed arti*, 97, 2 (1937–38), Classe di scienze morali e lettere (Venice, 1938), 113-40; G. B. Siragusa, *Il regno di Guglielmo I in Sicilia* (2nd ed.; Palermo, 1929), pp. 297 ff.

Recent researches show that Aristippus had never been a monk in Southern Italy, as some have supposed.—E. Jamison, *Admiral Eugenius*, cited in note 32 below, pp. xvii–xxi; L. Minio-Paluello, "Henri Aristippe, Guillaume de Moerbeke et les traductions latines médiévales des *Météorologiques* et du *De generatione et corruptione* d'Aristote," *Revue philosophique de Louvain*, 45 (1947), 206–35.

31 On Aristotle in the twelfth century, see G. Lacombe, *Corpus philosophorum medii aevi, Aristoteles Latinus*, 1 (Rome, 1939); 2 (Cambridge, Eng., 1955), who gives exhaustive bibliographies; M. Grabmann, "Aristoteles im zwölften Jahrhundert," *Mediaeval Studies*, 12 (1950), 123–62; H. J. D. Lulofs, ed., *Aristotelis de insomniis et de divinatione per somnum* (2 vols.; Leiden, 1947), with a Latin version of the twelfth century; E. Franceschini, "Aristotele nel medioevo latino," *Atti del ix congresso nazionale di filosofia*, Padova, 20–23 Settembre, 1934 (Padua, 1935), 189–207; B. Geyer, *Patristische und scholastische Philosophie, F. Ueberwegs Grundriss der Geschichte der Philosophie*, 2 (Basel, 1927), 343–50, lists works of Aristotle available in Latin in the twelfth century; *idem*, "Die alten lateinischen Uebersetzungen der aristotelischen Analytik, Topik und Elenchik," *Philosophisches Jahrbuch der Görres-Gesellschaft*, 30 (1917), 25–43.

On James, see L. Minio-Paluello, "Iacobus Veneticus Grecus, Canonist

and Translator of Aristotle," *Traditio*, 8 (1952), 265–304; *idem*, "Note sull'
Aristotele Latino medievale, 7. Manoscritti aristotelici latini del xii secolo
con note contemporanee: scolii greci alla 'Metafisica' tradotti in latino da
Giacomo Veneto," *Rivista di filosofia neo-scolastica*, 44 (1952), 485–95; E.
Franceschini, "Il contributo dell' Italia alla trasmissione del pensiero greco
in Occidente nei secoli xii-xiii e la questione di Giacomo Chierico di Vene-
zia," *Atti della xxvi riunione della Società Italiana per il progresso delle scienze,
Venezia*, 1937, 3, 2 (Rome, 1938), 287–310.

See also the papers and monographs in M. Grabmann, *Mittelalterliches
Geistesleben*, 3 vols. (Munich, 1926–56), with bibliography of Grabmann's
numerous publications on this subject, *ibid.*, 3, 10–35; F. Pelster, "Neuere
Forschungen über die Aristotelesübersetzungen des 12. und 13. Jahrhun-
derts. Eine kritische Übersicht," *Gregorianum*, 30 (1949), 46–77; R. Herval,
"Ecléctisme intellectuel," *Atti*, cited in note 26 above, Vol. 1, 73–104; J.
Storost, "La leggenda di Aristotele in Sicilia e in Normandia," *ibid.*, Vol. 1,
155–66.

32 E. Jamison, *Admiral Eugenius of Sicily, His Life and Work* (Oxford, 1957),
pp. 3–5, 21 ff., 302 f. Jamison, perhaps wisely, takes no notice of the conjecture of F. Bliemetzrieder, *Adelhard von Bath* (Munich, 1935), pp. 149–274,
that the unknown translator of the Almagest was Adelhard of Bath, *ca.* 1153–60.

33 C. H. Haskins, *Studies in the History of Mediaeval Science* (2nd ed.; Cambridge,
Mass., 1927), pp. 150, 202 ff.; cf. pp. 144, 145, 297 ff.

34 *Ibid.*, pp. 143, 178–82, 219 f. The text of a Latin translation of the twelfth
century has been edited by L. Delatte, *Textes latins et vieux français relatifs
aux Cyranides* (*Bibliothèque de la Faculté de Philosophie et Lettres de l'Université de
Liège*, 93 [1942]). H. Boese, ed., *Die mittelalterliche Übersetzung der Stoicheiosis
physike des Proclus* (*Deutsche Akademie der Wissenschaften, Arbeitsgruppe für hel-
lenistisch-römische Philosophie*, 6 [Berlin, 1958]): ca. 1160.

35 See note 80 below and R. Mols, "Burgundio de Pise," *Dictionnaire d'histoire
et de géographie ecclésiastiques*, 10 (Paris, 1938), 1363–69; M. Flecchia, "La
traduzione di Burgundio Pisano delle omelie di S. Giovanni Crisostomo
sopra Matteo," *Aevum*, 26 (1952), 113–30. For a portion of Burgundio's
version of Chrysostom, see H. F. Dondaine, *Recherches de théologie ancienne et
médiévale*, 19 (1952), 100–102. On the use of the Greek fathers, cf. Grabmann,
op. cit., note 29 above, 1, 76–116; 2, 81–94 and *passim*.

36 A. Dondaine, "Hugues Éthérien et Léon Toscan," *Archives d'histoire doctrinale
et littéraire du moyen âge*, 19 (1952), 67–134, with texts and bibliography;
cf. P. Classen, "Das Konzil von Konstantinopel 1166 und die Lateiner,"
Byzantinische Zeitschrift, 48 (1955), 339–68; A. Dondaine, "Hugues Éthérien
et le concile de Constantinople de 1166," *Historisches Jahrbuch*, 77 (1957),
473–83. See also note 148 below.

37 See the works of E. M. Buytaert, note 80 below, and A. B. Terebessy,
Translatio latina, cited, note 39 below.

38 Migne, *P.L.*, 184, 309A; J. M. Déchanet, *Guillaume de Saint-Thierry, l'homme
et son œuvre* (Bruges-Paris, 1942), pp. 200 ff. and index *s.v.*; *idem*, *Aux sources
de la spiritualité de Guillaume de Saint-Thierry* (Bruges, 1940); pp. 27–59. Cf.

M. M. Davy, *Un traité de la vie solitaire, Lettre aux frères du Mont-Dieu de Guillaume de Saint-Thierry* (Paris, 1946), pp. 191, 211, a translation based on the same author's Latin text (Paris, 1940). A valuable contribution on the impact of Greek thought upon the West has been made by Chenu, *La théologie*, cited, note 14 above, pp. 108–41, 274–308.

On Origen see J. Leclercq, "Nouveaux témoignages sur Origène au xiie siècle," *Mediaeval Studies*, 15 (1953), 104–6; *idem*, "Origène au xiie siècle," *Irénikon*, 24 (1951), 425–39; *idem*, "Saint Bernard et Origène d'après un manuscrit de Madrid," *Revue Bénédictine*, 59 (1949), 183–95. Cf. the anonymous *Ysagoge in Theologiam* (*ca.* 1148–52), ed. A. Landgraf, *Écrits théologiques de l'école d'Abélard* (*Spicilegium sacrum Lovaniense, Études et documents*, 14 [Louvain, 1934]), 270.2 ff.; *idem*, "Zum Werden der Theologie des zwölften Jahrhunderts," *Zeitschrift für katholische Theologie*, 79 (1957), 417–33, n.b. 418 ff.; and note 95 below.

Of the innumerable references to the Pseudo-Dionysius which occur in the twelfth century, cf. *idem*, *Spicilegium*, 14, 233.6 ff., 12 f.; P. Glorieux, "La somme 'Quoniam homines' d'Alain de Lille," *Archives d'histoire doctrinale et littéraire du moyen âge*, 20 (1953), 119, 120, 125, 127, 128, 131, 133, 135, 140, 213, 328; M. T. d'Alverny, "Le cosmos symbolique du xiie siècle," *ibid.*, 20 (1953), 31–81, on the *Clavis physicae* of Honorius of Autun; H. Weisweiler, "Die Ps.-Dionysiuskommentare 'In Coelestem Hierarchiam' des Skotus Eriugena und Hugos von St. Viktor," *Recherches de théologie ancienne et médiévale*, 19 (1952), 26–47; J. M. Parent, "Un nouveau témoin de la théologie dionysienne au xiie siècle" [an anonymous *Summa*], *Aus der Geisteswelt des Mittelalters* (*Beiträge zur Geschichte der Philosophie und Theologie des Mittelalters*, Supplementband 3, 1 [Münster i. W., 1935]), 289–309. Consult W. Völker, *Kontemplation und Ekstase bei Pseudo-Dionysius Areopagita* (Wiesbaden, 1958); and R. Roques, *L'univers dionysien* (Paris, 1954), for bibliography.

39 J. Daniélou, "Saint Bernard et les pères Grecs," *Analecta Sacri Ordinis Cisterciensis*, 9, fasc. 3–4 (1953), 46–55; cf. J. M. Déchanet, "Aux sources de la pensée philosophique de S. Bernard," *ibid.*, pp. 56–77; cf. *ibid.*, fasc. 1–2, 116–24 and *passim*; É. Gilson, "Maxime, Érigène, S. Bernard," *Aus der Geisteswelt des Mittelalters* (volume cited in previous note), pp. 188–95; *idem*, *La théologie mystique de Saint Bernard* (Paris, 1934). I have not seen E. Kleineidam, *Wissen, Wissenschaft, Theologie bei Bernard von Clairvaux* (*Erfurter Theologische Schriften*, 1 [Leipzig, 1955]), but cf. *idem, idem*, in *Bernhard von Clairvaux, Mönch und Mystiker* (*Veröffentlichungen des Instituts für Europäische Geschichte Mainz*, 6, ed. J. Lortz [*Wiesbaden*, 1955]), 128–67; E. von Ivánka, "Byzantinische Theologumena und hellenische Philosophumena in Zisterziensisch–Bernhardinischen Denken," *ibid.*, pp. 168–75.

On the translation of Maximus the Confessor by Cerbanus, see A. B. Terebessy, *Translatio latina sancti Maximi Confessoris* (*De caritate ad Elpidium L. i–iv) saeculo xii in Hungaria confecta* (Magyar Görög Tanulmányok, ed. G. Moravcsik, 25 [Budapest, 1944]).

40 N. M. Haring, "The Character and Range of the Influence of St. Cyril of

Alexandria on Latin Theology (430–1260)," *Mediaeval Studies*, 12 (1950), 1–19, n.b. 17.

41   G. Théry, "Documents concernant Jean Sarrazin," *Archives d'histoire doctrinale et littéraire du moyen âge*, 18 (1950–51), 45–87.

On genuine Platonism (as opposed to Neoplatonism of the Pseudo-Dionysian variety) see N. M. Haring, "The Creation and Creator of the World According to Thierry of Chartres and Clarenbaldus of Arras," *Archives d'histoire doctrinale et littéraire du moyen âge*, 22 (1955), 137–216, with texts and bibliography; M. D. Chenu, "Platon à Cîteaux," *ibid.*, 21 (1954), 99–106; *idem, La théologie*, note 14 above, pp. 108–41. Cf. R. Baron, *Science et sagesse chez Hugues de Saint-Victor* (Paris, 1957), pp. 73, 168–179.

42   On Abelard see G. Paré, A. Brunet, P. Tremblay, *La renaissance du xiie siècle, Les écoles et l'enseignement (Publications de l'Institut d'études médiévales d'Ottawa*, 3 [Paris-Ottawa, 1933]), 275–312; cf. for the method of Abelard and Gilbert, É. Lesne, *Les écoles de la fin du viiie siècle à la fin du xiie (Histoire de la propriété ecclésiastique en France*, 5 [Lille, 1940]), *s.v.;* J. Cottiaux, "La conception de la théologie chez Abélard," *Revue d'histoire ecclésiastique*, 28 (1932), 247–95, 533–51, 788–828, who concludes his survey by quoting from Abelard's *Epistola ad Heloissam:* "Nolo sic esse philosophus ut recalcitrem Paulo; non sic esse Aristoteles ut secludar a Christo."—ed. V. Cousin, *Petri Abaelardi opera*, 2 (Paris, 1849), 680; J. de Ghellinck, *Mouvement théologique*, pp. 171 ff., 466, 468, and *passim*, with bibliography.

On Abelard's knowledge of Plato and Aristotle, see the new edition of his *Dialectica*, ed. L. M. de Rijk (Assen, 1956), with list of sources, *ad fin.*; and P. Delhaye, "Un cas de transmission indirecte d'un thème philosophique grec," *Scholastica ratione historico-critica instauranda (Bibliotheca Pontificii Athenaei Antoniani*, 7 [Rome, 1951]), pp. 143–67. Cf. J. G. Sikes, *Peter Abailard* (Cambridge, Eng., 1932), 272 ff. An interesting summary of the proceedings of the councils of Soissons (1121) and Sens (1141) by which Abelard was unjustly condemned is to be found in C. J. Hefele and H. Leclercq, *Histoire des conciles*, 5, 1 (Paris, 1912), 593–602, 747–90.

On Gilbert, see the important observations by N. M. Haring, "The Case of Gilbert de la Porrée, Bishop of Poitiers (1142–1154)," *Mediaeval Studies*, 13 (1951), 1–40. Cf. also *idem*, "The Cistercian, Everard of Ypres, and his Appraisal of the Conflict Between St. Bernard and Gilbert of Poitiers," *ibid.*, 17 (1955), 143–72; *idem*, "A Latin Dialogue on the Doctrine of Gilbert of Poitiers," *ibid.*, 15 (1953), 243–89; de Ghellinck, *Mouvement théologique*, pp. 174–79, 230, 242 f., 402 f., 467 f. The rest of the literature can be located through the following: M. A. Schmidt, *Gottheit und Trinität nach dem Kommentar des Gilbert Porreta zu Boethius, De Trinitate (Studia philosophica, Jahrbuch der Schweizerischen philosophischen Gesellschaft*, Supplementum 7 [Basel, 1956]); S. V. Rovighi, "La filosofia di Gilberto Porretano," *Miscellanea del centro di studi medievali*, 1 *(Pubbl. dell' Università Cattolica del S. Cuore*, N.S., 58 [Milan, 1956]), 1–64; A. M. Landgraf, "Zur Lehre des Gilbert Porreta," *Zeitschrift für katholische Theologie*, 77 (1955), 331–37; *idem*, "Der Porretanismus der Homilien des Radulphus Ardens," *ibid.*, 64 (1940), 132–48; *idem,*

"Untersuchungen zu den Eigenlehren Gilberts de la Porrée," *ibid.*, 54 (1930), 180–213; *idem*, "Neue Funde zur Porretanerschule," *Collectanea Franciscana*, 6 (1936), 353–65; *idem*, "Mitteilungen zur Schule Gilberts de la Porrée," *ibid.*, 3 (1933), 182–208; V. Miano, "Il commento alle lettere di S. Paolo di Gilberto Porretano," *Scholastica . . . instauranda* (cited above), pp. 169–99. Announcement has been made of a book by H. C. van Elswijk entitled *Gilbert Porreta, sa vie, son œuvre, sa pensée*, which is to be published in the *Spicilegium sacrum Lovaniense*. Among the new editions of Gilbert's works, see, e.g., "The Commentaries of Gilbert, Bishop of Poitiers, . . . on the Two Boethian *opuscula sacra* on the Holy Trinity," ed. Haring in *Nine Mediaeval Thinkers*, ed. J. R. O'Donnell (Toronto, 1955), pp. 23–98; "The Commentary of Gilbert, Bishop of Poitiers, on Boethius' *Contra Eutychen et Nestorium*," ed. Haring, *Archives d'histoire doctrinale et littéraire du moyen âge*, 21 (1954), 241–357; Landgraf, ed. *Commentarius Porretanus in primam Epistolam ad Corinthios* (*Studi e Testi*, 117 [Vatican City, 1945]).

On Joachim of Flore see F. Foberti, *Gioacchino da Fiore* (Florence, 1934), pp. 75 f. and *passim*, who judges Joachim to have been orthodox; *contra* is P. Fournier, *Études sur Joachim de Flore* (Paris, 1909), pp. 32 f. and *passim*. N.b. the 211-page bibliography by F. Russo, *Bibliografia Gioachimita* (*Biblioteca di bibliografia italiana*, 28 [Florence, 1954]). Cf. B. Hirsch-Reich, "Eine Bibliographie über Joachim von Fiore und dessen Nachwirkung," *Recherches de théologie ancienne et médiévale*, 24 (1957), 27–44; M. W. Bloomfield and M. E. Reeves, "The Penetration of Joachism into Northern Europe," *Speculum*, 29 (1954), 772–93; Hefele and Leclercq, *Histoire des conciles*, 5, 2 (Paris, 1913), 1327–29. Note that the book of Foberti cited bears the subtitle, *Nuovi studi critici sulla mistica e la religiosità in Calabria*. It is to be distinguished from *idem, Gioacchino da Fiore e il Gioacchinismo antico e moderno* (Padua, 1942), which is devoted to proving that Joachim was not a heretic. To the above add M. W. Bloomfield, "Joachim of Flora, A Critical Survey of His Canon, Teaching, Sources, Biography and Influence," *Traditio*, 13 (1957), 249–311; reviewed by B. Hirsch-Reich, *loc. cit.*, 26 (1959), 128–37.

For hostile criticism of Abelard and Gilbert, see A. Michel, "Trinité," *Dictionnaire de théologie catholique*, 15, 2 (Paris, 1950), 1713–17.

43 On *Filioque*, cf. J. N. D. Kelly, *Early Christian Creeds* (London, 1950), pp. 358–67.

44 Migne erroneously prints Hugo's treatise under the title: "De haeresibus quas Graeci Latinos devolvunt libri tres, sive quod Spiritus Sanctus ex utroque, Patre scilicet et Filio, procedat, contra Graecos."—*P.L.*, 202, 229–396. But A. Dondaine, "Hugues Éthérien," note 36 above, pp. 93 ff., shows that this was the designation of a *Greek* polemic *against* the Latins, and that Hugo's work was entitled *De sancto et immortali Deo*.

For biographical details see *ibid.*, pp. 79 ff., 92; and R. Lechat, "La patristique grecque chez un théologien latin du xiie siècle, Hugues Éthérien," *Mélanges d'histoire offerts à Charles Moeller*, 1 (Université de Louvain, Recueil de Travaux, 40 [Louvain-Paris, 1914]), 485–507, who supplies a list of

references to the passages cited by Hugo from the Greek fathers of the
first eight centuries, but does not analyze what Hugo says or deal with the
later Byzantine theologians like Photius, Nicetas Byzantius, and Nicholas of
Methone, whom Hugo frequently names.

   In this section I summarize Hugo's principal arguments. But the subject
deserves more extended treatment, along with the Byzantine doctrine of the
Holy Spirit and the polemics of Latin theologians like Anselm of Aosta
(1033–1109) and Anselm of Havelberg (d. 1158), on the latter of whom
see note 52 below. M. Jugie has written on the Byzantine aspects of this
topic: *Theologia dogmatica Christianorum orientalium ab ecclesia catholica dissidentium*, 1 (Paris, 1926), 154–311; 2 (Paris, 1933), 296–326; and *De processione
Spiritus Sancti ex fontibus revelationis et secundum orientales dissidentes (Lateranum,
Nova series*, 2, no. 3–4 [Rome, 1936]), but a fuller and more critical study is
greatly needed. Cf. J. Hergenröther, *Photius, Patriarch von Constantinopel*,
3 (Regensburg, 1869), 175 ff., 791, 814 ff., 833 ff. See also *Tractatus contra
errores Graecorum*, ed. J. Basnage, *Thesaurus monumentorum ecclesiasticorum et
historicorum*, 4 (Amsterdam, 1725), 62–79, cf. 31 f.; Gerhoh's *Tractatus contra
Graecorum errorem negantium Spiritum s. a Filio procedere*, ed. F. Scheibelberger,
op. cit., note 89 below, pp. 341–57; Leo Tuscus, *De haeresibus et praevarica-
tionibus Graecorum*, ed. Dondaine, *loc. cit.*, note 36 above, pp. 116–19, 126 f.

45   P. Lamma, *Comneni e Staufer, ricerche sui rapporti fra Bisanzio e l'Occidente nel
      secolo xii*, 1 (see note 2 above), 165 ff. and *passim*; 2, *passim*; L. Bréhier,
      "Attempts at Reunion of the Greek and Latin Churches," *Cambridge
      Medieval History*, 4 (Cambridge, Eng., 1923), 600–603, 877 ff.; F. Chalandon,
      Les Comnène, 2 (Paris, 1912), 161–64, 227, 555–608; *idem, La domination nor-
      mande*, Vol. 2, pp. 195 ff., 204 ff., 211–19, 227 ff., 254–61, 299 ff., 356–59,
      368–73; W. Norden, *Das Papsttum und Byzanz* (Berlin, 1903), pp. 91–107.
      See bibliographical data in the papers cited in note 36 above.

46   Migne, *P.L.*, 202, 232D–233B.

47   *Ibid.*, 233A–B; for the date, see Lechat, "La patristique grecque," pp.
      488–92.

48   Migne, *P.L.*, 202, 229 f., 230B ("editum a me utraque lingua librum ac-
      cipite"); cf. 231A ("libros ... tam Graece quam Latine scriptos").

49   *Ibid.*, 227 ff., 233C–234D.

50   *Ibid.*, 235A–C.

51   *Ibid.*, 235C–236C.

52   *Ibid.*, 236D–238B. The original text of Nicholas of Methone is printed in
      Migne, *P.G.*, 102, 284 n. 33, 291 n. 89; A. K. Demetrakopulos, Ἐκκλησιασ-
      τικὴ Βιβλιοθήκη (Leipzig, 1866), 360, c. 1; cf. 366, c. 16. On Nicholas,
      cf. V. Grumel, *Dictionnaire de théologie catholique*, 11, 1 (Paris, 1931), 620 f.
      What Nicetas had to say on this subject is known to us only through the
      Dialogi of Anselm of Havelberg.—Migne, *P.L.*, 188, 1163A–1210B.
         On the important role played by Anselm during the controversy on the
      procession of the Holy Spirit, see K. Fina, "Anselm von Havelberg, Unter-
      suchungen zur Kirchen- und Geistesgeschichte des 12. Jahrhunderts,"
      Analecta Praemonstratensia, 32 (1956), 69–101, 193–227; 33 (1957), 5–39,

268–301 (still being continued), who gives the bibliography of the subject. Note especially G. Schreiber, "Anselm von Havelberg und die Ostkirche," *Zeitschrift für Kirchengeschichte*, 60 (3. Fol., 11, 1941), 354–411; J. Dräseke, "Bischof Anselm von Havelberg und seine Gesandtschaftsreisen nach Byzanz," *ibid.*, 21 (1900–1901), 160–85; E. Dombrowski, *Anselm von Havelberg* (Königsberg i. Pr., 1880).

53   Migne, *P.L.*, 202, 238C–D, 242D.

54   *Ibid.*, 244A–C; Nicetas Byzantius, *Capita syllogistica*, ed. J. Hergenroether, *Monumenta graeca ad Photium eiusque historiam pertinentia* (Ratisbonae [Regensburg], 1869), 92 f., 103.8 f.; cf. Photius, *De Sancti Spiritus mystagogia*, 61, Migne, *P.G.*, 102, 340B and notes. On Nicetas, see M. Gordillo, *Enciclopedia Cattolica*, 8 (1952), 1837.

55   Migne, *P.L.*, 202, 244C–246C.

56   *Ibid.*, 245D–246A.

57   *Ibid.*, 255C–D; Nicetas of Nicomedia *apud* Anselmum, *op. cit.*, Migne, *P.L.*, 188, 1170D. Cf. Nicetas Byzantius, ed. Hergenroether, 89.2 ff., 120.1 ff.; Photius, *op. cit.*, 6, Migne, *P.G.*, 102, 288B and n. 62.

58   Migne, *P.L.*, 202, 255D–256B.

59   *Ibid.*, 268D; Nicholas, ed. Demetrakopulos, 363, c. 6; and Migne, *P.G.*, 102, 281B–284D, with notes, especially n. 28.

60   Migne, *P.L.*, 202, 268D–272B.

61   *Ibid.*, 277 C–D. Nicetas Byzantius, ed. Hergenroether, 108 f., cf. 95; Migne, *P.G.*, 102, 288 f., n. 66.

62   Migne, *P.L.*, 202, 278A–279C.

63   *Ibid.*, 295B–298A. Hugo's statement that Archbishop Nicetas of Nicomedia was opposed to the compromise formula of the procession of the Spirit *ex Patre per filium* seems at first glance to contradict Anselm of Havelberg in *Dialogi*, 2, 27 (Migne, *P.L.*, 188, 1209 B–1210B), according to which Nicetas expressed full accord with Anselm in everything (*assentio etiam omnibus quae dixisti*). But Nicetas added, Anselm goes on to say, that since the Greek people were unfamiliar with the dogma of the procession of the Holy Spirit from the Son, it would be necessary to secure ratification of this doctrine by an oecumenical council of the Church under the authority of the Roman pope and with the sanction of the emperors. As soon as this conciliar definition was obtained, Nicetas promised, the Greeks would gladly join the Romans in proclaiming that the Holy Spirit proceeds from the Son. If we can trust Anselm's account, Nicetas was convinced by the Latin arguments and made what is represented as an unconditional surrender. Actually, however, he was only repeating the traditional Byzantine objection that the double procession was unacceptable since it had never been endorsed by a general council of the whole Church. He pretends that the Greeks would be willing to assent *after* such an oecumenical decision, but he knew very well that no Greek delegation would ever submit to a dogmatic decree authorizing the addition of *Filioque* to the creed. On this analysis, therefore, there is little difficulty in reconciling what Hugo says here with the *Dialogi* of Anselm, as can be seen from the text itself:

Nechites [Nicetas] archiepiscopus Nicomediae dixit: Tuam humilitatem, frater charissime, amplector, et eam devotionem quam habere videris ad veritatem fidei, admiror, et fateor: nequaquam possum non commoveri te loquente; assentio etiam omnibus quae dixisti, et accedo toto animo et toto corpore. Porro verba haec: *Spiritus sanctus procedit a Filio*, quoniam hactenus non sonuerunt publice in Ecclesiis Graecorum, nequaquam subito possunt induci, ut sine aliquo scandalo plebis vel aliquorum minus prudentium publice doceantur, vel scribantur; sed aliquod generale concilium occidentalis et orientalis Ecclesiae auctoritate sancti Romani pontificis, admittentibus piissimis imperatoribus celebrandum esset, ubi haec et nonnulla alia Catholicae Ecclesiae necessaria secundum Deum diffinirentur, ne forte vos vel nos in vacuum curreremus. Extunc omnes nos qui in partibus orientis Christiani sumus, una cum sancta Romana Ecclesia, et cum caeteris Ecclesiis quae sunt in occidente, communi voto et pari consensu sine aliquo nostrorum scandalo verbum hoc, *Spiritus sanctus procedit a Filio*, libenter susciperemus, et praedicaremus, et doceremus, et scriberemus, et in Ecclesiis orientis publice cantandum institueremus.

64 Migne, *P.G.*, 102, 317B and n. 24; ed. Demetrakopulos, 363 f., c. 7 f.

65 Migne, *P.L.*, 202, 302B–303A.

66 *Ibid.*, 317A–318 D; Migne, *P.G.*, 102, 284A–285B.

67 Migne, *P.L.*, 202, 318D–320B.

68 *Ibid.*, 320B–C. Information on these practices of the Greek church can be found in the following: R. Janin, *Les églises orientales et les rites orientaux* (4th ed.; Paris, 1955); F. Mercenier and F. Paris, *La prière des églises de rite byzantin*, 1 (2nd ed.; Amay-sur-Meuse, 1951); S. Salaville, *An Introduction to the Study of Eastern Liturgies*, ed. by J. M. T. Barton (London, 1938); F. Heiler, *Urkirche und Ostkirche* (Munich, 1937); N. Nilles, *Kalendarium manuale utriusque ecclesiae orientalis et occidentalis* (2 vols.; Innsbruck, 1896–97); F. E. Brightman, *Liturgies Eastern and Western*, 1 (Oxford, 1896); J. M. Neale, *A History of the Holy Eastern Church* (2 vols.; London, 1850); J. Goar, Εὐχολόγιον *sive rituale Graecorum* (in the edition of Paris, 1647, or that of Venice, 1730). Consult also the *Dictionnaire d'archéologie chrétienne et de liturgie* (30 vols.; Paris, 1907–53); *Jahrbuch für Liturgiewissenschaft* (15 vols.; 1921–41); *Archiv für Liturgiewissenschaft* (1950—); P. Hofmeister, *Die heiligen Öle in der morgen- und abendländischen Kirche* (*Das östliche Christentum*, N.F., 6–7 [Würzburg, 1948]).

69 Migne, *P.L.*, 202, 320D: "Nam licet solus nominetur Pater, subintelligitur omnino et Filius, eo quod absque medio de Patre non prodeat [*sc.* Spiritus], et cum nusquam Patrem dixisse reperiatur: Ego solus emitto Spiritum...." Cf. 321D.

70 *Ibid.*, 320D–321C.

71 *Ibid.*, 373B–375B.

72 *Ibid.*, 375B–378B.

73 *Ibid.*, 380A–384D.

74 *Ibid.*, 388B–393A. See A. Palmieri, "Niceta di Maronea e i suoi dialoghi

sulla Processione dello Spirito Santo," *Bessarione*, Anno 16, Vol. 28 (1912),
80–88; Nicetas' sixth treatise, which has not yet been published, contains
the specific passage to which Hugo alludes, as M. Jugie indicates, "Nicétas
de Maronée," *Dictionnaire de théologie catholique*, 11, 1 (1931), 475. But see the
fourth treatise, ed. N. Festa, *Bessarione*, 30 (1914), 72.14–16, for Nicetas'
view that the Spirit proceeds *from* (ἐx) the Father alone *through* (διά) the Son.

75 See references given by Lechat, "La patristique grecque," note 44 above,
pp. 500 f.

76 Migne, *P.L.*, 202, 394A–B; Migne, *P.G.*, 43, 29B–C: πνεῦμα τοῦ πατρὸς
καὶ πνεῦμα τοῦ υἱοῦ ... : 32C: ἄρα θεὸς ἐκ πατρὸς καὶ υἱοῦ τὸ πνεῦμα ....;
118A–B: τὸ δὲ ἅγιον πνεῦμα παρὰ ἀμφοτέρων (i.e., Father and Son), ed.
K. Holl, *Epiphanius*, 1 (Leipzig, 1915), 15.12–14, 16.11 f., 88.3–5. The last
of these texts was not identified by Lechat; and is accordingly absent from
his list.

77 Migne, *P.L.*, 202, 393A–C; Migne, *P.G.*, 68, 148A: εἴπερ ἐστὶ τοῦ θεοῦ καὶ
πατρός, καὶ μὴν καὶ τοῦ υἱοῦ, τὸ οὐσιωδῶς ἐξ ἀμφοῖν, ἤγουν ἐκ πατρὸς δι' υἱοῦ
προχεόμενον πνεῦμα. Migne, *P.G.*, 71, 377D: ἐξ αὐτοῦ (= τοῦ υἱοῦ).

78 Migne, *P.L.*, 202, 364D (not in Basil); *ibid.*, 328A; Migne, *P.G.*, 29, 656A
with n. 79; Lechat, "La patristique grecque," pp. 498 n. 6, 502 f. The Roman
Church justifies the addition: L. Lohn, "Doctrina S. Basilii M. de proces-
sionibus divinarum personarum," *Gregorianum*, 10 (1929), 329–64, 461–500;
but the list of MSS in D. Amand, "Essai d'une histoire critique des éditions
générales grecques et gréco-latines de S. Basile de Césarée," *Revue bénédictine*,
56 (1945–46), 135 f., 146 ff., shows that the Migne edition was based on
four codices of the eleventh century, which, as the editors remark in Migne,
P.G., 29, 656 n. 79, agree in omitting the passage quoted by Hugo. H. Dörries, *De spiritu sancto, der Beitrag des Basilius zum Abschluss des trinitarischen
Dogmas* (*Abhandlungen der Akademie der Wissenschaften in Göttingen, Philol.-Hist.
Kl.*, Dritte Folge, Nr. 39 [1956]), 11 n. 1, mentions but does not discuss the
problem. See the Acts of the Council of Ferrara-Florence, ed. J. Gill,
Concilium Florentinum, Series B, 5.2 (Rome, 1953), 262 n. 12, 328 and *passim*
(see index *s.v. Eunomius*); L. Mohler, *Kardinal Bessarion als Theologe, Humanist
und Staatsmann*, 1 (*Quellen und Forschungen aus dem Gebiete der Geschichte... der
Görres-Gesellschaft*, 20 [Paderborn, 1923]), 147 f., 206 f.; H. Vast, *Le Cardinal
Bessarion, 1403–72* (Paris, 1878), pp. 80 ff.

79 Migne, *P.L.*, 202, 394B–C; Migne, *P.G.*, 94, 832B–833A (Hugo erroneously
omits the words I have bracketed, although they are essential to his interpretation); Migne, *P.L.*, 202, 396A–B; Migne, *P.G.*, 96, 605B. Cf. Lechat,
"La patristique grecque," pp. 495 n. 2, 505 f.
On John's treatment of the procession of the Holy Spirit from the Father
alone, see J. Bilz, *Die Trinitätslehre des hl. Johannes von Damaskus* (*Forschungen
zur christlichen Literatur und Dogmengeschichte*, 9, 3 [Paderborn, 1909], 152 ff.
Hugo makes two other references to John, but they do not strengthen his
case: Migne, *P.L.*, 202, 292D (the Son is the *imago* of the Father, and the
Spirit is the *imago* of the Son); 364D (*per Filium datur Spiritus*).
The literature on John is listed by B. Studer, *Die theologische Arbeitsweise*

180   BYZANTINE INFLUENCE ON LATIN THOUGHT

des Johannes von Damaskus (Studia patristica et Byzantina, 2 [Ettal, 1956]).
F. Doelger, *Der griechische Barlaam-Roman ein Werk des h. Johannes von
Damaskos (ibid.,* 1 [Ettal, 1953]), maintains that the Greek version of the
famous tale of Barlaam and Joasaph in its present form was actually written
by John of Damascus, as had long been thought. D. M. Lang opposes this
view and derives the Greek text from the Buddhist original by way of successive derivation *via* Manichaean, Arabic, and Georgian recensions: "*The
Life of the Blessed Iodasaph:* a New Oriental Christian Version of the Barlaam
and Ioasaph Romance," *Bulletin of the School of Oriental and African Studies,* University of London, 20 (1957), 389–407; *idem, The Wisdom of Balahvar: A
Christian Legend of the Buddha* (London, 1957). More important for the subject
at hand is the fact that the story circulated widely throughout the West in a
Latin translation, of which a large number of codices were produced during
the twelfth century.—J. Sonet, *Le roman de Barlaam et Josaphat, 1: Recherches
sur la tradition manuscrite latine et française (Bibliothèque de la faculté de philosophie
et lettres de Namur,* 6 [Namur-Paris, 1949]), 76 ff.

80   *Saint John Damascene, De fide orthodoxa, Versions of Burgundio and Cerbanus
(Franciscan Institute Publications,* Text series, no. 8 [St. Bonaventure, N.Y.,
1955]). The facts and bibliography on the various translations are fully
set out in Buytaert's introduction.* I am greatly indebted to Professor Buytaert for this handsomely printed book and his four valuable articles on
John of Damascus: "Damascenus Latinus on Item 417 of Stegmueller's
Repertorium Commentariorum," Franciscan Studies, 13, 2–3 (1953), 37–70; "The
Apologeticus of Arno of Reichersberg," *ibid.,* 11 (1951), Nos. 3–4, Commemo-
rative volume, 1–47; "The Earliest Latin Translation of Damascene's De
orthodoxa fide III 1–8," *ibid.,* pp. 49–67; "St. John Damascene, Peter
Lombard and Gerhoh of Reichersberg," *ibid.,* 10 (1950), 323–43. See also
L. Callari, "Contributo allo studio della versione di Burgundio Pisano del
'De orthodoxa Fide' di Giovanni Damasceno," *Atti del Reale Istituto Veneto
di scienze, lettere ed arti,* 100, 2 (1940–41), Classe di scienze morali e lettere
(Venice, 1941), 197–246; H. Dausend, "Zur Übersetzungsweise Burgundios
von Pisa," *Wiener Studien, Zeitschrift für klassische Philologie,* 35 (1913), 353–69.

81   See Buytaert's papers cited in the previous note and de Ghellinck, *Mouvement théologique,* pp. 368–415.

82   F. Stegmüller, *Repertorium commentariorum in Sententias Petri Lombardi* (2 vols.;
Würzburg, 1947); and V. Doucet, *Commentaires sur les Sentences, Supplément
au Répertoire de M. Frédéric Stegmüller* (Ad Claras Aquas, 1954), reprinted
from the *Archivum Franciscanum historicum,* 47 (1954), provide impressive
testimony to the popularity and esteem which Peter the Lombard enjoyed.
See also J. de Ghellinck, "Pierre Lombard," *Dictionnaire de théologie catholique,*
12, 2 (Paris, 1935), 1941–2019; *idem, Mouvement théologique,* pp. 213–77,
374–86, 400–420.

83   H. Dausend, "Johannes Damascenus in der Chronik des Salimbene,"
Theologische Quartalschrift, 118 (1937), 173–92; I. Backes, *Die Christologie des
hl. Thomas v. Aquin und die griechischen Kirchenväter (Forschungen zur christlichen
Literatur- und Dogmengeschichte,* 17, 3–4 [Paderborn, 1931]), 44 ff.; P. Minges,

* See also note 149 below.

"Zum Gebrauch der Schrift 'De fide orthodoxa' des Joh. Damaszenus in der Scholastik," *Theologische Quartalschrift*, 96 (1914), 225–47; M. Duffo, "St. Jean Damascène, source de Saint Thomas," *Bulletin de littérature ecclésiastique* (1906), pp. 126–30.

84 See notes 106 f. below.

85 Ioannes de Walter, *Magistri Gandulphi Bononiensis Sententiarum libri quatuor* (Vienna and Breslau, 1924), p. lxviii; 1, 93, pp. 62 f.; 3, 35, p. 298; 3, 46, p. 305; 3, 58, p. 315; 3, 71, p. 321; 3, 73, p. 322; 3, 74, p. 324; 3, 92, p. 341; 3, 114, p. 360; see de Ghellinck, *Le mouvement théologique du xiie siècle*, pp. 335–46; A. M. Landgraf, *Dogmengeschichte der Frühscholastik*, 2, 2 (Regensburg, 1954), 153.

86 M. Chossat, *La Somme des Sentences, œuvre de Hugues de Mortagne vers 1155* (*Spicilegium sacrum Lovaniense, Études et documents*, 5 [Louvain-Paris, 1923]), 167 f.

87 A. M. Landgraf, ed., *Der Sentenzenkommentar des Kardinals Stephan Langton* (*Beiträge zur Geschichte der Philosophie und Theologie des Mittelalters*, 37, 1 [Münster i. W., 1952]), 105, 113.

88 Further research will uncover many other examples of this sort. See, e.g., N. M. Haring, ed., "The So-called *Apologia de Verbo Incarnato*," *Franciscan Studies*, 16 (1956), 102–43, n.b. 104, 108, 127.1, 131 n. 372, 134 n. 431; Landgraf, *Dogmengeschichte*, 2, 1, 162, 166; 2, 2, 141, 147 f., 155, 163 f., 171; 3, 2, 43, 45; de Ghellinck, *Mouvement théologique*, pp. 368–415 and *passim*.

89 *Liber contra duas haereses*, Migne, *P.L.*, 194, 1171A–C; *Liber de gloria et honore Filii hominis*, Migne, *P.L.*, 194, 1082D, 1114–15, 1140C; Buytaert, "St. John Damascene, Peter Lombard and Gerhoh of Reichersberg" (cited above, note 80), pp. 330 ff.; D. van den Eynde, *L'œuvre littéraire de Géroch de Reichersberg* (*Spicilegium Pontificii Athenaei Antoniani*, 11 [Rome, 1957]), 58 n. 5, 80 n. 5, 220, 228 n. 3, 297; D. and O. van den Eynde and A. Rijmersdael, *Gerhohi Praepositi Reichersbergensis opera inedita*, 1 (*ibid.*, 8 [Rome, 1955]), 294, 359 f. *Gerhohi Reichersbergensis Praepositi opera hactenus inedita*, ed. F. Scheibelberger, 1 (Linz, 1875), p. 275, contains one rather ambiguous reference to John of Damascus; cf. note 44 above.

90 See Buytaert, "The *Apologeticus* of Arno of Reichersberg" (note 80 above), for the identification of the passages from John of Damascus which he has located on pp. 45, 131, 150, 154 f., 162, 169, in the edition of C. Weichert, *Arnonis Reicherspergensis Apologeticus contra Folmarum* (Leipzig, 1888).

91 J. Warichez, ed., *Les Disputationes de Simon de Tournai* (*Spicilegium sacrum Lovaniense, Études et documents*, 12 [Louvain, 1932]), 38, 59, 140, 221, 237.

92 P. Glorieux, ed., "La somme 'Quoniam homines' d'Alain de Lille," *Archives d'histoire doctrinale et littéraire du moyen âge*, 20 (1953), 142, 143, 176, 192, 214, 249, 251.

93 Landgraf, *Dogmengeschichte*, 3, 2 (Regensburg, 1955), 36, prints a bit from the *Summa aurea* of William of Auxerre which utilizes the fourth book of the *De fide orthodoxa;* see also Landgraf, *ibid.*, 2, 1, 145 f.; 2, 2, 160; 3, 2, 307.

94 Buytaert, *Saint John Damascene, De fide orthodoxa* (see note 80 above), pp. xii f.

95   For Peter Lombard's position on the theological questions treated below, see O. Baltzer, *Die Sentenzen des Petrus Lombardus (Studien zur Geschichte der Theologie und der Kirche*, edd. N. Bonwetsch and R. Seeberg, 8, 3 [Leipzig, 1902]); idem, *Beiträge zur Geschichte des christologischen Dogmas im 11ten und 12ten Jahrhundert, ibid.*, 3, 1 (1898). Baltzer, however, has not attempted to scrutinize or evaluate Peter's dependence upon John of Damascus.

    J. de Ghellinck, *Mouvement théologique*, pp. 242 f., summarizes the statistics: Peter the Lombard cites Augustine nearly a thousand times, Hilary of Poitiers and Ambrose about 80 each. John of Damascus stands highest among the Greeks, with about 30 references. Athanasius, Didymus, and Cyril of Alexandria are used once each, the Pseudo-Dionysius twice, and Origen about a dozen times. For a full list of Peter's authorities, see the Quaracchi edition, cited in note 96 below, Vol. 2, pp. 1047 ff.

96   *Liber I. Sententiarum, Distinctio* 19, c. 9, *Petri Lombardi libri iv Sententiarum studio et cura PP. Collegii S. Bonaventurae*, 1 (2nd ed.; Ad Claras Aquas, 1916, the so-called Quaracchi edition), 132–34.

97   The *locus classicus* is the 38th Epistle of Basil of Caesarea, which was addressed to his brother, Gregory of Nyssa; cf. Epistle 8. For discussion and a collection of later passages, see R. Arnou, "Unité numérique et unité de nature chez les Pères, après le Concile de Nicée," *Gregorianum*, 15 (1934), 242–54; T. de Régnon, *Études de théologie positive sur la Sainte Trinité* (Première série; Paris, 1892), pp. 154–63. Some authorities attribute Epistle 38 to Gregory of Nyssa, and Epistle 8 to Evagrius Ponticus: see B. Altaner, *Patrologie* (5th ed.; Freiburg im Breisgau, 1958), p. 262.

98   *De fide orthodoxa*, 3, 6 (Migne, *P.G.*, 94, 1001C). I have verified all of Peter's references to John in the original, but have based my translations and paraphrases upon the Latin version, with only occasional corrections as required by the Greek text.

99   *Ibid.*, 3, 4 (Migne, *P.G.*, 94, 997A).

100 *Libri Sententiarum*, 1, *Dist.* 19, c. 9, *ed. cit.*, 1, note 96 above, 132 f. Walter of St. Victor, *loc. cit.*, note 16 above, p. 315 f., makes the same objection.

101 *Libri Sententiarum*, 1, 19, 3, *ed. cit.*, 1, 126; *De fid. orth.*, 3, 6 (Migne, *P.G.*, 94, 1004A).

102 1, 19, 9, *ed. cit.*, 1, 133 f.

103 Hugo, *De sacramentis*, 2, 1, 4 (Migne, *P.L.*, 176, 377A); Abelard, *Sic et non*, c. 8; *Theologia Christiana*, 4; *Introductio ad theologiam*, 2, 10 (Migne, *P.L.*, 178, 1360A–D, 1265A–B, 1057 f.).

104 Erigena, *De divisione naturae*, 1, 14 f., Migne, *P.L.*, 122, 461B, 463C. The Pseudo-Dionysius does not quite make this assertion in the same form, but the concept is deducible from his oft-repeated characterization of God as unknowable, supraessential (ὑπερούσιος), and beyond all being, who cannot be included within either the sensible (τὰ αἰσθητά) or the intelligible world (τὰ νοητά). The list of the Aristotelian categories given by Erigena as inapplicable to God roughly corresponds to that which appears in the *Theologia mystica*, pp. 4 f., of the Pseudo-Dionysius: Migne, *P. G.*, 3, 1040D, 1045D–1048B (fourteenth-century paraphrase by Pachy-

meres, *ibid.*, 1044A–1045C, 1057A–1064A). Cf. *De caelesti hierarchia*, 2, 3,
M⸗ne, *P.G.*, 3, 140C–141A (Pachymeres, 156A ff.). See also the de luxe
edition by P. Chevallier, *Dionysiaca*, 1 ([Paris], 1937), 594–602; 2 (n.p.,
n.d.), 753 ff., which contains the Greek text along with nine Latin versions.

The notion that God is not *genus, species,* or any of the categories is usually
traced back to the Neoplatonic exegesis of Plato's *Parmenides,* 141D–142A.—
F. M. Cornford, *Plato and Parmenides* (London, 1939), pp. 129 ff. But it was
first articulated in these words by Clement of Alexandria, *Stromata,* 5, 12
(Migne, *P.G.*, 9, 121A; ed. O. Stählin, *Clemens Alexandrinus,* 2 [Leipzig,
1906], 380.18–20; cf. Plato, *Timaeus,* 27c), apparently on the basis of
Philo. See H. A. Wolfson, *Philo,* 2 (Cambridge, Mass., 1948), 109 f., 113,
153 ff.; *idem,* "The Knowability and Describability of God in Plato and
Aristotle," *Harvard Studies in Classical Philology,* 56–57 (1947), 233–49.

The Neoplatonic affirmations of this principle are of considerable
interest because of their influence upon medieval thought.—Plotinus,
Enneads, 6, 2, 9; 6, 9, 4; Proclus, *In Platonis Parmenidem,* 7, ed. V. Cousin,
Procli philosophi Platonici opera inedita (Paris, 1864), 1181.8–24; cf. 1176.30–40,
1173.7 ff. Cf. L. J. Rosán, *The Philosophy of Proclus* (New York, 1949),
pp. 123 f., n.b. n. 22; note 38 above.

105 Peter Lombard, 1, 19, 10, *ed. cit.*, 1, 135.

106 *Sententiae Petri Pictaviensis,* 1 (*Publications in Mediaeval Studies,* edd. P. S.
Moore and M. Dulong [Notre Dame, 1943]), 282.10–283.46.

107 *Ibid.,* 284.47 ff. Alan of Lille, ed. P. Glorieux, *loc. cit.* in note 92 above,
249–51, discusses this point and concludes that the hypostases differ, not
*numero, sed numero personarum, id est [secundum] pluralitatem personalium proprieta-
tum.* This is what John meant, he says.

108 Peter Lombard, 1, 25, 3, *ed. cit.*, 1, 161–63; *De fid. orth.*, 3, 5 (Migne,
P.G., 94, 1000B).

109 1, 26, 1, *ed. cit.*, 1, 163 f.; cf. 3, 7, 1–2, *ed. cit.*, 2, 583; *De fid. orth.*, 3, 3
(Migne, *P.G.*, 94, 992A–B); Jerome, *Epistula* 15, 3 f. (Migne, *P.L.*, 22,
356 f.); Abelard, *Sic et non,* 9, Migne, *P.L.*, 178, 1366B–C. Cf. note 11 above.

110 1, 27, 3, *ed. cit.*, 1, 173; *De fid. orth.*, 3, 6 (Migne, *P.G.*, 94, 1001C); 3, 7
(Migne, *P.G.*, 94, 1008C).

111 For a good summary of Athanasian, Cappadocian, and other early
Christian theology on this point, see G. Bardy, "Trinité," *Dictionnaire de
théologie catholique,* 15, 2 (Paris, 1950), 1659–1702, with bibliography;
note 97 above.

112 *De fid. orth.*, 3, 5 (Migne, *P.G.*, 94, 1000B–D).

113 1, 33, 1, *ed. cit.*, 1, 207–10, quotation on p. 208. On the arguments of
Gilbert, see Haring, "The Case of Gilbert de la Porrée, Bishop of Poitiers,"
Mediaeval Studies, 13 (1951), 1–40, especially 20 ff.; cf. bibliography in
note 42 above.

114 Argument so summarized: 1, 33, 1, *ed. cit.*, 1, 209. See Haring, *loc. cit.*
in previous note. On Sabellianism, see E. Vagaggini, "Modalismo,"
Enciclopedia Cattolica, 8 (1952), 1162–65.

115 1, 33, 1, *ed. cit.*, 209 f.; *De fid. orth.*, 3, 6 (Migne, *P.G.*, 94, 1001C); cf.

note 110 above. Walter of St. Victor, *loc. cit.*, note 16 above, 319.13 ff., finds this passage from John useful against Sabellianism.

116   3, 2, 1, *ed. cit.*, 2, 554 f.; *De fid. orth.*, 3, 4 (Migne, *P.G.*, 94, 997A); 3, 3 (Migne, *P.G.*, 94, 992A–993A); 3, 6 (Migne, *P.G.*, 94, 1005A–B). The first of these excerpts from John of Damascus was quoted by John of Cornwall in his *Eulogium ad Alexandrum Papam tertium* (written just before the Third Lateran Council, which was held in 1179), ed. Haring, *Mediaeval Studies*, 13 (1951), 277 f. See notes 127 f. and 131 below.

117   For the principal passages on τὸ ἀπρόσληπτον ἀθεράπευτον (what was not assumed could not be cured), see E. Weigl, *Christologie vom Tode des Athanasius bis zum Ausbruch des Nestorianischen Streites (373–429)* (*Münchener Studien zur historischen Theologie*, 4 [Munich, 1925]), pp. 58–60 ff.; see bibliographies on the Cappadocians, including Amphilochius of Iconium, in Altaner, *Patrologie*, pp. 258–76; on Apollinarius, *ibid.*, pp. 280 f. The latest material on the Monophysites is to be found in A. Grillmeier and H. Bacht, *Das Konzil von Chalkedon* (3 vols.; Würzburg, 1951–54); n.b. the monograph by Joseph Lebon in Vol. 1, pp. 425–580.

118   Peter Lombard, 3, 2, 2, *ed. cit.*, 2, 555; *De fid. orth.*, 3, 6 (Migne, *P.G.*, 94, 1005B). Cf. Landgraf, *Dogmengeschichte*, 2, 1, 160 f.

119   3, 3, 1, *ed. cit.*, 2, 557–59; *De fid. orth.*, 3, 2 (Migne, *P.G.*, 94, 985B–988A).

120   3, 3, 4, *ed. cit.*, 2, 561 f.; *De fid. orth.*, 3, 7 (Migne, *P.G.*, 94, 1012B).

121   3, 5, 1, *ed. cit.*, 2, 566–70. Cf. Landgraf, *Dogmengeschichte*, 2, 1, 124 f., 116–37.

122   3, 5, 1, *ed cit.*, 567, sec. 25; 569 f., sec. 29.

123   *Ibid.*, pp. 569 f., sec. 29.

124   *Ibid.*, p. 570, sec. 30; *De fid. orth.*, 3, 6 (Migne, *P.G.*, 94, 1004B, 1008B–C). Immediately before the last sentence of his quotation from John, Peter interpolates "et unam naturam Dei Verbi incarnatam confitemur," which in the original Greek occurs, not at this point, but in the following chapter (3, 7, Migne, *P.G.*, 94, 1012B: καὶ μίαν δὲ φύσιν τοῦ Θεοῦ Λόγου σεσαρκωμένην ὁμολογοῦμεν). See note 120 above. John was misled by Cyril of Alexandria (Migne, *P.G.*, 76, 1212A; 77, 224D, 245A) into naming Athanasius here. The formula he cites is Apollinarian.—ed. H. Lietzmann, *Apollinaris von Laodicea und seine Schule*, 1 (Tübingen, 1904), 251.1 f. See Buytaert, *Saint John Damascene* (note 80 above), p. 190.

125   On the success of the Apollinarians in concealing the works of Apollinarius under the names of orthodox writers like Gregory Thaumaturgus, Athanasius, and Bishop Julius I of Rome, see H. Lietzmann, *Apollinaris*, pp. 108 ff. On Thomas Aquinas, see Backes, *op. cit.* (note 83 above), pp. 114 f., 150 f., 154, 293. On Justinian, cf. my article "The Immutability of Christ and Justinian's Condemnation of Theodore of Mopsuestia," *Dumbarton Oaks Papers*, 6 (1951), 159.

126   See Lietzmann, *Apollinaris*, pp. 108 ff.; and the author of *Adversus fraudes Apollinaristarum*, Migne, *P.G.*, 86, 2, 1948.

127   3, 6, 1–6; 3, 7, 1 f.; 3, 10, 1; *ed. cit.*, 2, 573–88, 593 f.; de Ghellinck, *Mouvement théologique*, pp. 250 ff., and works there cited; Hefele and Leclercq,

Histoire des conciles, 5, 2, 974–77; E. Portalié, "Adoptianisme," *Dictionnaire de théologie catholique*, 1, 1 (Paris, 1902), 414–18; Baltzer (see note 95 above), *Die Sentenzen*, pp. 84 ff.; *idem, Beiträge*, 65–67; J. Bach, *Die Dogmengeschichte des Mittelalters*, 2 (Vienna, 1875), 200–206, 208; J. A. Dorner, *History of the Development of the Doctrine of the Person of Christ*, 2.1 (Edinburgh, 1869), 313–19.

Note the attack on the third theory in the anonymous *Apologia de Verbo Incarnato* of *ca.* 1160 (note 88 above) and in John of Cornwall's *Eulogium*, the latter of whom converts two texts (note 116 above, note 131 below) from John of Damascus, *loc. cit.*, pp. 276–79, that had been quoted by his opponents into a buttress for his defense of the first theory. The second of these forms part of Peter's exposition of the second theory.

128 *Loc. cit.*, 116 above, pp. 265, 284; Migne, *P.L.*, 199, 1052C–D, 1053A–B, 1071B–C; n.b. introduction to the *Libri Sententiarum*, ed. *cit.*, 1, xlviii ff.; de Ghellinck, *Dictionnaire de théologie catholique*, 12, 2, 2003–5.

129 A. Michel, "Hypostatique (union)," *Dictionnaire de théologie catholique*, 7, 1 (Paris, 1921), 512 ff., n.b. 516. A catena of decisive passages from the fathers (n.b. Cyril) on the hypostatic union is to be found in *De incarnatione*, 3, 4, 10–17, *Dogmata theologica Dionysii Petavii*, ed. J. B. Fournials, 5 (Paris, 1866), 391 ff.

130 3, 6, 3, *ed. cit.*, 2, 577 f.; *De fid. orth.*, 3, 4 (Migne, *P.G.*, 94, 997B), 3, 7 (Migne, *P.G.*, 94, 1009A–B), 3, 3 (Migne, *P.G.*, 94, 993B–C). Leo, *Epistola* 28, Migne, *P.L.*, 54, 767B.

131 3, 7, 2, *ed. cit.*, 2, 585; *De fid. orth.*, 3, 3 (Migne, *P.G.*, 94, 988B–989A). Matching the penultimate clause of this sentence ("is perfect God and perfect man"), the Greek has only "perfect God," although "perfect man" is clearly implied by the context, and probably appeared in the Greek texts used by Cerbanus and Burgundio for their translations, which are identical at this point: "Deum perfectum et hominem perfectum eundem" (ed. Buytaert, *op. cit.*, note 80 above, 393.22 f., 174.25 f.). John of Cornwall uses this excerpt from John of Damascus to fortify his case in favor of the first theory, *loc. cit.*, note 116 above, 278.

132 3, 7, 2, *ed. cit.*, 2, 588; *De fid. orth.*, 3, 2 (Migne, *P.G.*, 94, 988A). On Adoptianism, cf. Landgraf, *Dogmengeschichte*, 2, 2, 24 ff.

133 3, 8, 2, *ed. cit.*, 2, 590; *De fid. orth.*, 3, 7 (Migne, *P.G.*, 94, 1009C). On the theological principles involved see, e.g., my "Immutability of Christ" (note 125 above), pp. 144–49.

134 3, 15, 1, *ed. cit.*, 2, 611; *De fid. orth.*, 3, 20 (Migne, *P.G.*, 94, 1081B). John is mentioned here only as *auctoritas*, not by name.

135 3, 9, 1, *ed. cit.*, 2, 591 f.; *De fid. orth.*, 3, 8 (Migne, *P.G.*, 94, 1013B–1016A). On the adoration (*latreia*) of Christ as of God, see the patristic excerpts collected in *De incarnatione*, 15, 3–4, *Dogmata theologica Dionysii Petavii*, ed. J. B. Fournials, 7 (Paris, 1867), 183 ff.; and on the comparison, Cyril, *Scholia de incarnatione unigeniti*, 10 (Migne, *P.G.*, 75, 1380A–B); H. A. Wolfson, *The Philosophy of the Church Fathers*, 1 (Cambridge, Mass., 1956), 384–417 *passim;* cf. Landgraf, *Dogmengeschichte*, 2, 2, 142–44, 147 f.

136   3, 22, 3, *ed. cit.*, 2, 653 f.; *De fid. orth.*, 3, 7 (Migne, *P.G.*, 94, 1012B–C). Cf. Michel, *loc. cit.*, note 129 above, p. 497; Tertullian, *Adversus Praxean,* 22, 10–11.

137   Edition cited in note 90 above, p. 154.

138   My own investigations confirm those of L. Ott, "Das Konzil von Chalkedon in der Frühscholastik," *Das Konzil von Chalkedon, op. cit.*, note 117 above, Vol. 2, pp. 873–922; *idem*, "Gratian und das Konzil von Chalcedon," *Studia Gratiana*, 1 (Bologna, 1953), 31–50. For a reference to the disciplinary canons of Chalcedon, see Landgraf, *Dogmengeschichte*, 2, 1, 18. Hugo, note 71 above, quotes a few words from the Chalcedonian symbol.

139   Peter Lombard, 1, 11, 1, *ed. cit.*, 1, 78 f. Actually, the so-called Niceno-Constantinopolitan Creed of 381, which is now designated as the Nicene Creed in the churches, first appears as an official document in the *Acta* of the Council of Chalcedon in 451.—J. N. D. Kelly, *Early Christian Creeds*, pp. 296 ff.

140   See the text edited by P. Glorieux, *loc. cit.*, note 16 above, p. 255.

141   *Ibid.*

142   On this vast subject I refer to the following, with bibliographical notes: E. F. Bruck, *Kirchenväter und soziales Erbrecht* (Berlin-Göttingen-Heidelberg, 1956), pp. 249–56, and *passim*; F. Calasso, E. Ewig, A. Steinwenter, A. V. Soloviev, "La sopravvivenza delle istituzioni giuridiche romane," *Comitato internazionale di scienze storiche, X congresso internazionale di scienze storiche*, Roma, 4–11 Settembre, 1955, *Relazioni*, 6 (Florence, 1955), 519–650; E. Genzmer, "Il diritto romano come fattore della civiltà europea," *Università degli studi di Trieste, Facoltà di giurisprudenza, Istituto di storia del diritto, Conferenze Romanistiche*, 3 (Trieste, 1954); *idem*, "Die iustinianische Kodifikation und die Glossatoren," *Atti del congresso internazionale di diritto romano, Bologna–Roma, 1933*, Bologna, 1 (Pavia, 1934), 345–430; *idem*, "Quare Glossatorum," *Gedächtnisschrift für Emil Seckel* (Berlin, 1927), pp. 1–69; G. Post, "*Philosophantes* and *Philosophi* in Roman and Canon Law," *Archives d'histoire doctrinale et littéraire du moyen âge*, 21 (1954), 135–38; P. S. Leicht, "Il processo italo-bizantino nell' Italia meridionale," *Atti del congresso internazionale di diritto romano e di storia del diritto*, Verona, 27–29 Settembre, 1948, 4 (Milan, 1953), 329–41; S. Kuttner, "New Studies on the Roman Law in Gratian's Decretum," *Seminar*, 11 (1953), 12–50; cf. *idem, Repertorium der Kanonistik (1140–1234) (Studi e Testi*, 71 [Vatican City, 1937]); *idem, Kanonistische Schuldlehre von Gratian bis auf die Dekretalen Gregors IX. (Studi e Testi*, 64 [Vatican City, 1935]); P. Koschaker, *Europa und das römische Recht* (Munich-Berlin, 1947 [1953 reprint]), pp. 55–76, 354 f., and *passim*; H. Kantorowicz, *Studies in the Glossators of the Roman Law, Newly Discovered Writings of the Twelfth Century* (Cambridge, Eng., 1938); W. Engelmann, *Die Wiedergeburt der Rechtskultur in Italien* (Leipzig, 1939); P. Vinogradoff, *Roman Law in Medieval Europe* (2nd ed.; Oxford, 1929); *Cambridge Medieval History*, 4 (Cambridge, Eng., 1923), 892 f.; H. Niese, *Die Gesetzgebung der normannischen Dynastie im Regnum Siciliae* (Halle a. S., 1910); L. S. Villanueva, *Diritto bizantino* (Milan, 1906), pp. 150 ff. (reprinted

from the *Enciclopedia Giuridica Italiana*); E. Seckel, *Beiträge zur Geschichte beider Rechte im Mittelalter* (2 vols.; Tübingen, 1898); F. Brandileone, *Il diritto romano nelle leggi normanne e sveve del regno di Sicilia* (Turin, 1884); F. C. von Savigny, *Geschichte des römischen Rechts im Mittelalter*, 2 (Heidelberg, 1834), 303–18, 494–99 (on Ivo of Chartres); 4 (2nd ed.; Heidelberg, 1850), on the twelfth century, pp. 394–410 on Burgundio. Mention should be made of the collected papers of G. Ferrari dalle Spade, *Scritti giuridici*, 3 vols. (Milan, 1953–56), which include a number of valuable studies on the transmission of Byzantine law to the West; see also F. Calasso, *Medio evo del diritto*, 1 (Milan, 1954).

143 The evidence is set forth in my paper, "Pletho, Strabo, and Columbus," *Annuaire de l'Institut de philologie et d'histoire orientales et slaves*, 12 (1952), 1–18. The best book on Pletho is by F. Masai, *Pléthon et le platonisme de Mistra* (Paris, 1956).

144 Hugo missed the point of Nicetas' argument, which was based on the Neoplatonic theory of a ladder of grades of being, descending from the highest to the lowest. According to this scheme, the One, the highest and most powerful cause in the universe, produced a being (i.e., an individual, whether spiritual or material) which was like it in many respects, but necessarily inferior to it because derived from it. This being, in turn, was the source of others, each of which was superior to that of which it itself was the cause. Thus, the more remote a being was from the One, the less directly it "participated" in the One, and the more inferior it was. That which is produced is said to "participate" in its cause, which is described as "the participated" and always stands higher than that which "participates." These principles were formulated with quasi-mathematical precision by the pagan philosopher Proclus (410–85), but exerted great influence upon the Pseudo-Dionysius and other Christian thinkers. See the critical edition of the Greek text, with English translation and commentary by E. R. Dodds, *Proclus, the Elements of Theology* (Oxford, 1933), propositions 7–9, 23 f., 36 f., 56 f., 126, 128, 130, 132.

ADDITIONAL NOTES

145 Gerhard Rohlfs, *Neue Beiträge zur Kenntnis der unteritalischen Gräzität* (*Sitzungsberichte der bayerischen Akademie der Wissenschaften, Philos.-hist. Klasse*, Heft 5 [Munich, 1962]): see Rohlfs' bibliography on the knowledge of Greek in Italy.

146 André Guillou, *Les actes grecs de S. Maria di Messina, enquête sur les populations grecques d'Italie du sud et de Sicile, XIe–XIVe s.* (*Istituto Siciliano di studi bizantini e neoellenici*, ed. Bruno Lavagnini, *Testi*, 8 [Palermo, 1963]), plus portfolio; *idem*, "Grecs d'Italie du sud et de Sicile au Moyen Âge: les moines," *Mélanges d'archéologie et d'histoire*, 75 (1963), 79–110; *idem* and W. Holtzmann, "Zwei Katepansurkunden aus Tricarico," *Quellen und Forschungen aus italienischen Archiven und Bibliotheken*, 41 (1961), 1–28; Léon-Robert Ménager,

Les actes latins di S. Maria di Messina, 1103–1250 (*Testi*, 9 [Palermo, 1963]).

147 Albert Siegmund, *Die Überlieferung der griechischen christlichen Literatur in der lateinischen Kirche bis zum zwölften Jahrhundert* (*Abhandlungen der bayerischen Benediktiner-Akademie*, 5 [Munich-Pasing, 1939]).

148 Cyril Mango, "The conciliar edict of 1166," *Dumbarton Oaks Papers*, 18 (1963), 313–30, with seven plates.

149 Despite a long and persistent search, I was unable to find, until after publication, E. Bertola, "Le citazioni di Giovanni Damasceno nel primo libro delle Sentenze Lombardiane," *Pier Lombardo*, 1 (1957), No. 3, 3–17, whose treatment of the subject is somewhat different from mine.

HISTORY OF SCIENCE

XIII

THE ALEXANDRIAN ORIGIN OF THE *CHRISTIAN TOPOGRAPHY* OF COSMAS INDICOPLEUSTES

This article, which is the first of a series of investigations on Cosmas, is a revised version of a short section of a paper read before the Symposium on Byzantine and Medieval Art and History conducted by Professor George La Piana at Dumbarton Oaks (April 29–May 1, 1943).

The remaining portion of this study, left unfinished on account of war work, contains an analysis of Cosmas's indebtedness to ancient science (Aristotle and Ptolemy) and a discussion of Cosmas's Nestorianism.

I am grateful to Professors R. P. Blake, W. R. W. Koehler, and George La Piana for advice, and to Miss Margaret Rathbone, Mrs. Nathalie Scheffer, Mrs. Eugene Bland, Miss M. H. Beale, and Miss Persis Mason for invaluable assistance. I am indebted to Dr. Joshua Starr for his kindness in verifying the reference to the *Life of Mar Aba* in note 34.

WHEN Montfaucon published the *editio princeps* of the *Christian Topography* in the *Collectio Nova Patrum et Scriptorum Graecorum*, he believed that it was written by Cosmas in Egypt.[1] A. Galland was also of this opinion,[2] as were Fabricius[3] and the chief representatives of early criticism.[4] But this theory was challenged in 1883 by H. Gelzer,[5] who asserted that near the end of his life Cosmas settled down in a monastery at Raithu[6] on the Sinai peninsula and there devoted himself to literary labors, of which the *Christian Topography* is the only surviving monument. Krumbacher[7] followed Gelzer here and found a warm supporter in Strzygowski,[8] who seized upon the statement of the Sinaitic authorship of Cosmas's work as proof of his theory of the Syrian origin of the famous Cosmas miniatures. In the meantime, however, J. W. McCrindle had brought out an English translation of the *Christian Topography*, and had stated that Cosmas returned to Alexandria after his travels and there[9] composed his only extant work [*ca.* 550].[10] He apparently regarded the matter as so certain that he did not feel the necessity of marshalling arguments to prove the point. E. O. Winstedt, the editor of the only critical text, belongs to the same school of thought.[11] But neither McCrindle nor Winstedt made use of Gelzer's researches. Indeed, Krumbacher in a review[12] reproaches McCrindle for failing to read and utilize Gelzer's article. The result, as one might expect, is chaos and confusion. Some contemporary writers pronounce boldly for the Alexandrian provenance,[13] others for the Sinaitic;[14] one group expresses perplexity or indecision,[15] and still another preserves a discreet silence.[16]

But there is no need for such uncertainty. Gelzer does not adduce any respectable support whatsoever for his theory. He argues[17] that the country about Sinai had been traversed so often by Cosmas that it had acquired a high emotional value in his sight and was for this reason chosen as a suitable place for his last days. He relies on the statement of Cosmas in the second book of the *Christian Topography* that his friend Menas, who had accompanied him on his archaeological expedition to Axum, had joined the monastic settlement at Raithu.[18] Gelzer makes much of the fact that Cosmas had an intimate knowledge of the topography and local traditions of the Sinai peninsula, that he was familiar with the Semitic inscriptions[19] found in that area, and that he had observed the wheel-ruts at Clysma, which he knew were regarded as mute witnesses of Pharaoh's charioteers and the miraculous defeat of the Egyptians during the flight of the chosen people across the Red Sea. But, to say nothing of the numerous medieval writers and pilgrims[20] who knew and revered these same Sinaitic monuments, none

76

of the passages cited by Gelzer bears out his hypothesis. Had Cosmas been a monk at Sinai, it is strange that his description of this region does not give the slightest hint that he had ever been more than a tourist there.[21]

The reason is, of course, that he was an Alexandrian and wrote the *Christian Topography* in Alexandria. There cannot be the slightest wavering or hesitancy about this. To begin with, in dedicating his book to Pamphilus, Cosmas writes of the time "when by the will of God you came to us here in Alexandria."[22] Further proof is to be found in the sixth book, which is of particular importance in view of the fact that Books 1–5 and 6–12 form separate entities.[23] In three passages[24] at this point Cosmas mentions the astronomical observations which he and the presbyter Stephen of Antioch had made in Alexandria. The texts are clear and decisive, and the adverb ἐνταῦθα is used in such a way as to leave no doubt that Cosmas means to say "here in Alexandria." Equally conclusive is his reference to the river Nile as τοῦ παρ' ἡμῖν Νείλου ποταμοῦ.[25] Moreover, in his general description of the extent of the world, Alexandria is always prominently mentioned.[26] The Mediterranean is ἡ ἡμετέρα θάλασσα,[27] and the Egyptian names of the months are used throughout.[28] Finally, in quoting excerpts from the sermons of the Patriarchs Timothy and Theodosius of Alexandria, he usually gives the exact date of the homily and the name of the church in which it was preached.[29] Not without interest in this connection is the fact that at the end of the seventh book of the *Christian Topography* Cosmas quotes two prayers (περὶ τῶν προσφερόντων and περὶ τῶν κεκοιμημένων) which seem to be derived from an early form of the Alexandrian rite, the *Liturgy of St. Mark*.[29a]

Having proved that the *Christian Topography* was written in Alexandria, we are now in a position to illuminate Cosmas's references to Patricius[30] (better known as Mar Aba, Catholicos of Persia from 540 to 552), who together with Thomas of Edessa gave a series of lectures on theology and cosmology which Cosmas must have attended. Cosmas himself tells us that he received

> oral instruction from Patricius, that very holy man and great teacher, . . . who came here from the land of the Chaldaeans together with Thomas of Edessa, . . . who . . . died in Constantinople.

O. Braun[31] wrongly took this passage to mean that Cosmas studied under Mar Aba at Constantinople. In so doing he seems to have led astray other scholars like Chabot, Baumstark, and Labourt,[32] all of whom failed to perceive that a few lines previously Cosmas had described himself as writing in Alexandria.[33] The non-Greek evidence accords perfectly with this fact, for we learn from the *Chronique de Séert*[34] that Mar Aba and Thomas of

Edessa visited Alexandria and offered what might be called a joint course on the works of Theodore of Mopsuestia. Mar Aba lectured in Syriac, and Thomas translated into Greek, until pressure from Alexandrian churchmen, who, as Monophysites, naturally resented the popularity and success of their Nestorian rivals, forced them to flee to Constantinople. Thomas died in the capital; [35] and Mar Aba, faced once more with persecution, took to flight again and escaped to Persia.

Cosmas may or may not have been a monk, as he is designated in the Mss.; [36] he says nothing about any personal experience he may have had with the monastic life. But there is no compelling reason to doubt, as some have done, that he actually bore the name Cosmas.[37] In any case, it is clear that our author, whether monk or not, and whatever his name may have been, wrote in Alexandria and not on Mount Sinai. It is to be hoped, therefore, that we shall hear no more of the alleged Sinaitic provenience of the *Christian Topography*. Strzygowski's followers, if such there be, will have to turn elsewhere for proof of their theory.

NOTES

1. Volume 2 (Paris, 1706), 113 ff. See the title page (reprinted in *MPG*, 88, 51); in *caput primum* of his preface Montfaucon refers to Cosmas as "Aegyptius Alexandrinus." Only a few unimportant fragments had been published before Montfaucon; see *MPG*, 88, 9 ff., and the literature cited in notes 4 and 16 *infra*.

2. *Bibliotheca Veterum Patrum*, 11 (Venice, 1776), xviii: *Cosmas Aegyptius, et quidem Alexandrinus*; Galland published the Greek text with a Latin translation.

3. *Bibliotheca Graeca*, ed. G. C. Harles, 4 (Hamburg, 1795, reprinted in *MPG*, 88, 23 f.), 253 n.h., 257.

4. R. Ceillier, *Histoire générale des auteurs sacrés et ecclésiastiques*, 2d. ed., 11 (Paris, 1862), 186; W. Cave, *Scriptorum ecclesiasticorum historia literaria*, 1 (Basel, 1741), 515. It has not seemed worthwhile to give references to all the older handbooks, encyclopaedias, and authorities (like Allatius, Assemani, Oudin, etc.), whose testimony, after all, matters little; the necessary bibliographical indications can be found in the works cited in my notes and also, in part, in U. Chevalier, *Répertoire des sources historiques du moyen âge, Bio-bibliographie*, 1 (Paris, 1905), 1056 f.

5. "Kosmas der Indienfahrer," *Jahrbücher für protestantische Theologie*, 9 (1883), 105–141.

6. *Ibid.*, 110 f.; on Cosmas's identification of Raithu as the ancient Elim (modern Tor), see L. Prévost, L. Dennefeld, etc., *Le Sinai hier . . . aujourd'hui*, an admirable little book (Paris, 1937), 161; and Winstedt's note *ad loc.*, 338 (see n. 18 *infra*); cf. also Lina Eckenstein, *History of Sinai* (London, 1921), 119 f. The contrary supposition of R. Weill, *La presqu'île du Sinai* (Paris, 1908), 225, that Cosmas never even visited Sinai, is groundless, as the note of Weill himself, *loc. cit.*, clearly demonstrates. Schiwietz, "Die altchristliche Tradition über den Berg Sinai und Kosmas Indikopleustes," *Der Katholik*, 4. Folge, 38 (1908), 9–30, does not concern himself with the provenance of the *Christian Topography*; cf. p. 26 on Elim. For full bibliographies see C. J. Jellouschek, "Eine Sinaifahrt," *Theologische Studien d. Österr. Leo-Gesellschaft*, 37 (Vienna, 1938), 6 f., 23 ff., and *passim*.

7. *Geschichte d. byzantinischen Litteratur*, 2d ed. (Munich, 1897), 412 ff.

78

8. *Der Bilderkreis des griechischen Physiologus, des Kosmas Indikopleustes u. Oktateuch,* *Byzantinisches Archiv,* Heft 2 (Leipzig, 1899), 54, 99 ff. In his review of C. Stornajolo, *Le* *miniature della Topografia Cristiana di Cosma I.* (Milan, 1908), *BZ,* 18 (1909), 672 f., Strzy-gowski mentions Stornajolo's view that Cosmas was an Alexandrian but does not comment further; see n. 13 *infra.*

9. London, 1897, ii, iv, viii.

10. The approximate date can be established by internal evidence. In Book II Cosmas says that his visit to Axum took place during the reign of Justin (518–27), roughly twenty-five years before the composition of the *Christian Topography:* E. O. Winstedt, ed., *Christian* *Topography of Cosmas Indicopleustes* (Cambridge, Eng., 1909), 72.25 ff. The eclipses men-tioned by Cosmas in Book VI (*op. cit.,* 232.18 ff.) are assigned to the year 547 by Jacob Krall, "Studien zur Geschichte des alten Aegypten," *Sitzungsb. der k. Ak. der Wiss., Philos.-hist.* *Cl.,* 121 (Vienna, 1890), Abh. 11, 72.

This evidence (cf. Winstedt, *op. cit.,* 5 f., 25 f.) would seem to indicate that the *C.T.* was written sometime between ca. 543 and 552. It should be noted, however, that Book VI, like Books VII-X (and perhaps XII), was written specifically to deal with special points arising out of the controversy provoked by Books I-V. This does not necessarily mean that Books I-V were written before 547, or that all of the material in Books VII-XII is to be dated after 547. Book XI (and possibly XII) seem to have been excerpted from a work or works by Cosmas which had no generic connection with the *C.T.* Occasional miscalculations like that of J. P. Junglas, *Leontius von Byzanz (Forschungen zur christlichen Lit. u. Dogmenge-schichte,* 7, Heft 3, Paderborn, 1908), 64, who dates the *C.T.* between 537 and 543, do not deserve consideration.

11. *Op. cit.,* 3. The Teubner edition by Georg Sieffert, announced in *BZ,* 4 (1895), 645, never appeared. For reviews of Winstedt's edition see *BZ,* 19 (1910), 605; 20 (1911), 312; 21 (1912–13), 246–8 (by Otto Stählin).

12. *BZ,* 8 (1899), 550 f.; Gelzer's paper is described as a *wichtige Abhandlung.*

13. The historians of art are almost unanimous: C. R. Morey, *Early Christian Art* (Prince-ton, 1942), 79 ff.; Kurt Weitzmann, *Die byzantinische Buchmalerei des 9. u. 10. Jahrhun-derts* (Berlin, 1935), 5 (see also the literature cited on p. 4); D. T. Rice, *Byzantine Art* (Ox-ford, 1935), 131 (Egypt); C. Diehl, *Manuel d'art byzantin,* 2d ed., 1 (Paris, 1925), 240 ff.; Stornajolo, *op. cit.,* 5 f. Cf. E. K. Rīedin, *Khristianskaĭa Topografiĭa Koz'my Indikoplova po* *grecheskim i russkim spiskam* (ed. D. V. Aĭnalov, Moscow, 1916), 34 ff.; N. Kondakoff, *His-toire de l'art byzantin considéré principalement dans les miniatures,* 1 (Paris, 1886), 141, and *idem, Puteshestvie na Sinaĭ (Zapiski Imp. Novorossīĭskago Universiteta,* 33, Odessa, 1882, pt. 3), 120, 137–43.

Here also belongs the excellent article by H. Leclercq in the *Dictionnaire d'archéologie* *chrétienne,* 8 (Paris, 1928), 820 f. Especially worthy of mention is J. Wittmann, *Sprachliche* *Untersuchungen zu Cosmas* (Borna-Leipzig, 1913), 1. Cf. A. A. Vasiliev, *Histoire de l'em-pire byzantin,* 1 (Paris, 1932), 215 ff.; L. Duchesne, *L'Église au viᵉ siècle* (Paris, 1925), 315 ff.; J. B. Bury, *History of the Later Roman Empire,* 2 (London, 1923), 319; and E. Mangenot in the *Dictionnaire de théologie catholique,* 3 (Paris, 1908), 1916.

14. A number of writers have followed Gelzer and Krumbacher on this point. The most important are: R. Hennig, *Terrae incognitae,* 2 (Leiden, 1937), 47; L. Bréhier in A. Fliche and V. Martin, *Histoire de l'Église,* 4 (Paris, 1937), 557; E. G. Pantelakes in Μεγάλη Ἑλληνικὴ Ἐγκυκλοπαίδεια, 14 (Athens, 1930), 949; Efron-Brockhaus, *Novyĭ Entsiklopedicheskiĭ Slo-var',* (Petrograd, n.d.), 111; J. L. Heiberg, "Et Christent Verdensbillede," *Studier fra Sprog-og Oldtidsforskning, Udgivne af Det Filologisk-Historiske Samfund, Nr. 138* (Copenhagen, 1926), 5. Wecker in Pauly-Wissowa-Kroll, *Real-encyclopädie,* 11 (Stuttgart, 1922), 1487; M. Jugie, "Abraham d'Éphèse et ses écrits," *BZ,* 22 (1913), 45; C. Diehl, *Justinien et la* *civilisation byzantine au viᵉ siècle* (Paris, 1901), xxiv.

15. O. Bardenhewer, *Geschichte der altkirchlichen Literatur,* 5 (Freiburg i. B., 1932), 95, regards the Sinaitic theory as *nicht ausreichend begründet;* so does F. X. Schühlein,

Lexikon für Theologie u. Kirche, 6 (Freiburg i. B., 1934), 219 f. See also O. M. Dalton, *East Christian art* (Oxford, 1925), 318, and the same writer's *Byzantine art and archaeology* (*ibid.*, 1911), 461 f. E. T. Charton, *Voyageurs anciens et modernes*, 2 (Paris, 1863), 1, hesitates between Alexandria and Jerusalem.

16. N. Iorga, *Histoire de la vie byzantine*, 1 (Bucharest, 1934), 183 f., but cf. 184; M. Thévenot, *Relations de divers voyages curieux*, 1 (Paris, 1696), nos. 13 and 14 (in the Library of Congress copy).

17. *Loc. cit.*, 111 ff.

18. References to the text of Cosmas will be preceded by W. (= Winstedt's edition, p.); thus, here, W. 72.31–73.2; cf. n. 6 *supra*.

19. On these inscriptions and on Cosmas's visit to Mt. Sinai in general, see the chapter by D. Gorce in L. Prévost, L. Dennefeld, etc., *Le Sinai hier . . . aujourd'hui* (Paris, 1937), 159 ff.; Lina Eckenstein, *op. cit.*, 87 ff.; further details on the inscriptions, with additional bibliographical material in A. Kammerer, *Pétra et la Nabatène* (Paris, 1929), 465 ff.; cf. also Gelzer, *loc. cit.*, 112 f.; C. Ritter, *Erdkunde*, 14 (Berlin, 1848), 28, 748 ff.; and n. 6 *supra*.

20. On Clysma itself (W. 138.5–9), see R. Devreesse, "Le christianisme dans la péninsule sinaïtique des origines à l'arrivée des Musulmans," *Revue Biblique*, 49 (1940), 209, and D. Gorce, *loc. cit.*, 160 ff. For the medieval writers and travelers who knew the wheel-ruts of Clysma at first hand, see McCrindle, *op. cit.*, 142, n. 1; Gelzer, *loc. cit.*, 111; and especially *Itinera Hierosolymitana saeculi iiii–viii*, ed. by P. Geyer, in *Corpus Scriptorum Ecclesiasticorum Latinorum*, 39 (Vienna, 1898), 115.21–116.18 (Petrus Diaconus and St. Silvia [see Devreesse, *loc. cit.*]), 187.13–18 (Antoninus Placentinus); cf. 46.19, 26; 47.2; 117.8–13; 188.9, 14. For additional details cf. the works cited by C. J. Jellouschek, *loc. cit.*

21. In the very passage Gelzer cites, Cosmas merely speaks of his observations when traveling through the country.

22. W. 51.25f.; cf. 52.8; this passage is summarized in the outline of Ms. 1186 published by V. N. Beneshevich, who, to judge from his heading, appreciated its significance: *Catalogus codicum manuscriptorum graecorum qui in monasterio Sanctae Catherinae in Monte Sina asservantur* (*Opisanie grecheskikh rukopiseĭ monastyriá Sviatoĭ Ekateriny na Sinaĭe*, 1, St. Petersburg, 1911), 433. In my use of Russian books, I owe much to the diligence and skill of Mrs. Nathalie Scheffer.

23. W. 231.20 ff., and cf. the prayer at the end of Book 5 on the same page. See note 10 *supra*.

24. W. 232.4 f.; 232.32 plus 233.4 (Cosmas speaks of Alexandria as being in the third κλίμα and then says ἐν τῷ τρίτῳ κλίματι . . . ἐνταῦθα).

25. W. 63.22 f.; 83.1, 3 (the Nile debouches into τὸν παρ' ἡμῖν κόλπον).

26. W. 37.23–38.5; 69.28 f.; 72.5 f. It is somewhat misleading, however, to quote W. 72.5 f. (ἔνθα καὶ τὴν ἐμπορίαν ποιούμεθα, οἱ ἀπὸ Ἀλεξανδρείας καὶ ἀπὸ Ἐλᾶ ἐμπορευόμενοι . . .), as Wittmann does (see n. 13 *supra* for reference), without discussion. For, if we were to judge by these words alone, it would be impossible to determine whether Cosmas was a citizen of Ela (modern Akabah, at the northernmost extremity of the Gulf of Akabah, an arm of the Red Sea; see the article *Aela* by S. Vailhé in *Dictionnaire d'histoire et de géographie ecclésiastiques*, 1 (1912), 647 f.), or of Alexandria, or both.

Cf. W. 47.33–48.3, where Cosmas points out that there have been earthquakes in Egypt (see W. *ad loc.* for other texts; I hope to discuss this matter in a paper on Cosmas's relation to Alexandrian science and philosophy); cf. W. 49.13–18 on the climate of the Thebaid.

27. W. 61.6; cf. 62.6 f. and 104.9 f.

28. W. 71.30; 138.25; 232.2, 5, 15, 19 f.; 315, 29; 316.3, 5, 25; 317.5.

29. W. 315.1 f., 24, 28 f.; 316.3, 5 f., 25; 317.4 f. On Timothy and Theodosius, see, in addition to the usual literature in encyclopaedias, etc.: B. Evetts, "History of the patriarchs of the Coptic Church of Alexandria," *Patrologia Orientalis*, 1 (Paris, 1907), fasc. 4, 451–69; E. W. Brooks, "Dates of the Alexandrine patriarchs . . . ," *BZ*, 12 (1903), 494–497; A.

80

Jülicher, "Die Liste der alexandrinischen Patriarchen im 6. u. 7. Jahrh.," *Festgabe, Karl Müller* (Tübingen, 1922), 23.

29a. See Erik Peterson, "Die alexandrinische Liturgie bei Kosmas Indikopleustes," *Ephemerides Liturgicae*, 46 (1932), 66–74; F. E. Brightman, *Liturgies Eastern and Western*, Oxford, 1896, 129.9 ff., 20 ff., and 170.32 ff.

30. W. 52.10 ff.; cf. 62.21; 135.17 f., etc. The identity of Mar Aba and Patricius, first recognized by G. S. Assemani, *Bibliotheca Orientalis*, 3.2 (Rome, 1728), 406, has never been disputed.

31. *Das Buch der Synhados nach einer Handschrift des Museo Borgiano übersetzt u. erläutert* (Stuttgart – Vienna, 1900), 383 f.

32. J. B. Chabot, *Littérature syriaque* (Paris, 1934), 53; A. Baumstark, *Geschichte der syrischen Literatur* (Bonn, 1922), 119; J. Labourt, *Le christianisme dans l'empire perse* (Paris, 1904), 165 f. R. Duval, *La littérature syriaque* (Paris, 1899), 67, mentions only the Alexandrian visit and does not allude to Cosmas; so Barhebraeus, *Chronicon Ecclesiasticum*, ed. J. B. Abbeloos et T. J. Lamy, 3 (Paris-Louvain, 1877), 89. The modern authors cited may have been confused by Mari ibn Soleiman (*De patriarchis ecclesiae orientalis* in *Maris Amri et Slibae de patriarchis Nestorianorum commentaria*, ed. H. Gismond, Rome, 1899, Pars prior, 44), who speaks of an expedition of Mar Aba and Thomas of Edessa to Constantinople but is silent about a sojourn in Alexandria. The evidence of Cosmas proves that the account in the *Chronique de Séert* (see *infra* and n. 34) is founded upon fact and is not merely a conflation of distinct Alexandrian and Constantinopolitan traditions of the same incident.

33. W. 51.26.

34. Arabic text and French translation by A. Scher in *Patrologia Orientalis*, 7 (Paris, 1911), fasc. 2, 154 ff. An anonymous *Life of Mar Aba* written in Syriac (ed. by P. Bedjan, *Histoire de Mar Jabalaha, de trois autres patriarches, . . . nestoriens*, 2nd ed. Paris, 1895, 217 f., 221) represents Mar Aba as visiting both Alexandria and Constantinople but gives no indication that he was accompanied by Thomas of Edessa. This *Life of Mar Aba*, which apparently dates from the latter half of the sixth century, has been translated by O. Braun, *Bibliothek d. Kirchenväter*, 22 (Kempten-Munich, 1915), 188–220.

35. Cosmas is the authority for the statement that Thomas died in Constantinople. According to other sources, Thomas fled from Constantinople with Mar Aba to Nisibis: *Chronique de Séert* (9th c. or later), *loc. cit.*, 156; M. ibn Soleiman (12th c.), *loc. cit.* This inconsistency is resolved by Baumstark, *op. cit.*, 121, who posits two Thomases, one of whom died in Constantinople, and the other of whom succeeded Mar Aba as Professor of Exegesis at the School of Nisibis. Cf. E. R. Hayes, *L'École d'Édesse* (Paris, 1930), 282; Braun, *op. cit.*, 192 ff.; and n. 32 *supra*.

36. See Winstedt's summary of the evidence of the MSS., *op cit.*, 3.

37. The argument is that, since Photius describes the *Christian Topography* merely as χριστιανοῦ βίβλος without naming the author (cod. 36), the name Cosmas, which appears in only one (*Laur. Plut. IX.28*) of the major MSS., is a descriptive appellative chosen by a late scribe as appropriate for a writer on cosmology. But the critics have not accepted this view (see W. 2 f., 19, with references and the works cited in notes 2–4 and 15 [Charton] *supra*). The name Cosmas was common enough in Byzantium; there were three Alexandrian patriarchs named Cosmas. See in addition F. Preisigke, *Namenbuch enthaltend alle griechischen, lateinischen, ägyptischen . . . Menschennamen, soweit sie in griechischen Urkunden (Papyri, Ostraka, Inschriften . . . usw.) Aegyptens sich vorfinden* (Heidelberg, 1922), 183: 20 instances are recorded, making Cosmas one of the commoner names.

Cod. Iberitan. 60, f. 191a (12th cent.), attributes to Cosmas Indicopleustes a number of works written in both Greek and Latin, including one on the names of the apostles, and describes him as the bishop of Tyre who suffered martyrdom during the reign of Julian. See R. A. Lipsius, *Die apokryphen Apostelgeschichten u. Apostellegenden*, 1 (Braunschweig, 1883), 195, and *Ergänzungsheft* (*ibid.*, 1890), 3, 15; W. 3. This is, of course, an obvious aberration (Cosmas has been confounded with the semi-legendary Dorotheos of Tyre) and is not to be taken seriously.

XIV

ARISTOTLE AND COSMAS INDICOPLEUSTES ON THE VOID
A NOTE ON THEOLOGY AND SCIENCE IN THE SIXTH CENTURY[1]

I

INTRODUCTION

In recent years, with the rebirth and new popularity of Byzantine studies in Europe and America, much has been done to advance our knowledge of Byzantine civilization. Contributions of the highest importance have been made by learned and productive scholars of modern Greece like Professor Kyriakides, whom it is a delight to honor in this volume of papers.

In the past, however, with few exceptions, the chief interest has been in archaeology and in political, social, and economic history. For the most part, intellectual history - πνευματικὴ ἱστορία or Geistesgeschichte - has been neglected. This is all the more regrettable in the Byzantine field because here, perhaps to a greater extent than elsewhere, a proper understanding of any single discipline depends heavily upon the results of research in all branches of Byzantinology — literature, philosophy, theology, science, politics, economics, and archaeology. This principle is, of course, most clearly demonstrable from the arts ; for there are few miniatures, mosaics, wall - paintings, or buildings that can be adequately appreciated without a careful appraisal of the entire cultural environment. But it applies with equal force to every phase of Byzantine activity.

Although by common consent the Emperor Justinian I (527-65)

---

1. This is an excerpt, somewhat revised, of a lecture read before the second Dumbarton Oaks Symposium held at Dumbarton Oaks, Harvard University, in Washington, D. C., in April, 1943, under the direction of Professor George La Piana, of Harvard University, to whom I owe a great debt of gratitude for innumerable kindnesses, both personal and academic. It is only a brief and preliminary version of my work on Cosmas and the intellectual history of the sixth century.

36

was one of the most important rulers of all time, the intellectual history of his reign has never attracted much attention. There is a huge literature on Justinian but very little has been done to investigate the literary, theological, philosophical, and scientific activity which flourished in the brilliant epoch which he dominated. Neither Charles Diehl in his famous but misnamed book, Justinien et la civilisation byzantine au VIᵉ siêcle (Paris, 1901), nor William G. Holmes, The age of Justinian and Theodora (2 vols., London, 1912), nor J. B. Bury, History of the Later Roman Empire from the death of Theodosius I. to the death of Justinian (2 vols., London, 1923), nor Ernst Stein, Histoire du Bas — Empire de la disparition de l'Empire d'Occident à la mort de Justinien (Paris - Brussels, 1949), nor the popular and unpretentious Justinian and his age, by Percy Ure (Penguin Books, 1951) makes any contribution to this vital aspect of the age of Justinian. Stein, it is true, does have a chapter on literary history, and there has been some work of value on the historiography[2] and poetry of this period[3]; but the subject as a whole is still all but completely ignored and unexplored.

This curious situation is not to be explained by dearth of material. The Emperor Justinian was an erudite theologian, and the proceedings of the Fifth Oecumenical Council of 553, as well as the developments leading thereto, require much fuller and more careful treatment than they have hitherto received.[4]

Moreover, the flourishing philosophical schools of Athens and Alexandria produced a large corpus of learned works, which are now available in excellent critical but little used editions. John Philoponus, the famous Monophysite scholar of Alexandria, wrote several theological treatises, including the περὶ ἀιδιότητος τοῦ κόσμου

---

2. We have, for example, a large, though scattered, literature on Procopius.

3. On poetry, see Franz Dölger, Die Byzantinische Dichtung in der Reinsprache (Berlin, 1948); C. A. Trypanis, Medieval and Modern Greek Poetry (Oxford, 1951); cf. Egon Wellesz, A history of Byzantine music and hymnography (Oxford, 1949).

4. I am now preparing a book on the theology of Justinian ; see my article on Theodore of Mopsuestia in Dumbarton Oaks Papers, No. 6 (Cambridge, Mass., 1951) 123-160.

and the περὶ κοσμοποιίας (the so-called De aeternitate mundi and
De opificio mundi well edited in the Bibliotheca Teubneriana by
Hugo Rabe and W. Reichardt respectively), and a number
of lengthy exegetical works on Aristotle (volumes 13 - 17 of
the Commentaria in Aristotelem Graeca).[5] No attempt has been
made to take advantage of this rich accumulation of texts, the
attribution of some of which has not yet been confirmed. We
are no better informed about such important contemporaries
of Philoponus as Damascius, Simplicius, Olympiodorus and
Priscian Lydus, whose writings have long been accessible to
scholars. Even the περὶ ἀρχῶν of John Lydus (De magistratibus, published in the Teubner series in 1903 by Richard
Wünsch), which has great importance for political and administrative history, still awaits an exegete, as do John's other
two works, the περὶ μηνῶν (De mensibus) and the περὶ διοση-
μειῶν (De ostentis).

II

Περὶ τοῦ κενοῦ

Another notable and undeservedly neglected figure of this
era is Cosmas Indicopleustes, whose Χριστιανικὴ Τοπογραφία[6]

5. The best information as yet available on the central philosophical
scholars of the sixth century are the articles in the Real-Encyclopädie
der classischen Altertumswissenschaft of Pauly-Wissowa. Basile Ta-
takis, La philosophie byzantine, in Émile Bréhier's Histoire de
philosophie, fascicule supplémentaire, 2 (Paris, 1949), devotes a few
pages to Philoponus but almost completely ignores Olympiodorus,
Simplicius, and the philosophical developments of the period as a whole.
Eduard Zeller, Die Philosophie der Griechen in ihrer geschichtli-
chen Entwicklung 3.2, Die nacharistotelische Philosophie (Leipzig, 1923),
is inadequate on the sixth century. On John Philoponus, see also Jean
Maspero, Histoire des patriarches d'Alexandrie... 518-616 (Bibliothèque de l'École des Hautes Études, 237 [Paris, 1923]) 7-11, 197-210,
Berthold Altaner, Patrologie (2d ed., Freiburg im Breisgau, 1950)
459. In the Mss the περὶ κοσμοποιίας is entitled τῶν εἰς τὴν Μωϋσέως κοσμο-
γονίαν ἐξηγητικῶν λόγοι ζ΄.
6. A critical edition which replaces that of MPG, 88, 51-476, was published by E. O. Winstedt (Cambridge, England, 1909) ; the English translation by J. W. McCrindle, The Christian Topography of Cosmas, an

provides valuable evidence for the dissemination of ancient learning
—scientific and philosophical—even in circles most hostile to pagan
culture. A devout merchant and traveler, who had wandered
perhaps as far as India[7] and reported many interesting tales about
commerce in Abyssinia and the esoteric flora and fauna of the
East, of which he seems to have had a first hand knowledge,
Cosmas was primarily concerned with salvation and Biblical
theology of a rather primitive sort. Because of his predilection
for what seems to us, as it undoubtedly also appeared to enlightened men of his own era,[8] a weird and ridiculous cosmology, it is
customary to dismiss Cosmas as a figure of little importance in
the history of thought. This attitude stems from Cosmas's fervor
in behalf of the Mosaic cosmology, to the defence and illustration
of which he devoted his Χριστιανικὴ Τοπογραφία. Cosmas's purpose
was both positive and negative. On the positive side, he seeks to
expound and demonstrate the Biblical theory of cosmogony.
Negatively, he refutes the pagans on this matter wherever they
conflict with what he takes to be Christian principles of science
and reason. In this polemic against the pagans, as scholars have
in the past failed to notice, Cosmas reveals a very considerable
knowledge of ancient philosophy. [9]

His own views are from the scientific point of view often deplo-
rable.He describes[10] the cosmos as comparable to a two-story house,

Egyptian monk (London, 1897), though based on Migne's text, is
excellent.

7. On Cosmas see the literature cited in Dumbarton Oaks Papers,
No. 3 (Cambridge, Mass., 1946) 77 ff.

8. The best medieval scholars did not believe that the earth was flat ;
see George H. T. Kimble, Geography in the Middle Ages (London,
1938), 35 f. ; Eva G. R. Taylor, Ideas of the shape and habitability
of the earth prior to the great age of discovery, History 22 (1937 - 38)
54 - 58 ; eadem, Some notes on early ideas of the form and size of the
earth , Geographical Journal 85 (1935) 65-68 ; John K. Wright, The
geographical lore of the time of the Crusades (American Geographical Society. Research series, No. 15 [N. Y., 1925] 15, 53 f., 383 f.

9. On the cosmographical opinions of the fathers, and of the later Middle
Ages see Winstedt, p. 7, n. 3 ; Pierre Duhem, Le système du monde
1 - 5 (Paris, 1913 - 17) ; and George Sarton, Introduction to the history
of science (3 vols. in 5, Baltimore, Md. 1927 - 47), passim.

10. See J. Zellinger, Die Genesishomilien des Bischofs Severian

the upper story of which, « the first heaven », rests on the firmament, which in turn constitutes «the second heaven», the sky of mortal men. The whole structure is set on a flat earth, regarded as resting at the bottom of the universe, which, according to him, is neither spherical nor in motion but is to be represented as a rectangular chamber roofed by a barrel vault. [11] The sun, moon, and the stars proceed in regular orbits according to the mandate of God, who can interrupt them in their courses at any time, as he did for Joshua (Joshua 10) and Hezekiah (II Kings, 20. 8-11 ; Isaiah, 38. 7 f.). The alteration of day and night is produced by a high range of mountains in the north, which cut off the rays of the sun from the part of the earth on the other side of the mountains; and the heavenly bodies do not move under their own power but owe their motion to the angels.

From this brief summary it is obvious that Cosmas comes into violent conflict with Greek thought at many points. But he was not in the slightest degree embarrassed by this breach with the past, and took pride in attacking ancient cosmology. His two major targets among the pagans were Aristotle and Ptolemy (the author of the Μαθηματικὴ Σύνταξις), whose views he constantly subjects to ridicule and scorn. In this brief paper, I can discuss only Cosmas's treatment of the void.

Cosmas does not usually identify his sources specifically in connection with the texts in which I believe that his knowledge of pagan learning can be discerned. The only exception to this rule

---

von Gabala (Alttestamentliche Abhandlungen 7, Heft 1 [Münster i. W., 1916]), for an analysis of the cosmology of Severianus and its influence on Cosmas. Cosmas transcribes several passages from Severianus in Book Ten of the Χριστιανικὴ Τοπογραφία (Winstedt, 301. 4 - 308. 25). Of interest also is the fact that the system of Cosmas was at several points identical with that of Theodore of Mopsuestia, whom Cosmas knew through Mar Aba (see below), if not directly also ; see the refutation of Theodore by John Philoponus in the latter's περὶ κοσμοποιίας, passim.

11. Reproductions of miniatures illustrating Cosmas's scheme can be found in Winstedt's edition, McCrindle's translation, MPG, 88, Cosimo Stornajolo, Le miniature della Topografia Cristiana di Cosma Indicopleuste, Codice Vaticano 699 (Milan, 1908); Josef Strzygowski, Der Bilderkreis des Griechischen Physiologus, des Kosmas Indikopleustes und Oktateuch, nach Handschriften der Bibliothek zu Smyrna (Byzantinisches Archiv, Heft 2 [Leipzig, 1899]).

occurs in the few pages in which he collects the witnesses for his own theories and triumphantly refers to the ancient writers (Ephorus, Pytheas of Marseille, and Xenophanes of Colophon) whom he regards as his predecessors.

In general, however, he either gives no indication of a source, as in the passage on the void here under consideration, or mentions principles which he says self—styled Christians adopted in imitation of pagan thinkers (κατὰ τοὺς ἔξωθεν φιλοσόφους). Occasionally, also, in various contexts not germane to the present article, he lists a few names of well known ancient authors. [12]

In describing the earth as fixed at the base of all things, Cosmas [13] says :

... Imagine an area one hundred cubits deep, filled with one of the heavier elements, like water, for example. If a man grasps a stone in his hand and casts it (into the water), how long will it take the stone to reach the bottom ? Assume that it will take four hours. Then if we suppose the area to be filled with a lighter element, like air, how much time will it take the stone to reach the bottom? Clearly less time, say two hours. If we assume a still lighter substance, we can say the stone will touch bottom in one hour. In an even lighter medium, the stone will arrive in half an hour. The finer the medium, the less time will be required, until the medium has been so far reduced as to become incorporeal. In that case, necessarily, time will disappear also. Thus, a weight dropped into a medium that is

---

12. W i n s t e d t , 81. 24 ff.; 39. 2f.; 95.28, 120.1, 123.12 ff., 326.22 f., cf. 117.30f. (a scholium).

13. Ed. Winstedt, p. 57.7 - 21 : ὥσπερ γάρ τις ὑπόθοιτο χῶρον ἕνα ἔχοντα βάθος πηχῶν ἑκατόν, γέμει δὲ ὁ χῶρος ἐκεῖνος σώματος παχυτέρου οἷον ὕδατος, κρατήσας δέ τις λίθον τῇ χειρὶ ἄνωθεν ἀπολύσει, πόσῳ διαστήματι χρόνου τὸ βάθος καταλήψεται ; ἐρεῖ τις πάλιν καθ' ὑπόθεσιν ὡρῶν τεσσάρων. Ἔτι δὲ λεπτοτέρου σώματος, ὑποθέμενος γέμειν τὸν χῶρον, οἷον ἀέρος, πόσῳ πάλιν διαστήματι χρόνου τὸ βάθος καταλήψεται ; δηλονότι βραχυτέρῳ, ὡσανεὶ ὡρῶν δύο. Πάλιν ἔτι λεπτοτέρου σώματος ὑποθέμενος, μιᾶς ὥρας εὑρήσει, καὶ ἔτι πάλιν λεπτοτέρου σώματος ὑποθέμενος ἡμιωρίου. Καὶ ἔτι πάλιν λεπτοτέρου [sic ego; codd. λεπτοτάτου], πάλιν βραχυτέρου εὑρήσει μέχρι καὶ τοῦ σώματος λεπτυνομένου καὶ εἰς ἀσώματον κατανοτήσαντος ἐξ ἀνάγκης καὶ ὁ χρόνος εἰς ἄχρονον λῆξαι. Οὕτως καὶ ἐνταῦθα ἐν οὐδενὶ σώματι παντελῶς, ἀλλ' ἀσωμάτῳ, ἀνάγκη ἀχρόνως καταλαμβάνειν τὸ βαρὺ σῶμα τοῦ παντὸς χώρου τὸ βάθος καὶ ἵστασθαι.

without substance and completely incorporeal will reach the bottom without passage of time and remain there.

McCrindle in the introduction to his translation (p. xvi) of Cosmas refers to this as « a very curious passage ». But neither McCrindle nor later students of Cosmas realized that Cosmas had done nothing here but apply quite literally a principle enunciated by Aristotle in the Fourth Book of the Physics : [14] A then will move through B in time Γ, and through Δ, which is thinner, in time E (if the length of B is equal to Δ), in proportion to the density of the hindering body. For let B be water and Δ air ; then by so much as air is thinner and more incorporeal than water, A will move through Δ faster than through B. Let the speed have the same ratio to the speed, then, that air has to water. Then if air is twice as thin, the body will traverse B in twice the time that it does Δ, and the time Γ will be twice the time E, and always, by so much as the medium is more incorporeal and less resistant and more easily traversed, the faster will be the movement.

Cosmas follows Aristotle very closely, positing like him water and a r successively as media for the falling object, which he assun s with Aristotle would pass over a given distance twice as rapidly in air than in water, the speed being inversely proportional to the density of the medium traversed.

---

14. W. D. Ross, ed., Aristotle's Physics, a revised text with introduction and commentary (Oxford, 1936) 4. 8, 215α 31ff. : τὸ δὴ ἐφ' οὖ Α οἰσθήσεται διὰ τοῦ Β τὶν ἐφ' ᾧ Γ χρόνον, διὰ δὲ τοῦ Δ λεπτοτέρου ὄντος τὸν ἐφ' ᾧ Ε, εἰ ἴσον τὸ μῆκος τὸ τοῦ Β τῷ Δ, κατὰ τὴν ἀναλογίαν τοῦ ἐμποδίζοντος σώματος. Ἔστω γὰρ τὸ μὲν Β ὕδωρ, τὸ δὲ Δ ἀήρ· ὅσῳ δὴ λεπτότερον ἀὴρ ὕδατος καὶ ἀσωματώτερον, τοσούτῳ θᾶττον τὸ Α διὰ τοῦ Δ οἰσθήσεται ἢ διὰ τοῦ Β. ἐχέτω δὴ τὸν αὐτὸν λόγον ὅνπερ διέστηκεν ἀὴρ πρὸς ὕδωρ, τὸ τάχος πρὸς τὸ τάχος. ὥστε εἰ διπλασίως λεπτόν, ἐν διπλασίῳ χρόνῳ τὴν τὸ Β δίεισιν ἢ τὴν τὸ Δ, καὶ ἔσται ὁ ἐφ' ᾧ Γ χρόνος διπλάσιος τοῦ ἐφ' ᾧ Ε. καὶ ἀεὶ δὴ ὅσῳ ἂν ᾖ ἀσωματώτερον καὶ ἧττον ἐμποδιστικὸν καὶ εὐδιαιρετώτερον δι' οὖ φέρεται, θᾶττον οἰσθήσεται. The translation is that of R. P. Hardie and R. K. Gaye (The works of Aristotle translated into English under the editorship of W. D. Ross, 2 [Oxford, 1930]). For Aristotle's views on the void, see W. D. Ross, Aristotle, 3rd ed. (London, 1937) 87-9 ; idem, Aristotle's Physics (Oxford, 1936) 590 ; idem, Aristotle's Metaphysics 2 (Oxford, 1924) 252.

Besides these points of agreement, however, there are also a few discrepancies between the two. Cosmas speaks of a stone as the object used in the experiment, although Aristotle does not do so, and he adds two additional but unimportant steps concerning media in which the stone would reach bottom in one hour and in one half hour. In one respect, moreover, without altering the form of the Aristotle's argument, he departs from his model, and sets forth a proposition which Aristotle himself had repudiated. For he carries the Aristotelian principle that movement is accelerated as the resistance offered by the medium is decreased to its logical end, and concludes that motion in a perfect vacuum would take place without the lapse of time. Aristotle, of course, had realized that this result would follow if there actually were such a thing as a void. But he rejects this possibility, preferring to deny that there is a void [15] or that there can be motion except in time. [16]

Aristotle's views on these matters are clearly and unambiguously stated, and were well understood by the Byzantine commentators, as can be seen from the paraphrases of Themistius (d. 388), Simplicius, and Cosmas's exact contemporary and fellow - townsman, John Philoponus of Alexandria. [17] Nevertheless, the last sentence in the above - quoted passage from Aristotle, taken by itself, does authorise Cosmas's deduction. Neither Themistius nor Simplicius reproduces these words, but

---

15. Physics, 4. 8, 214 β 12—4.9, 217 β 28. At the conclusion of this passage, Aristotle qualifies very slightly his denial of the existence of the void and suggests tentatively the possibility, which has no bearing upon the present problem, that the void might conceivably be the cause of motion : ἐκ δὴ τῶν εἰρημένων φανερὸν ὡς οὔτ' ἀποκεκριμένον κενὸν ἔστιν, οὔθ' ἁπλῶς οὔτ' ἐν τῷ μανῷ, οὔτε δυνάμει, εἰ μή τις βούλεται πάντως καλεῖν κενὸν τὸ αἴτιον τοῦ φέρεσθαι. οὕτω δ' ἡ τοῦ βαρέος καὶ κούφου ὕλη, ᾗ τοιαύτη, εἴη ἂν τὸ κενόν· τὸ γὰρ πυκνὸν καὶ τὸ μανὸν κατὰ ταύτην τὴν ἐναντίωσιν φορᾶς ποιητικά, κατὰ δὲ τὸ σκληρόν , καὶ μαλακὸν πάθους καὶ ἀπαθείας, καὶ οὐ φορᾶς ἀλλ' ἑτεροιώσεως μᾶλλον. καὶ περὶ μὲν κενοῦ, πῶς ἔστι καὶ πῶς οὐκ ἔστι, διωρίσθω τὸν τρόπον τοῦτον.

16. Ibid., 4. 14, 222 β 30 - 223 α 15.

17. Themistii in Aristotelis Physica paraphrasis, ed. H. Schenkl, Commentaria in Aristotelem Graeca (which I cite below as CIA) 5. 2 (Berlin, 1900) 130. 22 ff. ; Simplicii in Aristotelis Physicorum libros quattuor priores commentaria, ed. H. Diels, CIA, 9 (Berlin, 1882), 668, 7 ; Ioannis Philoponi, In Aristotelis Physicorum libros quinque posteriores commentaria, ed. H. Vitelli, CIA, 17 (Berlin, 1888), 652. 18-654. 12, 630. 6 ff..

John Philoponus does.[18] We are justified, therefore, in eliminating both Themistius and Simplicius as possible sources for Cosmas, both of whom can be excluded on other grounds also, Themistius because he refers to a gold or silver ball as the object used in the theoretical experiment, and Simplicius because he omits page 215a 31 ff. altogether from his analysis. Philoponus, on the other hand, who transcribes the entire text of Aristotle on these points practically verbatim, adds a full commentary and discussion (as does Themistius). It is difficult to imagine how Cosmas could have picked his way through Philoponus's exegesis and come out with a summary that is so succinct and so faithful to Aristotle. Furthermore, Philoponus makes it very clear throughout that Aristotle's purpose in this part of the Physics was to show that there was no void. So Cosmas could not have used Philoponus here..

It is more likely that Cosmas had had direct access to the actual text of Aristotle, either in its written form or via a public lecture or the school - room. This is the more plausible because Aristotle does not actually attack the theory of the void for somewhat more than two whole pages after the end of the passage quoted above. [19] In the paragraphs immediately following, he devotes himself to a number of arguments which do not necessarily in themselves repudiate the case for the void. Cosmas might well have failed to comprehend the conclusion to which Aristotle was leading ; or, more probably, while accepting Aristotle's analysis up to this point, he preferred to follow those who maintained that there was such a thing as a vacuum. Aristotle mentions several proponents of this doctrine, and Hero had produced a vacuum experimentally in Alexandria around the first century before Christ. [20]

---

18. CIA, 17, 653.17 - 22.
19. Physics 4. 8, 216 β 20 f.
20. Aristotle, Physics 4. 6, 213α 19 - 4. 7, 214 β 11 ; H e r o , Pneumatica. 1, introduction, ed. W i l h e l m S c h m i d t, Heronis Alexandrini opera quae supersunt omnia vol. 1 (Leipzig, 1899), 4 - 28 ; cf. ibid. 460. 10 ff. (Philo of Byzantium, De ingeniis spiritualibus, the Latin version, previously published by V a l e n t i n R o s e , Anecdota Graeca et Graecolatina, 2 [Berlin, 1870] 300. 12 ff.) ; C a r r a d e V a u x , Le livre des appareils pneumatiques et des machines hydrauliques par Philon de

44

There is no other known source which could have supplied
Cosmas with the materials of which he makes use. None of the
extant ancient or medieval manuals or compendia of ancient
philosophy, nor all of them together, can account for Cosmas's
knowledge of Aristotelianism. The discussion of Aristotle's theory
of the relationship of speed of motion to the resistance of the medium traversed is not to be found in the περὶ τῶν ἀρεσκόντων
φιλοσόφοις φυσικῶν δογμάτων (De placitis philosophorum) of the
Pseudo - Plutarch, or its epitome, or Diogenes Laertius, or the
Προπαρασκευὴ εὐαγγελικὴ (Praeparatio evangelica)[21] of Eusebius,
or the περὶ ψυχῆς (De anima) of Nemesius of Emesa,[22] or the
Ἑλληνικῶν θεραπευτικὴ παθημάτων (Graecarum affectionum curatio)
of Theodoretus,[23] or the Ἐκλογαὶ (Anthologium) of Stobaeus,
or any of the doxographic writers edited by Hermann Diels
in his Doxographi Graeci.[24]

Cosmas may possibly have imbibed some part of what he knew
about Aristotle from the discourses of Mar Aba, whom he calls
Patricius (Catholicos of Persia, 540—52) and Thomas of Edessa.
As he puts it himself, after stating that the Tabernacle of Moses
« was a model and outline of the universe » (τύπος ἦν καὶ ὑπογραφὴ
παντὸς τοῦ κόσμου), his view of these things was not original with
him but had been derived from a study of the Scriptures and from
the living voice of «Patricius, that very holy man and great teacher»
who, he says, communicated pious instruction and true learning. A

Byzance (Paris, 1902) c. 3, pp. 99 f.(the Arabic version) ; Lucretius, De rerum natura 1, 329 ff. For later medieval theories on this question, see
Harry A. Wolfson, Crescas' critique of Aristotle (Cambridge, Mass.,
1929) 54, 138 - 149, 178 - 185, 337 - 344, 356 (n. 79), 396 - 412 ; George
Sarton, Introduction to the history of science 3 (Baltimore, 1947)
148-150.

21. This conclusion is based on the excellent indices of E. H. Gifford,
in his edition, 2 vols. (Oxford, 1903).

22. On Nemesius, see Werner W. Jaeger, Nemesius von Emesa
(Berlin, 1914).

23. This I judge on the basis of the full indices in the edition by Joannes Raeder (Leipzig, 1904).

24. In his Doxographi Graeci (Berlin, 1879), Diels publishes the whole
of Hermias's Irrisio gentilium philosophorum plus a collection of doxographic texts, including fragments of Aetius, Arius Didymus, Theophrastus,
Cicero, Philodemus, Hippolytus, Plutarch, Epiphanius, and Galen.

little farther along in the same book Cosmas cites Patricius as one of his authorities for his knowledge of geography. Cosmas's testimony on this head is confirmed also by an important Arabic chronicle, the so-called Chronique de Séert, which records that Mar Aba and Thomas of Edessa visited Alexandria and offered what might be described as a joint course on Theodore of Mopsuestia and Christian theology, with Mar Aba lecturing in Syriac and Thomas translating into Greek. [25]

But whatever Cosmas may have learned from Mar Aba, it is difficult to believe that he could have been altogether isolated from contact with the Aristotelian scholars of Alexandria, where Ammonius, son of the Neo - Platonist Hermeias, at the beginning of the sixth century, established a lively school of Aristotelian studies, which included at one time or other such learned Aristotelians as Simplicius, Asclepius, Olympiodorus the younger, and John Philoponus.[26] In some such environment, with or without supplementary materials, oral or written along with the words of Aristotle discussed above, he may have heard or read that the more perfect the vacuum, the more rapid the motion. And in a perfect vacuum motion will take place without lapse of time. [27]

John Philoponus, who differed radically from Aristotle in his

---

25. Ed. Winstedt, 52. 5 ff.; 62. 20 ff.; Histoire Nestorienne (Chronique de Séert) ed. Addaï Scher, Patrologia Orientalis, 7. 2. (Paris, 1911), 155 ff. ; cf. Paul Peeters, Observations sur la vie syriaque de Mar Aba, Catholicos de l' Église Perse (540 - 552), Miscellanea Giovanni Mercati, 5, Studi e Testi, 125 (Vatican City, 1946), 69 ff., 73, 79 ff. On the currency of Aristotelian studies among the Nestorians and Syriac speaking people, see Khalil Georr, Les catégories d'Aristote dans leurs versions syro-arabes (Beyrouth, 1948), 1 - 32, who gives the bibliography of the subject.

26. On philosophical studies in Alexandria in the sixth century, see John E. Sandys, A history of classical scholarship 1 (Cambridge England, 1903) 367 ff. ; Jean Maspero, Histoires des patriarches d' Alexandrie, Bibliothèque de l' École des Hautes Études, 237 [Paris, 1923]), 6 ff., 40, 46 f., 81, 134, 197 ff.

27. Ed. Vitelli, CIA, 17, 645.17-19: καὶ εἰ ὅσῳ μεγαλομερῆ εἰσι τὰ κενά, τοσούτῳ θᾶττον ἡ κίνησις, ἐὰν ἄρα ὅλον ᾖ κενόν, ἀχρόνως ἐν αὐτῷ κινηθήσεται. Ibid., 654. 10ff. : ἐν οὐδενὶ ἄρα χρόνῳ διὰ τοῦ κενοῦ κινεῖται. Τοῦτο δὲ πάλιν ἀδύνατον· πᾶσα γὰρ κίνησις ἐν χρόνῳ. Οὐκ ἄρα ἐνδέχεται κίνησιν διὰ κενοῦ γενέσθαι. Cf. 656. 12-15, 649. 3 - 9.

theory about the void, [28] as I hope to show in detail on another occasion, actually makes this statement in so many words. But he does so only when, arguing q u a Aristotle against the proponents of the void, he seeks to demolish the case for the existence of the void by demonstrating its absurdity. The words cited merely form a part of a reductio ad absurdum. Nevertheless, here, too, as in the original passage from Aristotle, Cosmas may have read, or heard, or remembered these words isolated from their context. Or, as seems more likely, he may have tailored the argument to suit his own purposes, retaining and using only what he found acceptable.

III

COSMAS AND HIS OPPOSITION TO THE MONOPHYSITES

Though Cosmas was eager to confute and replace the cosmology of the ancient Greeks, his chief attack was not directed against actual pagan disputants. It was, to be sure, necessary for him to discredit the scientific notions of the non-Christian Greeks. But, in so doing, his principal aim was to admonish and convert the Christians who were so misguided as to adopt these pagan theories as their own. The Christians he had in mind, I think it can be demonstrated, were the Monophysites. To begin with, he was a devotee of the Nestorian Catholicos Mar Aba of Persia (see above), and under his guidance had taken over enthusiastically the doctrinal position of Theodore of Mopsuestia, whom recent investigation reveals to have been imbued with heretical ideas of what might anachronistically be termed a Nestorian tinge. [29] He condemns a number of heretics, including Eutyches, Marcion, Arius, the Manichaeans, and Apollinaris, [30] but is silent about Nestorius, whom he never mentions. On the other hand, he takes particular pains to emphasize the reality of Christ's human nature. [31] Moreover,

---

28. Ibid., 675. 12 - 695.8 ; cf. 639. 3ff.
29. See Dumbarton Oaks Papers, No. 6 (Cambridge, Mass., 1951) 156. In my book on Justinian I will examine the question of Cosmas's Nestorianism in detail.
30. Ed. Winstedt, 201. 23.
31. Apart from a host of references to Christ's activity κατὰ σάρκα, e.g., Winstedt, 136. 7, 137.19, 145.20, 149. 9, 155. 6, 20f., 157. 12f., 158. 11, 31,

he devotes considerable attention to the humanity of Christ in the tenth book of the Χριστιανικὴ Τοπογραφία. This book contains a number of texts - footnotes or pièces justificatives, we might call them, selected by Cosmas, as he tells us in the introduction to this book, to prove to his adversaries that the very patristic testimonies on which they themselves relied supported the metaphysical system set forth in the Χριστιανικὴ Τοπογραφία. [32]

These passages deal primarily with two subjects, cosmology and Christology. Most of the texts are concerned with former, and are cited by Cosmas in defence of his description of the universe from writers like Athanasius, Gregory of Nazianzus, John Chrysostom, Epiphanius, and Severianus of Gabala. But, some, concentrated at the end of the book, have to do with Christology and stress vigorously the human nature of Christ — his sufferings, hunger, thirst, and fatigue. One of these was taken from a homily of Philo, Bishop of Carpasia in Cyprus ca. 400.[33] The longest and most noteworthy are excerpts from the works of two Monophysite patriarchs of Alexandria, Theodosius (535-6), d. 556) and Timothy III (518 - 35). [34] In his introduction to the first quotation from Theodosius, Cosmas describes him as « a recent schismatic father of theirs, who is still alive » (καί τινος νέου ἀποσχίστου αὐτῶν πατρός, ἔτι καὶ νῦν ζῶντος).[35] In annotating Patriarch Theodosius's homily on Matthew 26. 39 (« Father, if it be possible, let it pass from me »),Cosmas exclaims, «How marvelous this is ! They say such things and yet they quarrel with us, dividing and oppressing the churches » (ἀποσχίζοντες τὰς ἐκκλησίας καὶ τυραννοῦντες). Then, after referring to Luke 22. 44 (on Christ's

---

159.5, 166. 6f., 169.19, 173.22, 174.1,186.18, (cf. 205.19), 208. 15, 209.13, 237.6, 16, 253.14, 264.25, and passim, Cosmas repeatedly insists that Christ was both human and divine : ibid., 181.15ff., 30 ff., 182. 11 ff., 229.29ff., 230.17, 239. 16 ff., 29 ff. He also lays emphasis on Christ's human nature by itself, without reference to his divinity : 241. 17 ff., 313. 23 ff., and in most of the material he quotes from Theodosius and Timothy, Monophysite partriarchs of Alexandria, p. 314. 12 - 317.16.

32. Winstedt, 294.7 - 28.
33. Ibid., 313. 23 - 26.
34. Ibid., 314.12 - 317.16.
35. Ibid., 314, 7 f.

48

agony), he asks: « How dare they quote this passage and still condemn those who are bold enough to interpret it ?» [36]

In summarizing the argument here, in the last paragraph of this book, Cosmas emphasizes the « harmony of those not in harmony with us, the involuntary agreement of the schismatics — the unwilling praise or assent of those who revile us ». From all this it is reasonable to infer that the Monophysites were Cosmas's principal foes. This may lead us a step farther in identification. In the proëm to Book Seven, Cosmas addresses himself to a request for enlightenment περὶ οὐρανοῦ which he had received from his friend, Anastasius.

You said [Cosmas writes] that one of those who boast of being a Christian wished to attack the pagans, but agreed with them, despite this intention, in supposing heaven to be a sphere that always revolves, although in his book he declares it to be dissoluble. I do not know what prompted him to make this assertion, and I am moved to wonder that the wisdom of a man of such great learning was blinded by his excessive desire for fame. [37]

This scholar (whom he does not name), Cosmas goes on to say, should have refuted the pagans on the sphericity of heaven and its motion.

This sounds very much like a reference to John Philoponus, whose two learned works on cosmology, written after his conversion, combine a modified Aristotelianism with Christianity. In the περὶ ἀιδιότητος τοῦ κόσμου, for example, he condemns the doctrine of the eternity of the cosmos, maintaining against Proclus that the universe was created and would also come to an end, because it was φθαρτὸς (corruptible, subject to decay). [38] At the same time, however, he clings to the Aristotelian notion of the sphericity of heaven [39] and its motion in a circle.[40]

---

36. Ibid., 315. 1, 11 ff.

37. Ibid., 242.6 ff. : ἔφησθα γὰρ ὥς τις τῶν χριστιανίζειν αὐχούντων βουλόμενος καθ᾽ Ἑλλήνων εἰπεῖν, ἔλαθεν ἑαυτὸν συνηγορῶν αὐτοῖς, σφαῖραν μὲν σὺν αὐτοῖς δοξάζων, ἀεὶ περιστρεφομένην, τὸν οὐρανόν, καταλυόμενον δὲ τοῦτον ἐν τῷ αὐτοῦ συγγράμματι κηρύττων.

38. Ed. Hugo Rabe (Leipzig, 1899) 272. 11 ff., 480. 12 - 14, 24 - 27, 493. 25 ff., 504. 28 - 505. 10.

39. Ibid., 287. 6 - 13, 423. 20 - 424. 4, 483. 21 ff.

40. Ibid., 256. 22 ff., 276. 6 - 10, 479. 16 ff., 480. 4- 11, et passim.

The unnamed writer was charged by Anastasius, as Cosmas tells us, with having believed that the heavens would never cease to revolve. This hypothesis, Cosmas rightly points out in his vigorous refutation of it, was inconsistent with the theory that the cosmos was of finite duration,[41] which this unknown author was also said to have espoused.

In this respect, it must be admitted, Cosmas's friend could hardly have been thinking of the περὶ ἀιδιότητος τοῦ κόσμου. For although Philoponus seems occasionally to be endorsing belief in endless motion,[42] he makes it clear in other contexts that he is opposed to this concept.[43] The matter in question may perhaps have been handled in the manner described by Cosmas in a no longer extant work of Philoponus on the same subject entitled ἀντιρρήσεις πρὸς 'Αριστοτέλη περὶ τῆς τοῦ κόσμου ἀιδιότητος.[44]

However this may be, Philoponus does say heaven is perpetually in motion in his περὶ κοσμοποιίας[45]: διὸ καί, ὡς ἔστιν εἰπεῖν, ἀεικίνητος ἔστηκεν ὁ οὐρανός, τὸ μὲν διὰ τὴν κυκλοφορίαν, τὸ δὲ διὰ τὸ μὴ τὸν ὅλον ἀμείβειν τόπον, ἀκινήτου μένοντος τοῦ κέντρου. This proposition would lead to a universe of infinite duration, as Cosmas observes, but this is not what Philoponus had in mind ; for he declares that heaven, which he deemed to be spherical in shape and endowed with circular motion, [46] was not everlasting, but like all created things subject to decay and dissolution.[47] Thus, though its title announces it to be an exegetical study on the Mosaic cosmogony and not, therefore, like the περὶ ἀιδιότητος τοῦ κόσμου a

---

41. Winstedt, 242. 18 : οὐδεὶς γὰρ τῶν εὐφρονούντων τὸ ἀεικίνητον φθαρτὸν καὶ καταλυόμενον, οὐδὲ τὸ φθαρτὸν καὶ καταλυόμενον ἀεικίνητον ἂν εἴποι· ἀλλὰ τὸ μὲν ἀεικίνητον, ὡς ἀεικίνητον, ἄφθαρτόν ἐστιν, τὸ δὲ μὴ ἀεὶ κινούμενον, καὶ καταλυόμενον, πάντως φθαρτόν ἐστιν, ἐπείπερ καὶ τῆς κινήσεως παύεται, διὸ οὐκ ἀεικίνητον. πῶς οὖν ὁ λογιώτατος ἀεικίνητον δεξάμενος τὸν οὐρανόν, οὐχ οὕτως τῇ θείᾳ Γραφῇ δοκοῦν, καταλυόμενον αὐτὸν ὁρίζεται ;
42. Ed. Rabe, 257. 1 ff.
43. Ibid., 258.22 - 259.10.
44. See G u d e m a n, s. v. Ioannes (no. 21), Pauly - Wissowa - Kroll, Real - Encyclopädie d. classischen Altertumswissenschaft 9 (Stuttgart, 1916) 1789, 47 ff.
45. Ed. Reichardt, 140. 18 ff.
46. Ibid., 120. 14 - 122.18, 127. 1ff.
47. Ibid., 222. 11 ff.

polemic against pagan philosophy, it is much concerned with Aristotelianism and touches upon all of the points mentioned by Cosmas.

Without a minute examination of both of these works and their sources, it is impossible to determine with finality whether either of them was the one to which Cosmas's friend had alluded. Even then, absolute certainty may be elusive. Nevertheless, on the basis of the above analysis, it is possible to conclude that it was either the latter of these or one very similar to it which prompted Anastasius's criticism and Cosmas's reply.

Despite the relative inconclusiveness of this attempt at identification, we have at least demonstrated that Cosmas's opponents were Monophysites partial to Aristotelian principles of science, and hostile to the Biblical cosmology favored by Cosmas and his spiritual ancestors, Severianus of Gabala and Theodore of Mopsuestia. John Philoponus repeatedly finds fault with the theological and cosmological views of Theodore, and rebukes followers of the latter for rejecting the sphericity and circular motion of the heavenly bodies,[48] and for their fantastic notion that night is caused by the disappearance of the sun behind high mountains in the north. [49]

There can be little doubt, therefore, that if John Philoponus himself was not the adversary of Cosmas and his friend, Anastasius, it was his disciples and associates whose views Cosmas was attacking.

Harvard University
Dumbarton Oaks Research Library
    and Collection

---

48. Ibid., 127. 1 ff., 131. 13 ff., cf. 141. 14 ff. ; see n. 10 above.
49. Ibid., 138. 3 ff.

XV

ΥΠΟΓΕΙΟΣ
a Byzantine term for perigee, and some Byzantine views of the date of perigee and apogee

ὑπόγειος.

The adjective ὑπόγειος, which is defined in the lexica as 'underground', 'subterranean', 'under the earth', 'at the nadir', and the like, occurs in two recently published scientific texts in the sense of 'at perigee', the term used by astronomers to describe the point or moment at which a celestial body, in this instance the sun, comes closest to the earth [2].

The first and earlier of these examples is to be found in the περὶ χρείας τῶν οὐρανίων σωμάτων (De utilitate corporum caelestium) [3] of Symeon Seth, the Byzantine scientist of the

[1] For invaluable advice and assistance, I am deeply indebted to Dr. Edgar W. Woolard of the U. S. Naval Observatory. I am grateful also for aid received from Professor George Sarton of Harvard University, Dr. Alexander Pogo of the Carnegie Institute, and Mrs. Hannah F. M. Hedrick, formerly of the U. S. Naval Observatory. The table of astronomical data in Part III is based upon the calculations of Mrs. Hedrick.

The subjects treated in the present article are not discussed in GINZEL, PAULY-WISSOWA (s. vv. Kalender, Jahreszeiten, etc.), or in any other work known to me.

[2] In modern parlance, with the emphasis on heliocentricity, perihelion and aphelion are more common than perigee and apogee.

[3] Admirably edited by A. DELATTE in the second volume of his Anecdota Atheniensia et alia. Tome II, textes grecs relatifs à l'histoire des sciences (Bibliothèque de la Faculté de Philosophie et Lettres de l'Université de Liége, Fasc. 88 [Liége-Paris, 1939]), 90 ff. On Seth, see Delatte, loc. cit., 1 ff ; George SARTON, Introduction to the history of science, 1 (Baltimore, 1927), 771, 741, 742, 744, 745; and Karl KRUMBACHER, Geschichte d. byzantinischen Literatur (2d. ed., Munich, 1897), 263, 270, 399, 615, 617, 896.

latter part of the eleventh century who translated the fables of Kalīla and Dimna from Arabic into Greek, and composed a number of works on medicine, botany, and general science. This usage is illustrated by the following passage (¹):

Διατί ὁ ἥλιός ποτε μὲν πλησιάζει,
ποτὲ δὲ ἀφίσταται τῆς γῆς.

Ἔχει δὲ ὁ ἥλιός ποτε ἀπόγειον καὶ ὑπόγειον, ὥσπερ καὶ οἱ πλανῆται καὶ ἡ σελήνη, καὶ τοῦτο σοφῇ οἰκονομίᾳ διαταχθέν· ὅταν γὰρ ἄρχηται τῷ θερινῷ τροπικῷ πλησιάζειν, ἀπόγειος γίνεται ἵνα μὴ διπλασιασθῇ ἡ ἐκ τούτου θερμότης διά τε τὸ πλησιάζειν τοῖς κατὰ κορυφὴν σημείοις καὶ τὸ πλησίον εἶναι τῆς γῆς, ἀλλ᾽ ὅταν ἄρχηται πλησιάζειν, τὴν μεγίστην ποιεῖται ἀπὸ τῆς γῆς ἀπόστασιν, φειδόμενος ὡσανεὶ τῶν ὑπ᾽ αὐτὸν ἵνα μὴ τῷ ὑπερβάλλοντι τῆς τῶν ἀκτίνων σφοδρότητος βλάψῃ ταῦτα· συνάπτει γοῦν τῇ γειτνιάσει ἀπόστασιν καὶ τῇ ἀποστάσει γειτνίασιν. ὅταν δὲ ἀφ᾽ ἡμῶν μηκύνῃ καὶ πρὸς τῷ χειμερινῷ τροπικῷ γένηται, ὑπόγειος γίνεται, ἵνα τὴν ἀπόστασιν ἀναπληρώσῃ διὰ τοῦ γενέσθαι ὑπόγειος. εἰ γὰρ τὸ ἀπόγειον αὐτοῦ ἦν ἐν τῷ Τοξότῃ, τὸ δ᾽ ὑπόγειον ἐν Διδύμοις, τὸ μὲν θέρος ἦν ἂν καὶ πάνυ ὑπερβολικὸν ἐν τοῖς καύμασι καὶ ὁ χειμὼν ὁμοίως ὑπερέχων ταῖς ψύξεσιν. ἀλλ᾽ ἡ θεία πρόνοια καὶ τούτου ὥσπερ τῶν ἄλλων προμηθουμένη, οὐ μόνον αὐτῷ τὴν κατὰ μῆκος καὶ πλάτος περιέθετο κίνησιν, ἀλλὰ καὶ τὴν κατὰ τὸ βάθος καὶ ταύτην ἀφορῶσαν πρὸς τὴν ἡμετέραν ὄνησιν. οὐ μὴν ἀλλὰ καὶ ἀνάλογον ποιεῖται αὐτὴν τῇ ἀποστάσει τῇ πρὸς τὰ τροπικὰ καὶ γειτνιάσει. οὐ γὰρ ἄφνω ἐξ ὑπογείου ἀπόγειος γίνεται, ἀλλὰ κατὰ μικρὸν προκόπτει ἀπὸ τοῦδε εἰς τόδε καὶ ἀνεπαισθήτως πλησιάζει τε καὶ ἀφίσταται διὰ τὸ μὴ ἀθρόας γίνεσθαι τὰς μεταβολάς (²), which I render as follows:

Why the sun sometimes approaches the earth,
and sometimes recedes from it.

Like the planets and the moon, the sun is sometimes at apogee and sometimes at perigee. This was wisely so ordained; for when the sun begins to approach the summer solstice it arrives at apogee,

---

(¹) DELATTE, op. cit. 116. 1-26. For another meaning of ὑπόγειος see pp. 391 f. infra, and also, with regard to the moon in this sense, *Catalogus codicum astrologorum Graecorum*, 11. 2, ed. C. O. ZURETTI (Brussels, 1934), 156. 9 ff., 164. 5 ff.

(²) These last few words, which occur also in PACHYMERES (see p. 389 n. 4 infra), are probably derived from Cleomedes.

so that its heat may not be doubled by its being close to the constellations at the zenith and close to the earth at the same time. So, as it begins to approach [the zenith], it recedes to its maximum distance from the earth, as if taking care not to do injury to the regions below it by undue violence of its rays. Thus it combines remoteness [from the earth] with proximity [to the zenith — in summer], and proximity [to the earth] with remoteness [from the zenith — in winter] (¹). And when it draws away from us [i. e., from our zenith] and comes near the winter solstice, it arrives at perigee, so as to make up for its remoteness [from the zenith] by being at its closest point to the earth. For if it were at apogee in *Toxotes* [*Sagittarios,* the zodiacal sign the sun enters in November], and at perigee in *Didymi* [*Gemini,* the sign the sun enters in May], summer would be intolerably hot and winter, likewise, intolerably cold. But divine Providence, providing for this, as for other things, gave the sun motion, not only in longitude [i. e., from solstice to solstice, or from equinox to equinox, or from sign to sign, and return] and in declination [i. e., angular distance north and south of the equator], but also in depth (²) [i. e., from apogee to perigee and *vice versa*], — the last of these out of consideration for our welfare.

(¹) Although συνάπτει-γειτνίασιν might, possibly, be translated:

' Thus it combines remoteness [from the earth] with proximity to [the zenith], and proximity [to the zenith] with remoteness [from the earth],

I prefer to take both ἀπόστασις and γειτνίασις here in two different senses, as the author does himself. In the sentence immediately preceding συνάπτει-γειτνίασιν, Seth defines ἀπόστασιν as distance from the earth (τὴν μεγίστην ποιεῖται ἀπὸ τῆς γῆς ἀπόστασιν) and combines it with proximity to the zenith, to describe the astronomical setting of summer. Consequently, since the clause, συνάπτει γοῦν τῇ γειτνιάσει ἀπόστασιν, summarizes the astronomical situation set forth in these words, ἀπόστασις must here apply to the linear distance of the earth from the sun. On the other hand, the phrase, καὶ τῇ ἀποστάσει γειτνίασιν, leads on to the following sentence, in which ἀπόστασιν clearly has reference to distance from the zenith, and must, therefore, be rendered in this sense.

(²) Since I find no trace in Symeon of the notion that the sun traveled along a circle slightly inclined to the eliptic, I understand motion κατὰ πλάτος as that between the northernmost and southernmost declination of the sun. For the theory concerning solar motion north and south of the ecliptic (also described as κατὰ πλάτος), espoused by Eudoxus but repudiated by both Hipparchus and Ptolemy, (on the history of which cf. Thomas HEATH, *Aristarchus of Samos* [Oxford, 1913], 198 ff.; J. L. E. DREYER, *History of the planetary systems from Thales to Kepler* [Cambridge, Eng., 1906], 93 ff., 163 f.), see THEON SMYRNAEUS, *Expositio rerum mathematicarum ad legendum Platonem utilium,* ed. E. HILLER (Leipzig, 1878), 172. 15 - 173. 16, cf. 134. 8 ff., 200. 13 ff.

388

Moreover, Providence establishes a reciprocal relation between the sun's motion [from perigee to apogee] and its remoteness from, and proximity to, [the zenith] at the solstices. For it does not move suddenly from perigee to apogee, but proceeds gradually from the former to the latter, and moves closer to and farther away from the earth imperceptibly, so as to avoid sudden changes.

The slight ambiguity involved in the author's use of ἀπόστασις and γειτνίασις to indicate both angular distance (remoteness from, and proximity to, the zenith) and linear distance (distance from, and closeness to, the earth) is dispelled by the obvious meaning here of ἀπόγειος and ὑπόγειος, both of which appear also in a discussion of the apogee and perigee of the moon ([1]). The translation of ἀφίσταται and πλησιάζει in the last sentence is determined by the context, as well as by the lemma, in which these words are construed with τῆς γῆς.

Symeon's analysis in the chapter translated makes it clear that, when he says, in a section on the obliquity of the ecliptic, that winter is caused διὰ τὴν τοῦ ἡλίου ἀπόστασιν, and summer, διὰ τὴν ἐγγύτητα ([2]), he is referring to the sun's remoteness from the zenith and not sanctioning the popular fallacy that the apogee of the sun falls in winter. Similarly applicable to angular distance from the zenith is his statement in another treatise, the Σύνοψις τῶν φυσικῶν (*Conspectus rerum naturalium*), formerly wrongly attributed to Psellus, that

when the sun reaches its maximum northern declination, it produces the summer solstice and comes close to us, inasmuch as our part of the world is in the northern hemisphere, as I have said..., and when it arrives at its maximum southern declination, it produces the winter solstice because of its great distance from us at that time ([3]).

The contrast between ἀπόγειος and ὑπόγειος, as apogee and perigee, respectively, recurs in the so-called *Quadrivium*

([1]) DELATTE, op. cit., 103. 20 ff.

([2]) Ibid., 111. 10 ff.

([3]) Ibid. 2, 49. 6 ff.: ὅταν δὲ τὸ τέρμα τῆς αὐτοῦ λοξώσεως τῆς πρὸς βορρᾶν καταλάβῃ, τὴν θερινὴν ἐργάζεται τροπὴν καὶ πλησιάζει ἡμῖν διὰ τὸ τὴν ἡμετέραν οἴκησιν ὡς ἔφαμεν βορειοτέραν εἶναι... καὶ ὅτε πρὸς τὸ ἔσχατον τῆς νοτίας αὐτοῦ λοξώσεως καταντήσῃ, τὴν χειμερινήν, διὰ τὸ τηνικαῦτα εἶναι πόρρωθεν ἡμῶν.

ὑπόγειος, a Byzantine term for perigee, and some Byzantine views... 389

(Σύνταγμα τῶν τεσσάρων μαθημάτων, ἀριθμητικῆς, μουσικῆς, γεωμε-
τρίας καὶ ἀστρονομίας) ([1]) of George Pachymeres (1262-ca. 1310),
the Byzantine historian and man of letters. In the astronomical section of this *Quadrivium* (which is, of course, a designation more common in the Latin West than in Byzantium),
Pachymeres says that the sun:

moves from apogee to perigee, being in the vicinity of apogee in
the summer, when it is said to attain its highest altitude, and then
reaching perigee when it is in the southern skies. For if it were at
apogee in *Toxotes* [*Sagittarius*], the cold would be excessive; similarly, if it were at perigee in *Didymi* [*Gemini*], the heat would
be excessive ([2]).

Pachymeres ascribes these astronomical phenomena to divine
Providence, which arranged things thus to avoid extremes
of heat and cold ([3]), and took care that the change in the
seasons should be gradual and not sudden ([4]).

From the passages cited from Pachymeres, we can see
that ὑπόγειος acquired the sense of 'at perigee' from the
circumstance that, in the skies of the northern hemisphere,
when the sun is closest to the earth (near the time of the

([1]) Edited sumptuously with a magnificent medieval portrait of Pachym-
eres in color, by P. TANNERY and E. STÉPHANOU, *Quadrivium de Georges
Pachymère* (*Studi e Testi*, 94 [Rome, 1940]). On Pachymeres, see KRUMBA-
CHER, op. cit., 288 ff.

([2]) Op. cit., 397. 11-14: ἔχει [*sc.* ὁ ἥλιος] δὲ κινήματα καὶ ἀπόγεια καὶ
ὑπόγεια, κατὰ μὲν τὸ θέρος ἀπόγεια, ὅτε καὶ ὕψωμα ὑψοῦσθαι λέγεται, ὅτε δὲ
ἐν τοῖς νοτίοις, ὑπόγειον ἐκτελεῖ κίνησιν· εἰ γὰρ ἦν ἀπόγειος ἐν Τοξότῃ, ἄμε-
τρον ὂν ἦν τὸ ψύχος, ὁμοίως δὲ καὶ εἰ ὑπόγειος ἐν τοῖς Διδύμοις, ἄμετρος ἂν
ἦν ἡ ἀλέα. Cf. ibid., 331. 3 ff., 23 ff. On the changing altitude of the sun and
its relation to the seasons, see ibid., 376. 7-19, 29-34, cf 390. 30-34, and
p. 390 n. 2 infra.

([3]) Ibid., 379. 2-6: ὅθεν καὶ οὐδὲ τὸ αὐτὸ ὕψος ἔχει ἀεὶ κινούμενος ὁ
Ἥλιος, ἀλλ' ἐν τοῖς κατὰ τοὺς Διδύμους τόποις, ὅπου καὶ αἱ μέγισται περιφέρειαι, ὑψοῦται, ἐν δὲ τοῖς κατὰ τὸν Τοξότην, ὅπου καὶ αἱ ἐλάχισται περιφέρειαι,
προσγειότερός ἐστι. καὶ τοῦτο καλῶς ὑπὸ τῆς Προνοίας ᾠκονομήθη, ὡς ἂν μήτε
ἐν τῷ καύματι λυπῇ προσεγγίζων, μήτε ἐν τῷ ψύχει ἀφιστάμενος.

([4]) Ibid., 378. 20 f.: δαιμονίως ἐργασαμένης ταῦτα τῆς Προνοίας, ὑπὲρ
τοῦ λεληθυίας ἀλλὰ μὴ ἀθρόας γίνεσθαι τὰς τῶν ὡρῶν μεταβολάς. These
words occur almost verbatim in CLEOMEDES, *De motu circulari corporum
caelestium*, ed. H. ZIEGLER (Leipzig, 1891), 52. 17-20, whence they were
presumably derived, either directly or through some intermediary. Cf. p. 386
n. 2 supra, and NICEPHORUS BLEMMYDES, *Epitome physica*, MPG, 142, 1288 D.

winter solstice), the sun rises, sets, and appears lower, i. e., farther south, than in summer. Hence it was considered to be nearer Egypt in the winter (¹) and therefore closer to the southern hemisphere at that season than it is to the north.

Accordingly, we find in astronomical texts that, from the point of view of an observer in the northern hemisphere, the sun is said to be 'highest' and farthest north at the time of the summer solstice, when it is traveling upon our summer solstice circle (ὁ παρ' ἡμῖν θερινὸς τροπικὸς κύκλος [Geminus, 56. 28 ff.], or what we should call the apparent diurnal path of the sun in summer). This is the season in which the sun attains its maximum northern declination (i. e., its greatest angular distance north of the celestial equator), and its greatest elevation above the horizon, rising, setting, and appearing in the sky farther north than at any other time. Conversely, again from the point of view of the northern hemisphere, it is said to be 'lowest' and farthest south at the winter solstice, when, traveling along what the Greeks called the χειμερινὸς τροπικὸς κύκλος (the apparent diurnal path of the sun in winter), it attains its maximum southern declination (its greatest angular distance south of the celestial equator), and its lowest elevation above the horizon, rising and setting farther south, and appearing lower over the horizon, than at any other time (²).

A well-recognized corollary of these propositions is that the seasons of the two hemispheres are exactly opposite. When it is winter in northern latitudes, it is summer south of the equator, and vice versa. When it is winter in the

---

(¹) HERODOTUS, 2, 24 f.; PSEUDO-PLUTARCH, De placitis philosophorum, 4. 1 (898 A); H. DIELS, Doxographi Graeci (Berlin, 1879), 385. 18-23.

(²) GEMINUS, Elementa astronomiae, ed. K. MANITIUS (Leipzig, 1898), 6. 4 - 8. 3, cf. 30. 2-13, 44. 12 - 46. 7, 23 ff., 48. 14-19; CLEOMEDES, De motu circulari, 48. 1 - 50. 10, 54. 19 - 56. 3, 44. 5 - 46. 28; Commentariorum in Aratum reliquiae, ed. E. MAASS (Berlin, 1898), 54. 12 ff., 56. 25 - 58. 23 (Achilles - 3rd cent.), cf. 64. 7 ff.; JOHN OF DAMASCUS, MPG, 94, 889 C 892 B; Anecdota Graeca, ed. J. A. CRAMER, 1 (Oxford, 1839), 376. 26 - 377. 19; BLEMMYDES, MPG, 142, 1285 A-D, 1288 A-D, 1289 B, 1308 C,. 1316 B-C; PACHYMERES, op. cit., 376. 10-19, 29-34, 379. 2-5, cf. 390. 22-34. Cf. CLAUDIUS PTOLEMAEUS, Opera quae exstant omnia, 3. 1, edd. F. BOLL and A. BOER (Leipzig, 1940), 43. 9 ff.; BASIL OF CAESAREA, MPG, 29, 136 A - 137 B. See also p. 391.

north and the sun is traveling upon ' our winter solstice circle ' (ὁ παρ' ἡμῖν χειμερινὸς τροπικὸς κύκλος), it is summer south of the equator, and the sun is moving upon what for the southern hemisphere is the ' summer solstice circle' (ὁ παρ' ἐκείνοις θερινὸς τροπικὸς κύκλος). At the summer solstice, the northern hemisphere has its longest days and shortest nights, while latitudes below the equator are having their shortest days and longest nights, the situation being reversed in the winter ([1]).

In what is winter for us, for example, the sun rises earlier and sets later at any given latitude south of the equator than it does at the corresponding latitude in the north. At any given north latitude, therefore, the sun, in our winter, is below the horizon part of the time that it is visible at the corresponding latitude in the southern hemisphere. And, in conformity with a well-recognized formula which designates the horizon as the line that divides τὸ ὑπὲρ γῆν ἡμισφαίριον ἀπὸ τοῦ ὑπὸ τὴν γῆν, the sun is then ὑπὸ τὴν γῆν Strictly speaking, of course, it is the terrestrial equator which makes an equal division of these two realms. But the horizon is also regarded as doing so, and celestial phenomena, like the *antarctica*, that are not visible on the horizon of observers north of the equator are dubbed ὑπὸ γῆν, while those that are visible are known as ὑπὲρ γῆν ([2]).

---

[1] GEMINUS, op. cit., 56. 26 - 58. 8, 174. 13-20, cf. 6. 10 - 8. 3, 44. 12 - 46. 7, 48. 27 - 52. 23, 70. 12 - 72. 20, 72. 21 - 76. 20, 76. 21 - 78. 24, 82. 15-27, 84. 1 - 86. 10; CLEOMEDES, op. cit., 26. 14 - 28. 15, 36. 17 ff., 44. 5 ff., 48. 1-13; E. MAASS, op. cit., 65. 15 - 66. 25, cf. 56. 30 - 58. 11; BLEMMYDES, MPG, 142, 1284 D, 1293 CD, 1296 A-C; PACHYMERES, op. cit., 381. 31 - 383. 2. Cf. PTO-LEMAEUS, op. cit., l. 1 (in following note), 17. 22 - 18. 4.

[2] AUTOLYCUS, *De ortibus et occasibus*, ed. F. HULTSCH (Leipzig, 1885), 66. 24-6, 68. 10 ff., 70. 16 ff., 100. 1 ff., and passim; *Eudoxi ars astronomica*, col. VI, ed. F. BLASS (Kiel 1887), 16 f.; HIPPARCHUS, *In Arati et Eudoxi Phaenomena commentariorum libri tres*, ed. K. MANITIUS (Leipzig, 1894), 144. 9-14, 26. 7 ff., 28. 8 ff., and passim; GEMINUS, op. cit., 48. 26 - 52. 25, 62. 11-21, 72. 21 ff., 76. 7 ff., 156. 1 ff., 158. 1 ff., and passim; CLAUDIUS PTO-LEMAEUS, op. cit., l. 1, *Syntaxis Mathematica*, ed. J. L. HEIBERG (Leipzig, 1898), 12. 12 f., 17. 9-14, 18. 12 ff., 20. 20 - 21. 6, 30. 4 ff., 101. 20 ff.; CLEO-MEDES, op. cit., 22. 11 - 26. 27, 40. 1 - 48. 13, 70. 18 f.; E. MAASS, op. cit., 53. 27 - 54. 6, 55. 3-6, 56. 30 - 58. 11, 73. 20 - 74. 15; THEON SMYRNAEUS, op. cit.'(p. 387 n. 2 supra), 131. 4 ff.; JOHN OF DAMASCUS, MPG, 94, 888 BC, 892 B;

Closely related to these conceptions is the language of astronomical geography which looks upen the southern hemisphere, viewed from north of the equator, as ὑπὸ γῆν and its inhabitants as ὑπόγειοι, antipodes, and the people 'down under' (οἱ κάτω), in distinction from the northern hemisphere and its inhabitants, which are, respectively, ὑπὲρ γῆν and ὑπέργειοι (¹).

Hence, though ὑπόγειος does not etymologically carry the meaning of 'close to the earth' or 'at perigee', it was taken over as an adjective to describe the sun at its closest approach to the earth, because the sun is at that time farthest south and at its greatest prominence (in intensity and duration of visibility) in the regions below the equator, to which the word ὑπόγειος is properly applied. Whether Symeon Seth was the first to transfer to this latter sense of ὑπόγειος the connotation of 'at perigee', I cannot say. Perhaps some reader of these *Mélanges* can supply the answer.

Perigee, apogee, and the cause of the seasons.

In correctly appreciating the relation of the perigee and apogee of the sun to the rotation of the seasons, Symeon and Pachymeres are witnesses to a Greek scientific tradition that goes back to the astronomer Hipparchus (fl. 125 B. C.), whose determinations of perigee and apogee are cited with

---

BLEMMYDES, MPG, 142, 1237 C, cf. 1276 BC, 1284 C, 1285 AD; PACHYMERES, op. cit., 330. 1 ff., 367. 5 ff., 375. 16 ff., 377. 1 ff., 27 ff. Cf. THEODOSIUS, *De habitationibus liber, De diebus et noctibus libri duo,* ed. R. FECHT (*Abhandlungen d. Gesellschaft d. Wiss. zu Göttingen,* Philolog.-hist. Kl., N. F. 19. 4 [1927]), 1-176, passim.

(¹) GEMINUS, op. cit., 56. 26 - 58. 3, 162, 15 - 164 2, 172. 7-11, 174. 13-18; CLEOMEDES, op. cit., 22. 11 - 28. 15; E. MAASS, op. cit., 65. 10 - 66. 25, 125. 4-10, 18-21, 133. 8-10, 421. 21-3; BLEMMYDES, MPG. 142, 1276 BC, 1277 A, 1293 BC. 1296 A; PACHYMERES, op. cit., 377. 1-12. Cf. COSMAS INDICOPLEUSTES, *Christian Topography,* ed. E. O. WINSTEDT (Cambridge, Eng., 1909), 45. 14 ff., 47. 5 ff., 92. 13 ff.; *Catalogus codicum astrologorum Graecorum,* 8. 1, ed. F. CUMONT (Brussels, 1929), 156 f. On ἀντίχθονες and ἀντίποδες see PAULY-WISSOWA, *Real-Encyclopädie,* 1 (1894), 2396 f., 2531-3; George SARTON, op. cit., indices, *s. vv.*

approval by Claudius Ptolemy (fl. 140) in his *Syntaxis Mathematica* (Μαθηματικὴ Σύνταξις, called the *Almagest* by the Arabs). According to these calculations, the accuracy of which Ptolemy demonstrates mathematically, the sun reaches apogee 24.5° before the summer solstice (i. e., *Didymi – Gemini* 5° 30′) and perigee in *Toxotes* (*Sagittarius*) 5° 30′) (¹). In another work, the Ἀποτελεσματικά, an astrological treatise, Ptolemy ascribes the heat of summer and the cold of winter to the sun's proximity to, and remoteness from, the zenith (²).

Roughly about the same time, Theon of Smyrna (fl. ca. 130) and Cleomedes, if he can be dated in this century, both independently of Ptolemy, the former (p. 401 n. 1 infra) under the influence of Adrastus (a contemporary philosopher of the Peripatetic School), the latter presumably following Posidonius, put apogee in *Didymi (Gemini)* and perigee in *Toxotes (Sagittarius)* (³).

Later on, Ptolemy's figures on apogee and perigee (cf. also Nicephorus Blemmydes, p. 398 n. 2 infra) were accepted by Theon of Alexandria (fl. 380) in his commentary on the *Syntaxis Mathematica*, and by Proclus, the Neoplatonist (410-85), in his *Hypotyposis astronomicarum positionum* (⁴). The Ptolemaic reasoning on the relation between the proximity of the sun to the zenith and the change of the seasons, but without mention of perigee and apogee, is applied to winter and summer by the author of the pseudo-Clementine *Recog-*

(¹) CLAUDIUS PTOLEMAEUS, op. cit., l. 1, 233. 1 ff., 255. 1 ff. ; on the accuracy of these computations, see *Commentaires de Pappus et de Théon d'Alexandrie sur l'Almageste*, ed. A. Rome, 3, THÉON D'ALEXANDRIE, *Commentaire sur les livres 3 et 4 de l'Almageste* (*Studi e Testi*, 106 [Rome, 1943]), 879 n. 5 ; K. MANITIUS, *Ptolemäus, Handbuch d. Astronomie*, 1 (Leipzig, 1912), 428 f. ; and Part III infra.

(²) CLAUDIUS PTOLEMAEUS, op. cit., 3. 1, 30. 11 ff.

(³) CLEOMEDES, op. cit. (p. 389 supra), 54. 22 ff : ...ὅθεν καὶ τοῦτον μὲν ἐν ἐλαχίστῳ διέρχεται χρόνῳ [sc. ὁ ἥλιος], τοὺς δὲ διδύμους ἐν μηκίστῳ, ἐνταῦθα μὲν ὑψηλότατος ὤν, ἐν δὲ τῷ τοξότῃ προσγειότατος, ἐν δὲ τοῖς ἄλλοις ἀναλόγως. THEON SMYRNAEUS, op. cit. (p. 387 supra), 157. 2-12, 168. 9 ff., 176. 8 ff. On Cleomedes and Theon of Smyrna, and their sources, see SARTON, op. cit., 1, 211 f., 267 f., 271 f.

(⁴) A. ROME, op. cit. (in n. 1 supra), 879. 6 ff. ; PROCLUS DIADOCHUS, *Hypotyposis astronomicarum positionum*, 3. 64 f., 7. 28 f., ed. Karl MANITIUS (Leipzig, 1909), 72. 9-19, 226. 16-24, 287 n. 6. See p. 401 n. 1 infra.

394

nitiones and by one of the anonymous commentators on the *Phaenomena* of Aratus ([1]), and to summer by Olympiodorus (fl. 525), who explains that the sun is hottest when it is near the zenith at the time of the summer solstice, in the sign of Καρκίνος (*Cancer*) ([2]). More detail is given by Basil of Caesarea in his *Homilia VI in Hexaemeron* and by Psellus (fl. 1070) in his Διδασκαλία παντοδαπή (*De omnifaria doctrina*), both of whom state that, when the sun moves north [of the celestial equator] and stands overhead it produces summer, and that when it moves to the south it produces winter ([3]).

Unfortunately, however, not all of the Greeks expressed themselves with equal clarity and precision on this subject, and some seem to put apogee in the winter and perigee in the summer. Even Geminus of Rhodes (fl. 70 B. C.), the author of an important astronomical treatise, the Εἰσαγωγὴ εἰς τὰ φαινόμενα (*Elementa astronomiae*), says that

the winter solstice comes at the time that the sun is farthest from our part of the world, when it stands lowest over the horizon, and follows its most southerly course, producing the shortest day and the longest night of the year,

and that the heat of summer is produced by the sun's approach ' towards us ' ([4]). About two centuries later, the

([1]) MPG, 1, 1393 A ; on Aratus, ed. E. MAASS, op. cit., 130. 26 - 131. 1.

([2]) *In Aristotelis Meteora commentaria*, ed. W. STÜVE (Berlin, 1900), 176. 30 ff.

([3]) BASIL, MPG, 29, 136 B, cf. 136 A - 137 B; more briefly in Psellus, MPG, 122, 748 D - 749 A: περὶ μέντοι γε θέρους ἢ χειμῶνος καὶ τῶν λοιπῶν ὡρῶν ἰστέον, ὡς ὅταν μὲν ὁ ἥλιος βόρειος ἡμῖν γένηται, καὶ ὑπὲρ κεφαλῆς κινοῖτο, θέρος ποιεῖ· ὅταν δὲ πρὸς νότον ἀπέλθῃ, χειμῶνα ἐργάζεται, καὶ ὅταν μὲν κατὰ τὸν Κριὸν τὸ ζῴδιον γένηται, ἰσημερίαν ποιεῖ· ὅταν δὲ κατ' ἄντικρυ διαπορεύηται τῶν Χηλῶν, μετοπώραν καὶ ἰσημερίαν αὖθις. Ptolemaic authority on the apogee of the sun is cited in pseudo-Psellus: Τοῦ σοφωτάτου Ψελλοῦ, σύνταγμα εὐσύνοπτον εἰς τὰς τέσσαρας μαθηματικὰς ἐπιστήμας, Ἀριθμητικὴν, Μουσικὴν, Γεωμετρίαν, καὶ Ἀστρονομίαν, ed. ARSENIUS, Archbishop of Monembasia (Venice, 1532), on which see G. SARTON, *Introduction*, 1, 750.

([4]) Ed. Karl MANITIUS (Leipzig, 1898), 6. 21 ff.: τροπὴ δέ ἐστι χειμερινή, ὅταν ὁ ἥλιος πορρωτάτω ἡμῶν τῆς οἰκήσεως γένηται καὶ ταπεινότατος ὡς πρὸς τὸν ὁρίζοντα καὶ νοτιώτατον κύκλον γράψῃ καὶ μεγίστην πασῶν τῶν ἐν τῷ ἐνιαυτῷ νύκτα ποιήσηται, ἐλαχίστην δὲ ἡμέραν. Ibid., 190. 20 f., 23 ff.: κατὰ τὸν συνεγγισμὸν τὸν πρὸς ἡμᾶς ἄρχεται [sc. ὁ ἥλιος] ἡμᾶς θερμαίνειν... μᾶλλον

learned Plutarch in a chapter on the Roman preference for January as the beginning of the year (under the heading, Διὰ τί τὸν Ἰανουάριον μῆνα νέου ἔτους ἀρχὴν λαμβάνουσι;) remarks:

They do best, however, who begin [the year] after the winter solstice, when the sun has ceased to move away, and turns about to retrace his course towards us. For this beginning of the year is in a sense natural to man, since it increases the length of the day for us, diminishes that of the night, and brings closer the lord and ruler of the whole world of flux (¹).

A portion of the first sentence of this text is repeated almost verbatim by the most celebrated pagans of Byzantium, the apostate Emperor Julian (²) (361-3) and the great classicist, George Gemistus Pletho (³) (ca. 1355-1452), as well as by Pletho's critic and opponent, Theodore of Gaza (⁴).

Not dissimilar are the views of two scholars of the third century, Achilles, the grammarian, and Alexander of Aphrodisias, the philosopher. The sun is hot at the time of the summer solstice (in the sign of Καρκίνος – *Cancer*), Achilles

---

ἀεὶ καὶ μᾶλλον συνεγγίζοντος τοῦ ἡλίου, ἐπαίσθησιν συμβαίνει τῆς θερμασίας γίνεσθαι. Cf. 190. 26 - 192. 9. I omit 6. 10 ff., a parallel passage to 6. 21 ff., because of the uncertain state of the text.

(¹) *Quaestiones Romanae*, 19 (268 D): ἄριστα δ' οἱ τὴν μετὰ τροπὰς χειμερινὰς λαμβάνοντες [sc. ἀρχὴν τοῦ ἔτους], ὁπηνίκα τοῦ πρόσω βαδίζειν πεπαυμένος ὁ ἥλιος ἐπιστρέφει καὶ ἀνακάμπτει πάλιν πρὸς ἡμᾶς· γίγνεται γὰρ ἀνθρώποις τρόπον τινὰ κατὰ φύσιν, τὸν μὲν τοῦ φωτὸς αὔξουσα χρόνον ἡμῖν, μειοῦσα δὲ τὸν τοῦ σκότους, ἐγγυτέρω δὲ ποιοῦσα τὸν κύριον καὶ ἡγεμόνα τῆς ῥευστῆς οὐσίας ἁπάσης. I have adopted the text, but not the translation, of F. C. BABBITT, *Plutarch's Moralia*, 4 (Cambridge, Mass., 1936), 32-4.

(²) Oratio IV, (156 A), ed. W. C. WRIGHT, *The Works of the Emperor Julian*, 1 (N. Y., 1930), 426: ὁπότε ὁ βασιλεὺς Ἥλιος αὖθις ἐπανάγει πρὸς ἡμᾶς ἀφεὶς τῆς μεσημβρίας τὰ ἔσχατα καὶ ὥσπερ περὶ νύσσαν τὸν Αἰγοκέρωτα κάμψας ἀπὸ τοῦ νότου πρὸς τὸν βορρᾶν ἔρχεται...

(³) In the twenty-first chapter of his: ἡ τῶν νόμων συγγραφή, ed. C. ALEXANDRE (Paris, 1858), 58. 4 ff.: τὰς ἡλίου τροπάς... τὰς χειμερινάς, ...ὅτε τὸ πλεῖστον ἡμῶν ὁ ἥλιος ἀποκεχωρηκὼς τῆς πρὸς ἡμᾶς αὖθις ἄρχεται προσόδου, on which see my monograph on PLETHO in *Dumbarton Oaks. Papers, No. 4*, now in press.

(⁴) *De mensibus*, 14, MPG, 19, 1200 D: Ῥωμαῖοι δὲ [sc. ἀρχὴν τοῦ ἐνιαυτοῦ] τὸν Ἰανουάριον, [sc. ἦγον] ὡς ἀπὸ τροπῶν χειμερινῶν, ...ἡνίκα δὴ ἥλιος, ὁ τῆς γενέσεως κύριος, τοῦ πρόσω ἰέναι λήγων ἀνακάμπτειν ἄρχεται ὡς ἡμᾶς, καὶ τὸν μὲν τοῦ φωτὸς αὔξει χρόνον, τὸν δὲ τοῦ σκότους μειοῖ. ὀρθῶς οὖν καὶ Νουμᾶς ἀρχὴν τοιαύτην Ῥωμαίοις τέταχε...

XV

396

says, because it is close to us (ἄτε πλησίον ἡμῶν ὤν), while winter comes (in the sign of Αἰγόκερως - *Capricornus*) when the sun is far away (πόῤῥω ἡμῶν). And Alexander, in commenting upon the *Meteorologica* of Aristotle, observes that the sun comes close in the summer, and that its proximity at that season brings increase to plants, which wither and wane when it departs. The same theory (τέτακται δὲ χειμὼν καὶ θέρος τῇ ἀποστάσει τοῦ ἡλίου καὶ τῷ πλησιάζειν ἡμῖν συνιστάμενα) is represented by John Philoponus (fl. 530), another commentator on the *Meteorologica*, although it is hazardous to generalize about Philoponus without a careful study of his voluminous works (as published in the *Commentaria in Aristotelem Graeca* and elsewhere) (¹). Likewise in the same vein, Suidas, the lexicographer of the tenth century, maintains that the sun is on its way towards us in the spring (²); and Eustathius of Thessalonica (fl. 1180), expounding the connection of January with janus (θύρα), explains that January ' brings back the sun to us from the south, terminates its outward course, and in a way ushers in the spring ', with its promise of fertility and vegetation, serving thus as a kind of door (³).

(¹) Achilles, ed. E. MAASS, op. cit., 54. 12 ff., 64. 8-23; ALEXANDER, *In Aristotelis Meteorologicorum libros commentarium,* ed. Michael HAYDUCK (Berlin, 1899), 59. 21 ff.: ὡς γὰρ τοῖς ζῴοις τε καὶ τοῖς ἐμψύχοις ἡ τοῦ ἡλίου περιφορὰ αἰτία αὐξήσεώς τε καὶ μειώσεως (προσιὼν μὲν γὰρ σωτηρίας τε καὶ αὐξήσεως, ἀπιὼν δὲ μειώσεώς τε καὶ φθορᾶς αἴτιος, ὡς δῆλον ἐκ τῶν ἐπετείων· ταῦτα γὰρ προσιόντος μὲν αὐτοῖς τοῦ ἡλίου αὔξεται, ἀπιόντος δὲ φθίνει τε καὶ φθείρεται) ὡς δ᾽ ἐπὶ τούτων, οὕτως καὶ ἐπὶ τῶν πολυχρονιωτέρων, ὧν ἡ αὔξησις πλείονι χρόνῳ καὶ ἡ φθίσις· ὧν γὰρ ἡ αὔξησις τοσαύταις ἡλίου προσόδοις, τούτων καὶ ἡ μείωσις καὶ ἡ φθίσις τοσαῖσδε ἀφόδοις. ὡς οὖν ταῦτα διὰ τὴν τοῦ ἡλίου περιφορὰν αὔξεταί τε καὶ φθίνει, οὕτω καὶ τὰ τῆς γῆς μέρη παρὰ τῆς προσόδου τε τοῦ ἡλίου καὶ ἀφόδου, καὶ ὅλως παρὰ τῆς ἐκείνου περιφορᾶς τήν τε ἀκμὴν καὶ τὴν παρακμὴν λαμβάνει... Ibid., 97. 23 ff : μετὰ μὲν οὖν τροπὰς θερινὰς καὶ κυνὸς ἀνατολὴν πνέουσιν, ὅτι πλησίον μὲν ὢν ὁ ἥλιος (ἔστι δὲ πλησίον προσιών τε ταῖς θεριναῖς τροπαῖς καὶ κατ᾽ αὐτὰς ὤν) διὰ τὴν ἐγγύτητα φθάνει ξηραίνων τὴν γῆν... ὀλίγον δὲ ἀπελθόντος σύμμετρος ἤδη γίνεται ἡ ἀπ᾽ αὐτοῦ θερμότης... JOANNES PHILOPONUS, *In Aristotelis Meteorologicorum librum primum commentarium,* ed. Michael HAYDUCK (Berlin, 1901), 45. 31-3.

(²) *Lexicon,* s. v. ἔαρ, ed. Ada ADLER, 2 (Leipzig, 1931), 188. 16 f.: ...ὥρα τοῦ ἔτους κατὰ τὴν πρὸς ἡμᾶς τοῦ ἡλίου πορείαν.

(³) *Opuscula,* ed. T. L. F. TAFEL (Francofurti ad Moenum, 1832): 316. 7 ff.: σεμνύνει δὲ καὶ ἄλλως τὸν καιρὸν τοῦτον ἐκεῖνος (sc. ὁ ᾽Ιανουάριος), ὅτι περ ἐκ τῶν νοτίων αὐτὸς ἡμῖν ἐπανάγει τὸν ἥλιον, καὶ τῆς μακρᾶς ἀποδημίας στήσας ἐπανακάμπτειν ποιεῖ, καὶ πως τὸ ἔαρ ἡμῖν ὑπανοίγει.

While it would be rash to attempt to make excuses for ambiguities or mistakes, it must be said that some of these texts deserve careful scrutiny. Even should we grant that Plutarch and some, or all, of the others have gone astray in this matter, there is good reason to hesitate before convicting a professional astronomer like Geminus of the same error. First of all, in the medieval Latin version of the *Elementa*, which seems to have been based upon an intermediary Arabic translation, the first of the passages quoted supra (p. 394 n. 4) is translated as follows:

Et conversio hyemalis est, quando sol est in sua ultimiore longitudine a sont [the medieval progenitor of our word zenith] capitum nostrorum in regione nostra et descendit ad partem orizontis septentrionis et pervenit in magis ultima suarum descensionum meridionalium et designat in suo cursu orbem in meridie et ponit noctem longiorem noctibus anni et diem breviorem diebus anni ([1]).

To judge from this, Geminus, considering the succession of the seasons in terms of the remoteness of the sun from our zenith, notes that in winter the sun is farther away from our zenith than at any other time. Moreover, he elucidates what he means by the sun's being ' farthest from our part of the world ' in winter, when he says:

Naturally and universally, in any part of the world, one would designate as the [apparent diurnal] path of the sun at the summer solstice that which comes closest to the region in which he lives. Accordingly, for those who live on the equator the [apparent diurnal] path of the sun at the summer solstice is the [celestial] equator. For that is the one on which the sun arrives at their zenith ([2]).

([1]) GEMINUS, op. cit., 287. 6 ff.; see also Manitius's discussion of the versions: ibid., XVIII ff., 285.

([2]) Ibid., 58. 8 ff.: φύσει γὰρ λέγοιτ' ἂν καὶ καθολικῶς πρὸς ἅπασαν τὴν οἰκουμένην θερινὸς τροπικὸς κύκλος ὑπάρχειν ὁ ἔγγιστα τῆς οἰκήσεως ὑπάρχων. δι' ἣν αἰτίαν τοῖς ὑπὸ τὸν ἰσημερινὸν οἰκοῦσι [ὁ] θερινὸς τροπικὸς κύκλος γίνεται ὁ ἰσημερινός. τότε γὰρ αὐτοῖς κατὰ κορυφὴν γίνεται ὁ ἥλιος. On the sun's being at the zenith over the equator at the equinoxes, see, *inter alios,* Achilles, ed. E. MAASS, op. cit., 67. 2 ff. The sun stands at the zenith of an observer on the equator twice a year, at what we in northern latitudes call the vernal and autumnal equinoxes. At the geographical equator, the celestial equator (the great circle in which the plane of the earth's equator intersects the celestial sphere) always passes through the observer's zenith;

398

In other words, by the diurnal path or circle that is closest to an observer at any given point Geminus understands that on which the observer sees the sun at, or most nearly at, his zenith. Conversely, the circle on which the observer sees the sun at its greatest elongation from his zenith is the one which Geminus would regard as the ' farthest ' away. To the same effect is his discussion of the relative heat of various tropical regions, in which he makes it clear that, when he writes of the sun's tarrying over certain parts of the world (οἰκήσεις) on their respective summer solstice circles, he is thinking of the sun as moving to [or close to] and away from the zenith of the observer (ἐπιμονῆς μὲν ⟨οὐ⟩ γινομένης ἐπὶ τοῦ κατὰ κορυφὴν σημείου [at the equator], ταχέως δὲ ἀποχωροῦντος τοῦ ἡλίου) (¹).

It may be that, despite this, Geminus did confuse angular distance from the zenith with linear distance from the earth in miles, conceiving proximity to the zenith to be identical with closeness to the earth. But such an adverse judgment is open to some doubt in view of the fact that authors like Cleomedes and Symeon Seth, both of whom, as we have already seen (pp. 386 ff. and p. 393 n. 3), were correctly informed with regard to the position of the sun's perigee and apogee, also write of summer as the time when the sun is closest to our part of the world (οἴκησις), and of winter as that in which the sun is farthest away (²), although it is

---

and on the days of the equinoxes (ca. Mar. 20-21, ca. Sept. 22-23) it is the great circle along which is described the sun's apparent diurnal motion. In other words, ' summer ' on the equator comes at the equinoxes, two times a year; and winter likewise comes twice annually, at what are for us in the northern hemisphere the summer and winter solstices, the sun being at its greatest angular distance from the zenith of an observer on the equator ca. June 21-22 and ca. December 21-22.

(¹) GEMINUS, op. cit., 178. 6 ff.

(²) See p. 388 nn. 2 f. supra. CLEOMEDES, op. cit., 48. 16 ff.: τροπὴν μὲν θερινὴν ποιεῖ [sc. ὁ ἥλιος], ὅταν ἔγγιστα τῆς οἰκήσεως ἡμῶν γενόμενος βορειότατον κύκλον γράψῃ... τροπὴν δὲ χειμερινὴν ποιεῖ, ὅταν ποῤῥωτάτω τῆς οἰκήσεως ἡμῶν γενόμενος καὶ ταπεινότατος ὡς πρὸς τὸν ὁρίζοντα νοτιώτατον γράψῃ κύκλον... Ibid., 44. 23 ff.: ὁπόταν δ' ἐφαψάμενος τοῦ χειμερινοῦ πρὸς ἡμᾶς πάλιν ὑποστρέφῃ [sc. ὁ ἥλιος]...

NICEPHORUS BLEMMYDES says (MPG, 142, 1285 A & D) that in summer the sun is closest to our part of the world (τῆς οἰκήσεως ἡμῶν γενόμενος

certain that, in so doing, they were thinking of the relation of the sun to the zenith, and not of the distance of the earth from the sun. Indeed, as the περὶ οἰκήσεων of Theodosius (ca. first century B. C.) and a number of passages in Geminus, Ptolemy, the commentators on Aratus, Pachymeres, and other writers show, οἴκησις is a *terminus technicus* for parallel of latitude, an equivalent for κλίμα and ' geographical position' in general (¹), so that references to the sun's being ' closest to our οἴκησις ' (²) are to be understood as indicating the sun's closest approach to the zenith at our latitude at the summer solstice, when the sun is visible above the horizon longer, and is more conspicuous in the heavens, than at any other time. Conversely, in the winter, when the opposite is true, it would be farthest from our zenith and hence ' farthest from our οἴκησις '.

ἔγγιστα) and in winter farthest away (τῆς οἰκήσεως ἡμῶν ποῤῥωτάτω γενόμενος), but qualifies these words somewhat in his section on the sun in Καρκίνος (*Cancer*, the sign of the summer solstice), where he may, perhaps, be understood as saying that the sun, *viewed vertically* (i. e., from the zenith), is closest to us in the summer, at the time that it starts out towards perigee (MPG, 142, 1316 C): καὶ διὰ τοῦτο καὶ κατὰ κορυφὴν ὢν ἡμῶν ἐκ τῆς τοῦ κόσμου ἐγκλίσεως καὶ προσγειότερος ἀρχόμενος γίνεσθαι, καὶ ἡμῶν ἐγγυτέρω κατὰ κάθετον, καὶ τὸ θερμότατον ἐν ζῳδίοις ἔχων ἐγγειτονοῦν, λέγω δὴ τὸν Λέοντα, μειζόνων γίνεται καυμάτων αἴτιος, ἢ ὅτε τὸ ὑπὸ τοὺς Διδύμους περιενόστει τμῆμα, τῆς οἰκείας σφαίρας τὸ ὑψηλότατον. But the text is ambiguous, and we cannot tell what Blemmydes really meant. Note also that in his transcription of the passage from Cleomedes on perigee he unaccountably suppresses what Cleomedes had to say on this subject (cf. MPG, 142, 1289 B, with CLEOMEDES, op. cit., 54. 22 ff. quoted in n. 3, p. 393 supra).

(¹) THEODOSIUS, *De habitationibus,* ed. Rudolf FECHT (see p. 392 supra), 14-52, n. b.: 16. 11 ff., 36. 19, 38. 35; GEMINUS, op. cit., 42. 16, 46. 14 f., 56. 5, 68. 9 f., 76. 2, 7-12, 162. 15 - 164. 8, 168. 21 ff., and index s. v.; PTOLEMAEUS, op. cit. (p. 391 n. 2 supra), 1. 1, 68. 7-9, 261. 10, and passim; E. MAASS, op. cit. (p. 390 n. 2 supra), 47. 16 f., 65. 17 ff., 66. 26 ff., 129. 4-6, 317. 1 f.; JOANNES PHILOPONUS, *De aeternitate mundi,* ed. H. RABE (Leipzig, 1899), 16. 6 ff.; IDEM, *De opificio mundi,* ed. W. REICHARDT (Leipzig, 1897). 138. 20 ff.; BLEMMYDES, MPG, 142, 1253 C, 1285 D, 1292 C ff.; PACHYMERES, op. cit., 330. 26 ff., 367. 2 ff., 375. 16-19, 378. 5 ff., 382. 5-8, 26 ff. On κλίμα, see ERNST HONIGMANN, *Die sieben Klimata u. die* πόλεις ἐπίσημοι (Heidelberg, 1929).

(²) In view of the astronomical texts discussed supra (Hipparchus, Ptolemy, etc.), it is ridiculous to say, as does IMMANUEL HOFFMANN, without proof (*Die Anschauungen d. Kirchenväter über Meteorologie* [Munich, 1907], 30 n. 1), that the ancients put aphelion [or, apogee] in the winter.

It seems reasonable to suppose, therefore, that the texts which mention the motion of the sun πρὸς ἡμᾶς and ἀφ᾽ ἡμῶν, or towards and away from our part of the world' (ἡ ἡμετέρα οἴκησις) (¹), etc., refer, not to the sun's passage between perigee and apogee, but to its varying angular distance from the zenith of the observer, and to its relative prominence in the skies at the various seasons of the year. Whether or not this reasoning be justified, it must be said that neither Geminus nor Plutarch nor any of the others who use these expressions, with the possible exception of Alexander Aphrodisiensis, goes beyond the language of Cleomedes and Symeon scrutinized and vindicated above. So far as I can determine, none of them says that the sun is farthest away from the *earth* in winter, or closest to the *earth* in summer (²). It may be objected, of course, that ambiguity is in itself reprehensible, especially when there is no actual proof that, in adopting this terminology, Plutarch and the others were really aware of its proper signification and did not erroneously take it in the sense of distance in miles between the earth and the sun. This is not impossible, although one would then have expected the use of the word γῆ — πρὸς τὴν γῆν, ἀπὸ τῆς γῆς, and the like — in at least one of the texts quoted from this group (pp. 394-7). The failure to use γῆ here may not amount to a vindication of these writers, but it does suggest that they should not be convicted of error without more incriminating evidence.

(¹) Pp. 386 II. 388 n. 3, 398 n. 2. Cf. also THEODORETUS, *Quaestiones in Genesin*, 1, 15, MPG, 80, 96 AB: ἀπὸ γὰρ τοῦ ἰσημερινοῦ τόπου πρὸς τὰ βόρεια μεταβαίνων, τὸ ἔαρ ποιεῖ [sc. ὁ ἥλιος]· εἶτα ἐκεῖθεν ἐπανιὼν μέχρι τούτων τῶν ὅρων, τὴν θερινὴν κατασκευάζει τροπήν, κτλ.

(²) Geminus's argument that the sun [in its diurnal] course around the earth is at all points equidistant from us (op. cit., 176. 10 ff.: αἱ δὲ ἀνατολαὶ τοῦ ἡλίου καὶ αἱ δύσεις γίνονται ἐκ τοῦ αἰθέρος καὶ εἰς τὸν αἰθέρα, διὰ παντὸς τοῦ ἡλίου ἴσον ἀπέχοντος τῆς γῆς), which has nothing to do with perigee and apogee, is part of his polemic against the theory of a flat earth, whose proponents held that the Ethiopians were burned by the sun because the sun, in this view, makes its closest approach to the earth at sunrise and sunset. when it was thought to be very near the east and the west, the land of sunrise and sunset, the supposed home of the Ethiopians. Cf. CLEOMEDES, op. cit., 120 ff.; BLEMMYDES, MPG. 142, 1253 AB.

Astronomical computations and conclusions.

All of the writers considered above who mention the perigee and apogee of the sun put the former in the zodiacal sign of *Toxotes* (*Sagittarius*) and the latter in the sign of *Didymi* (*Gemini*). Some are more precise and give their results in degrees and minutes of arc, as do Ptolemy, Theon of Alexandria, and Proclus, all three of whom locate apogee in *Didymi* 5° 30' (roughly five days after the entrance of the sun into this sign) and apogee in *Toxotes* 5° 30' (also ca. five days after the entry into the sign). Theon and Proclus derive these data from Ptolemy, but exactly the same figures occur in Theon of Smyrna (¹), who was dependent upon other sources.

Now Ptolemy's authority for fixing apogee (and perigee) at these points was Hipparchus, whose calculations he claims to have verified by independent observations of his own. Nevertheless, it has been shown that ca. 191 B. C. apogee fell in *Gemini* 5° 30', that by ca. 150 B. C., because of the precession of the equinoxes and other factors, it had advanced to *Gemini* 6° 12', and that in Ptolemy's day (140 of our era) it had reached *Gemini* 11° 12'. On this account some have

---

(¹) See pp. 292 f. supra. CLAUDIUS PTOLEMAEUS, op. cit., 1. 1, 233. 8 ff.: τὸ δ᾽ ἀπόγειον αὐτοῦ [sc. τοῦ ἡλίου] προηγούμενον τῆς θερινῆς τροπῆς [which then, as now, was regarded as occurring when the sun entered *Cancer*] τμήμασιν κδ̄L'ἔγγιστα. Ibid., 1. 1, 255. 19: τοῦ μὲν περιγείου, τουτέστιν τῶν τοῦ Τοξότου μοιρῶν ε̄L'... τοῦ δὲ ἀπογείου, τουτέστιν τῶν κατὰ τοὺς Διδύμους μοιρῶν ε̄λ̄.. THEON OF ALEXANDRIA, op. cit., 3. 879. 11 ff.: τὸ ἀπογειότατον σημεῖον προηγεῖται τοῦ θερινοῦ τροπικοῦ μοίρας κδL'... τουτέστιν ὅτι κατὰ τῆς τῶν Διδύμων πέμπτης καὶ ἡμισείας μοίρας πίπτει. Cf. ibid., 3, 905. 8 ff. Theon does not actually give the position of perigee. PROCLUS, op. cit., 72. 12 ff.: τὸ μὲν ἀπόγειον εἶναι τοῦ ἡλιακοῦ κύκλου μοιρῶν Διδύμων πέντε καὶ πρώτων ἑξηκοστῶν λ̄, τὸ δὲ περίγειον Τοξότου τῶν αὐτῶν. THEON SMYRNAEUS, op. cit., 168. 10 ff.: τὸ μὲν ἀπογειότατον ἔχων ὑπὸ τὸ α, ε΄ ς΄ μοῖραν τῶν Διδύμων, τὸ δὲ προσγειότατον ὑπὸ τὸ γ, ε΄ ς΄ μοῖραν τοῦ Τοξότου (n. b., ibid., 157. 2-9); ς΄ here is the editor's symbol for one half.

Since the sun moves 360° in a year (tropical year = 365ᵈ 5ʰ 48ᵐ 45ˢ. 98), it moves through the signs of the zodiac at very nearly one degree a day, actually a mean daily motion (in longitude) of 0.° 985647354.

402

argued that Ptolemy could not have checked Hipparchus personally, and that he did nothing but copy Hipparchus blindly without verification (¹).

Apologias for Ptolemy are not wanting (²). But, whether they are to be credited or not, it is obvious that the later writers who repeat these data uncritically can lay no claim here to regard as scientific astronomers. They are, in this respect, merely literary continuators of an astronomical tradition, who were satisfied to take their astronomy on faith. As the following table shows, the error accumulates so rapidly that by the time of Pachymeres, both apogee and perigee were more than 30⁰ (i. e., more than a whole zodiacal sign) ahead of the sign in which he had located them.

This is not to say that Byzantine scholars were wholly ignorant of the experimental method. Nicephoras Gregoras (³) did research which led him to anticipate the results of the Gregorian reform (1582) of the calendar; and George Gemistus Pletho in the fifteenth century made use of contemporary discoveries in his work on the geography of Strabo (⁴). But, generally speaking, it must be confessed that Byzantine science was rarely more than a phase of the study of the ancient classics, treated as literary texts and not as models for independent empirical investigation.

(¹) THEON, ed. A. ROME, 3, 879 n. 5. On the precession of the equinoxes, see George SARTON, op. cit., 1, 367, 403, and index s. v.; PIERRE M. M. DUHEM, *Le système du monde,* 2 (Paris, 1914), 180 ff.

(²) A. ROME, loc. cit.; Idem, " Les observations d'équinoxes et de solstices dans le chapitre 1 du livre 3 du Commentaire sur l'Almageste par Théon d'Alexandrie ", *Annales de la Société Scientifique de Bruxelles.* Série I, *Sciences mathématiques et physiques,* 57 (1937), 213-36; 58 (1938), 6-26.

(³) R. GUILLAND, *Essai sur Nicéphore Grégoras* (Paris, 1926), 282-5.

(⁴) See AUBREY Diller, ' A geographical treatise by PLETHO ', *Isis,* 27 (1937), 441-51, and my forthcoming article, " Pletho, Strabo, and Columbus '.

ὑπόγειος, a Byzantine term for perigee, and some Byzantine views... 403

Table of dates: Julian calendar, Greenwich Civil Time (¹).

Name and approximate date	1 True (mean) apogee	2 True (mean) perigee	3 Approximate date of this writer's apogee	4 Approximate date of this writer's perigee	5 Sun enters Cancer (summer solstice)	6 Sun enters Capricornus (winter solstice)	7 Sun enters Didymi (Gemini)	8 Sun enters Toxotes (Sagittarius)
Ptolemy (140)	June 3ᵈ 18ʰ	Dec. 3ᵈ 10ʰ	May 28	Nov. 28	June 23ᵈ 14ʰ	Dec. 21ᵈ 22ʰ	May 23ᵈ 3ʰ	Nov. 22ᵈ 12ʰ
Theon. Al (380)	June 6ᵈ 1ʰ	Dec. 5ᵈ 17ʰ	May 26	Nov. 26	June 21ᵈ 15ʰ	Dec. 20ᵈ 5ʰ	May 21ᵈ 3ʰ	Nov. 20ᵈ 19ʰ
Proclus (450)	June 7ᵈ 6ʰ	Dec. 6ᵈ 21ʰ	May 26	Nov. 26	June 21ᵈ 12ʰ	Dec. 20ᵈ 5ʰ	May 21ᵈ 1ʰ	Nov. 20ᵈ 19ʰ
Symeon 1070)	June 13ᵈ 5ʰ	Dec. 12ᵈ 20ʰ	May 21	Nov. 21	June 16ᵈ 8ʰ	Dec. 15ᵈ 18ʰ	May 15ᵈ 22ʰ	Nov 16ᵈ 8ʰ
Pachymeres (1300)	June 14ᵈ 22ʰ	Dec. 14ᵈ 13ʰ	May 19	Nov 19	June 13ᵈ 22ʰ	Dec. 13ᵈ 15ʰ	May 13ᵈ 12ʰ	Nov. 14ᵈ 4ʰ
1947	June 22ᵈ 10ʰ	Dec. 20ᵈ 6ʰ	—	—	June 9ᵈ 6ʰ	Dec. 9ᵈ 17ʰ	May 8ᵈ 22ʰ	Nov. 10ᵈ 4ʰ

(¹) The dates in the table can be converted to the Gregorian equivalents by the addition of 13 days for the twentieth century, 8 for the fourteenth (and for March-December, 1300), 6 for the eleventh, and 1 for the fifth and fourth. For the second century, the conversion can be made by subtracting one day from the Julian date: see Robert SCHRAM, *Kalendariographische u. chronologische Tafeln* (Leipzig, 1908), 36 ff.

The figures in columns 3 and 4 are obtained by adding approximately 5⁰ 30' (or almost five and a half days: see p. 401 n. 1 ad fin.) to the dates listed in columns 7 and 8.

Dumbarton Oaks.

XVI

PLETHO AND STRABO ON THE HABITABILITY OF THE TORRID ZONE[1]

Soon after his visit to Florence in 1439 Pletho prepared a number of excerpts[2] from Strabo with the hope of convincing his friends in Italy that the geographical system of Strabo, whose Γεωγραφικά were unknown in the Latin-speaking world,[3] was in many respects superior to Ptolemy's Γεωγραφικὴ ὑφήγησις, which had been circulating in a Latin translation by Jacobus Angelus from the time of its completion ca. 1406.[4] But despite this enthusiasm, Pletho found several points to criticize in Strabo and drew attention to them in a short treatise entitled Διόρθωσις ἐνίων τῶν οὐκ ὀρθῶς ὑπὸ Στράβωνος λεγομένων, which he wrote to accompany his excerpts. It is the second paragraph of this work which I offer here in English translation[5] with commentary, in honor of Professor Franz Dölger and his many significant contributions to Byzantine and Hellenic studies.

Furthermore, [Pletho says], Strabo is unjustified in holding that there is a torrid zone devoid of human habitation throughout its whole extent, for the entire belt between the tropics is known to be inhabited, except for occasional districts here and there in every part of this region which are unoccupied because of the lack of water. In this zone and even in the sections of the temperate zone bordering upon it, the plains[6] get very little rain, while the mountains have an abundant supply. Consequently, the mountains are inhabited and the plains, lacking water, are not, unless they are drained by rivers, as in Egypt. Accordingly, the whole tropical zone, as we have indicated, is inhabited. Thus, one Ethiopia stretches above Egypt to the Mountain

---

[1] This is a short section of my doctoral dissertation, Studies in Pletho (Harvard, 1940). A brief survey of Pletho's relation to Strabo and to the geographical theory of the Renaissance is scheduled to appear in the third volume of the Mélanges Grégoire (Brussels, 1951 [?]) under the title, "Pletho, Strabo and Columbus."

[2] I owe much to my friend, Professor Aubrey Diller of the University of Indiana, who generously sent me a copy of his valuable article, "A geographical treatise by Georgius Gemistus Pletho", Isis 27 (1937), 441-451. To Professor Diller belongs the credit for first raising the question which forms the subject of this paper.

[3] Details will be found in the article announced in n. 1 supra and in subsequent publications.

[4] A. Diller, loc. cit. 451; Joseph Fischer, Claudii Ptolemaei Geographiae Codex Urbinas Graecus 82 phototypice depictus. Tomus prodromus, pars prior, commentatio, Leiden-Leipzig 1932, 185 ff.

[5] For the original Greek, see A. Diller, loc. cit. 442-443. Diller's excellent edition is derived from Cod. Marcianus graecus 379 and replaces that published by Jo. Adam Goez, Anecdota Graeca, Nürnberg 1798, 90-96, which was based upon an inferior Ms.

[6] On Pletho's own geographical notions, as discussed in the course of this paragraph of the Diorthosis, I have written a short paper which I hope to submit for the next number of this admirable journal.

of the Moon, from which the Nile is fed. (This mountain is far south of the equator; for the Nile would probably not flood its banks during the course of our summer, unless it were then winter in the lands below the equator.) Another Ethiopia, the land of the Ethiopians that is called Agisymba, is represented as being even farther south than this mountain and lies at the other limit of this zone. Moreover, a part of the island of Taprobane is said to extend below the equator. Therefore no part of this zone is altogether uninhabited.

The question of the habitability of the torrid zone (ἡ διακεκαυμένη ζώνη) was much discussed by ancient and medieval scholars.[1] According to Strabo, Poseidonius (ca. 130–50 B. C.) believed that the torrid zone was uninhabitable except for the area directly on the equator, which he said was habitable.[2] Cleomedes (ca. second century of our era) was of the opinion that no part of the torrid zone could support human life, but Geminus (ca. 70 B. C.), the author of the Εἰσαγωγὴ εἰς τὰ φαινόμενα, repudiated this view, as did the geographer Ptolemy (ca. 140 of our era).

Diller names[3] Ptolemy as Pletho's principal source here, although it is not impossible that Pletho was influenced also by Geminus, with whose work there is some reason to suppose him to have been acquainted.[4] The crucial problem,[5] however, is what Strabo thought of the habitability of these regions. All of his references to the subject, when properly understood, show clearly and unequivocally that he believed the torrid zone to be uninhabitable.[6] But some passages[7] seem at first glance to support the contrary view, and must therefore be carefully examined. In one of these

---

[1] Texts from Geminus, Cleomedes and Achilles Tatius are quoted by E. Honigmann, Die sieben Klimata und die πόλεις ἐπίσημοι, Heidelberg 1929, 231 f.; and F. Jacoby, Die Fragmente der griechischen Historiker, 2. Teil C, Berlin 1926, 172 ff. Cf. Theodosius, De habitationibus liber, ed. R. Fecht, Abhandlungen d. Gesellschaft d. Wiss. zu Göttingen, Philolog.-hist. Kl., N. F. 19, 4 (1927), 16, 20 ff. See also J. Oliver Thomson, A history of ancient geography, London 1948, 117, 154, 163, 214 f., 217, 321–324, 328, 335, 359, 375, 382–384, 390–391; George H. T. Kimble, Geography in the Middle Ages, London 1938, 8, 84 f., 97 f., 144, 209, 213, 219, 229; C. Raymond Beazley, The dawn of modern geography, 3 vols., London 1897–1906, passim.

[2] Strabo 2, 2, 2–2, 3, 3; cf. 2, 5, 34: C. 95–97, cf. 132: Jones, vol. 1, 362–374, cf. 504; cf. J. O. Thomson, op. cit., 163, 213, 215, 335. E. Honigmann, op. cit., 231; maintains that Poseidonius „die Frage der Bewohnbarkeit der heißen Zone offen gelassen hat". Cf. also K. Reinhardt, Poseidonius, München 1921, 61 f.

[3] A. Diller, op. cit., 446–447.

[4] See my Pletho's calendar and liturgy (Dumbarton Oaks Papers, No. 4 [Cambridge, Mass. 1948]) 193.·

[5] Raised by A. Diller, op. cit., 442, 446.

[6] Strabo 2, 1, 13; 2, 2, 2f.; 2, 3, 1; 2, 5, 3; 2, 5, 5f.; 2, 5, 14f.; 2, 5, 34f.; 17, 3, 1: C. 72, 94f., 96, 111, 112f., 118ff., 132f., 824f.: Jones, vol. 1, 268–270, 360–366, 368–370, 424–426, 430–436, 454–460, 504–506; vol. 8, 154–156.
In all of my references to Strabo, as above, the first figures indicate the conventional divisions by book, chapter, and section; then comes the pagination of Casaubon (preceded by C.). Jones, followed by the number of the volume and the page, refers to the Loeb Library Strabo edited by Professor Horace Leonard Jones (London-New York, 1917–1932); a new critical edition is now being prepared by Professor Francesco Sbordone of the University of Naples.

[7] Strabo 2, 2, 2; 2, 5, 3: C. 94f., 111: Jones, vol. 1, 360ff., 428.

Strabo denies that any part of the earth is actually scorched or burned (οὔτ᾽ οὖν διακεκαυμένον χωρίον).[1] But, at this very same point, he unambiguously distinguishes between the habitable temperate zones and the zones which are uninhabitable because of heat or cold (εὐκράτους μὲν οὖν φασι τὰς οἰκεῖσθαι δυναμένας, ἀοικήτους δὲ τὰς ἄλλας, τὴν μὲν διὰ καῦμα, τὰς δὲ διὰ ψῦχος).[2] Actually he is only refusing to follow Poseidonius in taking διακεκαυμένη in the literal sense of the word.[3] There is a torrid zone (ἡ διακεκαυμένη ζώνη), he says, but no part of the earth is actually consumed by fire (οὔτ᾽ οὖν διακεκαυμένον χωρίον).

Confusion has arisen also because of Strabo's mention of Ethiopia in his analysis of the dimensions of the torrid zone and of the area between the two tropics of the torrid zone. Summarizing the cosmology of Poseidonius, Strabo says:

> By "torrid" is meant the region that is uninhabited on account of heat. More than half of the zone between the tropics is not inhabited, as we can infer from the Ethiopians who live south of Egypt, if [sc. as we will assume] each segment cut off by the equator is precisely one half of the entire zone [between the two tropics] . . .[4]

But this by no means answers or obviates Pletho's criticism. For Strabo's Ethiopia is in the environs of Meroe,[5] which he takes to be 11,800 stadia north of the equator[6] and 3,000 stadia north of the parallel of the Cinnamon-producing country, which lies on the co-ordinate by which he marks the northern boundary of the torrid zone and the most southerly limit of the inhabited world.[7] Strabo was not aware of the existence of the

---

[1] Strabo 2, 5, 3: C. 111: Jones, vol. 1, 428.9f.

[2] Ibid., Jones, vol. 1, 426. 6–8.

[3] Strabo 2, 2, 2: C. 94f.: Jones, vol. 1, 362.

[4] Ibid.: Jones, vol. 1, 362; my translation differs slightly from Jones's, but the final result is the same.

[5] Strabo 1, 2, 25: C. 32: Jones, vol. 1, 118, et passim.

[6] Strabo 2, 2, 2: C 95: Jones, vol. 1, 362–364. Strabo computes the breadth of the region between the two tropics (τὸ ἀμφίσκιον), from Syene in the north (the border line of the summer or northern tropic – north of the equator) to the winter or southern tropic – south of the equator, as 33, 600 stadia. This he does on the basis of the following calculations: a) Syene south to Meroe – 5,000 stadia; b) Meroe south to the parallel of the Cinnamon-producing country – 3,000 stadia; c) parallel of the Cinnamon-producing country south to the equator – 8,800 stadia. These 16,800 stadia represent one half the width of τὸ ἀμφίσκιον, for he assumes that the equator cuts the area enclosed by the two tropics exactly in half and that the same conditions, both climatic and spatial, prevail in both the northern and southern hemispheres. Similarly, he arrives at 17,600 stadia for the breadth of the torrid zone, 8,800 north, and 8,800 south, of the equator.

[7] Strabo 2, 1, 13: C. 72: Jones, vol. 1, 268, et passim. This is what Strabo actually says, and in modern drawings of "the inhabited world according to Strabo" (see frontispiece in Jones's edition, vol. 1; Bunbury, A history of ancient geography 2 [London 1879], opposite p. 238), Africa is terminated at the parallel of the Regio Cinnamomifera and is represented as facing upon the Mare Atlanticum sive Exterum sive Oceanus, although Strabo himself speaks of two temperate zones,

"second Ethiopia" (ἑτέρα Αἰθιοπία . . . 'Αγίσυμβα), located by Pletho, as by Ptolemy, south of the Mountain of the Moon, which was likewise thought by them to be below the equator.[1]

After a careful study of the Γεωγραφικά, I have found nothing to invalidate or impugn Pletho's criticism of Strabo's theory of the uninhabitability of the torrid zone. Strabo advocated a division of the terrestrial globe into five zones: two beneath the poles (the uninhabitable frigid zones), two temperate zones – one in the northern hemisphere and one in the southern, and the uninhabitable torrid zone, interposed between the two temperate zones and deemed to be cut into two equal divisions by the equator.[2] He refused to adopt the two additional narrow zones attributed to Poseidonius, who was thought to have conceived of them as lying under, and divided in half by, the tropic – one in the northern hemisphere under the northern or summer tropic that passed through Syene, and the other situated similarly in the southern hemisphere under the southern or winter tropic.[3] At one point he seems ready to concede that a narrow belt under the equator might be habitable. But he is careful to insist that the entire torrid zone, apart from this possible exception, was uninhabitable, and that the exempted area, itself of very limited compass, constituted a separate inhabited realm that did not form a part of our inhabited world: καὶ γὰρ εἰ οἰκήσιμα ταῦτά ἐστιν, ὥσπερ οἴονταί τινες, ἰδίᾳ γέ τις οἰκουμένη αὕτη ἐστί, διὰ μέσης τῆς ἀοικήτου διὰ καῦμα στενὴ τεταμένη, οὐκ οὖσα μέρος τῆς καθ' ἡμᾶς οἰκουμένης.[4]

---

one north of the equator and the other south of it, as well as of northern and southern hemispheres (Strabo 2, 2, 2–2, 3, 2; 2, 5, 3–2, 5, 7: C. 94–97, 111–114: Jones, vol. 1, 360–374, 424–440). Thus the modern cartographical sketches fail to give a true picture of Strabo's Africa, but they reflect the fact that Strabo disclaimed positive knowledge of the regions below the equator (2, 1, 13; 2, 5, 5; 2, 5, 34; 17, 3, 1: C. 72, 112f., 132, 824f.: Jones, vol. 1, 268f., 432, 502–506; vol. 8, 156, et passim).

[1] 4, 8 [9], 3, 5, 6: Claudii Ptolemaei Geographia, ed. C. F. A. Nobbe, Leipzig 1843, 283f. On Agisymba see J. O. Thomson, op. cit., 266f., 270, 275f., 281, 344f.; and R. Hennig, Terrae incognitae 1, Leiden 1936, 348f. As Bunbury points out, op. cit., vol. 2, 523 n. 1, Ptolemy speaks of two Agisymbas (1, 8, 5 and 4, 8 [9], 5: cf. 7, 5, 2); Pletho had reference to the second one of these, which, like Ptolemy, he placed at the southern end of the torrid zone.

[2] Strabo 2, 2, 2f.; 2, 3, 1f.; cf. 2, 5, 3–7, 37: C. 94–97, cf. 111–114, 132f.: Jones, vol. 1, 362–374, cf. 424–440, 508–510. Cf. p. 8 n. 2.

[3] Cf. E. Honigmann, op. cit., 26 ff., 231f.; F. Jacoby, loc. cit. (see p. 8 n. 1).

[4] Strabo 2, 5, 34; cf. 2, 3, 2f.: C. 132, cf. 97: Jones, vol. 1, 504, cf. 372–374.

XVII

Pletho, Strabo and Columbus [1]

I hope to show in the course of this paper that the geographical encyclopaedia of Strabo, designated *infra* as the *Geographika* (γεωγραφικά) to distinguish it from Ptolemy's *Cosmographia* (γεωγραφικὴ ὑφήγησις), came into prominence when it did because of the efforts of George Gemistus Pletho, the famous Byzantine humanist, who was almost one hundred years old at the time of his death in 1452 [2]. He was a man of prodigious learning and considerable versatility, and wrote on theology, history, government, philosophy, geometry, rhetoric, poetry, music, grammar, astronomy, and geography. Many of his works are in the form of excerpts which he made from ancient authors both for his own divertissement and for the use of his students [3].

One of the writers of whom he was especially fond was Strabo, the geographer. Pletho filled one hundred and eight folia with excerpts from Strabo's *Geographika* and added a brief critical essay entitled Διόρθωσις ἐνίων τῶν οὐκ ὀρθῶς ὑπὸ Στράβωνος λεγομένων (*A correction of certain errors made by Strabo*) [4]. The *Excerpts from Strabo* and the *Diorthosis*

---

(1) This communication is a brief summary of a chapter taken from my doctoral dissertation (Harvard, 1940) ; a much longer version, containing many additional details together with full documentation and analysis, is now being prepared.

(2) On the date of Pletho's death see Martin Jugie, ' La date de la mort de Gémistos Pléthon, ' *Échos d'Orient*, 34 (1935), 160 f. ; A. Dain, ' Sur un manuscrit grec de Salamanque, ' *Emerita*, 10 (Madrid, 1942), 8 ff.

(3) For the bibliography on Pletho, see my *Pletho's Calendar and Liturgy* (*Dumbarton Oaks Papers*, Number 4 [Cambridge, Mass., 1948]), 183 ff., 190 f.

(4) The latest and best edition of the Greek text is that of Aubrey Diller, ' A geographical treatise by Georgius Gemistus Pletho, ' *Isis*,

2

were both written around 1439, or shortly thereafter, as we can tell from a reference in the *Diorthosis* to Paolo Toscanelli, whom Pletho met while he was attending the Council of Florence. It is with these two works that I propose to deal in this paper.

The discussion is divided into four sections. First, there is a critical analysis of the *Excerpts* and the *Diorthosis*. Second, a survey is made of the facts which indicate that Pletho was the first to introduce Strabo to Western Europe at the end of the Middle Ages. Third, it is demonstrated that Pletho's introduction of Strabo to the West is all the more significant when it is recalled that the chief theoretical principles and a large number of the geographical co-ordinates recorded in Ptolemy's *Cosmographia* were available in Latin from the middle of the twelfth century, if not before. Fourth, it is then concluded that, in calling attention to Strabo, Pletho performed a service noteworthy not merely in the history of the transmission of an ancient text but also in the history of the geographical theory of the renaissance.

I. — The « Excerpts from Strabo » and the « Diorthosis».

Of the twenty-nine manuscripts known to me (^{1}) containing various portions of the Plethonic *Excerpts from Strabo*, twenty include the *Diorthosis* and nineteen, *Excerpt I*. The popularity of these two parts of the work is easily explained, for they

---

37 (1937), 441-51, which is based upon *Codex Marcianus Graecus*, 379. Diller's text supplants that of I. A. Goez, *Anecdota Graeca* (Nuremberg, 1798), 90-96.

(1) Not having a modern critical text of Strabo, I have had to rely upon the edition of Horace L. Jones (Loeb Library, 8 vols., 1917-32), and those of G. Kramer (3 vols., Berlin, 1844-52) and A. Meineke (3 vols., Leipzig, 1852-53). Important work on the text of Strabo has been done by Professor Aubrey Diller of the University of Indiana, and by Professor Francesco Sbordone of the University of Naples, the latter of whom hopes eventually to publish a scientific edition of the text. What I know of the *Excerpts from Strabo I* have learned from Kramer's introduction and the various catalogues of manuscripts.

both deal with the shape and extent of the inhabited world. This is a subject which interested Pletho very much ; and he often speculates on the habitability of unknown lands lying beyond the sea. The other *Excerpts from Strabo* treat of a great variety of subjects, but in the *Diorthosis* Pletho confines his attention almost exclusively to the sections that concern mathematical geography and the extent of the *oikumene*.

Free use of Pletho's text of Strabo has been made by various editors from Casaubon to Jones. In the absence of a printed edition, however, it is impossible to determine whether Pletho's emendations of the corrupt Strabonic text are of real value and reflect the niceties of textual criticism to be expected from one who spoke and wrote virtually pure Attic Greek, or whether they merely afford additional examples of the looseness and informality characterizing the attitude of renaissance scholars to the texts which they copied and excerpted.

The *Diorthosis* itself, though very short, is an intensely interesting document. Pletho here criticizes the views held by Strabo that the Caspian Sea is a gulf of the Ocean, that there is a torrid zone which is wholly uninhabitable on account of heat, that meridians may be represented satisfactorily on a plane surface by straight lines, and that the Nile is the boundary between Libya and Asia. He then goes on to recount what he had heard from reliable observers about the Island of Dateia (Scandinavia) and about the White Sea. Next he discusses the easternmost limits of the *oikumene* and expresses belief in the existence of an eastern sea and unknown lands east of India. Finally, after raising the question whether the Indian Ocean is a land-locked sea or not, he concludes with a few words of praise for Strabo, whose authority he does not regard as seriously impaired by a few errors.

A few points in this brief tractate call for attention. At first thought, it is strange that Pletho should have been ignorant of the voyages of renowned travelers like Marco Polo and Odorico da Pordenone. But this apparently singular lapse is the less remarkable when one reflects that Aeneas Sylvius Piccolomini, known during his pontificate (1458-64) as Pope Pius II, in the section on Asia in his *Historia rerum ubique gestarum locorumque descriptio* seems to have made

4

no use of the voyages of Marco Polo, despite the fact that the papal library had owned a copy of *Il Milione* at least as early as the pontificate of Eugene IV (1431-47) (¹).

As for Pletho's knowledge of Strabo, it can be shown that he had studied Strabo with care and did not limit himself altogether to the sections excerpted. In finding fault with certain aspects of Strabo, he did not ignore passages in which the statements reprehended might have been qualified or amended. Six of the ten paragraphs of the *Diorthosis* contain criticisms of Strabo. In regard to at least five of these, Pletho's judgment withstands analysis in every particular. Only once does he falter, although the case against him is far from clear. But even were we to resolve every question of doubt against Pletho and grant him no quarter whatsoever, he comes off with an average of 83.3, which, all things considered, if not excellent, is more than ordinarily tolerable in an age innocent of the printing press and the encyclopaedic concordance.

So much, then, for Pletho's use of Strabo. But what is to be said about his competence as a geographer? It is quite true that Pletho greatly exaggerated the merits of Strabo, if we are to apply the canons evolved in the course of the past five hundred years. But we must not make the mistake of judging Pletho's capacity as a critic from the point of view of modern geography. We cannot hold a scholar of the early fifteenth century to the standards and criteria of geographical research which obtain in the twentieth. The truth is that, when compared with his contemporaries, Pletho does not fare badly. Consider, for example, the world maps of Andreas Walsperger

---

(1) Eugène MÜNTZ and Paul FABRE, *La bibliothèque du Vatican au XVᵉ siècle* (*Bibliothèque des écoles françaises d'Athènes et de Rome*, 48 [Paris, 1887]), 6, 20 ; See Alfred BERG, *op. cit.* (p. 5 *infra*), 31. The *Il Milione* is not listed among the books owned by Pius II : Aeneas Piccolomini,' De codicibus Pii II et Pii III deque Bibliotheca ecclesiae cathedralis Senensis, ' *Bullettino Senese di Storia Patria*, 6 (1899), 483-96 ; Josephus Cugnoni, ' Aeneae Silvii Piccolomini Senensis qui postea fuit Pius II Pont. Max. opera inedita, ' *Atti della R. Accademia dei Lincei*, anno CCLXXX, S. 3a, *Memorie della classe di scienze morali, storiche e filologiche*, 8 (Rome, 1882-83), 333 ff.

and Fra Mauro, dated in 1448 and 1459 respectively ([1]). In spite of some slight use of empirical data based on the voyages of de' Conti to the extreme Orient, they are, from many points of view, inferior to Pletho.

All in all, considering his times, we must admit that Pletho had a fair knowledge of geography. Like most of the enlightened men of the Middle Ages, he knew the world was round, and abjured the fanciful geographical conceptions of the superstitious. He does not deal in weird monsters like the Sciapodes, nor does he harbor any delusions as to the realm of the mythical Prester John, whose curious history haunted the imaginations of men even later than the fifteenth century. On the contrary, he accepts enthusiastically the latest geographical information available. And, if he is behind the times in some respects, as for example in his ignorance of the exploits of Marco Polo, he outstrips the majority of his contemporaries in others (with regard to Dateia and Russia, concerning the latter of which, as previous investigators have failed to realize, he was probably informed by Isidore of Kiev, Russian delegate at the Council of Florence, and by Isidore's Russian companions). Moreover, to judge from his empirical approach to the authorities upon whom he relies, it is clear that, although he knew nothing of Niccolò de' Conti, he would not have taken Pope Pius II's skeptical attitude towards the account of de' Conti's far eastern voyages published by Poggio Bracciolini ([2]). It might, per-

(1) G. H. T. KIMBLE, Geography in the Middle Ages (London, 1938), 117-19, 198-200, pl. 12 and 16.

(2) On Isidore, etc., see Giovanni MERCATI, Scritti d'Isidoro, il Cardinale Ruteno (Studi e testi, 46 [Vat. C, 1926]) ; Ludwig MOHLER, Kardinal Bessarion als Theologe, Humanist u. Staatsmann, 1 (Paderborn, 1923), 117 f. ; C. F. HEFELE - H. LECLERCQ, Histoire des conciles, 7, 2. (Paris, 1916), 1080 f. ; PIERLING, La Russie et le Saint-Siège, 1 (Paris, 1896), 7 ff., 16 ff. ; Henri VAST, Le Cardinal Bessarion (1403-72), étude sur la chrétienté et la renaissance vers le milieu du XVe siècle (Paris, 1878), 107.

On Pius II, see Pii. II. Pon. Max. Asiae Europaeque elegantissima descriptio, mira festiuitate tum veterum, tum recentium res memoratu dignas complectens.... Accessit Henrici Glareani... compendiaria... (Paris, 1534), 18 f. ; cf. 28 f. See also Alfred BERG, Enea Silvio de'

6

haps, be too much to conclude that Pletho would not suffer in comparison with the leading scientists of his day. But in having an open mind, he was already in possession of the prime requisite of all scientific research, and could take his place with the most fearless and most enterprising intellects of the fifteenth century.

II. — Pletho's introduction of Strabo to the West.

In the *Diorthosis*, the principal emphasis is on Strabo. Indeed, in making the *Excerpts from Strabo* Pletho was undoubtedly seeking to introduce Strabo to a wider public. He recognized the merits of Ptolemy, but when confronted at the Council of Florence with the new cult of Ptolemy and with the humanists' unawareness of Strabo, he must have observed both to himself and to others that he could advance the study of geography by bringing forward a few of the more interesting sections of Strabo in handy form. For Ptolemy, it will be remembered, had been available in the Latin translation by Jacobus Angelus (Jacopo d'Angelo da Scarperia) dating from 1406 ; and Ptolemaic maps had been used as early as 1427 in a Latin version (1). The importance of Ptolemy was universally recognized, and the great influence which Ptolemy's *Cosmographia* was to exert upon the renaissance was already assured. What was necessary, Pletho felt, was to rejuvenate Strabo, whose geographical treatise had never really been given the attention it deserved, even in the lands in which Greek was read and understood.

It was in pursuit of this purpose, therefore, that Pletho

Piccolomini (*Papst Pius II.*) *in seiner Bedeutung als Geograph. Ein Beitrag zur Geschichte d. Erdkunde im Quattrocento* (Halle a. S., 1901) ; Georg VOIGT, *Enea Silvio de' Piccolomini, als Papst Pius d. Zweite, u. sein Zeitalter*, 2 (Berlin, 1862), 336. Cf. Waldemar SENS-BURG, *Poggio Bracciolini u. Nicolò de Conti in ihrer Bedeutung für die Geographie des Renaissance-Zeitalters* (Vienna, 1906).

(1) Joseph FISCHER, *Claudii Ptolemaei Geographiae Codex Urbinas Graecus 82 phototypice depictus*, 1, 1 (Leiden-Leipzig, 1932), 183 ff., 191, 201 ff., 213, 301 ff. ; Fischer's book, including 3 volumes and a large atlas, is the standard work on Ptolemy.

composed the *Excerpts* and the *Diorthosis*. We may be sure,
too, that he made the best of his opportunities at Florence to
initiate the geographers and classicists within his sphere of
influence into the mysteries of the Strabonic geography. He
says himself that he met in Florence men like Ugo Benzi and
the famous Paolo Toscanelli, whose letter to the Portuguese
canon, Fernão Martins, and correspondence with Christopher
Columbus are important literary monuments in the history
of the discovery of America (¹). Nor could he have failed to
have associated at the same time with Nicholas of Cusa and
Guarino da Verona, the latter of whom possibly first conceived
the project (completed in 1458) of translating Strabo into
Latin as a result of the stimulation and inspiration provided
by Pletho.

Pletho would have inevitably pointed out in the course
of the learned symposia he attended during his residence in
Florence that Ptolemy, admirable as he was, should be compared with his predecessor Strabo, whose *Geographika* sup-
plemented and complemented Ptolemy's work on the same
subject at many points. Among other things, he would
certainly have observed, as he does in the *Diorthosis*, that
Ptolemy's view of the Indian Ocean as landlocked was open
to serious question and that Africa, as Strabo taught, was
probably circumnavigable. This latter fact was of unusual
significance and may have exerted influence on the great
African voyages of the Portuguese in the third quarter of
the fifteenth century.

We must now inquire into the nature of the evidence for
the view just asserted, that before Pletho's sojourn in Italy
the Latin West had had no previous knowledge of Strabo.
I have found support for this proposition in three quarters :
a) in the history of medieval libraries, b) in the history of the
use of Strabo by Latin writers, and c) in the history of the
medieval tradition of the text of Strabo.

---

(1) *Diorthosis*, ed. Diller, *Isis*, 27 (1937), 443, 447 f. ; MPG, 160,
982B. On Toscanelli, see MORISON, *op. cit.* (p. 17 *infra*), vol. 1, 45-7,
56-8, 85-7, 102 ; VIGNAUD, *op. cit.* (p. 17 *infra*) ; Norbert SUMIEN,
*La correspondance du savant florentin Paolo dal Pozzo Toscanelli avec
Christophe Colomb* (Paris, 1927).

a) MEDIEVAL LIBRARIES.

It has not been possible to examine all of the many hundreds
of catalogues now available in print containing lists of books
found in various medieval collections. But is is clear from
the standard manuals on the contents of the libraries of the
Middle Ages and from the very considerable number of
catalogues of individual medieval libraries which I have consulted that no manuscript of Strabo found its way to the
west before the fifteenth century (¹). The only exception,
which is more apparent than real, is that of a Constantinopolitan palimpsest of the sixth century, which was preserved for
many years at the library of the monastery at Grottaferrata.
But this codex cannot be taken as representing a western
tradition of the text. For, to say nothing of its Constantinopolitan origin, its entire occidental history is confined to the
Greek monasteries of Southern Italy and Tusculum. Moreover,
at some early date in the Middle Ages, the text of Strabo was
erased and replaced by a Latin version of the Pentateuch (²).

b) USE OF STRABO BY LATIN WRITERS IN THE MIDDLE AGES.

In a field so vast, only a few preliminary tests could be
made at the points which seemed most promising. Accordingly, a study was undertaken of those authors in whom it was
thought on *a priori* grounds (their knowledge of Greek, e. g.,
or their interest in geography, or the encyclopaedic character

---

(1) My results are based upon the following works and upon a
study of a great many of the lists of the contents of medieval libraries
there cited : Theodor GOTTLIEB, *Ueber mittelalterliche Bibliotheken*
(Leipzig, 1890) ; Gustav BECKER, *Catalogi bibliothecarum antiqui*
(Bonn, 1885) ; B. ALTANER, ' Griechische codices in abendländischen
Bibliotheken des XIII. u. XIV. Jahrhunderts, ' *BZ*, 36 (1936), 32-5 ;
J. S. BEDDIE, ' The ancient classics in the mediaeval libraries, '
Speculum, 5 (1930), 1-20. See also Pearl KIBRE, ' The intellectual
interests reflected in the libraries of the fourteenth and fifteenth
centuries, ' *Journal of the history of ideas*, 7 (1946), 257-97.

(2) On this see Wolf ALY, *Der Strabon-Palimpsest, Vat. Gr. 2061A*
(*Sitzungsberichte d. Heidelberger Ak. d. Wiss., Philos-hist. Kl.*, 19
[1928-29]) ; *idem, Neue Beiträge zur Strabon- Ueberlieferung, ibid.*, 22
(1931-32).

of their work) that a reference to Strabo might possibly be expected.

According to some, Orosius' geographical introduction to the *Historiae adversum paganos* (*ca.* 419) shows the influence of Strabo, although Strabo is never actually mentioned. But there is no evidence whatever that the superficial similarities between Strabo and Orosius are not to be explained by the use of some other source. Strabo is named thrice in the ninth century (?) Latin translation (*Solutiones eorum de quibus dubitavit Chosroes Persarum Rex*) (¹) of a lost work written in Greek by Priscian Lydus, one of the scholars who fled to Persia with Damascius, Simplicius, and others after the closing of the Platonic Academy of Athens by Justinian in 529. Though none of these three passages (one of which lists Strabo among Priscian's authorities, and the other two of which allude to matters of local geography) deals with geography in a broad sense, it is conceivable that they may, nevertheless, have served to keep the memory of Strabo alive in the later Middle Ages. Charles Gidel very guardedly gives the impression that Strabo is cited in Eriugena's *De divisione naturae* ; but I can find no proof of this, and Cappuyns does not include Strabo in his careful catalogue of the authors cited by Eriugena (²).

Jordanes (*ca.* 551), borrowing no doubt from Cassiodorus, actually uses Strabo in dealing with some meteorological matters. But the references to Strabo in the *Memoria Seculorum* of Godfrey of Viterbo (*ca.* 1185), in the *De proprietatibus*

---

(1) KIMBLE, *op. cit.*, 20. Strabo is not listed by Karl Zangemeister in his *index scriptorum quibus Orosius usus est* : *Pauli Orosii Historiarum adversum paganos libri vii*, CSEL, 5 (Vienna, 1882). Cf. Friedrich WOTKE, *s. v.* Orosius, PAULY-WISSOWA-KROLL, *Real-Encyclopädie*, 18. 1 (1939), 1185-95 ; D. DETLEFSEN, *Ursprung, Einrichtung u. Bedeutung d. Erdkarte Agrippas* (*Quellen u. Forschungen zur alten Geschichte u. Geographie*, herausg. v. W. Sieglin, Heft 13 [Berlin, 1906]), 18, 21. *Prisciani Lydi quae extant*, ed. I. BYWATER (*Supplementum Aristotelicum*, 1, pars 2 [Berlin, 1886]), 42. 8 f., 71. 4, 91. 6, 11 ; Maïeul CAPPUYNS, *Jean Scot Érigène, sa vie, son oeuvre, sa pensée* (Louvain-Paris, 1933), 148 f.

(2) GIDEL, *Nouvelles études sur la littérature grecque moderne* (Paris, 1878), 179 ; CAPPUYNS, *op. cit.*

10

rerum of Bartholomaeus Anglicus (*ca.* 1230), and in the *Imago* mundi of Pierre d'Ailly (1350-1420), who merely reproduces Bartholomaeus Anglicus, are unimportant geographically and may in point of fact refer, not to Strabo the geographer, but to Walafrid Strabo, the grammarian ([1]). More interesting is the indubitable reminiscence of Strabo's etymology of the word βάρβαρος that occurs in the first book of the *Politica* of Albertus Magnus ([2]). But this allusion is philological, and was probably derived from a grammar or lexicon or some such work ; from the point of view of geography it is devoid of significance.

Enough has been said to prove that the cosmography of Strabo was not known in the West during the Middle Ages. The most we can find is a very few miscellaneous scraps of unconnected and unsystematic information on small points of detail. The main outlines and the general principles of geography enunciated by Strabo were wholly and completely inaccessible.

c) THE MEDIEVAL TRADITION OF THE TEXT OF STRABO.

At the outset, it is to be observed that there was no translation of Strabo previous to that completed in 1458 by Guarino da Verona. The translation by Gregory Tiphernas was begun after Guarino's ([3]).

(1) JORDANES, *Getica*, 2, 12, 14, ed. T. MOMMSEN, *Monumenta Germaniae Historica*, *Auctores Antiquissimi*, 5.1 (Berlin, 1882), xxx, XL ff., 56. 19-57. 2, 12 (Strabo, 4. 5. 2) ; Gotifredus Viterbiensis, MGH, *Scriptores*, 22 (Hanover, 1872), 95 ; Bartholomaeus Anglicus (Nuremberg, 1492), Liber 15, c. 112 (*De paradiso*) ; Edmond BURON, ed., *Ymago mundi de Pierre d'Ailly... texte latin et traduction française des quatres traités cosmographiques de d'Ailly et des notes marginales de Christophe Colomb*, 2 (Paris, 1930), 458 ff. and n. 342. Christopher Columbus found the passage from Bartholomaeus in Pierre d'AILLY, *loc. cit.*, and paraphrases it in the journal of his Third Voyage (August 11, 1498), *Raccolta* (p. 14 *infra*), 37.20 ff.

(2) *Politica*, ed. A. Borgnet, *B. Alberti Magni opera omnia*, 8 (Paris, 1891), 10 *i*; Strabo, 14.2.28. I owe this reference to Professor F. Edward Cranz of Connecticut College.

(3) Remigio SABBADINI, ' La traduzione guariniana di Strabone, ' *Il libro e la stampa*, N. S. 3 (1909), 5-16 : Tiphernas, who translated only Books 11-17, did not collaborate with Guarino, and finished his translation in 1456. Cf. R. Sabbadini, ed. *Epistolario di Guarino Ve-*

The facts concerning the principal Ms. can be summarized as follows (¹) :

1) None of the eight codices of Strabo which were transcribed between the tenth and the fourteenth centuries had any occidental circulation whatsoever before the beginning of the fifteenth century.

2) Three codices of Strabo had been imported from Greece during the first third of the fifteenth century, two by Giovanni Aurispa, and one by Francesco Filelfo (²). But they were bought in large lots together with a number of other classical texts, not separately for their own sakes, and none of them had borne progeny even as late as *ca.* 1459, the date of the first Greek manuscript of Strabo copied in the West that was not definitely related to Pletho's *Excerpts* and their earliest descendants.

3) None of the Greek manuscripts transcribed in the West can be dated before 1439 ; and a number of manuscripts exhibit a type of text that reproduces peculiarities found only in Pletho's *Excerpts*. These codices, therefore, may be regarded as part of the result of the impetus given Strabonic studies by Pletho and by Guarino's Latin translation.

On the basis of this evidence, we can only conclude that

ronese raccolto, ordinato, illustrato, 3 (*R. Deputazione di Storia Patria, Miscellanea di Storia Veneta*, Serie III, vol. 14 [1919]), 483-7.

(1) The manuscripts are for the most part those listed by the various editors in their editions. See also the valuable articles of Aubrey DILLER, ' Codex B of Strabo, ' *American Journal of Philology*, 56(1935), 97-102 ; 'The Vatopedi manuscript of Ptolemy and Strabo,' *ibid.*, 58 (1937), 174-84. I hope, with the aid of Professors Diller and Sbordone (see p. 2 *supra*), to base my final results upon a complete list of the extant manuscripts. At present, of course, the conclusions here summarized are of a tentative nature.

(2) See Remigio SABBADINI, *Le scoperte dei codici latini e greci ne' secoli XIV e XV*, (Florence, 1905), 46 ff. ; *idem*, ed.,. *Carteggio di Giovanni Aurispa* (*Fonti per la Storia d'Italia*, 70, [Rome, 1931]), IX, xv ff., 10 ff., 13.4 f. and n. 2, 73. 5-12, 97. 19-24, 127 n. 4 ; P. A. REVILLA, *Catálogo de los códices griegos de la Biblioteca de El Escorial*, 1 (Madrid, 1936), 471 ff. ; Aristide CALDERINI, ' Ricerche intorno alla biblioteca e alla cultura greca di Francesco Filelfo, ' *Studi italiani di filologia classica*, 20 (1913), 393-7.

12

the *Geographika* of Strabo as such was not available in the
Latin West until soon after 1439, when a demand arose for
reproductions of the Greek text. As we have seen, this new
interest in Strabo is directly associated with Pletho and his
zeal in persuading his friends to make a study of the *Geographika.*

III. — Knowledge of Ptolemy in the West.

It is usually maintained that the geography of Ptolemy
was unknown in the West during the Middle Ages. This is
quite true of the strictly cartographical sections of the treatise,
that is to say, of the maps and the formulation of the fundamentals of map projection set forth in the first book. But
in other respects, it can be shown, the *Cosmographia* could
claim some medieval circulation. An outline of Ptolemy's
chief theoretical principles and a not inconsiderable part of
his tables of latitude and longitude, often with marked im-
provements and rectifications, were accessible to all who
cared to use them. This is not to say that Ptolemy's theories
and figures were widely or correctly adopted for geographical
purposes. But they were available, and could have formed
the basis for plotting a fairly adequate map, in spite of the
fact that the Arabic and Latin versions are often inconsistent
in their use of Ptolemaic data (¹).

Among the Latins who were acquainted with Ptolemy's
geography in one form or another were Ammianus Marcellinus, Martianus Capella, Priscian Lydus (in the Latin version),
Cassiodorus, Jordanes, Eriugena, Alfred the Great, and Adam
of Bremen. In addition, there is a record in the twelfth
century of a request for a copy of *Ptolomaeum de cosmogra-*

---

(1) See Dana B. Durand, *The Vienna-Klosterneuburg map corpus
of the fifteenth century* (Leiden, 1939), a book of great value, the
publication of which has been delayed by the war ; John K. Wright,
The geographical lore of the time of the Crusades (N. Y., 1925) ; George
Sarton, *Introduction to the history of science*, 3 vols. in 5 (Baltimore,
1927-48) ; J. H. Kramers, *s. v. Djughrāfiyā*, *Encyclopaedia of Islam*,
Supplement (Leiden-London, 1934-6), 61-73.

phia (¹). The texts cited in the previous note show in varying degree that the tradition of Ptolemy's geography had not altogether perished in the West. But the greater part of what was known of Ptolemy in the Occident during the Middle Ages was derived from Arabic cosmographical and astronomical texts based upon Ptolemy, and made available in Latin by the translations of Gerard of Cremona, Plato of Tivoli, Robert of Chester, John of Seville, and John of Hollywood. Strabo, however, was not known by the Arabs, nor was any use made of his *Geographika* by Syriac writers.

IV. — Strabo and the Renaissance.

Pletho's judgment in preferring Strabo to Ptolemy was vindicated during the course of the renaissance. Strabo even beat Polemy to press and went through three editions (1469-73) before the appearance of the first printed version of Ptolemy in 1475 (²). Pius II definitely rejected the Ptolemaic conception of Africa in favor of the Strabonic (³) ; and, some-

---

(1) Martianus CAPELLA, *De nuptiis Philologiae et Mercurii*, ed. A. Dicks (Leipzig, 1925), Sec. 610, p. 301. 2-16, cf. Sec. 813, p. 430.5, on which cf. PTOLEMY, *Geographia*, ed. C.F.A. Nobbe,1 (Leipzig, 1843), Liber 1, c. 3, 7, and 11 ; Priscianus LYDUS, *Solutiones eorum de quibus dubitavit Chosroes Persarum Rex, ed. cit.* (p. 9 *supra*), 42. 11 f. ; *Cassiodori Senatoris institutiones*, ed. R.A.B. Mynors (Oxford, 1937), 66. 22 ff., cf. 184, 192 ; JORDANES, *Getica*, 3, 16-19, *ed. cit.* (p. 10 *supra*), 57. 17-58. 16 ; ERIUGENA, *De divisione naturae* (MPL, 122, 719A), ed. C. B. Schlüter (Münster, 1838), 279 (from Martianus CAPELLA, *loc.cit.* ; M. CAPPUYNS, *op. cit.* [p. 9 *supra*], 213, 215) ; G. BECKER, *Catalogi bibliothecarum*, 228, n⁰ 111, 1 (12th c.). C. R. BEAZLEY, *Dawn of modern geography*, 2 (London, 1901), 523, claims that Alfred the Great and Adam of Bremen had some acquaintance with Ptolemy. For Ammianus Marcellinus' knowledge of Ptolemy, see FISCHER, *op. cit.* (p. 6, n. 1 *supra*), 483 ff.

On the Arab use of Ptolemy's *Cosmographia* and on the transmission of Ptolemaic materials to the Latin West, chiefly in the form of astronomical tables containing Ptolemaic geographical data, see previous note.

(2) Arnold C. KLEBS, ' Incunabula scientifica et medica, ' *Osiris*, 4 (1938), 265 f., 311.

(3) Pii. II. Pont. (p. 5, n. 2 *supra*), pp. 6, 10 f.

14

what before, Pierre d'Ailly (1350-1420) had asserted, against
what he took to be the view of Ptolemy, that perhaps as
little as one seventh of the world is covered with water, not
so much as three fourths or five sixths (¹). Christopher
Columbus followed d'Ailly enthusiastically on this point and
regarded Bartholomew Diaz's accomplishment (1488) in roun-
ding the Cape of Good Hope as involving a repudiation of the
Ptolemaic description of the limits of the inhabited world (²).

Columbus cites Strabo in support of a belief in the existence
of other and as yet unknown inhabitable lands, and frequently
refers to his name in commenting upon Pius II's *Historia
rerum ubique gestarum locorumque descriptio* (³). But the
clearest and most definite statement of the use Columbus made
of Strabo is recorded in the biography of Columbus by his
son Fernando. According to Fernando, Strabo was one of
the chief authorities for the cosmography of Columbus. There
were, he tells us, two principal lines of documentary evidence
which led his father to believe that he could reach the Indies

---

(1) *Ymago mundi*, ed. Buron, 1, 206 ff.

Note, however, that in the *Cosmographia* Ptolemy makes no
statement on the percentage of the surface of the earth covered by
water. The passages on this subject attacked by d'Ailly and Columbus are cited from other writings of Ptolemy. On medieval theories
concerning the relative proportion of water and dry land, something,
but not very much, is to be found in Arnold NORLIND, *Das Problem
des gegenseitigen Verhältnisses von Land u. Wasser u. seine Behand-
lungen im Mittelalter* (*Lunds Universitets Årsskrift*, N. F., Avd. 1,
Bd. 14, Nr. 12 [Lund, 1918]).

(2) *Ymago mundi*, ed. Buron, 1, 206 ff. ; Cesare DE LOLLIS, *Scritti
di Cristoforo Colombo* (*Raccolta di documenti e studi pubblicati dalla
R. Commissione Colombiana pel quarto centenario della scoperta dell'
America*, Parte 1, vol. 2 [Rome, 1894]), 376 f. ; cf. 38. 30 ff., 39.4 ff.
Columbus' annotation is one of the many (898 on the *Ymago mundi*,
861 on Pius II's *Historia rerum ubique gestarum locorumque descriptio*, 366 on Marco Polo, 24 on the elder Pliny's *Naturalis historia*,
and 437 on Plutarch's *Vitae*) that he wrote in the margins of his
favorite books. All of these marginalia have been published by DE
LOLLIS, *op. cit.* Cf. BURON, *loc. cit.*, 27.

(3) Ed. Caddeo, 1, 96 (see following note) ; *Raccolta* (see previous
note), Parte 1, vol. 2, 291 n. 5, 292 n. 11, 306 n. 144, 307 nn. 150 f.,
308 n. 162, 309 n. 173, 310 n. 184, 313 n. 216, 316 n. 258, 324 n.
348, 328 n. 395, 332 n. 441, 336 n. 490, 345 n. 623, 360 n. 816.

by a new route. The first gave assurance that the sea to be
crossed was not inordinately wide, the second that it was
possible to reach the East by sailing due West. The quotations from Strabo on both of these points are unambiguous
and were, therefore, highly esteemed by Columbus.

Strabo is first mentioned by Fernando in a chapter entitled
*La principal cagione che mosse l'Ammiraglio a credere di poter
discoprir dette Indie*, to illuminate the discussion of the distance
between the Azores and India :

> Alla qual ragione s'aggiunge quel che dice Strabone nel xv
> libro della sua Cosmografia, niuno esser giunto con esercito
> al fine Orientale dell' India : il quale Ctesia scrive esser tanto
> grande, quanto tutta l'altra parte dell' Asia ; e Onesicrito
> afferma esser la terza parte della sfera ; e Nearco aver quattro
> mesi di cammino per pianura (¹).

The passage of Strabo Fernando had in mind here attributes
a great eastward extension to India (²). This was a matter
of the highest significance for the Admiral. Indeed, it was
his confidence in the projection of India into the east (and
the consequent diminution of the distance to be traversed by
sea from the western terminus of *terra firma*) that gave
Columbus courage to undertake his hazardous enterprise into
the unknown.

Strabo is named again in the seventh chapter (*La seconda
causa che mosse l'Ammiraglio a scoprire le Indie*), along with
Aristotle, Seneca, Marco Polo, and others, as one who maintained that it was possible to sail from Africa and Spain to
the Eastern terminus of India, and that the unknown ocean
was not of great extent :

> che dal fine occidentale dell' Africa e della Spagna potrebbe
> navigarsi per l'Occidente al fine orientale dell' India ; e che
> non era gran mare quello che in mezzo giaceva.

---

(1) *Le Historie della vita e dei fatti di Cristoforo Colombo per D.
Fernando Colombo, suo figlio*, ed. Rinaldo Caddeo, 1 (*Viaggi e scoperte
di navigatori ed esploratori italiani*, 11 [Milan, 1930]), 41 ff. The only
witness to the no longer extant Spanish text of Fernando Colón is the
Italian translation by Alfonso Ulloa (Venice, 1571).

(2) 1. 4. 6 ; 15. 1. 5 f., 10-12 (Casaubon, pp. 64 f., 686 f., 688-90).

16

Appeal is made to both the first and the second Books of
Strabo's *Geographia* :

> E Strabone nel primo libro della sua Cosmografia dice,
> che l'Oceano circonda tutta la terra : e che all' Oriente bagna
> l'India, e nell' Occidente la Spagna e la Mauritania : e che,
> se la grandezza dell' Atlantico non impedisse, si potrebbe
> navigare dall' uno all' altro luogo per uno istesso parallelo.
> E il medesimo torna a dire nel secondo libro (1).

The first (2) of these contains Strabo's summary of the
section in which Eratosthenes discusses the great extension
of the inhabitable world longitudinally (i.e., from east to
west) and expresses the opinion that the inhabited world

> forms a complete circle, itself meeting itself ; so that, if the
> immensity of the Atlantic Ocean did not prevent, we could
> sail from Iberia to India along one and the same parallel
> over the remainder of the circle.

Strabo quibbles over details but adds :

> It is possible that in the same temperate zone (*sc.* which
> we inhabit) there are actually two inhabited worlds, or even
> more, and particularly in the proximity of the parallel through
> Athens in the region of the Atlantic Ocean.

The second (3) is equally striking. There Strabo remarks that
Poseidonius did well to quote Plato's statement that there
was a possibility that the island of Atlantis had once actually
existed. He then goes on to say :

> And he (*sc.* Poseidonius) suspects that the length of the

---

(1) *Op. cit.*, 47, 50 ; n. b. Caddeo's analysis of the sources.
Christopher Columbus' use of Strabo is attested also by Fray Bartolo-
mé de Las Casas, who, like Fernando Colón, had had access to the
Admiral's log-book, letters, and papers, and made use of them in his
Historia de las Indias (Madrid, 1875, the *editio princeps* ; a new
critical text is now being prepared by Dr. Lewis Hanke, Chief of the
Hispanic Division of the Library of Congress, and Professor Agustín
Millares Carlo of the Colegio de México). Las Casas refers to Columbus's use of Strabo in Book 1, c. 5, vol. 1, 55 ff.
(2) Strabo, 1. 4. 6 (Casaubon, pp. 64 f.) ; here and *infra* I have
used the translation of Horace L. Jones with a few minor variations.
(3) Strabo, 2. 3. 6 (Casaubon, p. 102).

inhabited world, being about seventy thousand stadia, is half
of the entire circle on which it has been taken, so that, says
he, if you sail from the west in a straight course you will
reach India within the seventy thousand stadia.

None of these texts is quoted in the works of the other
authors studied and annotated by Christopher Columbus ([1]),
who must, therefore, have found them in the *Geographika* of
Strabo itself. At this point mention should be made of the
view of Henry Vignaud that all the cosmographical knowledge
and ancient lore displayed by Columbus in his writings and
recapitulated by his son and others were manufactured *post
eventum*. Vignaud contends that when Columbus set out in
1492 he had no intention of sailing to India. He was only
following the course, the secret of which had been bequeathed
to him by an « unknown pilot. » All the learned apparatus,
Vignaud argues, — the Strabo, the *Imago Mundi* of Pierre
d'Ailly and the rest, — were fabricated by Columbus after
his return from the first voyage in order to avoid recording
his debt to the « unknown pilot » and so as to create the
impression that his expedition across the Atlantic was the
logical conclusion of long and arduous research in both theoretical cosmography and practical navigation ([2]). But the mass
of evidence admirably summarized by Professor Samuel E.
Morison in his important book on Columbus ([3]), a great
thesaurus of Columbian learning, renders Vignaud's hypothesis
untenable.

Of course, it is possible that Columbus may have laid his
plans for an Atlantic crossing before reading Strabo, for he
was a man of action and leaned heavily upon actual nautical
experience. Nevertheless, the texts from Strabo offered him
not only confirmation and support to strenghten his own

(1) On Columbus's *postille*, see p. 14, nn. 2 f. *supra*.

(2) Henry VIGNAUD, *Histoire critique de la grande entreprise de
Christophe Colomb* (Paris, 1911), espec. 1, 211-50, 347 f. ; 2, 481-97 ;
IDEM, *Toscanelli and Columbus. The letter and chart of Toscanelli on
the route to the Indies by way of the west* (London, 1902), 99 ff., 267 ff.

(3) *Admiral of the Ocean Sea, a life of Christopher Columbus*, 2 vols.
(Boston, 1942). In the longer version of this article, which I am
now preparing, I hope to include a detailed criticism of Vignaud.

18

resolution and purpose but also a welcome learned authority to flaunt before the pedants appointed to scrutinize and report upon the feasibility of his scheme.

In conclusion, therefore, although no one would venture to credit Pletho with a share in the actual discovery of America, we must recognize that, in interesting the scholars of the West in the *Geographika* of Strabo, he made an important contribution to the development of the geographical theory of the renaissance, which reached itssupreme fulfilment in the great achievement of Columbus.

Dumbarton Oaks,
Harvard University.

INDEX

renovatio imperii:V 28
rescriptum:II 28
resurrection:I 442,443,447;X 186
Robert Grosseteste:XII 150
Robert of Melun:XII 132ff.,166 n.19
Roger II, king of Sicily (1101-54):
 XII 135
Roman Empire:V 24-28,32
Roman law, influence of:XII 163,
 186f. n.142
Romanos II,Emp.(959-63):III 205
Romanos III Argyros,Emp. (1028-
 34):III 197
Romanos IV,Emp. (1068-71):III 205
Rome:II 21;IV 8,11;V 21
rotundity of the earth:XVII 5
Russia:XVII 5

Sabellianism:XII 155
sacrifices,pagan:I 432-35
Sagittarius:XV 386ff. passim
St.Mary Blachernae, Church of:X 178
saints:X 181,186
 -as living images:X 181
salvation:I 438
Santa Maria in Trastevere:XII 137
Saracens:V 17
Sarrazin,John:XII 139
Satan:I 446
schism,Acacian:IV 4;IX 15
Sciapodes:XVII 5
scholarii:III 185,186
Scriptor incertus de Leone:XI 158
Scythian monks:IV 5
Sea of Tiberias:I 427,428
seasons:XV 390ff.
second coming (advent) of Christ:
 I 449;V 21,22,25
second crusade:XII 135
see of Rome:IV 8
senate:III 182,188,190-2,194-6
senate,Roman:I 448;II 40
Sibyl:XII 138
Sicily:VIII 38,39;IX passim
Sigisbert of Gembloux:VIII 13,14
silentiarii:III 184
Simplicius:XIV 42,43
Sinai:XIII 76,77,79 n.19
Socrates (church historian):
 I 423,425
Soda:I 440
Sol Invictus:II 40
solstices:XV 387ff.
sophia:I 441
soteriology:VII 138ff.;XII 161
sphericity of heaven:XIV 48,50
Stephen of Antioch:XIII 76
Stephen the Deacon:VIII 6,9,19,20

Stephen the Younger:VIII 6,9,10,12,
 19
Stephen II,Pope (752-57):IX 20
Stephen III,Pope (767-72): V 27
Stoicism:VI 126
Strabo:XV 402;XVI passim;XVII
 passim
substantia (substance, essence,usia):
 XII 140,152,154,165 n.11
Suidas (Suda):XV 396
Sulpicius Severus:V 20
Summa divinitas:II 38
sun:XV passim
 -eclipse of:I 445
Sylvester,Pope (314-35):V 37
Symeon Metaphrastes:VIII 19,20
Symeon Seth:XV passim
Synod of 727 (Roman):VIII 26
Syracuse:IX 25
Syene:XVI 9
Syrians:I 435

Taprobane:XVI 8
temperate zones:XVI 7-10
temples:I 436
Tereus:I 441
Tertullian: V 19
Thebes:XII 135
Themistius:V 15;XIV 42,43
Theocritus:III 187
Theodora,Empress (1042,1055-56):
 III 197-99
Theodore Lector:III 192
Theodore of Mopsuestia:V 22;VI 121;
 VII passim;XIII 77;XIV 46
Theodoretus of Cyprus:V 20,21;
 VI 140;VII 125;XV 400
Theodosius,geographer:XV 399
Theodosius of Alexandria,grammarian:
 XII 138
Theodosius,Patriarch of Alexandria
 (535-36):XIII 76;XIV 47
Theodosius,Bishop of Ephesus in
 754:X 177
Theodosius I,Emp.(379-95):II 22;
 V 15;XI 158
Theodosius II, Emp. (408-50):
 I 423;VI 140
Theodotion,recension of Daniel:
 V 31
Theodotus of Ancyra, associate
 of Cyril of Alexandria:X 183;XI
 155-57
Theon of Alexandria,4th century
 astronomer,father of Hypatia:
 XV 393
Theon Smyrnaeus,philosopher,fl.
 ca.150:XV 387ff.passim,393 passim

9

Theophanes,chronicler:III 192-194;
 VIII & IX passim;X 197
Theotokos:IV 5f.;VI 121-2,135
Thessalonike:XII 135,136
Thomas Aquinas:XII 180 n.83
Thomas of Edessa:V 23:XIII 76
Thracians:I 435
Three Chapters:VII 129,138
Tiberius (usurper,Petasius,ca.
 ca.730):VIII 33;IX 18
Tiberius II,Emp. (578-82):III 198
Tiberius III,Patriarch of Alexandria
 (518-35):XIII 76;XIV 47
Tiphernas,Gregory:XVII 10
torrid zone:XVI passim;XVII 3
Toscanelli,Paolo:XVII 2,7
toxotes:XV 386ff. passim
treptos, treptotēs:VII 125ff.,127,141,
 142ff.,156,158
Trinity:IV 3,5;VI 127;XII 139;
 152-55
tropics:XVI 7-10
Troy:I 443
Typos (of Justinian):VII 131
Twelve Anathemas (Cyril's)against
 Nestorius: IV 3,8;VI 119,123;
 VII 137,159
Two Natures in Christ:VII 129ff.,
 131;X 179,181;XII 158f.
Two Sons in Christ:VII 158ff.

Ulpian:II 31
"una natura Dei Verbi incarnata" see
 "mia physis tu theu logu sesarkō-
 menē"
uncircumscribable godhead (divinity):

III 203f.;X 180,188
union of two natures in Christ:
 VI 128,133
unity of Christ:VI 133
Urbicius:III 195
usia:VI passim;XII 133,140,154

Valentinian III,Emp. (425-55):
 I 423
Venice: VIII 27
 -San Marco:XII 136
Vetranio,Emp.(350):IIa 2-4
Victorinus:V 20
Vigilius Pope (£37-55):IV 11;
 VII 157
Virgin Mary:I 436;V 22;XII 157

Walsperger,Andreas:XVII 4
Walter of St. Victor:XII 134
White Sea:XVII 3
wealth:I 438,439
widow of emperor,role in selecting
 emperor:III 196-98
will,freedom of:VI 134
will of Christ:VI 133ff.
William of St. Thierre:XII 139
William I:XII 136

Zachariah,Pope (741-752):IX 18,19,
 29
Zeno,Emp. (474-91):III 195
Zeus:I 437
Zoe,Empress (1042-55):III 199
Zonaras:III 193,194,197;VIII 35;
 IX 20

INDEX

OF BIBLICAL CITATIONS

26.36f.: I 446
26.39: I 446
26.51: I 429
27.5: I 427
27.26f.: I 447
27.33: I 445

Mark
1.2f.: I 426
5.8f.: I 427
6.47f.: I 427
10.21: I 438
10.25: I 438
11.23: I 438
14.22f.: I 441
14.22-24: X 180
14.47: I 429
15.15f.: I 447
15.36: I 445

Luke
3.17: XII 133
5.31f.: I 439
8.31: I 427
12.33: I 438
17.21: V 33
18.22: I 438
18.25: I 438
22.15: XII 147
22.17-20: X 180
22.19f.: I 441
22.44: I 446
22.50: I 430

John
1.18: X 182
4.24: X 182
5.22f.: XII 146
5.37: X 182
5.46f.: I 434
6.19: I 427
6.53: I 440
8.28: VII 153
10.30: VII 150
10.34: I 436
11.34: VII 153
14.9: VII 145
14.10: VII 150
14.28: VII 131
15.26: XII 147
16.7: XII 146
16.15: VII 152
17.5: VII 147
18.10: I 429
19.29: I 445
20.28: VII 128
20.29: X 182

Acts
1.18: I 427
5.1-10: I 429
5.3: I 431
5.9: I 431
15.20: I 432
15.24: I 432 n.37
15.29: I 432

Romans
1.23: X 182
5.14f.: VI 128
7.12: I 432
7.14: I 432
8.9: VII 149
9.1: I 432
10.17: X 182
13.2: V 35
14.14-21: I 432 n.37
25b: X 182

I Corinthians
6.11: I 440
8.1-13: I 432 n.37
8.5f.: I 435,436
11.23f.: I 441
11.23-26: X 180
15.22: VI 128

II Corinthians
5.4c: X 184
5.16: X 182
8.9: VII 131,159

Galatians
2: I 429
3.1: I 432
3.10: I 432
5.3: I 432

Philippians
2.5f.: VII 144,153,159;X 183
2.5-11: VII 147
2.6-11: VI 136
2.6f.: VII 158
2.9: VII 146.147

I Thessalonians
4.16f.: I 449
4.17: I 449

Hebrews
2.9: VII 131,159
13.8: VII 148

I Peter
2.13-15: V 36